Aspects of English Protestantism

c. 1530—1700

MANCHESTER
UNIVERSITY PRESS

Politics, Culture and Society in Early Modern Britain

General Editors

PROFESSOR ANN HUGHES   DR ANTHONY MILTON   PROFESSOR PETER LAKE

This important series publishes monographs that take a fresh and challenging look at the interactions between politics, culture and society in Britain between 1500 and the mid-eighteenth century. It counteracts the fragmentation of current historiography through encouraging a variety of approaches which attempt to redefine the political, social and cultural worlds, and to explore their interconnection in a flexible and creative fashion. All the volumes in the series question and transcend traditional interdisciplinary boundaries, such as those between political history and literary studies, social history and divinity, urban history and anthropology. They thus contribute to a broader understanding of crucial developments in early modern Britain.

Further titles in preparation

Aspects of English Protestantism

c. 1530–1700

NICHOLAS TYACKE

Manchester
University Press

Manchester and New York

distributed exclusively in the USA by Palgrave

Published by Manchester University Press
Oxford Road, Manchester M13 9NR, UK
and Room 400, 175 Fifth Avenue, New York, NY 10010, USA
http://www.manchesteruniversitypress.co.uk

Distributed exclusively in the USA by
Palgrave, 175 Fifth Avenue, New York, NY 10010, USA

Distributed exclusively in Canada by
UBC Press, University of British Columbia, 2029 West Mall,
Vancouver, BC, Canada V6T 1Z2

British Library Cataloguing-in-Publication Data
A catalogue record for this book is available from the British Library

Library of Congress Cataloging-in-Publication Data applied for

ISBN 0 7190 5391 9 *hardback*
     0 7190 5392 7 *paperback*

First published 2001

10 09 08 07 06 05 04 03 02 01   10 9 8 7 6 5 4 3 2 1

Typeset in Scala with Pastonchi display
by Graphicraft Limited, Hong Kong

Printed in Great Britain
by Biddles Ltd, Guildford and King's Lynn

FOR SARAH

Contents

List of figures, map and tables

Preface

The essays collected together in this volume were originally published over a twenty-five year period (1973–98). Rather than attempt to rewrite them in the light of subsequent findings, I have addressed such matters by way of an introduction and some additional footnotes – the latter enclosed within square brackets. The aim has been both to preserve the historiographical integrity of the individual contributions and to indicate where they require updating. Although my work has been linked especially with a particular interpretation of the origins of the English Civil War, the concerns of the present book are much wider – namely English Protestantism considered from a variety of aspects and covering approximately the first 150 years of its existence. More general questions of this kind are also discussed in the introduction.

An emphasis throughout is on the role played by religious ideas, albeit operating within specific political and socioeconomic contexts. I am very conscious too of past writers, from the sixteenth century onwards, who have sought to make sense of some of the same material. Of particular relevance here is the Dominican friar Girolamo Pollini, whose *Storia Ecclesiastica della Rivoluzione d'Inghilterra* was published at Bologna in 1591. Pollini uses the term revolution in the modern sense of overturning the *status quo*, but with reference to the English Reformation as opposed to the Civil War. This Tudor revolution in religion began during the reign of Henry VIII, developed under Edward VI, and, after a Marian 'restituzione' of Roman Catholicism, was re-established following the accession of Elizabeth I. The fall-out from these momentous events provides my underlying theme.

Peter Lake and Vanessa Graham between them made this publishing venture possible. The former also commented on the introduction in draft, as did Kenneth Fincham. I thank all three of them.

N.T.
University College London

Acknowledgements

The essays which comprise this volume first appeared in the following places and are reprinted by kind permission of the original publishers.

1 N. Tyacke ed., *England's Long Reformation 1500–1800* (London, 1998), pp. 1–32. By permission of UCL Press.

2 O. P. Grell, J. I. Israel and N. Tyacke eds, *From Persecution to Toleration. The Glorious Revolution and Religion in England* Oxford, 1991), pp. 17–49. By permision of Oxford University Press.

3 P. Clark, A. G. R. Smith and N. Tyacke eds, *The English Commonwealth 1547–1640. Essays in Politics and Society presented to Joel Hurstfield* (Leicester, 1979), pp. 77–92, 229–33. By permission of Continuum.

4 N. Tyacke, *The Fortunes of English Puritanism, 1603–1640*, Friends of Dr Williams's Library Forty-Fourth Lecture (London, 1990). By permission of the Dr Williams's Trust.

5 C. Russell ed. *The Origins of the English Civil War* (London, 1973), pp. 119–43, 270–1. By permission of Macmillan Press Ltd.

Appendix. This was commissioned for a Blackwell encyclopaedia project which has since been discontinued. It appears here as written in 1993.

6 *Past and Present* 115 (1987), 201–16. By permission of the Past and Present Society, 175 Banbury Road, Oxford, England.

7 *Journal of British Studies* 35 (April 1996), 139–67. By permission of the North American Conference on British Studies.

8 K. Fincham ed., *The Early Stuart Church, 1603–1642* (Basingstoke, 1993), pp. 51–70, 256–8. By permission of Macmillan Press Ltd.

9 A. C. Duke and K. Tamse eds, *Church and State since the Reformation*, Britain and the Netherlands 7 (The Hague, 1981), pp. 94–117. By permission of Kluwer Academic Publishers.

10 D. Pennington and K. Thomas eds, *Puritans and Revolutionaries. Essays in Seventeenth-Century History presented to Christopher Hill* (Oxford, 1978), pp. 73–93. By permission of Oxford University Press.

11 N. Tyacke ed., *The History of the University of Oxford, IV: Seventeenth-Century Oxford* (Oxford, 1997), pp. 569–619. By permission of Oxford University Press.

12 S. Groenveld and M. Wintle eds, *The Exchange of Ideas. Religion, Scholarship and Art in Anglo-Dutch Relations in the Seventeenth Century*, Britain and the Netherlands 11 (Zutphen, 1994), pp. 68–83. By permission of the Walburg Press.

Abbreviations

APC   *Acts of the Privy Council*
Arber ed., *Transcript*   E. Arber ed. *A Transcript of the Registers of the Company of Stationers of London, 1554–1640* (London, 1875–94)
BIHR   *Bulletin of the Institute of Historical Research*
BL   British Library
Bodl.   Bodleian Library, Oxford
BRO   Berkshire RO
CL   Christ Church (Oxford) Library
Clark ed., *Register*   A. Clark ed. *The Register of the University of Oxford* (OHS, 1887–89), ii
CSPD   *Calendar of State Papers, Domestic*
CUA   Cambridge University Archives
CUL   Cambridge University Library
DNB   *Dictionary of National Biography*
EcHR   *Economic History Review*
EHR   *English Historical Review*
ESRO   East Sussex RO
GRO   Gloucestershire RO
HJ   *Historical Journal*
HMC   Historical Manuscripts Commission
HR   *Historical Research*
HRO   Hertfordshire RO
JBS   *Journal of British Studies*
JEH   *Journal of Ecclesiastical History*
Laud, *Works*   W. Laud, *Works* eds J. Bliss and W. Scott (Oxford, 1847–60)
NUL   Nottingham University Library
OHS   Oxford Historical Society
OUA   Oxford University Archives
P and P   *Past and Present*
PRO   Public Record Office
QCL   Queen's College (Oxford) Library
RO   Record Office
RSTC   *Revised Short Title Catalogue*, by W. A. Jackson, F. S. Ferguson and K. F. Pantzer (London, 1976–91)
SJL   St John's College (Oxford) Library
TCD   Trinity College Dublin
TRHS   *Transactions of the Royal Historical Society*
Tyacke, *Anti-Calvinists*   N. Tyacke, *Anti-Calvinists. The Rise of English Arminianism c. 1590–1640* (Oxford, 1987, 2nd edn 1990)
UCA   University College (Oxford) Archives
VCH   *Victoria County History*
WRO   Wiltshire RO
WSRO   West Sussex RO

FIGURE I Adam and Eve from the 1537 'Matthew' Bible

Introduction

***

WHY does someone become a historian? In my own case the die was probably cast early on, thanks especially to two remarkable school teachers: Christopher Bulteel and David Newsome each became headmasters later in their careers, but the latter also spent eleven years as fellow of a Cambridge college and has now written numerous books – mainly on aspects of the Victorian age. Both men were particularly interested in religious history and this undoubtedly made its mark on me.[1] Secondly the Oxford University which I entered in the autumn of 1959 could, at that time, legitimately claim to be *the* centre for seventeenth-century English historical studies. Thus the famous 'gentry controversy' about the socio-economic origins of the English Civil War was still reverberating, and most of the leading protagonists were resident academics: John Cooper, Lawrence Stone and Hugh Trevor-Roper.[2] My Balliol tutor Christopher Hill, although not directly involved in this debate, was clearly an interested party as doyen of the Marxist interpretation of the period. Moreover as a sixth former I had been much impressed by Trevor-Roper's *Historical Essays* (1957).

It was, however, Sir Richard Southern, perhaps despairing of me as a medievalist, who suggested at the end of my first undergraduate year that I should tackle the subject of Archbishop Laud for a college essay prize. My memory is that he actually had the original two volume edition of Laud's *Remains* (1695–1700) on his desk, and expressed deep dissatisfaction with the then standard biography of Laud by Trevor-Roper. Southern, almost certainly, was being more subversive than he realised because Trevor-Roper's *Archbishop Laud* and Hill's *The English Revolution 1640*, both originally published in 1940, are written from a similar point of view, namely that the English Civil War was a bourgeois revolution and that Laud is best understood as a leading light of the *ancien régime*. Only later did Trevor-Roper become a scourge of Marxist historians.[3]

Re-reading my 1961 essay on Laud, I am struck by the solitary reference to Arminianism as such.

> Within the Church of England, from the return of the Marian exiles onwards, there existed side by side two streams of thought, the one Calvinist basing itself on the *Institutes*, the other Anglican harking back to Cranmer's first

liturgy. (The later term Arminian Peter Heylyn compares to the linking of the western land mass with the name of Amerigo Vespucci.)

The passage does, however, go on to say that 'under Elizabeth the tendency is to the "left", reaching its height with the Lambeth Articles of 1595', whereas, so the conclusion runs, from 'Whitgift to Laud' there was a 'progression to the "right"' and 'the most obvious change was in the theory of predestination'. The essay also refers to ideas about episcopacy and the sacrament of communion, but attempts no overarching religious explanation. Yet the debt to Heylyn, the first biographer and near contemporary of Laud, already shows, not least in the choice of chronology – with the 1590s seen as a pivotal decade. Although the term 'Anglican' does occur, the concept of a *via media* is ignored. Furthermore the objection of Heylyn to the term Arminian was on grounds of origins rather than content, his own preferred description being Old English Protestant.[4]

Funded to pursue postgraduate research in the same subject area, and seeking to understand the religious changes of the period, I again found myself drawing on the work of Heylyn – who helped to provide a theological framework and, incidentally, the title of my eventual book *Anti-Calvinists*.[5] It is also important, however, to note here the influence of Harry Porter's *Reformation and Reaction in Tudor Cambridge*, published in 1958. Indeed David Newsome, a friend of Porter, had received a complimentary copy and I can remember him bringing it into class, but my serious engagement with the work only came some years later. The third and final section of *Reformation and Reaction*, entitled 'The Universe of Grace', served to open up fascinating new vistas. Apart from being a beautifully written and presented book, the author's apology for treating this 'forbidding' topic seemed quite unnecessary.

> Shelves and shelves of bulky, unread volumes, the stifling importance of great authors, the intricacies and confusions of scandals and controversies, have laid upon the theology of grace that inverted form of the Midas touch which kills all interest as dead as a doornail. The articles, the canons, the decrees, the points, the propositions – all these are distilled conclusions, without life, without passion. Yet the doctrines of grace and predestination, reflecting, in their immense complication, simple convictions about the sort of being God is and the kind of creature man is, concern not merely theology but all aspects of the human condition . . .[6]

Porter went on to analyse in detail the Cambridge University debates of the 1590s about predestination, but whereas Heylyn employed an essentially binary model, consisting of 'Calvinists' and their opponents, he argued for a third, Anglican, way. Nevertheless, in practice, it remains unclear how this last position differs from what comes to be known as sublapsarian Calvinism, the view that predestination, albeit unconditional, relates to humankind already fallen and therefore in a state of sin. Rather confusingly, Porter also suggested that the Thirty-nine Articles, the confession of faith of the English Church, are amenable to an Arminian interpretation. Thus he wrote that they 'left open the way for an insistence on faith and repentance as conditions of election', something asserted much more forcefully by Heylyn. At the same time Porter, like Heylyn, tended to equate Calvinism with Puritanism – seeing it, that is to say, as primarily the theology of those dissatisfied with the Elizabethan settlement of religion. Unlike Porter, however, Heylyn conceded that in practice Calvinism had come to dominate the late Elizabethan Church, from Archbishop Whitigift downwards.[7]

Since the whole topic of Calvinism and Arminianism has in recent years become bedevilled by disagreement over terminology, it is worth saying something more at this point about contemporary definitions.[8] One of the leading protagonists in Porter's account was Peter Baro, French *émigré* and Lady Margaret professor of divinity at Cambridge University, who provided a summary, in 1596, of what he regarded as the three main schools of thought on the predestinarian question, as held by members of the 'Protestant Church'. Regarding the first two opinions, Baro, although he does not use the actual terms, in effect rehearses the supralapsarian and sublapsarian views of predestination. As these labels imply, the difference hinges on whether God's absolute decree of election and reprobation has reference to humankind before or after the Fall. According to Baro, supralapsarians and sublapsarians agree that the elect 'can by no means avoid believing or fail of being saved' while the reprobate 'are not able to believe or to be saved'. Thus 'both these opinions impose on men an inevitable necessity' either of 'being saved' or of 'perishing'. Although sublapsarianism is seemingly 'milder', because it relates to sinful humankind, Baro concludes that 'in substance' it does not really differ from supralapsarianism.[9] Yet at the same time he links the supralapsarian school of thought especially with the names of John Calvin and Theodore Beza.[10]

Baro's 'third opinion' is 'that of the Fathers who flourished prior to the age of St Augustine', and among the moderns, preeminently, Philip Melancthon. This holds that predestination is conditional on faith. 'Whosoever believeth in Christ shall be saved; but he that believeth not shall be damned'. Therefore 'God hath predestinated such as he from all eternity foreknew would believe on Christ' and likewise 'reprobated all rebels, and such as contumaciously continue in sin'. The offer of saving grace is universal, and can be freely accepted or rejected since no necessity is imposed on the human will. Porter has rightly dubbed this third view, to which Baro himself subscribed, as Arminianism *'avant la lettre'*.[11]

Commenting on doctrines of predestination about a century after Baro, Archbishop John Tillotson offered a further refinement on his analysis and one which reflects developments during the interim. Albeit not naming them, he defines what are clearly the Calvinist and Arminian wings. The former teach that all who are 'converted and regenerated are wrought upon in an irresistible manner, and are merely passive in it; and that those who are not thus wrought upon, their repentance and conversion is impossible'. Conversely the latter hold that 'sufficient grace is offered to all, one time or another, who live under the gospel, which they may comply with or resist'; in consequence, 'if they be not brought to repentance their impenitency and ruin is the effect of their own choice, and God is free from the blood of all men'. Between these 'extremes', Tillotson went on to locate 'two middle opinions'. The first maintains that 'irresistible grace is afforded to all the elect, and sufficient grace to all others who live under the gospel . . . ; but then they say that none of those to whom this sufficient grace is afforded shall effectually comply with it, and be saved'. The second such 'middle opinion', and the one personally endorsed by Tillotson, is that 'some are converted in an irresistible manner when God pleaseth, and whom he designs to be extraordinary examples and instruments for the good of others, and that sufficient grace is afforded to others which is effectual to the salvation of many'.[12] Of these intermediate positions, the first is often referred to as 'hypothetical universalism' and found favour, for example, with some members of the British delegation to the Synod of Dort in 1618–19, while the second probably had an early advocate in Bishop John Overall and certainly was well established by the middle of the seventeenth century. It should be emphasised, however, that these two middle way doctrines have very close affinities with Calvinism and Arminianism respectively.[13]

Apropos the more general historiographical framework, my unpublished 1961 piece on Laud was set within a 'court and country' context of English politics. This was largely derived from Trevor-Roper, whose essay on 'James I and his Bishops' had particularly intrigued me.[14] Here he extended the model of a corrupt and venal Jacobean court, to office-holding within the English Church. From this it followed that the Puritans were the destroyers of a system the attempted reform of which by Laud had been too little and too late.[15] At bottom, however, this materialist interpretation left me unsatisfied. Also to the extent that R. H. Tawney's argument concerning the 'rise of the gentry' could be said to have tested Marxist assumptions empirically, the outcome seemed pretty damning.[16] Nevertheless, I only gradually came to confront such questions of interpretation. A milestone, in retrospect, was attending the 1962 Ford Lectures of Christopher Hill on 'Intellectual Origins of the English Revolution', and especially listening to what he had to say about the role of the English universities. Hill portrayed Oxford and Cambridge as bastions of Aristotelianism, and the academic counterpart of *ancien régime* institutions in church and state – even going so far as to claim that the Civil War was fought between Copernican parliamentarians and Ptolemaic royalists. The 'new philosophy' allegedly triumphed courtesy of the English Revolution. Subsequently working my way through the Oxford University Archives and seeking to vary an unrelieved diet of theological disputations, I chose to read more widely; in so doing, the picture of a very different pre-war world to that sketched by my erstwhile tutor began to emerge. The first fruits of this particular piece of truancy were not, however, to appear in print until the late 1970s.[17]

To suggest that religious ideas could have a historical import of their own was still very unfashionable in the early 1960s, all the more so when the views involved were those of the opponents of Puritanism. A further obstacle was the portrait painted, by those writing from an Anglican standpoint, of an early-modern English Church largely innocent of theology, especially of the continental Protestant variety.[18] Thus I was very fortunate to have a post-graduate supervisor prepared to indulge my heterodoxies in these matters. In the event Anne Whiteman was to oversee my labours for some six years and provided a meticulous training in research. Moreover almost at the outset she pointed me towards the records of the British delegation to the Synod of Dort, which condemned Arminianism in 1619, having initially surveyed the territory herself on my behalf. It is only right and proper, however, to add that Christopher Hill also read the successive chapters of the thesis in draft and, whatever his private reservations, he played a very supportive role throughout. My debt to him remains great.

Scepticism concerning materialist interpretations of history was also paralleled by growing doubts about Whig political history, notably of the constitutional variety. In this connection a particular target became Sir David Lindsay Keir's *The Constitutional History of Modern Britain since 1485*, although my youthful reaction to this rather sophisticated exposition now seems too extreme.[19] A principal objection to the constitutionalist approach was that the political realities tended to get squeezed out from a tale told in terms of legal precedents and one based moreover on progressive assumptions. Appointed an assistant lecturer in history at University College London in 1965, my teaching duties included contributing to a course on 'English Constitutional History' as part of the federal degree of the University of London. By 1972, however, I had persuaded a senior colleague, Joel Hurstfield, that we should thereafter cease teaching constitutional history, given the unsatisfactory nature of the subject. Two years later Conrad Russell, then of Bedford College, followed suit. Russell and I were already in process of planning a new joint special subject entitled 'Parliament and Society in England, 1603–1629', which was launched in 1974. Around this time Hurstfield also invited us both formally to join him in running the 'Tudor History' research seminar at the

Institute of Historical Research, which was rechristened 'English History, *c.* 1550–*c.* 1650'.[20]

The intellectual liason with Russell dated back to the completion of my Oxford D.Phil. thesis in 1969 ('Arminianism in England, in Religion and Politics, 1604 to 1640'), which survived the scrutiny of both Hill and Trevor-Roper as examiners.[21] Russell had distilled the findings of the thesis in his book *The Crisis of Parliaments*,[22] and it was logical that he should have thought of me as the author of a chapter in his planned 'Problems in Focus' volume for Macmillan – *The Origins of the English Civil War*. The introduction to this latter work, which was published in 1973, makes abundantly clear that the thrust of our collective enterprise involved a challenge to both Whig and Marxist thinking. While paying tribute to the scholarship of the great S. R. Gardiner, Russell wrote that he

> was of the generation most heavily influenced by Darwin, and held the view of society now described by anthropologists as 'evolutionary': that society was evolving towards some predestined end, and growing nearer to perfection at each stage of its development. For Gardiner, as *homo sapiens* was the ultimate perfection of biological evolution, so the British Constitution was the ultimate perfection of political evolution. He thought that 'the Parliament of England was the noblest monument ever reared by mortal man', and that the real cause of Charles's fall was his attempt to obstruct the inevitable development of the national will.

Russell went on to say:

> It is indeed time to begin to question those assumptions which nineteenth-century Whig and early twentieth-century Marxist historians have in common ... Both are products of the middle of the nineteenth century, when the notion of 'progress' was at its most fashionable. Both grew out of that intellectual climate of which Darwin was both a consequence and a cause, in which history was seen moving, by a series of inevitable stages, from the worse to the better, until it reached what Jeremy Bentham called 'this age, in which knowledge is rapidly advancing towards perfection'.

While Whigs and Marxists alike believed that 'the parliamentarians, because they won, were "progressive", and in some way stood for the future', by contrast 'one of the aims of this volume is to show the ways in which the parliamentarian gentry were the conservatives, standing for the outdated values of the Elizabethan world in which many of them had grown up'.[23] The original typescript of my own chapter in the Russell volume had also included a historiographical section on Gardiner, citing his 1886 obituary of Leopold von Ranke where he asked rhetorically 'is it not possible to do for history what Darwin has done for science?'. Three years earlier Frederick Engels, in his graveside oration for Karl Marx, had confidently claimed that 'just as Darwin discovered the law of development of organic nature, so Marx discovered the law of development of human history'.[24]

Russell located his remarks, about the affinity between Whig and Marxist paradigms, in the context of the gentry controversy. 'Social change explanations of the English Civil War must be regarded as having broken down'. But this did not mean returning to a Whig political interpretation, in terms of long-term constitutional developments. Rather it was the innovating religious policies of Charles I, against a background of deepening financial and administrative malaise, which provided the key. 'Financial issues made a constitutional crisis inevitable, but without the passion provided by the religious troubles, it would not have been inevitable that the constitutional crisis should end in war.' The 'collapse' of the government in 1640 'gave the discontented gentry their opportunity'. Above all it was the alienation of 'the main stream of English moderate Puritanism', due to the rise of Arminianism, that was crucial.[25]

Looking back, Russell's *Origins* can be seen to have blazed the trail for subsequent 'revisionist' explanations of the English Civil War.[26] Indeed its implications were rapidly grasped by Sir Geoffrey Elton, who in his review drew out the contrast with Lawrence Stone's *The Causes of the English Revolution 1529–1642* – which had been published the previous year, in 1972, and encapsulated the tradition against which Russell and his team were in revolt. In typically trenchant style, Elton wrote that

> Any historians who were depressed by the enthusiastic reception given to L. Stone's recent rehashing of outworn notions on the 'causes of the English Revolution' . . . may take heart. The New Look has arrived, only a few months later . . . What unites the contributors (all of whom belong to the younger generation of scholars) is their recognition that the 'origins of the Civil War' are not to be found in those famous long-term trends beloved by historians unwilling to study events, but in the immediate history of the reign of Charles I.

Russell 'concentrates convincingly on demolishing the Whig myth and on allowing the years 1625–40 the right to have produced their own effects – effects not predictable from what went before'. Elton was especially enthusiastic about my essay, as providing

> a forceful demonstration that Arminianism, not Puritanism, was the revolutionary and subversive creed of Charles's reign. At long last we have an historian who gets the so-called problem of Jacobean Puritanism right by seeing that what passes by that name was in fact the main-line Protestantism of the English Church.[27]

His overall conclusion was that 'what we have here is a truly welcome prospectus' for a 'very necessary revolution in historical thinking'.[28]

Russell was understandably reluctant in *Origins* to categorise the precise nature of the English Civil War, contenting himself with remarks such as: 'financial and administrative grievances' did not put people 'in fear for their lives or their souls' and that 'explanations of the Civil War' are 'led back to Puritanism'. My own chapter in the volume ended with a discussion of the battle standards flown by the cavalry captains on both sides and concluded that they 'suggest a high degree of religious motivation' among the parliamentarians.[29] Our cautiousness has not, however, prevented others making bolder claims. Thus Michael Watts cited *Origins* in 1978 as support for his statement that 'the Civil War was the English counterpart of the continental wars of religion'. This was subsequently and more famously formulated by John Morrill, in 1984, as 'the English Civil War was not the first European revolution: it was the last of the wars of religion'.[30] The danger with such a description, of course, is that it can give the false impression that the dispute was about religion and nothing else. Certainly Russell and I have continued to stress the multi-faceted nature of the conflict which broke out in 1642.[31]

At the same time there has been considerable speculation about the possible external factors which may have helped to produce the revisionist wave of the 1970s. David Cannadine, in colourful language, described the kind of history written by the likes of Lawrence Stone as a 'welfare-state version of the past'. It 'was the old Whig history of Britain's unique and privileged development dressed up in Butskellite guise'. Revisionists, by contrast, were 'new Tories', who had ceased to believe that British history was a 'success story'. Peter Lake, albeit in more measured tones, has similarly suggested that revisionism was 'recognisably a product of the same politico-ideological conjuncture that produced Thatcherism'. 'Modernisation theory' had ceased to make sense in the contemporary context of 'seemingly intractable national decline and economic crisis'.[32]

Speaking personally, however, the internal dynamics of the subject, as rehearsed above, were much more important. Shortly after the completion of my thesis I also undertook the rather quixotic task of trying to understand the nineteenth-century roots of history as an academic discipline, which involved a potentially massive reading programme. In this connexion I was contracted at one point, along with a UCL colleague, Negley Harte, to edit two volumes of inaugural lectures by British historians. One abiding interest of these writers concerned the nature of 'scientific' history. Furthermore my first head of department, Alfred Cobban, was the originator of modern revisionism as regards the French Revolution – a topic linked very closely with the idea of an 'English Revolution'.[33] Yet it was above all the upshot of the gentry controversy that, in my view, forced apprentice historians of the 1960s to reappraise the whole field of English Civil War studies.[34]

II

When researching and writing about the Arminian–Calvinist disputes of the early seventeenth century, the history of Puritanism, not surprisingly, kept on intruding. Here it was my good fortune to get to know Patrick Collinson in the final stages of the converting of his massive London Ph.D. thesis into book form. The last chapter of *The Elizabethan Puritan Movement* in fact dovetails with the first chapter of my thesis and subsequent book *Anti-Calvinists*.[35] In the late 1960s I was also contracted to contribute a volume to the Longmans 'Seminar Studies' series. It was to be called 'The Puritan Century 1560–1660', although this never progresed much further than an introduction. At this date the field was still dominated by William Haller's *The Rise of Puritanism* (1938), a work of the same vintage as the first writings of Hill and Trevor-Roper.

The combined Whig and literary approach of Haller struck me increasingly as doubly unfortunate. Moreover a particularly ironic feature of his book is that the sources principally consist of the licensed publications of the English printing press. In consequence Haller mainly defines Puritanism on the basis of ideas officially approved by the very episcopal authorities it was supposed to be against. Admittedly he does assume a largely hidden presbyterian agenda, running from the 1570s to the 1640s. 'The object of the Puritan reformers was the reorganisation of English society in the form of a church governed according to presbyterian principles.' But most of the book is taken up with an exposition of views the Puritan specificity of which remains unclear. Indeed it could be said that Haller employs a Laudian definition of Puritanism, in terms of Calvinist soteriology. 'The history of Puritan thought in England is primarily the history of the setting forth of the basic doctrine of predestination, in terms calculated to appeal to the English populace.' He went on to ascribe a 'spiritual equalitarianism' to predestinarian preaching and one which 'became the central force of revolutionary Puritanism'. The argument certainly has its attractions. Yet missing from this account is any discussion of doctrinal change; we are simply told that 'Anglicanism . . . moved steadily away from orthodox Calvinism'.[36]

Such is the background against which my first, 1973, venture into print should be set. 'Puritanism, Arminianism and Counter-Revolution' argues for a 'rise' of Arminianism rather than of Puritanism and that the former was more of a politically destabilising force in the early seventeenth-century situation. The essay also concentrates on the period from the accession of Charles I in 1625, when the Arminians increasingly came into their own. There are always dangers attendant upon the inverting of arguments and in this case an obvious criticism is that the independent existence of Puritanism risks becoming blurred almost to vanishing point or, as one colleague put it, being 'collapsed' into Calvinism. This is a justified complaint, which some of my later published work has endeavoured to remedy.[37] But I remain quite unrepentant in claiming that with the advent to power of Laud the doctrinal position of the English Church altered, and that this in turn helps to explain other religious changes of the period – notably as regards the treatment of the sacraments. On the other hand, my concentration on the 'single issue of predestination' does now seem excessive. Today I would wish to stress more that a nexus of associated orthodoxies were all coming under challenge at this same time.[38] The essay can also be criticised for insufficient analysis of the Calvinist hegemony against which the Arminians were reacting. But it now appears that the origins of this Calvinist or, more accurately, Reformed, dominance are traceable to the earliest days of the Protestant Reformation. Thus Diarmaid MacCulloch has demonstrated the predestinarian assumptions underlying the religious thought of Archbishop Thomas Cranmer, from the 1530s onwards. 'Justification was by faith through grace alone, within the framework of God's arbitrary predestination, without any foreseeing of individual human merit'. Moreover such views inform Cranmer's teaching on the sacraments and are incorporated into the Forty-two Articles of 1553, the basis in turn of the Thirty-nine Articles of 1563. Here in addition it appears highly significant that Edmund Bonner, Marian Bishop of London, seeking to repair the damage done by Edwardian Protestantism, began his *A Profitable and Necessarye Doctryne* of 1555 by refuting the doctrines of both justification by faith alone and unconditional predestination; he particularly censured those who believed themselves to be 'of the predestynates, whiche shall persever to the ende in their callyng'. Was Bonner perhaps aware too of the prayer used by Protector Somerset, in which he described himself as a 'vessel' of mercy 'written with the very bloud of Jesus' into 'the book of life' and expressed confidence that God's 'inestimable love will not cancell then my name'?[39]

Turning to the detailed steps in the argument of 'Puritanism, Arminianism and Counter-Revolution', it should be pointed out more clearly that my statement as regards a Calvinist 'majority' *c.* 1600 has reference to the university-educated elite – both clerical and lay. Hence too the emphasis on university theology. The evidence for Oxford can now be parallelled for Cambridge, also from the 1580s. In 1582 Humphrey Tyndall, future Dean of Ely, maintained as a doctoral thesis at the Cambridge Commencement that 'The eternal predestination of God does not depend on the foresight of either faith or works'. At the next Commencement, in 1583, Richard Wood defended the assertion that 'The faith of the saints never fails'. Such was the Calvinist tenor of English university teaching until the mid 1620s, mirrored as well in the licensed output of the printing press.[40] Yet there were always dissenters from these 'orthodoxies', and this deserved further elaboration by me. At the same time the notion of Calvinism as a 'common and ameliorating bond', helping to reconcile the differences between 'conformists and nonconformists, episcopalians and presbyterians', can be overdone. Archbishop Whitgift did in fact mount a formidable attack on Puritanism in the 1580s, and his public controversy with Cartwright was not only long but also bitter.[41] Nor is it convincing to assimilate the positions of John Pym and Francis Rous with that of Calvinist episcopalianism. Pym and Rous, together with many other opponents of Arminianism in the 1620s, were Puritan advocates of further reformation of the English Church.[42] Conversely evidence has since emerged that Archbishop Richard Bancroft was actually a Calvinist, while my distinction between his attitude towards Puritanism and that of Whitgift seems much exaggerated. The Puritan classical movement which he helped Whitgift to crush was no 'figment'. Nor had Puritanism more generally been eliminated as a genuine threat by the beginning of the seventeenth century.[43] None of which, however, detracts from the sense of alienation produced by the rise of Arminianism – especially among moderate Puritans.

On the other hand it was never my view that Arminianism in England owed much, apart from a name, to its Dutch counterpart. Why else adopt Porter's phrase Arminianism *avant la lettre*, in both my doctoral thesis and book, when discussing the Hampton Court Conference of 1604?[44] The use of the term in an English context denotes a similarity of doctrine, as regards the theology of grace, rather than a common source. Nevertheless the whole question of nomenclature has given rise to widespread confusion, from that day to this, not least in terms of spelling. Thus the first 'i' in Arminianism is vital. Armenians, as opposed to Arminians, originate from a place – Armenia. On this score Ben Jonson in his play *The Magnetic Lady*, licensed for the stage in 1632, has the following hilarious set of exchanges:

> *Mistress Polish* She would dispute with the doctors of divinity at her own table! And the spital preachers! And find out the Armenians.
> *Doctor Rut* The Arminians?
> *Mistress Polish* I say the Armenians.
> *Master Compass* Nay, I say so too!
> *Mistress Polish* So Master Polish called 'em, the Armenians!
> *Master Compass* And Medes, and Persians, did he not?
> *Mistress Polish* Yes, he knew 'em, and so did Mistress Steel! She was his pupil! The Armenians, he would say, were worse than Papists! And than [then] the Persians were our Puritans, had the fine piercing wit!
> *Master Compass* And who, the Medes?
> *Mistress Polish* The middle men, the lukewarm Protestants![45]

In similar vein Patrick Collinson has recorded that when I gave a lecture about Arminianism, at the University of Kent, 'three Arabs left after five minutes'.[46]

The difficulties with the term Arminianism, however, go much deeper, because many people would regard the views in question as quintessentially Christian. What could be more seemingly orthodox than to teach that Christ died to redeem the human race and, accordingly, that saving grace is freely available to all those who choose to take advantage of the offer? Certainly the Dutch theologian Jacobus Arminius of Leiden, who died in 1609, was not the inventor of this proposition. Arguably such teaching was normative prior to its denial by St Augustine during his controversy with the Pelagians, in the early fifth century.[47] It was these writings of Augustine, particularly his interpretation of the Pauline epistles in the New Testament, that exercised great influence on the first continental Protestant reformers.[48] A retreat, however, set in especially among second generation Lutherans by the middle of the sixteenth century. But the Reformed camp, to which England by and large belonged, tended to stand firm considerably longer. Among the Reformed it was Arminius who subsequently emerged as the most famous challenger. So it was both natural that his name should begin to be applied in an early seventeenth-century English context and understandable why those thus labelled would protest.[49] Indeed there exists a similar, if less acute, difficuty with the term Calvinist. For many of those described as such claimed to be following the Bible, at most with some help from Augustine. Yet from the early seventeenth century Arminian and Calvinist became the terms increasingly in vogue, and provided we are clear about definitions there is no good reason to avoid using them thenceforward.

The whole question of early Stuart ecclesiastical policy has now been more fully investigated by Kenneth Fincham and Peter Lake, and their joint insights need taking into account. They have plausibly argued that James I consciously aimed to drive a wedge between radical and moderate Puritans, but also sought to accommodate the emerging Arminian group – hence the fact that 'almost all the leading lights of the Caroline regime had enjoyed royal favour under James'. This Arminian presence was indeed necessary because of the related objective of wooing moderate Catholics, in the same way that evangelical Calvinists on the episcopal bench served to build bridges with moderate Puritans. On the subject of Jacobean Calvinism, Fincham and Lake conclude that 'theological propriety might allow divergences of private opinion, but the demands of political and ecclesiastical order would not allow open dispute, so the King suppressed public expression of anti-Calvinist theology'. Yet one unintended consequence of this overall policy was an increasingly volatile religious situation, matters coming to a head with the outbreak of the Thirty Years War in 1618 and a Calvinist call for England to head a crusade against the Habsburg powers. In these altered circumstances James leaned more towards the anti-Calvinists, who backed his attempt to resolve the international crisis by diplomatic as opposed to military means.[50]

None the less Fincham and Lake in their account of the subsequent direction taken by Caroline religious policy detect an 'emphatic shift from the Jacobean balance of ecclesiastical power', and one in favour of anti-Calvinists. At the same time they suggest that in the years 1625 to 1629 royal intentions remained 'ambiguous', not least because England was now engaged in fighting Spain and this made 'overt patronage of anti-Cavinists very dangerous indeed'. With the coming of peace in 1629–30, however, the situation changed markedly, as can be seen most obviously from the Arminian tenor of some of the sermons preached at the royal court during a decade when Calvinism, by contrast, was at a 'low ebb'.[51] Lake has also anatomised the 'Laudian style' which emerged at this time, while offering a broader definition of English Arminianism as Laudianism – in terms of a 'coherent, distinctive and polemically aggressive vision of the Church, the divine presence in the world and the appropriate ritual response to that presence'. Part and parcel of this was 'a greatly enhanced stress on the importance of the beauty of holiness, defined in both material and liturgical terms', along with the placing of the eucharist 'at the very centre of Christian piety and religion' and a new kind of priestly clericalism. Lake stresses that this package of views was both 'conservative and innovative' and had been 'canvassed among certain *avant garde* conformist divines since at least the 1590s'. Provided that the doctrinal aspect is not lost sight of, this more inclusive definition seems perfectly acceptable. Indeed it is worth recalling a passage from my 1973 essay where I wrote that, thanks to the Prayer Book, 'Arminianism in England emerged with an additional, sacramental dimension', the 'arbitrary grace of predestination' being replaced by a 'new found source of grace freely available in the sacraments'. 'Hence the preoccupation under Archbishop Laud with altars and private confession before receiving communion, as well as a belief in the absolute necessity of baptism.'[52]

Theory informed practice and as a consequence it will not do to argue, as some have, that doctrine was of little relevance to ordinary people. We are in fact dealing here with some of the intellectual underpinnings of popular religious observance. Furthermore, thanks to vernacular print, the ideas themselves had become widely dispersed. Granted that the 'niceties of academic theology' are not to be encountered in the writings of the Puritan artisan Nehemiah Wallington, the impress, however, on them of the Calvinist theology of grace remains unmistakeable.[53] In the opposite camp John Overall can be found both doing battle with the Calvinists in Elizabethan Cambridge, as Regius professor of divinity, and at the same time administering spiritual comfort to some of his Epping parishioners who 'could not be persuaded that Christ died for them'. The latter led to him preaching a sermon on the universality of grace, in which he referred to Christ as 'the sun of righteousness, the water of life, the heavenly medicine'. Such saving grace was most readily available via the sacrament of holy communion and here it is pertinent to turn to some notes on the Prayer Book by John Cosin, probably compiled soon after 1619 and as such reflecting the influence of Overall in whose employ he had been. Cosin, quoting from the 'ancient Fathers', described holy communion as 'medicamentum immortalitatis' and emphasised that the eucharist is a 'propitiatory sacrifice' for the sins of the 'whole world'. He was also adamant that communion should be reverently celebrated at an altar not a table, contrary to the objections of 'Puritans'.[54]

III

In the mid 1970s I was invited to contribute to a *festschrift* for Christopher Hill. Edited by Donald Pennington and Keith Thomas, the volume was on the theme of 'Puritans and Revolutionaries' – a word play on the title of Hill's first collection of essays *Puritanism and Revolution* (1958). With little hesitation, I offered 'Science and Religion at Oxford before the Civil War'. For the seeds sown by Hill's Ford lectures had continued to grow, especially due to the professional interest of my wife, Sarah Tyacke, in the history of early-modern cartography. Married in 1971, we attended the Polish quincentenary celebrations in 1973 of the birth of Nicholas Copernicus; more generally scholars such as E. G. R. Taylor and D. W. Waters, first encountered via Hill, now became household names and in the case of Waters a personal friend. The most controversial aspect of 'Intellectual Origins of the English Revolution' was the interpretation by Hill of the 'scientific revolution' of the seventeenth century. Much influenced by the historian and scientist Stephen Mason, he claimed that a positive link existed between Puritanism and the new 'bourgeois' science.[55] In this connexion Gresham College, in London, mercantile in orientation and allegedly Puritan, was deemed to have played a key role. By contrast the English universites were seen as reactionary backwaters, epitomised by Hill's dismissive account of the foundation of chairs of astronomy and geometry at Oxford by Sir Henry Savile, in 1619, which begins with the statement that 'the university has always been skilful at resisting reform and absorbing reformers'. My own conclusion was very different, namely that science at Laudian Oxford was in a flourishing state. But I did not ascribe this to Laudianism. On the contrary:

> close scrutiny . . . of scientific developments at Oxford, in the decades before the Civil War, indicates a negative correlation between religion and science. Despite Arminianism, the upward movement of science continued unabated . . . The religious background, however, remained pluralistic, embracing all manner of Protestants *and* Catholics.

Nor was an economic interpretation ruled out, 'for it was no accident that the countries moving into the commercial leadership of Europe were also those in the scientific vanguard'.[56]

John Bainbridge, Savilian professor of astronomy from 1621 until his death in 1643, emerged as the hero of my account of Oxford science before the Civil War. Although the Bainbridge papers at Trinity College Dublin had been listed in print, albeit very briefly, since 1900, no one before me apparently had investigated them.[57] The trip to Dublin in December 1975 was in many ways memorable; with all air flights from London grounded by fog I was forced instead to make my way by train from Euston to Holyhead, catching the night ferry and arriving a day late. But the Bainbridge papers turned out to be pure gold, including the discovery that an astronomical expedition to Latin America had been organised from Oxford in the 1630s. Moreover at this time the professors of astronomy and geometry at Gresham College, Henry Gellibrand and John Greaves, were both former pupils of Bainbridge. The surviving lecture notes of Bainbridge also reveal the up-to-date nature of his teaching. Far from this being an isolated exception, however, even Archbishop Laud can be found patronising Oxford science, while the printed university syllabus itself, of 1635, is graced with a Copernican motif.[58] Nevertheless today I would want to put more emphasis on the entrepreneurial partnership of Sir Thomas Bodley and Sir Henry Savile, as well as the neo-humanist intellectual environment, in explaining Oxford developments.[59] A symbolic illustration of the latter is the figure of Pallas Athene which tops Bodley's funeral monument.[60]

Shortly after completing the essay on Oxford science I first met Mordechai Feingold, then working on the doctoral thesis which became his book *The Mathematicians' Apprenticeship*. In this and more recent work Feingold has convincingly reevaluated the whole subject of university science, along with the role of Gresham College.[61] I returned again to the topic of science and religion in a paper given at the seventh Anglo-Dutch Historical Conference in 1979. Not content with simply proving a negative, 'Arminianism and English Culture' sets out, among other things, to investigate the 'wider philosophical implications of the Arminian controversy' and its possible affinities with Pyrrhonism and Epicureanism. But even here the suggestion that a connection existed between Arminianism and atomism was never designed as an alternative *religious* explanation of the rise of modern science.[62] The essay also explores Epicurean moral attitudes, in opposition to Calvinism and by extension Puritanism. This in turn links with another *festschrift* contribution of mine to a volume honouring Joel Hurstfield, which I edited along with Peter Clark and Alan Smith. Fear-God Barebone with his book of bawdy verse does indeed feature as a renegade Puritan in my account,[63] although the core concern of 'Popular Puritan Mentality in Late Elizabethan England' is with the sociology of Puritanism.[64]

Big claims have been made over the years concerning Puritan influence, yet the quarry itself has always proved somewhat elusive. Accordingly my idea was to trace Puritan parents through offspring on whom godly names had been bestowed in baptism, a chance reference in M. M. Knappen's *Tudor Puritanism* having led me to *Curiosities of Puritan Nomenclature* (1880) by C. W. Bardsley.[65] Early on in the research the county of Sussex emerged as prominent in the giving of such Puritan baptismal names, but it is worth spelling out the method of working. Having joined the Society of Genealogists specifically for the purpose, I proceeded county by county to examine index listings of names dating from the early seventeenth century. Evidence which has emerged since tends to confirm the finding of the essay that 'the heartland of Puritan nomenclature was undoubtedly east Sussex and the Kentish border'. Thus Edward Topsell in a sermon probably preached at Sevenoaks, in Kent, and published in 1596, defended the giving of 'holy and significant names', against charges of 'newnes and precisenesse', to put children 'in minde of their duetyes or to note the thankefulnes of their parents'. He instanced 'these names of rejoycing, thanksgiving, repentance, godlynes, mercy, constancie and such lyke'.[66] Again the identification of Dudley Fenner as 'the chief begetter nationally' is borne out by High Commission proceedings against him, where he is charged with having 'named or consented to naminge of certayne children in baptisme by these or the like names: Joye-agayne, From-above, More-fruicte, [and] Duste'. Fenner, while admitting that he had indeed been party to the giving of these names at Cranbrook, in Kent, replied that 'I fynde it the contynuall practise of the Churche in the Olde and Newe Testament to name their children with signifycant names in their owne tounge'.[67] We should also note that the Genevan Bible, from the first 1560 edition onwards, includes a 'Brief Table' on the interpretation of proper names in the Old Testament. 'Names of infants', it is claimed, 'shulde ever have some godlie advertisements in them and shulde be memorials and markes of the children of God received into his household'. Some of these Hebrew names as interpreted anticipate the later Puritan fashion, for example 'Jahalleel' (1 Chronicles, 4:16) meaning 'praising God', or 'Jeriel' (1 Chronicles, 7:2) 'the feare of God'. But most of the Puritan names in question do not appear to have a Hebrew equivalent, and cannot therefore be explained on this basis.[68]

My essay on Puritan names is a contribution to the now bourgeoning literature on Puritanism and social control.[69] It appeared the same year, 1979, as the classic study of the Essex village of Terling by Keith Wrightson and David Levine, but was designed to get round a methodological problem which seriously flaws their work. Wrightson and Levine essentially identify their Puritans on the basis of testamentary evidence, yet it is difficult to categorise even Protestants, let alone Puritans from their wills.[70] From the few passages which they quote, minimal Protestantism appears to equal Puritanism in their book. Moreover the further down the social scale the less religiously informative wills are. As a consequence everything appears to hang on the so-called 'will-making relationships', but these may not have been religiously determined. Thus it remains far from clear that the 'middling sort' in early seventeenth-century Terling were mainly Puritan, any more than they were in late Elizabethan Warbleton. Also, who in Terling reported the Puritan infractions of the law to the ecclesiastical authorities?[71] Apropos my own essay, one of the most striking facts to emerge was the existence of Puritan restrictions on the taking of interest as compared with the more frankly capitalistic attitudes of their non-Puritan neighbours. For the taking of interest, still pejoratively described as usury, is central to the argument of R. H. Tawney in his famous book *Religion and the Rise of Capitalism*; indeed it rates the biggest index entry. Whereas Max Weber invoked the idea of the Protestant ethic, fuelled by belief in predestination, as a driving force of early-modern capitalism, Tawney seems to have regarded the relaxation by Calvin of prohibitions on the taking of interest as being of at least equal significance. Ironically, however, by the mid seventeenth century English Arminian writers had become far more radical than Calvinists in such matters.[72]

IV

During the 1980s I was much preoccupied both with editing the seventeenth-century volume of *The History of University of Oxford*, inherited from Hugh Trevor-Roper in 1981, and getting the long-awaited monograph *Anti-Calvinists* into print. By then my 1973 essay in the Russell volume had begun to attract mounting criticism, which I was also concerned to take into account. Thus John Kenyon, in his *Stuart England*, published in 1978, dismissed Arminian-ism as a 'catch-all term of abuse'.[73] A much more sustained attempt at refutation, however, appeared in the journal *Past and Present* in 1983. The author, Peter White, was another of my former schoolmasters, but who had been assigned to teach me divinity not history, and I can still remember being asked by him to write an account of the teaching of St Paul on justification. Having recently encountered Gordon Rupp's *The Righteousness of God* (1953), the resulting exposition was couched in the Lutheran terms of justification by faith alone; although nothing was said explicitly, one got the distinct impression that the approach did not please. In the late 1960s I had returned to Wellington College to give a talk along the lines of my subsequent essay 'Puritanism, Arminianism and Counter-Revolution'. Afterwards White came up shaking his head and saying that he could not accept the argument. So his 1983 intervention in print should not have surprised me as much as it did.[74]

In the person of Peter White it could be said that the Anglican *via media* struck back. Indeed the idea of a Church of England middle way in doctrine was one of the original targets of my 1969 doctoral thesis, as can be seen most obviously from the official abstract.[75] Both a reply to White in *Past and Present* and the book *Anti-Calvinists* were published in 1987.[76] Meanwhile working on the history of Oxford University I had at last broken through the historiographical barrier of the mid seventeenth century.[77] The original commission from Trevor-Roper had simply been to write about 'new religious movements in Oxford, 1600–1630', but it seemed to me as editor that a much more worthwhile and also stimulating task would be to tackle the century as a whole. A UCL colleague, Jonathan Israel, also contributed to this re-education by inviting me to write about Puritanism in the context of the 1689 Toleration Act, as part of the tercentenary celebrations of the 1688 'Glorious Revolution'. In addition this provided a welcome opportunity to repair my previous neglect of Puritanism.

The resulting essay on toleration runs from 1571 to 1719, the keynote being that 'the time has come to restore Puritanism to its rightful place of political and religious importance'. While personally shouldering some of the blame for the previous deflation of Puritanism as a 'revolutionary force', the reference to its 'political' significance also alluded to recent accounts of Elizabethan and early Stuart parliaments.[78] Unfortunately the long timespan covered tended to diminish the impact of this essay and in particular the argument for the survival of Puritanism as 'an organised movement aiming at further reform of the English Church'.[79] Nevertheless I returned to the subject in my 1990 Friends of Dr Williams's Library lecture. This was published the same year as an important book by Jacqueline Eales on the Harleys of Brampton Bryan. Although Sir Robert Harley does not feature in my remarks, his own case history and religious circle more generally fits the argument for Puritan 'continuity' very well. In addition it is fascinating to note that Harley and Sir Thomas Wroth were on close religious terms by 1629, since the latter probably played a key role in the anti-episcopal agitation of 1640. Again some of the letters written to Harley during the early months of the Long Parliament and calling for radical ecclesiatical reform have striking similarities with parts of the surviving correspondence of Sir Edward Dering, Wroth's brother-in-law. At the same time, however, Eales points out how deeply offensive Arminian doctrine was both to Harley and his wife Lady Brilliana. Indeed she describes predestination as providing the 'core' and 'pivot' of their beliefs.[80]

'Money, organization and ideology give shape and substance to Puritanism under the early Stuarts' was the conclusion of 'The Fortunes of English Puritanism' (here chapter 4). Heading my list of donors was Sarah Venables and her bequest, in 1607, of over £2,500 on behalf of deprived clergy.

The will was contested in the Court of Exchequer, and it turns out that the bill, answer and final decree all survive.[81] The Attorney General, Sir Henry Hobart, argued on behalf of the crown that 'schisme in the Churche is noe lesse disturbance to the tranquilitie of quiet government of the state . . . then is sedition in the commonwealthe', and therefore 'in noe wise to be suffered, nor the persons infected therewithall to be countenanced'. Nevertheless those ministers, either suspended or deprived for nonconformity, are 'muche augmented in this theire obstinacie' by the financial support of 'certaine laie persons of theire secte and faction, whoe have them in admyracion as if they weare of extraordynarie purytie'. Whereas in the past such assistance came by 'pryvate and secret meanes' now 'it is growen by sufferance to suche a heade as that of late one Sara Venables, . . . transported in her affections' and with 'strange and intollerable presumption', has left the bulk of her estate – allegedly worth '£10,000 at the least' – to this cause. Hobart stressed the 'dangerous consequences that presidents [sic] of this kind will drawe on if private persons shall dare and be permytted' to maintain and reward schismatics. The court decreed that the money should go instead to poor 'conformable' clergy and the widows and orphans of nonconformists. But I was wrong to say that the 'relatives got nothing'; they in fact received £100.[82] The Venables case is also very important in the evolving concept at this time of an 'illegal charitable object'.[83]

Donations to Puritan clergy in trouble with the law can also, it transpires, be found earlier. Thus in 1588 Richard Walters, a London alderman, left £50 to such 'preachers as are put from their livings'. Two years later another London alderman, James Hewishe, bequeathed £20 for ministers who 'are or shal be silenced'.[84] Moreover if Stanley Gower, a protege of the Harleys, is to be believed, Lady Isabel Bowes, who died in 1622, spent £1,000 a year in support of Puritan clergy deprived for nonconformity. One of her pensioners apparently was Paul Baynes, the posthumous editing of whose works is discussed in 'Fortunes' (chapter 4). At the other end of the Jacobean scale was John Smith, rector of Clavering in Essex, who in 1616 left £20 to be divided between ten deprived clergy.[85] Meanwhile Sir Thomas Smith, some of whose Puritan patronage was revealed in 'Fortunes', persuaded the East India Company to disburse approximately £100 annually, between 1614 and 1621, to 'poore preachers'. He appears both to have initiated the scheme as governor and largely to have chosen the recipients. Although few names survive, in 1614 they included the '3 lecturers at St Antlins who have butt small meanes'.[86] The famous St Antholin's lectures had by 1628 been taken under the financial wing of the Puritan Feoffees for Impropriations. Suggestive, however, of their continued funding by the East India Company up to 1621, after which Smith ceased to be governor, is the fact that in 1622 the parishioners of St Antholin's petitioned the Court of Aldermen of the City of

London for 'some competent supply of maynteinance toward the dayly exercise of preachinge'. The committee of seven appointed to handle the matter included Sir Thomas Bennett and Sir Thomas Myddleton, the two surviving members of the group of four aldermen who in 1607 had so ostentatiously supported the Venables bequest on behalf of deprived ministers. The upshot was that from 1622 to 1629 the City contributed £40 a year to the St Antholin's lectures.[87]

Puritans also continued to meet during the reigns of both James I and Charles I, in order to plan strategy and tactics. In 1606, for example, there was a conference at the house of Lady Bowes, in Coventry, attended by, among others, Richard Bernard, John Dod and Arthur Hildersham. The additional presence at this conference of the future separatist John Smyth indicates that one of the aims was to prevent the fragmentation of the reform movement in the aftermath of the Puritan failure at the Hampton Court Conference. Similar agonising may have occurred in 1616 with the return to London of Henry Jacob from Dutch exile. Either individually or collectively Jacob consulted Dod, Richard Maunsell and Walter Travers, all deprived ministers, and allegedly received their approval for the setting up of an underground church – albeit in communion with the parish churches. Perhaps connected with this decision was the failure the previous year of another appeal to James I, when 'some discontented bretheren in London' had approached Peter Du Moulin 'with a bill of grevences to be represented to the King'. Renewed persecution under Charles I also encouraged such conferences, notably in 1633 at Ockley, in Surrey, on the eve of emigration to New England by John Cotton and Thomas Hooker. So the Midlands meeting of thirteen clergy in 1637, discussed in 'Fortunes', which Dod attended and which was concerned with subsequent New England developments, had clear antecedents.[88] In addition the whole question of the character of Puritan ecclesiology, whether congregational or presbyterian, continues to be debated.[89]

None of my essays so far discussed are biographical – a medium that has long seemed to me an unsatisfactory one for the historian to use, 'since the cycle from cradle to grave so easily becomes a substitute for explanation'.[90] In consequence I have always tended to work with a cast of many characters. A disadvantage of this, however, is that the intellectual development of an individual can come across as rather fragmented. Hence, in part, the decision to write at greater length about Archbishop Laud in another 'Problems in Focus' volume, this time edited by Kenneth Fincham on *The Early Stuart Church, 1603–1640* and published in 1993. The essay begins by seeking to distance itself from both the view of Laud as 'the greatest calamity ever visited upon the Church of England' and what is often seen as its alternative, namely that he was a fairly run-of-the-mill cleric of little originality.[91] More specifically my aim was to investigate the origins and evolution of the ideas of Laud, who like many other early Arminians appears to have begun with Calvinist convictions. At the same time it is clear that anti-Calvinism had deep roots, which in turn helps to explain Laud's own odyssey.[92] The essay furthermore makes the point that the attack in the 1630s on the previously dominant Calvinism was 'essentially secondary to the sacramental reorientation of English religious life now occurring'.[93] A missing dimension, however, is any discussion of the appeal which Laudianism undoubtedly had for some sections of lay society.[94]

Also in the course of working on 'religious controversy' at Oxford during the Restoration period, a question had arisen concerning parallel developments at Cambridge. My initial impression that the sources were poor for the other university was rapidly dispelled, thanks in particular to the splendid Joseph Beaumont archive at Peterhouse, Cambridge. This resulted in a comparative paper on 'Arminianism and the Theology of the Restoration Church', given at the eleventh Anglo-Dutch Historical Conference in 1991. Whereas the delicate balance of forces after 1660 at Oxford, between Calvinists and Arminians, apparently resulted in disputants there steering clear of the theology of grace, at Cambridge 'by the mid 1670s at the latest a full-blooded Arminianism emerged as the order of the day'. Of course predestination and its appendages was only one among a variety of Cambridge theological topics, but when such questions came up the Arminian position was regularly affirmed. Middleway doctrines, of the kind described by Archbishop Tillotson, do not seem to feature at all in this corpus of material. Moreover Beaumont himself was a product of the 1630s, having been at Peterhouse under Matthew Wren and John Cosin.[95]

The accuracy of the Cambridge picture which emerges from the papers of Beaumont is confirmed both by the published work of one of the disputants, whose theses he moderated as Regius professor of divinity, and by two surviving university sermons. In 1697 George Stanhope maintained as a Commencement thesis that the teaching of St Paul in Romans 8, 9 and 11 provided no support for the doctrine of unconditional predestination. Three years later, in 1700, he published at London a volume of his sermons treating of the 'change from an unregenerate to the truly Christian state' and with a dedication to Archbishop Thomas Tenison. In these sermons Stanhope discussed predestination at length and in an unmistakeably Arminian sense. Crucial here is sermon ix on 'The Nature of the Christian's Calling and Election, stated from the Parable of the Marriage Feast'. This takes as its text Matthew 22.14: 'For many are called, but few are chosen'. Stanhope's conclusion was 'that the election of God proceeds upon certain terms and qualifications, and although men are called by an act of mercy purely arbitrary, and without any respect to their behaviour, yet they are not chosen so'. Good works are 'the instrumental cause of our election and salvation'. Meanwhile at Cambridge on Commencement Sunday 1700 John Gaskarth preached in the morning and Offspring Blackall in the afternoon. Gaskarth drew a comparison between the 'unregenerate' and the 'truly Christian temper or state', and taught that God has put 'our happiness in our own hands, that thro the helps he has afforded us in his beloved Son we may obtain it to what degree we please'. Thus 'we lay the foundation of our after state . . . from our own behaviour.' Contrasted with this is any notion of an 'arbitrary' decree. Blackall in turn 'reconciled' the teaching of St Paul and St James, arguing that good works are a part of justification.[96] Taken together, Stanhope, Gaskarth and Blackall provide a remarkable chorus of support for the views of Beaumont in the year after his death in 1699.

Yet signs had been apparent much earlier that the days of Calvinism were numbered in the restored Church of England more generally. Evidence is cited below concerning the licensing activities of the chaplains of Archbishop Gilbert Sheldon, particularly as regards the anti-Calvinist works of George Bull which appeared in 1670 and 1676.[97] More high profile, however, was the involvement of the Archbishop in the publication of the works of Thomas Jackson, whom I have described elsewhere as 'the premier English Arminian theologian of the 1630s'. Jackson's collected works, consisting of three massive folios totalling over 3,000 pages and selling at £3 for the set, were published in 1673 with a dedication to Sheldon prefacing the whole. The editor, Barnabas Oley, singled out the Archbishop in this way both as a personal patron and, more importantly, as the literary executor of Jackson who had furnished the manuscript copies of books 10 and 11 of the latter's commentaries on the Apostles Creed.[98] These manuscripts had in fact first been published during the Interregnum, between 1653 and 1657, as part of an incomplete edition of Jackson's works and with a dedication to Sheldon in the third volume, which acknowledges his role and provides the additional information that the Arminian Henry Hammond had acted as an intermediary.[99]

Oley in his original 1653 'preface to the reader', reprinted in 1673, had sought to exonerate Jackson from the charge of Arminianism. He rather spoilt the effect, however, by going on to say that

> if the worst be given that this objection pretends to, the offence will be much asswaged if the ordinary reader do but know that the Lutheran, i.e. a consider-able part of the reformed church, is of that [Arminian] opinion, and that the other name is used mostly to inflame the *odium*.

Oley also singled out for special commendation the critique by Jackson of Calvinist teaching on 'assurance', a subject which had provided the flashpoint for the famous Calvinist disputes of the 1590s.[100] Moreover approximately a third of book 10 of Jackson's commentaries, as supplied by Sheldon, is taken up with the predestinarian question and in the first, 1654, edition this section is explicitly labelled 'Concerning Election and Reprobation'. While it is true that Jackson eschews the precise scholastic terms conventionally used in the Arminian dispute, he is quite categoric as regards election and reprobation that 'a great part of men, which have been baptised, are neither in the one state nor in the other'. They only become so in the course of their existence and according as to how they lead their lives, for the 'sons of God' by baptism may turn 'prodigal' and disinherit themselves. Jackson further argues, in book 11, that receiving the sacrament of holy communion is the chief means of repairing the inevitable lapses from grace which will occur.[101] Oley himself had been named in the early 1640s as 'a greate promoter' of Laudian 'innovations' at Cambridge, and his college, Clare, was said to have acquired the 'first altar in the university'.[102] The 1673 edition of the works of Jackson bears no *imprimatur*, probably because virtually all of it had been previously published, yet the implications of the very public associaton of Sheldon, Archbishop of Canterbury from 1663 to 1677, cannot have been lost on contemporaries. This after-life also contradicts the claim that Jackson rapidly 'faded from the limelight'.[103]

But what of Oxford University? 'Arminianism and the Theology of the Restoration Church' paints a picture of Oxford Calvinism grimly hanging on 'into the 1690s and beyond', most obviously in the person of Jonathan Edwards. Yet by 1711, when he published his *The Doctrine of Original Sin*, Edwards appears very much on the defensive. Thus, while affirming the existence of original sin against the Arminian Daniel Whitby, he was at pains to deny any attack on the 'Five Points' of Arminianism as such, and also distinguished the teachings of Arminius from those of later Remonstrants. In fact it was at approximately this same date that the crumbling walls of Oxford Calvinism seem finally to have fallen, with the publication there of *St Paul's Epistle to the Romans vindicated from Absolute or Unconditional Predestination* by Richard Roots.[104] Although as late as 1793 an edition of Edward Welchman's commentary on the Thirty-nine Articles was published at Oxford, in which the author concedes, as regards article 17 on predestination, that 'the grace of election is asserted in it' while adding that 'the severity of reprobation is left wholly untouch'd upon', the emergence of Calvinistic Methodism was to lead to an increasingly strident Oxford Arminianism from the end of the 1750s onwards. Authors such as William Hawkins and William Parker entered the lists in 1758 and 1759 respectively, the former writing of 'the absurdity of the doctrine of absolute predestination to life or death eternal' and the latter of 'enthusiastick writers' who fill people's minds with 'fantastick notions of their absolute predestination to life'. Moreover both Hawkins and Parker unhesitatingly interpreted the Thirty-nine Articles in an Arminian sense.[105] Similarly at Cambridge in 1759 Thomas Edwards attacked the 'absurd and uncouth doctrines of Calvinism', concerning 'irresistible grace' and 'absolute predestination'. Ten years later at Oxford succesive vice-chancellors, David Durell and Nathan Wetherell, and the Lady Margaret professor of divinity, Thomas Randolph, can be found publicly lending their authority to what had by now become something of an anti-Calvinist crusade.[106]

Whereas those writing about the Restoration religious scene tend to employ the descriptive labels 'High-Church' and 'Latitudinarian', the conclusion of 'Arminianism and the Theology of the Restoration Church' is that certainly prior to the Toleration Act of 1689 these terms are not very helpful. Many alleged Latitudinarians dragged their feet on the subject of absolute predestination and only espoused toleration late in the day. Indeed the enactment of religious toleration was a pragmatic rather than a principled response, as my earlier contribution to the tercentenary celebrations sought to demonstrate, if none the less crucial for all that. Furthermore the published proceedings of a conference held in 1987 on the subject of Latitudinarianism merely serve to reinforce such doubts. One of the editors, Richard Kroll, describes Latitudinarianism in his introduction as an 'excruciatingly vague' term, going on to recall that 'four days of often intense discussion yielded surprisingly little substantive or methodological agreement about the putative object of our pursuit'. The resulting essay, however, by Richard Ashcraft on 'Latitudinarianism and Toleration' in some ways complements mine, although the attempt to identify Dissent with rational theology seems a bridge too far.[107]

More generally *Philosophy, Science, and Religion in England 1640–1700*, edited by Kroll, Ashcraft and Perez Zagorin, like so much writing in the field, takes for granted that the English Civil War marks an intellectual watershed. Yet consideration of the century as a whole further encouraged me to question many of the assumed discontinuities. Hence when the time came to write the introduction to *Seventeenth-Century Oxford* it was the 'long-term pattern of development', in natural science and much else, that appeared especially striking.[108] Almost wherever one looked there were signs of growth, despite the political upheavals of the 1640s and 1650s. At the same time the impetus appeared to owe little to Puritanism as such. My own chapter on 'Religious Controversy' seeks to do justice to the variety of disputes involved, while identifying 'an obsession with Roman Catholicism' which 'was increasingly paralleled by alarm about a novel rationalizing tendency in religion'. Calvinist episcopalians are distinguished from Puritans, and Arminians from crypto-Catholics. On the other hand tackling a longer period served to connect the Arminian controversialist Richard Montagu, writing in the 1620s, with his Restoration equivalent George Bull. In between came Tristram Sugge, whose notebooks I effectively discovered at Christ

Church, Oxford, in 1986. Sugge, however, indulged in a form of religious brinkmanship which tends to set him apart. After 1660 Calvinist episcopalianism lived on in Thomas Barlow, and John Hall can be regarded as still representing the moderate Puritan tradition.[109]

V

But to play down the revolutionary intellectual results of mid seventeenth-century events in England does not commit one to the view of a static society, so much canvassed in certain revisionist quarters.[110] On the contrary, it serves to shift attention back to the changes of the sixteenth century and above all to the English Reformation. Here my role in organising a Neale Colloquium on the theme of 'England's Long Reformation, 1500–1800', which was held at UCL in 1996, provided the incentive to rethink the historiography in the light of the evidence. Confronted as a schoolboy with the choice between Sir Maurice Powicke's English Reformation as 'an act of state' and Gordon Rupp's Protestant-centred view, I had found the latter more convincing. Geoffrey Dickens' *English Reformation*, published in 1964, was broadly in the Rupp mould, but from the early 1980s a great raft of revisionist writing began to emerge – much of it a variation on the Powicke theme. Some of this work has been very salutory. Thus one hopes that the earlier caricatures of the medieval English Church and of Roman Catholicism more generally have been banished for ever, along with Whiggish assumptions about 'Protestantism and progress' and a profoundly biased reading of the reign of Mary Tudor. We should be duly grateful to revisionist historians for such lessons. Yet the new history of the English Reformation, with Protestantism largely left out, is in its own way as unsatisfactory as the old.[111]

Paradoxically, however, revisionist conclusions about the alienating effects of Protestantism highlight the novelty of the sixteenth century. For it was the English Reformation rather than the English Revolution a hundred years later that broke the mould. Indeed much of what happened in the mid-seventeenth century only makes sense in the context of previous developments. Whereas the religious radicalism spawned by the English Civil War has generated a specialist industry, Edwardian Protestantism remains by comparison sorely neglected. Nevertheless the 'commonwealth' group of the mid Tudor period clearly had a radical Protestant wing and one moreover which helped fire the rebellions of 1549; in the case of the East Anglian movement there appear to have been affinities too with the German Peasants' War of 1525.[112] This case is argued in my introduction to the Neale Colloquium volume, together with the more general proposition that the English Reformation needs to be understood in terms of a 'religious movement' as opposed to a series of high political manoeuvres.[113]

'Re-thinking the "English Reformation"' (here chapter 1) stresses the role of a 'clerical vanguard', emphasising the importance of Henrician Cambridge and a group there of reform-minded heads of house. The contrast with conservative Oxford broadly stands, although someone who escaped my notice was Robert Huick, fellow of Merton College, Oxford, and briefly principal of St Alban Hall in the years 1534–35. Huick had early on embraced the doctrine of justification by faith alone but clearly found Oxford a thoroughly uncongenial environment, describing it in 1537 as a place steeped in Pelagianism. He thereafter switched careers and by 1539 had re-emerged as a royal physician. Yet after his expulsion from the St Alban headship, in 1535, members of the hall petitioned Thomas Cromwell for his reinstatement; they claimed that his only crime was to have attacked scholasticism. Moreover two years later, in 1537, the Zurich reformer Rodolph Gualter on a visit to Oxford praised Magdalen College for its humanist and by implication evangelical sympathies. Long afterwards Gualter was also to recall that it was during this same Oxford visit that John Parkhurst of Merton, and a future Elizabethan bishop, began to profess 'pure faith in Christ'.[114] Again,

> in Lent 1539 an Oxford bookseller admitted that at least twenty fellows and scholars of Corpus Christi, Canterbury College, Oriel, Alban Hall, All Souls, King's [Christ Church], and Magdalen besides some townspeople had eaten flesh, which the authorities (including the chancellor) thought showed advanced Protestant leanings.

Parkhurst, now of St Alban Hall, featured among those named. Two other future Elizabethan bishops, Thomas Bickley and Thomas Bentham, were as fellows of Magdalen to disrupt Catholic services in the college chapel during 1548.[115] Despite such examples, however, Cambridge rather than Oxford provided the 'springboard' of reform, which in turn centred on south-east England and, above all, on London. Nor was it an accident that this area generated most resistance to the Marian restoration of Catholicism.[116]

Reformation teachings, however, not only challenged the premises of traditional Catholic religion but also introduced the possibility of choice. Whereas in the past heresy had been suppressed, in the sixteenth century a new marketplace of religious ideas emerged. Truth formerly one and indivisible was now fragmented into competing parts. Moreover repeated swings of the politico-religious pendulum favoured one group then another. The medium of print also played a transforming role; some seventeen editions of Tyndale's *New Testament* by 1536 may not sound very much,[117] yet for the reading public it was like water in a dry land. Given the duty to stamp out false beliefs, who, in an increasingly uncertain world, had the authority to judge? With state often pitted against church, others were able to enter the arena, and in consequence politics acquired a novel ideological dimension. The ending of

Roman Catholic monopoly meant that something of a Pandora's Box of aspirations was opened up. At its most extreme this might involve the right of resistance to the powers that be or a challenge to the existing social order – sometimes both. Albeit often repressive and intolerant, the new religion could also emanciptate.

Gain, however, usually involves loss. In his book *The Stripping of the Altars* (1992), Eamon Duffy has movingly reconstructed the 'traditional' religion of pre-Reformation England that was largely swept away during the sixteenth century. Nevertheless Protestant advance remained uneven and the religious situation generally in England by the accession of James I is far from clear. To what extent, for example, did so-called Prayer Book Protestantism[118] provide a new centre of gravity? Certainly the Elizabethan formularies were open to a wide variety of interpretation at both the popular and more elite levels. As regards the former a brand of residual Catholicism probably remained widespread, while among the Protestant intelligentsia the Calvinists and their Arminian critics came increasingly to vie for dominance. At the same time Puritans of various kinds continued to apply the logic of the Protestant appeal to the Bible, in the cause of further reformation.

Gradually English anti-Calvinists evolved into Laudians, being rechristened High-Churchmen from after about 1700, while Calvinist episcopalians were transmuted into Low-Churchmen or Latitudinarians – tending in the process to lose their original defining doctrinal characteristic. Puritanism, in its turn, hived off into Dissent. Yet the lines of development remain complex, with some Puritans surviving inside the established church, although at the parish level a form of Laudianism may well have become increasingly the order of the day from the later seventeenth century. More problematic still is the relationship between the disputes about predestination and the successor controversies concerning the Trinity. Granted a degree of overlap between Arminianism and Socinianism, apparently only in a small minority of cases did the one lead to the other. Yet a legacy of such debates was growing scepticism about the dogmatic claims of revealed religion, a frame of mind which has been deemed symptomatic of the English Enlightenment.[119] Protestantism would, indeed, prove a protean force.

NOTES

1 There was also the stimulus of my fellow pupils at Wellington College, who included the future historian Anthony Fletcher.

2 Taking as his starting point the model proposed by the mid seventeenth-century commentator James Harrington, R. H. Tawney claimed to have demonstrated that a shift in the balance of property holding, in favour of the gentry, had occurred before the Civil War and that this served largely to explain the subsequent conflict:

'Harrington's Interpretation of his Age', *Proceedings of the British Academy* 27 (1941), 199–223; 'The Rise of the Gentry, 1558–1640', *EcHR* 11 (1941), 1–38.

3 C. Hill, *The English Revolution 1640* (London, 1940, 3rd edn 1955), pp. 32–3; H. R. Trevor-Roper, *Archbishop Laud 1573–1645* (London, 1940, 2nd edn 1962), pp. 1–31; N. Tyacke, 'The Ambiguities of Early-Modern English Protestantism', *HJ* 34 (1991), 743–4.

4 The quotations are from a typescript in my possession, which is dated 13 May 1961; P. Heylyn, *Historia Quinqu-Articularis or a Declaration of the Judgement of the Western Churches, and more particularly of the Church of England, in the Five Controverted Points, reproched in these Last Times by the Name of Arminianism* (London, 1660), sig. Cv, pt i, p. 48. The Lambeth Articles (1595) were an attempt by Archbishop Whitgift to resolve a dispute about predestinarian teaching, which had broken out at Cambridge University.

5 N. Tyacke, *Anti-Calvinists. The Rise of English Arminianism c. 1590–1640* (Oxford, 1987, 2nd edn 1990); P. Heylyn, *Historia Quinqu-Articularis*, pt iii, p. 110.

6 H. C. Porter, *Reformation and Reaction in Tudor Cambridge* (Cambridge, 1958), p. 277.

7 Porter, *Reformation and Reaction*, pp. 338–41; P. Heylyn, *Cyprianus Anglicus or the History of the Life and Death of . . . William [Laud] . . . Archbishop of Canterbury* (London, 1671), pp. 28–9; Heylyn, *Historia Quinqu-Articularis*, pt iii, pp. 78–81, [89].

8 See also my 'Defining Arminianism', pp. 156–9 below.

9 Some present day commentators describe sublapsarians as holding a doctrine of 'single' as opposed to 'double' predestination, but this has always seemed to me highly misleading. For under this scheme the non-elect must still go to Hell, given God's unwillingness to save them.

10 J. Arminius, *Works*, ed. J. and W. Nichols (London, 1825–(75)), i, pp. 92–6.

11 The views of Baro are virtually indistinguishable from those of Arminius: *Works*, i, pp. 96–8, 549–93; Porter, *Reformation and Reaction*, p. 281; cf. S. F. Hughes, 'The Problem of "Calvinism": English Theologies of Predestination *c.* 1580–1630', in S. Wabuda and C. Litzenberger eds, *Belief and Practice in Reformation England: A Tribute to Patrick Collinson by his Students* (Aldershot, 1998), pp. 239–40.

12 J. Tillotson, *Works* (London, 1820), v, pp. 393–7.

13 Tyacke, *Anti-Calvinists*, pp. 24, 94–9; pp. 326–7 below. Arcane as such matters must at first sight appear, we need to remind ourselves of the key role ascribed to Calvinist teaching on predestination in Max Weber's extraordinarily influential work *The Protestant Ethic and the Spirit of Capitalism*, trans. T. Parsons (London, 1930).

14 During my Balliol scholarship interview, in January 1959, I had introduced this essay into a discussion with Hill on the origins of the English Civil War.

15 H. R. Trevor-Roper, *Historical Essays* (London, 1957), pp. 130–45. This account of the Jacobean Church was much later to receive its *coup de grace* at the hands of Kenneth Fincham: *Prelate as Pastor. The Episcopate of James I* (Oxford, 1990). Fincham's book began life as a London Ph.D. thesis, written under my supervision.

16 J. H. Hexter, 'Storm over the Gentry', in his *Reappraisals in History* (London, 1961), pp. 117–62. Having surveyed the wreckage of this controversy, however, Hexter in effect ended up calling for a return to the old Whig interpretation of the English Civil War as a struggle for liberty.

17 C. Hill, *Intellectual Origins of the English Revolution* (Oxford, 1965), p. 118; cf. B. Capp, *Astrology and the Popular Press. English Almanacs 1500–1800* (London, 1979), p. 194; see pp. 244–61 below. I was also well aware of the debate generated by Hill's lectures, conducted largely in the pages of the journal *Past and Present*: C. Webster ed., *The Intellectual Revolution of the Seventeenth Century* (London, 1974).

18 An example of this approach is T. M. Parker, 'Arminianism and Laudianism in Seventeenth-Century England', in C. W. Dugmore and C. Duggan eds, *Studies in Church History*, 1 (1964), 20–34.

19 The author of this standard work, first published in 1938 and which had reached an eighth edition by 1966, was master of Balliol and a benign presence during my time there.

20 These dates are derived from the printed course lists of the University of London School of History and Institute of Historical Research, the so-called 'White Pamphlet'. Sir John Neale, with whom Hurstfield had previously collaborated in running the 'Tudor History' seminar, died in September 1975.

21 I received a warm letter afterwards from Trevor-Roper, and in June 1970 he recruited me to write a chapter for the projected seventeenth-century volume in the then recently commissioned *History of the University of Oxford* series. (This volume finally saw the light of day, under my editorship, in 1997.) How far I convinced him may be judged by the essay 'Laudianism and Political Power', in his *Catholics, Anglicans and Puritans: Seventeenth Century Essays* (London, 1987), pp. 40–119. But certainly Hill remained more obdurate, as can be seen from the essay 'Archbishop Laud's Place in History', in his *A Nation of Change and Novelty. Radical Politics, Religion and Literature in Seventeenth-century England* (London, 1990), pp. 56–81.

22 C. Russell, *The Crisis of Parliaments. English History 1509–1660* (London, 1971), pp. 211–17.

23 C. Russell ed., *The Origins of the English Civil War* (London, 1973), pp. 5–6.

24 S. R. Gardiner, 'Leopold von Ranke', *The Academy*, 29 (1886), 380–1; K. Marx and F. Engels, *Selected Works. In One Volume* (London, 1968), p. 429. Ironically the Whig Gardiner had begun life as a Tory millenarian: N. Tyacke, 'An Unnoticed Work by Samuel Rawson Gardiner', *BIHR* 47 (1974), 244–5.

25 Russell, *Origins of the English Civil War*, pp. 8, 12, 17, 116.

26 Dare one suggest that this was the revisionist '*Ur-text*', for which Messrs John Morrill and Glenn Burgess have apparently sought in vain? J. Morrill, *Revolt in the Provinces. The People of England and the Tragedies of War 1630–1648* (London, 1976, 2nd edn 1999), pp. 1–10; G. Burgess, 'On Revisionism: An Analysis of Early Stuart Historiography in the the 1970s and 1980s', *HJ* 33 (1990), 609–27.

27 Elton was subsequently to become disenchanted with the notion of Arminianism, describing it as 'that mysterious entity which evades proper definition because it was really invented by Puritan controversialists of the seventeenth century and is too readily wheeled into the firing line by some modern historians'; Tyacke 'offers no really usable definition': G. R. Elton, 'Lancelot Andrewes', in his *Studies in Tudor and Stuart Politics and Government* (Cambridge, 1974–92), iv, pp. 167.

28 *HJ* 17 (1974), 213–15. For Elton's previous review of Stone, see *HJ* 16 (1973), 205–18.

29 Russell, *Origins of the English Civil War*, pp. 16, 19, 143. Some of the detail of my remarks about battle standards now needs revising in the light of I. Gentles, 'The

Iconography of Revolution: England 1642–1649', in I. Gentles, J. Morrill and B. Worden eds, *Soldiers, Writers and Statesmen of the English Revolution* (Cambridge, 1998), pp. 91–113.

30 M. Watts, *The Dissenters* (Oxford, 1978–95), i, p. 77; J. Morrill, 'The Religious Context of the English Civil War', *TRHS* 34 (1984), 178.

31 C. Russell, *The Causes of the English Civil War* (Oxford, 1990), *passim*; Tyacke, *Anti-Calvinists*, p. 245.

32 D. Cannadine, 'British History: Past, Present – and Future?', *P and P* 116 (1987), 171–3, 189–90; P. Lake, 'Wentworth's Political World in Revisionist and Post-Revisionist Perspective', in J. F. Merritt ed., *The Political World of Thomas Wentworth, Earl of Strafford, 1621–1641* (Cambridge, 1996), pp. 53–7.

33 A. Cobban, *The Social Interpretation of the French Revolution* (Cambridge, 1964). Cobban had earlier fired an opening salvo in his inaugural lecture of 1954, on 'The Myth of the French Revolution'; D. Johnson, *Guizot: Aspects of French History, 1787–1874* (London, 1963), pp. 321, 352–3.

34 The first postgraduate seminar that I attended at Oxford was conducted by Lawrence Stone, in the course of which he read us extracts from the draft of what became his famous *Crisis of the Aristocracy 1558–1641* (Oxford, 1965) – an obituary, in a sense, on the whole subject. Nevertheless, in terms of numbers, wealth and education the gentry themselves were transformed during the early-modern period.

35 P. Collinson, *The Elizabethan Puritan Movement* (London, 1967), pp. 448–67, 504, n. 38; N. Tyacke, 'Arminianism in England, in Religion and Politics, 1604 to 1640' (Oxford D. Phil., 1969), pp. 9–35; Tyacke, *Anti-Calvinists*, pp. 9–28.

36 W. Haller, *The Rise of Puritanism or The Way to the New Jerusalem as set forth in Pulpit and Press from Thomas Cartwright to John Lilburne and John Milton, 1570–1643* (New York, 1938, pbk edn 1957), pp. 21–2, 85–6, 173. His argument can, however, to some extent be rescued by defining 'Puritan' predestinarian teaching in so-called 'experimental' terms: R. T. Kendall, *Calvin and English Calvinism to 1649* (Oxford, 1979), pp. 5–9, 80. For my second thoughts more generally on Haller, see pp. 61–2 below.

37 P. Lake, 'The Significance of the Elizabethan Identification of the Pope as Antichrist', *JEH* 31 (1980), 178; see pp. 61–8, and pp. 111–31 below.

38 P. Lake, 'The Laudian Style: Order, Uniformity and the Pursuit of the Beauty of Holiness in the 1630s', in K. Fincham ed., *The Early Stuart Church, 1603–1642* (Basingstoke, 1993), p. 162; A. Milton, *Catholic and Reformed. The Roman and Protestant Churches in English Protestant Thought, 1600–1640* (Cambridge, 1995), *passim*; D. Hoyle, 'A Commons Investigation of Arminianism and Popery in Cambridge on the Eve of the Civil War', *HJ* 29 (1986), 419–25; cf. D. Oldridge, *Religion and Society in Early Stuart England* (Aldershot, 1998), who wants to separate 'theology' from 'church policy' and denies that an 'anti-Calvinist *coup*' occurred under Charles I: *ibid.* p. 23 and *passim*.

39 D. MacCulloch, *Thomas Cranmer. A Life* (Newhaven and London, 1996), pp. 210–11, 345, 405, 428; E. Bonner, *A Profitable and Necessarye Doctryne, with Certayne Homelies adioyned thereunto* (1555), sigs, Bii–Biv; J. Strype, *Ecclesiastical Memorials* (Oxford, 1822), ii, pt 2, p. 311; see also pp. 177–8 below.

40 See pp. 161–4 below; CUA, Misc. Collect. 10, Quaestiones Scholastice 1579–1584, p. 13. I am very grateful to Elizabeth Leedham-Green for providing me with a transcript

of this document. Tyndall was to play a leading role later in the suppression of Cambridge anti-Calvinism: Porter, *Reformation and Reaction*, pp. 364–5, 373; Tyacke, *Anti-Calvinists*, pp. 29–49, 58–81, 248–63.

41 See pp. 133–4 below; Collinson, *Elizabethan Puritan Movement*, pp. 243–88; P. Lake, *Anglicans and Puritans? Presbyterianism and English Conformist Thought from Whitgift to Hooker* (London, 1988), pp. 13–70.

42 See pp. 145–7 below; Tyacke, *Anti-Calvinists*, pp. 137–9; J. Eales, *Puritans and Roundheads. The Harleys of Brampton Bryan and the Outbreak of the English Civil War* (Cambridge, 1990), pp. 46–9, 52–3.

43 See p. 138 below; Tyacke, *Anti-Calvinists*, pp. 16–17; Collinson, *Elizabethan Puritan Movement*, pp. 313–14, 387, 452–4.

44 Tyacke, 'Arminianism in England', p. 9; Tyacke, *Anti-Calvinists*, p. 9.

45 B. Jonson, *The Magnetic Lady*, act 1, scene v, ll. 10–20; A. Barton, *Ben Jonson, Dramatist* (Cambridge, 1984), pp. xiv, 285–99. I owe this Jonson reference to Julie Sikkink. The middle way assumed in this passage is quite distinct from the Laudianism of the 1630s.

46 P. Collinson, *English Puritanism* (London, 1983), p. 42, n. 76. My own recollection is that all save one of these 'Arabs' realised their mistake before I started speaking. But were they actually Arabs? Turks, or even Armenians, would seem more likely.

47 A. E. McGrath, *Justicia Dei. A History of the Christian Doctrine of Justification* (Cambridge, 1986), i, pp. 17–23. For St Augustine's anti-Pelagian writings, see P. Schaff ed., *A Select Library of the Nicene and Post-Nicene Fathers of the Christian Church*, first ser. (New York, 1887), v.

48 A. E. McGrath, *The Intellectual Origins of the European Reformation* (Oxford, 1987), pp. 175–90.

49 See pp. 156–9 below.

50 K. Fincham and P. Lake, 'The Ecclesiastical Policies of James I and Charles I' in K. Fincham ed., *The Early Stuart Church, 1603–1642* (Basingstoke, 1993), pp. 23–4, 32; see also Fincham, *Prelate as Pastor*, pp. 248–93, P. E. McCullough, *Sermons at Court. Politics and Religion in Elizabethan and Jacobean Preaching* (Cambridge, 1998), pp. 101–55, and L. A. Ferrell, *Government by Polemic. James I, the King's Preachers, and the Rhetorics of Conformity, 1603–1625* (Stanford, 1998), pp. 113–66. The net effect of this more recent scholarship has been to emphasise the limits of any Jacobean 'consensus'.

51 Fincham and Lake, 'Ecclesiastical Policies of James I and Charles I', pp. 38–40.

52 P. Lake, 'The Laudian Style: Order, Uniformity and the Pursuit of the Beauty of Holines in the 1630s', in Fincham ed. *Early Stuart Church*, pp. 162, 168, 171, 181, 184; pp. 141–2 below. Ironically many of the sources cited by Lake were also quoted in my doctoral thesis, only to be sacrificed later in an attempt to produce a more streamlined account of Arminianism: Tyacke, 'Arminianism in England', pp. 237–76.

53 S. Doran and C. Durston, *Princes, Pastors and People: The Church and Religion in England 1529–1689* (London, 1991), p. 27; M. B. Young, *Charles I* (Basingstoke, 1997), p. 112; P. S. Seaver, *Wallington's World. A Puritan Artisan in Seventeenth-Century London* (Stanford, 1985), pp. 17–20, 35–44 and *passim*.

54 Porter, *Reformation and Reaction*, p. 408; J. Cosin, *Works*, ed. J. Sansom (Oxford, 1843–55), v, pp. 107–8, 119–20, 122. I am grateful to Kenneth Fincham for reminding me of the Epping incident.

55 Hill, *Intellectual Origins*, pp. viii, 5–7, 22–6; S. F. Mason, 'The Influence of the English Revolution upon the Development of Modern Science', *Modern Quarterly*, new ser. 4 (1949), pp. 169–77; S. F. Mason, *A History of the Sciences* (London, 1953), pp. viii, 138–50. (Both Hill and Mason can also be found writing sympathetically about T. D. Lysenko and the idea of 'proletarian' science: C. Hill, *Modern Quarterly*, new ser. 7 (1952), pp. 55–8; Mason, *History of the Sciences*, pp. 484–7.) The roots of this socio-religious interpretation of scientific developments can, of course, be traced back earlier: R. K. Merton, *Science, Technology and Society in Seventeenth-Century England* (Bruges, 1938, New York, 1970), p. 81 and *passim*.

56 Hill, *Intellectual Origins*, pp. 54–5, 301–14 and ch. 2 *passim*; pp. 254–7 below. Bizarrely, however, my essay has been described as 'arguing for links between High Church Anglicanism and science': J. Henry, *The Scientific Revolution and the Origins of Modern Science* (Basingstoke, 1997), pp. 82, 115.

57 T. K. Abbott, *Catalogue of the Manuscripts in the Library of Trinity College Dublin* (Dublin, 1900), pp. 59, 69, 129.

58 See p. 255 below; from my first 1973 essay onwards I have always tried to utilise visual evidence: p. 153 below.

59 See pp. 247–51 below; some of the Bainbridge material has now been published *in extenso* in J. Lorimer ed., *English and Irish Settlement on the River Amazon, 1550–1646* (Hakluyt Soc., second ser. 171, 1989), pp. 365–6, 385–6; N. Tyacke ed., *The History of the University of Oxford IV: Seventeenth-Century Oxford* (Oxford, 1997), pp. 1–3.

60 Tyacke, *Seventeenth-Century Oxford*, frontispiece.

61 M. Feingold, *The Mathematicians' Apprenticeship. Science, Universities and Society in England, 1560–1640* (Cambridge, 1984); M. Feingold, 'The Mathematical Sciences and New Philosophies' in Tyacke ed., *Seventeenth-century Oxford*, pp. 359–448. Unfortunately the second, 1997, edition of Hill's *Intellectual Origins* does not address any of the work published on the history of science since 1965. Moreover John Bainbridge has now been completely written out of the historical record since he appears as 'Jeremiah Bainbridge': *Intellectual Origins of the English Revolution Revisited* (Oxford, 1997), pp. 56, 279, 402.

62 Any more than the study by Charles Webster of the Towneley group in Lancashire commits him to a Catholic interpretation of the scientific revolution: C. Webster, 'Richard Towneley, 1629–1707, and the Towneley Group', *Transactions of the Historic Society of Lancashire and Cheshire*, 118 (1966), 51–76. At this stage Webster held out the possibility that the Towneley group 'may be representatives of a non-Puritan scientific movement of significant proportions': *ibid.* 76. Oddly, this interesting article goes unmentioned in Webster's *The Great Instauration. Science, Medicine and Reform 1626–1660* (London, 1975).

63 Fear-God Barebone was even more derivative than I realised, since the verses summing up his philosophy also occur in a manuscript of the late sixteenth century from the diocese of Ely. This also serves to correct my rendering of the third line which should read 'No woe to want' as opposed to 'No, no to want', and thus provides a more stoical flavour: D. M. Owen, *Ely Records. A Handlist of the Records of the Bishop and Archdeacon of Ely* (London, 1971), p. 31; cf. pp. 95, 105 below.

64 At the time of writing this essay, the classic study in the field, was Christopher Hill's *Society and Puritanism in Pre-Revolutionary England* (London, 1964).

65 M. M. Knappen, *Tudor Puritanism* (Chicago and London, 1939, Phoenix edn 1965), p. 462.

66 E. Topsell, *The Reward of Religion* (London, 1596), sig. * v, pp. 80–1. I owe this reference to Kenneth Fincham.

67 Northamptonshire Record Office, F.(M) P. 62. I owe this reference to Patrick Collinson. In his essay 'Cranbrook and the Fletchers: Popular and Unpopular Religion in the Kentish Weald', Collinson has suggested that Thomas Hely, the Puritan curate of Warbleton in Sussex, may have been the same person as Thomas Ely who appears earlier as curate of Cranbrook: P. Collinson, *Godly People. Essays on English Protestantism and Puritanism* (London, 1983), p. 416.

68 The quotations are from a facsimile version of the 1560 edition of the Genevan Bible. I am grateful to Michael Knibb for advice concerning Hebrew names; pp. 93–5 below. Confirmation of the comparative rarity of the type of Puritan name with which I was concerned is provided by S. Smith-Bannister, *Names and Naming Patterns in England, 1538–1700* (Oxford, 1997).

69 Some of this literature is reviewed in the revised edition of K. Wrightson and D. Levine, *Poverty and Piety in an English Village. Terling, 1525–1700* (London, 1979, Oxford, 1995), and the debt to Hill's *Society and Puritanism in Pre-Revolutionary England* (1964) is belatedly recognised: pp. 197–220. See also C. Hill, 'William Perkins and the Poor', in his *Puritanism and Revolution. Studies in the Interpretation of the English Revolution of the 17th century* (London, 1958), pp. 215–38.

70 For a recent example of the problems involved compare C. Litzenberger, *The English Reformation and the Laity. Gloucestershire, 1540–1580* (Cambridge, 1997), pp. 77, 121, 154, 168–78. See also a general critique in E. Duffy, *The Stripping of the Altars. Traditional Religion in England 1400–1580* (New Haven and London, 1992), pp. 504–23.

71 Wrightson and Levine, *Poverty and Piety*, pp. 158–62; pp. 98–102 below.

72 R. H. Tawney, *Religion and the Rise of Capitalism* (London, 1926, 1943), pp. 102–12, 175–6, 181, 210–11, 338 and *passim*; Weber, *Protestant Ethic*, pp. 95–154 and *passim*; C. J. Sommerville, 'The Anti-Puritan Work Ethic', *JBS* 20:2 (1981), 70–81.

73 J. P. Kenyon, *Stuart England* (London, 1978), pp. 99–100. Kenyon changed his mind in the second edition, stating that Laud and 'most of his clerical lieutenants clearly embraced the heresy of Arminius': *Stuart England* (London, 1985), pp. 9, 107–8. Only a year later, however, he contradicted himself in the second edition of his *Stuart Constitution* (Cambridge, 1966, 2nd edn 1986), pp. 131–4, which elaborates a more intransigent version of his original argument.

74 P. White, 'The Rise of Arminianism Reconsidered', *P and P* 101 (1983), 34–54.

75 Tyacke, 'Arminianism in England', p. i.

76 See pp. 160–75 below. A further reply to White was published in the *Journal of British Studies* for 1996: pp. 180–9 below. The foreword to the second (1990) edition of Tyacke, *Anti-Calvinists* also took up points raised by reviewers of the first (1987) edition: pp. vii–xv.

77 Historians of the British Isles, particularly as regards England in the early-modern period, are collectively guilty of an extreme narrowness of chronological coverage. Not

only are there Tudor and Stuart specialists, but these two centuries are further sub-divided. One consequence has been the establishment of a host of artificial distinctions.

78 G. R. Elton, *The Parliament of England 1559–1581* (Cambridge, 1986); C. Russell, *Parliaments and English Politics 1621–1629* (Oxford, 1979). Of course distinguished work continued to be carried out in the Puritan field, by historians such as J. T. Cliffe and Jacqueline Eales.

79 See p. 61 below.

80 J. Eales, *Puritans and Roundheads. The Harleys of Brampton Bryan and the Outbreak of the English Civil War* (Cambridge, 1990), pp. 39, 46–50, 61, 105–10; p. 127 below.

81 PRO, E 112/95/573b, E 126/1, fos 144v–45. I am most grateful to Simon Healy for having given me an induction course into this class of records, which does not yield its secrets easily.

82 *Ibid*; pp. 113–14 below.

83 G. Jones, *History of the Law of Charity, 1532–1827* (Cambridge, 1969), pp. 76–91.

84 D. Hickman, 'The Religious Allegiance of London's Ruling Elite, 1520–1603' (London Ph.D. 1996), pp. 263, 266–7.

85 C. M. Newman, '"An Honorable and Elect Lady": The Faith of Isabel, Lady Bowes', in D. Wood ed. *Life and Thought in the Northern Church* c. 1100–c. 1700 (Woodbridge, 1999), pp. 407, 415. Apropos the annual largesse of Lady Bowes to nonconformist clergy, Newman suggests that '£100 was probably far nearer the mark'; pp. 113–15 below; A. Wood, *Athenae Oxonienses*, ed. P. Bliss (London, 1813–20), ii, pp. 188–9.

86 BL, IOR B/5, pp. 243, 245; W. N. Sainsbury ed., *Calendar of State Papers Colonial. East Indies, China and Japan* (London, 1862–92), i, p. 439, ii. pp. 59, 214, 277, 311, 491, 493, 497, iii, pp. 179, 189.

87 D. A. Williams, 'Puritanism in the City Government 1610–1640', *Guildhall Miscellany* 1:4 (1952–59), pp. 5–8; p. 114 below. The committee of 1622 also included Sir Thomas Lowe, governor of the Levant Company (p. 5): A. C. Wood, *A History of the Levant Company* (Oxford, 1935), appendix iv.

88 Newman, '"An Honourable and Elect Lady"', p. 414; M. Tolmie, *The Triumph of the Saints. The Separate Churches of London 1616–1649* (Cambridge, 1977), pp. 7, 12–13; P. du Moulin, *A Letter of a French Protestant to a Scotishman of the Covenant* (London, 1640), p. 28; T. Webster, *Godly Clergy in Early Stuart England. The Caroline Puritan Movement*, c. 1620–1643 (Cambridge, 1977), pp. 58, 157–8.

89 S. Brachlow, *The Communion of the Saints. Radical Puritan Ecclesiology 1570–1625* (Oxford, 1988).

90 N. Tyacke, *History* 61 (1976), 288.

91 P. Collinson, *The Religion of Protestants. The Church in English Society 1559–1625* (Oxford, 1982), p. 90; K. Sharpe, 'Archbishop Laud', *History Today*, 33 (August 1983), 26–30.

92 Tyacke, *Anti-Calvinists*, pp. 60, 111–13; N. Tyacke, 'Lancelot Andrewes and the Myth of Anglicanism', in P. Lake and M. Questier eds, *Conformity and Orthodoxy in the English Church*, c. 1560–1660 (Woodbridge, 2000), pp. 9, 11–14.

93 See p. 218 below.

94 This last point will be developed in a book which I am writing jointly with Kenneth Fincham, under the working title *Altars Restored*.

95 See p. 4 above and pp. 331–2 below.

96 G. Stanhope, *Sermons preach'd upon Several Occasions* (London, 1700), pp. 252–308; J. Gaskarth, *A Description of the Unregenerate and the Truly Christian Temper or Estate* (Cambridge, 1700), pp. 28–9; O. Blackall, *St Paul and St James reconciled* (Cambridge, 1700). An even more striking example of Cambridge Arminianism is a sermon preached before the university by Robert Neville and published in 1682: *The Absolute and Peremptory Decree of Election to Eternal Glory Reprobated* (London, 1682). In this sermon Neville explicitly attacks the 'Contra-Remonstrants', that is to say the opponents of Dutch Aminianism (pp. 15–22).

97 See pp. 297, 307 below.

98 Tyacke, *Anti-Calvinists*, p. xiii; *Proposals Touching Subscriptions for Dr Thomas Jackson's Works Compleat* (London, 1672); T. Jackson, *Works* (1673), i, sigs (a)–(a)2; T. Jackson, *Works* (Oxford, 1844), i, p. xvii.

99 T. Jackson, *Maran Atha: or Dominus Veniet* (London, 1657), sigs A–A2v.

100 T, Jackson, *A Collection of the Works* (London, 1653), sigs [Av], ¶v–¶2; Jackson, *Works* (1673), i, sigs (b)v, (c)–(c)2; Porter, *Reformation and Reaction*, pp. 344–63.

101 T. Jackson, *An Exact Collection of the Works* (London, 1654), sig. ¶2; Jackson, *Works* (1673), iii, pp. 157–60, 174, 487–8.

102 BL, Harleian MS 7019, fo 84.

103 P. White, *Predestination, Policy and Polemic. Conflict and Consensus in the English Church from the Reformation to the Civil War* (Cambridge, 1992), p. 271.

104 D. Whitby, *A Discourse concerning the True Import of the Words Election and Reprobation* (London, 1710); J. Edwards, *The Doctrine of Original Sin* (Oxford, 1711), pp. 1–3, 12–13; in his reply, Whitby refers to the 'Calvinistick zeal' of Edwards: *A Full Answer to the Arguments of Dr Jonathan Edwards* (London, 1712), p. i; R. Roots, *St Paul's Epistle to the Romans vindicated from Absolute and Unconditional Predestination* (Oxford, ? 1711).

105 E. Welchman, *XXXIX Articuli Ecclesiae Anglicanae* (Oxford, 1793), p. 50; W. Hawkins, *Tracts in Divinity* (Oxford, 1758), i, pp. 159, 178, 182–7; W. Parker, *The Scripture Doctrine of Predestination stated and explained* (Oxford, 1759), pp. 6, 14, 38–44.

106 T. Edwards, *The Doctrine of Irresistible Grace proved to have no Foundation in the Writings of the New Testament* (Cambridge, 1759), pp. iii–iv, 3; T. Randolph, *The Witness of the Spirit* (Oxford, 1768), *imprimatur* by Durell, pp. 7–16; W. Hawkins, *The Pretences of Enthusiasts, as grounded in the Articles of the Church, considered and confuted* (Oxford, 1769), *imprimatur* by Wetherell, pp. 9–21; Wetherell in addition licensed the official answer to the Oxford Methodists, which also interpreted the Thirty-nine Articles in an Arminian sense: T. Nowell, *An Answer to a Pamphlet, entitled Pietas Oxoniensis* (Oxford, 1768), pp. 31, 103–18.

107 See pp. 76–7, 334–6 below; R. Kroll, R. Ashcraft, and P. Zagorin eds, *Philosophy, Science, and Religion in England 1640–1700* (Cambridge, 1992), pp. 2, 151–77.

108 The revolutionary results of the English Civil War lie elsewhere, most obviously in establishing the foundations of the fiscal-military state. Cf. J. Brewer, *The Sinews of Power* (London, 1989).

109 N. Tyacke ed., *Seventeenth-Century Oxford* (Oxford, 1997), pp. 1–24; pp. 262–319 below.

110 See especially J. C. D. Clark, *English Society 1688–1832. Ideology, Social Structure and Political Practice During the Ancien Regime* (Cambridge, 1985), and also his *Rebellion and Revolution. State and Society in England in the Seventeenth and Eighteenth Centuries* (Cambridge, 1986).

111 M. Powicke, *The Reformation in England* (London, 1941), p. 1; E. G. Rupp, *Studies in the Making of the English Protestant Tradition* (Cambridge, 1947); A. G. Dickens, *The English Reformation* (London, 1964); pp. 37–60 below. Nor should the concept of a 'Foxe-Dickens' interpretation of the English Reformation be allowed to pass unchallenged. Whatever may be the case as regards Geoffrey Dickens, to envisage John Foxe as 'Whig' is seriously misleading: C. Haigh, *The English Reformation Revised* (Cambridge, 1987), p. 2.

112 Some of the key documents have now been published by Ethan Shagan, who argues persuasively that Protector Somerset was engaged in a 'novel mode of popularity-politics': 'Protector Somerset and the 1549 Rebellions: New Sources and New Perspectives', *EHR* 114 (1999), 47, 53–63.

113 See pp. 37, 47–52 below.

114 *Letters and Papers . . . Henry VIII*, ix, no. 361, xii, pt i, no. 212, xiv, pt ii, no. 781, fos 78, 104b; P. Boesch, 'Rudolph Gwalthers Reise nach England im Jahr 1537', *Sonderabdruck aus Zwingliana*, 8 (1947), 452–3; H. Robinson ed. *The Zurich Letters (Second Series), 1558–1602* (Cambridge, 1845), p. 7.

115 C. Cross, 'Oxford and the Tudor State from the Accession of Henry VIII to the Death of Mary', in J. McConica ed., *The History of the University of Oxford III: The Collegiate University* (Oxford, 1986), pp. 131–2; *Letters and Papers . . . Henry VIII*, xiv, pt i, no. 684; J. R. Bloxham ed., *A Register of . . . Magdalen College* (Oxford, 1857), ii, p. xliii.

116 C. Haigh, *English Reformations. Religion, Politics and Society under the Tudors* (Oxford, 1993), pp. 207–8; R. Hutton, 'The Local Impact of the Tudor Reformation', in C. Haigh ed., *The English Reformation Revised* (Cambridge, 1987), p. 128; p. 40 below.

117 See p. 43 below.

118 J. Maltby, *Prayer Book and People in Elizabethan and Early Stuart England* (Cambridge, 1998).

119 H. R. Trevor-Roper, *Religion, the Reformation and Social Change* (London, 1967), pp. 193–236; E. Gibbon, *The History of the Decline and Fall of the Roman Empire*, ed. D. Womersley (London, 1995), iii, pp. 436–9; N. Tyacke, 'Ways out of (and into) Barbarism', *Times Literary Supplement*, no. 5058 (10 March, 2000), pp. 8–9.

Chapter 1

◆

Re-thinking
the 'English Reformation'

I

HISTORIANS of continental Europe are accustomed to taking a long-term view of the Reformation. Thus the modern discussion of its 'success and failure' ranges across both the sixteenth and seventeenth centuries, while Jean Delumeau's seminal treatment of the Counter-Reformation employs an even wider time frame.[1] The case as regards England, however, is somewhat different, where the Reformation remains largely corralled in the mid-sixteenth century and the recent revisionist accounts seek only to edge forward a few decades. Part of the explanation for this historiographical contrast lies in the still dominant English tradition of political interpretation, which treats the subject as first and foremost a succession of legislative enactments – culminating under Elizabeth I and followed by a fairly rapid collapse of Catholicism.[2] Continental historians, on the other hand, have been more willing to see the Reformation as a religious movement, and one furthermore that continued to be strongly contested.

Apart from this difference of approach, the English model requires glossing over a number of problems. Catholicism may have withered away, but how did a religion of the word (Protestantism) fare in a predominantly illiterate society? At least according to one account, itself a notable exception to the historiographic rule, magical beliefs came partly to fill the gap.[3] Related to this question are the deep divisions among Protestants, which resulted during the seventeenth century in the temporary destruction of the Elizabethan settlement of religion, with the Puritans and their Dissenter successors claiming to be the true heirs of the Reformation – a conflict of interpretation which the 1689 Toleration Act only served to institutionalise. There are indeed analogies to be drawn here between this internecine Protestant strife and the struggle on the continent between reformers and counter-reformers.

Moreover, the subsequent Enlightenment critique of all such bands of competing Christians, mounted during the eighteenth century, also owed a debt
to English thinkers.

Nevertheless, considerations of this kind are far removed from those of
most historians of the Reformation in England, where since the 1970s much
energy has been consumed in a prolonged bout of revisionist enthuslasm.[4]
According to this new account, the Reformation was imposed from above
upon an unwilling people, by a process both officially inspired and markedly
piecemeal; religious change came about only gradually and largely because
of the manoeuvrings of a section of the political elite; such was the enduring
strength of Catholicism that Protestantism remained for long a sickly plant,
its survival far from assured. These views are associated especially with the
historians Christopher Haigh and J. J. Scarisbrick, although they have received
powerful reinforcement from Eamon Duffy whose book concentrates more
on the fifteenth century. While the centre of gravity of Scarisbrick's *The
Reformation and the English People* is the earlier sixteenth century and the
focus of Haigh's various writings is rather later, they are two parts of a
related argument about Tudor religious developments. The thesis appears
firmly grounded on the evidence of bountiful Catholic religious giving as
recorded in the wills of the period, the building and adornment of churches
right up to the Reformation, items of expenditure in churchwardens' accounts
during the first half of the sixteenth century, flourishing lay confraternities
almost until the moment of their statutory abolition, and the high clerical
standards revealed by pre-Reformation episcopal visitations. All in all, the
English Church emerges from these documents as being in excellent shape
at the accession of Henry VIII. Hence revisionists reject what they see as an
essentially Protestant and triumphalist story of events thereafter, portraying
them instead as an accidental by-product of Tudor politics.[5]

Closer inspection, however, reveals this new interpretation to be an old
one resurrected. Specifically, it is a Catholic version propagated at the beginning of the twentieth century by Cardinal Aidan Gasquet and his protégé
H. N. Birt. Gasquet's book *The Eve of the Reformation*, published back in
1900, now seems remarkably prescient, drawing as it did on wills, churchwardens' accounts, records of lay confraternities, and visitation materials,
among other sources, to illustrate the healthy state of the pre-Reformation
English Church. Gasquet also suggested that the importance of anti-clericalism
had been much exaggerated, and this argument too has recently been revived.
But his main contention was that 'up to the very eve of the [Reformation]
changes the old religion had not lost its hold upon the minds and affections of the people at large'.[6] On the other hand, the concern of Birt, in his
1907 publication *The Elizabethan Religious Settlement*, was with the fate of
Catholicism under Queen Elizabeth. His conclusion was that

as in the case of the clergy, so in that of the laity, while some without doubt heartily embraced the change of religion, the majority of them were not favourable to it, but acquiesced outwardly for the sake of peace, not fully understanding the details of the differences between Protestantism and Catholicism.

At the same time, so Birt claimed, large numbers of Marian priests refused to submit to the Elizabethan regime, ministering instead to the Catholic laity, whom he characterised as numerically 'not only considerable, but formidable, far into the reign'. Readers will be struck here by the distinct anticipations of Haigh's arguments especially about the 'continuity of Catholicism' across the Reformation, and the merging of the old Marian priests with the younger generation of seminarians trained abroad, as well as the alleged religious conservatism of many nominal Protestants.[7]

There is, of course, nothing shameful about following in the footsteps of previous historians, even if it does rather detract from revisionist claims to novelty. Nor is a Catholic version of events inherently any worse than a supposedly Protestant one, although it may be no better. Yet doubts arise, particularly concerning the *relevance* of the type of evidence used by Gasquet and his modern equivalents to understanding the Reformation process. Revisionist historians usually distinguish the Reformation in England from that elsewhere, but similar signs of Catholic health can be found in many parts of continental Europe which were to turn Protestant.[8] Here indeed the original Gasquet version was distinctly superior, allowing as it did for a 'Lutheran invasion' concurrent with the Henrician break from Rome, whereas Luther does not rate a single mention in Scarisbrick's index – a telling, if extreme, example.[9]

Haigh offers us a stark choice between conceiving of the English Reformation as either 'from above' or 'from below'. Despite a further subdivision into 'fast' and 'slow', these are the basic options.[10] Reformation from below is linked pre-eminently, in this scenario, with the name of A. G. Dickens, who attempted the praiseworthy task of trying to provide a popular dimension to more traditional political accounts, along with emphasising 'the development and spread of Protestantism'.[11] But this Haighian 'choice' is largely illusory. Thus the concept of a Reformation from below, which we are asked to reject, is something of a revisionist straw man. In comparative continental terms it implies a broad popular movement only really conceivable if some kind of peasant revolt,[12] as in Germany, had interacted with the early stages of the English Reformation, yet even then the attitude of the magistrate would still have been decisive in the long run. Conversely Haigh's Reformation from above is defined extremely narrowly, in the high political terms of court faction. As a consequence a whole range of other possibilities are ruled out.

What, for example, of the intelligentsia and the role of ideas more generally? As on the continent, we need to take into account the very important part played by a clerical vanguard. Increasing signs of alarm were also registered by the English authorities over the influx of printed heretical literature. Thus May 1521 saw the formal burning of Luther's works at St Paul's Cross in London, with an accompanying sermon from Bishop Fisher of Rochester which sought, among other things, to refute the doctrine of justification by faith alone. There were similar book-burnings in Oxford and Cambridge at this time, as part of a nationwide campaign.[13] Yet by the mid-1520s a heretical network had developed, which embraced London and both universities. The upper echelons included at least two heads of Cambridge colleges, Thomas Forman of Queens' and William Sowode of Corpus Christi. Forman master-minded a trade in forbidden books from his London parish of All Hallows, Honey Lane. Arrested in 1528, he died the same year – his 'Lutheran' views on justification recorded for posterity in the hostile pages of Thomas More. Nevertheless the successors of Forman at Queens', Simon Heynes (1528) and William May (1537), turned out to be of a similar religious persuasion to him, as was Matthew Parker who followed Sowode at Corpus Christi in 1544. By this last date St John's (John Taylor: 1538) and Pembroke (Nicholas Ridley: 1540) had joined the roster of colleges with reformist heads. We should probably add to the list Peterhouse, where the master, John Edmunds, died a secretly married man in 1544, and Christ's whose master, Henry Lockwood, sponsored the performance that year of a Lutheran play. In addition, between 1528 and 1538 King's had a reformist provost in the person of Edward Fox.[14] Fellows of like mind can be found across the university as a whole and heretical works regularly show up in the inventories of individual Cambridge scholars from the 1530s onwards. During the same decade William Turner of Pembroke College was translating, for English publication, continental propaganda in favour of the 'new' religion. Oxford undoubtedly lagged behind, only acquiring a clearly reformist head with Richard Cox, already in trouble for his religious views in the late 1520s, as Dean of Christ Church in 1546, and continental reformed theology seems to have been much less widely available there'.[15] Even one English university, however, was springboard enough.

By the beginning of the 1530s the authorities had condemned over twenty heretical works in English and many more in Latin.[16] Whereas a few years earlier it had been thought sufficient to catalogue the errors of Luther, now this treatment was extended to his fellow reformers as well as to a new breed of English language authors. From the mid-1520s some of the most intrepid English evangelists had journeyed to Luther's Wittenberg itself, while a favoured port of call by the later 1530s was Bullinger's Zurich, this last with the personal blessing of Archbishop Thomas Cranmer. Also during the 1530s works by Bullinger and Luther became available in English, along with others by Bucer, Lambert and Osiander; Melanchthon and Zwingli were added to the list in the early 1540s.[17] Here, however, revisionists are able to counter that the bulk of the population was illiterate. Yet the spoken word is not constrained by such barriers and, as on the continent so in England, preaching proved central to the spread of what retrospectively was called Protestantism. The amount of preaching is unquantifiable, but we can cite as indirect evidence an instruction on this subject issued by Archbishop Cranmer in 1534. It appears to have been triggered by the reformist sermons of Hugh Latimer at Bristol but clearly had a much wider reference, other foci for example being the similar preaching of John Bale at Doncaster and that of Thomas Rose at Hadleigh in Suffolk. Cranmer stipulated that no one for a year should preach either for or against 'purgatory, honouring of saints, that priests may have wives, that faith only justifieth', the making of 'pilgrimages' and the working of 'miracles', since these 'things have caused dissension amongst the subjects of this realm already'.[18] But that the orthodox Catholic view should now be a matter of doubt shows just how rapidly ideas were changing, courtesy in part of the pulpit.

Revisionists usually couch their accounts of the English Reformation in terms of the history of parliamentary legislation, yet this produces a very distorted picture. At the official level indeed it remains vital to distinguish between the Henrician and Edwardian Reformations, because only after 1547 was Protestantism established. Nevertheless there is an underlying trajectory of evangelical activity from the 1520s and through into the 1550s. At this unofficial level the allegedly piecemeal nature of the Henrician Reformation makes much less sense. Granted considerable wells of indifference or plain muddle, plenty of evidence also exists of growing polarisation between the advocates of the 'new learning' as opposed to the 'old learning', by which is meant religion. (The contemporary state papers are littered with such references.) Compared with this, the leading parliamentary issues of the 1530s, such as the royal supremacy and the dissolution of the monasteries, were relatively uncontentious matters. Therefore the argument that the Reformation crept up unnoticed on the educated classes presupposes an extraordinary insensitivity on their part to what was happening under their noses.[19] Take, for instance, the electrifying sermons preached to the Convocation of Canterbury, in June 1536, by Latimer. Having previously been accused of 'erroneous preaching' on purgatory and the veneration of images, he now daringly threw the charges back in the faces of the assembled clergy. Even more boldly he bracketed his own case with that of William Tracy, a Gloucestershire gentleman who was posthumously burned in 1531 for having made an heretical will. Speaking of 'purgatory pick-purse' and 'deceitful and juggling images', Latimer invoked instead 'Christ's faithful and lively images' – the poor – lying 'wrapped in all wretchedness'. Originally preached in Latin, the sermons were published in English translation the following year.[20]

It is true that royal proclamations against the publication and sale of heretical books continued to be issued until the end of Henry VIII's reign. In practice, however, during the 1530s it became much easier to publish such works in England. For example *The Parable of the Wicked Mammon* by William Tyndale, originally printed at Antwerp in 1528, came out openly in a London edition of 1536 and moreover under his own name. Teaching 'just-ification by faith only' in combination with a powerful statement concerning the necessity of charitable 'deeds' by the righteous, this book had previously been condemned by royal proclamation'.[21] Similarly London editions of works by Luther himself now appeared, albeit not identifying the author. One key figure here was the printer James Nicholson of Southwark. There was also a range of quasi-official publications, which propagated the thinking of con-tinental reformers. A treatise by Martin Bucer, arguing against the placing of images in churches, was printed at London in 1535, the translator William Marshall being a publicist regularly employed by the royal minister Thomas Cromwell. The latter was also the dedicatee next year of an English transla-tion of the Augsburg Confession – the Lutheran formulary of faith.[22]

Most striking of all, however, is the so-called 'Matthew' Bible published in 1537 under royal licence. Largely the work of Tyndale, this not only included his notorious prologue to the Epistle to the Romans, and other heretical marginalia, but was further supplemented with a 'table' of 'principal matters' lifted wholesale from the first French Protestant Bible of 1535. This table, by the unacknowledged 'Matthieu Gramelin', provided a conspectus of reformed teaching which was quite uncompromising in its message. The 'mass', for example, is condemned as not to be found in the Bible, the reader being cross-referenced to 'supper of our Lord' which is defined as 'an holy memory and giving of thanks for the death of Christ'. 'Free will' is rejected as equally unscriptural, religious 'images' are described as 'abominations', and there is a ringing declaration that 'we are all priests to God'. Dismissed too are auricular confession, ceremonies, holy days, merit, purgatory and traditions. Justification by faith alone is affirmed, and a predestinarian strand runs throughout the whole. This was the Bible, published by Richard Grafton and Edward Whitchurch, about which Cranmer wrote to Cromwell that the news of its licensing was more welcome than the gift of a thousand pounds. Drawing on both French and German sources, the work is truly international in character. As for 'Matthieu Gramelin', he was in reality Thomas Malingre, pastor of Neuchâtel, which perhaps best explains why the English compiler John Rogers chose the pseudonym Thomas Matthew.[23]

Between 1534 and 1538 annual numbers of English reformist publications, printed both at home and abroad but omitting Bibles and prayer books, rose from about four to ten, at which point they heavily outnumbered equivalent works of Catholic orthodoxy. Moreover by 1536 Tyndale's New Testament had gone through at least seventeen editions, published abroad and smuggled into England; with its notes and prologues partly derived from Luther, this was one of the most important sources of reformed teaching available. (As early as November 1526 Archbishop Warham had complained of the 'great number' of Tyndale New Testaments circulating in the province of Canterbury.)[24] The widening opportunities in the 1530s for English reformers, whether in press, pulpit or academe, undoubtedly owed a great deal to the benevolent patronage of Queen Anne Boleyn, Cromwell and to a lesser extent Cranmer.[25] Conversely the 'reaction' which set in from 1539 is graphically illustrated by the history of religious publication. Reformed output collapsed that year, with only some three possible candidates and remained at around this level until 1543 when numbers briefly surpassed the previous peak of 1538. For the rest of Henry VIII's reign the figure averaged about six books, although they were now generally published abroad. It was also during these last years, however, that Parker at Cambridge and Cox at Oxford were moving into strategic university positions, as vice-chancellor (1544–45) and Dean of Christ Church respectively. Cox was to become chancellor of Oxford in 1547, when Parker was again elected vice-chancellor of Cambridge.

A fascinating glimpse of the febrile religious situation at late Henrician Cambridge comes from a letter which has been ascribed to early 1545, written by Roger Ascham of St John's College to Cranmer. Ascham reported that 'the doctrines of original sin and predestination' were being debated between supporters of the modern Catholic theologian Albertus Pighius on the one hand and the followers of St Augustine on the other – among whom he numbered himself. But what he did not spell out was that the two principal targets of Pighius's book were Luther and Calvin.[26] At about the same time Christ's College had staged a performance of a play by Thomas Kirchmeyer, entitled *Pammachius*. A full-blooded attack on Catholic teaching from the Lutheran standpoint, this had been published at Wittenberg in 1538 with dedications to both Cranmer and Luther. Despite certain cuts having been made in the original, Stephen Gardiner, the university chancellor and a leading religious conservative, was still furious. Nevertheless Parker, as vice-chancellor, stood his ground, claiming that 'none . . . were offended with any thing that now they remember was then spoken'.[27]

Historians are understandably hesitant about using the word 'Protestant' in the early phase of the Reformation, because of the fluidity of the situation. They prefer instead the term 'evangelical'. But the problem still remains how far the first generation of English evangelicals developed out of orthodox Catholicism or were recruited instead from a still-living heretical tradition. Thus the significance of Lollardy has been much debated. The work of

Dickens, among others, has clearly demonstrated the continued existence of Lollards, often wrongly categorized as Lutherans by the ecclesiastical authorities. There are also recorded instances of Lollards making contact with the new continental reforming current, and literally discarding their old Wycliffite Bibles for Tyndale's New Testament. In addition, they played some part in the distribution of illegal printed literature.[28] Yet it would appear, on the face of it, that the intellectually deracinated nature of Lollardy made for a fairly limited role by the time of the Reformation. Academic Lollardy had been effectively wiped out during the first half of the fifteenth century, and it is striking that the majority of Lollard writings which survive do so in manuscripts dating from the same early period. Nevertheless there exists at least one reference to an apparently Lollard scriptorium, or writing shop, in Henrician London. More tantalizing still is the possibility of Lollard involvement in the production of Tyndale's New Testament.[29] Lollards may also have participated in the growing popular iconoclasm, which is detectable from the late 1520s. This involved both the destruction of wayside crosses and the burning of roods, although these outbreaks seem to have been stimulated by radical preachers such as Thomas Bilney and Thomas Rose. Some of the heat was subsequently taken out of the situation, when the Henrician government itself embarked on a policy of limited iconoclasm in the 1530s.[30]

Anticlericalism is an especial *bête noire* of the revisionists. They are quite correct that most parishioners seem to have been satisfied with their local clergy. There is also the obvious point that clerics spearheaded the Reformation. Yet in seeking to reduce anticlericalism to the grievances of common lawyers, hungry for the business of church courts, revisionists are in danger of scoring an own goal. For it is precisely the legal fraternity that one would expect to produce a challenge to the near-monopoly of learning exercised by the upper ranks of the late medieval clergy. Not for nothing have the London Inns of Court been called the 'third university' of England, and only in the course of the fifteenth century was the previous clerical dominance of the central government bureaucracy undermined by members of the laity.[31] Some of the earliest and most committed lay support for the Reformation was in fact to come from lawyers. Here a particularly interesting group comprised James Baynham, Simon Fish and Richard Tracy. Tracy's father William was, as we have already remarked, posthumously burnt as a heretic in 1531. Tyndale, who knew the family, later remarked that Tracy senior 'was better seen in the works of St. Austin [Augustine] twenty years before he died than ever I knew doctor in England'. The son followed in his father's religious footsteps, while Baynham who was William Tracy's nephew, and like Richard a member of the Inner Temple, was burnt to death as a heretic in 1532. Baynham had also married the widow of Simon Fish of Gray's Inn – author of the notorious *Supplicacyon for the Beggers* (1529), which attacked the doctrine of purgatory, monasticism and the clerical estate in general.[32] Fish was in addition involved in importing the earliest editions of Tyndale's New Testament from abroad and in their sale in England. Not surprisingly merchants too were crucial in this clandestine enterprise, and one very important early figure was Richard Harman of Antwerp, London and Cranbrook in Kent, operative from about 1526.[33]

Revisionists are prone to belittle the power of ideas in bringing about the Reformation, emphasising what they see as almost the irrelevance of theology. Yet this is seriously to neglect the subversive potential particularly of the doctrine of justification by faith alone, undermining as it did the whole panoply of medieval Catholic teaching and practice built on the notion of spiritual good works. Reformation teaching had the effect of making largely irrelevant the great round of masses, prayers, penances, pilgrimages and related observances. It also radically reduced the role of both priests and ecclesiastical institutions. At the same time material grievances against the clergy certainly existed, and in the early 1530s cases as far apart as Devon and Lancashire can be found of literally murderous assaults on priests seeking to levy mortuary or burial fees. Resistance on this issue, however, appears to have been greatest in London.[34] There too the question of church tithes provided a long-running dispute, particularly from the late 1520s to the mid-1540s, and one initially linking up with attacks on Cardinal Wolsey. Religious reformers were not slow to capitalise on such material grievances, some of which spilled over into the Parliament which met in 1529.[35]

For much of the 1530s the evangelicals appeared to be riding high, their aims increasingly coinciding with official government policy. Yet it was always something of a marriage of convenience, influenced by the exigencies of the international situation, and Henry VIII was never truly won over. But although the reformers failed in the event to capture the Henrician regime, they were not dislodged from their English strongholds. Susan Brigden, for example, has drawn attention to 'the activities of a band of more than fifty reforming clergy in London in Henry's last years'. Like the London printers of reformist works, most lived to fight another day and indeed attracted new recruits to their ranks.[36] Moreover even in 1542 an almost despairing note crept into a draft proclamation against heretical books in English which have 'increased to an infinite number and unknown diversities of titles and names'. Meanwhile at Norwich, the second city of the kingdom, in February 1539 the conservative Bishop Rugge had been publicly refuted by the evangelical Robert Watson in a classic continental-style debate on the freedom of the will, as a result of which Watson apparently won over the mayor and corporation to his views.[37] With the change of monarch, both cities witnessed religious reform at the parish level running ahead of government orders. In London images began to come down almost immediately on Edward VI's accession in 1547, and by September iconoclasm was far advanced. Similarly, on 17 September 1547, the Norwich Mayor's Court debated

> a great matter . . . concerning diverse curates and other idle persons within the city, which hath unlawfully and without authority and commandment enterprised to rifle churches, pulling down images and bearing them away.[38]

The same month, in what threatened to become a major scandal, the pyx over the altar at St John's College, Cambridge was desecrated. That October the parishioners of Great St Mary's, the Cambridge University church, voted to sell their silver-gilt crucifix.[39]

Also unauthorized was the subsequent attack on the mass, London preachers and printers weighing in along with 'irreverent talkers' and 'revilers' more generally. A rash of books and ballads appeared on this subject in 1548, some of them extremely scabrous. While the government moved forward rather gingerly, Londoners especially were making a much faster pace – emboldened by the knowledge that Protector Somerset and his circle favoured change.[40] At Cambridge too the evangelicals can be found straining at the leash. Thus in late 1547 a group of reformist fellows at St John's College held a disputation on whether the 'mass' and the 'supper of the Lord' were the same thing. Proceedings were then transferred to the divinity schools, until halted by anxious university authorities. In these circumstances Ascham put pen to paper, excoriating the 'Romish abuses' of the eucharist and proclaiming 'behold the mass of the Pope which takes away the supper of the Lord'.[41] Not until mid-1549 was the mass formally condemned by the universities, the year when altars began to be demolished in Norwich – again in advance of official instructions.[42]

Yet between 1547 and 1549 a Protestant Church was established in England. During the summer of 1547 a Book of Homilies was issued, the central reformist message of which was that works played no part in justification. Chantries were abolished that December, the parliamentary statute including an explicit attack on the doctrine of purgatory. This was followed by an Order of Communion, introduced in April 1548 and subsequently expanded into the Prayer Book of 1549. As regards the latter, Eamon Duffy has commented that it represents a 'radical discontinuity with traditional religion', eliminating 'almost everything that had till then been central to lay eucharistic piety'. These and other changes were enforced by accompanying visitations, commissions and injunctions. In February 1548 the Privy Council ordered all images to be removed from churches and, on the evidence of surviving churchwardens' accounts, the process of iconoclasm would appear to have been 'virtually complete' by the end of the year. The same source indicates that windows were reglazed and walls whitewashed, as part of the purge. Although parishes were slow to acquire the Book of Homilies, purchase of the Prayer Book, published by Grafton and Whitchurch, was enforced effectively – the old Catholic service books being either destroyed or sold. More generally, Ronald Hutton concludes that at this time there 'crashed a whole world of popular religion'.[43] In addition, from 1549 priests were allowed to be married. At Oxford and Cambridge Peter Martyr and Martin Bucer were installed respectively as Regius professors of divinity – thus bringing continental reformed theology more directly to bear on the English universities. Meanwhile reformist literature poured off the London printing presses. Along with the greatly expanded numbers of works by English and continental writers now being published, Matthew Bibles and Tyndale New Testaments became much more widely available in various sizes, and on a sliding scale of prices.[44]

II

In the course of 1549, however, England was wracked by social disturbances, some of which escalated into full-scale rebellions. That in the west country took the religious form of Catholic opposition to the liturgical changes introduced by the Edwardian regime. But, as Diarmaid MacCulloch has noted, the 'further east one goes, the more positive enthusiasm for the new religion one finds' among the protesters. This is especially the case as regards Essex, Norfolk and Suffolk. We know from the reply of the Privy Council that the Essex rebels buttressed their grievances with biblical texts, and claimed to 'greatly hunger' for 'the Gospel'. Other letters to the Norfolk and Suffolk rebels speak of them 'professing Christ's doctrine in words', while showing 'the contrary fruit' by their deeds.[45] Given the combined influence of Cambridge, Norwich and London, the distinctive religious tone of social protest in this part of England is perhaps not surprising. The sole surviving list of articles from these three counties is that drawn up by the group of Norfolk rebels led by Robert Kett, and camped on Mousehold Heath outside Norwich. It was A. F. Pollard, today a deeply unfashionable historian, who suggested a possible link between the Kett list of requests and the Twelve Articles of Memmingen produced in 1525 during the German Peasants' War. Comparison of the two documents tends to bear Pollard out, especially if allowance is made for the different socio-economic context and the more polished nature of the Memmingen articles.[46]

Both the Kett list of requests and Memmingen articles combine calls for change in religion and society, each asking for clergy to be *chosen* by their parishioners and able to preach the 'word of God' (Kett no. 8) or 'holy gospel' (Memmingen no. 1). The Kett list of requests elaborates further on the imperative for a resident minister, to give religious instruction (nos. 15 and 20). The two lists also share a desire to limit tithe payments (Kett no. 22 and

47

Memmingen no. 2). As regards secular grievances, there is a mutual concern with the need to reduce rents (Kett nos. 5, 6 and 14 and Memmingen no. 8), the restoration of rights to common land (Kett nos. 3, 11 and 13 and Memmingen no. 10), freedom of river fishing (Kett no. 17 and Memmingen no. 4), and the abolition of serfdom – albeit there was only a remnant left in England (Kett no. 16 and Memmingen no. 3). At the same time the Kett list of requests exhibits many specific differences from that of Memmingen, not least because the former itemised more than twice as many grievances. Moreover unlike the Memmingen articles, which speak of 'Christian justice', those produced by the Norfolk rebels do not enunciate any underlying philosophy.[47]

Contemporary rumours existed concerning 'Anabaptist' involvement in East Anglia, yet the rebels seem to have taken their cue from more mainstream reformers. Interestingly Cranmer, in a sermon preached at the height of the disturbances in 1549, spoke not of Anabaptists but rather of a report 'that there be many among these unlawful assemblies that pretend knowledge of the gospel and will needs be called gospellers'. On the other hand it is important to remind ourselves that barely a decade previously the government had nipped in the bud a Norfolk conspiracy which involved similar social grievances, although combined on this earlier occasion with Catholic opposition to religious change. Among those then executed were a number of priests.[48] During 1549 a servant of the Catholic Princess Mary was said to be active in Suffolk and a Catholic priest, John Chandler, seems to have played a leading role in the rebel camp outside King's Lynn in Norfolk.[49] The rebels, however, under Kett's captaincy were ministered to religiously by reformers such as John Barret, Thomas Conyers, Matthew Parker and Robert Watson. After the event these clergy were keen to explain their role exclusively in terms of attempting to persuade the rebels to rely on the goodwill of central government and go home quietly. But some of them may have had a hand in formulating, and possibly toning down, the list of grievances.[50]

The rebellions of 1549 took place against a background of galloping price inflation, fuelled by the government's own policy of debasing the coinage, and in the context of what many contemporary commentators perceived as a loss of social cohesion due to the rise of unfettered economic individualism, which they characterised in the traditional terms of 'avarice', 'covetousness' and 'greed'. Moreover by the eve of the rebellions a printed literature on the subject was already in existence, among the best known examples being *An Informacion and Peticion agaynst the Oppressours of the Pore Commons of this Realme*, written by Robert Crowley and published probably as early as 1547. Crowley was at this date a layman and reformist London printer, subsequently being ordained in 1551. Ostensibly addressing Parliament, Crowley put the case for social reform in terms of Christian stewardship. 'Take me not here that I should go about to persuade men to make all things common', but 'if the possessioners would consider themselves to be but stewards, and not lords over their possessions, this oppression would soon be redressed'. Such, says Crowley, is the teaching of the Bible, and he compares himself to a prophet sent by God, quoting Isaiah 5.8: 'Woe be unto you therefore that do join house unto house, and couple one field to another, so long as there is any ground to be had'. Landlords were lashed by Crowley as 'murderers' of the 'impotent', who died 'for lack of necessaries', and 'causers' of 'stealing, robbing and revenge', by withholding the earth from the 'sturdy' who 'should dig and plough their living'. He was equally unsparing of the 'hireling' clergy. Particularly arresting, however, is the following passage from his conclusion:

> Wishing unto you (most worthy councillors) the same spirit that in the primitive church gave unto the multitude of believers one heart, one mind, and to esteem nothing of this world as their own, *ministering unto every one according to his necessities.*

Crowley and his like trod a narrow path here between permitted criticism and social subversion, as his disclaimer of communism makes plain.[51]

The genealogy of the ideas expressed in Crowley's *An Informacion and Peticion* can be traced back to the earliest writings of the English reformers and via them to the very beginnings of the continental Reformation. Such social teaching was indeed much older, but had been recast by the reformers in the light of their attack on Catholic views concerning good works. Not only does faith alone justify, but the works which are its necessary fruit differ. Essentially one should give to the poor and not to the Church. The reformers aimed to transfer the urgency with which Catholics strove for a place in heaven to the living of a truly Christian life on earth. This twin-track agenda is evident, for example, in Tyndale's *Parable of the Wicked Mammon* (1528). 'Deeds are the fruits of love, and love is the fruit of faith.' These deeds 'testify' to faith and relate above all to the manner in which Christians treat their neighbours. 'Among Christian men, love maketh all things common; every man is other's debtor, and every man is bound to minister to his neighbours, and to supply his neighbour's lack of that wherewith God hath endowed him.' Furthermore, 'Christ is Lord over all; and every Christian is heir annexed with Christ, and therefore Lord of all; and every one Lord of whatsoever another bath'. This line of argument can also be found in *The Summe of the Holye Scrypture*, a translation of about 1529 by Simon Fish from a Dutch original of 1523. Moreover the social teaching of both works was explicitly condemned by the English Catholic authorities in 1530. By 1548 the *Parable* and the *Summe* were in their fifth and seventh editions respectively.[52]

Similar views had now penetrated the government itself, most famously in the case of John Hales, Clerk of the Hanaper, who was appointed to a commission set up in 1548 to enforce the existing legislation against enclosures.

Hales and five others were made responsible for the counties of Bedfordshire, Berkshire, Buckinghamshire, Leicestershire, Oxfordshire, Northamptonshire and Warwickshire. The actual commission, dated 1 June 1548, talks of 'the corruption and infection of private lucre grown universally among our subjects'. On 24 July and near the end of the first tour of these seven counties, Hales can be found writing to Protector Somerset that 'the people . . . have a great hope that the iron world is now at an end, and the golden is returning again'. He also made clear the intimate connection in his own mind between the social and religious programmes of the government.

> If there be any way or policy of man to make the people receive, embrace and love God's word, it is only this – when they shall see that it bringeth forth so goodly fruit, that men seek not their own wealth, nor their private commodity, but, as good members, the universal wealth of the whole body. Surely God's word is that precious balm that must increase comfort, and cherish that godly charity between man and man, which is the sinews that tie and hold together the members of every Christian commonwealth, and maketh one of us to be glad of another.

The ideal held up is that all 'shall live in a due temperament and harmony, without one having too much, and a great many nothing at all, as at this present it appeareth plainly they have'.[53]

Only a few weeks later, on 12 August, Hales had to defend himself, in a letter to the Earl of Warwick, from the accusation that he 'should by hortations set the commons against the nobility and the gentlemen'. While rebutting the charge, Hales none the less adjured Warwick to 'remember the poor, have mercy and compassion on them, go not about to hinder them'. Reading his later account of the proceedings of this commission, written up in the summer of 1549, one can understand why the arguments used by Hales generated alarm among members of the propertied classes. As he explained, in his meetings with 'the people' Hales had provided an exposition of the commission and accompanying instructions from the government. His local audiences were in effect treated to sermons on the social ills of the day. He spoke of 'the great dropsy and the insatiable desire of riches of some men . . . this most hurtful disease of the commonwealth, private profit', while making plain his credentials as a religious reformer. Masses and prayers for the dead will not save the uncharitable rich from damnation. Hales also glossed the oath taken by the juries of presentment as being 'not by all saints, but as you trust to be saved by the merits of Christ's passion'. Now, in this time of the Gospel, men must be doers as well as 'talkers of God's word'. Hales hammered away remorselessly at his central theme, 'to remove the self love that is in many men' and to restore a charitable 'mean', backed up by threats of divine judgement. Like Crowley, he too quoted Isaiah, concluding 'let it not appear that we have received the grace of God, and the knowledge of his word, in vain'. Only at the very end of his harangue did Hales warn the aggrieved not to take matters into their own hands, and 'go about . . . to cut up men's hedges and to put down their enclosures'. In retrospect he denied any responsibility for the ensuing collapse of law and order, laying the blame on 'Papists' and 'Anabaptists', along with the failure of the local rulers to implement government orders.[54] But the sermonizing of Hales and others is likely to have produced both a general heightening of expectations, and an enhanced sense of mismatch between ideal and reality in a county such as Norfolk, where no enclosure commission appears to have been at work.

Enclosure became a great symbol during the 1549 rebellions, although in much of East Anglia overstocking of the commons by landlords was the leading agrarian issue. Certainly this is true of the list of grievances drawn up by the rebels under Kett. It was the principal concern too at Landbeach, in Cambridgeshire, which has been described as Kett's Rebellion 'in miniature', with the crucial difference, however, that here matters were resolved peacefully, whereas in Norfolk the situation developed into a pitched battle. In this village an archetypal grasping landlord, Richard Kirby, had come into conflict with the tenants of Corpus Christi College, Cambridge. The master of the college, the reformist Matthew Parker, was also rector of the parish. Having failed to pacify the rebels on Mousehold Heath, Parker secured agreement at Landbeach.[55] Anti-enclosure riots actually broke out in the immediate vicinity of Cambridge at this time, but order was restored by the mayor and vice-chancellor with little use of force. A set of verses relating to this episode survives, which takes the side of the rioters and expresses sentiments not unlike Crowley and Hales. This is especially true of some lines spoken by Harry Clowte:

> Good conscience should them move
> Their neighbours quietly to love,
> And thus not for to wrinch,
> The commons still for to pinch,
> To take into their hands
> That be other men's lands.[56]

The events of 1549 in East Anglia would seem to have involved an upsurge of popular religious fervour not so far removed after all from Haigh's concept of a Reformation 'from below'. It is all the more remarkable that this occurred in one of the heartlands of late medieval Catholic piety. Nor did social criticism, by religious reformers, die away in the aftermath of the rebellions. Crowley, for example, continued to hold forth as loudly as ever on the subject of oppression, while John Hooper's treatise on the Ten Commandments expounded 'Thou shalt not steal' partly with reference to 'avarice'. Likewise

some of the fiercest denunciations of greed by Latimer postdate the rebellions, when he also denied that preaching against 'covetousness' had been
the cause of the troubles. Moreover such teachings also informed the official
Edwardian Primer of 1553, especially as regards the prayer for landlords:

> We heartily pray thee . . . that they, remembering themselves to be thy tenants,
> may not rack and stretch out the rents of their houses and lands, nor yet take
> unreasonable fines and incomes after the manner of covetous worldlings,
> . . . and not join house to house, nor couple land to land, to the impoverish-
> ment of other.

Again one hears the echo of Isaiah. The accompanying prayer for the clergy
includes the request 'Take away from us, O Lord, all such wicked ministers
as deface thy glory, corrupt thy blessed word, despise they flock, and feed
themselves, and not thy sheep'.[57]

MacCulloch has plausibly argued that the 'evangelical establishment group-
ing knew from the start in 1547 exactly what Reformation it wanted' and, as
a consequence, 'there was an essential continuity of purpose in a graduated
series of religious changes over seven years'. Hence the second Edwardian
Prayer Book of 1552, primer, catechism and Articles of Religion of 1553 represent the elaboration of an original intention rather than a radical redirection
of religious effort. During 1550 all stone altars were ordered to be demolished,
and Cranmer published his *Defence of the True and Catholike Doctrine of the
Sacrament* which developed the view that 'only the faithful consume the body
of Christ' and, as he put it, 'with the heart, not with the teeth'. This teaching
informed the communion service in the new Prayer Book. The catechism
and Articles are also notable for including fairly uncompromising statements of unconditional predestination. But, possibly as a balance to the anti-
landlordism of the primer, one of the Articles was devoted to condemning
'Anabaptist' teaching on 'the riches and goods of Christians'. These are
'not common . . . notwithstanding every man ought, of such things as he
possesseth, liberally to give alms to the poor, *according to his ability*'.[58] At the
parish level altars were generally removed and the Prayer Book again bought.[59]
Time, however, was running out for the regime, as Edward VI became
increasingly ill and the Catholic Princess Mary waited in the wings. Moreover
the evangelical preachers began to turn the edge of their social criticism
against the government itself – now led by Northumberland (the former
Warwick), after the fall of Somerset. The context was the continuing plunder
of what remained of ecclesiastical wealth, for private profit. Northumberland
was, in addition, still remembered as the butcher of the Norfolk rebels in
1549, and this may partly explain why Mary was able to win crucial support
in East Anglia, during 1553, when successfully resisting diversion of the royal
succession to Queen Jane.[60]

III

Under Mary, between 1553 and 1558, Roman Catholicism was restored. Revisionist historians have rightly taught us that there existed no intrinsic reason why this reversal should not have endured, save only that Mary was in turn succeeded by her Protestant half-sister Elizabeth. The grass-roots evidence of Catholic restoration, as detailed by Duffy and Hutton, is especially impressive.[61] Yet it remains worth pondering that when, at the end of October 1553, the Marian regime introduced a composite parliamentary bill repealing the Edwardian religious legislation a quarter of MPs present in the Commons voted against it, and the debates were drawn out for a week. These eighty or so dissenters appear to represent the kind of significant minority commitment that the history of the Reformation elsewhere would lead one to expect. They may also link ideologically, if not in direct terms of personnel, with Sir Thomas Wyatt's rebellion of the following year in Kent. An insurrection, predominantly of the gentry, aimed at deposing Mary, the inner ring of conspirators does seem to have consisted mainly of evangelicals.[62]

In the counties the commissions of the peace had already been purged of politically unreliable and, by implication, evangelically inclined gentry. As early as 13 and 16 August 1553 respectively all clergy in the City of London and Norwich diocese were inhibited, by the Privy Council, from preaching without special royal licence. At Cambridge, in marked contrast to Oxford, nearly all the heads of colleges were removed, either by deprivation or resignation, and there was also a loss of college fellows – including over twenty from St John's. Some went into exile abroad, but others stayed in England unreconciled to the official changes. (Northumberland had been chancellor of Cambridge University, and was in fact arrested there in 1553, along with the vice-chancellor Edwin Sandys.)[63] In London, by Easter 1554 approximately a third of all benefices 'had been emptied by the deprivation, resignation, or imprisonment of their Edwardian reformist incumbents'. Although some Londoners fled, the city continued to be religiously divided, the bravest evangelicals going underground and forming a secret church.[64] During 1554, the 'poor men' and 'lovers of Christ's true religion in Norfolk and Suffolk' went so far as to petition the Marian commissioners not to restore the mass. Meanwhile at Norwich itself the irrepressible reformer Robert Watson was for a time imprisoned, but the civic authorities seem as far as possible to have turned a blind eye to the undoubted religious diversity in their midst. More generally there was probably widespread resort in England to 'Nicodemism', that is to say, dissembling of one's true beliefs.[65] Of course, the situation to the north and west differed, where reformers were thin on the ground – notoriously so in counties such as Lancashire or Devon and Cornwall. But this constituted no mere aborted English Reformation 'from above'. Furthermore in the war of printed propaganda, the reformers maintained their lead even during Mary's reign.[66]

The undoubted strength of Marian Catholicism, however, proved inadequate defence against the lottery of hereditary royal succession. During the years 1558 to 1563 the Edwardian Church of the reformers was in effect restored, courtesy of Queen Elizabeth. Catholics were thenceforward faced with the choice of either compromising with the new religious establishment, and ultimately being absorbed by it, or retreating into the ecclesiastical wilderness. Despite their far greater numbers, in the longer term they were in no better position than the 'Protestants' under the Marian dispensation. Yet we are still here only at the start of the Reformation process, with probably a large majority of the population remaining to be won. Moreover it was not a question of a once for all conversion, let alone of simply waiting for those who had known a fully functioning Catholic Church to die off. Each new generation required to be nurtured afresh.[67] Nevertheless it was also from this point on that a fault line present at the outset between radical and moderate religious reformers became more prominent. Whereas under Edward VI both Somerset and Northumberland had backed a programme of unequivocally Protestant change, Elizabeth revealed herself as a conservative unhappy even with Edwardian developments at the official level. The tensions this created were compounded by the direct experience of continental reform on the part of the former Marian exiles. Puritan attempts at further reformation are discussed below, yet mainstream Edwardian Protestantism too was to face an increasing challenge from those who regretted its uncompromising nature.[68]

A good illustration here of the ambiguity at the very heart of the Elizabethan establishment and one full of import for the future is provided by the Injunctions of 1559. As compared with their Edwardian predecessors they exhibit a less thoroughgoing iconoclasm, which is further reflected in the Homilies of 1563. Although the visitors charged with implementing these Injunctions in fact launched an attack on 'all images', Elizabeth subsequently intervened to protect those in glass windows. The Queen also tried but failed to have the images on rood screens restored.[69] A comparable tussle occurred over the position of the communion table, for the Injunctions of 1559 modified the rubric in the Prayer Book issued the same year. This rubric followed that in the Edwardian Prayer Book of 1552 and assumed a communion table permanently aligned east and west, i.e. longways. By contrast the Injunctions ordered that, out of time of communion, tables should stand on the site and in the position of pre-Reformation altars. Moreover Elizabeth intimated that there was no objection in principle to the retention of the stone altars which were currently being demolished.[70] This disagreement at the outset of her reign was to furnish important precedents for the Laudians in the early seventeenth century, when the issue reemerged – but now involving doctrine as well as practice.

It may also be significant that only in 1563, more than four years into the reign, was an adaptation of the Edwardian Forty-two Articles introduced. These Thirty-nine Articles reiterate the doctrine of unconditional predestination, God's 'sentence', although not before an agitation had been mounted by a group of 'free-will men'. At about the same date the orthodoxy of Elizabeth herself on this issue was questioned by none other than Bishop Richard Cox, who during the Marian exile had defended the Prayer Book against John Knox and his followers. Certainly during the predestinarian disputes of the 1590s the Queen was to come down against the Calvinist expositors of Church of England teaching.[71] Accordingly the pedigree of English anti-Calvinism, in its various aspects, can be said to derive in part from the personal idiosyncrasies of Queen Elizabeth.

NOTES

This essay seeks to open up debate on the early stages of the English Reformation. I am grateful to Diarmaid MacCulloch for his comments on earlier draft versions, and to Philip Broadhead and Christopher Coleman for advice concerning particular points.

1 G. Strauss, 'Success and Failure in the German Reformation', *P and P* 67 (1975), 30–63; G. Parker, 'Success and Failure during the First Century of the Reformation', *P and P* 136 (1992), 43–82; J. Delumeau, *Catholicism from Luther to Voltaire* (London, 1977).

2 C. Haigh, *English Reformations: Religion, Politics and Society under the Tudors* (Oxford, 1993). This is the most recent general statement of the revisionist position, and is rather more nuanced than C. Haigh ed., *The English Reformation Revised* (Cambridge, 1987).

3 K. Thomas, *Religion and the Decline of Magic: Studies in Popular Beliefs in Sixteenth- and Seventeenth-century England* (London, 1971); cf. R. Hutton, 'The English Reformation and the Evidence of Folklore', *P and P* 148 (1995), 89–116.

4 In retrospect, Haigh's book *Reformation and Resistance in Tudor Lancashire* (Cambridge, 1975) can be seen to have adumbrated the agenda of subsequent revisionist accounts of the English Reformation.

5 Haigh, *English Reformations* and Haigh ed., *The English Reformation Revised*; J. J. Scarisbrick, *The Reformation and the English People* (Oxford, 1984); E. Duffy, *The Stripping of the Altars: Traditional Religion in England c. 1400–1580* (New Haven and London, 1992). Of these three historians, Haigh has proved by far the most combative and my remarks about revisionism relate primarily to his work.

6 F. A. Gasquet, *The Eve of the Reformation: Studies in the Religious Life and Thought of the English People in the Period Preceding the Rejection of the Roman Jurisdiction by Henry VIII* (London, 1900), pp. 13, 43, 119, 323–415. For the famous controversy concerning Gasquet's scholarship, see M. D. Knowles, *Cardinal Gasquet as an Historian* (Creighton Lecture, London, 1957); cf. Haigh ed., *The English Reformation Revised*, pp. 56–74.

7 H. N. Birt, *The Elizabethan Religious Settlement: a Study of Contemporary Documents* (London, 1907), pp. xi, 191, 537; cf. Haigh ed., *The English Reformation Revised*, pp. 176–208 and C. Haigh, 'From Monopoly to Minority: Catholicism in Early Modern England', *TRHS* 5th series 31 (1981), 129–47. Birt was in part responding to H. Gee, *The Elizabethan Clergy and the Settlement of Religion 1558–1564* (Oxford, 1898). Whereas Gee put the figure for deprived priests in the early years of Elizabeth at about 200 (p. 247), Birt upped this to approximately 2,000 – defined as those 'who abandoned their livings from conscientious inability to conform' (p. 203). Ironically, the larger the number the more profound the religious break with Catholicism produced by the Elizabethan settlement.

8 B. Moeller, 'Piety in Germany around 1500', in S. E. Ozment ed., *The Reformation in Medieval Perspective* (Chicago, 1971), pp. 50–75; cf. Haigh, *English Reformations*, pp. 12–13.

9 Gasquet, *The Eve of the Reformation*, pp. 208–35; Scarisbrick, *The Reformation and the English People*, pp. 197–203. Another absentee is Tyndale.

10 Haigh ed., *The English Reformation Revised*, pp. 19–33.

11 A. G. Dickens, *The English Reformation* (London, 1964), p. v. In the second edition of this book (London, 1989), Dickens defends his argument.

12 For analogies, however, between Kett's rebellion of 1549 and the German Peasants' War of 1525, see pp. 47–8 above.

13 R. Rex, *The Theology of John Fisher* (Cambridge, 1991), p. 80 and R. Rex, 'The English Campaign against Luther in the 1520s', *TRHS* 5th series 39 (1989), 86.

14 J. Fines, *A Biographical Register of Early English Protestants and Others Opposed to the Roman Catholic Church*, pt. 2, unpublished typescript (West Sussex Institute of Education, 1985), F 10, G 3–4, G 12, S 25, H 18–19, M 12, P 4–5, T 2–3, R 7–8, F 13. I have used the copy at the Institute of Historical Research, University of London; C. H. and T. Cooper, *Athenae Cantabrigienses* (Cambridge, 1858), i, p. 86; for the Lutheran play performed at Christ's College in 1544, see p. 43 above; J. Le Neve, *Fasti Ecclesiae Anglicanae*, ed. T. D. Hardy (Oxford, 1854), iii, pp. 685, 681, 692, 674, 668, 690, 683.

15 E. S. Leedham-Green ed., *Books in Cambridge Inventories* (Cambridge, 1986), i, pp. xxi, 1–3, 9–11, 16–18, 20, 22, 29–30, 32, 39–42, 51, 57, 62–6, 71, 82–6; W. R. D. Jones, *William Turner, Tudor Naturalist, Physician and Divine* (London and New York, 1988), pp. 10–11; J. Fines, *A Biographical Register of Early English Protestants and Others Opposed to the Roman Catholic Church 1525–1558*, pt. i (Abingdon, 1981), 'Cox, Richard'. Professor Fines very kindly supplied me with a copy of this part; R. J. Fehrenbach and E. S. Leedham-Green eds, *Private Libraries in Renaissance England* (Marlborough, 1993), ii, pp. 265–75. Cf. p. 26 above.

16 J. Foxe, *The Acts and Monuments*, ed. S. R. Cattley and G. Townsend (London, 1837), iv, pp. 666–70, 679.

17 C. E. Foerstemann ed., *Album Academiae Vitenbergensis* (1502–1560), (Leipzig, 1841), i, pp. 125b, 149b, 186a; D. MacCulloch, *Thomas Cranmer: a Life* (New Haven and London, 1996), pp. 176–7; *RSTC* nos. 4054, 16962, 16979.7, 16999, 24238, 15179, 18878, 17793, 17798, 26138.

18 J. E. Cox ed., *Miscellaneous Writings and Letters of Thomas Cranmer* (Cambridge, 1846), pp. 460–1; M. C. Skeeters, *Community and Clergy: Bristol and the Reformation c. 1530–1570* (Oxford, 1993), pp. 38–47, 229; A. G. Dickens, *Lollards and Protestants in the*

Diocese of York 1509–1558 (Oxford, 1959), pp. 140–3; MacCulloch, *Thomas Cranmer*, p. 110.

19 R. Rex, 'The New Learning', *JEH* 44 (1993), 26–44; J. Gairdner ed., *Letters and Papers, Foreign and Domestic, of the Reign of Henry VIII* (London, 1891), xii, pt. ii, pp. 593, 643; cf. Haigh ed., *The English Reformation Revised*, pp. 6–7, 10–11, 15–17.

20 G. E. Corrie ed., *Sermons and Remains of Hugh Latimer* (Cambridge, 1845), pp. 218–20; G. E. Corrie ed., *Sermons by Hugh Latimer* (Cambridge, 1844), pp. 36–7, 46, 50, 55; *RSTC*, nos. 15285, 15286.

21 P. L. Hughes and J. F. Larkin eds, *Tudor Royal Proclamations* (New Haven and London, 1964), i, nos 122, 129 *(Parable of the Wicked Mammon)*, 186, 272; *RSTC*, nos. 24454, 24455.

22 *RSTC*, nos. 16962, 16999, 17000, 24238, 908. M. Aston, *England's Iconoclasts* (Oxford, 1988), pp. 203–10; J. K. McConica, *English Humanists and Reformation Politics under Henry VIII and Edward VI* (Oxford, 1956), p. 170.

23 *RSTC*, no. 2066, *La Bible qui est toute la saincte escripture* (Neuchâtel, 1535), fos. 95–105v at end; MacCulloch, *Thomas Cranmer*, pp. 196–7; A. L. Herminjard ed., *Correspondance des réformateurs dans les pays de langue française* (Geneva, 1870), iii, pp. 257n. 289n. 290n. Gramelin is an anagram for Malingre, although Matthieu works less well for Thomas (Mathos). This French Bible was the work of Pierre Robert (Olivétan) and includes prefatory material by John Calvin. To the best of my knowledge, I am the first to offer this explanation of the name Thomas Matthew.

24 It should be emphasised that the publication figures given in this paragraph are only my rough calculations, based on *RSTC*; D. Wilkins ed., *Concilia Magnae Britanniae et Hiberniae* (London, 1737), iii, p. 706.

25 M. Dowling, 'Anne Boleyn and Reform', *JEH* 35 (1984), 30–46; E. W. Ives, 'Anne Boleyn and the Early Reformation in England: The Contemporary Evidence', *HJ* 37 (1994), 389–499; S. Brigden, 'Thomas Cromwell and the Brethren', in C. Cross, D. Loades and J. J. Scarisbrick eds, *Law and Government under the Tudors*, (Cambridge, 1988), pp. 31–49; MacCulloch, *Thomas Cranmer*, pp. 173–236, cf. G. Bernard, 'Anne Boleyn's Religion', *HJ* 36 (1993), 1–20.

26 L. V. Ryan, *Roger Ascham* (Stanford, 1963), pp. 45–6; J. A. Giles ed., *The Whole Works of Roger Ascham* (London, 1865), i, p. 68; A. Pighius, *De Libero Hominis Arbitrio et Divina Gratia* (Cologne, 1542).

27 T. Naogeorgus [Kirchmeyer], *Pammachius* (Wittenberg, 1538); T. T. Perowne ed., *Correspondence of Matthew Parker* (Cambridge, 1853), pp. 20–9.

28 Dickens, *Lollards and Protestants*; Dickens, *The English Reformation* (2nd edn, London, 1989), pp. 52, 56–7.

29 A. Hudson, *The Premature Reformation: Wycliffite Texts and Lollard History* (Oxford, 1988), pp. 17–18. Hudson, however, draws attention to 'a number of early sixteenth-century copies' of Lollard works (p. 17); S. Brigden, *London and the Reformation* (Oxford, 1989), pp. 106–9.

30 Aston, *England's Iconoclasts*, pp. 210–19.

31 Haigh ed., *The English Reformation Revised*, pp. 56–74, and Haigh, *English Reformations*, pp. 72–87; R. L. Storey, 'Gentlemen Bureaucrats', in C. H. Clough ed., *Profession, Vocation and Culture in Later Medieval England* (Liverpool, 1982), pp. 90–129.

32 J. Craig and C. Litzenberger, 'Wills as Religious Propaganda: The Testament of William Tracy', *JEH* 44 (1993), 421–5; H. Walter ed., *An Answer to Sir Thomas More's Dialogue, . . . and Wm. Tracy's Testament Expounded, by William Tyndale* (Cambridge, 1850), p. 279; *RSTC*, no. 10883; radical lawyers in turn overlapped with gentry of the same ilk, Baynham being visited in prison by the brothers William and Ralph Morice, along with William's brother-in-law Edward Isaac: Corrie ed., *Sermons and Remains of Hugh Latimer*, pp. 221–2.

33 Fines, *A Biographical Register*, pt. ii, F 6, H 10; E. F. Rogers, *The Letters of Sir John Hackett 1526–1534* (Morgantown, 1971), pp. 156, 161, 173–4.

34 R. Whiting, *The Blind Devotion of the People: Popular Religion and the English Reformation* (Cambridge, 1989), p. 225; Haigh, *Reformation and Resistance in Tudor Lancashire*, pp. 35–6; S. E. Lehmberg, *The Reformation Parliament 1529–1536* (Cambridge, 1970), pp. 6–7, 81–2.

35 S. Brigden, 'Tithe Controversy in Reformation London', *JEH* 32 (1981), 285–301; Brigden, *London and the Reformation*, pp. 49–52; Lehmberg, *The Reformation Parliament*, pp. 76–104.

36 Brigden, *London and the Reformation*, pp. 399–404, 345–6.

37 J. Gairdner and R. H. Brodie, *Letters and Papers, Foreign and Domestic, of the Reign of Henry VIII* (London, 1900), xvii, p. 79; G. R. Elton, *Policy and Police: The Enforcement of the Reformation in the Age of Thomas Cromwell* (Cambridge, 1972), pp. 138–9.

38 Brigden, *London and the Reformation*, pp. 424, 430; M. C. McClendon, 'The Quiet Reformation: Norwich Magistrates and the Coming of Protestantism, 1520–1575' (Stanford Ph.D., 1990), p. 125.

39 Ryan, *Roger Ascham*, p. 92; J. E. Foster ed., *Churchwardens' Accounts of St Mary the Great Cambridge from 1504 to 1635* (Cambridge, 1905), pp. 114, 117.

40 Brigden, *London and the Reformation*, pp. 433–9.

41 Ryan, *Roger Ascham*, pp. 92–6.

42 C. H. Cooper, *Annals of Cambridge* (Cambridge, 1843), ii, p. 31; J. K. McConica ed., *The History of the University of Oxford, III: the Collegiate University* (Oxford, 1986), pp. 369–72; McClendon, 'The Quiet Reformation', pp. 58–9 and M. C. McClendon, 'Discipline and Punish? Magistrates and Clergy in Early Reformation Norwich', in E. J. Carlson ed., *Religion and the English People 1500–1640* (Kirksville, Mo, 1998).

43 MacCulloch, *Thomas Cranmer*, pp. 369–75, 384–6, 410–12; Duffy, *The Stripping of the Altars*, pp. 454, 464; R. Hutton, 'The Local Impact of the Tudor Reformations', in Haigh ed., *The English Reformation Revised*, pp. 120–5.

44 *Statutes of the Realm* (London, 1819), iv, p. 67; McConica ed., *The Collegiate University*, pp. 134–5, 318–19; 368–74; C. Hopf, *Martin Bucer and the English Reformation* (Oxford, 1946), pp. 12–29, P. M. Took, 'Government and the Printing Trade, 1540–60' (London Ph.D., 1979), pp. 134–223, 343–5.

45 MacCulloch, *Thomas Cranmer*, pp. 432–3; BL, Add. MS 48018, fos 388, 389v, 391.

46 A. F. Pollard, *The History of England from the Accession of Edward VI to the Death of Elizabeth (1547–1603)* (London, 1919), pp. 33–4. Pollard was sensitised to this issue having written a chapter on 'Social Revolution and Catholic Reaction in Germany', for *The Cambridge Modern History* (Cambridge, 1907), ii, pp. 174–205. It remains unclear

whether a copy of the Memmingen articles was actually available to the leaders of Kett's rebellion, or whether the link was more indirect. There would appear, however, to have been a common ideological context.

47 A. Fletcher, *Tudor Rebellions* (3rd edn, London, 1983), pp. 120–3; P. Blickle, *The Revolution of 1525: The German Peasants' War from a New Perspective* (Baltimore, 1988), pp. 195–201.

48 Cox ed., *Miscellaneous Writings and Letters of Thomas Cranmer*, p. 195; Elton, *Policy and Police*, pp. 144–51.

49 D. MacCulloch, 'Kett's Rebellion in Context', *P and P* 84 (1979), 49, 58. This article is the essential modern starting point for discussion of Kett's rebellion; Norfolk Record Office, NCC will (John Chandler) 1553, 22 Wilkins (MF 49). This will, hitherto unnoticed and dated 1550/1, establishes Chandler's Catholicism; B. L. Beer, *Rebellion and Riot: Popular Disorder in England during the Reign of Edward VI* (Kent, Ohio, 1982), pp. 141–2.

50 MacCulloch, *Thomas Cranmer*, pp. 433–4; J. Cornwall, *Revolt of the Peasantry 1549* (London, 1977), pp. 149–50; McClendon, 'The Quiet Reformation', p. 125.

51 C. E. Challis, 'The Debasement of the Coinage', *Ec HR*, 2nd series 20 (1967), 441–66; J. M. Cowper ed., *The Select Works of Robert Crowley* (London, 1872), pp. 154, 156–7, 161, 164, 175. My italics. Crowley refers to the Act of Six Articles as still unrepealed, which dates his writing to before December 1547 (p. 170).

52 H. Walter ed., *Doctrinal Treatises and Introductions to Different Portions of the Holy Scriptures by William Tyndale* (Cambridge, 1848), pp. 57, 59, 95, 97; *RSTC*, no. 3036; Wilkins, *Concilia Magnae Britanniae et Hibernia*, iii, pp. 728, 731–2; for the related teaching of Zwingli, see L. P. Wandel *Always Among Us: Images of the Poor in Zwingli's Zurich* (Cambridge, 1990), pp. 36–76; cf. also S. Brigden, 'Popular Disturbance and the Fall of Thomas Cormwell and the Reformers, 1539–1540', *HJ* 24 (1981), 270–2.

53 J. Strype, *Ecclesiastical Memorials Relating Chiefly to Religion . . . under King Henry VIII, King Edward VI and Queen Mary I* (Oxford, 1822), ii, pt. ii, p. 349; P. F. Tytler, *England under the Reigns of Edward VI and Mary* (London, 1839), pp. 114–16.

54 BL, Lansdowne MS 238, fos 322r–v, Strype, *Ecclesiastical Memorials Relating Chiefly to Religion . . .* , ii, pt. ii, pp. 352–8, 364; E. Lamond ed., *A Discourse of the Common Weal of this Realm of England* (Cambridge, 1954), pp. lvi–lix.

55 MacCulloch, 'Kett's Rebellion in Context', pp. 50–3; J. R. Ravensdale, 'Landbeach in 1549: Kett's Rebellion in Miniature', in L. M. Munby ed., *East Anglian Studies* (Cambridge, 1968), pp. 94–116.

56 Beer, *Rebellion and Riot*, pp. 143–4; Cooper, *Annals of Cambridge*, ii, pp. 36–44. Pyrse Plowman says (p. 41): 'I wonder at this covetous nation | That scrat and get all out of fashion'.

57 Cowper ed., *The Select Works of Robert Crowley*, pp. 131–50; S. Carr ed., *Early Writings of John Hooper . . .* (Cambridge, 1843), pp. 387–404; Corrie ed., *Sermons by Hugh Latimer*, pp. 246–50; J. Ketley ed., *The Two Liturgies . . . with Other Documents Set Forth by Authority in the Reign of King Edward VI* (Cambridge, 1844), pp. 457–8. Cf. also the prayer 'for rich men' (p. 460). These prayers are in fact taken from T. Becon, *The Flower of Godly Prayers* (London, c. 1550).

58 MacCulloch, *Thomas Cranmer*, pp. 365–6, 458, 463–4, 504–12; Ketley ed., *The Two Liturgies*, pp. 511–13; E. Cardwell ed., *Synodalia* i (Oxford, 1842), pp. 96–7, 105. My italics.

59 Hutton, 'The Local Impact of the Tudor Reformations', pp. 125–6.

60 MacCulloch, *Thomas Cranmer*, pp. 531–3; D. MacCulloch, 'Debate: Kett's Rebellion in Context', *P and P* 93 (1981), 172–3.

61 Duffy, *The Stripping of the Altars*, pp. 524–63; Hutton, 'The Local Impact of the Tudor Reformations', pp. 128–31.

62 J. Loach, *Parliament and the Crown in the Reign of Mary Tudor* (Oxford, 1986), pp. 77–8; M. R. Thorp, 'Religion and the Wyatt Rebellion of 1554', *Church History* 47 (1978), 363–80; P. Clark, *English Provincial Society from the Reformation to the Revolution: Religion, Politics and Society in Kent, 1500–1640* (Hassocks, 1977), pp. 87–98.

63 D. MacCulloch, *Suffolk and the Tudors: Politics and Religion in an English County 1500–1600* (Oxford, 1986), pp. 232–3, 416; *APC 1552–1554*, pp. 317, 321; Cooper, *Annals of Cambridge*, ii, pp. 83–4; Le Neve, *Fasti Ecclesiae Anglicanae*, iii, pp. 668, 671, 674, 679, 681, 683, 685, 687, 688, 690, 692, 699; H. C. Porter, *Reformation and Reaction in Tudor Cambridge* (Cambridge, 1958), pp. 75–6.

64 Brigden, *London and the Reformation*, pp. 575–6.

65 Foxe, *The Acts and Monuments*, ed. Cattley and Townsend (London, 1839), viii, pp. 121–30. The petitioners emphasised their loyalty to Mary in 1553. My dating of this document disagrees with Foxe; McClendon, 'The Quiet Reformation', pp. 176–8; A. Pettegree, *Marian Protestantism: Six Studies* (Aldershot, 1996), pp. 86–117.

66 Haigh, *Reformation and Resistance in Tudor Lancashire*; Whiting, *The Blind Devotion of the People*; E. J. Baskerville, *A Chronological Bibliography of Propaganda and Polemic, Published in English between 1553 and 1558, from the Death of Edward VI to the Death of Mary I* (Philadelphia, 1979), pp. 5–10.

67 At this point the original text went on to discuss the contributions to *England's Long Reformation 1500–1800* (London, 1998), of which it formed the introduction. What follows is new in this edition.

68 See pp. 61–8 below; D. MacCulloch, *Tudor Church Militant. Edward VI and the Protestant Reformation* (London, 1999), pp. 191–222.

69 Aston, *England's Iconoclasts*, pp. 299–304, 316, 320–4.

70 W. P. Haugaard, *Elizabeth and the English Reformation. The Struggle for a Stable Settlement of Religion* (Cambridge, 1968), pp. 112–13, 148; E. Cardwell ed., *Documentary Annals of the Reformed Church of England* (Oxford, 1844), i, pp. 233–4.

71 E. Cardwell ed., *Synodalia* (Oxford, 1842), i, pp. 23–4, 63–4; Haugaard, *Elizabeth and the English Reformation*, pp. 239, 250, 283–4; J. Strype, *Annals of the Reformation* (Oxford, 1824), i, pt i, pp. 494–8, 540–1; Porter, *Reformation and Reaction*, pp. 373–4.

Chapter 2

The 'Rise of Puritanism' and the legalising of Dissent, 1571–1719

I

THE title of this essay recalls an additional anniversary to that of the 1689 Toleration Act. For it is now fifty years since the publication of an epoch-making book – William Haller's *The Rise of Puritanism*. An American professor of English literature, Haller came to the study of Puritanism via John Milton and a three-volume work entitled *Tracts on Liberty in the Puritan Revolution*. He went on to co-edit a volume of *Leveller Tracts* and to write a sequel to his earlier book: *Liberty and Reformation in the Puritan Revolution*.[1] Haller indeed would have had no difficulty in understanding why someone should want to write about Puritanism in the context of the Williamite Revolution, given his assumption that Milton was the voice of the future and 'freedom' the end result.[2] This thinking is, of course, in the great Whig tradition which runs from Macaulay to Trevelyan, the latter opining that toleration was 'the true road of Puritan development in England'.[3] Or, as Haller put it, the upshot was 'not the New Jerusalem but something like the modern English state'.[4]

Recent years, however, have witnessed a retreat from such confident certainties, by scholars more interested in short-term reality and generally suspicious of what they regard as teleology. In the process, Puritanism has been deflated as revolutionary force. But, as so often with historiographical fashion, what began as a sensible attempt at redressing the balance now threatens to turn into a caricature.[5] Arguably, then, the time has come to restore Puritanism to its rightful place of political and religious importance. For an organised movement aiming at further reform of the English Church, and one which contemporaries christened 'Puritan', is traceable from the earliest years of Queen Elizabeth. Although the movement was largely clerical in leadership, the laity nevertheless played a vital role, both as patrons and as advocates of the Puritan cause. From the vestments' controversy of the 1560s to the Millenary Petition of 1603, the programme remained basically the same.[6] It resurfaced again in more muted form at the accession of Charles I, gathered strength during the 1630s, and erupted in 1640.[7] The strategy was two-pronged throughout: a revised religious settlement, but toleration meanwhile for those unable to live with the status quo.

These objectives survived into the changed world of the Restoration, but with the emphasis increasingly on 'indulgence' – that is to say toleration of Protestants outside the Established Church. Yet even then the notion of 'comprehension', in some minds at least, still involved shifting the entire English Church in a more Protestant direction.[8] Toleration remained for many at best half a loaf, the guarantee of survival not the ultimate goal. Moreover, a clue to the high ancestry of this policy lies embedded in the 1689 Toleration Act itself. Thus the section of the act concerning Dissenting ministers refers to the 'Articles of Religion mentioned in the statute made in the thirteenth yeare of the raigne of the late Queen Elizabeth'. (These are the famous Thirty-nine Articles, passed by convocation in 1563.) The 1689 act then goes on explicitly to waive subscription to articles 34, 35, and 36, and part of article 20 – covering church traditions, the homilies, the consecration of bishops and ministers, and rites and ceremonies.[9] In so doing it sanctioned a form of modified clerical subscription, which Puritans had been seeking to establish by law for well over a hundred years.

The penal legislation of the Restoration period also refers to the statute of 13 Elizabeth chapter 12, and assumes that it had simply enshrined the Thirty-nine Articles in a parliamentary act.[10] An alternative view, however, exists that this 1571 act was in origin a Puritan measure, designed for the ease of scrupulous consciences but subsequently subverted by the ecclesiastical authorities. The crucial passage in the Elizabethan act runs that the clergy are henceforth to subscribe to those articles which '*onely* concerne the confession of the true Christian faithe and the doctrine of the sacraments'. Furthermore, we know that Puritan Members of Parliament wished at this time to exclude 'the articles for the homilyes, consecrating of bishops and such like' from any proposed legislation.[11] But why, then, should Elizabeth have allowed such a Puritan bill to become law? The most likely explanation is that it was part of a package of anti-Catholic legislation, in the wake of the Northern Rebellion and the papal excommunication of the Queen.

Thus the first clause of the 1571 act seeks to detect crypto-Catholics, by imposing subscription on any minister not ordained according to either the Edwardian or the Elizabethan Protestant formularies. Radical Protestants ordained abroad, however, might also have been caught in this snare. Hence the limiting formula. Nevertheless, a further clause of the act makes this same modified subscription the test for all future ordinands.[12] On the face of it this was a remarkable victory for parliamentary Puritanism, albeit dependent on a wider spectrum of support. But the triumph was hollow, in that much depended on the attitude adopted by the bishops. This potential clash of interpretation came to a head during the 1580s, with Archbishop Whitgift's imposition of a much more rigorous form of clerical subscription – including approbation of the Prayer Book.[13] One consequence was that the year 1586 saw the first of a long line of parliamentary bills designed to secure the benefits of the 1571 act. Similarly, two years earlier, in 1584, the Puritan lawyer Thomas Norton can be found urging the 'toleration' of ministers with scruples about subscribing.[14]

One should not, however, be misled by the moderate tone that Puritans sometimes chose to adopt. The 1571 Parliament, which saw the passage of what may be called a first toleration act, also witnessed a full-scale critique of the Elizabethan Prayer Book. The grievances rehearsed by William Strickland, on this occasion, were almost identical to those which would be presented some thirty years later to James I. Strickland's subsequent treatment by the Privy Council led to a classic debate about the 'liberty' of the House of Commons.[15] With the *Admonition to Parliament* in 1572, bishops as such came under attack. By now English Puritanism had acquired a presbyterian dimension, which it was never again completely to lose. Episcopal government was dubbed 'Antichristian' and 'contrarye to the Scriptures'. Nevertheless, an associated parliamentary measure of the same date, designed to make use of the existing Prayer Book optional, spoke of the variety of practice permitted by 'some godlie bishops and ordinaries'. This bill 'concerning rites and ceremonies' commanded widespread support in the Commons, and an amended version would almost certainly have been passed had Elizabeth not personally intervened.[16]

Even more striking evidence of lay support for Puritanism comes from the 1584–85 Parliament. In December 1584 the Commons submitted a petition to the Lords, which included provisions that subscription be 'onely' as 'expresly prescribed by the statutes of this realme' and that ministers be excused 'for omissions or changes of some portions or ryte' in the Prayer Book. This was backed up by county petitions from Essex, Leicestershire, Lincolnshire, Sussex and Warwickshire. It also brought to the fore competing jurisdictional views, members of the Commons claiming that the Church was subject to Parliament, and led to a remarkable rebuke from Elizabeth. Stressing her unwillingess to 'tolerate newfangledness', she added: 'I must pronounce them dangerous to a kingly rule: to have every man, according to his own censure, to make a doom of the validity and privity of his prince's government, with a common veil and cover of God's word, whose followers must not be judged but by private men's expositions.'[17]

It remains necessary to distinguish between the moderate and radical wings of Puritanism. The latter, in its presbyterian form, was much less popular. But the distinction was not an absolute one, as is clear from the initial success of Anthony Cope's presbyterian bill in the Parliament of 1586–87.[18] The leading theoreticians of Elizabethan Puritanism, like Thomas Cartwright, were also presbyterians. There is indeed a sense in which presbyterianism represents the logical resolution of difficulties encountered by more pragmatic exponents of further reformation. Rather than tinker with existing arrangements, why not opt for a completely new system? The former approach, however, remained more realistic. At the same time, the royal veto on the handling of religious matters in Parliament is liable to give an impression that the Puritan reform movement was in decline by the end of the sixteenth century. Yet, given what happened immediately after the Queen's death in 1603, we should perhaps think more in terms of a tactical postponement.[19] For, within days of the accession of James I, a nation-wide Puritan agitation was launched from London. Draft petitions were dispatched into the localities, while emissaries went north to lobby the new King.[20] The organisational effort involved was at least as impressive as that deployed during the previous high point of political activity in the 1580s. Moreover, the religious remedies requested were old Elizabethan ones, as can be seen from the Millenary Petition presented to James that April. Purporting to be in the name of 'more than a thousand' clergy, the petition spelt out the case for reform, especially as regards the Prayer Book. There was also a sting in the tail, the petitioners requesting that 'discipline and excommunication may be administered according to Christ's own institution' – for discipline was a word with which to conjure, implying at least a measure of 'presbytery in episcopacy'.[21]

The ensuing conference, to which James agreed, was something which the Puritans had requested for many years. As we know, it achieved very little.[22] Less familiar, however, are the subsequent developments in the new Parliament, which met in March 1604. When contemporaries claimed that three-quarters of the House of Commons were Puritans, they scarcely exaggerated.[23] The Millenary programme, having been rejected by James, was now reintroduced into the Commons, and it met with an enthusiastic reception. Unlike Elizabeth, James did not seek to cut off the debates. Indeed, he permitted the Commons to confer with the Lords about church reform, and then himself addressed them in conciliatory fashion. Further joint conferences followed, until torpedoed by a vote in Convocation that the 'liberties of the Church' were being infringed. This in turn led to the Commons drawing up a petition to the King, for 'dispensation' of 'some godly ministers in matters indifferent and of ceremony'. The Member of Parliament chosen to present the petition, and also the leading Puritan in the Commons at this date, was Sir Francis Hastings.[24] So far as is known, this petition was never actually presented, the prorogation of Parliament supervening. The epilogue, six months later, was the personal disgrace of Hastings for drawing up a petition on behalf of the suspended Northamptonshire ministers.[25]

Unabashed, when Parliament reconvened, Hastings introduced a bill for the 'restoring of deprived ministers'. This received its first reading in February 1606. Ultimately, however, the Commons proceeded to petition the King on the subject, via the Speaker. A year later, in June 1607, a similar petition was only prevented by the direct intervention of James. The preceding May the Commons had passed a bill limiting subscription to the terms of the 1571 Act. They did so again in June 1610, following it up with another appeal to the King on behalf of the 'deprived and silenced ministers'.[26] After the first session of 1604 the Puritans in Parliament were on the defensive, but their initial aims clearly included Prayer Book reform. Moreover, they tended to link the fate of the Puritan ministers with the threat of Catholicism.[27]

A related pamphlet literature was also generated in these years. It includes *An Humble Supplication for Toleration* of 1609, by Henry Jacob. The author had been among the organisers of the Millenary Petition, and claims to speak for 'some of the late silenced and deprived ministers and people consenting in judgement with them'. Since Jacob requests an 'entier exemption' from the 'prelates', it is clear that the 'toleration' being sought here was outside the Established Church. The point is underlined by his citing with approval the situation obtaining in France, under the terms of the Edict of Nantes. This pamphlet, therefore, marks something of an intellectual benchmark, anticipating as it does the toleration achieved eighty years later. Nevertheless, the bulk of Puritan nonconformists before the Civil War wanted to remain within the existing Church, seeking a relaxation of the rules to this end. Jacob also explicitly rejects presbyterianism, and can plausibly be seen as a founding father of independency or congregationalism. Although he disowns the separatists, his position in fact overlaps with them.[28] But it has to be said that his views pale beside those now being developed by the Baptists. As early as 1612 Thomas Helwys can be found arguing that 'men's religion' is 'betwixt God and themselves'. There exists no right of compulsion, 'let them be heretikes, Turcks, Jewes or whatsoever'. Furthermore, Helwys and his co-religionists were able to realize their dream in Dutch exile.[29] Intolerance, however, remained the English order of the day.

During the Addled Parliament of 1614 a subscription bill also received a first reading in the Commons, although there is no trace of such measures in the Parliaments of 1621 and 1624.[30] The last decade of James I's reign in fact recalls that of the 1590s, with at least a superficial dying down of Puritan activity. Significantly, this changed with the accession of Charles I. Thus the Parliament of 1625 saw both the introduction of a subscription bill into the

Commons, and moves on behalf of the silenced ministers. A clause concerning their plight was included in a petition to Charles, which was, however, mainly taken up with 'the dangerous consequences of the increase of Popery'.[31] Subscription bills similarly featured in the Parliaments of 1626 and 1628. The unusually full record of debate for 1628 reveals a Puritan group, including John Pym, whose members were dissatisfied with the existing Prayer Book.[32] But by now the religious situation was becoming increasingly complicated, with the rise to power of an Arminian or anti-Calvinist faction within the English Church.[33]

Parliament remained the vehicle of Puritan legal aspirations. Yet these activities seem a far cry from the literature analysed by Haller in *The Rise of Puritanism*. Frustrated in their attempts to bring about institutional reform, so it has been said, Puritan preachers concentrated their efforts under the early Stuarts on the spiritual regeneration of the individual.[34] This, however, had always been a major preoccupation, and the extent of the shift should not be exaggerated. More debatable is the role of censorship, because most of the printed Puritan output was licensed by the episcopal authorities. Despite this, some of these publications do indicate the grounds of continuing Puritan objections to the ceremonial requirements of the Prayer Book. A good illustration is provided by Arthur Hildersham of Ashby-de-la-Zouch, in Leicestershire. Kinsman and protégé of the Hastings family, as well as a literary executor of Cartwright, Hildersham, during a long career stretching back to Elizabethan days, was regularly in trouble for nonconformity.[35] At Ashby in 1630 he can still be found teaching that 'in nothing are we so precisely tied to the direction of the word, as in the matters of the worship of God'. He went on to argue from Deuteronomy 12. 32 that 'puritie' of worship requires doing neither more nor less than God commands. 'What thing soever I command you, that shall ye observe to do: thou shalt not add thereto, nor diminish from it.'[36]

A more extended treatment of this subject, from the same point of view, is to be found in *A Plain and Familiar Exposition of the Ten Commandments* by John Dod and Robert Cleaver. One of the deductions drawn from the second commandment is that we must 'stand for God's pure worship against . . . all manner of superstition'. Worship ought not to be 'after the inventions of flesh and blood' but according to the Bible. Papists 'are most guilty in this point'. Among other things 'they have added the crosse' in baptism, which is both 'wicked and abominable'. (So, too, by implication, is the usage of the Church of England.) The radical thrust of the volume emerges even more clearly from a set of prefatory verses where those with parish churches served by 'blind and lazie faithlesse droanes' are encouraged to go elsewhere.[37] Moreover, between 1603 and 1635 *A Plain and Familiar Exposition* went through nineteen English editions. Dod was himself a leading nonconformist and, like Hildersham, one of Cartwright's executors. During the 1630s Dod ministered to a congregation at Fawsley in Northamptonshire, which included John Pym.[38]

Dod and Hildersham are representatives of hardline nonconformity. Other Puritans, however, were prepared to concede that the disputed ceremonies were in the final analysis matters 'indifferent', and that it was better to conform than to be deprived. Their objections sprang from the Popish 'abuse' of ceremonies as opposed to any intrinsic unlawfulness. Ceremonies, like the use of the cross in baptism and the surplice, were best abolished, because they proved offensive to fellow brethren and also encouraged backsliding among religious waverers.[39] Clearly such grounds for nonconformity were less compelling than the alleged breach of God's commandment. Nevertheless this divergence of opinion among Puritans, instead of producing a schism, in fact engendered an attitude of mutal forbearance. As Hildersham put it, in a sermon of 1610:

> Some hold the ceremonies to be unlawfull, others hold them to bee lawfull and fit. And this difference in judgement hath wrought great alienation of heart and affection among God's servants. But this ought not to be so. We should reverence and esteem one another, so many as we see to be able and painfull, and godly men . . . The odious termes of Puritans, or Formalists, of Schismatickes, or Time-Servers ought not to be heard amongst brethern.

It is not entirely fanciful to see opening up here a limited field of toleration, although one produced by particular circumstances, and which to some extent anticipates the later resolution of disagreements over church government when bishops were abolished in the 1640s.[40]

The writings of Hildersham are also imbued with the spirit of evangelical Calvinism. His very last extant sermon, dated 27 December 1631, ends with a defence of preaching as the means whereby the grain is winnowed from the chaff. 'The elect of God are made the better and the rest the worse by it, and God will be glorified in them both.' For the grace of God is free. 'Neither the good workes he fore-saw we should doe, nor the faith he fore-saw we should have, moved him at the first to finde out this way for our salvation and to purpose to bestow this gift upon us, but his owne good pleasure onely.' Christ is said to be the 'saviour of the world' with reference to 'the elect onely that are scattered throughout the world'. Christians should seek to obtain personal 'assurance' of their salvation, taking comfort in the knowledge that one who is 'truly regenerate shall never fall finally nor totally'.[41]

It was not so much that the rise of Arminianism made converts to Puritanism, although there are apparent instances of this,[42] but rather that those already of Puritan inclination were jolted into reassessing their attitude to the Established Church. Up until the 1620s it had been conventional for

Puritans and their opponents to assume a basic doctrinal agreement. Hence, among other things, Puritan willingness to subscribe to the doctrinal part of the Thirty-nine Articles. With the attempted suppression of Calvinism, however, in the first years of Charles's reign, all this changed.[43] The consequences can be graphically illustrated from the writings of the Puritan layman William Prynne. Between his books *Anti-Arminianisme* (1630) and *The Unbishoping of Timothy and Titus* (1636), Prynne moved from a position of moderate nonconformity to one of virtual presbyterianism.[44]

Moreover, for anyone of nonconformist scruples, the new ceremonial requirements of the 1630s, especially as regards the communion service, are likely to have been deeply disturbing. Matters were further compounded by the new liturgy of 1637 imposed on Scotland, in which the compilers had reverted to the eucharistic wording of the first Edwardian Prayer Book.[45] Certainly the failure of Charles to suppress the Scottish rebellion, and his resulting appeal to Parliament in 1640 for money, provided the Puritans with a golden opportunity. Criticism of Arminian or Laudian innovations rapidly developed into a call for more sweeping changes, articulated by way of petitions which came flowing into the Long Parliament. There are distinct echoes here of earlier Puritan campaigns, notably on 23 January 1641 when Sir Robert Harley preferred a petition with 'neare upon a thousand ministers names to it, and a remonstrance with it desiring a reformation in matters of religion and government'.[46]

Already the previous month, however, a more radical London petition calling for the 'root-and-branch' extirpation of episcopacy had been presented. This was followed by a series of county petitions, some of them clearly modelled upon it. Long-standing nonconformist grievances now jostled with newer ones concerning Arminianism.[47] During the 1640s, partly under Scottish pressure, bishops and Prayer Book were to be swept away. On paper at least they were replaced by a Presbyterian system of church government and a new directory for worship.[48] But by 1643 disagreements had arisen among the members of the Westminster Assembly, convened by Parliament to draft a new religious settlement, with a minority of Independents opposed to the Presbyterians over the question of church government. In the ensuing pamphlet controversy, certain Independents developed a theory of religious toleration which revived ideas formulated earlier by Jacob and Helwys.[49]

II

An Apologeticall Narration (1643), produced by the Independents in the Westminster Assembly, is one of the tracts which Haller chose to edit. The central plea of this rather modest document is that the authors be allowed the 'peaceable practises of our consciences' in following a 'middle way' between 'Brownisme' – that is to say full-blown separatism – and the 'authoritative Presbyteriall government'.[50] More daring are the subsequent elaborations of this claim, by two fellow Independents – Henry Burton and John Goodwin. Between them they envisage Independent gathered congregations of 'visible saints', existing alongside a national Presbyterian church, and generally reject compulsion in religious matters. 'Prisons and swords are no church-officers.' Especially subversive was Goodwin's claim that men ran 'the hazard of fighting against God in suppressing any way, doctrine or practice, concerning which they know not certainly whether it be from God or no'.[51] Unlike Baptist writers, however, Burton and Goodwin restricted toleration to varieties of Protestantism. It can be argued that such authors are giving theoretical expression to an inherent centrifugal tendency within Puritanism, first manifested in Elizabethan separatism. But the earliest separatists, notably the followers of Henry Barrow, had, by contrast, been markedly intolerant.[52]

From the mid-1640s the fortunes of the Independents, and those of religious toleration as a whole, rose broadly in unison with the growing influence of the New Model Army in politics. Thus the Army, which had become something of a haven for sectaries, included a request for toleration in their Heads of Proposals of 1647.[53] The Heads in turn were to provide the basis of the Instrument of Government – the constitution of the Protectorate, after the Rump Parliament had been ousted by military force. On the other hand, we do well to remind ourselves, in the words of the modern historian of the Rump, that 'more often than not in Puritan England toleration was a dirty word' and that 'the Long Parliament consistently used the term pejoratively'. In 1650 the Rump passed what may be called a second toleration act, prodded into doing so by a group of Army officers.[54] This repealed the Elizabethan laws enforcing church attendance. Yet it left unrepealed the draconian Blasphemy Ordinance of 1648, which, among many other offences, punished by imprisonment anyone maintaining that 'government by Presbytery' or 'baptizing of infants' is 'unlawfull' – aimed respectively at Independents and Baptists.[55] Similarly silent about the earlier ordinance was the extremely generous provision of the Instrument of Government in 1653, that 'such as profess faith in God by Jesus Christ (though differing in judgement from the doctrine, worship or discipline publicly held forth) shall not be restrained from, but shall be protected in, the profession of the faith and exercise of their religion'. Also 'Popery' and 'Prelacy' were explicitly excluded from this liberty, and use of the Prayer Book remained illegal.[56]

None the less the Cromwellian Church, as it emerged, remains a novel and remarkable experiment. A loose confederation of Presbyterians, Independents, and some Baptists, with a great variety of permitted sectarian activity beyond its fringes, this new English Church was an attempt to translate into practice Baptist principles as adapted by Independents in the 1640s. Its federalism is most apparent in the operation of the Commission of Triers, which vetted would-be parish clergy.[57] Moreover, many episcopalians continued to hold church benefices, and the notion of 'prelacy' did not completely rule out bishops. During the 1640s Archbishop Ussher had adumbrated a version of the limited episcopacy which continued to find favour with moderate Presbyterians like Richard Baxter.[58] Those Protestants who remained beyond the official pale of toleration were the Socinians or anti-Trinitarians and the Quakers, the latter especially because of their refusal to pay tithes.[59]

But the Baptists continued to argue against any such limitations, incorporating this view into at least one of their confessions of faith, which states:

> That it is the will and mind of God (in these gospel times) that all men should have the free liberty of their own conscience in matters of religion, or worship, without the least oppression or persecution, as simply upon that account; and that for any in authority otherwise to act, we confidently believe is expressly contrary to the mind of Christ, who requires that whatsoever men would that others should do unto them, they should even so do unto others, Matthew 7. 12, and that the tares and the wheat should grow together in the field (which is the world) until the harvest (which is the end of the world), Matthew 13. 29–30, 38–9.[60]

A section of the Baptists had also broken with Calvinism and embraced Arminianism, as early as the second decade of the seventeenth century. About 1650 they were joined in this by the Independent John Goodwin.[61]

Meanwhile the freedom to publish in Cromwellian England was in fact almost unbounded, approaching very near to the ideal advanced by John Milton in his *Areopagitica* of 1644.[62] Last but not least, what made the Interregnum religious experiment possible was the benevolent attitude of the Lord Protector himself. When dissolving his first Parliament in January 1655, Oliver Cromwell asked rhetorically: 'Is it ingenuous to ask liberty and not to give it? What greater hypocrisy than for those who were oppressed by the bishops to become the greatest oppressors themselves, as soon as their yoke was removed?' The Presbyterians especially were already trying to whittle away the toleration guaranteed by the Instrument of Government. Milton, in the immediate aftermath of Cromwell's death, while arguing that 'it is not lawfull for any power on earth to compell in matters of religion', also acknowledged the 'Christian liberty which we enjoy'. His *Treatise of Civil Power in Ecclesiastical Causes* is, among other things, an epitaph on the 1650s.[63]

At this point it is appropriate to mention another distinguished American scholar, the third volume of whose four-volume history of religious toleration in England was also published fifty years ago. Wilbur K. Jordan completed this particular labour at a time when, as he wrote, 'the fragile vessel of freedom' was under attack by 'contemporary totalitarian philosophy'. Jordan's study ends in 1660, with monarchy restored in the person of Charles II, and assumes that by then 'the mass of responsible opinion' was convinced of 'the necessity of religious toleration'. Thereafter, so Jordan says, there only remained the admittedly 'difficult' task of making the requisite 'institutional adaptations'. He reached this conclusion having incorporated into his history studies of both episcopalian and Catholic writers on toleration, notably Jeremy Taylor and John Austin.[64] A markedly different Restoration perspective is, however, possible, whether from the point of view of John Bunyan imprisoned in Bedford gaol or that of more moderate Dissenters.[65]

III

Under Cromwell the main body of Puritans had tasted power. It was hardly to be expected that for the future such people would enthusiastically embrace the status of a tolerated sect. Indeed March 1660 had seen a last-ditch attempt, by the briefly restored Long Parliament, to legislate Presbyterianism back into existence.[66] In the event the Puritans got a persecuting episcopalianism, despite the fact that Charles II had himself declared a 'liberty to tender consciences'.[67] As a direct consequence of the 1662 Act of Uniformity, over nine hundred clergy were ejected for their unwillingness, among other things, 'to symbolize with the superstitious rites and inventions of men'. This compares with less than a hundred deprived at the beginning of James I's reign, and made for a much greater chorus of complaint.[68] Yet throughout the 1660s the Nonconformist sympathizers in the Cavalier Parliament were heavily outvoted. The years 1661 to 1665 saw the enactment of a series of punitive measures against Dissenters, collectively known as the Clarendon Code.[69] A tentative government move in 1668 to introduce a comprehension bill, aimed at reuniting the ejected ministers to the Established Church, met with a generally hostile reception and in 1670 the Clarendon Code was itself topped up with a further Conventicle Act.[70]

Within three years, however, essentially the same House of Commons had performed an about-turn, passing in March 1673 a bill 'for the ease of His Majesty's Protestant subjects, Dissenters from the Church of England'. This bill foreshadows the toleration established by law in 1689, the main difference being that in 1673 no provisions were made for Baptists and Quakers.[71] Members of Parliament were quite frank in debate about the main reason for their change of heart. As Sir Thomas Meres, chairman of the committee for the bill, put it: 'What is it that makes us now so zealous in this question, but our fears of Popery?' The 1672 royal Declaration of Indulgence, which granted toleration to both Dissenters *and* Catholics, was predominantly responsible for this realignment. While the old allegation can still be found in these debates that 'Presbyterians will ever be for a Commonwealth', the claim of Charles II to suspend penal statutes now took centre stage. The Commons both denied this royal power and distinguished the cause of the Dissenters from that of the Catholics.[72] In consequence their proposed bill was doubly unattractive to Charles. All the more so since this parliamentary session also produced a Test Act, aimed against Catholic office-holders and originally entitled a bill 'to prevent the growth of Popery'.[73]

Indeed one can scarcely exaggerate the importance of the anti-Catholic factor in these years. The link between foreign policy and the domestic toleration of Catholicism raised up the spectre of absolutism, much as it had before the Civil War – with France now playing the role of Spain. While the Catholic clauses of the 1670 Treaty of Dover remained secret, the French alliance was official. There was also an increasing awareness that James, Duke of York, the heir to the throne, had converted to Catholicism.[74] Matters were further compounded by the growing perception of a French commercial threat, which served to redirect English hostility away from the Dutch.[75] By 1673, therefore, toleration courtesy of the royal prerogative had become deeply suspect.

The fate, in the House of Lords, of the bill for ease of Protestant Dissenters is instructive. There it was radically altered in two respects. First, the actual implementation of the proposed Act was, as amended by the Lords, to be left to the discretion of the monarch. This in effect confirmed the royal suspending power. Secondly, the obligation on Dissenting ministers to take the oaths of supremacy and allegiance, and to subscribe to the doctrinal part of the Thirty-nine Articles, was removed by the Lords from the bill. The Commons retorted that, on this basis, 'liberty might be given to Popery, and all heresies and sects whatsoever'. They added that their proposed 'tests will put a difference between the Popish and Protestant Dissenters, which were never sufficiently distinguished by any law yet extant; and . . . will be of great benefit and advantage to the Church of England, and conduce very much to the preservation and security of the Protestant religion'. In the event neither house proved willing to budge from its respective position, and talks were getting nowhere when the session was adjourned and subsequently prorogued.[76]

The debates in the Commons on the bill for ease of Protestant Dissenters also highlight the role of economic considerations at this time. For some years indeed these had provided a plank in the Dissenter case for toleration. Thus in 1670 the Independent clergyman John Owen had argued against the renewal of the Conventicle Act, largely on economic grounds. He claimed that the victims would be mainly 'merchants, clothiers, operators in our manufactures, and occupants of land, with the like furtherers and promoters of trade'. Their 'ruin' will cause 'a distressing general poverty'.[77] This theme was more fully developed, however, in a work of the following year by Slingsby Bethell. He was also an Independent, but a layman and retired merchant. In *The Present Interest of England Stated* (1671), Bethell maintained that 'imposing upon conscience, in matters of religion, is a mischief unto trade transcending all others whatsoever'. Countries like Spain have 'split upon' this 'rock'. Bethell also produced a striking piece of sociological generalisation. There is, he wrote, 'a kind of natural unaptness in the Popish religion to business, whereas on the contrary among the reformed the greater their zeal the greater their inclination to trade and industry, as holding idleness unlawful'. Protestant Dissenters were the 'soberest and most industrious sort'.[78]

But Dissenters had no monopoly of such views. Someone of a very different religious outlook, who likewise argued publicly for the economic benefits of toleration at this time, was Sir William Temple. His *Observations upon the United Provinces of the Netherlands* was published in 1673, and includes related chapters on religion and trade. Temple takes as his premiss that 'the great and general end of all religion, next to men's happiness hereafter, is their happiness here'. Since 'the way to our future happiness has been perpetually disputed throughout the world, and must be left at last to the impressions made upon every man's belief and conscience', our 'happiness here' is alone of public concern. The rulers of the United Provinces have grasped this basic axiom and the country has prospered accordingly. There

> men live together like citizens of the world, associated by the common ties of humanity and by the bonds of peace, under the impartial protection of indifferent laws, with equal encouragement of all art and industry and equal freedom of speculation and enquiry, . . . wherein will appear to consist chiefly the vast growth of their trade and riches, and consequently the strength and greatness of their state.[79]

Back in 1668 Colonel John Birch, a leading member of the Dissenter lobby in the Commons, can be found arguing that 'toleration' is to the 'advantage of trade'. He reiterated this view in 1673, but now it found much more general support among Members of Parliament.[80] Lord St John, eldest son of the Marquess of Winchester, went so far as to say that 'it is the intention of the bill [for ease of Protestant Dissenters] to bring people and manufactures into the nation, and to keep those here we have'. Likewise Sir Charles Harbord instanced Temple's newly published *Observations*, which 'tells you that mighty things have been done there by what you intend in this act'. By contrast, the decline of Spain was held up as an object lesson in the results of persecution.[81] At a time when fighting the Dutch was proving increasingly unsuccessful, alternative mercantilist approaches such as religious toleration acquired new relevance.[82] It was left to Edmund Waller, the poet, to articulate a more general theory of toleration during these discussions in the Commons, maintaining that coercion of belief merely breeds hypocrisy.[83]

For the fullest exposition of toleration in a parliamentary context, however, we need to turn to George Villiers, second Duke of Buckingham, who introduced an abortive toleration bill into the House of Lords during November 1675. The moment was particularly inauspicious because the two Houses were involved in a jurisdictional dispute, but this does not affect the interest of the ideas expressed. Moreover Buckingham was closely allied with Shaftesbury. The latter held similar views concerning toleration, and during the 1650s had served as a member of the Council of State established by the Instrument of Government. Also, since the late 1660s John Locke had been a member of the Shaftesbury household, writing 'An Essay concerning Toleration' in 1667.[84] Buckingham, in 1675, located 'indulgence to all Protestant Dissenters' firmly in the context of 'a thing called Liberty'. Our 'fellow subjects' are 'daily abused, divested of their liberties and birthrights, and miserably thrown out of their possessions and freeholds, only because they cannot agree with others in some opinions and niceties of religion'. Persecution is both incompatible with the 'improvement of our trade and increase of the wealth, strength and greatness of this nation', and also wrong-headed. For it makes 'every man's safety' depend upon 'uncertain opinions of religion' rather than upon 'living well toward the civil government established by law', and is, in addition, 'positively against the express doctrine and example of Jesus Christ'.[85] The preamble of the surviving bill covers much the same ground, adding that penal laws are 'altogether ineffectual to convince the understandings of men, to alter their faith, or to deter others from believing what their reason leads them to'.[86]

With Temple and Waller, Buckingham represents what has been called a new 'secularizing tendency'.[87] Long gone were the days when Puritans could hope to win parliamentary majorities on the intrinsic merits of their case, the experience of the Civil War and Interregnum having largely dissipated that earlier fund of goodwill. Even before 1640, however, anti-Catholicism was already an important factor, and the idea of a Popish Plot featured prominently in the early debates of the Long Parliament.[88] But the failure of the 1673 bill, and the withdrawal by Charles II of his Declaration of Indulgence, produced a political stalemate regarding toleration. Not until 1680, as a result of the Exclusion Crisis, were there any further moves in the Commons. The latter reflect an attempt to reach a compromise between the Whigs, bent on excluding the Catholic James, Duke of York, from the succession, and those who favoured less draconian means of securing the future of Protestantism.[89]

Indicative of the change of mood since 1673 is that in November 1680 a Commons committee was appointed to prepare a bill 'for the better uniting of all His Majesty's Protestant subjects'.[90] Faced with the prospect of a Catholic king, comprehension rather than toleration recommended itself to the leaders of the Commons. The object was a broad Protestant front, against the 'common enemy'. But the committee also spawned a toleration bill, designed to meet the needs of Independents and others whom it would be very difficult to comprehend within anything like the existing establishment. These two bills, of comprehension and indulgence, are the immediate precursors of the bills introduced in 1689. Both of the 1680 bills entailed clergy subscribing to the doctrinal part of the Thirty-nine Articles, the only difference being that in the toleration measure part of article 27 was also omitted on behalf of Baptists. The oaths of supremacy and allegiance, and a declaration against 'Popery', were also obligations common to the two bills. The comprehension bill accepted the validity of Presbyterian ordination received prior to 1660 and repealed various other requirements of the Act of Uniformity, such as the 'assent and consent' to the Prayer Book. A black gown replaced the surplice for use in parish churches, and the ceremonies of signing with the cross in baptism and kneeling at communion were made optional.[91]

The draft toleration bill of 1680 largely anticipates the act of 1689, guaranteeing freedom of worship in return for limited clerical subscription. Both contain provisions dispensing Quakers from taking the oaths.[92] As with the later measure, the existing civil disabilities and the obligation to pay tithes remained. Moreover, by 1680 there would appear to have been more support for toleration than for comprehension. Indeed, ever since large numbers of Dissenters had taken out licences in 1672, under the terms of the Declaration of Indulgence, their position had tended to become institutionalised.[93] Subsequent events, however, were to show that comprehension remained attractive at least to some Presbyterians.[94] Neither bill passed beyond a second reading in 1680, because of the dissolution of the Parliament. Although reintroduced into the new Parliament of 1681, their fate then was even more summary, and for the same reason.[95] But the necessary conditions of success were by now clear. While sincere believers in the principle of toleration manifestly existed, they were too few to win the argument in Parliament. A coalition of anti-Catholic interests pointed the way forward, although one of the hardest tasks would be to convince the bishops in the Lords. Still more problematic was the position of the monarch. Meanwhile, toleration by royal prerogative remained a possible alternative.

Rather surprisingly, the economic argument for toleration is absent from the recorded debates of the Commons in 1680. Part of the explanation here may be that population loss through emigration was slowing down. Moreover, England was soon to experience renewed foreign Protestant immigration on a considerable scale and extending over several decades.[96] Nor did anti-Catholicism remain a constant. For during the early 1680s Charles II repaired royal relations with the Established Church to such good effect that the Parliament summoned in 1685, by his successor James II, proved at least as loyalist as the Cavalier Parliament in its heyday. The principal victims of this *rapprochement* were the Dissenters.[97] But, just as the 1672 Declaration of Indulgence had served earlier to weaken the alliance of church and king, so James's much greater commitment to Catholicism proved even more destructive. In the spring of 1686 the Dissenters again became a stalking-horse for the toleration of Catholics, culminating the next year with the issue of a new Declaration of Indulgence.[98]

IV

The years 1686 to 1688 saw the Dissenters being wooed by both James II and the Protestant leaders of the Church of England. Yet the olive branch proffered by the bishops came remarkably late, in May 1688. While rejecting the royal order to publish the Declaration of Indulgence, they explained that this did not stem from 'any want of due tenderness to Dissenters, in relation to whom they were willing to come to such a temper as shall be thought fit, when that matter shall be settled in Parliament and Convocation'.[99] A frontal challenge to the monopoly of the Church of England, by a Catholicising ruler, had induced this concessionary mood. The flight of James later in the year, however, led to a renewed hardening of episcopal attitudes. William and Mary were increasingly identified with the Dissenter cause, and the threat of Popery was replaced by fears of resurgent Puritanism.[100]

Even in 1689 the passing of the Toleration Act was to prove a close run thing, barely carried on the crest of reaction to James II. Much of the credit for success must be ascribed to the Tory Daniel Finch, Earl of Nottingham. It was Nottingham, before his accession to the peerage, who had masterminded the parliamentary proceedings on toleration and comprehension in 1680. Again in February and March 1689 he introduced similar bills into the Lords.[101] But now there was a rise in Dissenter expectations, involving the abolition of civil as well as religious disabilities. The consequent attempt to repeal the relevant sections of the Corporation and Test Acts, despite the public backing of William, ended in defeat. Overambition also helps to explain the failure of the comprehension measure, the Dissenters sponsoring a rival and more radical bill to that of Nottingham.[102] Nevertheless the toleration bill was passed, apparently as part of a political deal between Whigs and Tories whereby the question of comprehension was referred to Convocation. There the clergy subsequently killed it, despite preparatory work by a specially appointed royal commission.[103] Furthermore, at a crucial moment in the Commons – a time-limit on toleration having been proposed – news was announced of a substantial financial loan to the crown by the Dissenters and the amendment was defeated.[104]

With the abandonment of comprehension died the last chance of fulfilling the original Puritan aim of further reform of the English Church. But what of the Toleration Act? Opinions have varied considerably as to its significance. For example, play has been made on the fact that the Act was officially entitled 'for exempting Their Majesties' Protestant subjects, dissenting from the Church of England, from the penalties of certain laws'. Nowhere is the word 'toleration' mentioned.[105] Yet examination of the journals of the Lords and Commons reveals a great variety of usage. At various stages in both houses the draft proposals on this subject are described as being for 'toleration'. In addition the manuscript House of Lords Committee Book refers to the measure throughout under the rubric of 'E. Nottingham Tolleracion'.[106] Nor, given the wish to distinguish between Catholics and Protestants, is it clear what alternative form the legislation could have taken. More to the point is the disadvantageous comparison with the previous Declarations of Indulgence. They did indeed declare a general toleration, but flew in the face of parliamentary hostility. Their authors also exhibited an alarming inconstancy of purpose, Charles II reverting to a policy of persecution from the mid–1670s and one which James II himself pursued initially.[107] After 1685 there was in addition the grim reminder of the Revocation of the Edict of Nantes. Although there was no such thing as a cast-iron guarantee, a parliamentary statute represented the next best thing.

It was a compromise – but the Toleration Act none the less compares well with the more principled measures of the Interregnum, which had officially excluded the episcopalian majority and failed to protect the Quakers. Also it gave Dissenters what many Independents, generally suspicious of establishment, had been requesting all along. Judged of course by John Locke's *Letter concerning Toleration* (1689), which envisages complete disestablishment and the virtual abolition of all doctrinal tests,[108] the Toleration Act falls far short. In the real world, however, of late seventeenth-century England the practical achievement was remarkable. Presbyterians, Independents, Baptists and Quakers all gained the right, by law, to worship freely. Paradoxically fear of Popery had proved necessary to break the monopoly of the Church of England, and Catholics were the losers.[109] But among Protestants the only group not to benefit was the anti-Trinitarians, although even here 'the check was only temporary'.[110] Jettisoning as it did the old idea of religious unity in favour of a pluralism guaranteed by the state, the Toleration Act truly merits the term revolutionary.

Particularly interesting here is the reaction of Locke himself. Writing in June 1689, to the Dutch Remonstrant Philip van Limborch, he comments:

Toleration has now at last been established by law in our country. Not perhaps so wide in scope as might be wished for by you and those like you, who are true Christians and free from ambition or envy. Still, it is something to have progressed so far. I hope that, with these beginnings, the foundations have been laid of that liberty and peace in which the church of Christ is one day to be established.

By contrast, Locke showed no enthusiasm for the comprehension bill. 'Men will always differ on religious questions and rival parties will continue to quarrel and wage war on each other, unless the establishment of equal liberty for all provides a bond of mutual charity by which all may be brought together into one body.'[111]

Locke tended to draw the line, however, at tolerating Catholics. William III, on the other hand, was publicly committed to granting them some measure of relief.[112] Thus royal wishes probably lie behind the attempt in December 1689 to enlarge the scope of the Toleration Act to include Catholics, 'so as the same extend not to the *public* exercise of the Popish religion'. Under the terms of the proposed bill, Catholics were obliged to take an oath of allegiance, which also involved abjuring the papal deposing power. In return, as well as being allowed to worship privately, they were to be freed from the financial and other penalties of recusancy. Entitled 'an act for exempting Their Majesties' Popish subjects from the penalties of certain laws', it received a first reading in the Lords on 19 December. After a second reading on 30 December it was referred to a select committee. Reported on 31 December, the bill was recommitted and did not re-emerge. To judge from the amended draft, the most controversial aspect was the inclusion of Catholics under the terms of the Toleration Act. But in the end no legal relief of any kind was forthcoming.[113]

In March 1689 the King had also sought to remove the civil disabilities under which Dissenters suffered – something never at this time proposed for Catholics. As we have noted, this move by William failed. But the toleration bill as originally introduced into the Lords had itself been significantly more generous, in that it permitted the licensing of Dissenter schoolmasters on the same terms as clergy ministering to a congregation. The clause was lost, however, in committee.[114] As a consequence a question mark still hung over the future of Dissenter education. Dissenter schoolmasters remained liable to legal prosecution, although a body of case law on the whole favourable to them and dating from 1670 onwards continued to build up. Prosecutions brought against such schoolmasters in the ecclesiastical courts were usually removed, by a writ of prohibition, to the common-law jurisdiction. The influence of the crown, under William, was also used on their behalf.[115]

The Dissenter academies especially provided a crucial training ground for future generations of clergy, and were viewed with deepening hostility as

Nonconformity prospered in the aftermath of the Toleration Act. (By 1718 there were almost two thousand Dissenter congregations in England and Wales.)[116] Meanwhile, since the Corporation and Test Acts continued to apply to Dissenters, recourse was regularly made to the device of Occasional Conformity, whereby Dissenters qualified themselves for office in such a way as to make a mockery of the existing legislation. The situation as regards the Corporation of London was especially notorious. Thus in 1697 the Lord Mayor, Sir Humphrey Edwin, went so far as to attend St Paul's Cathedral and a Dissenter meeting-house on the same day, in full regalia on both occasions.[117] Matters came to a head on these issues with the accession of Queen Anne in 1702 and the resurgence of Tory hopes, the years 1702 to 1704 seeing a succession of parliamentary bills aimed at stamping out Occasional Conformity.[118] Also in 1703 the editors of Clarendon's *History of the Rebellion*, dedicating the second volume to the new Queen, asked rhetorically: 'what can be the meaning of the several seminaries, and as it were universities, set up in divers parts of the kingdom, by more than ordinary industry, contrary to law, supported by large contributions, where the youth is bred up in principles directly contrary to monarchical and episcopal government?' The following year, in a similar dedication of the third volume, they added 'irreligion' to their catalogue of woe. 'When many who have been in authority have not, on several accounts, been heartily affected to the support of the Church established by law, there has crept in, little by little, a liberty against all religion'.[119] From this perspective the Dissenters and their Whig allies had glossed the 1689 Toleration Act so broadly as seriously to endanger the Established Church – a view articulated most famously of course in the sermons of Henry Sacheverell. Yet the parliamentary debates and associated pamphleteering on the Occasional Conformity bills reveal very similar sentiments. 'Are we afraid', enquired Sir John Pakington in 1703, 'to disoblige a party of men that are against the church and government' and 'whose principles of hatred and malice to the family of the Stuarts descends to them by inheritance?' He went on to say that 'by the benefit of this Occasional Conformity the Dissenters will come to be the majority of this house, and then I will venture to pronounce the days of the Church of England few'. Pakington's fellow Member of Parliament, Sir Humphrey Mackworth, asked more sinisterly:

are the Dissenters secure that there are no lurking Deists, no Socinian politicians behind the curtain, who are striving for power and dominion under the specious pretence of liberty and conscience . . . making use of the Dissenters as tools and scaffolds to raise themselves, destroy our constitution and extirpate the true Christian religion out of the kingdom?[120]

The years after 1689 had indeed seen an upsurge in the publishing of heterodox views, which the law seemed powerless to control. This despite the passing of a Blasphemy Act in 1698. Equally alarming was the growth of popular irreligion, for many parishioners seem to have taken advantage of the Toleration Act to stay away from any place of worship whatsoever.[121] There was in addition the running sore of Scottish episcopalianism, bishops having been abolished in Scotland during 1689 and the episcopalian clergy systematically removed from their livings.[122] Moreover, the prospect of Anglo-Scottish union in the early years of Anne's reign served to highlight the religious situation north of the border. Such was the immediate background to the parliamentary debates in 1705 on the 'Church in danger' and the publication the same year of *The Memorial of the Church of England*. While not the author, Mackworth apparently had a hand in distributing this anonymous Tory pamphlet.[123] According to *The Memorial*, there was a 'hectick feavour lurking in the very bowels' of the English Church, which 'if not timely cur'd will infect all the humours and at length destroy the very being of it'. Dissenters and Scottish Presbyterians threatened the Church from the outside, while Occasional Conformists undermined it from within. The latter were abetted by 'Deists, Socinians and Latitudinarians', as well as by 'Low Church-Men'. *The Memorial* also expressed fears for the religious consequences of a Hanoverian succession, and attacked bishops who still had their 'heads vainly filled with chimerical notions of an impracticable comprehension'. It concluded by raising the spectre of war between Scotland and England.[124]

Published in July 1705, *The Memorial* proved a *cause célèbre* – its reverberarions were still felt a year later. A hunt began almost immediately for the author, printer and publisher. That September *The Memorial* was burnt by the common hangman, having been presented by the London and Middlesex grand jury as a 'false, scandalous and traiterous libel'.[125] At the opening of Parliament in October it was alluded to in Queen Anne's speech and was cited in a royal proclamation issued on 20 December. The Lords and Commons having voted that the Church of England was 'in a most safe and flourishing condition, and that whosoever goes about to suggest and insinuate that the Church is in danger under Her Majestie's Administration is an enemy to the Queen, the Church and Kingdom', the proclamation gave teeth to this resolution. The 'utmost severity the law will allow' was to be used against the 'authors or spreaders of the said seditious and scandalous reports'. Law officers were to 'take effectual care for the speedy apprehension, prosecution and punishment of all such persons', and the general public were ordered to assist them. The proclamation then went on to offer a £200 reward for the 'discovery' of the author of *The Memorial*, describing it as a 'malicious and seditious libel'.[126]

Three days later, on 23 December 1705, Henry Sacheverell preached a sermon before the assembled University of Oxford, 'upon "in perills amongst false bretheren", in the prosecution of which words he did with a great deal of courage and boldness shew the great danger the Church is in at present – notwithstanding the Parliament has voted it to be in none'. Thomas Hearne, the source of this information, later noted that 'this is the very sermon that he preach'd afterwards in London, November 5 1709', and 'for which he was impeach'd and punished'.[127] So much is well known, but the existence of the proclamation of 20 December has slipped from historical view.[128] The fact that Sacheverell was apparently quite unscathed on this first occasion, despite such a direct challenge to authority, can only have encouraged him in the view that he was invulnerable. Nevertheless the years from 1706 to 1709 do seem to have witnessed a dying down of agitation against the Dissenters. Partly this was because of continuing divisions among the Tories and partly because of a feeling that the extremists had overreached themselves. What changed the situation was a dawning prospect of European peace and the resultant opportunity to break the increasing stranglehold of the Whigs. There was an element of the fortuitous, however, in the catalytic role that the repreaching by Sacheverell of his 1705 sermon came to play.[129]

In the course of this sermon, at least in the November 1709 version, Sacheverell referred to the Toleration Act as an 'indulgence the government has condescended to give' to 'consciences truly scrupulous'. By contrast he spoke of 'false bretheren' who 'defend toleration and liberty of conscience'.[130] This was to provide one of the impeachment charges against him, when he compounded matters by further claiming that 'upon the most diligent enquiry' he had 'not been able to inform himself that a Toleration hath been granted by law'.[131] The Sacheverell trial of 1710 in fact provides a *locus classicus* for the divergent interpretations of the Toleration Act which had by now clearly emerged. The Whig prosecution was adamant that a 'Toleration Act' had been passed in 1689 and that to speak of 'indulgence' rather than 'toleration' was a meaningless distinction. They produced extensive evidence, including a speech by Queen Anne, in support of what they claimed was normal usage. The defence, on the other hand, continued to argue that 'there is no such thing as a Toleration granted by law'. But they also said that Sacheverell's pejorative remarks were to be understood of 'an universal general toleration', as opposed to the much more modest 1689 measure. In addition the defence claimed that many existing Dissenter congregations were in breach of the law, having failed to register their existence. Finally, they justified the assertion of Sacheverell that all Dissenters were guilty of 'schism' according to the law of the English Church.[132]

Although found guilty on this and the other charge, Sacheverell received a minimal sentence and the trial boomeranged on its promoters. At the general election in the autumn of 1710 the Tories secured a resounding majority of 151 Members of Parliament, and a new ministry was formed under Sir

Robert Harley – a descendant of his Puritan namesake and future Earl of Oxford. Symbolic of the changed political atmosphere was the unopposed reprinting in 1711 of *The Memorial*, and the successful passage into law of an Occasional Conformity Act. (In fact the bill only passed the Lords due to a somewhat bizarre alliance between Nottingham and the Whigs, the latter trying to prevent a European peace settlement.) Also indicative of Tory pressure is the repeal by this same Parliament, in 1712, of the Act of General Naturalisation. Conversely, Scottish episcopalians were granted toleration.[133] The general election of 1713 produced an even heftier Tory majority in the Commons, followed by the 1714 Schism Act aimed against Dissenter education. During the debate in the Lords the Earl of Anglesey stated that the Dissenters had 'rendered themselves unworthy of the indulgence the Church of England granted them at the Revolution, by endeavouring to engross the education of youth'.[134] Despite the moderating influence of both Harley and Queen Anne, the religious drift of these years is clear. The net effect was the narrowest possible interpretation of toleration, short of actually rescinding the 1689 act.

Yet the collapse of the Tory party following on the accession of George I in 1714 did not lead to the rapid repeal of either the Occasional Conformity Act or the Schism Act, in spite of assurances from Hanover during Anne's lifetime.[135] The explanation would appear to lie in the politically unstable situation which George inherited, marked by widespread signs of popular disaffection – much of it directed against Dissenters. The extent of English Jacobitism was unclear to the government.[136] Distrustful of the Tories, they nevertheless wished so far as possible to placate the Church of England clergy, who, led by Archbishop William Wake from 1716, were mainly against repeal.[137] Matters were further complicated by factional divisions among the Whig leadership.[138] Not until November 1717 did George make any public move on behalf of the Dissenters, urging 'some proper method for the greater strengthening the Protestant interest', by 'the union and mutual charity of all Protestants'.[139] Even then it was not until over a year later that Earl Stanhope introduced a bill into the Lords, in December 1718, entitled an act 'for strengthening the Protestant interest in these kingdoms'.

The bill was a composite one, designed to repeal both the Occasional Conformity Act and the Schism Act. As first introduced, it also sought to remove the civil disabilities of Dissenters. This was to be achieved on the basis of a rather complicated formula, under which certified refusal of the sacrament by a Church of England clergyman to a declared Dissenter would qualify him for office. It is an interesting question whether Stanhope and the Earl of Sunderland, who was also closely involved, ever thought this most controversial aspect of the bill could succeed. At any rate the clause was quickly abandoned, and the rest of the bill became law in 1719.[140] Thus the legal position of Dissenters reverted to that of mid–1689. But what originally had been a bipartisan measure was now clearly identified with the Whigs and their more principled wing at that, for Sir Robert Walpole had publicly opposed Stanhope's bill even as amended.[141] From 1719 onwards, however, toleration was to prove safe in Whig hands, while largely leaving behind its Puritan roots and becoming grafted into a different philosophical tradition.

NOTES

This essay was originally delivered as a lecture in November 1988, at a London conference held under the auspices of the William and Mary Tercentenary Trust.

1 W. Haller, *The Rise of Puritanism; or the Way to the New Jerusalem as Set forth in Pulpit and Press from Thomas Cartwright to John Lilburne and John Milton* (New York, 1938, pbk edn 1957); ed., *The Works of John Milton* (New York, 1931–38), iv–vi; ed., *Tracts on Liberty in the Puritan Revolution, 1638–1647* (New York, 1933–34); and G. Davies eds, *The Leveller Tracts, 1647–1653* (New York, 1944); *Liberty and Reformation in the Puritan Revolution* (New York, 1955).

2 Haller, *Rise of Puritanism*, pp. 289, 362–3.

3 G. M. Trevelyan, *England under the Stuarts* (London, 1949), p. 170.

4 Haller, *Liberty and Reformation*, p. xv.

5 My own work on the history of English Arminianism must bear some responsibility for the modern neglect of Puritanism: Tyacke, *Anti-Calvinists*.

6 P. Collinson, *The Elizabethan Puritan Movement* (London, 1967); J. H. Primus, *The Vestments Controversy: An Historical Study of the Earliest Tensions within the Church of England in the Reigns of Edward VI and Elizabeth* (Kampen, 1960); S. B. Babbage, *Puritanism and Richard Bancroft* (London, 1962); L. J. Trinterud, *Elizabethan Puritanism* (New York, 1971), pp. 7–8.

7 See pp. 65–8 above.

8 R. Thomas, 'Comprehension and Indulgence', in G. F. Nuttall and O. Chadwick eds, *From Uniformity to Unity, 1662–1962* (London, 1962), p. 244.

9 *The Statutes of the Realm* (London, 1810–28), vi, pp. 74–6.

10 *Ibid.*, v, pp. 367–8.

11 *Ibid.*, iv, 546. My italics; T. E. Hartley ed., *Proceedings in the Parliaments of Elizabeth I* (Leicester, 1981), i, p. 432. Cf. G. R. Elton, *The Parliament of England, 1559–1581* (Cambridge, 1986), pp. 210–14.

12 *Statutes of the Realm*, iv, pp. 546–7.

13 Collinson, *Elizabethan Puritan Movement*, pp. 244–5.

14 A. Peel ed., *The Seconde Parte of a Register* (Cambridge, 1915), i, p. 195; ii, p. 198.

15 Hartley ed., *Proceedings*, i, pp. 200, 220, 225, 238–9; J. P. Kenyon ed., *The Stuart Constitution* (2nd edn, Cambridge, 1986), p. 118.

16 W. H. Frere and C. E. Douglas, *Puritan Manifestos* (London, 1907), pp. 30, 149–52; Hartley, ed., *Proceedings*, i, pp. 362–3, 368–70; J. E. Neale, *Elizabeth I and her Parliaments, 1559–1581* (London, 1953), pp. 297–303.

17 J. Strype, *The Life and Acts of John Whitgift* (Oxford, 1822), iii, pp. 120–1; J. E. Neale, *Elizabeth I and her Parliaments, 1584–1601* (London, 1957), pp. 61, 64, 100.

18 Collinson, *Elizabethan Puritan Movement*, pp. 303–16.

19 Cf. Neale, *Elizabeth and her Parliaments, 1584–1601*, pp. 394–410.

20 Collinson, *Elizabethan Puritan Movement*, pp. 448–54; Babbage, *Puritanism and Richard Bancroft*, pp. 43–73; PRO, SP 14/10, no. 62.

21 Kenyon ed., *Stuart Constitution*, p. 118; pp. 111–12 below.

22 P. Collinson, 'The Jacobean Religious Settlement: The Hampton Court Conference', in H. Tomlinson ed., *Before the English Civil War* (London, 1983), pp. 27–51.

23 PRO, SP 14/7, no. 2.

24 *Commons Journals*, i, pp. 153, 172–6, 199–200, 214, 224, 235, 238, 240–1; Babbage, *Puritanism and Richard Bancroft*, ch. 8.

25 C. Cross ed., *The Letters of Sir Francis Hastings, 1574–1609* (Somerset Recd. Soc., 69, 1969), pp. 88–97.

26 D. Willson ed., *The Parliamentary Diary of Robert Bowyer, 1606–1607* (Minneapolis, 1931), pp. 56, 167–70, 342; HMC House of Lords, NS ii, pp. 11–12, 127; E. R. Foster ed., *Proceedings in Parliament, 1610* (New Haven, 1966), ii, pp. 255–6.

27 Babbage, *Puritanism and Richard Bancroft*, pp. 237, 243–4.

28 H. Jacob, *To the Right High and Mightie Prince, James, an Humble Supplication for Toleration and Libertie to Enjoy and Observe the Ordinances of Christ Jesus in th'Administration of His Churches in Lieu of Humane Constitutions* (Middleburg, 1609), pp. 8, 13, 20, 23, 28, 48.

29 T. Helwys, *A Short Declaration of the Mistery of Iniquity* (Amsterdam, 1612), p. 69; K. L. Sprunger, *Dutch Puritanism: A History of English and Scottish Churches of the Netherlands in the Sixteenth and Seventeenth Centuries* (Studies in the History of Christian Thought, 21; Leiden, 1982), pp. 76–90.

30 M. J. Jansson ed., *Proceedings in Parliament, 1614 (House of Commons)*, (Philadelphia, 1988), p. 75; C. Russell, *Parliaments and English Politics, 1621–1629* (Oxford, 1979), p. 231.

31 S. R. Gardiner ed., *Debates in the House of Commons in 1625* (Camden Soc. NS 6; 1873), pp. 26, 289; J. Rushworth, *Historical Collections* (London, 1659–1701), i, pp. 182–3; Russell, *Parliaments and English Politics*, p. 231.

32 Russell, *Parliaments and English Politics*, p. 307; R. C. Johnson, M. F. Keeler, M. J. Cole, and W. B. Bidwell eds, *Commons Debates 1628* (New Haven, 1977–83), iii, pp. 513–22.

33 Tyacke, *Anti-Calvinists*, pp. 106–80.

34 Haller, *Rise of Puritanism*, p. 50; C. Hill, *Society and Puritanism in Pre-Revolutionary England* (London, 1964), p. 502.

35 S. Clarke, *The Lives of Thirty-two English Divines* (London, 1677), pp. 114–24; A. F. Scott Pearson, *Thomas Cartwright and Elizabethan Puritanism, 1535–1603* (Cambridge, 1925), p. 392.

36 A. Hildersham, *CLII Lectures upon Psalm LI* (London, 1642), p. 652.

37 J. Dod and R. Cleaver, *A Plaine and Familiar Exposition of the Ten Commandments* (London, 1604), sig. A3v, pp. 59, 76, 80.

38 Scott Pearson, *Thomas Cartwright*, p. 392; J. T. Cliffe, *The Puritan Gentry* (London, 1984), pp. 180–3; C. Russell, 'The Parliamentary Career of John Pym', in P. Clark, A. G. R. Smith, and N. Tyacke eds, *The English Commonwealth, 1547–1640* (Leicester, 1979), pp. 148, 249.

39 P. Lake, *Moderate Puritans and the Elizabethan Church* (Cambridge, 1982), pp. 242–68.

40 A. Hildersham, *CVIII Lectures upon the Fourth of John* (London, 1632), p. 301; see above, pp. 68–70.

41 Hildersham, *CLII Lectures*, p. 735; *CVIII Lectures*, sig. a2v, pp. 13, 329, 339.

42 Cornelius Burges would seem to be a case in point: A. Wood, *Athenae Oxonienses*, ed., P. Bliss (Oxford, 1913–20), iii, p. 682.

43 Tyacke, *Anti-Calvinists*, pp. 181–8.

44 *Ibid.* 225–6; W. Prynne, *Anti-Arminianisme or the Church of England's Old Antithesis to New Arminianisme* (London, 1630), sigs. oo*2–qq*4.

45 G. Donaldson, *The Making of the Scottish Prayer Book of 1637* (Edinburgh, 1954), pp. 52, 200–1.

46 W. Notestein ed., *The Journal of Sir Simonds D'Ewes from the Beginning of the Long Parliament* (New Haven, 1923), p. 277.

47 A. Fletcher, *The Outbreak of the English Civil War* (London, 1981), pp. 91–2, 96; S. R. Gardiner ed., *The Constitutional Documents of the Puritan Revolution, 1625–1660* (Oxford, 1962), pp. 137–44.

48 C. H. Firth and R. S. Rait ed., *Acts and Ordinances of the Interregnum, 1642–1660* (London, 1911), i, pp. 582–607, 749–57, 879–83.

49 *Complete Prose Works of John Milton* (New Haven, 1953–82), ii, pp. 65–120; cf. A. Zakai, 'Religious Toleration and its Enemies: The Independent Divines and the Issue of Toleration during the Civil War', *Albion* 21 (1989), 1–38. From the 1640s onwards it is customary to capitalise the initial letter of Independency and Presbyterianism, because of their emergence as distinct denominations.

50 Haller, *Tracts on Liberty*, ii, pp. 332–3.

51 *Ibid.* iii, p. 34; H. Burton, *A Vindication of Churches Commonly Called Independent* (London, 1644), pp. 70–1.

52 W. L. Lumpkin ed., *Baptist Confessions of Faith* (Philadelphia, 1959), pp. 90–4. I owe this reference to Barrie White.

53 Kenyon ed., *Stuart Constitution*, p. 271.

54 B. Worden, 'Toleration and the Cromwellian Protectorate', in W. J. Sheils ed., *Persecution and Toleration* (Studies in Church History, 21; Oxford, 1984), p. 200; *The Rump Parliament, 1648–1653* (Cambridge, 1974), p. 201.

55 *Acts and Ordinances*, i, p. 1135; ii, pp. 423–5.

56 Kenyon ed., *Stuart Constitution*, pp. 312–13.

57 M. R. Watts, *The Dissenters: from the Reformation to the French Revolution* (Oxford, 1978–95), i, pp. 151–68.

58 A. G. Matthews, *Walker Revised* (Oxford, 1988), pp. xvii–xviii; C. G. Bolam, J. Goring, H. L. Short, and R. Thomas, *The English Presbyterians* (London, 1968), pp. 60–3.

59 H. J. McLachlan, *Socinianism in Seventeenth-Century England* (Oxford, 1951), pp. 202–13; H. Barbour, *The Quakers in Puritan England* (New Haven, 1964), 194–202.

60 E. B. Underhill ed., *Confessions of Faith, and other Public Documents Illustrative of the History of the Baptist Churches of England in the Seventeenth Century* (Hanserd Knollys Society, 1854), p. 118.

61 Lumpkin ed., *Baptist Confessions*, pp. 100–1; J. Goodwin, *Redemption Redeemed* (London, 1651).

62 I base this statement on the great range of religious and political opinion to be found among the Thomason Tracts: G. K. Fortescue ed., *Catalogue of the Pamphlets, Books, Newspapers and Manuscripts . . . Collected by George Thomason, 1640–1661* (London, 1908).

63 W. C. Abbott ed., *The Writings and Speeches of Oliver Cromwell* (Cambridge, Mass., 1937–47), iii, p. 586; *Complete Prose Works of John Milton*, vii, pp. 238, 241.

64 W. K. Jordan, *The Development of Religious Toleration in England* (London, 1932–40), iii, pp. 9–10; iv, pp. 10, 378–409, 446–5, 468–9. Jordan, however, fails to deal with Taylor's behaviour after 1660. Nor is it at all clear that Austin was typical of Catholic opinion.

65 C. Hill, *A Turbulent, Seditious, and Factious People: John Bunyan and his Church, 1628–1688* (Oxford, 1988), pp. 105–24; Watts, *The Dissenters*, pp. 221–62.

66 *Acts and Ordinances*, ii, pp. 1461–2.

67 Watts, *The Dissenters*, pp. 221–49; A. Fletcher, 'The Enforcement of the Conventicle Acts 1664–1679', in Sheils ed., *Persecution and Toleration*, pp. 235–46.

68 A. G. Matthews, *Calamy Revised* (Oxford, 1934), pp. xii–xiii; G. F. Nuttall, 'The First Nonconformists', in Nuttall and Chadwick eds, *From Uniformity to Unity*, p. 160; Babbage, *Puritanism and Richard Bancroft*, p. 217.

69 Watts, *The Dissenters*, pp. 221–7.

70 Thomas, 'Comprehension and Indulgence', pp. 198–206; D. R. Lacey, *Dissent and Parliamentary Politics in England, 1661–1689* (New Brunswick, 1969), pp. 56–60.

71 *Commons Journals*, ix, pp. 254, 271; Bodl., Tanner MS, 43, fos 191–4.

72 A. Grey, *Debates of the House of Commons, from the Year 1667 to the Year 1694* (London, 1769), ii, pp. 33, 41; Kenyon ed., *Stuart Constitution*, pp. 382–3. John Evelyn described the 1672 Declaration of Indulgence as being for 'an universal tolleration' (E. S. de Beer ed., *The Diary of John Evelyn* (Oxford, 1955), iii, p. 607).

73 *Commons Journals*, ix, p. 263.

74 J. Miller, *Popery and Politics in England, 1660–1688* (Cambridge, 1978), pp. 124–5 and *passim*.

75 M. Priestley, 'London Merchants and Opposition Politics in Charles II's Reign', *BIHR* 29 (1956), 205–19.

76 Bodl., Tanner MS, 43, fos. 189–90; *Lords Journals*, xii, pp. 579–80, 584.

77 J. Owen, *Works*, ed. W. H. Goold (London, 1850–5), xiii, pp. 576, 583–6.

78 S. Bethell, *The Present Interest of England Stated* (London, 1671), pp. 13–14, 17, 23–4.

79 W. Temple, *Observations upon the United Provinces of the Netherlands*, ed. G. N. Clark (Oxford, 1972), pp. 99–100, 106–7.

80 C. Robbins ed., *The Diary of John Milward ... September, 1666 to May, 1668* (Cambridge, 1938), p. 248; Grey, *Debates*, ii, p. 12.

81 Grey, *Debates*, ii, pp. 133, 164.

82 K. H. D. Haley, *The First Earl of Shaftesbury* (Oxford, 1968), pp. 257–8.

83 Grey, *Debates*, ii, p. 132.

84 Haley, *Shaftesbury*, pp. 77–8, 224–6. J. Locke, *A Letter concerning Toleration*, ed. J. H. Tully (Indianapolis, 1983), pp. 1–16.

85 G. Villiers, *Two Speeches* (Amsterdam, 1675), pp. 12–13.

86 HMC Ninth Report, ii, p. 68.

87 G. N. Clark, *The Later Stuarts, 1660–1714* (Oxford, 1955), p. 35.

88 Fletcher, *Outbreak of the English Civil War*, pp. xix–xxv.

89 H. Horwitz, *Revolution Politicks: The Career of Daniel Finch, Second Earl of Nottingham, 1647–1730* (Cambridge, 1968), pp. 28–9; 'Protestant Reconciliation in the Exclusion Crisis', *JEH* 15 (1964), 201–17.

90 *Commons Journals*, ix, p. 645.

91 Thomas, 'Comprehension and Indulgence', pp. 226–7.

92 Horwitz, 'Protestant Reconciliation', p. 210.

93 Thomas, 'Comprehension and Indulgence', pp. 229–30; Watts, *The Dissenters*, pp. 248–9.

94 Thomas, 'Comprehension and Indulgence', p. 244.

95 *Commons Journals*, ix, p. 711.

96 E. A. Wrigley and R. S. Schofield, *The Population History of England, 1541–1871* (London, 1981), pp. 186, 224; D. Cressy, *Coming Over: Migration and Communication between England and New England in the Seventeenth Century* (Cambridge, 1987), pp. 50–1, 68–9: I owe these references to Julian Hoppit.

97 J. Miller, *James II: A Study in Kingship* (London, 1978), pp. 111–19, 134–7.

98 Kenyon ed., *Stuart Constitution*, pp. 389–91. Like the 1672 Declaration, this contains a brief reference to the economic benefits of religious toleration.

99 *Ibid.*, p. 407.

100 Thomas, 'Comprehension and Indulgence', pp. 248–5.

101 Horwitz, *Revolution Politicks*, p. 87.

102 Horwitz, *Revolution Politicks*, pp. 88–92; Thomas, 'Comprehension and Indulgence', pp. 247–50.

103 Horwitz, *Revolution Politicks*, pp. 92–3; N. Sykes, *From Sheldon to Secker: Aspects of English Church History, 1660–1768* (Cambridge, 1959), pp. 87–8.

104 Lacey, *Dissent and Parliamentary Politics*, p. 237. More general economic arguments for religious toleration are absent in 1689, as they had been in 1680.

105 Sykes, *From Sheldon to Secker*, pp. 89–90; G. Holmes, *Religion and Party in Stuart England* (London, 1975), pp. 12–13; *The Trial of Doctor Sacheverell* (London, 1973), pp. 24, 35–6.

106 *Lords Journals*, xiv, pp. 175, 178; *Commons Journals*, x, p. 87; House of Lords Record Office, Committee Books, iv (1688–90), fos 28–31.

107 Watts, *The Dissenters*, pp. 250–7.

108 Locke, *Letter concerning Toleration*, ed. Tully.

109 For the *de facto* toleration of Catholicism, however, see J. Bossy, 'English Catholics after 1688', in O. P. Grell, J. I. Israel and N. Tyacke eds, *From Persecution to Toleration. The Glorious Revolution and Religion in England* (Oxford, 1991), pp. 367–87.

110 McLachlan, *Socinianism*, pp. 334–5; R. N. Stromberg, *Religious Liberalism in Eighteenth-Century England* (Oxford, 1954).

111 E. S. de Beer ed., *Correspondence of John Locke* (Oxford, 1976–), iii, pp. 633, 689. The claim that Locke 'would have preferred comprehension' appears to be without foundation: John Locke, *The Second Treatise of Government . . . and Letter concerning Toleration*, ed. J. W. Gough (Oxford, 1976), p. xliii.

112 E. N. Williams ed., *The Eighteenth Century Constitution* (Cambridge, 1960), p. 16.

113 HMC Twelfth Report, vi, pp. 385–8. My italics. This abortive measure has escaped the attention of modern commentators.

114 *Ibid.*, p. 35.

115 J. E. G. de Montmorency, *State Intervention in English Education* (Cambridge, 1902), pp. 170–6; Sykes, *From Sheldon to Secker*, pp. 92–3.

116 Watts, *The Dissenters*, pp. 267–9.

117 G. S. de Krey, *A Fractured Society: The Politics of London in the First Age of Party* (Oxford, 1985), pp. 114–15.

118 J. Flaningham, 'The Occasional Conformity Controversy: Ideology and Party Politics, 1697–1711', *JBS* 17: 2 (1977), 38–62.

119 W. D. Macray ed., *The History of the Rebellion . . . by Edward, Earl of Clarendon* (Oxford, 1888), i, pp. xliii, liv–lv.

120 R. Chandler, *The History and Proceedings of the House of Commons from the Restoration to the Present Time* (London, 1742), iii, pp. 281–3; H. Mackworth, *Peace at Home* (London, 1703), pp. 14–15. Both Pakington and Mackworth had links with Sacheverell. Holmes, *Trial of Doctor Sacheverell*, p. 18; G. V. Bennett, 'The Era of Party Zeal, 1702–14', in L. S. Sutherland and L. G. Mitchell eds, *The History of the University of Oxford, V: the Eighteenth Century* (Oxford, 1986), pp. 75–6.

121 G. V. Bennett, *The Tory Crisis in Church and State: The Career of Francis Atterbury, Bishop of Rochester* (Oxford, 1975), pp. 11–12, 16–20; Holmes, *Trial of Doctor Sacheverell*, pp. 25–7.

122 F. Goldie, *A Short History of the Episcopal Church in Scotland, from the Restoration to the Present Time* (London, 1951), pp. 26–42.

123 P. W. J. Riley, *The Union of England and Scotland* (Manchester, 1978), pp. 114–61; Holmes, *Trial of Doctor Sacheverell*, pp. 43–6; J. A. Downie, *Robert Harley and the Press: Propaganda and Public Opinion in the Age of Swift and Defoe* (Cambridge, 1979), pp. 80–100.

124 *The Memorial of the Church of England* (London, 1705), pp. 3–5, 15, 17–20, 27–30. According to the second edition, this was a joint work by J. Drake and H. Poley. *The Memorial* (London, 1711), p. iii.

125 C. E. Doble, D. W. Ronnie, and H. E. Salter ed., *Remarks and Collections of Thomas Hearne* (OHS, 1884–1921), i, pp. 3–4, 6, 10–11, 40, 170, 332; A. Boyer, *The History of the Reign of Queen Anne* (1703–12), iv, p. 176.

126 *Lords Journals*, xviii, pp. 8, 43–4, 48–9; *The London Gazette*, 4186 (20–24 Dec. 1705); I am grateful to Clyve Jones for pointing out this source for the text of royal proclamations.

127 *Remarks and Collections of Thomas Hearne*, i, pp. 138–9.

128 Thus it receives no mention in the standard account by Geoffrey Holmes.

129 Holmes, *Trial of Doctor Sacheverell*, p. 47; Bennett, *The Tory Crisis*, pp. 81–110.

130 H. Sacheverell, *The Perils of False Brethren, both in Church and State* (London, 1710), pp. 10, 19.

131 T. B. Howell ed., *A Complete Collection of State Trials* (London, 1816–28), xv, p. 44. The preamble to the articles of impeachment cites the royal proclamation of 20 December 1705 (*ibid.*, p. 38).

132 *Ibid.*, pp. 136, 153, 293–4, 298–9.

133 W. A. Speck, *Tory and Whig: The Struggle in the Constituencies, 1701–1715* (London, 1970), p. 123; Horwitz, *Revolution Politicks*, pp. 219, 233–4; G. Holmes, *British Politics in the Age of Anne* (London, 1987), pp. 105–6; D. Szechi, 'The Politics of "Persecution": Scots Episcopalian Toleration and the Harley Ministry, 1710–12', in Sheils ed., *Persecution and Toleration*, pp. 275–87. The preface of the 1711 edition of *The Memorial* identifies its stance with that of the 'new' ministry (pp. x–xi).

134 Speck, *Tory and Whig*, p. 123; Holmes, *British Politics in the Age of Anne*, pp. 54–5; *Debates and Speeches in both Houses of Parliament, concerning the Schism Bill* (London, 1715), p. 9.

135 E. Calamy, *An Historical Account of my Own Life*, ed. J. T. Rutt (London, 1830), ii, pp. 245–6.

136 N. Rogers, 'Riot and Popular Jacobitism in Early Hanoverian England', in E. Cruickshanks ed., *Ideology and Conspiracy: Aspects of Jacobitism, 1689–1759* (Edinburgh, 1982), pp. 70–88.

137 N. Sykes, *William Wake: Archbishop of Canterbury, 1657–1737* (Cambridge, 1957), ii, pp. 115–29.

138 J. H. Plumb, *Sir Robert Walpole* (London, 1956–), i, pp. 243–92.

139 *Lords Journals*, xx, p. 555; xxi, p. 24.

140 *Ibid.*, xxi, pp. 30, 74; G. M. Townend, 'Religious Radicalism and Conservatism in the Whig Party under George I: The Repeal of the Occasional Conformity and Schism Acts', *Parliamentary History* 7 (1988), 24–44.

141 Plumb, *Sir Robert Walpole*, pp. 249, 269–70; B. Williams, *Stanhope: A Study in Eighteenth-Century War and Diplomacy* (London, 1932), pp. 136–7, 385, 390–8.

Chapter 3

———◆———

Popular Puritan mentality
in late Elizabethan England

I

'I WISH I had been able to penetrate more deeply into the thoughts and feelings of the mass of the nation. Nothing is, however, more difficult than to descend below the surface to the depths of society: nothing more easy than to be led astray into imagining the chance utterance of some poetaster or pamphleteer to be the echo of the popular mind'. So wrote the founding father of English seventeenth-century historical studies, S. R. Gardiner, pausing amidst his labours on the history of the 'Puritan Revolution'. But, with the best of intentions, can an historian of Puritanism ever hope to descend Cousteau-like beneath the waves of sermon and similar literature? For Puritans constituted neither a church nor a sect and there seems no satisfactory means of collectively identifying them. Instead the subject appears fated to lead a more or less 'surface' existence. Yet one possible and certainly neglected approach lies via the Puritan baptismal names – names like Fear-God, which emerged during the late sixteenth century. Assuming that such names are a genuine echo of Puritan mentality, lay as well as clerical, then the children may be able to lead us to their parents, who they were, and what they thought and did.[1]

Everyone has heard of Praise-God Barebone after whom is called the nominated parliament of 1653, and students of English literature at least are familiar with the peculiar names that Ben Jonson gives to some of his characters in *The Alchemist* (1610) and *Bartholomew Fair* (1614): Tribulation Wholesome, Zeal-of-the-land Busy and Win-the-fight Littlewit. Jonson's most likely source was William Camden, his former schoolmaster, who had earlier remarked in print on the 'new names', including Tribulation, given 'upon some singular and precise conceit'. More specific as to the religious context was Richard Bancroft, the future Archbishop. In his *Dangerous Positions*

. . . practised . . . for the Presbyterial Discipline, he asked rhetorically 'whence else do these new names and fancies proceed: The-Lord-is-near, More-trial, Reformation, Discipline, Joy-again, Sufficient, From-above, Free-gift, More-fruit, Dust and many other such like?' According to him they were an outgrowth of 'English Scotizing'. While both Camden and Bancroft agree in assigning the origin of these Puritan baptismal names to the later years of Queen Elizabeth neither gives any indication of whereabouts in England they occurred.[2]

The first person seriously to investigate Puritan nomenclature was the Victorian vicar C. W. Bardsley, who made a very important distinction between what he called the 'Hebraic invasion' of English parish registers by Old Testament names, dating from the 1560s, and a later crop of baptismal names consisting of 'scriptural phrases, pious ejaculations, or godly admonitions'. This second stage Bardsley linked to the English presbyterian movement of the 1580s, and there are good grounds for thinking him correct. Untenable, however, are his further claims that the new baptismal fashion of the 1580s lasted until the Civil War and moreover spread into every English county 'south of Trent'.[3] In fact the giving of such names was much more delimited than Bardsley thought, both in time and space.

Historiographically these 'scriptural phrases, pious ejaculations, or godly admonitions' came to be associated particularly with the county of Sussex. Thus wide publicity was given by David Hume in his *History* to a list of seventeenth-century Sussex jurymen, all endowed with names like Redeemed Compton of Battle.[4] This and a similar published list together yield twenty-three identifiable Sussex parishes.[5] All of them are in the eastern part of the county and the possible significance of this can be tested against the extant west Sussex protestation returns of 1642. The latter indicate a total absence of Puritan baptismal names originating in west Sussex.[6] A similar east–west contrast exists between names recorded in the archdeaconries of Lewes and Chichester, both of testators and applicants for marriage licences. On the basis of the Lewes wills and marriage licences we can add twenty-two more east Sussex parishes to our original twenty-three.[7] Finally three other parishes, which have come to my notice, need to be included.[8]

Examination of the relevant parish registers, where available, reveals eighteen east Sussex parishes in which Puritan baptismal names were being given during the last two decades of the sixteenth century; fifteen of these parishes are contiguous, running in an arc from Salehurst on the Kent border to Alfriston on the South Downs.[9] The names occur earliest in a triangle formed by the parishes of Heathfield, Warbleton and Burwash, although the highest concentration of names in any of the eighteen parishes is at Warbleton. Between 1587 and 1590 more than half of the children baptised each year at Warbleton received Puritan names.[10] The charismatic element seems to have

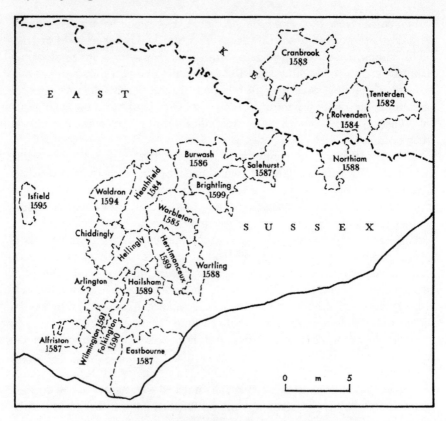

MAP   First appearance of Puritan baptismal names in
East Sussex and the Kentish Weald

been provided by the local curate, Thomas Hely, who in November 1585 christened his son Much-mercy. This was the second child at Warbleton to be given one of the new names, the practice being inaugurated in July 1585 when Goddard Hepden's son was baptised Return. At neighbouring Heathfield two children had been given Puritan names even earlier: in March 1584 Richard Fuller's son was baptised Obedient and in April 1585 Roger Luff's son was baptised Zealous.

The Vicar of Heathfield, John Miles, was childless but apparently sympathetic to this novel style in names. Certainly he and Hely had close links; in 1591, for example, Miles witnessed the will of Hely's mother-in-law.[11] The other witness was Humphrey Sommer, schoolmaster at Heathfield, who in October 1588 called his daughter Flee-sin. Also associated with Hely was William Hopkinson, Rector of Warbleton and Vicar of Salehurst. At Salehurst, between November 1587 and February 1592, Hopkinson named his children Endure, Renewed and Safe-on-high. Hely and Miles were both men of property in their own right by the early 1590s, being assessed for purpose of subsidy on respectively £2 worth of lands and £4 10s. worth of lands. None of the three clergy had a university degree. Of the earliest Sussex laity to adopt the new nomenclature, Fuller and Hepden were each substantial yeomen, while Luff was a husbandman unable as a witness to sign his own name.[12]

Puritan nomenclature did not however originate in Sussex. The chief begetter nationally was almost certainly Dudley Fenner, curate at Cranbrook in Kent by the early 1580s. Fenner previously had been in Antwerp with Thomas Cartwright, one of the 'principal ideologues of the English presbyterian movement'.[13] At Cranbrook, in December 1583, Fenner named his daughter More-fruit and was most likely involved in the earlier naming, in March 1583, of From-above Hendley, gentleman. From-above was the son of Thomas Hendley, esquire, of Corshorne near Cranbrook, and the nephew of Sir Henry Bowyer of Cuckfield Park in Sussex. Fenner too was of gentry stock and, interestingly, from Sussex. For this may help explain why the giving of Puritan names spread from Cranbrook and the nearby parishes of Tenterden and Rolvenden south-west into Sussex rather than north into other parts of Kent.[14]

Fenner states that 'the father's duty is . . . to present the child for the first sacrament, and there to give a name in the mother tongue, which may have some godly signification, . . . so the Greeks in Greek, as Timothy: the fear of God'. Further light is shed by his remarks on the sacrament of baptism and the biblical teaching of Matthew 28.19, which is usually rendered as 'go ye therefore, and teach all nations, baptising them *in the name* of the Father, and of the Son, and of the Holy Ghost'. Translating literally from the original Greek, Fenner writes that:

> we are segregated from the world to have fellowship with one God in three persons, as a wife with an husband, which is noted by this *'into the name'*, that is to bear the name in being one with these three persons by faith, and by hanging on them for all government, blessing etc. Whereof it cometh that as the wife is called by the name of the husband, and to bear the man's name . . . so to be into the name of God, to bear his name, is to be separated and dedicated to him as his spouse.[15]

The practice seems analogous to the taking of a saint's name by those entering on a monastic vocation, in this case with the new born child being 'separated and dedicated' as the 'spouse' of God.

When Walter Travers, probably advised by Cartwright, drew up the Book of Discipline in the mid-1580s, baptismal names were recommended 'chiefly such whereof there are examples in the Holy Scriptures in the names of those who are reported in them to have been godly and virtuous'. No support was given to the kind of name favoured by Fenner and the reason, I would suggest, was a dislike of their separatist tenor. Yet, as Patrick Collinson has pointed out, preachers by distinguishing between 'the godly' and the rest inevitably divided parishes against themselves. 'Hath not Ely set Tenterden, his parish, together by the ears, which before was quiet', asked a hostile contemporary, and 'what broil and contention hath Fenner made in Cranbrook, and all the rest likewise, in their several cures?' George Ely, Vicar of Tenterden, did not adopt the new Puritan nomenclature for his children although Fenner, in recommending names of 'godly signification', was only taking a few more steps along the same religious road that led, among other things, to congregationalism.[16]

By 1586 Fenner was in exile at Middelburg where he died the next year. At Cranbrook the type of baptismal name that he had popularised continued to be given by a small group of families, all laymen, until the turn of the century. Most remarkable was Thomas Starr who between 1589 and 1600 called his children Comfort, No-strength, More-gift, Mercy, Sure-trust, and Stand-well. Thereafter the family moved to Ashford in the same county, Comfort Starr emigrating as a surgeon to New England in the 1630s. In other parts of Kent the practice seems only to have survived with any vigour at Eastwell, where Josias Nicholls was Vicar. Nicholls, in January 1583, named his daughter Above-hope and as late as March 1595 called his son Repent, although few parishioners followed his example. He eventually married Fenner's widow and the two men may have been collaborating closely in the early 1580s.[17]

The heartland of Puritan nomenclature was undoubtedly east Sussex and the Kentish border. In other areas, like Essex and Suffolk,[18] the new names never became fashionable. Elsewhere only in Northamptonshire, around Daventry, do Puritan names appear to have established a foothold. This was mainly under the influence of John Penry, the future separatist martyr. His wife came from Northampton and in June 1589, at All Saints church, his daughter was christened Deliverance. Earlier at nearby Daventry, in January 1589, the baptism is also recorded of Deliverance Wilton. Thus these Northamptonshire Puritans celebrated the defeat of the Spanish Armada and England's deliverance from Antichrist. Penry's other three children, all girls, were named Comfort, Safety and Sure-hope. He was on the move during these last years, because of his clandestine publishing activities, and the Elizabethan authorities finally captured him in March 1593. Executed in May, Penry had formally declared for separatism the previous year, and his defection would seem dramatically to have fulfilled the worst possible fears of the English presbyterian leadership about the new baptismal names. To what extent Penry was influenced by Fenner is unclear although they were both educated, within a few years of each other, at Peterhouse, Cambridge.[19]

In so far as Penry had a Northamptonshire successor this looks to have been John Barebone, Rector of Charwelton. The Charwelton parish registers do not survive, but John Barebone was most likely the father of the famous Praise-God. The origins of Praise-God Barebone have never been traced back beyond his appearance in London as a freeman of the Leathersellers' Company in 1623; from a statement made late in life his birth has been dated to about 1596. The vital clue, however, is the existence of a Fear-God Barebone living at Daventry in the early seventeenth century, for in August 1594 John Barebone had married Mary Roper of Daventry. It is possible to go further and suggest why John Barebone chose these specific names for his sons, because the Elizabethan Prayer Book defines the first cause for which marriage was ordained as 'the procreation of children, to be brought up *in the fear ... and praise of God'*. If the father was a logical man, this would make Fear-God the elder of the two boys.[20]

John Barebone was deprived for nonconformity in 1605, and Praise-God Barebone became a separatist. Fear-God Barebone, on the other hand, rebelled against his upbringing. We only know of his existence because there survives a collection of verses made by him in the early seventeenth century. The verses are decidedly bawdy and Fear-God writes, in the third person, that he collected them 'for the mending of his hand in writing than worse to bestow his time'. Examples are the lines which begin:

> I dreamed my love lay in her bed
> And twas my chance to take her,

or the refrain:

> Tumble, tumble, tumble, tumble,
> Up and down the green meadow.

He also sums up his own philosophy of life in the following quatrain:

> No foe to fortune,
> No friend to faith,
> No, no to want,
> So Fear-God Barebone saith.

For him the god Jehovah had apparently been displaced by the goddess Fortuna, faith and fortune proving antipathetic.[21]

II

While Puritan names clearly tell us nothing definite about the recipients, how far can we be certain concerning the outlook of those who gave them?

At Warbleton, in Sussex, ninety-three children were given Puritan names during the years 1586 to 1596 inclusive.[22] Over the same period at Warbleton 124 children were given non-Puritan names.[23] A small group of families, nineteen to be exact, gave their children both Puritan and non-Puritan names. Apart from these, there are 100 Warbleton families who were consistent in the choice of baptismal names between 1586 and 1596. In this eleven-year period forty-two families consistently chose Puritan names, while fifty-eight families consistently chose non-Puritan names.

We do not know the relative influence of minister and parents, father and mother, in the giving of these names. Certainly a measure of free choice was exercised by parents because where the local incumbent was unsympathetic, for example at Eastbourne,[24] Puritan names none the less occur in the register of baptisms. With regard to the roles of father and mother, Fenner, as already noted, states that it is 'the father's duty' to name his child, and he assumes moreover a family relationship in which the husband is the 'chief or foregovernor . . . over all persons and matters in the house'. From October 1585 to October 1591 Hely, as curate of Warbleton, called his children Much-mercy, Increased, Sin-deny, Fear-not and Constance. Hely was also the leading nonconformist of the parish; in 1583 he crossed swords with Archbishop Whitgift on the subject of clerical subscription and in 1592 he was summoned to appear before the archdeacon's court for failing to use the sign of the cross in baptism and for not observing holy days.[25] Ultimately he was to be deprived. The likelihood is that those of his parishioners who consistently chose Puritan names for their children were some of the parents closest to him in matters of religion generally. Conversely those who declined to give names of 'godly signification' in baptism probably included the Warbleton parents least affected by Hely's ministrations.

But if Puritan nomenclature is to provide any kind of key to the sociology of Puritanism, then both the geographical and chronological limitations of the data need stressing. East Sussex is patently not England. Furthermore there is an important distinction to be drawn between rural and urban environments because Puritan names never, so far as I am aware, became popular either in London or in any other major town. As for chronology, Puritan baptismal names generally fade out after 1600. Thus we are talking about a late Elizabeth phenomenon, in the context mainly of the Sussex Weald. For there, especially at Warbleton, the highest proportions of Puritan names are found.

In agricultural terms Wealden Sussex was a wood-pasture economy of scattered farms and enclosed fields.[26] Warbleton is a parish of nine square miles and as late as the 1930s half the area was pasture and a sixth was woodland; the population in the late sixteenth century numbered some 400 persons.[27] It had no market, unlike the adjoining parishes of Heathfield and Burwash. Iron-working was carried on in the locality and a conveyance of 1617 mentions Rushlake furnace, Warbleton, with its 'water-courses, water-lays, ponds, bays, banks, pens, dams, flood-gates, sluices, ways, workmen's houses, coal places, mine places and other grounds adjoining'. Industrial plant of this kind must have provided some full-time employment and the reference to 'workmen's houses' indicates as much. The local iron industry also meant useful by-employment, digging ore and making charcoal. Most people however seem to have been chiefly engaged in agriculture. Unfortunately very few inventories survive for east Sussex, but a will of 1586 gives some idea of the type of farming practised in the region: William Dungate, of Warbleton, bequeaths to his wife 'all my cattle whatsoever, as kine, steers, twelvemonthings and weaners, and my hogs and all my poultry, and also my corn and hay.'[28]

County gentlemen, defined as potential or actual JPs, were thin on the ground and the upper ranks of this society are best described as 'yeomanly gentry', to borrow a later term from Celia Fiennes.[29] Typical representatives of such yeomanly gentry were the brothers Thomas and Goddard Hepden. When their father John Hepden, of Burwash, made his will in 1586 he styled himself yeoman, although one of his two executors was a gentlemen. Both sons, at this stage referred to as yeomen, sired children during the 1580s and 1590s. Between 1586 and 1596 Thomas, the elder brother, named his offspring Martha, Constance, John, Elizabeth, William and Herbert. By contrast Goddard Hepden, between 1585 and 1596, chose the names Return, Good-gift, Hope-still, Fear-not, Thankful and Constant.[30] During this same period Goddard took to signing his name 'Godward', apparently in line with his choice of baptismal names, and in 1591 he was reported by the vicar of Burwash for failing to receive communion there for over a year. By 1609 Thomas Hepden was being called gentleman and Goddard was similarly described the previous year, as a member of the grand jury. The house that Goddard Hepden built at Burwash, Holmshurst, still stands; it is constructed of brick with stone dressings, and has the initials G. H. and the date 1610 carved on the lintel. He describes it in his will of 1632 as 'my house called Holmehurst' and, styling himself gentleman, he had by this stage reverted to signing his name as 'Goddard' Hepden. In the religious preamble to his will he acknowledges 'the days of my pilgrimage to be both few and evil' and speaks of 'the small estate and substance which God hath lent me'. He goes on to mention freehold lands in Heathfield and Mayfield, and copyhold land in Brightling, as well as property in Burwash. Two gentlemen of Brightling, 'my loving friends' Thomas Collins and Nehemiah Panton, are appointed overseers. Significant, however, of Goddard Hepden's continuing agricultural horizons, is that he arranges for Goddard junior to assist his stepmother in 'her husbanddry'.[31]

Other Wealden families of yeomanly gentry, who also gave their children puritan names, were the Bishops of Northiam and the Collinses of Brightling. Tradition has it that when Queen Elizabeth passed through Northiam in 1573 she was entertained by the Bishop family. George Bishop senior, although his brother John was a Catholic recusant, named his son Thankful in 1589. When he came to make a will in 1605 he avoided using any status description and began with an elaborate confession of faith concerning God's 'testimony . . . to my conscience that I am his elect vessel and chosen child'. He mentions lands in Battle, Bexhill, Northiam and Westfield, and specifies two legacies of £140 each. His eldest son George Bishop styles himself gentleman in his will of 1614 whereas Thankful Bishop, the younger brother, is called yeoman in 1617. Thomas Collins of Brightling, between 1599 and 1606, named his children Changed, Increase and Patience. Like George Bishop senior he avoided a status description in his will of 1612, and like Goddard Hepden referred to the lands and goods which God 'in this life hath lent me'. These included the manor of Socknersh and a blast-furnace. His daughter, Changed, was bequeathed a marriage portion of £500. Thomas Collins junior was, as we have seen, described as a gentleman in Goddard Hepden's will of 1632, and both the Collinses and the Hepdens are included in the heralds' visitation of Sussex in the 1630s.[32]

The term yeomanly gentry implies a blurring of status distinctions which also occured further down the social scale. In his study of east Sussex during the century 1540 to 1640, Colin Brent has written of the Wealden area that 'the distinction between family farmer and smallholder, between smallholder and cottager, and between craftsman and agriculturalist, must often have been difficult to make'. At Warbleton it has proved possible to find status descriptions for fourteen laymen who consistently gave their children either Puritan or non-Puritan names in the period 1586–96. They consist of six 'yeomen', six 'husbandmen' and two 'tailors'. Of the six yeomen only James Brown and Goddard Hepden, who is called yeoman during the 1590s, gave their children Puritan names.[33] This situation is reversed with the husband-men, four out of the six, William Dorant, Roger Luff, Richard Reve and John Weeks, having given their children Puritan names.[34] Of the two tailors one, Roger Elliard, gave his children Puritan names, while the other, Timothy Pettet, did not.[35] It would be rash, however, to conclude that Puritanism, even at Warbleton, was predominantly the religion of husbandmen. Quite apart from the small numbers involved, the terms yeoman and husbandman are lacking in precision. We need to check them, where possible, against testamentary evidence, and in any case rather more wills survive than do status descriptions.

Seventeen wills exist for laymen who were consistent in the choice of baptismal names at Warbleton during the years 1586–96. Taking the ten

TABLE 1   Wills of non-Puritan fathers at Warbleton, 1586–96

Name	Date	Status	Land	Money	Interest rate	Poor relief
Henry Stroker	1588			£21		
John Hobeme	1591		Freehold and copyhold	£40	'most profit'	6s. 8d.
Richard Browne	1593			£90	'most profit'	3s. 4d.
William Hobeme	1593	Husbandman		£22		
John Medherst	1596		House and lands			1s.
William Stace *alias* Shether	1597	Yeoman		£40		3s. 4d.
James Busse	1603		House and tenement	£11 3s. 4d.	'most advantage'	
John Pettet	1606		Lands	£52 + £5 annuity	'best advantage'	£2
William Avery	1607	Yeoman	46 acres	£40		6s.
Ambrose Hunt	1631			4s.		

non-Puritan wills first (see Table 1), the earliest dates from 1588 and is that of Henry Stroker. Henry junior receives £11 and three daughters are each bequeathed five marks, two ewes and two lambs. John Hobeme's will, made in 1591, suggests someone economically much more prosperous than Stroker. Hobeme mentions freehold land in Warbleton and copyhold land in Heathfield, and bequeaths a portion of £40 to his daughter Anne; rent from the copyhold is to 'be put out unto the most profit' for the benefit of his son William. He also gives 6s. 8d. to the poor and 3s. 4d. for the church fabric. Next in time is the will of Richard Browne, dated January 1593. Richard junior receives £50, 'to be put out unto the most profit', and other cash bequests total £40, plus 3s. 4d. for the poor. The second son, Caleb Browne, is described as a carpenter in 1606. William Hobeme, husbandman, made his will in November 1593 and legacies come to £22. John Medherst, in his will of 1596, speaks of a house and lands, bequeaths to his son Richard 'one acre of wheat of the best', and the poor receive one shilling. The following year, 1597, William Stace alias Shether, yeoman, made his will. Portions, all to his daughters, total £40 and the poor receive 3s. 4d. No land is mentioned but Thomas Stolion, gentleman, is named as one of the two overseers. From 1603 comes the will of James Busse. He bequeaths to his wife a house and tenement with 'the stables and shops'. Cash bequests amount to £11 3s. 4d., those to his nieces 'to be put out to the most advantage'.[36]

With John Pettet's will of 1606 we seem to be moving among the yeomanly gentry, albeit of the non-Puritan variety, No status is given, but he refers to

TABLE 2   Wills of Puritan fathers at Warbleton, 1586–96

Name	Date	Status	Land	Money	Interest rate	Poor relief
Edmund Gower	1601			£57		
John Jennings	1603			£64 10s.	'meet'	
Roger Elliard	1603	Tailor		£92	'reasonable increase'	13s. 4d.
Richard Morris	1606					
John Weeks	1610	Husbandman				
Roger Luff	1619	Husbandman		£63 10s.		5s.
Goddard Hepden	1632 (c. 1590)	Gentleman (yeoman)	Freehold and copyhold (£4 subsidyman)	£183 5s. + £23 annuities		£2 10s.

'my brother' Thomas Stolion, either the 'gentleman' of ten years earlier or his son, and the Warbleton poor receive £2. Pettet mentions lands in Heathfield, Hellingly, Herstmonceux, Warbleton and Westham, and other money bequests add up to £52 plus an annuity of £5. The £20 which he wills to his god-daughter is to be 'employed . . . for her best advantage'. William Avery, yeoman, made his will in 1607. Avery is unusual in that he actually gives the acreage of his lands; located in Ashburnham, Warbleton and Wartling, they comprised forty-six acres. He bequeaths to his wife all his cattle and 'seven acres of corn on the ground'. Legacies come to £40 plus 6s. to the poor. Lastly, there is the will of Ambrose Hunt, dated 1631. He was by then living at Brightling, but the names of his children indicate that it is the same man who lived at Warbleton in the 1590s. Four children are bequeathed 1s. each and his major wealth seems to consist of 'eleven pounds of linen ready spun'.[37]

Turning now to the seven Puritan wills (see Table 2), the earliest is that of Edmund Gower, dated 1601, and cash bequests total £57. In May 1588 he had named a son Be-thankful. Of comparable wealth appears to have been John Jennings, who made his will in April 1603. His legacies come to £64 10s., and his son-in-law receives four bushels of wheat. Between January 1587 and July 1591, his children were christened Faint-not, Increased and Good-gift. Jennings entrusts their portions to John Creasy of Wartling 'and he to give for the use . . . that my overseers and executor shall think meet'. From June 1603 dates the will of Roger Elliard, tailor. He gives 13s. 4d. to the poor and further money bequests amount to £92, including sums to his grandchildren which he specifies are 'to be put to some reasonable increase' and 'reasonable profit'. Elliard leaves to his wife 'nine pounds of fleece wool and all the hemp in my house, and seven pounds of linen yarn'. Less expected is the further bequest to her of two kine, one weaner, one heifer, one bullock, 'my best barrow hog and my second sow', 'one goose and six young geese, one crock of six quarts of butter and two cheeses', as well as seams of 'oaten malt' and oats, and two quarters of wheat. Other stock is mentioned, and Elliard's case serves to illustrate the over-simplifications of a status description; if he was a tailor he was also a farmer. In addition to having called his children Unfained and Confidence in April 1586 and January 1588, he speaks in his will of 'my beloved in Christ' Thomas Stolion the younger and Richard Stolion. These presumably were the sons of Thomas Stolion, gentleman.[38]

In apparent contrast to the wealth of Gower, Jennings and Elliard is the situation revealed by Richard Morris's will of 1606; no money or land is mentioned and his son, Thomas, receives two ewes and two lambs. His son Fear-not, baptised in November 1594, was presumably dead. Similarly poor, to judge from his will of 1610, was John Weeks, husbandman. His five children, including Refrain, baptised in May 1595, each receive one ewe and one lamb and nothing else. Seemingly a much more prosperous husbandman was Roger Luff, who made his will in 1619. From March 1588 to November 1594 he had named his children More-fruit, Be-thankful, Sin-deny and Preserved. These four children were all baptised at Warbleton, although an earlier child, Zealous Luff, was baptised at Heathfield and in his will Roger describes himself as of Heathfield. Cash bequests come to £63 10s. and the poor receive 5s. Goddard Hepden did not make his will until 1632, and as evidence for his position in society thirty years earlier it is likely to be misleading. By 1632 he had for many years, as we have seen, been calling himself gentleman and was now possessed of land in three parishes. His money bequests amount to £183 5s. and a further £23 in annuities, plus £2 10s. for the poor. Back in the 1590s, when he was called a yeoman, he had been assessed, for purposes of subsidy, on £4 worth of lands.[39] What then can these wills tell us about lay Puritanism?

The wills confirm that yeomen were, in the main, more prosperous than husbandmen and to that extent they underline the preponderance of yeomen over husbandmen among the non-Puritans. Taking each group as a whole, in money terms the Puritans were twice as wealthy as the rest, although this figure is probably inflated by Goddard Hepden's upward mobility, from yeoman to gentleman. Against this greater Puritan liquidity, however, is the imponderable element of land values, for half the non-Puritans mention land compared with the solitary Puritan instance of Goddard Hepden. There is the additional and insoluble problem of the possible failure by testators to record significant assets. As to individual cases, the Puritans Richard Morris and John Weeks have no close counterparts among the non-Puritans save Ambrose Hunt, who may have been even poorer; in 1594 Hunt was described as 'labouring' in Dallington, a parish adjacent to Warbleton.[40] Apart from a few sheep, men like Morris and Weeks appear to have owned only household goods. More generally, the donations to poor relief do not seem to indicate any very clear differences – the Puritans gave more *in toto*, while more non-Puritans gave something.

Wills can also, of course, shed light on literacy. Although the inability to sign one's name, when in good health, does not necessarily mean complete illiteracy – a person can read without being able to write – at the very least it points to semi-literacy. Marks made by testators may simply reflect illness, and in consequence are best ignored, but we commented earlier on the mark made by the Puritan husbandman, Roger Luff, as a witness to a will in 1613. Similarly the non-Puritan William Avery, yeoman, revealed his inability to write as a deponent in 1607.[41] There are no references to books in any of these Warbleton wills. Nor, with the exception of Goddard Hepden, do any of these testators begin with more than a formal statement of religious belief.

The foregoing evidence seems to indicate that Puritan and non-Puritan name groups were broadly similar in socio-economic terms, and that the acceptance or rejection of Puritanism at Warbleton tended to divide the community along vertical rather than horizontal lines. There are, however, two other differences which run deeper. For the dates at which the wills were made imply that the Puritans were in general younger, and this is lent support by the fact that Puritan births are more closely spaced than non-Puritan ones in the period 1586 to 1596.[42] At the same time there is a marked divergence in attitudes towards the taking of interest. The non-Puritans John Hobeme, Richard Browne, James Busse and John Pettet specify, as we have seen, that their money bequests be 'put out unto the most profit' or 'the most advantage', whereas the Puritans Roger Elliard and John Jennings speak of 'reasonable increase' and that which is 'meet'. The reality of this distinction is borne out by the will of Humphrey Sommer, the Puritan schoolmaster at Heathfield, 'written with my own hand' in 1598. One of his overseers was John Miles, Vicar of Heathfield, to whom he willed the 'book between the archbishop and Mr. Cartwright' and 'Mr. Fenner's *Divinity*'. But what matters for immediate purposes is that Sommer bequeathed to his four daughters, Restored, Flee-sin, Constant and Susanna, £10 each 'to be employed by my executors *in such sort as the word of God will warrant*'. Thus the Warbleton Puritans stand revealed as young conservatives, unwilling simply to endorse the statutory maximum interest rate of 10 per cent on money lent.[43]

III

Yet something more can be said about the mental and physical universe of those who, in late Elizabethan England, chose either to accept or to reject the gospel according to Fenner and his ilk. For the 1580s saw both an upsurge of invasion panic and the worst harvest since 1562. Rumour flourished even more luxuriantly than usual, and at its most extreme took the form of predictions that the world was due to end in 1588. Prophecies also were current of Queen Elizabeth's violent death. By May 1586 the Privy Council was talking in terms of 'a general dearth of corn and victual' and the previous month rioters at Framilode, in Gloucestershire, had seized a cargo of malt, claiming that they had been driven to feed their children on cats, dogs and nettle roots. At about the same time there was rioting at Romsey, in Hampshire, which by July had escalated into a conspiracy to fire the beacons and during the ensuing chaos to rob the houses of the local gentry. Then in August 1586 broke the news of the Babington plot, and with it came the final act in the long-drawn-out drama of Mary Queen of Scots. Meanwhile, month by month, the prospect of an invasion attempt by Spain became more certain. [44]

Against this background of fear and hardship, the nonconformist preachers and their lay allies were experiencing a crisis of their own. Ever since the appointment of Whitgift to the archbishopric of Canterbury in 1583 they had been under growing pressure to conform and partly as a reaction to this there had sprung up the presbyterian movement. November 1586 saw a renewed, and more extreme, presbyterian campaign in Parliament, which culminated in the imprisonment in March 1587 of Peter Wentworth and his fellow parliamentary agitators. The late 1580s also saw an attempt to secure nationwide approval for the Book of Discipline and one of the stumbling blocks to this was perhaps the subject of baptismal names. For a basic question was after what fashion the new discipline should be erected, with Puritan nomenclature arguably constituting one of the 'tokens of an incipient congregationalism'. [45] It may be in this light that we can best understand the baptising at Daventry, in August 1589, of Discipline Brookbank – as a call for the setting up of communities of visible saints, loosely affiliated, rather than a presbyterian national church.

The giving of Puritan names was at its height, in Sussex, Kent and Northamptonshire, during the six-year period 1587–92. Only at Warbleton, however, did a majority of the children baptised in any year receive such names. Elsewhere the proportion was at most a third, as at Northiam in 1592, and a more usual ratio even at the peak was about 1:6, as at Heathfield in 1591. Moreover only at Warbleton can any pattern be detected in the choice of names. There in 1586, out of nine Puritan names, three children were called Repent and two Refrain. From January to May of 1587 Be-thankful or Give-thanks account for three out of seven Puritan names, with Repent or Repentance and Obey or Obedience predominating for the rest of the year. Throughout 1588 the names Be-thankful and Good-gift were between them the most popular. The next year, 1589, from January to April three children were baptised Sin-deny, and from May to October three others were baptised Fear-not. January 1590 was characterised by the name Sin-deny or Sorry-for-sin, with Be-thankful the most popular name from February to July. The year 1591 began on the note Repent, which from June turned into Be-thankful, these names together constituting four out of an annual total of six Puritan names. This was followed by a final burst of Sin-denys in 1592 – three out of seven Puritan names, and thereafter no pattern is discernible.[46]

The most likely explanation of this pattern of Puritan names is that it represents a recurring religious cycle of repentance on account of sin followed by thanksgiving for the withdrawal of God's wrath. No examples survive of sermons preached at this time by Hely and like-minded Sussex ministers. Nevertheless there are the strident pamphlets of John Penry who, as we have noted, called his children Deliverance, Comfort, Safety and Sure-hope, and his writings suggest some of the assumptions shared by those who gave their children Puritan names. In his pamphlet of 1587, the *Aequity*, Penry is concerned with the evangelisation of Wales, as a matter of spiritual life or death for his fellow countrymen. The lack of a Welsh preaching ministry is a crying sin, which must be remedied by the action of Queen and Parliament; already God's displeasure at their delay has been made plain.

> We feel the Lord's hand many ways against us at this time in regard of the scarcity of all things, and especially of victuals . . . The unseasonable harvest 1585 yielded very little corn. Therefore many were able to sow nothing the last year, because they had not bread corn, much less seed. The winter 1585 destroyed all their cattle well near, so that now the very sinew of their maintenance is gone . . . This famine is for our sins, and the Lord without our repentance saith it shall continue.

After a spell in prison, Penry returned to the theme of Welsh evangelisation in his *Exhortation* of 1588. Now with invasion imminent, he prophesies that the Spaniards will 'prevail against this land unless another course be taken for God's glory in Wales . . . than hitherto hath been'. The following year, 1589, appeared the *Supplication* where Penry explicitly associates himself with concurrent attempts to reform the Established Church in England, and he warns against misinterpreting the meaning of England's recent victory over the Spanish Armada. 'The Lord by that deliverance gave us warning that he passed by us, but so as unless the corruptions of his service be clean done away, with speed . . . [he] meaneth to pass by us no more, but to suffer his whole displeasure to fall upon us.'[47]

But if some parents gave their children names like Deliverance or Pre-served,[48] in memory of Spain's defeat, others revealed much more personal concerns. For instance at Isfield in Sussex, in August 1595, Edward Goodman called his daughter Joy-in-sorrow, his son Caleb having died the previous month. We have already suggested that the names Fear-God and Praise-God originated in contemporary marital teaching and the same is probably true of the name Comfort, for the Elizabethan Prayer Book defines the third cause for which marriage was ordained as 'the mutual society, help and *comfort* that the one ought to have for the other'.[49] More difficult to gauge are significant names when bestowed on children born out of wedlock. Of three bastards baptised at Warbleton between 1589–91 only Repent Rowly received a Puritan name, which implies that in this case the parents, or one of them, wished to be absolved in the eyes of the godly.

'Sin' for Penry however was pre-eminently a matter of 'wicked ecclesiastical constitutions', and his writings convey a sense of growing desperation at the failure to achieve religious reform. The type of baptismal name that he chose for his children had never found favour with the majority of nonconformist ministers, and the fashion was probably killed more by internal criticism than anything else. Thus John Frewen, Rector of Northiam in Sussex, having baptised his two eldest sons Accepted and Thankful, from January 1594 chose the names John and Joseph for his subsequent sons. The gradual abandonment of Puritan names during the 1590s perhaps also reflects a collapse of eschatological hopes; the reform programme remained unfulfilled, and God had failed to come in final judgment. From 1597 it became obligatory for parishes to make regular returns to their diocesan registries of all baptisms, marriages and burials and this unaccustomed limelight may further have hastened the demise of Puritan nomenclature. Although Puritan names did not entirely die out, as part of a religious movement their end is symbolised by the baptism in March 1606, at Isfield, of Deprived Winsbury. For deprivation from their ministries was indeed the fate by this time of Thomas Hely in Sussex, Josias Nicholls in Kent, and John Barebone in Northamptonshire.[50]

At one level Puritan baptismal names provide the stuff of endless ribaldry. Yet they also permit us to enter the world of those who were engaged, at this time, in 'rediscovering' the Bible 'as a code of private and public behaviour'. In so far as such names represent an extreme manifestation of popular Puritanism they accentuate rather than distort the ethos of a movement which, it has been said, 'constituted a threat . . . to culture as a whole'.[51] Dividing both family and community, Puritan counter-culture, in Sussex, was certainly no friend to economic individualism.[52] Indeed, if like Goddard Hepden one conceived of man's life as a spiritual 'pilgrimage', material goods were *ipso facto* of secondary importance. While over against this Puritan realm stands Fear-God Barebone, with his firm 'no, no to want' and evident distaste for 'faith'; a poetaster, he may nevertheless be allowed to speak for a very different facet of the popular mind.

NOTES

The research on which this essay is based would have been impossible without membership of the Society of Genealogists and consequent access to their unrivalled collection of parish register copies; the latter are listed in *Parish Register Copies, Pt I: Society of Genealogists Collection* (London, 1975). For making available to me parish registers, either originals or copies, and other records in their keeping, I am grateful to the staffs of the East Sussex, Essex, Kent, Northamptonshire and West Sussex Record Offices, the Sussex Archaeological Society, Messrs Phillimore and Co. Ltd, and also to Rev. D. R. Corfe (Eastwell) and Rev. D. Shacklock (Northiam). Advice and information on various points has been generously given by Michael Burchall, Claire Cross, Richard Cust, Jeremy Goring, Geoffrey Nuttall, Bill Sheils, David Thomas and Andrew Watson. I am indebted to the members of Jack Fisher's Seminar for their stringent criticisms, and to David Coleman, Patrick Collinson, Jeremy Goring, Negley Harte and Conrad Russell for reading the essay, or part of it, in draft. Finally I must thank my wife, Sarah Tyacke, for her unfailing encouragement.

1 S. R. Gardiner, *The Personal Government of Charles I* (London, 1877), i, p. ix. An alternative approach to that adopted here would be to investigate a parish, or parishes, where religious differences brought large numbers of parishioners before the ecclesiastical courts, both as plaintiffs and defendants.

2 W. Camden, *Remains of a Greater Work* (London, 1605), p. 33; R. Bancroft, *Dangerous Positions* (London, 1593), p. 104. [The name Sindefy also occurs in the play *Eastward Ho!*, a joint work written by George Chapman, Ben Jonson and John Marston, and licensed in 1605.]

3 C. W. Bardsley, *Curiosities of Puritan Nomenclature* (London, 1880). For a memoir of Bardsley see his posthumously published *Dictionary of English and Welsh Surnames* (London, 1901), pp. v–xi.

4 D. Hume, *The History of Great Britain* (London, 1754–57), ii, p. 51. These names were probably extracted from the quarter sessions rolls. Hume was of course mistaken in regarding them as names assumed in adult life.

5 M. A. Lower, *English Surnames* (London, 1842), pp. 134–7. The twenty-three parishes are Battle, Brightling, Burwash, Chiddingly, Crowhurst, Cuckfield, Ewhurst, Hailsham, Heathfield, Hellingly, East Hoathly, Lewes, Northiam, Pevensey, Rye, Salehurst, Shoreham, Uckfield, Waldron, Warbleton, Wartling, Westham and Withyam.

6 R. G. Rice ed., *West Sussex Protestaion Returns* (Sussex Rec. Soc., v, 1906). The only two puritan names recorded are Desire Smith and Free-gift Collins, both of St Peter the Great, Chichester. Neither is to be found among the St Peter the Great baptisms.

7 W. H. Hall ed., *Calendar of Wills and Administrations ... Lewes, 1541–1660* (British Rec. Soc., xxiv, 1901); E. A. Fry ed., *Calendar of Wills ... Chichester, 1482–1800* (British Rec. Soc., xlix, 1915); E. H. W. Dunkin ed., *Calendar of Sussex Marriage Licences ... Lewes, 1586–1643* (Sussex Rec. Soc., i, 1902); and *idem* ed., *Calendar of Sussex Marriage Licences ... Chichester, 1575–1730* (Sussex Rec. Soc., ix, 1909). The twenty-two parishes are Arlington, Beddingham, Bexhill, Bishopstone, Brede, Brighton, Eastbourne, West Firle, Folkington, Framfield, Frant, Hastings, Little Horsted, Lullington, Maresfield, Ninfield, Playden, Seaford, Southover, Ticehurst, Wilmington and Wivelsfield.

8 Alfriston, Herstmonceux and Isfield.

9 See map. Where no date is given this is because, lacking a contemporary register, Puritan baptismal names have been inferred from the later clustering of such names among those married *c.* 1620. An invaluable guide to the existence and whereabouts of east Sussex parish registers is M. J. Burchall, *Index of East Sussex Parish Records, 1275–1870* (London, 1975).

10 1587: 14/20; 1588: 13/22; 1589: 13/23; 1590: 13/23.

11 ESRO, Lewes Wills, Bk A 9, fo 10. Miles, in his will of 1601, bequeathed to Hely his 'best gown' and Rheims Testament: PRO, PROB 11/98/51. [The attitude of Thomas Parish, curate of Burwash, remains unclear.]

12 WSRO, Ep.ii/5/5. fo 198v.; PRO, E 179/190/332, Hawksborough Hundred; BL, Add, MS. 39326, Biographies of Sussex Clergy; ESRO, Lewes Wills, Bks A8, fos 341v–2v, A14, fo 114, A17, fo 39r–v. [William Hopkinson may in fact be the same person who graduated from St John's College, Cambridge, in 1568.]

13 A. F. Scott Pearson, *Thomas Cartwright and Elizabethan Puritanism, 1535–1603* (London, 1925), p. 274; P. Collinson, *The Elizabethan Puritan Movement* (London, 1967), p. 294.

14 J. Comber, *Sussex Genealogies: Ardingly Centre* (London, 1932), p. 233; F. W. T. Attree ed., *Notes of Post Mortem Inquisitions . . . Sussex* (Sussex Rec. Soc., xiv, 1912), p. 89. I owe this reference to Michael Burchall. As indicated on the map, Puritan names leap-frog from the Cranbrook area to that of Warbleton and a further clue may be Hely's own Kentish origins, for he was ordained in 1574–5 by Richard Rogers, suffragan Bishop of Dover, and in his will of 1605 refers to a brother, Stephen Hely, at Maidstone: BL, Add. MS 39326 (46), fo 1394; PRO, PROB 11/106/71. See also p. 33, n. 67 above.

15 D. Fenner, *The Arts of Logic and Rhetoric* (Middelburg, ? 1588), sigs F5v–F6, and *The Whole Doctrine of the Sacraments* (Middelburg, 1588), sigs C2r–v. My italics.

16 *A Directory of Church Government* (London, 1644), sig. B2; P. Collinson, 'The Godly: Aspects of Popular Protestantism in Elizabethan England' (papers presented to the *Past and Present* Conference on Popular Religion, 1966), p. 6 and *passim*. Between December 1581 and March 1591, George Ely called his children Obadiah, Lydia, Daniel and Abigail.

17 B. P. Starr, *A History of the Starr Family of New England* (Hartford, Conn., 1879), pp. i–iv. Faint-not Fenner, in her will of 1604, refers to Josias Nicholls as 'father-in-law' i.e. stepfather: PRO, PROB 11/104/85.

18 F. G. Emmison ed., *Wills at Chelmsford, 1620–1720* (British Rec. Soc., lxxix, 1959–60); C. E. Banks ed., *Able Men of Suffolk, 1638* (Boston, Mass., 1931).

19 W. Pierce, *John Penry* (London, 1923), pp. 207, 367–72, 385, 416.

20 *DNB*, s.n. Barebone, Praise-God, and H. I. Longden, *Northamptonshire and Rutland Clergy* (London, 1938), i, p. 179. My italics.

21 BL, Harleian MS 7332, fos 41, 47v, 48 and 49v. cf. p. 32, n. 63 above.

22 These Puritan names, in order of popularity, are Sin-deny (10), Be-thankful (9), Repent (9), Patience (7), Free-gift (5), Good-gift (5), Refrain (5), Fear-not (4), Abuse-not (2), Constance (2), Depend (2), Faint-not (2), Give-thanks (2), Increased (2), Magnify (2), Much-mercy (2), Obedient (2), Preserved (2), Renewed (2), Be-steadfast (1), Confidence (1), Eschew-evil (1), Faithful (1), Fear-God (1), Indued (1), Lament (1),

Learn-wisdom (1), More-fruit (1), No-merit (1), Obey (1), Repentance (1), Return (1), Silence (1), Sorry-for-sin (1), Unfeigned (1) and Zealous (1).

23 These non-Puritan names, in order of popularity, are Mary (16), Thomas (16), John (10), Richard (9), Elizabeth (8), Edward (5), William (5), Anne (4), Joan (4), Margaret (4), Samuel (4), Sara (3), Susan (3), Dorothy (2), Ellen (2), George (2), Lydia (2), Priscilla (2), Stephen (2), Abel (1), Abraham (1), Agnes (1), Alice (1), Ananias (1), Anthony (1), Benjamin (1), Cornelius (1), Denys (1), Edmond (1), Effagina (1), Henry (1), Judith (1), Michael (1), Obadiah (1), Odiane (1), Rebecca (1), Roger (1), Silas (1), Silvester (1) and Winifred (1). The popularity of the name Mary is especially striking given that a modern authority has written that it 'suffered an eclipse after the Reformation and was seldom used during Elizabeth's reign': E. G. Withycombe, *The Oxford Dictionary of English Christian Names* (London, 1977), p. 211.

24 Between March 1590 and September 1602, Richard Vernon, Vicar of Eastbourne, called his children Mary, George, Caesar, Margaret, Elizabeth and John.

25 Fenner, *The Arts of Logic and Rhetoric*, sig. E8; A. Peel ed., *The Seconde Parte of a Register* (London, 1915), i, p. 214. William Hopkinson, Rector of Warbleton, was also a member of the 1583 Sussex delegation to Whitgift: *ibid.*; WSRO, Ep.II/9/6, fo 57.

26 I have found particularly helpful C. Brent, 'Employment, Land Tenure and Population in East Sussex, 1540–1640' (Sussex Ph.D., 1974) and J. L. M. Gulley, 'The Wealden Landscape in the Early Seventeenth Century' (London Ph.D., 1960).

27 Brent, 'Employment, Land Tenure and Population', p. 65; *VCH*, Sussex, ix, pp. 204, 206. My population figure represents the median annual number of deaths (thirteen) in the period 1570–1600, multiplied by thirty-one.

28 Gulley, 'The Wealden Landscape', pp. 190, 521–3; BL, Add. charter 30920, and E. Straker, *Wealden Iron* (London, 1931), pp. 359–61, 377–80; ESRO, Lewes Wills, Bk A8, fos 27v–8.

29 C. Morris ed., *The Journeys of Celia Fiennes* (London, 1947), p. 136. The term is used apropos Goudhurst, in the Kentish Weald and adjacent to Cranbrook.

30 PRO, PROB 11/66/20 and St Ch 5/M16/22; WSRO, Ep.ii/5/5, fo 342v.

31 ESRO, Lewes Wills, Bks A11, fo 19 and A22, fos 89–96. The originals of these wills are extant; WSRO, Ep.ii/9/5 fo 305r–v; Dunkin (Sussex Rec. Soc., i, 1902), p. 67 and J. S. Cockburn ed., *Calendar of Assize Records: Sussex Indictments James I* (London, 1975) p. 21; *VCH*, Sussex, ix, p. 195, where the name is given incorrectly as 'Hepburn'.

32 A. L. Frewen, *A History of Brickwall in Sussex and of the Parishes of Northiam and Brede* (London, 1909), p. 45; J. Bishop, *A Courteous Conference with the English Catholics Roman* (1598), sig. A2v; PRO, PROB 11/106/55; ESRO, Lewes Wills, Bk A14, fo 197. This is calendared incorrectly as the will of 'John' Bishop. Hall (British Rec. Soc., xxiv, 1901), p. 163; Dunkin (Sussex Rec. Soc., i, 1902), p. 105; PRO, PROB 11/120/75; W. B. Bannerman ed., *The Visitations of the County of Sussex . . . 1633–4* (Harleian Soc., liii, 1905), pp. 133, 169–70.

33 Brent, 'Employment, Land Tenure and Population', p. 226. The other four Warbleton yeomen are William Avery, John Delve, William Stace alias Shether and George Wattell: ESRO, Lewes Wills, Bks A10, fo 103r–v, A12, fos 248–9; WSRO, Ep.ii/5/3, fo 38v, Ep.ii/5/8, fo 21v; Dunkin (Sussex Rec. Soc., i, 1902), p. 20.

34 The other two Warbleton husbandmen are Thomas Breach and William Hobeme: ESRO, Lewes Wills, Bks A9, fo 227r–v, A16, fo 113, A17, fo 39r–v and QR/E/3, fo 82. For help with Sussex quarter sessions material I am grateful to Christopher Whittick; WSRO, Ep.ii/5/1, fo 144v; Dunkin (Sussex Rec. Soc., i, 1902), p. 40.

35 ESRO, Lewes Wills, Bk A11, fos 233–4; Dunkin (Sussex Rec. Soc., i, 1902), p. 23.

36 ESRO, Lewes Wills, Bks A8, fo 446, A9, fos 114v–15, 174v–5, 227r–v, A10, fos 41r–v, 103r–v, A12, fos 6v–7, and QR/E/7, fo 29.

37 ESRO, Lewes Wills, Bks A12, fos 148–9, 248–9, A21, fos 101v–2.

38 ESRO, Lewes Wills, Bk A11, fos 99r–v, 215v, 223–4.

39 ESRO, Lewes Wills, Bks A12, fo 156v, A16, fo 113, A17, fo 39r–v, A22, fos 89–96; PRO, E 179/190/332, Hawksborough Hundred.

40 WSRO, Ep.ii/9/7, fo 119v.

41 M. Spufford, 'The Schooling of the Peasantry in Cambridgeshire, 1575–1700', in J. Thirsk ed., *Land, Church and People* (London, 1970), pp. 121–2, 134–6; WSRO, Ep.ii/5/8, fo 22v.

42 Out of eleven Puritan families the mean baptismal interval is 28.4 months (median: 27.2) whereas out of twenty non-Puritan families the mean baptismal interval is 33.6 months (median: 30).

43 PRO, PROB 11/91/42. My italics. The language of these testators has to be understood in the light of contemporary views concerning usury. Many ordinary people regarded the 1571 statute 'as sanctioning interest up to ten per cent' while 'theologians and moralists' *all* glossed it in a more restrictive sense. The Warbleton Puritans here followed their religious teachers: R. H. Tawney ed., *A Discourse upon Usury . . . by Thomas Wilson* (London, 1925), pp. 118–19, 165, 170. The nature of the Warbleton evidence moreover suggests that, in a rural context, a major solvent of traditional attitudes towards usury was the experience of inflation; it must have become increasingly obvious that cash bequests payable some years hence, to children on reaching their majorities, would by then be worth less in real terms. See also p. 17 above.

44 W. G. Hoskins, 'Harvest Fluctuations and English Economic History, 1480–1619', *Agricultural History Review*, 12 (1964), 39; W. Perkins, 'A Fruitful Dialogue Concerning the End of the World', in *Works* (London, 1608–9), iii, pp. 467–77; *APC 1586–87*, pp. 91, 119; *CSPD 1581–90*, pp. 323, 326, 340, 343–4, 347, 364 and index references to 'Armada'. For unrest in 1587 see P. Clark, 'Popular Protest and Disturbance in Kent, 1558–1640', *EcHR*, 29 (1976), 367.

45 Collinson, *The Elizabethan Puritan Movement*, pp. 291–329, 333.

46 Cf. n. 10 above.

47 D. Williams ed., *Three Treatises Concerning Wales [by John Penry]* (London, 1960), pp. xviii, 41–2, 162.

48 Preserved Holman was christened at Warbleton on 1 August 1588. To my knowledge this is the first use of Preserved as a baptismal name.

49 In addition to Comfort Starr and Comfort Penry, Comfort Tamkin was christened at Wartling, Sussex, in April 1600. My italics.

50 R. B. Manning, *Religion and Society in Elizabethan Sussex* (London, 1969), pp. 201, 211; P. Clark, 'Josias Nicholls and Religious Radicalism, 1553–1639', JEH 28 (1977), 145; Longden, *Northamptonshire and Rutland Clergy*, i, p. 179.

51 J. Hurstfield, *Freedom, Corruption and Government in Elizabethan England* (London, 1973), pp. 68–9.

52 R. H. Tawney, *Religion and the Rise of Capitalism* (London, 1926), pp. 175–93.

Chapter 4

◆

The fortunes
of English Puritanism, 1603–40

I

S HORTLY after the accession of James I, a darkness seems to descend over the history of Puritanism, or, to switch metaphors, the old roads appear to peter out and new ones only emerge on the eve of the Civil War. With good reason, the events surrounding the famous Hampton Court Conference in January 1604 have been described as the 'end of a movement'. The movement in question, of course, is the concerted Elizabethan attempt to remodel the English Church along more Protestant lines. From the 1560s onwards the Puritans had campaigned for further reformation; beginning with criticisms of the Prayer Book, some of them had proceeded to attack bishops as such. Increasingly frustrated in the attempt to impose their will from above, through Parliament, the more radical among them had sought to presbyterianise the ecclesiastical structure from below. Thus groups of clergy can be found meeting during the 1580s, in numerous clandestine conferences or *classes*. It was to these meetings that a draft form of presbyterian government, the Book of Discipline, had been circulated for approval. Police action by the authorities, however, had put an end to this particular design, and thenceforward reformist hopes were concentrated on the presumed heir to the throne – James VI of Scotland.[1]

Yet the death of Queen Elizabeth, in March 1603, revealed that the Puritan reform movement more generally was far from dead. Above all the capacity to organise on a nation-wide basis remained, as evidenced by the petitioning campaign which now ensued. One obvious result of this activity was the conference at Hampton Court, presided over by the new King. Nevertheless these proceedings are liable to give a false impression of moderation, for the Puritan spokesmen on this occasion were royal appointees not delegates.[2] In parallel with the Hampton Court Conference, a London meeting of regional

representatives had spelt out the Puritan requests in much more uncompromising fashion:

> The use of the surplice, cope, cross in baptism, kneeling at communion . . . ,
> imposition of hands in confirmation, ring in marriage, and sundry other
> offensive ceremonies in our Church, is not indifferent but simply unlawful in
> the public worship and divine service of God.

They also asked that the Prayer Book might 'be corrected according to the
Word', that is to say the Bible. Moreover, many of the petitions in circulation
at this time called for the introduction of the 'discipline, as it was delivered
by our saviour Christ and his holy apostles', and 'agreeable to the example
of other reformed churches'. At the very least, this would have involved
granting powers of excommunication to the parish clergy and probably the
introduction of lay elders as well. But most revealing is the statement in the
so-called 'advices', issued by the Puritan organizers, that petitioners should
'not *expressly* desire the removal of bishops'.[3]

The implication is that the radicals still favoured abolishing the episcopal
system in its entirety. On the other hand, even the moderate requests put to
King James produced negligible results. Hence there followed a fresh resort
to Parliament, especially in the years 1604 to 1610.[4] Reformism, however,
was rapidly overshadowed by the fate of ministers now threatened with
deprivation, for refusing subscription to Prayer Book and bishops. According
to the Puritan campaign managers some thousand clergy sympathised with
their aims, to the extent of being willing to sign petitions. The claim is lent
credence by a numerical breakdown for London and twenty-four counties,
which they published in 1605. This list totals approximately 750 clergy,
leaving a further 250 clergy for the rest of England. On this basis, about 10
per cent of clerical personnel can be considered as some shade or other of
Puritan. While less than a hundred of these men were actually to suffer
deprivation from their benefices, it does not necessarily follow that this 1 per
cent comprised a hard core of radicals.[5] Beneficed clergy were in practice
more vulnerable than either donative curates or stipendiary lecturers, the
latter who had begun to proliferate in the Elizabethan period. Nor is there
any simple correlation between the names of activists in 1603–4 and those
subsequently deprived. How far the Puritan majority at this time was truly
moderate remains open to question.

This problem also links with the fate of presbyterianism. In so far as
Elizabethan theory had been translated into practice it was largely at the parish
level, by Puritan parsons and like-minded churchwardens. The *classes* had
never established effective control over individual congregations, remaining
instead in a merely advisory role. Therefore the demise of the Puritan conferences may be of less significance than has often been assumed. Indeed

much hinges here on our interpretation of a pamphlet published in 1605, with the challenging title *English Puritanisme*. The author was William Bradshaw, who emerged in the aftermath of the Hampton Court Conference as a leading spokesman for what he himself terms the 'rigidest sort' of Puritans. In *English Puritanisme*, Bradshaw asserts the autonomy of individual congregations. 'No other churches or spiritual church officers have, by any warrant from the Word of God, power to censure, punish, or control the same, but are only to counsel and advise'.[6] Bradshaw's apparent repudiation of synodical power marks a major theoretical break with the Book of Discipline. But the position adopted in *English Puritanisme* was arguably even more radical than the earlier presbyterianism, given its closer proximity to separatism; each congregation was independent, albeit subject to the civil magistrate. Meanwhile, since no fellow Puritan ventured publicly to contradict him, Bradshaw was left in possession of the field.

Like a number of other radical Puritans, Bradshaw had already been silenced under Queen Elizabeth. Thereafter he found employment as chaplain to a Derbyshire gentry family, at the same time functioning as a more-or-less unsalaried preacher in the locality. This looks to have been a fairly common pattern for those unable to make what Bradshaw called a 'politique subscription'.[7] Another possibility was schoolmastering, although that too technically required subscription in order to obtain a license, while a last resort was emigration, initially to the Netherlands and from the late 1620s to New England as well. Loss of benefice, curacy or lectureship almost always involved hardship, especially if dependents were involved. Many gentry and merchants helped cushion such blows by individual acts of charity. Much less well known, however, are the joint endeavours to the same end, which also serve to illustrate the new organisational forms that Puritanism was now taking. Particular interest attaches to London events in the years 1606–7, when the subscription campaign was at its height and large numbers of Puritan ministers feared for their future livelihoods. Against this background Sarah Venables, the wealthy widow of a London merchant tailor, came to make her will. According to the later testimony of her aggrieved relations, she did so under the influence of a group of clergy threatened with deprivation.[8] By her will of July 1606, Mrs Venables left the bulk of her estate to be 'distributed unto and amongst such poor ministers as are, or shall be, put from their places and livings, which I see are grievously distressed, by such portions as the necessity or charge of children of them shall require, according to the discretion of mine executors.'

Any clergyman 'within the realm of England' was entitled to benefit, and subsequent calculations indicated that slightly in excess of £2,500 was available. The four executors included two Puritan clergy, Anthony Wotton and Edward Buckland. Two other Puritan ministers, Stephen Egerton and Edmund

Snape, were named as possible substitutes. Egerton in particular had played a major part in the recent petitioning movement, although Snape was not far behind in importance. Yet in some ways even more interesting are the names of the two overseers: Sir John Savile, a baron of the Court of Exchequer, and Sir Thomas Myddleton, a leading London alderman. By the time Mrs Venables died, in October 1607, Savile was dead and had been replaced by another Exchequer baron, Sir Nowell Sotherton. Since the will was contested the following November in the Court of Exchequer, the choice of overseers strongly suggests a preemptive move, by the testator and her advisers, to evade a legal challenge.

As matters turned out it was the government, in the person of the Attorney General, Sir Henry Hobart, rather than the relatives, who actually instituted legal proceedings. Thanks to a deposition by the brother-in-law of Mrs Venables, we can reconstruct the immediately preceding events. John Chalkhill, to his patent surprise, was summoned to a meeting at the Guildhall, on 12 October, where the will was 'published . . . with much ostentation before divers aldermen and many strangers, who gave countenance to the same'. But these proceedings having come to the attention of Archbishop Bancroft, he in turn alerted Lord Treasurer Dorset and other privy councillors. Probate was stayed, and a bill exhibited in the Court of Exchequer. In consequence the Puritans Wotton and Buckland were forbidden to act as executors, and the court determined that the money should be distributed to 'such preaching conformable ministers as stood in need thereof, and to the wives and children of such deprived and silenced inconformable ministers as were dead'. The relatives got nothing and the alternative of outright confiscation, as at one point mooted, was also avoided.[9] Instead, the remaining executors were left with considerable freedom of manoeuvre. If not a Puritan victory, nor was it a total defeat. Yet a question remains concerning the identity of the aldermen and others present at the Guildhall, for the reading of Mrs Venables's will. The names are in fact listed with the register copy of the will, and include four, aldermen: Sir Thomas Bennett, Sir Thomas Cambell, Sir Thomas Myddleton and Sir William Romney.[10] The presumption must be that we are here in the presence of both the London great and the godly. Moreover the link is most likely provided by another name on the list, that of 'Mr William Charke', who was a silenced minister and leading radical from Elizabethan days. One of the original disciples of the famous Thomas Cartwright, as early as 1572 he had preached against episcopacy as being the invention of Satan.[11] Charke was also the brother-in-law of Sir William Romney.

Judging from the phraseology of their surviving wills, Romney was the most committed Puritan among the four aldermen associated with this highly ambitious attempt to aid the deprived and silenced clergy. The religious preamble to his will of 1611 is unusually long and also includes a number of idiosyncratic features. In particular, Romney speaks of men on earth as 'pilgrims and strangers, looking for a city whose builder is God eternal in the heavens'. His overseers included William Charke and Sir Thomas Myddleton. Among other tasks, they were to distribute £50 to 'godly poor preachers that are in want'.[12] This was a mere bagatelle, however, compared to the £1,000 bequeathed for the same purpose by William Jones, in 1615. Jones, who died a bachelor at Hamburg, was a merchant adventurer and haberdasher like Romney. Distribution of the money, to 'poor preachers in England', was left to the deputy of the Merchant Adventurers at Hamburg, and the ministers Stephen Egerton and Richard Sedgwick. The last named is described as 'our preacher here in Hamburg' and had fled England as a nonconformist in about 1601. Furthermore the Hamburg church, over which Sedgwick presided, operated along fully reformed lines and Jones himself had apparently served as an elder.[13] Another £1,000 was bequeathed to 'godly, painful and poor preachers' in 1623, by Lady Mary Weld, the widow of Alderman Sir Humphrey Weld. In this case the executors responsible were headed by her son-in-law Sir Robert Brooke, a well known patron of Puritan clergy.[14]

The foregoing examples are sufficient to indicate that sizeable sums of money were being channelled, during these years, in the direction of clergy who must count as Puritan even on the strictest definition. Occasionally it is possible to document the complete transaction, as with the £50 bequeathed for the 'relief of poor ministers and preachers of the gospel', by John Swayne of Staffordshire, in 1623. The intermediary in this case was Arthur Hildersham, one of Cartwright's literary executors and regularly in trouble for his nonconformity. Among the recipients of Swayne's bounty was Walter Travers, co-author with Cartwright of the Book of Discipline and long since silenced. Swayne's will survives and so does a related receipt from Travers to Hildersham for £5.[15] It is probably no accident that the names of William Charke and Stephen Egerton both feature prominently in such schemes. The city connections of Charke look to have been particularly important, and his eldest son Benjamin was to become a haberdasher. But back in the 1570s and 1580s Charke had been successively lecturer at Gray's Inn and Lincoln's Inn, with a very different lawyer and gentry clientéle. When he died in 1617 both Alderman Sir Thomas Myddleton and Sir Thomas Smith, 'my dear landlord', were remembered in Charke's will. Smith was indeed a governor of the East India Company, yet in 1626 his widow was to marry the Earl of Leicester and his brother, Sir Richard Smith, resided part of the time at Leeds Castle in Kent. Charke himself remains a rather elusive figure. Something of his outlook, however, can be deduced from the remarkable coat of arms and motto, which he acquired in 1604 when registering his claims to gentility. The motto, in Greek, is taken from Matthew 7.13: 'Enter ye in at the strait gate, for wide is the gate and broad is the way that leadeth to destruction, and many there be which go in thereat'. Both the crest and principal device selected by Charke consist of a Y or gamma, symbolising the choice between the broad way of destruction and the narrow path of salvation. Undoubtedly for Charke, the true worship of God was intimately bound up with the pursuit of that narrow path.[16] By comparison, Stephen Egerton seems to have adopted a rather less absolutist stance. Nevertheless he too had been a very prominent figure in the Elizabethan classical movement, and his parish of St Anne's, Blackfriars, was a veritable epicentre of Puritan activity in the early years of King James. An unrepentant nonconformist, Egerton gave up his lectureship in 1607 but continued as curate at St Anne's until his death in 1622. From about 1609 he was assisted by William Gouge, who had been recommended by Arthur Hildersham and was also a nonconformist – if less extreme.[17] Between them Egerton and Gouge were to span a period of seventy years at Blackfriars, from 1583 to 1653.

II

The study of wills enables us to reconstruct part of the network of Puritan relationships which once existed. So too does a systematic examination of the products of the printing press. An especially illuminating instance is provided by the publications of Paul Baynes who died in 1617. Baynes was a radical Puritan, who had been suspended from his Cambridge lectureship in 1608[18] and published almost nothing during his lifetime. Between 1617 and 1621, however, fourteen posthumous works appeared. With one exception, they were all printed at London. The principal editor signs himself variously as E. C. or Ez. Ch. This turns out to be Ezekiel Charke, son of William, who relinquished his fellowship at King's College, Cambridge, in 1617. Since Baynes had continued to reside mainly in Cambridge after his suspension and apparently died there, he may well have personally entrusted Ezekiel Charke with his manuscripts. A number of different London publishers were employed, but Baynes's writings were chiefly handled by Nathaniel Newbery. Somewhat unusually Newbery himself wrote and signed a number of the dedications, and was clearly religiously committed to the enterprise. None of these London publications was clandestine and all are recorded in the Stationers Registers as being licensed. Nevertheless, in every case save one the editors went to the same licenser: Daniel Featley. Although now chaplain to Archbishop Abbot, Featley was a protégé of the leading Oxford Puritan and chief spokesman at the Hampton Court Conference – John Rainolds.[19] The impression is that Featley remained sympathetic to Puritan publishing and would not make unnecessary difficulties.

Nearly all Baynes's posthumous publications are furnished with a personal dedication. Those selected as dedicatees tended to be London notables, which is partly a reflection of the Charke family's circle of acquaintance, and not surprisingly they include names already encountered: Lady Rebecca Romney, widow of Sir William, Sir Thomas Smith and Lady Mary Weld. It emerges from Ezekiel Charke's dedication to Smith of *Two Godly and Fruitful Treatises*, in 1619, that this merchant prince was a patron in a very real sense. The Charkes and the Smiths were London neighbours, living in the same parish of St Dionis Backchurch, and Ezekiel writes of his desire 'not only to be thankful to you for myself, but much more for the many and great kindnesses a long time continued to my dear parents'. He also describes his own editorial efforts as being intended for the benefit of the 'Church of God'.[20] That the patronage of this particular Puritan family, by Smith, was not an isolated act can be shown from another dedication to him, also in 1619. Again the work was posthumous, by William Negus and edited by his son Jonathan. William Negus had been deprived, for nonconformity, of an Essex benefice in 1609, continuing to live nearby in retirement until his death. The dedication recalls Smith's 'good affection and respect' for the father and the 'liberal allowance' for 'some years' granted to the son. This suggests that Smith had been subsidising the studies of Jonathan Negus at King's College, Cambridge. Entitled *Man's Active Obedience, or the Power of Godliness*, the book is also graced with a preface to the reader by Stephen Egerton, who describes the author as having been one of the 'worthies of God's Israel'.[21]

Meanwhile the publication which Ezekiel Charke chose to dedicate to his aunt Lady Romney, in 1618, was a catechism by Baynes, and it too carried a preface by Egerton. Two years later, in 1620, Lady Weld was yoked with her sister and fellow widow Lady Lennard, as joint dedicatee of Baynes's *Christian Letters*, a treatise of spiritual counsel based on genuine case histories. 'As you are sisters in nature, so you are nearer sisters in grace', wrote Charke.[22] Earlier, in 1618, Charke singled out a Cambridge contemporary, Robert Clavering, for the dedication of *A Caveat for Cold Christians* by Baynes. Clavering, now town clerk of Newcastle, had also been a fellow of King's College, Cambridge, and one or other of them may actually have tutored young Jonathan Negus. King's College is not normally thought of as an especially Puritan institution, yet the dedication hints at the godly society which Charke and Clavering had enjoyed, the 'comfortable loving and living together', and the 'wonted sweet intercourse of speech'. Charke writes that God 'hath begun the good work some years ago in you', and signs himself as 'yours in surest bond'.[23]

Also in 1618 the publisher Nathaniel Newbery dedicated three further writings by Baynes to Sir William Craven and William Halliday, both London aldermen, and to Nicholas Jordan, a leading member of the Sussex gentry and a brother-in-law of Baynes.[24] The sermon dedicated to Craven is described on the title-page as having been preached 'at Cranbrook, in Kent, 1617', the year Baynes died still apparently under suspension. Therefore this sermon was technically illegal. The presence of Baynes at Cranbrook on this and no doubt many other occasions is to be explained by the fact that his wife was related to a local clothier dynasty – the Sheafes.[25] Moreover two other posthumous works by Baynes have a Cranbrook association, being edited by J. E., 'at the free-school in Cranbrook'. This was John Elmstone, master of the local grammar school, who also wrote some commemorative verses on the author, including the following stanza:

> Rare is a faithful, zealous Christian;
> More rare good conscience and great learning meet.
> One of a thousand proves a godly man.
> A learned scribe, a skilfull, a discrete,
> A watchful pastor, teacher excellent,
> Such who can find, unless Paul Baynes be meant?

Elmstone dedicated his editorial labours to the heads of two leading gentry families in the parish, Sir Thomas Roberts and Sir Henry Baker.[26] Again the publisher was Nathaniel Newbery, which indicates that this was part of the same collective enterprise.

But to describe John Elmstone simply as a Puritan schoolmaster is at best a misleading half-truth, since he was in addition almost certainly a deprived minister. Thus in 1602 a John Elmstone M.A. was licensed as minister of Aldington in Kent, where he had been replaced by late 1607. In January 1612 our John Elmstone M.A. was licensed to teach at Cranbrook. What virtually clinches the case for them being the same person is that according to the register he was licensed 'without oath or subscription', a remarkable concession and one which points to scruples of conscience. Elmstone lived on at Cranbrook for another forty-nine years, not dying until 1661, a radical Puritan and increasingly patriarchal presence in this major Wealden town.[27] As we shall see, he was also to play a key role in the religious politics of 1640. All of which calls for considerable revision of our understanding of events in this much studied locality, and the worsening relations of the Vicar of Cranbrook, Robert Abbot, with a group of his parishioners. Up until now Abbot's difficulties have been ascribed to an upsurge of separatism during the 1630s. Yet there are likely to have been serious tensions present from the moment that Abbot arrived at Cranbrook in 1616. What he made of Baynes using his pulpit we do not know, although Abbot's belief in the 'aristocratical' government of the English Church by 'bishops and ministers' sharply distinguished their two positions.[28]

The works by Baynes mentioned so far were comparatively short pieces and involved little financial risk for the publisher. Of a different order, however, was his *Commentary* on Ephesians. Indeed only the commentary on the first chapter saw print at this time, but even it ran to over 400 quarto pages. Published in 1618, the same year as the Synod of Dort, the work was geared to the highly topical subject of Arminianism, Baynes having taken a predictably Calvinist line. Ezekiel Charke dedicated it to Sir Henry Yelverton, the current Attorney General, and the publisher this time was Robert Milbourne. Yelverton appears to have been a relative stranger to Charke, the real link being Richard Sibbes, who provided a preface. Sibbes owed his religious conversion to Baynes, at Cambridge, and his position as lecturer at Gray's Inn was largely thanks to Yelverton. According to Sibbes, Baynes 'left large notes of no chapter but this' of Ephesians.[29] Nevertheless the full commentary was to appear in 1643, from the same publisher and in a folio edition of over 800 pages. An explanation of the delay either in terms of a lack of finance or the incompleteness of the manuscript is unsatisfactory, because from the second chapter of Ephesians onwards Baynes's commentary was liable to have offended the censor in 1618. For example, he writes of religious ceremonies:

> If of God, they do both serve to be bonds of unity and walls of separation from those without; if of man, they do bind such together as receive them and are a wall twixt such and others who cannot yield to entertain them. I would it were not too apparent that they, from their first admission, were occasion and prop of difference, and now Christians are subdivided by them into conformable and unconformable.

He also maintains that the church ministry laid down in the New Testament consists of 'pastors and teachers', who are tied to a particular congregation.[30] The wraps really come off, however, with *The Diocesans Tryall* by Baynes, published at Amsterdam in 1621 and edited by the exiled radical William Ames. In this Baynes argues at length that the only churches instituted by Christ or the apostles are parochial and that all ministers are equal. Perhaps by design, *The Diocesans Tryall* was the last of this particular clutch of writings to be printed. Whereas Baynes is simply described in his other posthumous publications as 'sometime preacher of God's word at St Andrew's in Cambridge', Ames here recounts his sufferings at episcopal hands.[31]

Ames himself had been driven out of Cambridge some two years after the suspension of Baynes, and shortly arrived in the Netherlands. One of his first actions was to produce a Latin version of Bradshaw's pamphlet *English Puritanisme*, translated as *Puritanismus Anglicanus* and published at Frankfurt in 1610. Between then and his death in 1633, Ames kept the foreign printing presses supplied with a regular stream of his own writings, many of them against the worship and polity of the English Church. In the process he emerged both as the chief voice of the religious exiles and of radical Puritanism more generally. His most important work was the *Medulla* or *Marrow of Sacred Divinity*. Running through four Latin editions between 1627 and 1630, the *Medulla* is, among other things, a handbook for Puritan revolutionaries. In it, Ames defines a particular visible church as 'a society of believers joined together by a special bond among themselves, for the constant exercise of the communion of saints'. This 'bond is a covenant, either express or implicit, whereby believers do particularly bind themselves to perform all those duties, both towards God and one toward another, which pertain to the respect and edification of the church'. It is the function of those 'elected' as ministers to preach the word and administer the sacraments. Ecclesiastical 'discipline' is an 'adjunct' to this, in which 'the elders have the chief parts'. The churches ordained by God are neither 'national, provincial or diocesan' but 'parochial'. Particular churches 'may and oftentimes also ought to enter into a mutual confederacy and fellowship amongst themselves in *classes* and synods', although this does not take away their 'liberty and power'. As for the episcopal hierarchy, this derives from the 'Roman Antichrist himself'. The mode of Christian worship is also divinely instituted and 'nothing must here be added, taken away or changed'.[32] Remarkably, there were two London printings of the *Medulla* in 1629 and 1630. Not apparently until July 1635 were the English ecclesiastical authorities fully aroused as to the danger posed by the writings of Ames.[33]

III

In exile Ames had benefitted from some powerful patronage. Between 1611 and 1619, he had been chaplain to Sir Horace Vere, commander of the English forces in the Netherlands. When this chaplaincy was terminated, due to pressure from England, Vere's fellow colonel Sir Edward Harwood came to the rescue. Thanks to Harwood's intervention with the stadholder, Prince Maurice, Ames had been appointed professor of divinity at Franeker University.[34] An intellectual rather than a man of action, the ideas of Ames none the less underlie one of the most striking Puritan developments during the 1620s – the creation of an English synod or *classis* of the Netherlands. The number of English churches and garrison chaplaincies in the Netherlands had been steadily growing, and a rational argument could be made for greater supervision. Certainly that was how the matter was presented to King James, in seeking his permission. But the churches in question had all departed from the English ecclesiastical model, largely abandoning the Prayer Book and setting up forms of congregational discipline. If James thought to bring them back into line, he was almost doomed to disappointment. What emerged instead was an increasing affront to episcopal sensibilities. Indeed in some respects the English synod of the 1620s marks a revival of the conference system of the 1580s, albeit abroad and with official authorisation. The organising genius was John Forbes, an exiled Scottish presbyterian who had come under the intellectual influence of Ames. He and his colleagues argued that, since they received financial support from the Dutch magistracy, they were bound to follow Dutch religious practices. The synod met on an annual basis between 1622 and 1631, and as well as licensing ministers it began to undertake the ordination of new clergy.[35]

Not surprisingly, there was a growing concern in English government circles that the synod had become a front organisation for radical Puritanism. William Laud, the future Archbishop of Canterbury, was among the first to sound the alarm and effectively prevented the synod from meeting after 1631.[36] It was Laud also who helped to quash another major Puritan initiative of the 1620s – the English-based activities of a group known to history as the Feoffees for Impropriations. Most of our knowledge of this body comes from the successful prosecution mounted against it in the Court of Exchequer during the years 1632–33. Although the existence of the feoffees allegedly dated back to about 1612, all the evidence produced in court was from 1625 onwards. They were a committee of clergy, lawyers and merchants, who, by their own account, had engaged in the innocent and indeed praiseworthy task of raising money to buy back church tithes which had been alienated into lay hands. Yet these impropriations once re-acquired were not simply given back to the parishes concerned; rather the income was devoted to a variety of religious uses, at the discretion of the feoffees. The essence of the prosecution case was that the money had been misappropriated, in that it was mainly spent on hiring preachers and not on endowing vicarages. There was little suggestion during the trial itself that the feoffees were Puritans, but the surviving comments of Laud are much less restrained. He noted in his diary, on the day of the dissolution of the feoffees, that 'they were the main instrument for the Puritan faction to undo the Church'. Elsewhere Laud added that 'most of the men they put in were persons disaffected to the discipline, if not the doctrine too, of the Church of England'. Morever 'no small part was given to schoolmasters, to season youth *ab ovo* for their party, and to young students in the universities, to purchase them and their judgements on their side, against their coming abroad into the church'.[37]

One of the precedents cited by the prosecution during the trial of the feoffees was the Venables case of 1607 and, while they did not draw out the implications, the comparison does not appear unduly strained.[38] There are also echoes more generally of earlier Puritan benefactions, as well as some overlaps of individuals. For example the feoffee George Harwood, a haber-dasher and brother of Sir Edward, is probably the same person named by

Lady Weld as an overseer in her will of 1623.[39] Another feoffee was William
Gouge, the former assistant to Stephen Egerton at Blackfriars. Alderman
Rowland Heylyn, the senior city member among the early feoffees, provides
continuity of another kind. Together with Sir Thomas Myddleton, an overseer
of the Venables will, he subsidised the first popular edition of the Bible in
Welsh, published as an octavo in 1630. These two leading Londoners are thus
part of a tradition of Welsh evangelism which runs from the Elizabethan
separatist John Penry to the Cromwellian fifth-monarchist Vavasour Powell.
More specifically, the propagation of the gospel in the 'dark corners' of the
land was one of the objects of the feoffees.[40] Furthermore, in his will of 1631,
Alderman Heylyn bequeathed £300 to 'poor ministers and schoolmasters',
part of which was to be administered on the advice, among others, of Julines
Herring. The latter was lecturer at St. Alkmund's, Shrewsbury, a post partly
funded by Heylyn. Herring was also an extreme Puritan, who had studied
for the ministry with the deprived clergyman Humphrey Fenn and had got
round subscription by being ordained at the hands of an Irish bishop. During
the 1630s he was to migrate to the Netherlands.[41] Herring was preceded
there by two other refugee clergy, one a feoffee and the other closely associated with the scheme, John Davenport and Hugh Peter.

Clearly we must resist the temptation to define the feoffees in terms of
their most radical element. Outwardly much more moderate were the two
leading clerical members, William Gouge and Richard Sibbes. Yet Gouge
had received his early religious training from his uncle, Ezekiel Culverwell,
who was to be deprived in 1609. Both Gouge and Sibbes provided prefaces
to Culverwell's *Treatise of Faith*, published in 1623. Preaching at the funeral
of Gouge in 1653, his successor at Blackfriars recalled how he had been a
'sweet refreshing shade and shelter' to the 'old godly Puritans', by 'admitting
them to the lord's supper', when they 'could not either atall or at least purely,
in regard of superstitious gestures, genuflections, etc., enjoy that ordinance at
home'.[42] Although Richard Sibbes was apparently a conformist, his voluminous published writings include a definition of the visible church which sounds
extraordinarily similar to that of Bradshaw and Ames.

> Every particular church and congregation under one pastor, their meeting is
> the church of God, a several church independent. Our national church, that
> is the Church of England, because it is under a government civil, which is
> not dependent upon any foreign prince, it is a particular church from other
> nations.

Most of his works were published posthumously, but in 1630 Sibbes dedicated
a volume of sermons to Sir Horace and Lady Mary Vere. As we have already
illustrated, the Veres were major patrons of refugee Puritan clergy in the
Netherlands. Moreover the main editors of the writings of Sibbes, following

his death in 1635, were the two radical Puritans Thomas Goodwin and Philip Nye, who subsequently fled to the Netherlands in 1639, joining the English church at Arnhem.[43] Further radical links can also be inferred from Sibbes's will, one of the overseers for instance being Sir Nathaniel Barnardiston whose parish of Kedington, in Suffolk, was a virtual Puritan fiefdom. There the nonconformist Samuel Fairclough remained unharmed throughout the 1630s.[44]

Turning to the lawyers among the feoffees, both Christopher Sherland and his successor Sir Thomas Crewe remembered John Dod in their wills, respectively of 1632 and 1634. Dod had been deprived back in 1607 and finally found a safe haven at Fawsley, in Northamptonshire, which became in consequence almost a Puritan shrine during the 1630s. The godly went on pilgrimage there and sometimes even to die.[45] Arguably the most formidable of all the feoffees, however, was the lawyer John White. In the first years of the Long Parliament, as chairman of the committee for scandalous ministers, he would come to strike terror into the heart of many a parson. Another expatriate Welshman, White has been plausibly associated with the evangelising efforts of Myddleton and Heylyn. At the same time he appears to have been driven by an especially militant Puritanism, which came to the fore in 1640. Like many of the feoffees, White was in addition associated with New England colonisation.[46] Whereas the activities of the feoffees can be understood as an attempt to work the existing English ecclesiastical system in the interests of Puritan preachers, America offered on a far grander scale than the Netherlands the opportunity to rebuild from the foundations. Indeed, with the collapse of the English synod and of the feoffees in rapid succession, godly hopes came to be concentrated on this remaining avenue for advance.

Recent scholarship has reminded us just how mixed were the motives of emigrants to New England. Nevertheless, it remains true that many of the leaders did wish to create a society religiously very different from England.[47] The New England 'way', as it developed, was to acquire a number of idiosyncratic features, notably the making of church membership dependent on visible sanctity, but there is widespread agreement that the ideas of William Ames were a major source of inspiration. When Ames died in 1633 his wife and son sold up in the Netherlands and sailed across the Atlantic. They were soon followed by John Davenport and Hugh Peter. During the last year of his life, Ames had become co-pastor with Peter at the English church in Rotterdam and Peter was to act as his literary executor. The Rotterdam church can be regarded as a prototype for New England ecclesiastical developments, having been reconstituted on the basis of a covenant in 1633 and with stringent tests for membership. Subsequently the claims of this type of congregationalism were to split the Puritan reform movement, although it is noticeable that both parties in the 1640s claimed to be the true heirs of Ames.[48]

An unusual window onto how Puritans regarded these events in their beginning is provided by a surviving cache of letters from the early 1630s. The letters were seized by the English authorities in 1635, during a combined raid on the studies of two clergymen: John Stoughton, curate of St. Mary Aldermanbury, in London, and John White, Rector of Holy Trinity, Dorchester, who is not to be confused with his lawyer namesake. Whether or not we call Stoughton and White Puritans, some of their correspondents certainly were. Today the letters are to be found scattered chronologically through State Papers Domestic and State Papers Colonial in the Public Record Office. Again the trail starts with money in the form of a bequest by a west country widow, Mrs Philippa Pitt, who left £100 for 'good uses', to be distributed at the discretion of Stoughton and White.[49] It was rumours about this and other cash that led to their appearance before the Court of High Commission and, ultimately, to our being able to recover something of the mood at the time. John White of Dorchester was himself a pioneer of North American colonisation and John Stoughton's brother Israel had emigrated to New England in 1630. Most of the correspondence is addressed to Stoughton, and straddles the North Sea as well as the Atlantic. Three letters are from James Forbes, son of the John Forbes who had masterminded the English synod during the 1620s. Written from Delft, the then Dutch headquarters of the English Merchant Adventurers, they refer both to continuing conformist pressure from England on the exiled Puritan communities and to the growing disagreement within their own ranks about the nature of true church order. The great importance attached to the writings of William Ames comes across very clearly. At the same time Forbes sounds a prophetic note. Although right religion is now retreating from 'these parts', he hopes that 'God will find out a place, where his saints may have the freedom of the gospel in the purity and integrity of it'.[50] Written in April 1634, this letter finds an answering call in one from New England that December, where Stoughton's son-in-law, James Cudworth, extols the setting up of the first New England churches and their appointment of 'pastors' and 'teachers'. The 'Lord hath brought me to see that which my forefathers desired to see but could not . . . so many churches walking in the way and order of the gospel, [and] enjoying that Christian liberty that Christ has purchased for us'.[51] In stark contrast, however, is the letter sent to Stoughton the following September 1635. The author was Sir Thomas Wroth, who resided both in Somerset and in the London parish of St Stephen's, Coleman Street. Writing via his widowed sister Lady Elizabeth Clere, who also lived in Coleman Street, Wroth lamented that 'all things go on from worse to worse'. Yet 'now is the time to shew our courage' and 'stand to our captain Christ Jesus'. It 'will argue some patience if we quietly suffer *usque ad rerum amissionem*, but it will be a great evidence of Christian resolution if we suffer *usque ad sanguinis effusionem*, for preservation of faith and a good conscience'.[52] Whether Wroth was really advocating armed resistance remains unclear, but his sense of dismay at the turn of religious affairs in England is unmistakeable.

For most of those among Stoughton's correspondents New England seemed to be a single ray of light shining through the otherwise encircling gloom. Nevertheless as news filtered back of revolutionary religious doings across the ocean, some members of the Puritan old guard grew increasingly worried. It was partly that the compromises often forced on Puritans in England came to look shabby by comparison with the freedom allowed in the American colonies. More fundamentally, however, such Puritans believed they were faced with the large-scale revival of separatism masquerading as a national church. Although these disputes have been studied largely with reference to the 1640s there is an important prehistory, especially as regards the collective response by a group of English clergy in 1637, whose names are recorded in a letter now preserved at the Boston Public Library in Massachusetts.[53] This list of thirteen signatories, criticising their New England brethren, is headed by the octogenarian John Dod and the septuagenarian Robert Cleaver, both of whom had been deprived in 1607. Dod, as we have noted, was currently based at Fawsley and Cleaver was probably living nearby at Canons Ashby. At least three of the other signatories were also Northamptonshire clergy: Timothy Dod, son of John, John Winston and Nathaniel Cotton. Winston and Cotton indeed appear to have been sons-in-law of Cleaver.[54] Yet this was not simply a local or even familial Northamptonshire response, since the other names include Simeon Ashe and Ephraim Huitt of Warwickshire, John Ball of Staffordshire, William Bourne and Thomas Paget of Lancashire, and Julines Herring now of Cheshire. All of them were nonconformists, Ball for example, along with Herring, having been ordained by a sympathetic Irish bishop.[55] In 1637 these eleven, plus Thomas Langley and Ralph Shearard, addressed a series of questions to the New England clergy, claiming to have jointly 'maintained the purity of worship against corruptions, both on the right hand and on the left', while 'we lived together in the same kingdom'. They were particularly concerned to know whether their former colleagues taught that a 'stinted form of prayer and set liturgy is unlawful', and that the godly should not 'join in prayer' or 'receive the sacraments' where such 'a stinted liturgy is used'. New England developments, they feared, lent substance to the allegation that 'nonconformists in practice are separatists in heart'.[56]

How then are these thirteen English clergy, meeting together in 1637, best categorised? To call them a synod seems unduly formal, although there are some similarities with the Puritan conferences of high Elizabethan days and one of their number, John Ball, was subsequently commissioned by them to reply to the answer received from New England. None the less they look more like a gathering of refugees from persecution, thrown together rather haphazardly. Certainly the group was soon scattered, Herring and Paget going to Amsterdam and Huitt, somewhat ironically, emigrating to New England. Ball died in 1640 and Cleaver perhaps even earlier. Yet between 1637 and 1640 the situation in which English Puritans found themselves was dramatically transformed, because of events in Scotland which up until this point appears to have featured hardly at all in their thinking. For after the religious changes introduced by James I, Scotland had increasingly become a place for the godly to flee from rather than to. Thus the Scottish rebellion, triggered by Charles I's attempted introduction of a new Prayer Book in 1637, and even more the abolition of bishops there in late 1638 was largely unanticipated in Puritan circles. But once these developments north of the border began to unfold so those in England, who had never been truly reconciled to the existing ecclesiastical polity, were able to grasp the opportunity now presented. The essential means was a parliament, with which to bring pressure to bear on the monarch and for which a coalition of opposition interests manoeuvred as the Scottish crisis deepened. By October 1640 and the meeting of the Long Parliament, all other options available to Charles had been exhausted. At the same time he was obliged to negotiate with his critics from a position of unprecedented weakness.

IV

Historians are unclear to what extent the call for the 'root and branch' abolition of episcopacy, which emerged that autumn, was a Scottish import grafted onto relatively recent English discontent or the expression of a radical Puritan tradition which had never died out since Elizabethan times. Archbishop Laud especially has been blamed for the recrudescence of a largely moribund Puritan movement, due to his imposition of a package of religious policies going under the label of Arminianism as well as the harsh treatment of nonconformity.[57] Without wishing to belittle the reaction provoked by Laud, the evidence reviewed up to this point also confirms the existence of a radical Puritan continuum. This is not, however, to resurrect the notion of an inevitable rise and triumph of Puritanism, since it was only the collapse of Caroline policies in Scotland which opened the door to radical religious aspirations in England. Not surprisingly the religious opponents of Charles in both kingdoms made common cause, but the English were never less than equal partners. The nature of the relationship is well conveyed by the London letters sent home by the Scottish treaty commissioner Robert Baillie, during November and December 1640. As a clergyman, Baillie was particularly sensitive to the state of religious affairs in the capital. On 18 November, he wrote that 'the town of London . . . minds to present a petition, which I have seen, for the abolition of bishops, deans and all their appurtenances'. Three weeks later, on 12 December, he reported that

> yesterday a world of honest citizens, in their best apparrel, in a very modest way, went to the House of Commons [and] sent in two aldermen with their petition, subscribed as we hear by 15,000 hands, for removing episcopacy, the service book, and all other such scandals out of their Church.

Although Baillie and the Scots were clearly well-informed, they were certainly not orchestrating these events. Indeed, Baillie shared the widespread view that the London petitioners had acted with undue haste.[58]

The London root and branch petition was presented to the Commons by Alderman Isaac Pennington, member for the City of London, and it has long been assumed that his parish of St Stephen's, Coleman Street, constituted the organisational centre of the anti-episcopal agitation at this time. The radical and sometime feoffee John Davenport had been Vicar there between 1625 and 1633, and was succeeded by John Goodwin who emerged during the early 1640s as a leading congregationalist. Furthermore, Goodwin dedicated his first book to Pennington in August 1640.[59] But a very important additional piece of the jigsaw, missing until now, is probably provided by Sir Thomas Wroth. The latter, as we have seen, was a resident of Coleman Street, where he had been born in 1584.[60] An extreme Puritan, he was also the brother-in-law of Sir Edward Dering, member for Kent at the beginning of the Long Parliament. It was Dering who presented the first county petition calling for the root and branch abolition of bishops, in January 1641, and who also sponsored the root and branch bill to the same effect in May. At the beginning of December 1640, however, and before the London root and branch petition was actually presented, a group of his constituents had forwarded a version to Dering with a roll of Kentish signatories. There was an accompanying letter with it from John Elmstone, schoolmaster of Cranbrook, asking for Dering's support in their endeavour 'to lay low the high tower of our lordly church prelacy'. The petition and probably the letter too were delivered to Dering by a Cranbrook clothier, Richard Rabson. Among Elmstone's other Kentish associates was a suspended minister Thomas Wilson, who can be found writing to Dering the following February. Urging ecclesiastical reformation on him, Wilson quoted from the *Medulla* of William Ames.[61] Meanwhile at Westminster, as the parliamentary attack on bishops gathered momentum, John White, lawyer and former feoffee, emerged as one of the most principled advocates of abolition, his notorious book *The First Century of Scandalous and Malignant Priests* providing an inverse image of the evangelism which Puritans still aimed to promote.[62]

Money, organisation and ideology give shape and substance to Puritanism under the early Stuarts. Although the symmetry of the Elizabethan classical movement was lacking, the variety of responses called forth by new circumstances more than compensated. The individual parish or congregation was now emphasised as the basic unit of reformation and the local support of the laity became increasingly crucial. Moreover religious constraints at home were offset by the growing possibilities for experiment abroad, especially in the Netherlands and New England. If the price was a certain incoherence, nevertheless radicals of different views stood shoulder to shoulder in 1640 – united in their determination to break down the barriers which for so long had blocked the path to the promised land.

NOTES

This essay was delivered as a lecture at the Dr Williams's Library in October 1990. I am grateful to the following for their help: Michael Crawford, Carlotta Dionisotti, Kenneth Fincham, Peter Lake, Norman Pettit and Conrad Russell.

1 P. Collinson, *The Elizabethan Puritan Movement* (London, 1967), pt. 8 and *passim*.

2 P. Collinson, 'The Jacobean Religious Settlement: the Hampton Court Conference', in H. Tomlinson ed., *Before the Civil War* (London, 1983), pp. 27–51.

3 HMC Beaulieu, pp. 33–4; R. G. Usher, *The Reconstruction of the English Church* (London, 1910), i, pp. 296–7, ii, p. 358. My italics.

4 S. B. Babbage, *Puritanism and Richard Bancroft* (London, 1962), ch. 8.

5 *An Abridgement of the Booke which the Ministers of Lincoln Diocess delivered to his Majestie* (London, 1605), p. 52. K. Fincham, *Prelate as Pastor: the Episcopate of James I* (Oxford, 1990), Appendix VI.

6 W. Bradshaw, *English Puritanisme* (London, 1605), pp. 5–6.

7 P. Lake, *Moderate Puritans and the Elizabethan Church* (Cambridge, 1982), pp. 267–8; *DNB, s.n.* Bradshaw, William.

8 The following account is based on PRO, SP 14/37, fos 222–37.

9 I. M. Calder ed., *Activities of the Puritan Faction of the Church of England, 1625–33,* (London, 1957), p. 63; PRO, SP 14/45, fo 206. [Strictly speaking it was a petition not a deposition by Chalkhill.]

10 PRO, PROB 11/112, fo 9. [The recording of such additional information with a will is extremely unusual.]

11 H. C. Porter, *Reformation and Reaction in Tudor Cambridge* (Cambridge, 1958), p. 141.

12 PRO, PROB 11/117, fos 335v–38.

13 PRO, PROB 11/126, fos 408v–409; S. Clarke, *The Lives of Thirty-Two English Divines* (London, 1677), p. 159.

14 PRO, PROB 11/141, fos 228v, 233v; J. T. Cliffe, *The Puritan Gentry: the Great Puritan Families of Early Stuart England* (London, 1984), p. 38.

15 PRO, PROB 11/141, fo 143; BL Add. MS 4276, fo 157.

16 W. R. Prest, *The Inns of Court under Elizabeth I and the Early Stuarts* (London, 1972), pp. 189–94; PRO, PROB 11/130, fo 169v; J. T. Howard and J. L. Chester ed., *The Visitation of London, 1633–35* (Harleian Soc. 15, 1880), i, p. 154. I am indebted to Michael Crawford and Carlotta Dionisotti for advice on Charke's coat of arms and motto. [Technically a capital letter 'Y' is not a gamma.]

17 P. Seaver, *The Puritan Lectureships: the Politics of Religious Dissent, 1560–1662* (Stanford, 1970), pp. 225–6.

18 Fincham, *Prelate as Pastor*, p. 21.

19 Tyacke, *Anti-Calvinists*, pp. 64–5; *DNB, s.n.* Featley, Daniel. [Arber ed., *Transcript*, iii, fos 286b, 289b, 290, 290b, 291, 291b, 292b, 293, 297b, 305b, 308, 311.]

20 P. Baynes, *Two Godly and Fruitfull Treatises* (London, 1619), sigs A3v, A4v; J. L. Chester ed., *The Reiester Booke of Saynte De'nis Backchurch Parishe* (Harleian Soc. Registers iii, 1878), pp. 97, 206, 210, 212–14.

21 W. Negus, *Man's Active Obedience, or the Power of Godliness* (London, 1619), sigs A3v–A4 [Again Newbery was the publisher and Featley the licenser: Arber ed., *Transcript*, iii, fo 293.]; Fincham, *Prelate as Pastor*, p. 325; *DNB, s.n.* Negus, William.

22 P. Baynes, *A Helpe to True Happinesse* (London, 1618), *Christian Letters* (London, 1620), sig. ꓛC4.

23 P. Baynes, *A Caveat for Cold Christians* (London, 1618), sig. A3.

24 P. Baynes, *A Counterbane against Earthly Carefulness* (London, 1618), *Holy Soliloquies* (London, 1618), *Briefe Directions unto a Godly Life* (London, 1618).

25 Clarke, *The Lives of Thirty-Two English Divines*, p. 24.

26 P. Baynes, *The Mirrour or Miracle of God's Love unto the World of his Elect* (London, 1619) [p. 72], *An Epitome of Man's Misery and Deliverie* (London, 1619).

27 A. J. Willis ed., *Canterbury Licenses (General), 1568–1646* (Chichester, 1972), pp. 14, 55, 57. John Elmstone's death is recorded in the Cranbrook parish registers, of which there is a transcript at the Society of Genealogists.

28 P. Collinson, 'Cranbrook and the Fletchers: Popular and Unpopular Religion in the Kentish Weald', in P. N. Brooks ed., *Reformation Principle and Practice* (London, 1980), pp. 201–2; R. Abbot, *The Danger of Popery* (London, 1625), p. 20.

29 P. Baynes, *A Commentarie upon the First Chapter of the Epistle to the Ephesians* (London, 1618), sig. Av; *DNB, s.n.* Sibbes, Richard.

30 P. Baynes, *An Entire Commentary upon the Whole Epistle of the Apostle Paul to the Ephesians* (London, 1643), pp. 292, 350–1, 481–3.

31 P. Baynes, *The Diocesans Tryall* (Amsterdam, 1621), sigs A2v–A4.

32 W. Ames, *Medulla S.S. Theologiae* (London, 1630), pp. 168–9, 200, 204, 215–17, 335–6. I have followed the English translation of 1642.

33 PRO, SP 16/261, fo 257v. [There is no record, not surprisingly, that the *Medulla* was ever licensed for publication in England.]

34 K. L. Sprunger, *The Learned Doctor William Ames: Dutch Backgrounds of English and American Puritanism* (Urbana, 1972), pp. 30, 73.

35 K. L. Sprunger, *Dutch Puritanism: a History of English and Scottish Churches of the Netherlands in the Sixteenth and Seventeenth Centuries* (Leiden, 1982), pp. 285–306.

36 Sprunger, *Dutch Puritanism*, p. 306.

37 Calder ed., *Activities of the Puritan Faction, passim*; Laud, *Works*, iii, pp. 216–17, iv, p. 304.

38 Calder ed., *Activities of the Puritan Faction*, pp. 63, 98, 113. See p. 278 below.

39 PRO, PROB 11/141, fo 233v.

40 J. Ballinger, *The Bible in Wales* (London, 1906), pp. 26–8; *The Advice of that Worthy Commander Sir Edward Harwood, Colonel* (Harleian Misc. iv, 1809), p. 279.

41 PRO, PROB 11/161, fo 180; H. Owen and J. B. Blakeway, *A History of Shrewsbury* (London, 1825), ii, pp. 270, 279; Clarke, *The Lives of Thirty-Two English Divines*, p. 190; Sprunger, *Dutch Puritanism*, p. 120.

42 *DNB*, s.n. Gouge, William; W. Jenkyn, *A Shock of Corn* (London, 1654), p. 42.

43 R. Sibbes, *A Breathing after God* (London, 1638), p. 94; *The Bruised Reede and Smoaking Flax* (London, 1630); Sprunger, *Dutch Puritanism*, pp. 227–8.

44 PRO, PROB 11/168, fo 284v; *DNB*, s.n. Fairclough, Samuel.

45 PRO, PROB 11/161, fo 81v, PROB 11/165, fo 357; Cliffe, *The Puritan Gentry*, pp. 182–3. It was John Preston who chose to die at Fawsley in 1628. Space does not permit a discussion here of the important part played by Preston during the 1620s.

46 C. Hill, 'Puritanism and the "Dark Corners" of the Land', *TRHS*, 5th series, 13 (1963), 92; Calder ed., *Activities of the Puritan Faction*, p. xxiv.

47 D. Cressy, *Coming Over: Migration and Communication between England and New England in the Seventeenth Century* (Cambridge, 1987), ch. 3.

48 Sprunger, *The Learned Doctor William Ames*, pp. 200–6, 250–2; idem, *Dutch Puritanism*, pp. 164–5; D. D. Hall, *The Faithful Shepherd: a History of the New England Ministry in the Seventeenth Century* (Chapel Hill, Conn., 1972), pp. 46–7, 81–2.

49 PRO, SP 16/290, fo 25.

50 PRO, SP 16/265, fo 70. For the other two letters by Forbes, see SP 16/258, fos 154–5 and SP 16/308, fo 67r–v.

51 PRO, CO 1/8, fo 110v.

52 PRO, SP 16/297, fo 204. For the will of Lady Clere, proved in 1645, see PRO, PROB 11/194, fos 53v–55.

53 Boston Public Library, Prince Collection, Cotton Papers, pt. 2, no. 9. The published version of this letter omits the signatories. I owe a special debt of gratitude to Norman Pettit, of Boston University, who telephoned the names to me from the United States.

54 Fincham, *Prelate as Pastor*, p. 325; PRO, PROB 11/187, fos 62v–63.

55 Clarke, *The Lives of Thirty-Two English Divines*, p. 148.

56 *A Letter of Many Ministers in Old England . . . Writen Anno Dom. 1637* (London, 1643), sig. A2v. Julines Herring left England on 15 September 1637: Sprunger, *Dutch Puritanism*, p. 120.

57 See pp. 132–55 below; N. Tyacke, *Anti-Calvinists*, ch. 8. [This self-criticism deserves emphasising.]

58 R. Baillie, *The Letters and Journals . . . 1637–62*, ed. D. Laing (Edinburgh, 1841–42), i, pp. 273–4, 280.

59 V. Pearl, *London and the Outbreak of the Puritan Revolution: City Government and National Politics, 1625–43* (Oxford, 1961), pp. 183–4; J. Goodwin, *The Saints' Interest in God* (London, 1640). The other alderman involved in presenting the root and branch petition was apparently Thomas Soames.

60 For the biography of Sir Thomas Wroth, I have relied mainly on the excellent *DNB* article and the unpublished records of St Stephen's, Coleman Street, at the Guildhall Library.

61 NRA, Dering, p. 120; L. B. Larking ed., *Proceedings, principally in the County of Kent, in connection with the Parliament called in 1640* (Camden Soc., 1st ser., 80, 1862), pp. 25–42. My identification of Richard Rabson (*sic*) is based on the Cranbrook parish registers.

62 *A Speech of Mr. John White made in the House of Commons, concerning Episcopacy* (London, 1641); J. White, *The First Century of Scandalous and Malignant Priests* (London, 1643).

Chapter 5

Puritanism, Arminianism
and counter-revolution

I

HISTORIANS of the English Civil War all agree that Puritanism had a role
to play in its origins. Beyond this however agreement ceases. For some,
particularly the Marxists, Puritanism was the ideology of the newly emergent
middle classes or *bourgeoisie*, as they are sometimes called. Puritan ideas, it is
argued, complemented and encouraged the capitalist activities of 'progressive'
gentry, merchants and artisans alike. On the assumption, again made by
those most under the influence of Marxism, that the English Civil War was a
'bourgeois revolution' the Puritans are naturally to be found fighting against
King Charles and his old-world followers. An alternative and widely held
interpretation sees Puritanism as a religious fifth column within the Church
of England, and one whose numbers dramatically increased during the first
decades of the seventeenth century; by the early 1640s, with the collapse
of the central government and its repressive system of church courts, the
Puritans were thus able to take over at least in the religious sphere. These
two schools of thought, the Marxist and the fifth-columnist, are best represented by the writings respectively of Christopher Hill and William Haller.

In the following essay however a different view will be put forward, to the
effect that religion became an issue in the Civil War crisis due primarily to
the rise to power of Arminianism in the 1620s. The essence of Arminianism
was a belief in God's universal grace and the freewill of all men to obtain
salvation. Therefore Arminians rejected the teaching of Calvinism that the
world was divided into elect and reprobate whom God had arbitrarily predestinated, the one to Heaven and the other to Hell. It is difficult for us to grasp
how great a revolution this involved for a society as steeped in Calvinist
theology as was England before the Civil War. But whether or not we agree
with the arguments of Christopher Hill, it is clear that the Puritan ideas to

which he ascribes so much importance for the development of modern, capitalist society are in the main predestinarian ones. Similarly with Haller's thesis concerning the growth of Puritanism, the message preached with such success from Puritan pulpits was rooted in the Calvinist theology of grace.[1]

At the beginning of the seventeenth century, a majority of the clergy from the Archbishop of Canterbury downwards were Calvinists in doctrine, and the same was probably true of the more educated laity. So Puritanism in this Calvinist sense was not then seen as a political threat. Only when predestinarian teaching came to be outlawed by the leaders of the established church, as was the case under Archbishop William Laud, would its exponents find themselves in opposition to the government. Any doubts that the Church of England was doctrinally Calvinist, before Laud took control, can be resolved by reading the extant doctoral theses in divinity maintained at Oxford University from the 1580s to the 1620s. There, year after year predestinarian teaching was formally endorsed, and its opposite denied. The following are a representative selection of such theses, translated from the original Latin and listed in chronological order: 'No one who is elect can perish' (1582); 'God of his own volition will repudiate some people' (1596); 'According to the eternal predestination of God some are ordained to life and others to death' (1597); 'Man's spiritual will is not itself capable of achieving true good' (1602); 'The saints cannot fall from grace' (1608); 'Is grace sufficient for salvation granted to all men? No.' (1612); 'Does man's will only play a passive role in his initial conversion? Yes' (1618); 'Is faith and the righteousness of faith the exclusive property of the elect? Yes' (1619); and 'Has original sin utterly extinguished free will in Adam and his posterity? Yes' (1622). The licensed publications of the English press tell the same Calvinist story, albeit in a more popular vein, as do many religious preambles to wills where the testator confidently affirms belief in his divine election. A good example of this type of Calvinist will is that made by Lord Treasurer Dorset, who died in 1608; George Abbot, future Archbishop of Canterbury, was so impressed by Dorset's claim to be an elect saint that he quoted the will verbatim when preaching his funeral sermon in Westminster Abbey. Calvinism at the time was clearly establishment orthodoxy, and contemporaries would have found any suggestion that Calvinists were Puritans completely incomprehensible.[2]

Puritanism around the year 1600, and for more than two decades subsequently, was thought of in terms either of a refusal to conform with the religious rites and ceremonies of the English Church, or as a presbyterian rejection of church government by bishops. At that date conformists and nonconformists, episcopalians and presbyterians all had in common Calvinist predestinarian ideas. Here however we come to the crux of the matter, for Calvinism also helped to reconcile the differences between them. Thus the late Elizabethan Archbishop of Canterbury, John Whitgift, who was a Calvinist in doctrine, regarded Puritan nonconformity in a different light from that of the Arminian Archbishop Laud. This did not stop Whitgift as Archbishop from attacking nonconformists, especially with Queen Elizabeth hard on his heels, but it did impose important limits on the extent of his persecution. Before the advent of Laud, nonconformists and even presbyterians were never regarded as being totally beyond the pale; they were seen instead as aberrant brethren deserving of some indulgence. Symbolic of the pre-Laudian state of affairs is that in the 1560s Whitgift had been a nonconformist and Thomas Cartwright, the later presbyterian, a candidate for an Irish archbishopric and, despite a long history of public controversy between them, they ended up on good terms in the 1590s. Calvinist doctrine provided a common and ameliorating bond that was only to be destroyed by the rise of Arminianism. As a result of this destruction, during the 1620s, Puritanism came to be redefined in terms which included the very Calvinism that previously had linked nonconformists to the leaders of the established church, and the nonconformist element in the former Calvinist partership was driven into an unprecedented radicalism. The Arminians and their patron King Charles were undoubtedly the religious revolutionaries in the first instance. Opposed to them were the Calvinists, initially conservative and counter-revolutionary, of whom the typical lay representative was John Pym. These are the developments which we must now consider in detail. First however something more needs saying about the definition of a Puritan.[3]

One possibility would be to define Puritanism in terms of Calvinist predestinarian teachings, and certainly many modern writers agree in labelling this body of ideas as in some sense Puritan. We have already noted that such labelling involves the paradox of making Archbishop Whitgift and most of his fellow bishops into Puritans. Doctrinal Calvinism does not however explain why Elizabethan Protestants became nonconformists, presbyterians, and sometimes separatists. Here what seems to have been critical was a difference in attitude to the authority of the Bible as a religious model, although the distinction is by no means clear cut. Indeed the point needs making that it is extremely artificial to start drawing hard and fast lines between Puritans and 'Anglicans' in the Elizabethan and Jacobean periods. There are far too many cases which defy categorisation. For example in a sermon collection published in 1585, Archbishop Sandys of York asserted that 'in the scriptures . . . is contained all that is good, and all that which God requireth or accepteth of', and that this was no empty claim is clear from his will, dated two years later, where he wrote 'concerning rites and ceremonies by political constitutions authorised amongst us, . . . in the church reformed, and in all this time of the gospel (wherein the seed of the scripture hath so long been sown), they may better be disused by little and little'. Despite these declared views Archbishop Sandys himself conformed, and was prepared on occasion to prosecute in the church courts those who did not. At the other extreme however the separatist leader Henry Barrow, writing in 1591, justified his separation from the Church of England on the grounds that 'every part of the Scripture is alike true, inspired of God, given to our direction and instruction in all things'.[4]

But if Calvinism did not cause Puritan nonconformity there was as we have said a willingness among predestinarians to tolerate such aberrations, or at least not to regard them in a very serious light. This can be illustrated by a visitation sermon preached in 1605 about 'the lawful use of things indifferent'. The author was a doctrinal Calvinist, Sebastian Benefield, who later as Lady Margaret professor of divinity at Oxford became well known for his attacks on Arminian heresy. In his sermon of 1605 he took as his model St. Paul, who became 'all things to all men' that he might 'by all means save some', and placed ceremonial conformity firmly in the context of the elect's calling to salvation by the sowing of 'the immortal seed of the word of God'. Preaching he described as the human means 'whereby the foreknown of God from all eternity, and the predestinated to life of God's pure favour, are effectually called from the state of servitude to liberty'. This task of preaching took priority over any conscientious scruples about wearing surplices and the like, and it was the duty of a minister to conform rather than be silenced. On the other hand, although Benefield did not explicitly make the point, those in authority logically should exercise great restraint in applying ultimate sanctions against nonconformists lest their evangelising services be lost. Another doctrinal Calvinist whose writings exhibit an even more marked ambiguity than do Benefield's as regards nonconformity, was Samuel Gardiner. His theology can readily be deduced from a series of surviving sermons which he preached in 1611 on the subject of God's eternal predestination. Earlier, in 1605, he had published a work in dialogue form concerning 'the rites and ceremonies of the Church of England,' in the course of which the conformist admits to his opponent that 'if the laws had not been in these cases already made, I should never, for my own part, wish to have them made.' But for the present ceremonies were to be tolerated until 'it shall seem good by higher powers, they may as superfluous or little profitable, grow out of use.' The views of Benefield and Gardiner are highly relevant for understanding official attitudes to Puritan nonconformity before the time of Laud, because both men became chaplains to George Abbot, Archbishop of Canterbury from 1611 to 1633. Abbot, a committed predestinarian, was chided by King James in 1613 for advancing 'one of the puritans' arguments', when he maintained that 'Scripture doth directly or by consequence contain in it sufficient matter to decide all controversies, especially in things appertaining to the church.' This links Abbot with Archbishop Sandys, who, as we have seen, believed that the rites and ceremonies of the Church of England needed further reformation.[5]

In the light of such evidence it should already be apparent that the first decades of the seventeenth century in England did not witness any straight-forward contest between an 'Anglican' hierarchy on the one hand and the serried ranks of Puritanism on the other. This becomes even clearer if we take the case of William Perkins, whom Christopher Hill has described as 'the dominant influence in Puritan thought for the forty years after his death' in 1602. His funeral sermon was preached by James Montagu, shortly to become Dean of the Chapel Royal and subsequently Bishop of Winchester, and the chief critic of Perkins's works was answered in print by Bishop Robert Abbot of Salisbury, whose intellectual position was identical to that of his brother the Archbishop. While this blurring of religious differences seems characteristic of the period, a further complicating factor was the religious stand-point of the monarch, as supreme governor of the English Church. James I was much more sympathetic to Calvinist doctrine than his predecessor Elizabeth, and to that extent those Puritan nonconformists were correct who hoped for better things on the Queen's death in 1603. The proof of the King's Calvinist affinities was conveniently published as a pamphlet in 1626, by Francis Rous, who was the step-brother of John Pym and an outspoken parliamentary critic of Arminianism. Two examples of this royal Calvinism must suffice. In 1604 James was officially quoted as saying that 'predestina-tion and election dependeth not upon any qualities, actions or works of man, which be mutable, but upon God his eternal and immutable decree and purpose'. Similarly in 1619 he wrote that 'God draws by his effectual grace, out of that attainted and corrupt mass [mankind], whom he pleaseth for the work of his mercy, leaving the rest to their own ways which all lead to perdition.' Yet having demonstrated James's Calvinism, and therefore the existence of a common and potentially reconciling bond with Puritan non-conformists, one is faced with the problem of his celebrated outbursts against Puritans – as for instance when he described them in March 1604 as a 'sect unable to be suffered in any well-governed commonwealth', and the depriva-tions for nonconformity which occurred during his first years on the throne. The explanation, however, would seem to lie in *raison d'état*, as that was interpreted by the King. His exposure in Scotland at an early age to Calvinist theology had left him favourably disposed towards its teachings, yet his experi-ence there of religious rebellion had also made him politically suspicious of anything remotely akin to presbyterianism. Whereas for Elizabeth political considerations had complemented her religious antipathies, with James there was thus something of a conflict. The preface to the 1603 edition of his book *Basilikon Doron*, where James withdrew some earlier unflattering comments about Puritans, has often been seen as propaganda aimed at smoothing the path of his succession to the English throne. But the same sentiments recur, notably in some royal remarks paraphrased by Robert Cecil during a Star Chamber speech in 1605. 'For the puritans . . . [the King] would go half way to meet them, and he loved and reverenced many of them, and if they would leave their [nonconformist] opinions, there were some of them he would prefer to the best bishoprics that were void.' King James himself put the dichotomy more succinctly in July of the previous year. 'To discreet men I say, they shall obtain their desires by grace, but to all I profess, they shall extort nothing by violence.'[6]

These distinctions would be rather academic had James's fear of Puritan nonconformity continued to dominate him as much as it did during the earliest years of his English reign. Increasingly however, a countervailing political factor emerged in the shape of an intensified fear of Catholicism. This was particularly the case between 1608 and 1615, a period in which the King himself wrote as many as three works on the subject of the oath of allegiance. The latter was a modified form of the supremacy oath, enacted by statute during the aftermath of Gunpowder Plot in an attempt to isolate politically disloyal Catholics. Any chance of success which the scheme might have had was effectively wrecked by strong papal opposition and an ensuing pamphlet war. Almost inevitably Puritanism benefited from this redirection of government energies. Religious differences among the various royal champions who entered the lists were subsumed in a cloud of zeal against the common Papist enemy. Catholic charges that Puritans differed on doctrinal grounds from the established church were publicly denied even by emergent Arminians like Bishop Andrewes, and there was a widespread campaign to ban the use of the term Puritan completely. Suggestive also is the fact that from 1611 until 1618 no work directed specifically against Puritanism, either in its nonconformist or presbyterian guises, is recorded in the Stationers' Registers as being licensed for the press.[7]

In part symptomatic of the altered climate was George Abbot's own promotion to Canterbury in 1611. The Jesuit Father Coffin wrote of the new primate as 'a brutal and fierce man, and a sworn enemy of the very name of Catholic'. Certainly his elevation occurred during a two-year period which witnessed a third of all the Catholic martyrdoms under James. The supposition that these events were linked is further strengthened by the terms in which the appointment of Toby Matthew to the archbishopric of York had been canvassed back in 1606. Already at that date there was alarm in government circles over conditions in the north, as an area 'overpestered with Popery and not with Puritanism'. Cecil was urged to promote the appointment of 'a painful and preaching successor' to Archbishop Hutton and one 'industrious against Papists'. Policy however was often inextricably interwoven with patronage; just as Cecil was Matthew's patron, so Abbot had been recommended as Archbishop by the current royal favourite Dunbar. Abbot, as Dunbar's chaplain, had been instrumental in helping reconcile the Scottish Church to episcopacy, and his Puritan proclivities almost certainly contributed to the success of that enterprise. Compared with his Protestant predecessors at Canterbury, Abbot in his general outlook seems most to have resembled Edmund Grindal. The latter has recently been described by Patrick Collinson as 'one of the very few Elizabethan bishops who enjoyed the full approval of the Protestant governing class and the equal confidence of all but a small embittered minority of the godly preaching ministers.'[8]

By contrast, the archiepiscopal predecessor whom Abbot least resembled was the man he immediately succeeded. This was Richard Bancroft, whose policies more than those of any other churchman prior to the Arminian Laud drove Puritan nonconformists to extremes. Bancroft's loathing of Puritanism amounted almost to paranoia, and his espionage methods threatened to make real the Puritan conspiracy which originated largely as a figment of his own imagination. He was also among the first Protestant churchmen in England to disassociate himself from the predestinarian teachings of Calvinism, and therefore lacked the restraining influence of a theology shared with his nonconformist opponents. Fortunately, from the point of view of political stability, Bancroft's extremism was kept in check by King James. Indeed the appointment of Bancroft to Canterbury in 1604 was a Jacobean anomaly; his Elizabethan record of severity against Puritans apparently recommended him as the man of the hour, when nonconformist clergy, backed by gentry support, seemed to pose a serious political threat. As Archbishop, Bancroft had from the start been a rather isolated figure. Those who succeeded him in the bishopric of London, a post which administratively ranked second only to Canterbury, were all Calvinists during his lifetime. One of them, Richard Vaughan, who was Bishop of London from 1604 to 1607, became well known for his tolerance of Puritan deviation from the strict letter of the law. Moreover in 1608 Bancroft was forced to acquiesce in the publication of an official Calvinist commentary on The Thirty-nine Articles – the Church of England's confession of faith. After his death in 1610 Calvinist dominance became even more marked, and the combined religious and political atmosphere generally favoured a *modus vivendi* with Puritan nonconformity. In addition to government attacks on Catholicism, which distracted attention from dis- agreements among Protestants, the chief posts in the church were filled by men whose views at many important points merged with those of their nonconformist brethren. Both Archbishop Abbot and John King, Bishop of London from 1611 to 1621, had been lecturers in the 1590s, and the former expressed the hope during a parliamentary debate in 1610 that he would die in the pulpit. They were also sabbatarians, Abbot successfully intervening in 1618 to preserve the Puritan Sunday from the threat of the royal Book of

Sports. A third very powerful Jacobean cleric was Bishop James Montagu of Winchester, editor of King James's collected works and a Privy Councillor. He had been the first master of Sidney Sussex College in Cambridge where he had not enforced conformity, and we have noted his connexion with the 'Puritan' theologian William Perkins. His brother, Sir Edward Montagu, had been a prominent spokesman on behalf of nonconformist Puritans during the parliament of 1604. All three bishops were Calvinists, Montagu assuming a watching brief for doctrinal orthodoxy at Cambridge and Abbot placing his brother Robert and his chaplain Benefield, respectively in the Regius and Lady Margaret chairs of divinity at Oxford. At the same time, with royal fears of Catholicism still in the ascendant, these churchmen had the support of the new favourite Buckingham. Archbishop Abbot was on sufficiently familiar terms in 1616 to call him 'my George', being dubbed 'father' in return, and Montagu, who died in 1618, described Buckingham in his will as 'the most faithful friend that ever I had'. In Montagu's view the period since the accession of King James in 1603 had on the whole been one of 'harmony' with the Puritans.[9]

This impression of comparative calm receives some statistical confirmation from a recent study of Puritan lecturers in London by Paul Seaver. Between 1604 and 1606 out of twenty identifiable Puritan lecturers only six came before the church courts, and of these six only one was permanently suspended from preaching. From 1607 to 1609 the pattern was 'much the same'. During the second decade of the seventeenth century prosecutions for nonconformity were even fewer and Seaver conjectures that 'at a time when controversy was at a minimum, when no great issues divided public opinion . . . some puritanically inclined ministers might have found little cause for militancy and small reason not to conform'. A situation similar to that in London existed in the northern province, under Archbishop Toby Matthew, where citations for nonconformity were rare despite the existence of many potential offenders. According to Ronald Marchant's account of Puritanism in the diocese of York, a 'general policy of toleration' prevailed there until the late 1620s. Matthew was a Calvinist and employed at least one moderate nonconformist, John Favour, as his chaplain, as well as being an indefatigable preacher himself. With archbishops like Matthew and Abbot in command, Puritanism presented no real problem.[10]

There was however an element of uncertainty in the situation, since much could depend on the vagaries of international politics and the shifting sands of court favour. Just as the oath of allegiance controversy, and its associated anti-Catholic attitudes, had worked to the benefit of Puritan nonconformity, so with plans for marrying Prince Charles to a Catholic Spanish infanta the process seemed about to go into reverse. By 1618 there was talk of tolerating Catholicism, as a condition of the Spanish marriage. The concomitant of this would be a slump in demand for polemic against the Popish Antichrist, and tighter government control over the diversity of Protestant practice. That this threat did not materialise was mainly due to a political crisis in the Low Countries, which was deemed to affect England's foreign policy interests. In the United Provinces, Oldenbarnveldt and Prince Maurice were engaged in a struggle for power, and had enlisted on their respective sides the rival Dutch church parties of Arminian and Calvinist. King James, for reasons which included theology, supported Maurice and the Calvinists, and in late 1618 sent a delegation, under Bishop Carleton of Llandaff, to participate in an international synod at Dort. This gathering proceeded to condemn the Arminian theology of grace, and affirm its Calvinist converse, and was an event which has never received the emphasis it deserves from students of English religious history. For the Calvinist doctrines at issue in the United Provinces were fundamental to English Puritanism before the Civil War, in a way that ceremonies and discipline were not. Calvinist predestinarian teaching was, as we have indicated, a crucial common assumption, shared by a majority of the hierarchy and virtually all its nonconformist opponents, during the Elizabethan and Jacobean periods. Indeed it is not too much to say that for many people in the early seventeenth century the basic issue as between Protestantism and Catholicism was that of divine determinism versus human freewill. Calvinist affinities between the bishops and their critics lent substance to claims that rites and ceremonies were matters of indifference. Accordingly the assertion of predestinarian Calvinism made by the Synod of Dort, with English delegates participating and its published proceedings dedicated to King James, served to emphasise afresh the theology binding conformist and nonconformist together, and the limits which that common bond imposed on persecution.

Hindsight is often the curse of the historian, and none more so in attempting to reconstruct the religious history of the pre-Civil War era. The battle lines of 1640–2 were not drawn by the early 1620s in this any more than other spheres. The Parliaments of 1621 and 1624 were remarkable for a dearth of religious grievances. 'Godly reformation' was limited to allegations of corrupt practices by certain ecclesiastical officials, and requests that the recusancy laws be more strictly enforced. Among the clergy an appeal from Bermuda in 1617 by the presbyterian Lewis Hughes, to avoid persecution by emigration, fell on deaf ears. Moreover in 1621 Hughes's own form of catechism concerning 'public exercises of religion', as well as a tract on strict sabbath observance, were licensed for publication by one of Archbishop Abbot's chaplains. When therefore the Spanish marriage negotiations finally collapsed in 1624 it was natural for the favourite Buckingham to cultivate closer relations with John Preston, at that date 'leader of the Puritan party', again to quote Christopher Hill. Two years before, Buckingham had secured for Preston the mastership of Emmanuel College, Cambridge, and now held out promises of further preferment. Preston was a Calvinist conformist and the Cambridge protégé of John Davenant, who had been a delegate to the Synod of Dort and was now bishop of Salisbury. Far from being an untypical eccentric, Davenant was in the mainstream of Calvinist episcopalianism, and that Preston also found favour was of a piece with Jacobean religious developments. Indeed Preston might well have ended up adorning the episcopal bench. This was the context in which John Pym, during the Parliament of 1621, rejected 'that odious and factious name of Puritans' which a fellow member had tried to fasten on the promoters of a bill for the better observance of Sunday. Pym thought that the speech was especially reprehensible in that it tended to 'divide us amongst our selves . . . or at least would make the world believe we were divided'. As it turned out however Preston died in the ecclesiastical wilderness in 1628, and a doctrinal revolution took place within the established church which shattered the Jacobean dispensation. The two events were intimately connected, for during the 1620s the Calvinist heritage was overthrown and with it the prerequisite of English Protestant unity. The result was a polarisation of extremes unknown since the Reformation, and one which rendered earlier compromises unworkable. It is this triumph of Arminianism, and its divisive consequences, which we must now consider.[11]

II

England in the early seventeenth century was doctrinally a part of Calvinist Europe, and it is within this ambience that the teachings of the Dutch theologian Arminius at Leiden have to be seen. During the first decade of the century, Arminius elaborated a critique of doctrinal Calvinism so systematic as to give his name to an international movement, namely Arminianism. He was concerned to refute the teachings on divine grace associated with the followers of Calvin, but he spoke as a member of the fully reformed and presbyterian Dutch Church, whereas his doctrinal equivalents in England were part of a different ecclesiastical tradition. There the most notable survivor of the English Reformation, apart from episcopacy, was the Prayer Book which, as its critics were pleased to point out, was an adapted version of the old Catholic mass book. Consequently Arminianism in England emerged with an additional, sacramental dimension to that in the United Provinces. Arminius was read with approval by anti-Calvinists in England but adapted to the local situation. English Arminians came to balance their rejection of the arbitrary grace of predestination with a new found source of grace freely available in the sacraments, which Calvinists had belittled. Hence the preoccupation under Archbishop Laud with altars and private confession before receiving communion, as well as a belief in the absolute necessity of baptism.

By the 1620s the Church of England had been Calvinist in doctrine for approximately sixty years. There had, however, always been a minority of dissidents, who led a more-or-less clandestine existence; in so far as these had a collective designation in the Elizabethan period they were known as 'Lutherans', after the second-generation followers of Luther who had rejected Calvinist predestinarian teaching. Not until Bancroft did the English 'Lutherans' find a champion holding high office and, as we have noted, not even he was strong enough to swim against the Calvinist tide. But after Bancroft's death in 1610 other lesser figures emerged to lead what it now becomes proper to call the Arminian party within the Church of England. The most powerful member of this early Arminian leadership was Bishop Richard Neile, although it also included Bishops Andrewes, Buckeridge and Overall; Laud was still a relatively obscure figure, dependent on Neile's patronage. They were not allowed to air their Arminian views in print, but managed to register them in a variety of covert ways. For example, in 1617, Neile, on his translation to the bishopric of Durham, had the communion table transformed into an altar at the east end of the cathedral and supported Laud in a like action the same year at Gloucester, where the latter was Dean. A few years later Overall and Andrewes can be found advocating the novel practice of private confession before receiving the communion. As Laud was to say, during the 1630s, 'the altar is the greatest place of God's residence upon earth, greater than the pulpit; for there 'tis *Hoc est corpus meum*, This is my body; but in the other it is at most but *Hoc est verbum meum*, This is my word.' Such a view involved the replacement of preaching as the normal vehicle of saving grace, and one restricted in its application to the elect saints, by sacraments which conferred grace indiscriminately; baptism of all infants, without qualification, began the process of salvation, and this was to be followed by the regular receiving of communion as a result of which all partakers, provided they confessed past sins, were renewed in grace. This flank attack on predestinarian Calvinism has misled historians into thinking that the Dutch and English Arminian movements were unconnected. In fact both Arminian parties considered themselves to be engaged in a mutual duel with Calvinism; as early as 1605 the views of Arminius were being cited with approval by anti-Calvinists in Cambridge, and the Dutch Arminians can be found from 1613 until the eve of the Synod of Dort appealing for help to Arminian bishops like Andrewes and Overall. But the latter were powerless to intervene in the United Provinces, engaged as they were in their own English struggle for survival.

If the situation was ever to alter in favour of the English Arminians, their best hope lay in trying to capture the mind of the King or at least that of the royal favourite. This was the course on which they embarked, during the aftermath of the Synod of Dort. Neile was the chief intermediary between the Arminians and King James, while Laud came to play an equivalent role in Buckingham's entourage. Apart from direct theological argument in favour of Arminianism, one powerful lever was to suggest that Calvinist conformists were Puritans at heart and as such politically subversive, or again that predestinarian Calvinism lent itself to so much popular misunderstanding that its widespread propagation inevitably led to religious conflict. By 1624 arguments of this kind seem to have affected adversely James's attitude towards Calvinism. Fear of approaching death may also have helped sap his confidence in deterministic teaching, for should doubt as to whether one was an elect saint ever become unbearable, there was always the Arminian possibility of denying that the predestinarian scheme was true. As regards Buckingham, opportunism was the most effective argument for his listening sympathetically to the Arminians. In 1624 he was identified with war against Spain, and was temporarily the hero of the parliamentary and ultra-Protestant camp. Buckingham was well aware however that the situation could rapidly change and a need arise for new allies. His willingness to support the Arminian Laud, while at the same time patronising the 'Puritan' Preston, was part of a double insurance policy for the future.

It was in this more hopeful atmosphere that the Arminian party decided on a test case. This took the form of publishing a book in 1624, by the Arminian Richard Montagu, which while ostensibly answering Roman Catholic criticisms of the Church of England also rejected predestinarian Calvinism, on the ground that this was no part of the teaching enshrined in the Thirty-nine Articles. The interpretation of these articles was and still is debatable, but not only were Bishop Neile and his chaplains able to get Montagu's book, *A New Gagg*, past the censor; they also managed to prevent its subsequent suppression. In terms of previous Arminian experience in England this was a dramatic breakthrough. Outraged Calvinist clergy appealed to Parliament; John Pym took up their cause in the House of Commons, and Archbishop Abbot made representations to King James. The only result was a royal request that Richard Montagu clarify his views by writing a second book. Yet it soon became clear that the final arbiter of England's theological fate would be the heir to the throne, Prince Charles. Prior to his accession some observers considered Charles to be inclined towards Puritanism, but those closer to him, among them the Arminian Matthew Wren, claimed the reverse was true and that on this score his reign would contrast with James's. Wren's prediction was to prove abundantly true, for King Charles became the architect of an Arminian revolution which had at most been dimly foreshadowed in the last year of his father's reign. As the House of Commons was to complain in 1629: 'some prelates, near the King, having gotten the chief administration of ecclesiastical affairs under his Majesty, have discountenanced and hindered the preferment of those that are orthodox [i.e. Calvinist], and favoured such as are contrary.'[12]

The suddenness of James's death in March 1625 seems to have taken most people by surprise. Buckingham survived as royal favourite, but it was now Charles who increasingly made the religious pace. The new King had never apparently been a Calvinist; certainly a decisive bias in favour of Arminianism became clear during the first few months of his reign. Calvinist bishops were excluded from the royal counsels, and in July 1625 the Arminian Richard Montagu was placed under Charles's personal protection. In February of the following year Buckingham, clearly acting with the approval of Charles, chaired a debate at York House on the subject of Montagu's writings, in the course of which he made plain his Arminian sympathies. The Arminian Bishop Buckeridge was pitted against the Calvinist Bishop Morton, and during their exchanges the question arose as to how pre-destinarian doctrine could be reconciled with Prayer Book teaching on the sacraments of baptism and communion. 'What,' exclaimed Morton, 'will you have the grace of God tied to sacraments?' Buckeridge's seconder, Dean White of Carlisle, replied that all baptised infants were 'made the sons of God by adoption', and Buckingham told Morton that he 'disparaged his own ministry, and did . . . debase the sacrament'. White further argued that the Synod of Dort, by limiting Christ's redemption to the elect, had overthrown the sacrament of communion; he asked how on such predestinarian assumptions could ministers 'say to all communicants whatsoever, "The Body of our Lord which was given for thee", as we are bound to say? Let the opinion of the Dortists be admitted, and the tenth person in the Church shall not have been redeemed.' This clash of interpretation underlines the sacramental emphasis of the English Arminian rejection of Calvinism, whereby the Prayer Book was thrown into the scales against the Calvinist interpretation of the Thirty-nine Articles which had been so prevalent in Elizabethan and Jacobean times.[13]

The York House Conference was however far from being a mere wrangle among theologians. It had been called at the request of Viscount Saye and the Earl of Warwick, who were two of the government's most prominent critics and subsequently leaders of the parliamentary party in the Civil War. Moreover Bishop Morton's seconder at the conference was the 'Puritan' John Preston, and their ability to collaborate in this fashion exemplified the sixty-year-old shared Calvinist assumptions which were now at risk. Immediately after the conference, the Arminian John Cosin was reporting that the King 'swears his perpetual patronage of our cause', and the rebuff that Calvinism received at York House was the signal for the House of Commons to begin impeachment proceedings against Buckingham for alleged gross misman-agement of the government. The fiction was maintained by the opposition that Buckingham's policies were distinct from those of the crown, but this became increasingly unconvincing especially as regards religion. In June

1626 Buckingham was foisted on Cambridge University as chancellor, and all predestinarian teaching was forthwith forbidden. This was backed up by a royal proclamation which effectively outlawed Calvinism on a national basis. The London and Cambridge printing presses rapidly succumbed. At Oxford University however under the chancellorship of the Calvinist third Earl of Pembroke predestinarian views were preached and printed for another two years. But even Oxford yielded when in late 1628 Charles reissued the Thirty-nine Articles with a prefatory declaration which insisted on their 'literal and grammatical' sense and commanded 'that all further curious search be laid aside, and these disputes shut up in God's promises, as they be generally set forth to us in holy scriptures'. As Prideaux the Oxford Regius professor of divinity put it, 'we are concluded under an anathema to stand to the Synod of Dort against the Arminians'.[14]

Reaction in Parliament to this Arminianisation of the Church of England became increasingly strident, and the situation was made worse by the readiness of the Arminians to brand their Calvinist opponents as Puritans. We know from Laud's diary that in 1626 he had been promised the succession to Canterbury, and from this date he comes into prominence as the chief religious spokesman of the government. His sermon at the opening of Charles's second Parliament in February 1626 was remarkable for its aggressive tone. He conjured up the vision of a presbyterian conspiracy, aiming at the overthrow of church and state. 'They, whoever they be, that would overthrow *sedes ecclesia*, the seats of ecclesiastical government, will not spare (if ever they get power) to have a pluck at the throne of David. And there is not a man that is for parity, all fellows in the church, but he is not for monarchy in the state'. The reply of Pym and numerous other Calvinist members of the House of Commons was that on the contrary they were the true orthodox loyalists and that the new Arminian religion was both heterodox and the means of introducing Roman Catholicism into England. Some went further and claimed that the denouement would be the murder of the king at the hands of Jesuit-inspired plotters. They took particular exception to Richard Montagu's use of the term Puritan – a use shared by Laud who in 1624 had written on the subject of 'doctrinal Puritanism'. A Commons committee reported in 1625 that Montagu 'saith there are Puritans in heart' and that 'bishops may be Puritans'; since Montagu also defined predestinarian Calvinists as Puritans, the committee were quite correct to conclude that 'by his opinion we may be all Puritans'. More generally the Commons appealed to recent history in justification of their Calvinist exposition of English religion.[15]

Arminianism was of course only one among a number of reasons for the breakdown of relations between Charles and his Parliaments in the late 1620s, but some idea of its relative importance is conveyed by the last Parliament before the Personal Rule, that of 1628–29. The first session was largely taken up with the Petition of Right, in an attempt to prevent any future resort by the crown to forced loans, but the second session saw Arminianism as an issue taking precedence over other questions; charges of heterodoxy were levelled at Neile and Laud, who had both been made Privy Councillors in early 1627, and it was claimed the path of ecclesiastical preferment was blocked to all but men of their persuasion. The debate on Arminianism was opened on 26 January 1629 by Francis Rous. The issue he said was 'right of religion . . . and this right, in the name of this nation, I this day claim, and desire that there may be a deep and serious consideration of the violation of it'. The violations, he thought, reduced to two, consisting of both a growth of Catholicism and Arminianism, the latter being 'an error that maketh the grace of God lackey it after the will of man, that maketh the sheep to keep the shepherd, that maketh mortal seed of an immortal God'. Moreover he claimed that the two phenomena were biologically connected, 'for an Arminian is the spawn of a Papist', and it was now high time for the Commons to covenant together in defence of true religion. Arminianism and the more mundane subject of tunnage and poundage were the main items of the session until it was forcibly terminated on 2 March. Rous and all the other contributors to the debate on religion, with one Arminian exception, spoke as Calvinist episcopalians. The rise of Arminianism was seen as a function of clerical pretentiousness, but was not yet considered to discredit the episcopal order as such. Indeed Sir John Eliot, speaking of Richard Montagu who had been consecrated a bishop in August 1628, said 'I reverence the order, I honour not the man'. But this reverence was subject to the continued existence of other bishops 'that openly show their hearts to the Truth'.[16]

John Pym was not given to the rhetoric of Eliot and Rous, but he more than any other M.P. inspired the Commons' case against Arminianism. From 1624 to 1629 he can be found chairing committees, delivering reports, and preparing impeachment charges on the Arminian question. Like many of his fellow M.P.s, Pym had imbibed Calvinism both in the home and at university. For them cynical calculations of the kind made by Buckingham were not a primary motive, nor in most cases did their religious stance disguise materialistic hopes of stripping the church of its remaining wealth. Nevertheless speeches on the floor of the House of Commons were not made *in vacuo*, and it is therefore particularly interesting to penetrate where possible behind the public image. While this cannot on present material be done for Pym, considerable evidence has survived for Oliver St. John who was to inherit the leadership of the Long Parliament on Pym's death in 1643. St. John, who was about fourteen years younger than Pym, had been a pupil of Preston at Cambridge, and there still exists a religious commonplace book which he kept during the 1620s and early 1630s. This allows for a reconstruction of his beliefs before the Civil War experience intervened, and an illuminating portrait emerges. He appears quite prepared to accept the order of episcopacy and has no objection to ceremonial conformity, in both cases quoting with approval the views of Bishop Davenant. Especially noticeable however is his dominating concern with predestinarian theology, Calvinist views being listed at length and their opposites labelled as 'heterodox'. Although he seems to agree with William Prynne's hostile views on the subject of bowing at the name of Jesus, so did Archbishop Abbot. The only other signs of Puritanism are some doubts about whether clergymen might hold civil office, and strong disapproval of men growing their hair long or any similar marks of what St. John calls 'effeminacy'.[17]

All the indications are that Pym's brand of Puritanism was much the same as that of St. John. This is supported by a mass of material relating to the fourth Earl of Bedford, who was both St. John's employer and Pym's close associate. The evidence, again consisting of commonplace books, has only recently become available to historians and investigation is not yet complete. Like St. John, Bedford appears to be a firm Calvinist and much exercised about the predestinarian controversy. At the same time he does not think of himself as a Puritan, whom at one point he dismisses as a person who 'will eat his red herring on Christmas day, and his roast beef on Good Friday'. He sees Arminianism leading logically to Catholicism, writing of the former as 'the little thief put into the window of the church to unlock the door', and cites Bishop Williams against the altar-wise position of the communion table. Unfortunately such entries cannot be dated as accurately as those from St. John, and the *terminus ad quem* is Bedford's death from smallpox in 1641. Thus it is not clear from how long before the Long Parliament dates his dislike of lordly bishops. He writes, or quotes from some anonymous authority, that 'lordship [was] forbidden to the apostles, Matthew, 20.25, therefore dars't thou assume it?' But he also notes that when the Hussites thrust out bishops there was left 'neither bishop nor earl'. His general social conservatism and concern to preserve the aristocratic order are revealed in a number of passages, as for instance when considering the rise of favourites or quoting Viscount Saye on the ambitions of plebeians. Bedford perhaps carried the greatest weight among the leaders of the opposition to Charles I. His religious views seem to have been fairly typical of the opposition leadership as a whole, although Saye, his son Nathaniel Fiennes, and Lord Brooke all held more radical beliefs. Their families, who tended to intermarry, sometimes had formidable Calvinist matriarchs in the background like Elizabeth Clinton, Countess of Lincoln. It was she who campaigned against the upper class practice of putting children out to wet nurses on the ground, among others, that the infant might be 'one of God's very elect . . . to whom to be a nursing mother, is a queen's honour'. Her son, the fourth Earl of Lincoln, was also a pupil of the 'Puritan' Preston at Cambridge, and married a daughter of Viscount Saye. He distinguished himself by raising troops to fight for the recovery of the Palatinate, and in 1626 refused to contribute to the forced loan. Not very surprisingly he ended by siding against the King in the Civil War. Another Calvinist bluestocking, this time from the upper gentry, was Lady Mary Vere, wife of the hero of the siege of Mannheim and instrumental in securing the archbishopric of Armagh for James Ussher in 1624. Ussher was a close friend of some of the leading Puritan nonconformists, and his scheme for limited episcopacy put forward in the first months of the Long Parliament looked briefly like proving an acceptable compromise. With the subsequent destruction of the hierarchy he was appointed, at the instigation of St. John, lecturer at Lincoln's Inn. Indeed the 'godly bishop' long remained a legitimate Puritan aspiration.[18]

Among the clergy in the late 1620s, as with the laity, the hallmark of opposition to the Arminian policy of the government was still Calvinist episcopalianism. Puritan nonconformity although subsumed within this Calvinist episcopalianism was not the question at issue. As for presbyterianism, it was a negligible element in the situation, being confined to a handful of survivors from Elizabethan days. Nevertheless, it has been argued by Christopher Hill that English Puritanism in the first decades of the seventeenth century was taking on a new and looser institutional form, along the lines of congregationalism *within* episcopacy. In so far as this was the case, it still implies a compatibility of religious approach prior to the Arminian 1630s. The continued failure however of Calvinist episcopalianism to withstand the pressures of Arminianism was bound in the longer term to result in its being discredited as a viable church system. Charles's decision in 1629 to rule without parliament brought that time nearer, for it meant there was now no court of Calvinist appeal left. In 1630 died the third Earl of Pembroke, who had been the most influential Calvinist among the King's Privy Councillors. He was moreover succeeded as chancellor of Oxford by Laud, who since 1628 had been controlling the London printing press as Bishop of London. The York primacy had been filled with a succession of Arminians since the Calvinist Matthew's death in 1628, and from 1632 was occupied by Neile. At Canterbury the Calvinist Abbot, in disgrace ever since refusing to license a sermon in support of forced loans in 1627, lingered on until 1633 when he was succeeded by Laud. By this process the court increasingly isolated itself from Calvinist opinion in the country. Arminian doctrines were now freely published while Calvinism languished in silence. An instance of the lengths to which propaganda went is supplied by the 1633 edition of the standard Latin–English Dictionary, compiled by Francis Holyoke. Published at London and dedicated to Laud, this new edition contained for the first time the word *Praedestinatiani*, who were defined as 'a kind of heretics that held fatal predestination of every particular matter person or action, and that all things came to passe, and fell out necessarily; especially touching the salvation and damnation of particular men'. While Calvinists would regard this as misrepresenting their views, the definition was clearly aimed at them. This is confirmed by its citation in a book of 1635 by the Arminian Edmund Reeve, called *The Communion Booke Catechisme*. Dedicating the work to Bishop Wright of Coventry and Lichfield, he claimed Bishops Overall and Buckeridge as his mentors. The exposition, which grew from the needs of his congregation at Hayes in Middlesex, contains an explicit refutation of predestinarian Calvinism and is a typical product of the decade.[19]

Theory went hand in hand with practice. In November 1633, three months after Laud became Archbishop of Canterbury, King Charles by act of Privy Council established the precedent that all parochial churches should follow the by then general cathedral practice of placing communion tables altar-wise at the east end of chancels. We have already had cause to comment on the sacramental undermining by English Arminians of the Calvinist theology of grace, and on the basis of this Privy Council ruling Arminianism during the 1630s was made manifest throughout every parish in England, the sacrament of the altar becoming henceforth a propitiation for the sins of all partakers. These were the years too which saw an unprecedented onslaught on the lecturing movement, the *cause célèbre* being the dissolution of the Feoffees for Impropriations in 1633. The feoffees were a trust, administered by a group of clergy, lawyers and merchants, and set up in an attempt to improve the level of clerical incomes. Laud, supported by Charles, claimed that a plot was involved to destroy episcopal jurisdiction. This sinister inter-pretation was not however shared by bishops like Morton, who in 1630 can be found recommending an impoverished curate to the charity of the feoffees. Morton was, as we have seen, a Calvinist, and did not agree with Laud's dictum that the altar took precedence over the pulpit. The attitude of the hierarchy to lecturers was in fact largely a matter of theological perspective. From a Calvinist standpoint preaching, whether by a beneficed incumbent or a lecturer, was the chief means of salvation. Only an episcopate dominated by Arminians could contemplate with equanimity, and indeed pleasure, a diminution in the number of sermons preached. Similarly Arminian bishops had little compunction in silencing nonconforming lecturers, whereas their Calvinist predecessors had so far as possible avoided this extreme.[20]

This change in attitude was not confined to the treatment of lecturers, but extended to nonconformity in general, and not only did the breaking of the Calvinist theological bond lead to the stricter enforcement of conformity: non-conformity itself acquired a much wider definition. Nonconformist offences now included expounding the Thirty-nine Articles in a Calvinist sense or any form of predestinarian preaching, objecting to the new ceremonies associated with the transformation of communion tables into altars, and refusal to

implement the Book of Sports which was reissued by Charles in 1633. The
surviving Calvinist bishops found themselves in an alien world, and were
distrusted by their colleagues; the Arminian Laud went so far as to put a spy
on the tail of the Calvinist Morton. We have already noted that the English
Arminians redefined Puritanism so as to include doctrinal Calvinism and
this elicited from Bishop Davenant of Salisbury the anguished complaint:
'Why that should now be esteemed Puritan doctrine, which those held who
have done our Church the greatest service in beating down Puritanism, or
why men should be restrained from teaching that doctrine hereafter, which
hitherto has been generally and publicly maintained, (wiser men perhaps
may) but I cannot understand.' When however in 1633 the Calvinist Davenant,
who was also a sabbatarian, had to discipline the recorder of Salisbury, Henry
Sherfield, for destroying an allegedly idolatrous window in a church, doubts
were expressed by his cathedral dean as to whether he would take a sufficiently
firm line. Hardly surprisingly the 1630s as a whole saw a great increase in
the number of prosecutions for Puritanism, an indirect measure of this being
the large scale emigration to New England. In addition to creating widespread
resentment of the episcopal hierarchy, these persecuting activities generated
a Puritan militancy which in the early 1640s was to erupt in the shape of
presbyterianism and congregationalism.[21]

Arminian clerics also revealed themselves as very hostile to lay intervention in church matters. This was partly because parliament had proved so
antagonistic, and they were in any case completely dependent on royal protection, but there was also a novel sacerdotal element in their teaching whereby
the priestly replaced the preaching function. Evidence exists to suggest that
one of the factors involved here was a desire to compensate for a sense of
social inferiority. Certainly the Calvinist bishops had better blood relations
with the gentry and aldermanic classes than did their Arminian successors,
and there was some substance to Lord Brooke's derogatory remarks in 1641
about lowborn prelates.[22] At the same time the reassertion of sacramental
grace lent itself to the view that clerics were almost a caste apart, but because
of their magical not their preaching roles. Indeed many English Arminians
consciously regarded themselves as engaged in a counter-reforming movement dedicated to undoing the Protestant damage of the Reformation.

While English Arminianism did not automatically result in the theoretical
advancement of royal absolutism in the secular sphere, the injunction 'render
unto Caesar' might seem a fitting counterpart to the idea of a holy priesthood
with consecrated property rights. The Calvinist opposition however conveniently forgot that during the debates on the Petition of Right the Arminian
Bishop Harsnett had spoken out in defence of the subject's liberties, and
instead they remembered the stance of Archbishop Abbot, in condemning
the arguments of Sibthorpe and Mainwaring for unparliamentary taxation.

Indeed as early as the 1590s Abbot had taught that 'God is better pleased, when good things shall be commanded, first by the highest in place, and then after it shall be added, by the Lords spiritual and temporal, and by the assent of the commons. And Princes which are gracious do never grieve at this, and wise men do love that style, when all is not appropriated to one, but there is a kind of parting.' Yet a decade or so earlier Archbishop Sandys, a man of similar theological colour to Abbot, had preached that taxation was a tribute due to the King and not a gift freely given. Thus there was an element of accident in the Arminian and royalist partnership. But in practice the religious policy of King Charles meant that during the Personal Rule absolutism and Arminianism became closely identified in the popular mind.[23]

On the future parliamentarian side there did however exist a positive link with Calvinism, concerning the right of political resistance. Calvinists held no monopoly of such views, but among Protestants they had developed the most explicit body of teaching on the subject. In England by far the most important vehicle of their thought was the Genevan annotated version of the Bible, which among other things had a predestinarian catechism bound up with it. Not always entirely consistent and stopping considerably short of an outright doctrine of tyrannicide, the Genevan commentators were prepared to admit the legitimacy of resistance to magistrates in certain circumstances, especially when the issue was religion. Their medium was biblical history, notably that contained in the Old Testament, and the use they made of it led King James to insist that the new Authorised translation of the Bible should contain no marginalia at all, apart from variant readings and cross-references. Illustrative of the political tendency of the Genevan annotations is that Ecclesiastes, 8. 3. had been glossed as 'withdraw not thy self lightly from the obedience of thy prince,' and the famous opening verse of Romans 13, 'Let every soul be subject unto the higher powers . . .' was described as relating to a 'private man', thus in principle leaving inferior magistrates free to act against erring superiors.[24]

Despite the existence of an official rival from 1611 onwards, the Genevan Bible long retained its popularity, being printed latterly in the Low Countries with the fictitious date 1599 on its title page. In origin the Genevan version was the work of a group of Marian exiles. They had included Goodman and Knox, who were both authors of works advocating the right of armed defence, particularly against heretical and persecuting rulers. Although the product of a specific exilic situation, ideas of this type survived the turn of the century, by which date however they were usually confined to discussions about continental Protestantism. Thus in 1603 Robert Abbot, brother of the future Archbishop, dedicated a book to King James which contained a defence of both Dutch and French Protestant rebels. At the same time there existed a competing body of passive-resistance theory, against which the only regular antidote was the Genevan Bible. With the subsequent rise of English Arminianism, Calvinist ideas of resistance took on new domestic relevance; as early as 1632 a Puritan lecturer, Nathaniel Barnard, dared to make the connection in a sermon. After the actual outbreak of hostilities, one of those to be found defending the parliamentary cause on religious grounds was Stephen Marshall, who has been described as 'the most famous political parson of the revolution'. Eschewing legal arguments, Marshall cited biblical precedent and among more recent authorities Bishop Abbot.[25]

Perhaps even without a rebellion in Scotland the finances of the Personal Rule would have foundered on their own inadequacies, and a parliament have had to be summoned. What however until recently has largely gone unnoticed, is the part played in the Scottish disturbances by Arminianism. The Scots at this time are usually thought of as intransigent presbyterians for whom Charles's attempt to impose an English-style prayer book was simply an excuse to throw off the whole episcopalian system. But it has been pointed out that many of the members of the Glasgow Assembly, which in 1638 abolished bishops, had never known a fully presbyterian church. Moreover someone like Robert Baillie, who is traditionally thought of as a presbyterian diehard, was even at that date not prepared to deny that a form of episcopacy had scriptural warrant. Arminianism, however, appears to have been the deciding factor. The Glasgow Assembly explicitly modelled itself on the Synod of Dort and listened to a series of harangues on the Arminian question. What really seems to have rankled was not so much the office of bishop but that the hierarchy were mostly Arminians. Again and again this charge features in the indictments, and heterodox teaching on predestination clearly is meant. The dual association with unpopular royalist policies in the secular field and with Arminianism in the religious meant that episcopacy went down even faster in Scotland than it was to in England where the system was more indigenous.[26]

The Short Parliament of 1640, called to subsidise the suppression of the Scottish rebellion, did not last long enough for the religious question fully to come out in the open, although 'innovations in matters of religion' were high on Pym's list of grievances. The fact that after the dissolution of Parliament the Convocation of Clergy continued in session and proceeded to enact a series of canons which included a strong statement of royal absolutism, all fostered a mounting hostility to the episcopate. Nor was the example of Scotland lost on the English opposition, and increasingly too a presbyterian model in religion became the price of Scottish support. When the Long Parliament assembled later in the year more radical pressures were brought to bear by the London populace, and the root and branch petition of December, which called for the abolition of bishops, in part represented such interests. Even here however it was the woeful results of episcopacy, with Arminianism taking a prominent place, that were stressed rather than the essential unlawfulness of the order. Moreover, Calvinists like Archbishop Ussher and Bishop Morton meeting in committee during March 1641 with Puritan ministers such as Marshall and Calamy looked like agreeing on a common reformist platform. But the basic Arminian intransigence of King Charles, combined with the sheer speed of events, made religious compromises of this kind unworkable. Conciliation was overtaken by the drift to war.[27]

As an old man looking back on the Civil War at the end of the century, Philip fourth Lord Wharton, who had fought against the King, claimed that 'a hundred to one of the Calvinists ... joined the parliamentarians'. The process which had brought this alleged situation about was highly complex, and even Wharton would not have seriously maintained that all they were fighting about was Calvinism. At the same time the propaganda put out by parliamentary army officers in the early stages of the war does suggest a high degree of religious motivation. This declaration of sentiments took the visual form of battle standards flown by the captains of each cavalry troop, who incidentally all claimed to be gentlemen. While Magna Carta and a blood-stained head, probably Strafford's, were occasionally chosen as symbols, the dominating motif was the Bible with accompanying slogans such as 'Verbum Dei', 'Sacra Scriptura' and 'Jehova Nisi'. Also depicted were bishops tumbling from their thrones with the caption 'Antichrist Must Down', a lethal rain of arrows labelled 'Contra Impios' and cloud-wreathed anchors illustrating the assertion 'Only in Heaven'. Comparable propaganda on the Royalist side was of a much more secular kind, displaying the insignia of monarchy or satirising the 'roundhead' opposition. One popular emblem was a pack of hounds all barking 'Pym'. Revealingly, Charles described his opponents as consisting mainly of 'Brownists, Anabaptists and Atheists'. Such was the gulf of misunderstanding that had opened up between the Arminian king and his Calvinist subjects.[28]

In terms of English Protestant history the charge in 1640 that King Charles and Archbishop Laud were religious innovators is irrefutable. The reaction provoked however by the Arminian revolution was of such violence that it could be transformed with relative ease into a call for 'root and branch' remedies, and presbyterianism emerge as the cure of Arminian disease. Thus what had begun as a counter-revolution itself became radicalised.

NOTES

For some of the shortcomings of this essay see my remarks in the Introduction, pp. 9–11 above.

1 C. Hill, *Society and Puritanism in Pre-Revolutionary England* (London, 1964); W. Haller, *The Rise of Puritanism* (New York, 1938).

2 Clark ed., *Register OHS*, pt i, pp. 194–217. [For a revised and much fuller listing of Calvinist theses maintained at Oxford University, see Tyacke, *Anti-Calvinists*, pp. 60–81]; G. Abbot, *A Sermon preached at Westminster* (London, 1608), pp. 19–20.

3 H. C. Porter, *Reformation and Reaction in Tudor Cambridge* (Cambridge, 1958), pp. 365–75; P. Collinson, 'The "Nott Conformytye" of the Young John Whitgift', *JEH* 15 (1964), 192–200; A. F. Scott Pearson, *Thomas Cartwright and Elizabethan Puritanism, 1535–1603* (Cambridge, 1925), pp. 22–3, 396.

4 J. Ayre ed., *The Sermons of Edwin Sandys* (Cambridge, 1842), pp. 223, 448; R. A. Marchant, *The Puritans and the Church Courts in the Diocese of York, 1560–1642* (London, 1960), pp. 18–21; L. Carlson ed., *The Writings of Henry Barrow, 1590–1642* (London, 1966), p. 62.

5 S. Benefield, *A Sermon preached at Wotton under Edge* (Oxford, 1613); [S. Gardiner, *The Foundation of the Faythfull* (London, 1611); *The Way to Heaven* (London, 1611)]; S. Gardiner, *A Dialogue* (London, 1605), sigs E3v, B4; W. Scott ed., *Somers Tracts* (London, 1809), ii, pp. 307–8, 311. [My remarks in this paragraph blur some important differences within the ranks of the Jacobean episcopate. At the very least one needs to distinguish the attitude of evangelical bishops from others: K. Fincham, *Prelate as Pastor. The Episcopate of James I* (Oxford, 1990), pp. 257–61.]

6 C. Hill, *Puritanism and Revolution* (London, 1958), pp. 216, 238; R. Abbot, *A Defence of the Reformed Catholic of W. Perkins* (London, 1611); F. Rous, *Testis Veritatis* (London, 1626), pp. 2–3; C. H. McIlwain ed., *The Political Works of James I* (Cambridge, Mass., 1918), p. 274; W. P. Baildon ed., *Les Reportes . . . in Camera Stellata, 1593 to 1609* (London, 1894), p. 191; J. P. Kenyon ed., *The Stuart Constitution, 1603–1688* (Cambridge, 1966), p. 41.

7 [McIlwain ed. *Political Works of James I*, pp. 71–168. In fact James I only wrote two works about the oath of allegiance.]; L. Andrewes, *Responsio* (London, 1610), p. 123; T. G. Crippen ed., 'Of the Name of Puritans', *Transactions of the Congregational Historical Society*, 6 (1913–15), 83; Arber ed., Transcript, iii.

8 H. Foley ed., *Records of the English Province of the Society of Jesus* (London, 1877–83), i, p. 70; M. Tierney ed., *Dodd's Church History* (London, 1839–43), iv, pp. 179–80; HMC *Salisbury*, xviii, p. 21; A. G. R. Smith, *The Government of Elizabethan England* (London, 1967), p. 65; P. Collinson, *The Elizabethan Puritan Movement* (London, 1967), p. 159.

9 R. Bancroft, *Dangerous Positions and Proceedings . . . under Pretence of Reformation* (London, 1593); M. Knappen ed., *Two Elizabethan Diaries* (Chicago, 1933), p. 32; T. Rogers *The Faith, Doctrine and Religion professed and protected in . . . England* (Cambridge, 1607); E. R. Foster ed., *Proceedings in Parliament, 1610* (New Haven, Conn., 1966), ii, p. 78; G. Goodman, *The Court of James I* (London, 1839), ii, pp. 160–1; P. Hembry, *The Bishops of Bath and Wells* (London, 1967). p. 211; *The Works of [King] James* (London, 1616), sig. e. For much of the information in this and succeeding paragraphs, see Tyacke *Anti-Calvinists*. [On the question of sabbatarianism now see K. L. Parker, *The English Sabbath. A Study of Doctrine and Discipline from the Reformation to the Civil War* (Cambridge, 1988), pp. 111, 120, 132–3, 160 and *passim*, but cf. N. Tyacke in *EHR* 106 (1991), 1002–3.]

10 P. Seaver, *The Puritan Lectureships . . . 1560–1662* (Stanford, CA, 1970), pp. 224–9; Marchant, *Puritans and Church Courts*, p. 43.

11 Manchester MSS (formerly at PRO), Hughes to Nathaniel Rich, 19 May 1617; L. Hughes, *A Plain and True Relation of . . . the Summer Islands* (London, 1621); Hill, *Puritanism and Revolution*, p. 146; I. Morgan, *Prince Charles's Puritan Chaplain* (London, 1957); W. Notestein ed., *Commons' Debates 1621* (New Haven, Conn., 1935), iv, p. 63.

12 W. Notestein ed., *Commons Debates for 1629* (Minneapolis, 1921), p. 100.

13 J. Sansom ed., *The Works of John Cosin* (Oxford, 1843–55), ii, pp. 61–4.

14 *Ibid.*, p. 74; Kenyon ed., *Stuart Constitution*, pp. 154–5; S. R. Gardiner ed., *The Constitutional Documents of the Puritan Revolution, 1625–1660* (Oxford, 1906), p. 76. [The operation of press censorship was more complicated than my remarks imply. Thus Calvinist views continued to be printed at least until the death of Archbishop Abbot in mid-1633, thanks to the licensing activities of his various chaplains. See also pp. 276–7 below.]

15 Kenyon ed., *Stuart Constitution*, pp. 153–4; S. R. Gardiner ed., *Debates in the House of Commons for 1625* (Camden Soc., N. S. vi, 1873), p. 49.

16 Notestein ed., *Commons Debates for 1629*, pp. 12–15, 27.

17 BL, Add. MS 25, 285. I owe my knowledge of this volume to Valerie Pearl. [For Archbishop Abbot's views on bowing at the name of Jesus, see Laud, *Works*, v, pp. 39–40, 205–7. They are to be distinguished from those of Prynne.]

18 Woburn Abbey, Bedford MS xi, 96, 100, 158, 248, 1236, 1293. [These references were kindly supplied by Conrad Russell. Bedford's remark about Arminianism is in fact a direct quotation from Francis Rous: *Testis Veritatis*, p. 105.]; W. Fiennes, Viscount Saye, *Two Speeches* (London, 1641), pp. 13–14; N. Fiennes, *A Speech . . . concerning Bishops* (London, 1641); R. Greville, Lord Brooke, *A Discourse opening the Nature of . . . Episcopacy* (London, 1641); E. Clinton, *Countess of Lincoln's Nurserie* (London, 1622), p. 17; G. E. Cockayne, *The Complete Peerage* (London, 1910–59), vii, pp. 696–7; Morgan, *Prince Charles's Puritan Chaplain*, p. 43; D. Underdown, *Pride's Purge* (Oxford, 1971), p. 20.

[19 Hill, *Society and Puritanium*, pp. 501–6; E. Reeve, *The Communion Booke Catechisme* (London, 1635), pp. 47–9, 61–7.]

20 [Cf. Tyacke, *Anti-Calvinists*, pp. 199–216]; I. M. Calder, *Activities of the Puritan Faction . . . 1625–1633* (London, 1957), p. xxii; cf. pp. 121–3 above, 278–9 below.

21 R. Howell, *Newcastle-upon-Tyne and the Puritan Revolution* (Oxford, 1966), p. 112; *CSPD 1631–3*, p. 571. [Hill, *Society and Puritanium*, p. 163]

[22 Today I would be more cautious in drawing any such social distinctions between Arminian and Calvinist bishops.]

23 R. F. Williams ed., *Court and Times of Charles I* (London, 1848), i, p. 347; G. Abbot, *An Exposition on the Prophet Jonah* (London, 1613), pp. 436–7; Ayre ed., *Sermons of Edwin Sandys*, p. 199.

24. *The Geneva Bible* (facsimile of first edition, Wisconsin, 1969).

25 R. Abbot, *Antichristi Demonstratio* (London, 1603), pp. 92–3; S. Marshall, *Copy of a Letter* (London, 1643), pp. 11, 20; H. R. Trevor-Roper ed., *Essays in British History* (London, 1965), p. 89.

26 M. C. Kitshoff, 'Aspects of Arminianism in Scotland' (St Andrews M. Th., 1968).

27 Kenyon ed., *Stuart Constitution*, pp. 167–8, 172, 198; W. A. Shaw, *A History of the English Church . . . 1640–60* (London, 1900), i, pp. 65–76.

28 G. F. T. Jones, *Saw-Pit Wharton* (Sydney, 1967), p. 50; Dr Williams's Library, MSS Modern Folios 12.7; BL, Add. MS 5247, Harleian MS 986; *Old Parliamentary History* (London, 1760–3), xi, p. 435.

APPENDIX: DEFINING ARMINIANISM

The subject of Arminianism is full of pitfalls for the unwary. Although the term derives from the Latinised name of the Dutch Protestant theologian Jacobus Arminius (Jacob Harmensz), who died in 1609, the teachings concerned are much older. We are in fact dealing here with a recurring debate throughout much of Christian history, about the relationship between divine grace and human free will, its particular Arminian manifestation representing a doctrinal split within the ranks of the Dutch Reformed or Calvinist Church. Moreover very similar doctrines were held by many contemporary Catholics and Lutherans. Thus it only really makes sense to talk of Arminianism in a Calvinist context. Even in the United Provinces, however, Arminius had various precursors, a reflection in part of the diverse origins of Dutch Protestantism; but as Calvinist orthodoxy hardened, particularly under the influence of the Genevan Theodore Beza, such dissenters were increasingly at risk. By way of reaction Arminius himself, during the 1590s, adopted the views of the Lutheran Philip Melancthon and his Danish disciple Niels Hemmingsen.[1] Indeed, what comes to be called Arminianism is virtually indistinguishable from the Melancthonian brand of Lutheranism.

The dispute centred on the manner in which individual members of fallen humanity achieved salvation. Granted that faith is essential, do we believe because God has already chosen us or are we chosen in the light of our belief? This was how Hemmingsen, subsequently to be quoted by Arminius, summed up the issue.[2] Both men maintained the latter position, namely that God's choice or election is conditional on faith. Arminius first formulated his own anti-Calvinist ideas while expounding St Paul's epistle to the Romans, when serving as pastor at Amsterdam.[3] It was not, however, until he became professor at Leiden University in 1603 that Arminius clashed publicly with Calvinist orthodoxy, matters coming to a head the following year on the subject of predestination. The predestination of the elect, according to Arminius, has reference to believers. He now felt compelled to write a series of defences of his teaching, culminating with the *Declaration of Sentiments* in 1608. Much of this is taken up with refuting Calvinist views, but it also contains the following key statement. God has 'decreed to receive into favour those who repent and believe, and, in Christ, for his sake and through him, to effect the salvation of such penitents and believers as persevered to the end, but [to] leave in sin and under wrath all impenitent persons and unbelievers, and to damn them as alien from Christ'.[4]

Arminianism, however, acquired its classic definition in 1610, the year after the death of Arminius, when his Dutch followers formulated their doctrines under five headings in the form of a *Remonstrance*. As a result of this document Dutch Arminians came to be known as Remonstrants and their opponents as Counter-Remonstrants. The five points of the remonstrance comprised predestination, redemption, free will, grace and perseverance[5]. Eight years later, in 1618–19, the Synod of Dort proceeded to condemn Arminianism under approximately the same five heads. Against the Arminians, the Calvinists asserted that predestination was not conditional on faith, redemption was limited in its saving efficacy to the elect, on whose corrupt will grace worked infallibly, and lastly that the perseverance of true believers was guaranteed.[6]

Most parts of Europe considered at the time to fall within the Calvinist orbit were invited to send representatives to the Synod of Dort, and the subsequent rulings came to be widely adopted as an international standard. The Dutch Arminians were driven from the Established Church and initially subjected to persecution, many of the clergy going into exile. Outside the United Provinces what little support existed for Arminianism within the Calvinist Churches was generally suppressed. In France, for example, Daniel Tilenus was deposed from the Calvinist ministry, although somewhat ironically the Dutch Arminian leaders found a temporary haven there courtesy of the Catholic government.[7] The major exception, however, was England, whose King, James I, had sent representatives to Dort but where Calvinism rapidly went into eclipse during the 1620s. There existed a long-standing anti-Calvinist or Lutheran tradition in England, but Calvinism had achieved a position of dominance by the end of the sixteenth century – especially at the universities of Oxford and Cambridge. This ascendancy had been won the more easily because of the part played by the Reformed theologians Martin Bucer and Peter Martyr in the original Protestantisation of England.[8] Yet it was a Calvinism with important differences from that on the continent, not least because the English Church possessed a Prayer Book the sacramental teaching of which sat uneasily with the doctrine of unconditional predestination.[9]

What now seems mainly to have tipped the balance against Calvinism in England was the religious policy pursued by Charles I, from 1625 onwards. English Arminianism itself derived from a variety of sources, owing something to Lutheranism, and Hemmingsen in particular, while the early Christian writers, notably Chrysostom, were very important too.[10] A leading exponent in the 1620s was Richard Montagu, who apparently developed his ideas quite independently of the Dutch; nor was he a systematic theologian. Nevertheless, albeit by a different route and method, Montagu arrived at the same result. In two polemical pamphlets published during the years 1624 and 1625, he denied among other things that the English Church was Calvinist in its theology. Like the Dutch Arminians, Montagu argued that predestination was conditional, the offer of grace was unrestricted and its working on the will not infallible, and that justifying faith could be lost.[11] As well as receiving royal support, Montagu had some powerful clerical backers, including William Laud, the future Archbishop of Canterbury, who privately endorsed his views on predestination and the related points. None the less public discussion of these questions was discouraged thereafter, not least due to the enduring strength of Calvinism. Apart from Montagu, the other leading anti-Calvinist theologian in England at this time was Thomas Jackson. Such ideas also underpinned many of the outward religious changes in England during the 1630s, associated with the eucharist – in particular the widespread conversion of communion tables into altars.[12]

In both England and the United Provinces, the Arminian controversy was intimately connected with politics. The stadholder Prince Maurice had backed the Dutch Calvinists in his political struggle with Oldenbarneveldt and the States of Holland, but after the death of Maurice, and the succession of Frederick Henry to the stadholderate in 1625, it became possible for the Dutch Arminian exiles to return home. Arminian or Remonstrant churches were opened in Amsterdam and Rotterdam, among other places, as well as an academy. In this newly tolerant atmosphere, Arminians from other parts of Europe tended to gravitate to the United Provinces, for example Etienne de Courcelles and later Jean Le Clerc. Although the numbers of church members declined during the seventeenth century, the Dutch Remonstrants continued to produce distinguished theologians, such as Philip van Limborch, and to exercise an international influence.[13] It was also the second generation of Dutch Arminians who developed a full-blown theory of toleration, the writings of Simon Episcopius being particularly significant in this respect.[14]

Whereas in the United Provinces the Arminians separated from the Established Church, in England they remained closely associated with monarchy and episcopacy. During the English Civil War, and under the republican regimes of the 1650s, Calvinism came back into favour, but after 1660, when king and bishops were restored, Arminian teaching made rapid gains. Cambridge University led the way under Peter Gunning and Joseph Beaumont, with the development of a more systematic Arminian theology, while Calvinists conducted a rearguard action at Oxford.[15] The position of the latter, however, was greatly weakened by the hiving off of so many Calvinists into the ranks of the Dissenters. Works such as *The Whole Duty of Man* (1658) also helped to propagate Arminianism more generally. Yet only belatedly did the causes of Arminianism and toleration merge in England, associated with the growth of Latitudinarianism during the 1690s. In other parts of Calvinist Europe the spread of what is called Amyraldism, a modified form of Calvinism, should not be confused with Arminianism. Moïse Amyraut, a professor at the Academy of Saumur, who died in 1664 and gave his name to the movement, attempted to reconcile unconditional predestination with the universality of redemptive grace. His views were especially influential in France and Geneva.[16]

It is England which remains the great Arminian success story, even if some modern commentators are reluctant to use this particular religious label.[17] They correctly point out that Dutch and English developments were largely independent of one another, but have greater difficulty in explaining away the shared Reformed or Calvinist legacy in both countries. We need, however, to remember that England was neither a physical nor an intellectual island for, in addition to influences from Scotland, English Protestantism owed a direct debt to continental Reformed theology; Calvin's own teachings were subsequently grafted on to these roots. Therefore the invitation to send English representatives to the Synod of Dort was not so much an accident of international politics as a recognition of genuine doctrinal affinities. With reference to England, anti-Calvinism is, strictly speaking, a more accurate description than Arminianism, yet to insist upon it seems unduly pedantic.

APPENDIX NOTES

1 J. and W. Nichols eds, *The Works of James Arminius* (London, 1825–75), i, pp. 30–1.

2 *Ibid.*, i, pp. 578–9.

3 C. Bangs, *Arminius. A Study in the Dutch Reformation* (Nashville, 1971), pp. 193–205.

4 Nichols eds, *Works of James Arminius*, i, p. 589.

5 A. W. Harrison, *The Beginnings of Arminianism to the Synod of Dort* (London, 1926), pp. 150–1.

6 *Ibid.*, pp. 347–75.

7 A. W. Harrison, *Arminius* (London, 1937), pp. 97–109.

8 P. White, *Predestination, Policy and Polemic. Conflict and Consensus in the English Church from the Reformation to the Civil War* (Cambridge, 1992), pp. 44–52.

9 Tyacke, *Anti-Calvinists*, pp. 3–4, 29–36, 58–62, and *passim*.

10 White, *Predestination, Policy and Polemic*, pp. 89–90, 216–17.

11 R. Montagu, *Appello Caesarem. A Just Appeal from Two Unjust Informers* (London, 1625), pp. 56–74.

12 Tyacke, *Anti-Calvinists*, pp. 159–60, 198–209, 266–7.

13 L. Simonutti, 'Reason and Toleration. Henry More and Philip van Limborch', in S. Hutton ed., *Henry More (1614–1687). Tercentenary Studies* (Dordrecht, 1990), pp. 201–18.

14 D. Nobbs, *Theocracy and Toleration. A Study of the Disputes in Dutch Calvinism from 1600 to 1650* (Cambridge, 1938), pp. 91–107.

15 See pp. 323–33 below.

16 B. G. Armstrong, *Calvinism and the Amyraut Heresy. Protestant Scholasticism and Humanism in Seventeenth-Century France* (Madison, 1969).

17 White, *Predestination, Policy and Polemic*.

Chapter 6

───────◆───────

The rise of Arminianism
reconsidered

I

WISE historians think twice before entering a *Past and Present* debate. But my continued silence as regards the published views of Peter White might be misconstrued, given the source of many of the ideas in dispute.[1] White's central contention is very simple. There was *no* 'rise of Arminianism' in early seventeenth-century England. Historians who so argue are, he claims, the dupes of Puritan propaganda. For the English Church had always embraced 'a spectrum of views on the doctrine of predestination'. As a consequence, it is improper to describe either the Elizabethan or Jacobean Church as Calvinist. Moreover 'a *via media* between extremes' remained intrinsic to Church of England theology from the Elizabethan settlement onwards. The 'outlook was essentially patristic, irenic, comprehensive and if necessary properly agnostic'. Not even the notorious Richard Montagu turns out to be, in this scenario, 'a genuine Arminian'. Similarly, the notion that James I ever held Calvinist beliefs is, we are told, another 'myth'. What made Arminianism temporarily an issue in the 1620s was, says White, the international situation. The 'Thirty Years War . . . unleashed a renewal of militant Protestantism'. Allegations of Arminianism at this time are therefore best understood as a kind of foreign-policy reflex. Accordingly, with the return of peace during the 1630s concern about Arminianism died away, and it was not an issue in the Civil War crisis.[2]

At one level this is a piece of ultra-revisionism. Paradoxically, however, White also seeks to rehabilitate the categories of Anglican and Puritan as the most appropriate terms in which to analyse religious developments under the early Stuarts. That said, there are a number of specific difficulties with his account, perhaps the most serious being an apparent unwillingness to recognise that the Church of England was liable to change over time both in its doctrine and practice. As a supporter of Archbishop Laud put it, in an officially licensed work of 1637, the 'faith of England is not in the sole dead letter of our Articles and Church Booke etc., but in the living spirit and consent of the fathers of the Church [the bishops] ... *determining the sense*'.[3] It would indeed be surprising if the collective thinking of the English church leadership had stood still during the eighty years which separate the Elizabethan settlement from the Caroline canons of 1640, quite apart from the vagaries of three monarchs and six archbishops of Canterbury.

Manifestly by the 1590s Calvinism was dominant in the highest reaches of the Established Church. This is most clearly evident from the operation of press censorship. Under the terms of the 1586 Star Chamber decree, all London religious publications had to be licensed by either the Archbishop of Canterbury or the Bishop of London.[4] On the whole they tended to delegate this task. Nevertheless in a minority of cases Bishops John Aylmer and Richard Bancroft of London, and Archbishop John Whitgift of Canterbury, can be found personally licensing books. The doctrines to which they thus gave their approval are very revealing. In 1590 Bishop Aylmer licensed *A Golden Chaine* by William Perkins.[5] Predestination provides the principal theme of this book, and Perkins defined it as 'the decree of God by which he hath ordeined all men to a certain and everlasting estate, that is either to salvation or condemnation for his own glory'. Opposed to this view are those who ascribe any role to 'men's foreseen preparations'. Furthermore the death of Christ is a 'propitiation' for 'the elect' and not 'all the world'.[6] A year later, in 1591, Archbishop Whitgift licensed a Paul's Cross sermon by Gervase Babington.[7] (The author was consecrated bishop the same year.) Babington taught that 'all men [were] at the first before the Lord in his eternall counsell, to receive an end or use according to his will'. They 'onely beleeve which are ordayned ... which because many, yea the most part of men, are not therefore they beleeve not'. Christ is to the 'cursed castawaies ... a stone to stumble at and a rock of offence, they being disobedient and even ordeigned to this thing'.[8]

Bancroft became Bishop of London in 1597. The following year he licensed the English version of a four-hundred-page Calvinist treatise, by Jacobus Kimedoncius of Heidelberg.[9] Kimedoncius defended two basic contentions: 'No reason but the onely will of God can be given why this man is elected and that man is reprobated' and 'Christ effectually died for the elect and faithfull onely'.[10] It must be emphasised that the licensing of these Calvinist works did not comprise part of an even-handed policy under which alternative views could also be printed. On the contrary, anti-Calvinist doctrine was suppressed. This happened to writings by both Peter Baro and Richard Thomson during the 1590s.[11] University religious publishing, controlled by the vice-chancellors of Oxford and Cambridge, was likewise monopolised at this time by Calvinists. Successive Oxford editions of *The Summe of Christian Religion* by Zacharias Ursinus, another Heidelberg divine, maintained that 'election' and 'reprobation' are according to 'the eternall counsell of God', and not dependent on whether 'a man is worthy'; while at Cambridge Robert Some's *Three Questions* included the proposition that 'Christ died effectually for the elect alone' and 'therefore not for every severall man'.[12] In addition, whenever such topics were treated at the Oxford Act and Cambridge Commencement, Calvinist orthodoxy invariably prevailed, the conclusions having been approved in advance by the university authorities. For example, at Oxford in 1596 it was affirmed that 'God of his own volition will repudiate some people', and at Cambridge the previous year 'universal redemption' was denied.[13] Calvinism has been aptly described as the 'regnant teaching' of the day.[14]

Whether we call this teaching Calvinist is of no great moment.[15] An alternative description would be Augustinian, and certainly St Augustine was the author most usually cited by Calvinists.[16] What matters is the body of doctrine so described. (The same holds true of the term Arminian.) On the basis of the writings cited above, this Calvinist doctrine can be summarised as follows. God's predestination consists of a double and absolute decree, whereby both election and reprobation are unconditional. Concomitantly saving grace is only granted to the elect. The questions at issue here cannot be dismissed, in White's phrase, as 'finer points'.[17] Rather they are fundamental. Hence the importance of the famous Lambeth Articles of 1595, which sought to quash emergent English anti-Calvinism – especially in the person of Peter Baro who, like the Dutch Arminius later, was an advocate of *conditional* predestination. Baro held that 'God has predestined such as he from all eternity foreknew would believe on Christ', and 'hath likewise from all eternity reprobated all rebels and such as contumaciously continue in sin'.[18] Accordingly election and reprobation are conditional respectively on faith and sin, saving grace being universal, and Baro has rightly been called an 'Arminian *avant la lettre*'.[19] White is incorrect in claiming that the Lambeth Articles state 'reprobation' to be 'on account of sin'. They in fact say that 'those not predestined to salvation [the reprobate] are inevitably *condemned* on account of their sins'.[20] This reflects the then orthodox Calvinist distinction between reprobation and damnation, sin being the cause only of the latter.[21] It follows that the Lambeth Articles embody the doctrine of double and absolute predestination, which largely explains the profound distaste felt for them by English Arminians.[22]

Queen Elizabeth objected to the Lambeth Articles.[23] But more striking, in this connection, is the Calvinist unanimity of the clerical leadership of the English Church. For Archbishop Whitgift was assisted in drawing up the Lambeth Articles by Bishop Richard Fletcher of London, while his fellow archbishop, Matthew Hutton of York, both endorsed them and wrote a Calvinist treatise on the subject.[24] Are these events really best understood, *à la* White, as a Puritan plot?[25] In an international context, the Lambeth Articles underlined the fact that the theology of the Church of England derived from the Swiss rather than the German Reformation. More specifically, they registered a seismic tremor originating from the Colloquy of Montbéliard in 1586. Predestination had been only one of a number of subjects discussed at Montbéliard, between rival Lutheran and Calvinist delegations led respectively by Jacob Andreae of Tübingen and Theodore Beza of Geneva.[26] It was this topic, however, which proved the most contentious, driving a deeper wedge between Lutherans and Calvinists and revealing divisions within the Calvinist camp itself.

The Colloquy of Montbéliard led Samuel Huber, a Bernese pastor, to launch a wide-ranging assault on Calvinist predestinarian teaching. Particularly important was his book entitled *Theses Christum Jesum*, of about 1590, which sought to demonstrate the universality of saving grace.[27] Perkins quoted from Beza's account of the Colloquy of Montbéliard in his *A Golden Chaine*.[28] Huber himself was coming under English attack by 1594, and three years later his views were rebutted in a sermon at Paul's Cross.[29] Huber's *Theses* had already been subjected to a detailed refutation by Kimedoncius in his *De Redemptione Generis Humani* of 1592.[30] Translated as *Of the Redemption of Mankind*, this is the book which Bishop Bancroft licensed in 1598. Linked with Huber, by English critics, were the Frieslander Gellius Snecanus and the Danish Neils Hemmingsen.[31] Snecanus was arguably the most significant Dutch precursor of Arminius, advancing views soon to be called Arminian in his *Methodica Descriptio* of 1591.[32] But in terms of positively influencing English theology, Hemmingsen probably counted for more than either Huber or Snecanus. The full extent of Hemmingsen's dissent from Calvinism only emerged with the publication in 1591 of his *Tractatus de Gratia Universali*.[33]

Andrew Willet commented in 1594 that the teaching of Hemmingsen and Snecanus on conditional predestination 'already hath gotten some patrons and defenders in our Church'.[34] Certainly Peter Baro can be found writing to Hemmingsen in 1596, as a religious ally against Calvinism.[35] On the other hand, one should not exaggerate the derivative nature of Baro's theology, which deserves more study than it has yet received. The unpublished writings of Baro during the 1590s are more radical than anything he had said earlier in print.[36] But this may reflect censorship rather than intellectual evolution. The same interplay between English and foreign influences can be seen in the later reception of Dutch Arminianism. Richard or 'Dutch' Thomson resided for a time in Holland and knew Arminius personally, while John Overall corresponded with Hugo Grotius.[37] By 1613 the writings of Arminius were circulating among English sympathisers.[38] Conversely Richard

Montagu, according to his own account, had never read a word of Arminius until 1625.[39] Montagu was, in point of fact, just old enough to have picked up some of his theological ideas from other continental sources during the late 1590s. Nevertheless there had always been English dissenters from Calvinism.[40] The difference, however, between the anti-Calvinist challenge of the 1590s and that of the 1620s is that on the first occasion Calvinism remained firmly in the saddle, whereas at the second attempt it was toppled.

Calvinist dominance of the Church of England continued during the first two decades of the seventeenth century. Bancroft, whose personal licensing of Calvinist doctrine we have already noted, succeeded Whitgift as Archbishop of Canterbury in 1604. In the diocese of London, Calvinist bishop followed Calvinist bishop – Richard Vaughan (1604–7), Thomas Ravis (1607–9), George Abbot (1610–11) and John King (1611–21). In 1611 the Calvinist George Abbot was promoted to Canterbury. Vaughan, who had also helped Whitgift to compile the Lambeth Articles, licensed in 1606 the English translation of the *Institutiones Theologicae* by Gulielmus Bucanus of Lausanne.[41] Predestination is there defined as 'the eternal purpose of God whereby, according to the good pleasure of his will [and] before the foundations of the world were laid, he hath determined to glorifie himselfe by ordeining some men to grace and salvation [and] others to displeasure and eternall destruction'. Moreover Christ's 'death was sufficient for all ... but effectual onely for the elect'. (The translator also recalled the recommending by Archbishop Whitgift, to 'us students' of Cambridge University, of Calvin's *Institutes*.)[42] Ravis was the author of a characteristically Calvinist will, describing himself as confident of enjoying 'eternall lief among the sainctes and holy elect'.[43] Abbot, in his own published sermons of the 1590s, had distinguished between the 'reprobate, appointed and predestinated before hand unto evill', and the elect, 'booked in the register of the saints'.[44] Finally King, in 1611, licensed *The Repentance of Peter and Judas* by Charles Richardson.[45] This work is largely taken up with demonstrating that 'God will not suffer his children to perish in their sins'. For they 'can never fall totally nor finally from the grace of God'.[46] Under the stewardship of these archbishops and bishops, a regular stream of Calvinist works came off the London printing presses.[47] Similarly, official teaching at the universities of Oxford and Cambridge remained Calvinist.[48]

II

The foregoing provides scant evidence of an Anglican *via media* on the subject of predestination. Here White's case hinges on the typicality, or otherwise, of Bishop Overall's views. Demonstrably the position of Overall differed from that of the British delegation at the Synod of Dort in 1619, as well as from all other English Calvinists.[49] He did indeed espouse an intermediate predestinarian position, which enabled both Calvinists and Arminians to quote him – albeit selectively. Overall envisaged two categories of persons, the one unconditionally elect and the other consisting of those whose destiny depended on how they applied God's graces.[50] Yet, in practice, he tended to side with the Arminians and it is far from clear why his idiosyncratic formulation of the theology of grace should be considered normative, even among anti-Calvinists.[51] Thus among his contemporaries Lancelot Andrewes and Samuel Harsnett, as well as Peter Baro, maintained the full Arminian doctrine.[52] So too did Richard Montagu during the 1620s. White writes that Montagu's book of 1624, *A New Gagg*, 'followed what had been the sure recipe for ecclesiastical preferment: a defence of the Church of England against the Papist calumny . . . that the doctrines of the Church of England were those of extreme Calvinism'.[53] In reality, however, *A New Gagg* was without precedent. Previous English Protestant polemicists against Roman Catholicism had assumed a Calvinist consensus among members of the Church of England.[54] The concept of 'doctrinal Puritanism', as deployed by Montagu to describe Calvinism, was a neologism therefore of revolutionary significance. Furthermore his diocesan, Bishop George Carleton of Chichester, had no doubt that Montagu held Arminian views. 'In the doctrine of pre-destination he attempteth to bring in a decree respective', teaching 'that God's will herein is directed by somewhat fore-seene in men'.[55] Carleton had headed the British delegation to Dort and was in a good position to judge Arminianism.

Montagu wrote, in *A New Gagg*, that the Church of England was 'opposed' to the doctrine that:

> Peter was saved because that God would have him saved absolutely, and resolved to save him necessarily because hee would so and no further; that Judas was damned as necessarily because that God, as absolute to decree as omnipotent to effect, did primarily so resolve concerning him and so deter-mine touching him, without respect of anything but his owne will. Insomuch that Peter could not perish though he would nor Judas be saved doo what he could.

Despite conflating reprobation and damnation, and generally presenting Calvinist teaching in an unfavourable light, Montagu clearly rejected an absolute decree both of election and reprobation. He reiterated this view in his subsequent apologia of 1625, *Appello Caesarem*, denying what he called 'that absolute decree of predestination'.[56] Montagu also asserted that 'the learnedst in the Church of England' taught that justifying faith 'may be lost totally and finally'.[57]

Moreover Montagu claimed to have had the support of King James I.[58] Among Montagu's opponents, Francis Rous in particular took up this point.

The avowed purpose of Rous, in his *Testis Veritatis* of 1626, was to demonstrate the opposition of the late King to 'Arminianisme'.[59] Naturally Rous described James's views in terms of 'Catholic' rather than Calvinist orthodoxy, deeming the two to be indistinguishable.[60] None the less he was able to show, by direct quotation, that as late as 1619 King James had publicly endorsed the doctrines of absolute election and absolute reprobation. 'God drawes by his effectuall grace, out of that attainted and corrupt masse [of fallen mankind], whom he pleaseth for the work of his mercy, leaving the rest to their owne wayes which all leade to perdition'.[61] The key word here is 'pleaseth'. White himself, although unwittingly, provides further evidence of the King's Calvinism, in his quotation from *A Brotherly Perswasion* by Thomas Sparke. This book was licensed for publication by Bishop Vaughan of London in 1607.[62] Sparke there records that at the Hampton Court Conference of 1604, King James had 'graunted' that the sixteenth of the Thirty-nine Articles, 'touching falling from grace of regeneration, should be explayned, by addition of some such words, as whereby plainly it might appeare that it taught not that the regenerate and justified either totally or finally fall at any time from the same'.[63] This teaching on the perseverance of the saints went even further than the Lambeth Articles of 1595 and anticipates the Irish Articles of 1615, by speaking not simply of 'the elect' but of 'the regenerate and justified'.[64] As such it indicates a thoroughgoing royal Calvinism.

The signs are, however, that during the last few years of his life James sought increasingly to distance himself from Calvinism. A number of possible reasons can be adduced for this, including a genuine change of mind on the King's part. But it was never my argument that this alteration occurred because James had gone 'senile'.[65] Perhaps the most convincing explanation is that he came at this time to perceive Calvinism as a direct threat to his scheme for an Anglo-Spanish marriage alliance, under the terms of which the Elector Frederick would be restored to the Palatinate without recourse to war. Calvinist clerics, from Archbishop Abbot downwards, were opposed to this pacific foreign policy with its feared corollary of a toleration for Catholicism.[66] It gave Montagu's episcopal backers their chance to challenge the previously dominant Calvinists, and they met with at least a measure of royal support. Up until now such anti-Calvinist bishops had been compelled generally to keep silence on the subject of predestination, leaving the Calvinists as a consequence in possession of the field. The Thirty Years War therefore made *Calvinism* into a political issue, which is the reverse of White's argument.[67] This shift in the balance of theological power, at the end of the reign of James, gathered further momentum after the accession of King Charles in 1625, and it was no accident that in 1628 the House of Commons named Bishops William Laud and Richard Neile as 'Arminians'.[68] They had been made Privy Councillors the previous year.[69]

On the basis of a royal proclamation in June 1626 and a subsequent declaration in November 1628 Calvinism was suppressed.[70] According to White, this represents a return to the Anglican *via media*, which had been briefly disrupted by the exaggerated fears of militant English Protestants who saw Arminianism where no such thing existed.[71] The outlawing of Calvinism, however, is real enough. Thus, on the basis of the 1626 proclamation, Calvinist predestinarian teaching was immediately banned from the Cambridge Commencement, and a similar embargo on Calvinist printing was imposed in the capital when Laud became bishop of London in July 1628.[72] The Cambridge order arrived via Bishop Neile, acting on the instructions of King Charles, and snuffed out a Calvinist tradition there which can be traced back to the 1590s, when records begin.[73] As for London, the Calvinist doctrine which Laud caused to be suppressed had a printing history dating from the period of the Elizabethan settlement onwards.[74] Calvinism also disappeared from the Oxford Act after 1631, in the wake of Laud becoming chancellor of the university, ending in this case a Calvinist tradition traceable since the 1570s.[75] Conversely, in the late 1620s other English Arminian writings apart from those of Montagu began to be published. Among the earliest were the books of Thomas Jackson, who up until 1628 had not dared to air his anti-Calvinist views in print. It is indicative of the changed publishing climate that he now felt emboldened to do so in his *Divine Essence and Attributes.*[76]

While disclaiming Arminianism, as Montagu had done, Jackson went on to attack Calvinist teaching on predestination. Of a more philosophic bent than Montagu, he sought to reconcile God's 'eternal and immutable decree' with the 'contingent actions of men'. As part of his argument, Jackson asserted God's 'universall' love while denying the Augustinian and Calvinist 'restrictions' on divine grace. He also in effect abolished the absolute decree of predestination, claiming that men '*become* reprobates' and that God is 'free to recompense every man according to his present wayes'. Indeed Jackson explicitly criticised 'the doctrine and uses of God's *absolute* decree for electing some and reprobating most' which, he admitted, had been 'generally taught' for 'these forty yeares last past'.[77] His book, like Montagu's *Appello Caesarem*, was licensed by a deputy of Bishop George Montaigne of London.[78]

Charles himself had probably decided against Calvinism, as Prince Wales, at the time of his abortive journey to Spain in 1623. Attempts were then made to convert him to Catholicism and this seems a likely occasion for the future King to have pondered the nature of his Christian beliefs. Assuming that Charles agreed with the arguments subsequently advanced by Laud, his motives were both religious and political. For Laud deemed Calvinism to be incompatible with 'the practice of piety and obedience'. On this view, the arrogant certainty of divine election led men equally to despise the 'external ministry' of the Church and to challenge 'civil government in the common-wealth'.[79] It was also implied that Calvinists subscribed to a theory of dominion through grace.[80] Together this constituted an Arminian version, with a vengeance, of the dictum 'no bishop, no king'. The anti-Calvinism of Charles, however, only emerged after he ascended the throne. One of the first intimations of his real beliefs was the York House Conference in February 1626, called to discuss the writings of Richard Montagu. This was chaired by the royal favourite Buckingham, who opened proceedings by announcing his 'good opinion' of Montagu's religious 'soundness'.[81] Buckingham spoke here to a brief supplied by the supporters of Montagu among the bishops and, it can be assumed, with the approbation of Charles.[82]

White writes of the 'absence of any "Puritan" account' of the York House Conference and appears unaware of the versions compiled by John Preston, who was a leading participant at the second session on 17 February.[83] During this second session Preston hammered home the charge of Arminianism against Montagu, especially his maintaining 'election out of foresight or to be a respective condicionall decree'.[84] According to White, 'the published replies to Montagu . . . were more concerned with his alleged Popery' than with 'the charge of Arminianism'.[85] But Bishop Carleton's answer is entirely taken up with Arminianism, as are the contributions of William Prynne and Francis Rous.[86] Between 80 and 90 per cent of Henry Burton's *Plea to an Appeale* and John Yates's *Ibis ad Caesarem* concentrate on Arminianism.[87] *A Second Parallel*, by Daniel Featley, treats of Arminianism and Popery at almost exactly equal length.[88] White's statement only holds true of *A Dangerous Plot*, by Anthony Wotton, where approximately a third of the book is about Arminianism.[89]

By 1629 the question of Arminianism had become a major issue in the House of Commons, and John Pym had established a reputation as the leading expert on the subject among his fellow MPs.[90] Yet, if we are to believe White, no connection exists between this concern about Arminianism and the attack ten years later on the religious policies of the Caroline regime. Laud's archiepiscopate allegedly epitomized the spirit of the Anglican *via media*, and presumably the religious débâcle of 1640 should be understood in terms of Puritan exploitation of the Scottish rebellion. Hence English events are explained by the need to fight a war with Scotland and on the basis of a historical tradition which sees Archbishop Laud and like-minded bishops, during the 1630s, as essentially engaged in a belated stand against Puritanism. The villain of the piece, from this point of view, is the allegedly lax Archbishop Abbot (1611–33). In this perspective the Puritan Abbot, not the Arminian Laud, figures as the odd man out.[91]

There is a danger here of ascribing too much religious significance to particular individuals, even if they happen to be archbishops. None the less

White says almost nothing about Laud's theology. Was Laud in fact an Arminian in his beliefs? Clearly White thinks not. But without doubt Laud was a passionate anti-Calvinist, who denounced the Lambeth Articles as containing 'fatal opinions'. He also condemned Calvinist teaching on reprobation and perseverance. Calvinism, claimed Laud, makes God 'to be the most unreasonable tyrant in the world' and 'teareth up the very foundations of religion'.[92] Such were the views of the man who became Archbishop of Canterbury in 1633, having been promised the job by King Charles as early as 1626.[93] The theology of Laud looks to have been at variance with all his predecessors at Canterbury since the Elizabethan settlement.[94] At the same time, it is important not to underestimate the cautious approach favoured by Laud, compared with some of his rasher Arminian colleagues such as Richard Montagu. Laud would probably have been content simply to suppress all overt discussion of predestinarian theology, so causing Calvinism to wither away by default. In practice, however, Arminian views continued to be licensed for publication during the 1630s, at London, Oxford and Cambridge, thus emphasising the break with the Calvinist past. The authors included Edward Boughen, Thomas Browne, Thomas Chown, John Gore, Thomas Laurence, Edmund Reeve, Robert Shelford and Oliver Whitbie. Between them they taught that saving grace was universal and that both predestination and perseverance were conditional.[95]

The Scottish rebellion did indeed set in train a succession of events which allowed English Calvinists to fight back. Bishop John Davenant was now able to publish his reply to an English Arminian treatise of 1633.[96] His fellow Calvinist episcopalians, chronicling the 'innovations' of the 1630s, claimed that 'some have defended the whole grosse substance of Arminianisme: that "election is from faith forseen", that the act of conversion depends upon the concurrence of man's free will, that the justified man may fall finally and totally from grace', and that 'universal grace' is 'imparted as much to reprobates as to the elect'.[97] The rise of Arminianism, however, also helped to discredit episcopacy as an institution. Thus Arminianism was to the forefront of the 'root and branch' petition of December 1640, calling for the abolition of bishops. The petitioners complained of 'the faintheartedness of ministers to preach the truth of God, lest they should displease the prelates, as namely the doctrine of predestination, of free grace, of perseverance' and 'against universal grace, election for faith forseen [and] freewill'.[98] Furthermore Arminianism featured prominently in the official parliamentary history of Laud's trial.[99] Yet for many people the practical implications of the recent Arminian triumph had been the most alarming – novel ceremonies, attacks on preaching and a resurgent clericalism.[100] There was, too, a tendency to subsume allegations of Arminianism under the general charge of Popery. This lent further potency to the idea of a Popish Plot, in terms of which Charles's opponents increasingly articulated their grievances, both secular and religious.[101] Certainly it is difficult to avoid the conclusion that the Arminian or anti-Calvinist movement was a destabilising force in early seventeenth-century England.

NOTES

I am grateful to Kenneth Fincham and Sears McGee for commenting on my remarks in draft.

1 P. White, 'The Rise of Arminianism Reconsidered', *P and P*, 101 (1983), 34–54; see pp. 132–55 above. For aspects of White's argument, not discussed in the present contribution, see P. Lake, 'Calvinism and the English Church, 1570–1635', *P and P*, 114 (1987), 32–76.

2 White, 'Rise of Arminianism Reconsidered', pp. 35, 39, 44–5, 48, 54.

3 J. Buck, *A Treatise of the Beatitudes* (London, 1637), pp. 283–4. My italics. Arber ed., *Transcript*, iv, p. 349.

4 W. W. Greg ed., *A Companion to Arber* (Oxford, 1967), p. 41.

5 Arber ed., *Transcript*, ii, fo 264.

6 W. Perkins, *A Golden Chaine . . . containing the Order of the Causes of Salvation and Damnation* (London, 1591), sigs A2, B4, T8.

7 Arber ed., *Transcript*, ii, fo 279.

8 G. Babington, *A Sermon preached at Paules Crosse* (London, 1591), pp. 2–3, 8, 14.

9 Arber ed., *Transcript*, iii, fo 43b. This evidence especially has forced a radical alteration of my earlier view of Bancroft: cf. pp. 138, 142 above. The conclusion is inescapable that Bancroft was a 'credal' Calvinist: Lake, 'Calvinism and the English Church', p. 40, n. 19.

10 J. Kimedoncius, *Of the Redemption of Mankind* (London, 1598), pp. 38, 270.

11 J. and W. Nichols eds, *The Works of James Arminius* (London, 1825–75), i, p. 92; R. Abbot, *De Gratia et Perseverantia Sanctorum* (London, 1618), sig. C4v.

12 Z. Ursinus, *The Summe of Christian Religion* (Oxford, 1587), p. 637; R. Some, *Three Questions* (Cambridge, 1596), p. 20.

13 Clark ed., *Register*, pt. i., p. 197; BL, Harleian MS 7038, p. 80. These are my translations from the Latin. For a listing of relevant divinity theses, see Tyacke, *Anti-Calvinists*, pp. 33–48, 60–81. This evidence, together will that of licensing policy, is ignored by White.

14 D. D. Wallace, *Puritans and Predestination: Grace in English Protestant Theology, 1525–1695* (Chapel Hill, 1982), p. 66.

15 Heavy weather has been made by many modern commentators over the Calvinism of John Calvin. Nevertheless Calvin is quite clear that election and reprobation are unconditional, and that God does not will the salvation of all men. J. Calvin, *Institutes of the Christian Religion*, ed. H. Beveridge (London, 1957), ii, pp. 202–58. The passage

concerning 'all men' is to be found on pp. 254–5 of this edition. Unlike most of his followers Calvin allows that in some sense Christ died for all mankind, although this does not alter the unconditional nature of divine predestination: R. T. Kendall, *Calvin and English Calvinism to 1649* (Oxford, 1979), pp. 13–28.

16 Terminological agreement does not, however, appear to lie down this road, because St Augustine changed his mind about predestination and it is therefore possible to quote the earlier writings against the later.

17 White, 'Rise of Arminianism Reconsidered', p. 36.

18 Nichols eds, *Works of James Arminius*, i, p. 96. For the identical views of Arminius, see p. 589.

19 H. C. Porter, *Reformation and Reaction in Tudor Cambridge* (Cambridge, 1958), p. 281. This is the 'simple definition of Arminianism'. Cf. White, 'Rise of Arminianism Reconsidered', p. 41, n. 25.

20 White, 'Rise of Arminianism Reconsidered', p. 37; Porter, *Reformation and Reaction in Tudor Cambridge*, p. 371. My italics.

21 Kimedoncius, *Redemption of Mankind*, pp. 304–5; Ursinus, *Summe of Christian Religion*, p. 643.

22 J. P. Kenyon ed., *The Stuart Constitution* (2nd edn, Cambridge, 1986), p. 137.

23 Porter, *Reformation and Reaction in Tudor Cambridge*, pp. 373–4.

24 J. Strype, *The Life and Acts of John Whitgift* (Oxford, 1822), ii, pp. 280–1; M. Hutton, *Brevis et Dilucida Explicatio . . . de Electione, Praedestinatione ac Reprobatione* (Harderwijk, 1613).

25 White, 'Rise of Arminianism Reconsidered', p. 50.

26 Andreae and Beza ritually refused to shake hands at the conclusion of the Colloquy of Montbéliard and published rival versions of the proceedings. *Acta Colloquii Montis Belligartensis* (Tübingen, 1587); T. Beza, *Ad Acta Colloquii Montisbelgartensis* (Geneva, 1587).

27 In the 1592 edition of this book Huber refers to a first edition of two years earlier. S. Huber, *Theses Christum Jesum esse Mortuum pro Peccatis Totius Generis Humani . . . accessit quoque Confutatio Thesium Kimedoncii* (Tübingen, 1592), sig.):(2. The dedication is dated 26 August 1592.

28 Perkins, *Golden Chaine*, sigs X2–X7.

29 A. Willet, *Synopsis Papismi* (London, 1594), pp. 839–40; J. Dove, *A Sermon preached at Paules Crosse* (London, 1597), pp. 31, 42, 64–5, 71, 74.

30 J. Kimedoncius, *De Redemptione Generis Humani* (Heidelberg, 1592), pp. 58–442. The dedication is dated 12 March 1592.

31 Willet, *Synopsis Papismi*, pp. 839–40.

32 G. Snecanus, *Methodica Descriptio sive Fundamentum Praecipuorum Locorum Communionium, aut Dogmatum S. Scripturae de Cognitione Dei et Hominis huiusque* (Harlem, 1591). Sections eleven and twelve of the *Methodica* are entitled respectively 'De praedestinatione' and 'De distributio causarum salutis et damnationis'. For the influence of Snecanus on Arminius, see C. Bangs, *Arminius: A Study in the Dutch Reformation* (Nashville, Tenn., 1971), pp. 193–4.

33 N. Hemmingsen, *Tractatus de Gratia Universali seu Salutari Omnibus Hominibus* (Copenhagen, 1591). This also includes a piece entitled 'De libero arbitrio'.

34 Willet, *Synopsis Papismi*, p. 841.

35 Nichols eds, *Works of James Arminius*, i, pp. 91–2. Baro also cites Snecanus (p. 96).

36 *Ibid.*, pp. 91–100. For the fullest discussion to date of Baro's views, see Porter, *Reformation and Reaction in Tudor Cambridge*, pp. 376–90.

37 D. Baudius, *Epistolarum Centuriae Tres* (Leiden, 1620), p. 731; I. Casaubon, *Epistolae* (Rotterdam, 1709), nos. 12–13; P. C. Molhuysen and B. L. Meulenbroek eds, *Briefwisseling van Hugo Grotius* (The Hague, 1928–81), i, pp. 240–4, 607.

38 OUA, Hyp. B. 20, fos 18r–v, Tyacke, *Anti-Calvinists*, pp. 65–7.

39 G. Ornsby ed., *The Correspondence of John Cosin* (Surtees Soc., lii, lv, 1869–72), i. pp. 68, 90.

40 Wallace, *Puritans and Predestination*, pp. 20–4, 31, 35, 38–40.

41 T. Fuller, *The Church History of Britain*, ed. J. S. Brewer (Oxford, 1845), v, p. 219; Arber ed., *Transcript*, iii, fo 136b.

42 G. Bucanus, *Institutions of Christian Religion* (London, 1606), sig. A7, pp. 431, 433–4.

43 PRO, PROB 11/115, fo 60v.

44 G. Abbot, *An Exposition upon the Prophet Jonah* (London, 1600), p. 230.

45 Arber ed., *Transcript of the Registers of the Company of Stationers*, iii, fo 213b.

46 C. Richardson, *The Repentance of Peter and Judas* (London, 1612), pp. 51, 98.

47 For a systematic analysis of some of this printed material, see Tyacke, *Anti-Calvinists*, pp. 248–65.

48 *Ibid.*, pp. 33–48, 60–81.

49 *The Collegiat Suffrage of Great Britaine* (London, 1629); Tyacke, *Anti-Calvinists*, pp. 87–105. Cf. White, 'Rise of Arminianism Reconsidered', p. 44.

50 An English translation of Overall's Latin commentary on the Arminian controversy is to be found in W. Goode, *The Doctrine of the Church of England as to the Effects of Baptism in the Case of Infants* (London, 1850), pp. 127–30. [Mine certainly seems the most plausible interpretation of Overall's views concerning predestination.]

51 Molhuysen and Meulenbroek eds, *Briefwisseling van Hugo Grotius*, i, pp. 240–4, 607.

52 J. P. Wilson and J. Bliss eds, *The Works of Lancelot Andrewes* (Oxford, 1841–54), vi, pp. 296–8; [N. Tyacke, 'Lancelot Andrewes and the Myth of Anglicanism', in P. Lake and M. Questier eds, *Conformity and Orthodoxy in the English Church, c. 1560–1660* (Woodridge, 2000), pp. 12–14, 18.] S. Harsnett, *A Fourth Sermon*, appended to Richard Steward, *Three Sermons* (London, 1656), pp. 154–5.

53 White, 'Rise of Arminianism Reconsidered', p. 45.

54 An example of the genre is Matthew Sutcliffe. 'Papistes' say 'that men are predestinated for their merites' and 'reprobated for their sinnes foreseene before': M. Sutcliffe, *An Abridgement or Survey of Poperie* (London, 1606), pp. 2, 9.

55 G. Carleton, *An Examination of those Things wherein the Author of the Late Appeale [Richard Montagu] holdeth the Doctrines of the Pelagians and Arminians to be the Doctrines of the Church of England* (London, 1626), pp. 1, 14. According to White, Bishop Carleton

was part of the Anglican consensus: White, 'Rise of Arminianism Reconsidered', p. 45. Carleton, it is true, preferred to speak of absolute 'dereliction' rather than 'reprobation', but this did not affect the inevitable condemnation of the non-elect (*Examination*, p. 24).

56 R. Montagu, *A Gagg for the New Gospell? No, a New Gagg for an Old Goose* (London, 1624), p. 179; *Appello Caesarem: A Just Appeale from Two Unjust Informers* (London, 1625), pp. 49, 58.

57 Montagu, *New Gagg for an Old Goose*, p. 158.

58 Montagu, *Appello Caesarem*, sig. a3r–v.

59 F. Rous, *Testis Veritatis: The Doctrine of King James . . . of the Church of England* [and] *of the Catholicke Church, plainely showed to bee One in the Points of Praedestination, Free-Will* [and] *Certaintie of Salvation* (London, 1626), sig. A2.

60 Cf. White, 'Rise of Arminianism Reconsidered', pp. 47–8.

61 Rous, *Testis Veritatis*, pp. 2–3.

62 Arber ed., *Transcript*, iii, fo 147b.

63 T. Sparke, *A Brotherly Perswasion to Unitie and Uniformitie* (London, 1607), p. 3.

64 P. Schaff ed., *The History of the Creeds* (London, 1877–78), iii, pp. 523–4, 534.

65 White, 'Rise of Arminianism Reconsidered', p. 34. My exact words were: 'fear of approaching death may also have helped sap his [James's] confidence in deterministic teaching': see p. 143 above. *Timor mortis* and senility are not normally considered the same thing.

66 K. Fincham and P. Lake, 'The Ecclesiastical Policy of King James I', *JBS Studies*, 24 (1985), 202–6.

67 White, 'Rise of Arminianism Reconsidered', pp. 45–8.

68 R. C. Johnson, M. F. Keeler, M. J. Cole and W. B. Bidwell eds, *Commons Debates, 1628* (New Haven, 1977–78), iv, p. 313.

69 *APC 1627*, p. 253. Cf. White, 'Rise of Arminianism Reconsidered', p. 51.

70 Kenyon ed., *Stuart Constitution*, pp. 138–9; S. R. Gardiner ed., *The Constitutional Documents of the Puritan Revolution* (Oxford, 1906), pp. 75–6.

71 White, 'Rise of Arminianism Reconsidered', pp. 50–1.

72 Tyacke, *Anti-Calvinists*, pp. 48, 249. [The 'embargo' relates to Paul's Cross sermons.]

73 BL, Harleian MS. 7038, p. 80 [now see p. 10 above]. For a discussion of Neile's own theological views, see Tyacke, *Anti-Calvinists*, pp. 111–13.

74 Wallace, *Puritans and Predestination*, pp. 38–9.

75 Tyacke, *Anti-Calvinists*, p. 81; Clark ed., *Register of the University of Oxford*, ii, pt. i, p. 194.

76 Tyacke, *Anti-Calvinists*, pp. 66–7, 121.

77 T. Jackson, *A Treatise of the Divine Essence and Attributes* (London, 1628), sig. *3r–v, pp. 120, 125, 165–72, 180, 201. My italics. See also pp. 22–3 above.

78 Arber ed., *Transcript*, iv, pp. 98, 150. Bishop Montaigne had thrown in his lot with the Arminian party by 1625. More to the point, perhaps, is that both Thomas Jackson

and Richard Montagu were the protégés of Bishop Neile: Tyacke, *Anti-Calvinists*, pp. 120–1.

79 Kenyon ed., *Stuart Constitution*, p. 137. Cf. p. 144 above.

80 At the Oxford Act in 1639, Thomas Weekes denied that 'temporal dominion is founded in grace': OUA, NEP/*Supra*/16, register Q, fo 180 (my translation from Latin). Weekes was a chaplain of Bishop William Juxon of London and fellow of St John's College, Oxford. His thesis most probably has reference to the Scottish rebellion.

81 J. Sansom ed., *The Works of John Cosin* (Oxford, 1843–55), ii, p. 22.

82 Laud, *Works*, vi, p. 249.

83 White, 'Rise of Arminianism Reconsidered', p. 49; T. Ball, *The Life of the Renowned Dr Preston*, ed. E. W. Harcourt (London, 1885), pp. 118–41.

84 BL, Harleian MS. 6866, fos 77r–v.

85 White, 'Rise of Arminianism Reconsidered', p. 47.

86 Carleton, *Examination*; W. Prynne, *The Perpetuitie of a Regenerate Man's Estate* (London, 1626); Rous, *Testis Veritatis*.

87 H. Burton, *A Plea to an Appeale, traversed Dialogue Wise* (London, 1626), pp. 13–93; J. Yates, *Ibis ad Caesarem: or, A Submissive Appearance before Caesar, in Answer to Mr Montague's Appeal in the Points of Arminianisme and Popery, maintained and defended by Him, against the Doctrine of the Church of England* (London, 1626), pt. i, pp. 1–95, pt. ii, pp. 1–168.

88 D. Featley, *A Second Parallel together with a Writ of Error sued against the Appealer* (London, 1626), pt. 1, pp. 1–95 (Arminianism), pt. 2, pp. 1–97 (Popery).

89 A. Wotton, *A Dangerous Plot discovered . . . wherein is proved that R. Mountague . . . laboureth to bring in the Faith of Rome and Arminius* (London, 1626), pt. 1, pp. 52–83, pt. 2, pp. 37–80, 126–68.

90 Tyacke, *Anti-Calvinists*, pp. 154, 160–3.

91 This interpretation, like much of the ultra-revisionist case, can be found in Clarendon's *History of the Rebellion and Civil Wars in England*, ed. W. D. Macray (Oxford, 1888), i, pp. 118–19, 126. The most recent assessment of Archbishop Abbot, however, suggests a high degree of continuity between his rule and that of Archbishop Bancroft. Moreover Bancroft regarded the religious proclivities of Laud's circle generally as deeply suspect. Fincham and Lake, 'Ecclesiastical Policy of King James I', pp. 188–9; K. Fincham, 'Prelacy and Politics: Archbishop Abbot's Defence of Protestant Orthodoxy', *HR* 61 (1988), 36–64.

92 Kenyon ed., *Stuart Constitution*, p. 137; Laud, *Works*, vi, pp. 132–3. The views of Laud on these matters are discussed in Tyacke, *Anti-Calvinists*, pp. 70, 266–70. His remarks indicate that he rejected 'credal' as well as 'experimental' Calvinism. For this distinction, see Lake, 'Calvinism and the English Church', pp. 39–41.

93 Laud, *Works*, iii, p. 196.

94 For Archbishop Matthew Parker, see the Calvinist marginalia in the officially authorized Bishop's Bible of 1568, especially relating to Romans ix. This particular note reads that 'the will and purpose of God is the cause of . . . election and reprobation. For his mercy and calling through Christ are the means of salvation and the withdrawing of his mercy is the cause of damnation'. B. F. Westcott, *A General View of the English*

Bible (London, 1905), pp. 96–7, 244. Parker exercised general editorial control over this project. The Calvinism of Archbishop Edmund Grindal emerges most clearly from his surviving correspondence: Wallace, *Puritans and Predestination*, pp. 34–5.

95 Tyacke, *Anti-Calvinists*, pp. 53, 83, 184–5, 216–19.

96 J. Davenant, *Animadversions upon a Treatise intitled God's Love to Mankind* (Cambridge, 1641). This was a reply to S. Hoard and H. Mason, *God's Love to Mankind, manifested by disprooving his Absolute Decree for their Damnation* ([London], 1633). Davenant, who had been a member of the British delegation to the Synod of Dort, is one of White's so-called Anglicans: White, 'Rise of Arminianism Reconsidered', p. 45. But see Lake, 'Calvinism and the English Church', pp. 63–5.

97 W. A. Shaw, *A History of the English Church during the Civil Wars and under the Commonwealth, 1640–1660* (London, 1900), ii, p. 288. This passage is partly my translation from Latin.

98 Gardiner ed., *Constitutional Documents of the Puritan Revolution*, p. 138.

99 W. Prynne, *Canterburies Doome: or, The First Part of a Compleat History of the Commitment, Charge, Tryall, Condemnation [and] Execution of William Laud, Late Archbishop of Canterbury* (London, 1646), pp. 155–78, 219–20, 303–13. Cf. White, 'Rise of Arminianism Reconsidered', pp. 53–4.

100 Tyacke, *Anti-Calvinists*, pp. 181–244. Particularly important was the sacramental dimension to English Arminianism which led, among other things, to the widespread conversion of communion tables into altars.

101 *Ibid.*, pp. 235–8, 242–4.

Chapter 7

———————◆———————

Anglican attitudes: some recent writings on English religious history, from the Reformation to the Civil War

I

I T remains a commonplace that what historians write bears some relation to their own time and particular angle of vision. Less often remarked, however, is the tendency for historical interpretations to acquire lives of their own, at least partly independent of the original circumstances that produced them, and to enter as it were the intellectual bloodstream of subsequent generations. A good illustration of this latter proposition is afforded by the history of the English Church. For, since at least the seventeenth century, the very radicalism of the Reformation has proved a continuing source of embarrassment to a section of Church of England opinion; rather than frankly admit their own dissent from the views of many of the Tudor founding fathers, they have regularly sought to rewrite the past in the light of the present. This conservative vision has come to be expressed in terms of a so-called *via media*, which is deemed to have characterised the English or 'Anglican' way of religious reform.[1]

Until quite recently, the historiography was heavily influenced by these same Anglican insiders, other historians being prepared largely to take on trust their claims – especially as regards theological change. Moreover, willingness to follow what is in effect a party line has now received powerful reinforcement from certain revisionist historians, who discern a congruence between the alleged moderation of Anglicanism and their own commitment to a consensual model of English politics in the decades before the Civil War. The old idea of the English Church as epitomising a mean between the extremes of Protestantism and Catholicism is once more being pressed into service. Thus a new historiographical alliance has been created, between those concerned primarily to defend a particular reading of English religious history and others who emphasise the play of the contingent and unforeseen in explaining the crisis of 1640–42. Both these components are to some extent present in the wide-ranging article by George Bernard, published in the journal *History* during 1990.[2]

At one level Bernard provides a classic, if rather exaggerated, example of old-style Anglican apologetic. Ostensibly writing about the English Church from *c.* 1529 to *c.* 1642, he none the less omits the crucial reign of Edward VI; conversely, no real distinction is drawn between religious developments under Henry VIII and later. Yet England became a Protestant country at the official level only after the death of Henry VIII in 1547, moving thereafter fairly rapidly toward a Reformed position – influenced especially by the Continental theologians Martin Bucer and Peter Martyr, who were installed at Cambridge and Oxford, respectively. The liturgies and other formularies produced during the years 1547–53 mark a clear break with what had gone before, despite some continuity of personnel – notably, Archbishop Thomas Cranmer. Furthermore, the officially sponsored iconoclasm from cathedral down to parish level can have left people in little doubt that they were living through a time of drastic change. After the brief Marian restoration of Catholicism, it was essentially the Edwardian Church which came back under Elizabeth in 1558.[3] Bernard, however, like his historiographical forbears, proceeds to read off the Elizabethan settlement of religion in terms of its purported *Henrician* antecedents. At the same time, he invokes the notion of a 'monarchical church', as serving to define the nature of the English Reformation. From this point of view, it was the jurisdictional break with Rome and not the ensuing religious changes that mattered. The priorities of England's monarchical church were political stability rather than Protestantism and, hence, what Bernard sees as recurring attempts to balance competing religious interests. We are in fact presented here with a politically driven concept of the Anglican middle way, but one which appears to depend on abolishing Protestantism from the historical record.

There is too an underlying confusion, between the obvious desire of any regime to promote stability and the particular brand of Christianity obtaining in a given part of Europe from the sixteenth century onward. Bernard's main purpose, however, is to argue against the proposition that the English Church went through a Calvinist phase. The implication is that given the political imperatives of the monarchical church any such development was logically impossible. Nevertheless, historical reality has a way of defying the strict rules of logic, all the more so when the initial premise is in doubt. Bernard complains that those who have argued for a period of Calvinist dominance in the English Church begin their accounts '*in medias res*' – that is to say, the 1590s. Let us then take up his challenge and return *ad fontes*. Elizabethan doctrinal developments, as we have already indicated, must be understood in terms of an Edwardian legacy. While much is often made of the fact that Elizabeth's first Archbishop of Canterbury, Matthew Parker, was uncontaminated by Marian exile, it is conveniently forgotten that he had been the Cambridge intimate of Bucer. As early as 1536, in a work dedicated to Cranmer, Bucer had expounded predestination and the theology of grace more generally along lines later to be called Calvinist. In his lectures as Regius professor of divinity, at Edwardian Cambridge, Bucer reiterated this doctrine. Meanwhile at Edwardian Oxford, also as Regius professor, Martyr can be found lecturing in similar vein.[4] Again, the famous Elizabethan Thirty-nine Articles are a revised version of the Edwardian Forty-two Articles of 1553. In the latter context, what is noteworthy is not their skirting around the doctrine of reprobation – God's 'sentence' – but that unconditional predestination has a long article devoted entirely to it at so early a date.[5] While the teaching of Bucer and Martyr exercised no monopoly among English protestants, the indications are that it was becoming increasingly influential by the death of Edward VI.

Unlike some later commentators, leading Elizabethan Protestants were proud to acknowledge how much they owed to Bucer and Martyr. Walter Haddon, writing at the behest of the English government in 1563, went out of his way to acknowledge that debt and at the same time did not hesitate to defend predestination – both double and absolute.[6] Back in 1551, Haddon had delivered the oration at Bucer's funeral and Parker the sermon. Moreover, the continuing pamphlet exchanges during the 1560s between Haddon and the Catholic controversialist Jerome Osorio came to turn increasingly on predestination. After the death of Haddon, John Foxe took up the uncompleted task of replying, and a joint work was published in 1577 – with some hundred pages devoted to maintaining absolute predestination.[7] Such Reformed teaching did not, however, go uncontested, and for the first two decades of Elizabeth's reign Lutheran treatises, either in Latin or English translation, propagated an alternative doctrine. The most important author in this context was the Danish Lutheran Neils Hemmingsen. Nevertheless, after about 1580 anti-Calvinist views (as we may now call them) apparently ceased to be printed in England, probably reflecting a tightening of religious censorship.[8] Some of those concurrently in the forefront of making Calvinist doctrine available in translation were undoubtedly Puritans, such as John Field. At the same time, however, dedicatees of these books included Archbishop Edmund Grindal.[9] The foregoing story has never been investigated in any detail, but enough is already known to suggest that the mid-1590s saw a somewhat desperate attempt by English Lutherans (for want of a better term) to fight back. Although this episode, which produced the notorious Lambeth Articles, is still much disputed by historians, it would be difficult to argue that the Lutherans then regained ground previously lost.

The Anglican school, with which Bernard chooses here to identify, has always objected strongly to the employment of such continental religious terminology in an English context, but it is incontestable that much of the Elizabethan debate on subjects like predestination was conducted through the medium of foreign authors – either Latin re-publications or English translations. Bernard also proves surprisingly slapdash in his account of the argument that he wishes to refute. Thus we are told that the present writer has claimed that 'the dominant doctrine in the early seventeenth-century Church of England was predestination', subsequently coming under attack from 'a group of Arminians ... who allegedly followed the teaching of the Dutch theologian Arminius', and I am chided for neglecting the 'realities of religious life in the parishes'.[10] It would indeed be a rash historian who claimed to have isolated the 'dominant doctrine' purveyed countrywide, at this or any other period, although such religious teaching is likely to have been fairly platitudinous and certainly nothing so relatively esoteric as pre-destination. The 'dominance' in question relates to that formulation of the theology of grace most favored by the clerical leadership at various dates. (It is important, however, to emphasise that the early modern disputes about predestination did revolve around the central topic of salvation.) Nor are English anti-Calvinists deemed by me to have '*followed* the teaching' of Arminius.[11] Furthermore, the concept of dominance itself implies the continued existence of different, less influential teaching. None the less, it is becoming increasingly clear that English and Dutch anti-Calvinists shared a common ancestor in second-generation Lutheranism, specifically involving the work of Hemmingsen.[12]

Bernard and a number of other historians, notably, Sheila Lambert, seek in addition to undermine the notion of Calvinist dominance, prior to the 1620s, by reference to the undisputed fact that some anti-Calvinists became Jacobean bishops. The fallacy, however, of such arguments is that they fail to distinguish the key appointments, to Canterbury and London, and how power was actually exercised.[13] Regardless of the precise religious sympathies of James I, the *de facto* situation was that until the 1620s Calvinists generally controlled the English licensing of religious books, under the aegis of Canterbury and London in the capital, and the determination of orthodoxy in university disputations.[14] The evidence on both these counts seems over-whelming and has certainly not been adequately addressed by would-be critics. It was a balance of forces which shifted only in the last years of James. Nevertheless, for Bernard, and those who think like him, the religious policies pursued by Charles I were continuous with those of his predecessor and indeed the Tudor Church. Significantly, he has little to say about the doctrines at issue in the controversy surrounding the publications of Richard Montagu, during the 1620s. But the teaching of Montagu, as we shall see, especially in his *Appello Caesarem* of 1625, was actually more dogmatically anti-Calvinist than either Arminius himself or the *Remonstrance* drawn up by his Dutch followers in 1610. Montagu dared to say things they had left unsaid.[15] Moreover, the upshot of the Montagu controversy was to end a period of Calvinist dominance, traceable from at least the 1580s. Despite his stress on contextualisation, Bernard fails to consider either this point or its bearing on the question of Puritanism. For, with the English Church now increasingly seen as purveying false doctrine, a new and destabilizing element had been introduced. Purity of doctrine, after all, was one of the conventional marks of a true church.

Part and parcel of Bernard's case, and that of other revisionists, is that no serious religious tensions existed in England before the Scottish rebellion of the late 1630s. The latter, like some *deus ex machina*, is seen as a sufficient explanation of all that followed thereafter. To this end, these revisionists play down the importance both of Puritanism and of ceremonial innovation during the 1630s – the imposition of what contemporaries called the 'new' as opposed to the 'old conformity'. The numbers of Puritans are deemed insignificant, and much of the ceremonial change that occurred is ascribed to local rather than central initiatives. Also denied is any link between doctrine and outward forms, especially the alterations to communion tables in parish churches.[16] Indeed, the rise of Arminianism itself is written off as a myth put about by a handful of Puritans, led by the infamous William Prynne. Those attracted especially by this last argument are now able to cite a book-length study by Peter White, which traverses the same chronological ground as Bernard but concentrates almost exclusively on doctrinal developments.

II

White is the leading spokesman for the Anglican wing of the revisionist alliance of Civil War historians. His avowed purpose is to reaffirm the continued existence of an Anglican *via media* in doctrine, stretching from the days of Henry VIII to those of Charles I. White's book, *Predestination, Policy and Polemic*, consists of a series of case studies devoted to a number of theological writers, interspersed with expositions of particular episodes and periods. The alliteration of the title refers both to the interconnectedness of religion and politics and to what the author regards as the polemical distortions of a middle ground normally inhabited by most theologians. Indeed, White goes so far as to define theology proper as consisting in 'the resolution of the great antinomies, of nature and grace, of freedom and necessity, of faith and works', thus effectively privileging his own conception of a doctrinal *via media*. A further consequence is that whole swathes of religious writing can be dismissed as theologically irrelevant because essentially polemical.

Perhaps unsurprisingly, White claims to find few Calvinists or Arminians in pre-Civil War England. Not content, however, with this loading of the dice, he proceeds to define his doctrinal terms in such a way as to eliminate most contenders. Despite the fact that English Calvinists by the early seventeenth century were generally sublapsarians, who conceived of fallen man as the object of predestination, we are presented with a *creabilitarian* definition of Calvinism: 'the doctrine that the decree to predestinate is logically prior . . . to the decree to create'. This is, of course, an even more extreme doctrinal position than the usual supralapsarian alternative to sublapsarianism: 'the doctrine that the decree to predestinate was logically prior to the decree to permit the fall'. Creabilitarianism is a complete red herring.[17]

On the subject of Arminianism, the attempt of White at definition is so opaque as to leave the reader with no real criterion by which to judge particular allegations. Arminius, however, conveniently summed up the difference between himself and his opponents, in the form of the following double-barrelled question: 'Do we believe because we have been elected, or are we elected because we believe?' What is more, this formulation is an acknowledged borrowing from Hemmingsen. White, however, both fails to quote this passage and denies that Arminius had 'any direct link with Lutheranism'. Nevertheless, Petrus Bertius, in his funeral oration of 1609, indicated that Arminius abandoned Calvinism under the influence of Philipp Melanchthon and Hemmingsen. Moreover, Hemmingsen and Arminius answered their own question in terms usually expressed as predestination *ex praevisa fide* – from foresight of faith. A handy source of Dutch Arminian doctrine, although one not used by White, is also provided by their *Remonstrance* of 1610. This maintains that predestination is conditional on faith, the offer of grace unrestricted, and its working on the will not infallible.[18]

Clearly White regards himself as specially equipped theologically, at various points alluding to the alleged incompetence of others. We are also encouraged in this opinion by the very flattering pre-reviews printed on the dust jacket. This book, John Guy tells us, is 'a brilliant, and breathtakingly learned, exposition'. According to John Morrill, it exhibits a 'rare ambition and authority'. All the more disappointing then that White provides such a careless analysis of the views he seeks to discredit, in the following terms: 'Doctrinally, it is asserted, the English Church was *uniformly* "Calvinist" from the beginning of the reign of Elizabeth'; not, 'it is argued, until the 1590s' was Calvinism '*first* challenged' in England, involving an '*Arminian assertion of "the free will of all men to obtain salvation"*'; nevertheless, 'the majority of the clergy and probably *most of the laity*' remained 'convinced predestinarians'; this Calvinist 'consensus' was only overthrown after the accession of Charles I, and the 'English Civil War is . . . seen as *primarily* the result'.[19] Unfortunately much of the foregoing (as indicated by italics) is a caricature of the historical argument actually advanced. It also involves at least two serious misquotations from a twenty-year-old essay of mine. What I then wrote was that 'the essence of Arminianism was a belief in God's *universal grace* and the free will of all men to obtain salvation', and that 'at the beginning of the seventeenth century, a majority of the clergy . . . were Calvinist in doctrine, and the same was probably true of the *more educated laity*'.[20] Since most of the population were illiterate at the time, this last point is no mere pedantry. Worse, the mangled quotation about free will implies that the present writer does not understand the difference between Arminianism and Pelagianism, the latter denying a need for grace. None of this augurs well for White's likely treatment of sixteenth- and seventeenth-century authors.

True to his Anglican paradigm, White early on glosses official Edwardian doctrine in terms of its Henrician antecedents. This proves all the more necessary because of the damaging admissions he feels compelled to make about the unconditional predestinarianism of Bucer and Martyr. But the King's Book of 1543, produced at the height of the Henrician Catholic reaction, and the Forty-two Articles of 1553 are in reality worlds apart. The former inculcates, among other things, transubstantiation and justification by works as well as faith, in addition to emphasising free will in a way that many Edwardian Protestants would find deeply offensive. White rightly points out that some of the Edwardian leaders, preeminently John Hooper and Hugh Latimer, held views on predestination very different from Bucer and Martyr. Latimer was pretty clearly what in later parlance would be called an Arminian.[21] The question, however, remains as to where the theological center of gravity had come to rest by the death of Edward VI. Remarkably, we still lack a modern and authoritative account of the Edwardian Reformation that might enable us to answer that question with confidence. Yet the role of Cranmer appears crucial, particularly in the formulation of the Forty-two Articles – produced at the very end of the reign. Given the likely competing pressures on him, the fairly uncompromising stance on predestination, of article 17, is all the more striking. Thus there is no suggestion that election – 'predestination to life' – is conditional on faith. On the contrary, 'such as have so excellent a benefit of God given unto them, be called according to God's purpose, by his spirit working in due season, they through grace obey the calling, they be justified freely, they be made sons by adoption, they be made like the image of God's only begotten son Jesus Christ, they walk religiously in good works, and at length by God's mercy, they attain to everlasting felicity'. The word 'reprobation' is not used as such, although it occurs in the associated *Reformatio Legum Ecclesiasticarum*. Nevertheless, the article does refer to the pastoral danger that consideration of the 'sentence of God's predestination' may drive 'curious and carnal persons, lacking the spirit of Christ', to 'desperation or into recklessness of most unclean living'. At the very least, we are dealing here with a concept of non-election – the negative counterpart to 'the everlasting purpose of God . . . to deliver from curse and damnation those whom he hath chosen out of mankind'.[22]

With some very slight changes, the Edwardian article on predestination was incorporated into the Elizabethan Thirty-nine Articles of 1563. Meanwhile, the related Oxford and Cambridge lectures of Martyr and Bucer were published in the years immediately preceding; those by Martyr came out in 1559, dedicated to Sir Anthony Cooke, while Bucer's appeared in 1562, dedicated by the editor to Sir Nicholas Throckmorton.[23] We have already noted the 1563 exchange between Haddon and Osorio on the same subject. Apparently unaware of these developments, White chooses to discuss instead the views of the Elizabethan Protestant apologist John Jewel. In the light of the well-known close personal links between Jewel and Martyr, we might have expected them to hold similar theological views. White, however, uses Jewel's published sermons on Thessalonians in order to deny this. Yet, employing the same source, it is possible to reach a different conclusion and one more in line with our initial expectations. Jewel speaks of the 'company of the faithful', their 'names written in the book of life', the 'elect', who 'shall never perish'. He cites St Augustine that to one 'it is given to believe, to the other it is not given'. God 'only disposeth the ways of men' and 'knoweth whom he will bring to be of his fold'. As for the 'wicked', this 'is a token of God's heavy displeasure upon them that they repent not of their former evils, but grow worse and worse'. Those who Antichrist will deceive are they 'whose names are not written in the book of life'. But 'God hath chosen you from the beginning; his election is sure for ever'. You 'shall not fall from grace, you shall not perish'. None of these passages, however, are quoted by White. Moreover, looking ahead, he concludes that there is 'nothing' in Jewel 'which would have helped the Cambridge opponents of Baro and Barrett in the conflict that led to the Lambeth Articles'. His deduction is the more extraordinary because Peter Baro, like Arminius, taught predestination *ex praevisa fide*.[24]

Appropriately enough, White then turns to a consideration of Henry Bullinger, whose *Decades* acquired a quasi-official status in Elizabethan England. The discussion which follows, however, is very confused, with contrary positions being ascribed to Bullinger in successive paragraphs. First we are told that Bullinger's teaching on 'election' is a 'remarkable and explicit anticipation of what was later called Arminianism'. But then we learn that Bullinger taught that 'faith is the *result* of election'. A possible explanation might be that Bullinger had changed his mind, yet White assures us that he 'never withdrew' his earlier remarks. In fact, the doctrine of the *Decades* is compatible with what comes to be known as sublapsarian Calvinism. Here and elsewhere, White appears to mix up the latter with what he calls 'single predestination', although no definition is provided.[25] Moreover, on the face of it, rather surprising is that, among other continental theologians 'popular' in Elizabethan England, Hemmingsen rates less than two pages. Can this be because Hemmingsen's strong endorsement of conditional predestinarian views undermines the concept of a doctrinal 'spectrum' so much canvassed by White? Equally sketchy is the treatment afforded the sermon preached by Samuel Harsnett at Paul's Cross, in 1584. The context of this anti-Calvinist sermon, which nearly ruined Harsnett's career, cries out for investigation. According to White, however, it was not the doctrinal content of what Harsnett preached that got him into trouble with Archbishop John Whitgift, but making 'Geneva his target'. This seems highly unlikely, not least because of the type of predestinarian teaching that Whitgift can be found personally licensing only a few years afterward.[26]

While it is indeed the case that the doctrinal controversies of the 1590s, culminating in the Lambeth Articles, need to be viewed in the light of the contemporary Puritan vogue for supralapsarian teaching on predestination, it does not follow that the disputes were simply Puritan-inspired. A major contributor, for instance, was Bishop Gervase Babington.[27] White also signally fails to recognise the three-cornered nature of these debates, involving Arminians *avant la lettre* and Calvinists of both supralapsarian and sublapsarian varieties. He resolutely refuses to accept that the archbishops of Canterbury and York, Whitgift and Matthew Hutton, were either of them 'in any meaningful sense a Calvinist', and sees the Lambeth Articles as intended 'to put a rein on both Calvinists and anti-Calvinists' alike. This interpretation, however, is only possible because of White's exclusive definition of Calvinism. In actuality, both Whitgift and Hutton, as well as the Lambeth Articles, are best understood as speaking the language of *sublapsarian* Calvinism. Albeit positing fallen man as the object of predestination, such Calvinists still taught an unconditional form of double predestination. Just how much turns on this point can be illustrated by the fact that the canons of the Synod of Dort, which condemned Arminianism in 1619, similarly enshrined sublapsarian Calvinism. Furthermore, underlying the Cambridge crisis in 1595 were the teachings of Peter Baro – the Lady Margaret professor of divinity. Here it is vital to grasp that Baro, like Hemmingsen and Arminius, taught predestination *ex praevisa fide* – that is, election was conditional on belief. To describe the Arminianism of Baro, albeit *avant la lettre*, as coming across as rather muffled in White's account would be an understatement. But, as even White concedes, Baro was the main 'target' of the Cambridge Calvinists. A final irony is that in outlining the doctrinal position of Archbishop Hutton, White actually provides a working definition of sublapsarian Calvinism, although he seems quite unaware of this. 'Election refers to the purpose of God to separate in Christ those he has chosen out of the corrupt mass. The reprobate are those who are left in the mass.'[28]

In the Anglican tradition, Richard Hooker is regarded as a kind of keeper of the lamp – the theologian whose writings above all illuminate the *via media*. Understandably, White objects strongly to the recent demonstration, at the hands of Peter Lake, of just how *avant-garde* Hooker was. Hooker matters, so Lake argues, not so much for his implicit anti-Calvinism as for his articulation of a new style of sacrament-centered piety that came to its full fruition during the Laudian ascendancy. Lake has now gone on to trace these Hookerian developments in the Jacobean Church, particularly in the thought and practice of those two seminal figures Lancelot Andrewes and John Buckeridge.[29] White, by contrast, reiterates the conventional view of Hooker as spokesman for a middle way, which continued to characterise the English Church after the accession of James I. Yet at the Hampton Court Conference of 1604, the Puritans sought to press home the attack on Arminianism *avant la lettre*. Granted that they failed in their bid to have the teaching of the Thirty-nine Articles tightened up as regards predestination, a revised commentary on the articles by Archbishop Richard Bancroft's chaplain, Thomas Rogers, was published in 1607. White remains adamant that Rogers did not take 'a "Calvinist" stance on the matters in dispute at Cambridge in the 1590s'. Again, however, the text is capable of yielding a different and Calvinist answer. The first point to make is that Rogers quite explicitly interprets article 17, on predestination, in the light of the Second Helvetic, Gallican, and Belgic Reformed confessions of faith. Second, Rogers maintains that both election and reprobation are unconditional: 'Of the mere will and purpose of God some men in Christ Jesus are elected, *and not others*, unto salvation.' Opposed to this is the view that 'God beheld in every man whether he would use his grace well, and believe the gospel or no; and as he saw a man affected, so he did predestinate, choose, or *refuse* him.' Furthermore, another error is that 'no certain company be foredestined unto eternal condemnation'. There is no suggestion in Rogers that anyone other than the elect can achieve salvation. Nor should we be surprised that Rogers was chaplain to Bancroft, since the latter as bishop of London can be found personally licensing a full-blooded Calvinist treatise in 1598.[30]

Even when confronted with so obvious a Jacobean Calvinist as Robert Abbot, brother of the archbishop of Canterbury, White seeks to distinguish between his eirenical and polemical 'faces'. Only the former is deemed to represent genuine 'theology'. But since the distinction hinges on Abbot's being a sublapsarian Calvinist, which is manifest throughout his published work, it appears meaningless.[31] The treatment, however, of the anti-Calvinists John Overall and Richard Thomson, as alleged exponents of the Anglican middle way, calls for more discussion here. In Overall, at least, we have a genuine *single* predestinarian, that is to say someone who apparently taught that there existed a special category of unconditionally elect side by side with others, probably a majority, who might or might not with the assistance of God's grace achieve salvation. This is quite different from the sublapsarian Calvinist view that the reprobate are condemned as a consequence of original sin. By contrast, Overall's formulation granted the essence of the Arminian case, namely, that the 'promise of the Gospel' is 'conditional'.[32] Richard Thomson may also have been a single predestinarian. Certainly Overall helped to arrange for the posthumous publication abroad of Thomson's treatise *De Amissione et Intercisione Gratiae*, in 1616. Nevertheless, what must strike any reader who compares Thomson's *De Amissione* with the *De Sanctorum Perseverantia et Apostasia* of the Dutch Arminian Petrus Bertius, first published in 1610, is how closely allied they are. Indeed, apart from the choice of title by Bertius, his views on falling from grace seem almost indistinguishable from those of Thomson. Both teach that the truly justified may fall, temporarily or permanently. Apropos the falls of the elect, Thomson speaks of 'intercision' rather than 'apostasy'. Neither taught that the elect could fall finally; this would anyway have involved a contradiction as regards election *ex praevisa fide*, which assumes faith at the last. None of this is explained by White or, in the case of Bertius, even mentioned. Instead, we are told that 'no theologian in the Church of England taught that the elect might fall finally in this period'. Yet, even on White's own previous showing, neither did Arminius.[33] Such are some of the foundations of the purported *via media* in doctrine.

The participation of a British delegation at the Synod of Dort, which condemned Arminianism in 1619, has always posed a potential problem for those writing from an Anglican standpoint. Until recently they tended to ignore it. Since this is no longer possible, they are now obliged to explain Dort away. But, rather than ascribe these events to the international exigencies of the time, White questions the Calvinism of the delegation itself. Indeed he goes further, claiming that the Dort debates 'confirmed' the 'thrust of English theology' as 'a middle way', that 'concentrated on fundamentals and avoided extremes, but nevertheless was comprehensive and eirenic'. The fact that the delegation included no anti-Calvinists is, however, ignored. Furthermore, the joint *Suffrage* which the British delegates produced was quite clear in its repudiation of the main Arminian points at issue. This despite the fact that John Davenant and Samuel Ward subscribed to what is known as a hypothetical universalist view of Christ's atonement, which attempted to reconcile universal redemption with unconditional predestination. We can acknowledge the comparative moderation of the British delegation without having to deny their Calvinism. Moreover, it is a Calvinism which, contrary to White, has clear affinities with that of the Lambeth Articles drawn up almost a quarter of a century earlier. Most obviously, this involves a shared sublapsarianism.[34] Nevertheless, the ensuing anti-Calvinist reaction of the 1620s was more marked than that of the 1590s, and with very different end results. Cambridge was again a focus. Matters came to a head there during the Commencement in 1622, revealing, in White's words, 'very significant support' for the Dutch Arminians. A Calvinist following, led by the Dort delegate Samuel Ward, confronted an Arminian group headed by Leonard Mawe. Ward was the Lady Margaret professor and Mawe the vice chancellor, and each backed rival theological spokesmen.[35]

Having himself drawn attention to the extent of this doctrinal division, White then rapidly moves to play it down. There 'were on both sides moderates looking for a middle way; the reality was a spectrum and not merely polarities'. The exemplars of moderation singled out in this context by White, Walter Balcanqual and Jerome Beale, are however very odd. Balcanqual had been one of the hard-liners among the British delegation to Dort, who sought to restrict the benefits of Christ's atonement to the elect. As for Beale, by the late 1620s he can be found interpreting the teaching of the Thirty-nine Articles in terms of predestination *ex praevisa fide*. The Cambridge disputes of July 1622 almost certainly contributed to the issuing that August of royal directions restricting preaching on predestination.[36] But it is above all the Montagu controversy, which broke out two years later in 1624, that has rightly exercised historians. Was Richard Montagu an Arminian, and why did James I support him? That Montagu and his immediate backers were all Cambridge men is probably not coincidental. At the same time, it is widely agreed that the changing international situation, in particular James's pursuit of a Spanish alliance, benefited the anti-Calvinists. Sheila Lambert, in the article already mentioned, has recently reviewed the evidence. She is quite correct to stress the private royal backing for Montagu's book, *A New Gagg*, in advance of publication, and has convincingly redated some of the surviving letters. But the book as printed exhibits a number of odd features, not least its lack of any dedication. Again, neither she nor White are able to instance any comparable previous publication. It is also unclear just how much James actually read in manuscript of *A New Gagg* or of Montagu's subsequent defense – *Appello Caesarem*.[37] Yet the very fact that the supporters of Montagu, notably Bishop Richard Neile, sought advance royal approval for what in origin purported to be merely an anti-Catholic pamphlet indicates just how much was at issue. Montagu indeed looks to have been the stalking horse for a court-based faction of leading clergy, who sought not merely to counteract the effects of Dort but fundamentally to alter the doctrinal stance of the English Church concerning predestination and much else.

The extreme distaste with which Montagu regarded Calvinism is revealed in a surviving manuscript commonplace book, where he refers to the 'execrable impiety' of 'Calvin's opinion concerning the antecedent immutable decree of predestination'.[38] *A New Gagg*, however, compared with *Appello Caesarem*, is a relatively cautious book; so much so that not only the Calvinist Joseph

Hall but even the Puritan Henry Burton, at least initially, felt able to judge it charitably.[39] On the basis of the first book it was possible to argue that Montagu, like Overall before him, taught a form of single predestination. Yet in *Appello Caesarem* he abandoned any such pretense, teaching predestination *ex praevisa fide* without qualification. Moreover, in maintaining there that the truly justified can fall both totally and finally, Montagu went beyond Arminius and embraced the same position as Bertius. Arminius himself had only gone as far as to say that 'there are passages of scripture which seem to me to wear this aspect'. Similarly, the Arminian *Remonstrance* of 1610 concluded that the possibility of falling from grace 'must be more particularly determined out of holy scripture, before we ourselves can teach it with the full persuasion of our mind'.[40] Unless we are to assume that they misunderstood Montagu, it is remarkable that five English bishops felt able to affirm in January 1626 that he 'hath not affirmed anything to be the doctrine of the Church of England but that which in our opinions is the doctrine of the Church of England, or agreeable thereunto'.[41] Although Montagu's *Appello Caesarem* was eventually suppressed, on the basis of a royal proclamation in 1629, by then the controversy had served its purpose.

Despite paraphrasing the teaching of Montagu in Arminian terms, that 'predestination to life was the work of God to draw out of misery those who will take hold of his mercy', White exonerates him from the charge of Arminianism. However, a few pages later, we are told that at the York House Conference, in February 1626, Montagu 'was obliged to admit that he had gone too far in asserting that the Church of England had determined against irrespective election'. Nor does White adequately ponder the implication of the fact that despite rejecting his father's foreign policy Charles I did not abandon Montagu. Although the court remained far from monolithic in its religious views, the Calvinists had none the less lost out by the end of the 1620s. William Herbert, third Earl of Pembroke, whom White confuses with his brother Philip, fourth Earl of Pembroke, was at best able to conduct a rearguard action on their behalf. As early as June 1626, when, preaching before the King, the Calvinist Archbishop James Ussher protested against the trend of religious policy. That October, following on the death of Lancelot Andrewes, William Laud was promised the succession to Canterbury – still occupied by the Calvinist Archbishop George Abbot. Meanwhile, Laud became Dean of the Chapel Royal. Calvinist professors at Oxford and Cambridge, as a consequence of the royal declaration of 1628 silencing controversy, were obliged to adapt their teaching. The same year Laud put an end to Calvinist preaching from the famous Paul's Cross pulpit in London, terminating indeed an 'unchallenged Calvinist oration' there stretching back to the 1580s. Montagu was also promoted to the episcopate in 1628, although the rumor that he had recanted Arminianism seems to have been wishful thinking on the part of Calvinists.[42]

Both in the immediate future and the longer term, the doctrinal changes of the 1620s were to prove decisive – not as White would have it with the establishment of a 'judicious agnosticism', but in the eclipse of Calvinism. Here university teaching is the most obvious litmus test of the changing concept of orthodoxy, Calvinism disappearing from the Cambridge Commencement in the mid-1620s and from the Oxford Act after 1631. Catholics and Puritans were each to comment on the alteration which involved much more than simply the theology of grace.[43] Symptomatic of the new theological tendency are the publications of Thomas Jackson, whose Arminianism White characteristically denies although noting his agreement with Hemmingsen. One of the striking things, however, about the published teaching of Jackson is the marked change from 1628 onward, reflecting almost certainly a climate more favorable to his true views. Meanwhile, Jackson's critics were obliged to publish abroad.[44] As regards the Arminian sympathies of Laud and Neile, it is very important to grasp that their views had changed over time. Thus the fact that Neile's denial of Arminianism, in 1629, was phrased in the past tense appears highly significant. Laud's own condemnation of the Lambeth Articles, in 1625, is dismissed by White as mere 'anti-Calvinist polemic'. By contrast, he describes even so stridently an anti-Calvinist work as Edmund Reeve's *Communion Booke Catechisme*, of 1635, as containing 'nothing' that 'any communicant would no have heard countless times in his parish church at any time since the accession of Elizabeth'. As well as citing Jackson on predestination, Reeve couched his argument in terms of the 'old doctrine' of the Prayer Book versus the 'new' teaching of the Calvinists and sought to demonstrate the incompatibility of the latter with sacramental grace. Reeve also wrote of the desirability of doing reverence to the altar – God's 'mercy seat'.[45] White, however, ignores such ceremonial matters. By contrast, they are of central concern to Julian Davies in his book *The Caroline Captivity of the Church*.[46]

III

Davies, like White, regards the rise of English Arminianism as a fiction and devotes a rather short chapter to this theme. He is unwilling to concede that even Richard Montagu was a genuine Arminian, writing of his 'near-Arminian views on foreseen faith and falling from grace'. Davies claims that Laud and the other supporters of Montagu were single predestinarians, because they concentrated their criticisms on the doctrine of reprobation. This, however, was a standard anti-Calvinist ploy and by itself proves nothing. More specifically, his assertion that the hostile reference by Buckeridge, John Howson, and Laud, in 1625, to the 'fatal opinions' contained in the Lambeth Articles must by definition refer to 'reprobation' can be refuted on the basis of a quotation from Hemmingsen – conveniently supplied by Peter White. Hemmingsen adjured 'that we seek not our assurance of faith or hope in the tablets of the fates'.[47] Unconditional election, from an anti-Calvinist point of view, could thus be equally 'fatal'. In addition, Davies fails to distinguish the earlier views of Laud from those which he later espoused, compounding matters by mistranslating 'renatos' as 'elect' instead of regenerate. What Laud actually wrote, in a comment probably dating from the first decade of the seventeenth century, was that the 'regenerate' – a much broader category – cannot fall into final impenitency. As White has written, in another context, the difference is 'fundamental', and had Laud still held this view in the mid-1620s his support for Montagu would indeed be difficult to explain.[48] Davies also says that the royal declaration of 1628, far from proscribing 'single predestinarian Calvinism', actually 'endorsed' it, although he fails to explain why the moderate Calvinist Bishop Davenant was so severely reprimanded for merely touching on the doctrine of election in a court sermon of 1630. Not only is the very concept of 'single predestinarian *Calvinism*' a contradiction in terms, but the reader may well be unaware that in this context Davies quotes from the Thirty-nine Articles rather than the declaration itself. The latter purported to silence all parties.[49]

Like White too, Davies writes from an Anglican standpoint. Nevertheless, there are some very important differences. The Caroline 'captivity' of the book's title refers to what Davies sees as the distortion of Anglicanism by Charles I. Although he also refers rather vaguely to Laud's attempted 'recatholicisation' of the English Church, it is Charles who occupies the center stage in this account. Essentially we are offered a challenging, but deeply flawed, political interpretation of religious change, in terms of something called 'Carolinism' and the concept of 'caesaro-sacramentalism'. In the eyes of Charles the altarwise communion table was, says Davies, a 'visual and mnemonic means of impressing a greater respect for his pretensions to divine right among the people'. The King allegedly sought to diffuse 'his own cult and apotheosis – an *imago dei*, which found its most disturbing icon in the face of Christ, commissioned by [Bishop] John Williams in 1631 for the east window of his new chapel at Lincoln College, Oxford'. This somewhat cryptic last remark refers to the picture on the dust jacket (not reproduced in the book), which shows a Charles-faced Jesus presiding over the last supper. 'Through the manipulation of divine worship and its setting, Charles I's pretensions to sacramental kingship received not only visual expression but the cloak of divine respectability'.[50] Apart from the Lincoln College window, the main evidence adduced in this connection is a handful of sermons preached during the 1630s. Why, however, these should represent the views of Charles rather than of the preachers concerned is unclear. In order to inculcate reverence to the altar, Thomas Laurence and others drew an analogy between it and the chair of state in the royal presence chamber. But they did not confuse the two, and Laurence indeed went out of his way to distinguish. 'Nor is all this to insinuate the derivation of God's honour upon any besides God. (God divert that damnable idolatry as far from me, as hee hath done from the church of God.)' This denial is not quoted by Davies, who writes instead of 'Caroline idolatry' being destroyed in the 1640s.[51] More dubious still is his attempt to show that 'Calvinists' also were 'prepared to practise and vindicate the novel modes of worship'. Here we are told that the Calvinist Walter Balcanqual 'stressed the exemplar of Charles's approach to the [communion] table'. Yet the passage cited has nothing to do with either Charles or communion tables and relates instead to kneeling at prayer. Equally malapropos are the references to the Calvinist Daniel Featley, who refused to turn the communion table altarwise in Lambeth parish church, and the Calvinist Dean John Young who had to defend himself from the charge of 'not bowing to the altare' in Winchester cathedral.[52] Thus the evidence for caesaro-sacramentalism appears to reduce to a piece of flattery by Bishop Williams, but even he did not seek to identify King Charles with the crucified Christ.

Davies repeatedly accuses the present writer of introducing a wrongheaded 'Weberian polarity between grace and predestination', into modern accounts of the early Stuart Church. This, however, misstates my original proposition, which does not moreover depend on Max Weber. By the end of the sixteenth century, the relationship between the grace of election and that which came via the sacraments was a well-worn theme in debates between Calvinists and Lutherans, surfacing for example at the Colloquy of Montbéliard in 1586. Like the continental Lutherans, English anti-Calvinists came to argue that a true valuation of the sacraments was incompatible with absolute predestination. During the 1630s they made a further linkage, while urging reverence to the altar – often itself a recently converted communion table. Thus there are frequent references to the altar as God's 'mercy-seat'. When Laurence, Reeve, and Robert Shelford use this phrase, it seems reasonable to assume they mean the merciful grace of God mediated to all penitent sinners through the eucharist.[53] But here Davies plays what he evidently regards as a trump card, claiming that one of the most vigorous enforcers of the altar changes in the 1630s was the Calvinist Bishop John Davenant of Salisbury – although paradoxically conceding that 'there is reason to believe that he would rather they had not been introduced'. Nevertheless, Davies is only able to produce a single early case of enforcement under Davenant, that of Edington, Wiltshire, in October 1635. Even on his own showing there were untypical features to the Edington case, not least the apparently unique requirement to 'rail in the font' as well as the communion table. In reality the initiative was almost certainly that of Lady Anne Beauchamp, sister to the Earl of Dorset and a close friend of Secretary Francis Windebank, who had recently erected a monument to her late husband in the chancel of Edington church. This monument too appears originally to have had a rail around it. Davies fails to alert the reader to the fact that Lady Anne is actually mentioned in the court record. Nor does her name feature at all in his account.[54] Yet more damaging to Davies's argument concerning Bishop Davenant are events at Newbury, Berkshire. In 1634 the Newbury churchwardens reportedly had been ordered by Laud's vicar-general, at the metropolitical visitation, to move their communion table. They had still not done so by June 1637, when the case disappears from view. The court latterly responsible was that of Archdeacon Edward Davenant, the bishop's nephew.[55] Davies also has an odd way with statistics, deducing compliance from silence. Not in fact until the years 1637 and 1638 is there much evidence of communion tables being either moved or railed, in Salisbury diocese.[56] By this time, most dioceses bear witness to the impact of the Caroline altar policy.

IV

The implausible attempt to portray Bishop Davenant as a Calvinist ceremonialist is, however, part of a much wider endeavor by Davies to dissociate Archbishop Laud from the religious policy of Charles I. He purports indeed to have discovered no less than six different ceremonial strategies being pursued during the 1630s in the various dioceses of England and Wales. Rather than talk of an altar policy, he writes of the 'table of separation' and weaves a complex web in terms of the positioning and railing of communion tables as well as the place where communicants knelt. Nevertheless, many of his distinctions can be shown to be spurious. For example, his assertion that in the diocese of London, under Bishop William Juxon, the altarwise position was not enforced is based on a misreading of the surviving records. Misled by subsequent abbreviations, Davies neglects to note that all parishes in the archdeaconry of St Albans were instructed by Laud's vicar-general in 1637 'to remove theire communion table to the upper end of theire chancell and place it *alonge* the east wall; and compasse it with a convenient and decent rail'. By the end of the year all twenty-six parishes had certified obedience.[57] Again, we are told that in Canterbury diocese Laud did not enforce reception at the rails; but the records tell a different story. Thus, in December 1637, the minister at St James's Dover was ordered to remain 'within' the rail when administering communion – according to the vicar-general's charge *'throughout the diocese at the last ordinary visitation'*.[58] Similarly, the claim that Laud did not advocate an altarwise position for communion tables flies in the face of the archbishop's reiterated assertion that this was still a binding requirement under the Elizabethan injunctions.[59] Davies also makes extensive use of a deposition by William Stackhouse, a parishioner involved in the famou St Gregory's, London, case of 1633, concerning the position of the communion table, and appears to regard it as reliable. Yet he conceals Stackhouse's statement that in 1633 Laud had argued, against both King Charles and Archbishop Richard Neile, in favor of a *permanent* altarwise position for the communion table.[60] Granted the complexity of the evolution of Caroline altar policy, Davies has done a serious disservice by sowing so much confusion. Furthermore, attention is distracted from the very real quarrel between Laud and Bishop Williams, which may date back to the late 1620s and the activities of one of Laud's archdeacons, Thomas Rayment of St Albans, as rector of Ashwell within Williams's own diocese of Lincoln. Although Davies obfuscates matters, Williams recommended an east–west position for parish communion tables as opposed to a north–south or altarwise one. Laud appears always to have favored the latter.[61]

The cautiousness – even the statesmanlike qualities – of Laud's handling of religious matters during the 1630s are not in question. But was Laud really the unwilling executant of royal policy? Much is made by Davies of the influence on Charles of Lancelot Andrewes as Dean of the Chapel Royal, yet the King chose Laud as successor to Andrewes in 1626. If Charles had truly been the moving force behind the altar policy, we would have expected some official sanction like the declaration concerning Sunday sports. What Davies rather grandly calls the 'metropolitical order' has, however, a degree of informality about it that savors more of Laud than the King. Moreover, there is the important fact that these instructions regarding communion tables were issued in the archbishop's name.[62] Nor will it really do to shift responsibility onto other clerics – in particular the overzealous Matthew Wren, who is portrayed by Davies as the true heir of Andrewes. Laud too was a disciple of Andrewes and modeled his own religious practices on him.[63] Finally, in the 'history' of his troubles and trial, Laud made no attempt to claim *à la* Davies that he had pursued a different altar policy to that of his master King Charles – an obvious defence, were it true.

V

The two wings of the revisionist alliance come together most clearly in Kevin Sharpe's massive book – *The Personal Rule of Charles I*. Although published the same year as White and Davies, Sharpe has been able to take account of their findings prior to publication and finds them jointly to have produced 'a full and persuasive new account'. But Sharpe is his own man; the conclusions which he has reached as regards the religious development of the 1630s are 'based on my own research'.[64] We would be premature to deliver a final verdict on Sharpe's book as a whole. Time will tell how far it comes to look like some great beached leviathan, stranded by the receding tides of revisionism. For present purposes, however, there are two key chapters in this near thousand-page excursus. The first, chapter 6, treats the 'Reformation of the Church' under Charles I and Laud. In it the King is portrayed as being motivated by a psychologically based obsession with 'order', and Archbishop Laud as the 'executor rather than deviser of royal policy'. Sharpe correctly points out that on a number of occasions the archbishop denied being an Arminian. Yet Laud did not say what he meant by the term. The present writer has never claimed that, to quote Bernard, Laud or Richard Montagu were Arminians 'in the strict sense of someone influenced by Arminius'. When applied in an English context, the description usually refers to a similarity of doctrine. Nevertheless, Sharpe declines to discuss the evidence for Laud's anti-Calvinist views.[65] Similarly, in a section revealingly entitled 'Theological Wrangles', instead of examining the published teaching of Montagu, he provides a pastiche derived from the apologia written by Francis White for having licensed *Appello Caesarem*. White did indeed shelter behind quotations culled from the sublapsarian Calvinist Robert Abbot and the *Suffrage* of the British delegation to Dort, but their rehearsal by Sharpe is no substitute for an analysis of *Appello Caesarem* itself. As regards the York House Conference, we are simply told that 'the attempt to prove that Montagu was unorthodox on the subject of predestination failed'. Sharpe concludes this section with the baffling statement that 'the religion of most protestants, as we shall see, had very little to do with quarrels about supralapsarianism'. Four pages earlier he defines 'supralapsarianism' as 'the doctrine that election and damnation predated the fall'.[66] But no one has seriously suggested that *supralapsarian* Calvinism was the doctrine at issue in the early seventeenth-century controversy about Arminianism.

While the references by Sharpe to the predestinarian dispute suggest a certain lack of comprehension on his part, he manages to produce an unmitigated muddle over the subject of ceremonies – specifically with reference to 'bowing', whether at the name of Jesus or toward the altar. The distinction matters a great deal, because the former was a canonical requirement and the latter not. His discussion here gets off to a particularly bad start from which it never recovers. According to Sharpe, Laud in 1631 opposed the publication of a 'defence of bowing to the altar'. In fact this book, by William Page, was *A Treatise or Justification of Bowing at the Name of Jesus*; it was Archbishop Abbot who opposed publication, while Laud encouraged it. Sharpe subsequently fails to distinguish between the different types of bowing, although Laud advocated both.[67] Turning to the 'Altar Controversies', Sharpe misses the point that the dispute centered on where the communion table should generally stand in parish churches. Thus the metropolitical visitation articles of Laud do not conflict with the archbishop's parallel claim that under the terms of the Elizabethan injunctions the communion table should be set 'altarwise'; they merely left open the possibility that it might be moved at the time of administering communion. In practice, however, there is scant evidence that Laud favored any such peripatetic principle. We also know that from at least the summer of 1635 Laud's vicar-general was instructing parish authorities to place their communion tables altarwise. Sharpe also appears to confuse 'indifferency' with freedom of choice.[68] Laud did not mean the latter when he described the siting of communion tables as being a matter of indifference, and his position was emphatically not the same as Bishop Williams. Nevertheless, Sharpe claims that the argument of Williams in *The Holy Table: Name and Thing* 'was close to Laud's own practice'. In fact, Williams recommended an east–west as opposed to a north–south (altarwise) placing of parish communion tables.[69]

Like Davies, Sharpe seeks to portray the Calvinist Bishop Davenant as more 'Laudian' than Laud – but adds a further dimension by introducing the case of Henry Sherfield, who was prosecuted in Star Chamber for breaking an allegedly idolatrous church window at St Edmund's, Salisbury. According to Sharpe, Davenant was the prime instigator of this prosecution. 'Sherfield had challenged the bishop's authority – an authority which the Calvinist Davenant was as determined to preserve as Laud.' Sharpe, however, suppresses (the word does not seem too strong) a key set of documents among the State Papers concerning the role of the Dean of Salisbury, Edmund Mason. These reveal Mason, in March 1633, pressing for a much harsher form of recantation by the Puritan Sherfield than that sanctioned by Davenant and expressing grave doubts about the Bishop's own firmness against 'the faction that now domineers in his diocese'. Davenant 'in this, as in all other busynesses of ecclesiastical defence, casts backward and retyres himselfe into caution and sylence'. Mason wanted Sherfield to confess to having cast a 'reproch and scandall' on 'the blessed reformation of true religion from superstitious Popery, together with the whole government both of state and church in England'. The Dean also forwarded to Secretary Windebank a petition from Davenant's chancellor, who was seeking to recover his costs for prosecuting Sherfield in Star Chamber, and similarly invoked the support of Laud.[70] Not one word of this is revealed by Sharpe, despite entitling his account a 'Case Study in Complexities'. Davenant indeed would appear to have been caught in the cross-fire between a group of *avant-garde* conformists based on Salisbury cathedral close and the city Puritans. Moreover, both Laud and Neile used their speeches against Sherfield, in Star Chamber, to defend religious imagery in churches – especially pictures of Christ.[71] Again, this goes unremarked by Sharpe.

'Puritanism and Opposition' is the subject of Sharpe's chapter 12. He rightly remarks that the 'radical potential of puritanism' has been 'wrongly downplayed in recent years' by many historians but does not venture far in redressing the balance – presumably for fear of bringing his own revisionist edifice tumbling down.[72] Puritans such as John Pym still appear out of virtually nowhere in 1640. Nor is any real explanation offered as to why, for instance, the former Clerk of the Closet to Prince Charles (Henry Burton) or someone on visiting terms at Lambeth Palace under Archbishop Abbot (William Prynne) were driven to Puritan extremism during the 1630s. In the account which is offered, however, the term 'separatist' is used with reckless abandon. Among those so described are the perpetual curate of St Mary, Aldermanbury, Dr John Stoughton, and the eminently respectable Sir Humphrey Lynde, the latter on the basis of a Catholic satire which Sharpe culpably assumes to be a genuine work by Lynde.[73] At the same time, the only real novelty which Sharpe sees in the religious situation under Charles I is the stricter enforcement of conformity to the existing rules. The numbers of Puritans, he suggests, were 'small' and 'radical Puritans were a tiny sect'. A mixture of governmental mistakes and sheer bad luck from 1637 onward was what, in his view, 'began to change the climate, to radicalize the moderates and to bring a measure of public sympathy to their cause'. According to Sharpe, the same goes for secular grievances such as ship money.[74] Enormous weight, therefore, is put on the Scottish rebellion and its political consequences. Sharpe in fact wishes to elevate short-termism to an unprecedented height among revisionist accounts of the origins of the English Civil War.

The present writer has argued that 'religion was a major contributory cause' of the armed conflict which broke out in 1642. But to say this does not, as Julian Davies assumes, preclude other causes. Thus I have never myself jibbed at the term 'absolutist' to describe certain tendencies in early Stuart government. It is true that stress on the role of Arminianism has had the unfortunate consequence of distracting attention from Puritanism – something which my own recent work has endeavoured to correct.[75] The important religious changes during the reign of Charles I, which served further to alienate Puritans, also need to be seen in a much longer perspective. What resurfaced in the early seventeenth century under the guise of Arminianism clearly had a prehistory in the Elizabethan struggle for dominance between Calvinists and Lutherans. Nevertheless, it was the fusion of religious and secular discontents that was always potentially the most dangerous. Although there are traces of this under Elizabeth, the external threat from Spain was a limiting factor on any Protestant opposition. Peace and the failure of financial reform after the accession of James I, however, led to a deteriorating political situation. The pursuit of a Spanish alliance abroad produced allegations of Popery at home, and the financial straits of the government led increasingly to the adoption of arguably unconstitutional solutions. By the end of the

1620s a particularly virulent form of Popish Plot theory had come into exist-ence, which combined secular and religious grievances in an all-embracing explanation. This situation is all the more striking because England was by now fighting both Spain and France, the two major Catholic powers. Here continued royal support for the anti-Calvinist faction within the English Church looks to have been the key element, yet clearly much more was involved than simply the theology of grace. In this context we might well adapt Davies's notion of a 'recatholicisation' of the English Church. Nothing indeed appeared sacrosanct. Even the cardinal doctrine of justification by faith alone was to come under attack, while the idea of what constituted idolatry was more and more restricted and communion tables were turned back into altars. At the same time, the secularisation of church property, consequent upon the Reformation, seemed increasingly at risk. The net effect was that by 1640 the earlier charge of Arminianism had escalated into the much more damaging one of Popery.[76]

How close the Caroline government ever came to solving its financial problems remains unclear.[77] Yet the need to suppress the Scottish rebellion rapidly exhausted existing funds and, hence, the recourse to Parliament. Undoubtedly it was the Scottish crisis that enabled the domestic opponents of royal policy to make themselves heard. Similarly the point is well made that some two years elapsed between the meeting of the Long Parliament and the actual outbreak of fighting. That granted, however, we must also take into account certain prior changes. The origins of the emerging opposition program in 1640–42 are traceable not only to the 1620s but in some respects back to the reign of Queen Elizabeth. Neither the monarchy nor the English Church had stood still during the interim, any more than had the Puritans and other critics. It is less a question of apportioning blame for what happened – a rather sterile task at the best of times – than of trying to dis-cern the long-term pattern of developments. In this connection the idea of an unchanging Anglican *via media* remains deeply unhelpful, as does that of a flourishing Stuart regime brought down by a Scottish bolt from the blue.

NOTES

I am grateful to the following for commenting on a draft version of this essay: Kenneth Fincham, Peter Lake, Diarmaid MacCulloch and Fred Trott.

The works discussed in this review are G. Bernard, 'The Church of England, *c.* 1529–*c.* 1642'. *History* 75 (1990), 183–206; S. Lambert, 'Richard Montagu, Arminianism and Censorship', *P and P* 124 (1989), 38–42; P. White, *Predestination, Policy and Polemic. Conflict and Consensus in the English Church from the Reformation to the Civil War* (Cambridge, 1992); J. Davies, *The Caroline Captivity of the Church. Charles I and the Remoulding of Anglicanism* (Oxford, 1992); and K. Sharpe, *The Personal Rule of Charles I* (New Haven and London, 1992).

1 For a related argument, see D. MacCulloch, 'The Myth of the English Reformation', *JBS* 30 (1991), 1–19.

2 G. W. Bernard, 'The Church of England, *c.* 1529–*c.* 1642', *History* 75 (1990), 183–206. Bernard, like his colleague Kevin Sharpe, would appear to be attracted by an 'Anglican' version of religious events primarily because of its innately revisionist thrust: see pp. 193–6 above.

3 D. MacCulloch, *The Later Reformation in England, 1547–1603* (Basingstoke, 1990); M. Aston, *England's Iconoclasts* (Oxford, 1988), esp. ch. 6.

4 Bernard, 'The Church of England', p. 184; M. Bucer, *Metaphrases et Enarrationes Perpetuae Epistolarum D. Pauli Apostoli . . . Tomus Primus . . . ad Romanos* (Strasbourg, 1536); M. Bucer, *Praelectiones . . . in Epistolam . . . ad Ephesios* (Basel, 1562); D. F. Wright ed., *Common Places of Martin Bucer* (Abingdon, 1972), pp. 95–118; P. Martyr, *In Epistolam S. Pauli Apostoli ad Romanos* (Zurich, 1559), esp. pp. 682–743.

5 E. Cardwell ed., *Synodalia* (Oxford, 1842), i, pp. 23–4; P. Schaff ed., *A History of the Creeds of Christendom* (London, 1877), iii, pp. 193–516; see pp. 182–3 above.

6 W. Haddon, *A Sight of the Portugall Pearle* (London, ?1565), sigs Biiii, Cvii–Diii. This is a translation of the original Latin edition, which is not known to survive; L. V. Ryan, 'The Haddon-Osorio Controversy (1563–1583)', *Church History* 22 (1953), 142–54. My attention was drawn to this important article by Tom Freeman.

7 M. Bucer, *Scripta Anglicana* (Basel, 1577), pp. 876–99; J. Foxe, *Contra Hieron. Osorium* (London, 1577), fos 153v–210.

8 N. Hemmingsen, *The Epistle of . . . Saint Paul to the Ephesians* (London, 1580), esp. pp. 53–72. This was among the last of Hemmingsen's works to be published in England and is also the most overtly anti-Calvinist.

9 J. Calvin, *Thirteen Sermons . . . entreating of the Free Election of God in Jacob, and of Reprobation in Esau*, trans. J. Field (London, 1579); J. Calvin, *Sermons . . . upon . . . Ephesians* (London, 1577), dedicated by the translator, Arthur Golding, to Archbishop Grindal. Golding writes of 'the doctrine of election and predestination' as 'being the chief groundwoorke of this epistle to the Ephesians': sig. *ii.

10 Bernard, 'The Church of England', pp. 183, 195–6.

11 N. Tyacke, *Anti-Calvinists*, p. 245.

12 *Ibid.*, pp. 20, 39, 59; pp. 156 and 181 above.

13 Bernard, 'The Church of England', p. 194; S. Lambert, 'Richard Montagu, Arminianism and Censorship', *P and P* 124 (1989), 38–42. Bernard and Lambert also fail to distinguish between 'court bishops' and the rest: K. Fincham, *Prelate as Pastor: The Episcopate of James I* (Oxford, 1990), pp. 41–57.

14 See pp. 161–2, 164, 167 above; Bernard, especially, does not appear to understand how religious censorship worked, writing of Laud's 'chaplains' licensing books at 'Oxford' (ibid., p. 197), where the relevant authority was, of course, the vice-chancellor.

15 See p. 188 above.

16 Compare, however, K. Fincham, 'Episcopal Government, 1603–1640', in K. Fincham ed., *The Early Stuart Church, 1603–1642* (Basingstoke, 1993), pp. 71–91.

17 P. White, *Predestination, Policy and Polemic. Conflict and Consensus in the English Church from the Reformation to the Civil War* (Cambridge, 1992), pp. 5, 16.

18 White, *Predestination*, pp. 22–38; J. and W. Nichols ed., *The Works of James Arminius* (London, 1825–75), i, pp. 30, 578–79; Schaff ed., *History of the Creeds*, iii, pp. 545–9.

19 White, *Predestination*, pp. x, 1.

20 See pp. 132–3 above. My italics.

21 White, *Predestination*, pp. 39–52, 54, 56; C. Lloyd ed., *The King's Book* (London, 1932), pp. 10–13, 50–1, 147–63.

22 Cardwell ed., *Synodalia*, i, pp. 23–4; White, *Predestination*, pp. 57–9; E. Cardwell ed., *The Reformation of the Ecclesiastical Laws* (Oxford, 1850), p. 21.

23 Cardwell, ed., *Synodalia*, i, pp. 63–4; see n. 4 above.

24 White, *Predestination*, pp. 72–4; J. Ayre ed., *The Works of John Jewel* (Cambridge, 1845–50), ii, pp. 819, 821–2, 828, 841, 923, 933; H. C. Porter, *Reformation and Reaction in Tudor Cambridge* (Cambridge, 1958), pp. 386–9.

25 White, *Predestination*, pp. 74–5. My italics; T. Harding ed., *The Decades of Henry Bullinger* (Cambridge, 1841–52), iii, pp. 185–95; see pp. 185–6 below.

26 White, *Predestination*, pp. 89–90, 99–100; Tyacke, *Anti-Calvinists*, pp. 32, 164–5, 251–2; his surviving library suggests that Harsnett was in touch with Lutheran teaching: G. Goodwin, *A Catalogue of the Harsnett Library at Colchester* (London, 1888), pp. 5, 12, 120, 163. [The dating of Harsnett's sermon is insecure: F. W. Brownlow, *Shakespeare, Harsnett and the Devils of Denham* (Cranbury N.J., 1993), p. 42.]

27 Tyacke, *Anti-Calvinists*, pp. 29, 31, 38, 251–2; P. Lake, *Moderate Puritans and the Elizabethan Church* (Cambridge, 1982), p. 150; G. Babington, *A Sermon preached at Paules Crosse* (London, 1591); compare White, *Predestination*, pp. 95–7.

28 White, *Predestination*, ch. 6; Tyacke, *Anti-Calvinists*, pp. 30–3; Schaff ed., *History of the Creeds*, iii, pp. 581–5.

29 White, *Predestination*, ch. 7; P. Lake, *Anglicans and Puritans? Presbyterianism and English Conformist Thought from Whitgift to Hooker* (London, 1988), ch. 4; P. Lake, 'Lancelot Andrewes, John Buckeridge and *Avant-Garde* Conformity at the Court of James I', in L. Peck ed., *The Mental World of the Jacobean Court* (Cambridge, 1991), pp. 113–33.

30 White, *Predestination*, pp. 150–2; T. Rogers, *The Catholic Doctrine of the Church of England*, ed. J. J. S. Perowne (Cambridge, 1854), pp. 147–9. My italics; see p. 161 above.

31 White, *Predestination*, pp. 157–9, 169. White also refers to Robert Abbot indulging in 'polemic' for 'the benefit of undergraduates', although his 'students' would in reality have been pursuing a postgraduate course in theology: *ibid.*, p. 157.

32 White, *Predestination*, pp. 165–6; W. Goode, *The Doctrine of the Church of England as to the Effects of Baptism in the Case of Infants* (London, 1850), pp. 126–30.

33 Tyacke, *Anti-Calvinists*, p. 36; White, *Predestination*, pp. 36–7, 167–74; R. Thomson, *Diatriba de Amissione et Intercisione Gratiae et Justificationis* (Leiden, 1616); P. Bertius, *Hymenaeus Desertor, sive de Sanctorum Perseverantia et Apostasia* (Leiden, 1610).

34 White, *Predestination*, p. 202; *The Collegiate Suffrage of the Divines of Great Britaine concerning the Five Articles controverted in the Low Countries* (London, 1629); Tyacke, *Anti-Calvinists*, ch. 4.

35 White, *Predestination*, pp. 208–9; Tyacke, *Anti-Calvinists*, pp. 46–7.

36 White, *Predestination*, p. 209; Tyacke, *Anti-Calvinists*, pp. 50–1, 96–7, 102–3. White's treatment here of the surviving Beale–Ward correspondence is particularly unsatisfactory: White, *Predestination*, p. 234, n. 107.

37 Lambert, 'Richard Montagu', pp. 42–50.

38 Archbishop Marsh's Library, Dublin, MS Z. 4.2.10, fos 151v–52.

39 P. Wynter ed., *The Works of . . . Joseph Hall* (Oxford, 1863), i, pp. xliii–xliv; ix, pp. 489–516; H. Burton, *Truth's Triumph over Trent* (London, 1629), pp. 341–3. On internal evidence, this book was written when James I was still alive: *ibid.*, pp. 314–15.

40 R. Montagu, *Appello Caesarem* (London, 1625), pp. 21–2, 28–30, 56–9, 64–5, 73–4; Nichols eds, *The Works of James Arminius*, i, p. 603; Schaff ed., *History of the Creeds*, iii, pp. 548–9; see above, pp. 185–6.

41 *Laud Works*, vi, p. 249.

42 White, *Predestination*, pp. 221, 229, 250, and index refs. to 'Pembroke'; Tyacke, *Anti-Calvinists*, pp. 49, 50–1, 76–9, 249, 261; p. 214 below; compare Porter, *Reformation and Reaction*, p. 287, quoted by Bernard, 'The Church of England', p. 192.

43 White, *Predestination*, p. 254; Tyacke, *Anti-Calvinists*, pp. 48–9, 81, 224, 227; see also pp. 320–39 below.

44 White, *Predestination*, p. 270; Tyacke, *Anti-Calvinists*, p. 121; W. Twisse, *A Discovery of D. Jackson's Vanitie* (Amsterdam, 1631); S. Rutherford, *Exercitationes Apologeticae pro Divina Gratia* (Amsterdam, 1636), pp. 351–5.

45 White, *Predestination*, pp. 242, 274, 297; Tyacke, *Anti-Calvinists*, pp. 109–13, 266–8; pp. 209–11, below E. Reeve, *The Communion Booke Catechisme Expounded* (London, 1635), sig. C2r–v, pp. 48, 66–7, 132–7.

46 J. Davies, *The Caroline Captivity of the Church: Charles I and the Remoulding of Anglicanism* (Oxford, 1992).

47 *Ibid.*, pp. 95–7; White, *Predestination*, p. 270; Tyacke, *Anti-Calvinists*, pp. 266–7.

48 Davies, *Caroline Captivity*, p. 96; p. 209 below; White, *Predestination*, p. 108.

49 Davies, *Caroline Captivity*, pp. 117–18; White, *Predestination*, pp. 251–2, 299–300. As with White, Davies never makes clear what he means by 'single' predestination.

50 Davies, *Caroline Captivity*, pp. 15, 206, 299.

51 *Ibid.*, pp. 18–19, 317; T. Laurence, *A Sermon preached before the King's Majesty at Whitehall* (London, 1637), p. 25.

52 Davies, *Caroline Captivity*, pp. 19–20; W. Balcanqual, *The Honour of Christian Churches* (London, 1633), p. 12; D. Featley, *The Gentle Lash or the Vindication of Dr. Featley* (London, 1644), p. 10; F. R. Goodman ed., *The Diary of John Young* (London, 1928), pp. 108–9.

53 Davies, *Caroline Captivity*, pp. 50, 92, 122, 299; Tyacke, *Anti-Calvinists*, pp. 10, 39, 52, 55, 175–6; J. Raitt, *The Colloquy of Montbéliard: Religion and Politics in the Sixteenth Century* (New York, 1993), ch. 5; T. Laurence, *Two Sermons* (Oxford, 1635), i, p. 37; Reeve, *Communion Booke Catechisme*, pp. 132–7; R. Shelford, *Five Pious and Learned Discourses* (Cambridge, 1635), pp. 4, 15.

54 Davies, *Caroline Captivity*, pp. 223–5; WRO, D1/41/1/2, Citations 1635; *VCH, Wiltshire* 8 (1965), 248; C. E. Ponting, 'Edington Church', *Wiltshire Archaeological and Natural History Magazine* 25 (1891), 224; *CSPD, 1635–6*, p. 378.

55 BRO, D/A2/c.77, *Acta* (Berkshire Archdeaconry), 1635–6, fo 81v–82, D/A2/c.78, *Acta* (Berkshire Archdeaconry), 1636–7, fo 255v. The rector of Newbury was the famous Calvinist William Twisse – future prolocutor of the Westminster Assembly. Davies does not discuss this case, although it features anonymously and repeatedly in his footnotes as evidence of 'enforcement': Davies, *Caroline Captivity*, p. 224, nn. 76, 80.

56 WRO, D2/4/1/16, *Acta* (Salisbury Archdeaconry), 1636–41, fos 32, 65v, 113v, D3/4/7, *Acta* (Wiltshire Archdeaconry), 1632–42, fo 56v. It was in March 1638, not December 1637 (Davies, p. 225), that the churchwardens of Fifield were ordered to move and rail their communion table 'as in other churches the same is done': D3/4/7, fo 56v. I have discussed elsewhere the Aldbourne, Wiltshire, case of May 1637: Tyacke, *Anti-Calvinists*, pp. 210–12.

57 Davies, *Caroline Captivity*, pp. 218, 227–29, and ch. 6 generally; HRO, Hertford, ASA7/31, *Acta* (St. Albans Archdeaconry), 1636–38, fos 36v–37. My italics. Although Davies misinterprets this document in a diocesan context, strictly speaking it illustrates the local impact of metropolitical instructions.

58 Canterbury Cathedral Archives, Canterbury, Z.4.6, *Acta* (Canterbury Consistory), 1636–40, fo 127. My italics. There are similar references at fos 127v and 150. All are ignored by Davies.

59 Laud, *Works*, iv, pp. 121, 225; vi, pp. 59–60. Instead, Davies relies on an obscure reference during Laud's trial to the 'indifferency' of how communion tables should be placed: Davies, *Caroline Captivity*, p. 231, n. 119; see p. 195 above.

60 Davies, *Caroline Captivity*, p. 208, n. 16, p. 211, nn. 23, 27–8, p. 213, n. 35; PRO, SP16/499/42.

61 Tyacke, *Anti-Calvinists*, pp. 199, 209.

62 Davies, *Caroline Captivity*, p. 218. It should be pointed out here that the earliest surviving version of the so-called metropolitical order dates from June 1635 and was issued for Gloucester diocese. This says nothing about *where* communicants should receive, which Davies claims was an essential component. GRO, Gloucester, GDR189, fos 8v–9. I owe this reference to Kenneth Fincham.

63 Davies, *Caroline Captivity*, pp. 215–16; Laud, *Works*, iv, pp. 203, 210, 247.

64 K. Sharpe, *The Personal Rule of Charles I* (New Haven and London, 1992), p. 275, n. 1.

65 *Ibid.*, pp. 279, 285–7; Bernard, 'The Church of England', p. 197; Tyacke, *Anti-Calvinists*, pp. x–xi, 266–70; pp. 210–11 below.

66 Sharpe, *Personal Rule*, pp. 293–4, 296–7, 300; see p. 188 above.

67 Sharpe, *Personal Rule*, pp. 287, 328–32; Laud, *Works*, v, pp. 39–40, 205–7.

68 Sharpe, *Personal Rule*, pp. 333–5; Laud, *Works*, v, p. 421; vi, p. 60; see n. 62 above; for the doctrine of religious things 'indifferent' – i.e., not ordained by God, but which can still be legally binding – see B. J. Verkamp, *The Indifferent Mean: Adiaphorism in the English Reformation to 1554* (Athens, Ohio, 1977), esp. ch. 7.

69 Sharpe, *Personal Rule*, pp. 334, 338; Tyacke, *Anti-Calvinists*, p. 209.

70 Sharpe, *Personal Rule*, pp. 345–8; PRO, SP16/233/88, see also p. 150 above.

71 T. B. Howell and T. J. Howell eds, *A Complete Collection of State Trials* (London, 1816–28), iii, pp. 548–53, 557–9.

72 Sharpe, *Personal Rule*, pp. 694, 731–2. For an attempt to redress the balance, see pp. 61–8, 111–31 above.

73 Sharpe, *Personal Rule*, pp. 734, 740; [J. Floyd?], *A Letter of Sir Humfrey Linde* [St Omer] (1634). Daniel Featley preached Lynde's funeral sermon in 1638, while Stoughton died in post during 1639.

74 Sharpe, *Personal Rule*, pp. 292, 729–30, 757.

75 Tyacke, *Anti-Calvinists*, pp. 159, 245; Davies, *Caroline Captivity*, pp. 1–4, 49–50, 313–18; see n. 72 above.

76 Tyacke, *Anti-Calvinists*, pp. 54, 139, 157–9, 192–4, 198–216; D. Hoyle, 'A Commons Investigation of Arminianism and Popery in Cambridge on the Eve of the Civil War', *HJ* 29 (1986), 419–25; C. Hill, *Economic Problems of the Church: From Archbishop Whitgift to the Long Parliament* (Oxford, 1956), esp. ch. 14.

77 P. K. O'Brien and P. A. Hunt, 'The Rise of a Fiscal State in England, 1485–1815', *HR* 66 (1993), 151, 154.

Chapter 8

◆

Archbishop Laud

I

WILLIAM Laud deserves to rank among the greatest archbishops of Canterbury since the Reformation. Indeed one is hard pressed to think of others in the same league, save the obvious Thomas Cranmer. But to say this does not necessarily imply approval. Rather it acknowledges the fact that both men made a major contribution to the future of the English Church. Although Cranmer was burnt to death as a heretic and Laud was executed for treason, their respective legacies lived on. In the case of Laud the time-lag was greater, yet just as the Elizabethan Church owed much to Cranmer so did the Restoration Church to Laud. Thus commentators in the 1660s were clear that it was the religious supporters of Laud and not his opponents who had won through. Whereas in the early seventeenth century 'the current of the Church of England ran the Calvinist way' now 'Arminianism' is 'received amongst our clergy', as are similar innovations: 'the communion table set altarwise', when 'it ought to be in the body of the church', and 'bowing' practised towards it.[1] This hostile evaluation, made by Sir Thomas Littleton during a parliamentary debate in March 1668, serves to indicate, albeit in shorthand form, some of the longer-term consequences of the 'Laudian' movement for both doctrine and worship. Our concern in this essay, however, is with the beginnings of that story and more specifically the contribution made by Laud himself.

While Archbishop Laud has never lacked for biographers, the modern historiography begins in 1940. Since then the pendulum has swung from the frankly materialistic interpretation of Hugh Trevor-Roper to the psychological portrait painted recently by Charles Carlton. Writing against the background of the 1930s, Trevor-Roper defined religion as 'the ideal expression of a particular social and political organisation' and saw Laud as the religious representative of those elements in society opposed to the forces of nascent capitalism. For Carlton, by contrast, the key to Laud lies in his 'insecurity', arising from his allegedly 'humble origins' and supposed homosexuality. Meanwhile, to others, Laud remains the epitome of 'Anglicanism'. All three of these interpretations, not least the last mentioned, depart fairly radically from seventeenth-century assessments. Moreover, they ring their changes on the same basic body of evidence.[2]

On the face of it, the sources for the study of Laud are both abundant and accessible; the nineteenth-century edition of his collected works runs to seven volumes and there are literally thousands of references to him in the published calendars of *State Papers Domestic*. Closer inspection, however, reveals a less satisfactory situation. Only a fairly small proportion of this material is concerned with religious as opposed to administrative matters. Furthermore, there is virtually nothing at all before the second decade of the seventeenth century. Laud was born in 1573, and this means that his formative years are very difficult to reconstruct. Hence the heavy reliance by historians on the near-contemporary life of Laud, written by Peter Heylyn and first published in 1668. (Heylyn was twenty-seven years younger than Laud, but had worked quite closely with him during the 1630s.) It is Heylyn, for example, who supplies the details of Laud's early clashes with his fellow Oxford theologians at the turn of the century. Clearly there is a possibility that our view of Laud has been unduly coloured by Heylyn, who may have read his own later preoccupations into the record.

This type of criticism also applies to the historical background, as sketched by Heylyn in his biography and elsewhere. Laud is depicted as struggling almost single-handedly against a dominant Calvinism in Oxford and in the English Church more generally *circa* 1600: 'two or three' in the face of an 'army'. Heylyn is quite clear that Laud was effectively a revolutionary, overturning what had become the religious *status quo*. But, according to Heylyn, Laud had right on his side. In this scenario Laud, unlike most of his contemporaries, was true to the Elizabethan settlement of religion. For, so the argument runs, only during the later sixteenth century was the English Church swamped by a rising tide of Calvinism. Heylyn stresses that he is not simply talking about the Elizabethan Puritan challenge to the Prayer Book and the bishops, but something much more pervasive. By 'Calvinism' he means the type of teaching, on subjects like predestination, contained within the pages of John Calvin's famous book – *The Institutes of Christian Religion*.[3]

Arguably, however, far from later historians paying too much attention to Heylyn, and thus misconstruing Laud's role, they have on the contrary failed to take sufficiently seriously what he says. Certainly the current picture of Laud tends to be one of an ecclesiastical administrator rather than a theologian, highly efficient but no innovator. Yet it, in turn, has created a problem of interpretation, because if Laud was such an ordinary ecclesiastic why did his archiepiscopate prove so controversial? Various strategies have been evolved to meet this difficulty. Firstly there has been an attempt to shift attention away from Archbishop Laud to King Charles I. Laud, it is said, was simply obeying orders, and the initiative for change was that of the King. But if the direct evidence for Laud's religious views is less than abundant that for Charles is almost non-existent, and to substitute the one for the other solves nothing. Alternatively there is the argument that little central direction existed and thus Laud cannot be held responsible for the innovatory religious policies of individual bishops. Nevertheless this anarchic view of the 1630s remains unconvincing, particularly given the activities of Laud's own officials.[4]

Again it has been claimed that Laud was the victim of a Puritan backlash, due to his attempt to take up the task of ecclesiastical reconstruction left uncompleted by Archbishop Bancroft in 1610. Here the blame is attached to Laud's immediate predecessor at Canterbury – Archbishop George Abbot, who at worst was himself a Puritan and at best was a lax administrator. For over twenty years (1611–33), this version has it, Abbot let things slide; conformity was only intermittently enforced and nothing done to improve the financial lot of the parish clergy. This, however, is a very partial reading both of Heylyn and of the historical record, abolishing as it does any real difference between Laud and most of his predecessors at Canterbury, and making Abbot not Laud the true exception. Undoubtedly the churchmanship of Archbishop Abbot had its idiosyncratic features, notably his virulent anti-Catholicism, although there is little sign that the death of Archbishop Bancroft led to a resurgence of Puritanism. Nor were efforts abandoned under Abbot to solve the economic problems of the English Church.[5] Moreover the logical implication of Heylyn's view of Laud, as an isolated opponent of Calvinism, is that not only Archbishop Abbot but also Archbishop Bancroft and Archbishop Whitgift, not to mention Archbishop Grindal and perhaps Archbishop Parker too, were all Calvinists. The evidence suggests that this was indeed the case, and that the mature theology of Laud differed from that of his predecessors at Canterbury from at least Grindal onwards. Investigation of official university teachings and the licensed publications of the printing press also substantiates the claim about Calvinist dominance.[6]

Confidence in Heylyn's grasp of the overall pattern of English religious developments in the later sixteenth century does not, of course, obviate the need for further research into the career of Laud, especially the early phase. Heylyn's Laud, apart from the supposed influence of his tutor John Buckeridge, at St John's College, Oxford, comes essentially out of an intellectual vacuum. Laud himself, however, does provide one further clue, noting in his diary the fact of his ordination as deacon and priest, in 1601, by Bishop

John Young of Rochester. On its own this would be without significance, since the bishopric of Oxford was vacant at the time. Nevertheless another tradition, recorded by David Lloyd in his *Memoires* of 1668, has Bishop Young prophesying of Laud that, 'if he lived, he would be an instrument of restoring the Church from the narrow and private principles of modern times, to the more free, large and public sentiments of the purest and first ages', because 'finding his study raised above the systems and opinions of the [present] age' and 'upon the nobler foundations of the fathers, councils and ecclesiastical historians'.[7]

We might still dismiss this simply as embroidery after the event, were it not that Bishop Young was also a long-standing critic of the Calvinist theology of grace. Preaching before Queen Elizabeth, in 1576, Young had spoken of the 'profane curiosity' of those who moved 'unnecessary questions' about 'election' and 'reprobation'. Furthermore there are some traces of a Rochester connection of like-minded St John's College men. Laud's Oxford tutor Buckeridge was a prebendary of Rochester, during the 1590s, while another former St John's College fellow, Henry Bearblock, was Vicar of Strood next door to Rochester. Bearblock and Buckeridge can be found acting together in 1602 against the Puritan William Bradshaw, who at the time was lecturer at Chatham. Bradshaw responded by criticising in turn the religious teaching of Bearblock. Thus he characterised his sermons as being 'full of charity towards adulterers, drunkards, blasphemers and other sinners that swarm in the Church', and 'none that hear you but they are God's faithfull children ... though they be foul, grievous sinners, yet they are repentant and God's mercy belongs unto them; that no man is without sin, but the best and holiest is unclean'. At issue here seemingly were divergent views of the original sin of Adam and its consequences for mankind generally. Could all Christians aspire to Heaven, as Bearblock implied, or was this the prerogative only of a predestined minority of elect saints who were not like ordinary mortals? As a Puritan Bradshaw was particularly concerned to distinguish the godly from the rest, although he apparently recognised an anti-Calvinist tendency in Bearblock's preaching that many in ecclesiastical authority would also have found offensive.[8]

In a published work of four years later (1606), Bradshaw went on to accuse some conformist members of the Church of England of a recent falling away from what 'heretofore hath been constantly and generally held by our Church'. Instead they now teach 'things which have been accounted and are in truth Popish or Lutheran errors, viz. touching general grace and the death of Christ for every particular person, against particular election and reprobation, for images in churches ..., that the pope is not Antichrist ..., also the necessity of baptism [and] auricular confession'. (Interestingly the official reply to Bradshaw denied all these charges.) The most likely target of his remarks was certain Cambridge theologians who, during the 1590s, mounted an abortive counter-attack against the dominant Calvinists.[9] Bradshaw had been a fellow of Sidney Sussex College at the time. But he may in addition have been alluding to his more recent encounter with the Oxonians from St John's College. Much later Laud was to recall how shocked he had been by a book published in 1605, which claimed that the Pope was as certainly Antichrist as Jesus Christ was the son of God. Laud had also caused a furore in 1604 at Oxford when, for one of his bachelor's theses in divinity, he maintained the necessity of baptism, and he certainly came to hold most of the other views itemised by Bradshaw.[10]

The likelihood is that the religion of Laud reflects, in part, the ethos of his particular Oxford college. St John's was a Roman Catholic foundation, dating from the reign of Queen Mary. The Catholic founder, a merchant called Thomas White, continued to oversee the college until his death in 1567. As late as 1573 five fellows, including the future Jesuit Edmund Campion, defected to Rome. 'Owing to this exodus', it has been said, the university authorities 'were suspicious of the religion of all the members of the college'. Similarly, for us historians, the nature of the Protestantism of those others who continued in the Church of England remains in some doubt. But unlike the Marian parish priests who conformed under Elizabeth, their combinations of old and new largely dying with them, a college environment could provide some continuity of religious beliefs. This is not, however, to imply that Laud's tutor Buckeridge was a crypto-Catholic. For Buckeridge entered St John's in 1578, five years after the Catholic exodus and one year after the arrival of Bearblock.[11]

Yet we may surmise that the Protestantism of many of the fellowship owed comparatively little to the thought of continental reformers. Although the Thirty-nine Articles – the English confession of faith – clearly denied a number of central Roman Catholic teachings, such as purgatory and transubstantiation, the Elizabethan Prayer Book still lent itself to a variety of possible interpretations on many other doctrinal issues. Moreover during the second half of the sixteenth century the continental followers of Luther and Calvin were becoming increasingly estranged from one another. In these circumstances the existence of a measure of English resistance to Calvinism is unsurprising. At the same time these years saw a reviving interest in the early Christian writers or Church Fathers, as they are known. The Greek Fathers especially provided a powerful court of appeal from certain aspects of modern Protestantism. Hence the significance of the following passage from the earliest extant publication of John Buckeridge. Preaching against Scottish presbyterianism in 1606, he said that 'in a reformation [of the Church] we should conform ourselves . . . to the rule of the ancient scriptures, apostles and fathers: Chrysostom, Nazianzen, Basil, Ambrose, Jerome, Augustine,

Gregory and the like, rather than after the new cut of those who have not above the life of a man on their backs, sixty or seventy years'. This perhaps sounds innocuous enough until we recall the grave reservations entertained by some Elizabethan bishops about the orthodoxy of the Greek Fathers, notably Chrysostom, on the subject of predestination.[12]

II

William Laud went up to Oxford in 1589, and was the only child of a substantial Reading clothier. When his father died in 1594 he left money and stock worth £1,200, as well as three properties. The widow, who died in 1600, had a life interest in half of the estate. Her brother Sir William Webb was a lord mayor of London, who bequeathed his nephew William Laud £100 in 1599. All of which is difficult to reconcile with the notion of 'humble origins'. On the contrary, Laud was unusual among his fellow clergy both as regards his means and his connections.[13] Nor is it at all clear that his sexuality was significant for his career. But why did he go to university, rather than into business? The fact that his half-brother William Robinson also became a clergyman suggests that parental wishes were important here. As we have noted, there is a tendency among historians to see Laud as primarily an administrator – a bureaucrat whose holy orders were necessary to his career. Yet if this was his ambition he set about it in a very odd way. Within only a few years of ordination Laud had become embroiled in religious controversy at Oxford. Far from attracting the favourable attention of superiors, it could be argued that this endangered his early prospects. Because Laud chose not to publish his views in print this has obscured the truth that he first appeared on the public stage as a controversial *theologian*.

Laud seems very early to have developed an extremely exalted view of episcopacy, both as divinely instituted and an essential mark of the true Church. The effect of this was to redress the denominational balance in favour of Roman Catholicism, at the expense of the Protestant non-episcopal Churches. It was also apparently the original occasion of Laud's clash with George Abbot, the future Archbishop, who like many other English Protestants derived the historical succession of the true Church partly via various medieval heretical groups. According to Laud, the English Church stemmed from that of Rome – the transition only occurring at the Reformation. These rival theories had particular practical application when it came to foreign policy, clergy of Abbot's stamp believing in a pan-Protestant cause and looking askance at any alliance with a Catholic power. Furthermore the true radicalism of Laud's views on episcopacy has eluded historians. For the claim that bishops were *iure divino* was something of a Jacobean commonplace. But Laud went much further, arguing that 'only a bishop can confer orders'.

This was one of his Oxford doctoral theses in 1608 and the effect was to unchurch most European and also Scottish Protestants, denying as it did the legitimacy of their clergy.[14]

We should not, however, assume that the ideas of the mature Laud were all fully fledged by the time of his ordination. Nor is Buckeridge likely to have been the sole intellectual influence on him. During the 1630s, Laud was to comment on the damage done to students by too early exposure to Calvin's *Institutes*, and his remarks may be partly autobiographical – for there is evidence that he himself went through a Calvinist phase. Central for understanding the intellectual development of Laud are his surviving manuscript annotations to a three-volume set of Cardinal Bellarmine's *Disputationes*, published between 1596 and 1599. These annotations have never been properly studied and present considerable problems of interpretation. They include entries made as late as 1618. On the other hand some are probably much earlier. Of greatest interest here is Laud's comment on a section where Bellarmine maintains, against Calvin, that faith once had can be lost. Laud notes, in support of Calvin, that 'the regenerate' cannot fall into final impenitency. The implication of this remark is that Laud originally accepted the Calvinist doctrine of double and absolute predestination, because the unregenerate are by definition incapable of salvation. It also helps to explain how he was able to become chaplain in 1603 to the Calvinist, not to say Puritan, Earl of Devon.[15]

Devon died three years later in disgrace for having married the divorced Lady Penelope Rich, her first husband still living, which was in breach of canon law. Laud had performed the marriage ceremony and was thus implicated in the scandal. Again, his annotations on Bellarmine indicate the religious reasons with which he justified his action. The ensuing *débâcle*, however, looks to have precipitated an intellectual crisis, leading Laud fundamentally to rethink his theological position. Two years later, in 1608, he became chaplain to Bishop Richard Neile, and this relationship was to prove very, important for his subsequent career. Neile had considerable influence at court, as Clerk of the Closet; moreover he too looks to have broken with an earlier Calvinism. By 1615 Laud definitely had come to be identified as an anti-Calvinist. Clearly Neile and Laud were both ambitious men, although it was not only the fruits of office which they wanted. Laud especially sought power with a particular end in mind, namely to translate into practice his ideal of the kind of organisation the Church of England should be. This vision included a wealthier Church and one more independent of the laity, to be achieved by an even closer alliance with the monarchy than already existed. The example held forth is that of King David in the Old Testament. Meanwhile, according to Laud, priests continue to live in a 'mean' condition and the Church lies 'basely', both the victims of 'sacrilege'.[16]

Laud elaborated on this conception in a number of surviving sermons from the 1620s. A recurrent theme is that of the 'unity' of Jerusalem, the ancient temple and city standing for the English Church and state. 'Commonwealth and Church', he preached in 1621, 'are collective bodies made up of many into one, and both so near allied that the one, the Church, can never subsist but in the other, the Commonwealth, nay so near that the same men, which in a temporal respect make the Commonwealth do in a spiritual make the Church'. Laud goes on quite explicitly to blur the distinction, made famous by St Augustine, between 'grace' and 'nature', the city of God and that of the world. There was little or no room in this scheme for a godly elite distinct from earthly hierarchies. The Church was, or ought to be, the nation at prayer and according to set forms, worship being built around the sacrament of holy communion rather than preaching.[17]

One of these sermons also sheds very important light on the position of Laud *vis-à-vis* what, in the aftermath of the Synod of Dort in 1619, we can call Arminianism. (At Dort the Dutch Arminians, who rejected Calvinist teaching on predestination, were condemned by an international gathering which included English representatives.) Preaching before King James in March 1622, Laud ventured some remarks on the question of individual 'assurance' or certainty of salvation. He chose his words carefully, in expounding the second part of his text: 'Because the king [David] trusteth in the Lord, and in the mercy of the most High, he shall not miscarry' (Psalms 21.7). According to Laud, these words are not to be understood in an 'absolute' sense. There is a 'double condition' involving on David's part a 'religious heart to God that cannot but trust in Him', and on God's part a 'merciful providence' which 'knows not how to forsake till it be forsaken, if it do then'. The safest course is to rely on God's mercy, 'for that holds firm when men break'. Yet mercy 'will not profit any man that doth not believe and trust in it'. At a time when Calvinism still passed for orthodoxy and King James had as yet given no public signal to the contrary, Laud was obliged to tread warily. Nevertheless he does raise the possibility of God's *forsaking* David, and therefore of the non-perseverance even of the elect, while covering himself with the additional statement that faith and hope are 'due only' to God's mercy.[18]

That, however, is far from exhausting the relevance of this sermon of 1622 by Laud. For in the same section which discusses Christian assurance he cites approvingly a passage on free will from the *Collationes* of John Cassian. By the seventeenth century Cassian was notorious as the founder of what is called Semi-Pelagianism – a theological half-way house between Augustine and Pelagius on the subject of predestination and free will, elaborated during the first decades of the fifth century. Cassian had been ordained by Chrysostom and drew intellectually on the Greek Fathers, in combating the thoroughgoing predestinarian teaching of Augustine against the Pelagians.

Never formally condemned, Cassian remained a vital source for anyone who wished to break away from the Augustinianism of the Protestant Reformation. Semi-Pelagianism is in fact an early Christian equivalent of Arminianism.[19]

We do not know when Laud first read Cassian or the extent to which he agreed with him, although the library of St John's College, Oxford, acquired a copy of the *Collationes* in 1608.[20] Yet for Laud to cite Cassian, in such a doctrinal context, when preaching before the King appears a remarkable piece of boldness, and suggests that he was confident of support. Certainly the sermon was subsequently printed by royal command, and that August James I issued directions prohibiting all 'popular' preaching about the pros and cons of predestination. It has been convincingly argued that in these last years of his reign James, partly for political reasons, was moving away from his previous support of the Calvinists.[21] As for Laud, his sermon of 1622 constitutes a declaration of Arminian sympathies.

Laud had become a bishop in 1621, but only of St David's. Not until 1633, aged sixty, was he in a position as Archbishop fully to apply his ideas at national level. It would be something of an exaggeration to describe the first two decades of the seventeenth century as the wilderness years of Laud. He did become head of his Oxford college, in 1611, and Dean of Gloucester, in 1616. These were, however, years of relative obscurity, which also partly explains the lack of surviving evidence. One of the earliest episodes which can be documented independently of Heylyn is Laud's intervention at Gloucester Cathedral, as newly, appointed Dean. On arrival there he found the communion table positioned in the middle of the choir, and in early 1617 ordered that it be placed altarwise at the east end. There were a variety of cathedral practices at the time, although this initiative by Laud implies a very un-Calvinist view of the eucharist or holy communion, as a source of grace to all receivers. Indeed he was later to describe the altar as 'the greatest place of God's residence upon earth'. The year 1617 also saw the altarwise repositioning of the communion table at Durham Cathedral, where his patron Neile was Bishop. Again at about the same time Laud's old tutor and mentor John Buckeridge, now a bishop, apparently commissioned a remarkable new chalice for his private chapel. This chalice survives, having been bequeathed by Buckeridge to St John's College, Oxford, and has been dated on the basis of the maker's mark. Modelled on the design of pre-Reformation chalices, it also depicts Christ as the 'good shepherd' – the sheep on his shoulders representing a sinner gone astray. Under Queen Elizabeth most chalices had been melted down and turned into communion cups. Buckeridge's chalice is the earliest extant example of a subsequent renaissance, the actual image of the good shepherd deriving from early Christian sources.[22]

Very much more was involved here than simply aesthetic considerations. This is clear both from a discourse on kneeling at communion, published by Buckeridge in 1618, and from his surviving will of 1631. Buckeridge describes himself in this latter document as the 'most unworthy Bishop of Ely', beseeching God to 'wash me thoroughly in the blood of thy son . . . and though my sins be as crimson yet let it please thee to make them as white as snow'. This is a highly unusual will for the period, and it certainly does not mean that Buckeridge had led an especially immoral life. There are echoes here of the teaching of Henry Bearblock in the 1590s – 'no man is without sin, but the best and holiest is unclean', and also of Buckeridge's own discourse, where he describes prospective communicants as 'vile and base . . . mortal and sinful' and invokes the image of the prodigal son. Traces too of this attitude can be found in the will made by Laud in 1644, where he calls himself 'a most prodigal son' and speaks of his 'many great and grievous transgressions'.[23] Calvinist wills of the period tend to be very different, the testators confidently affirming their belief that they are elect saints and often with no reference at all to personal sinfulness. By contrast in the anti-Calvinist economy of salvation, now being evolved by Buckeridge, Laud and their like, the sacrament of holy communion played a crucial role. Salvation came via the grace which it conferred, penitent sinners being washed by the blood of Christ.

The same association of ideas can be found present in Laud's volume of private devotions. Especially striking is the eucharistic section, where Laud prays before receiving the elements of bread and wine:

> O Lord, I am thy son, thy most unkind, prodigal, run-away son, yet thy son . . . O Lord, in thy grace I return to thee; and though I have eaten draff with all the unclean swine in the world, in my hungry absence from thee, yet now Lord, upon my humble return to thee, give me I beseech thee the bread of life, the body and blood of my Saviour.

Having received the sacrament of holy communion, Laud concludes: 'enrich me with all those graces which come from that precious body and blood, even till I be possessed of eternal life in Christ'.[24] Herein lies the remedy for sin, as opposed to an arbitrary decree of divine election. Such views are also a very important dimension to the ceremonial changes characteristic of the 1630s, when Laud was actually in the saddle.

Behind Laud and Buckeridge, however, stands another English religious figure – that of Lancelot Andrewes. When Andrewes died in September 1626, Laud described him as 'the great light of the Christian world'. Preaching at the funeral, Buckeridge said 'I loved and honoured him for above thirty years space'. He and Laud were appointed by Charles I to edit the collected sermons of Andrewes, which appeared as a handsome folio volume in 1629 and with a dedication to the King. The third edition, of 1635, also includes an analytical subject index. Some of these index entries provide important pointers to the thinking of Andrewes and, by extension, that of his editors. 'Eucharist . . . the conduit-pipe of grace', 'Grace offered to all', 'Perseverance and falling back', 'Prayer . . . the chief part of God's service', 'Reprobation not absolute' and 'Sermons . . . not the chief exercise of religion'.[25]

Andrewes was an anti-Calvinist veteran of the 1590s. Yet his central role has been obscured by the misdating of a key sermon preached before Queen Elizabeth, at Hampton Court, on 6 March 1595. This sermon relates to the predestinarian controversy at Cambridge University, where Andrewes was master of Pembroke Hall. On the text 'Remember Lot's wife' (Luke 7.32), it was not published until 1629 but repays close study. The wife of Lot is described as an example of 'imperseverant and relapsing righteous persons'. Andrewes distinguishes between 'two sorts', the one 'in state of sin that are wrong' and the other 'in state of grace that are well, if so they can keep them'. For the latter are always in danger of turning back, like Lot's wife, and finally perishing. Perseverance is, of course, the coping stone of Calvinist predestinarian teaching, the crown laid up for God's elect. But the clear message of Andrewes in 1595 was that no one can rest safe.[26]

It may well be significant that this is the only extant sermon of Andrewes which treats at length of perseverance or any related predestinarian theme and, as we have said, it remained unpublished in his lifetime. Was he warned off the subject? Certainly that happened to him under King James. Nevertheless, in the wake of the religious crisis at Cambridge, Andrewes ventured some further private comments. Among other things, he stated that 'almost all' the Fathers maintained that the decree of election was due to 'faith foreseen'. Therefore according to them election, like reprobation, was not absolute. Instead, both were conditional. Andrewes did not 'dare', so he wrote, to 'condemn' this view. But anti-Calvinist teaching on the theology of grace was only part of his legacy. Andrewes also possessed a chalice, 'having on the outside of the bowl Christ with the lost sheep on his shoulders', which sounds identical to that later bequeathed by Buckeridge to St John's College, Oxford. In his will Andrewes spoke of himself as a 'most wretched and unworthy sinner', to some extent anticipating Buckeridge and Laud. Similarly his collection of private devotions includes a eucharistic prayer reminiscent of that used by Laud, and in this case taken from Chrysostom.

> As thou didst not repel even the harlot like me, the sinner, coming to thee and touching thee; as thou didst not abhor her filthy mouth and polluted, . . . in like sort vouchsafe to accept me withal the inveterate, miserable, the singular great sinner to the touch and partaking of the immaculate, awful, quickening and saving mysteries of thine allholy body and precious blood.[27]

Both prayers abolish any real distinction between election and reprobation, all mankind being plunged into an abyss of habitual sin and from which the only escape is via the eucharistic sacrifice. They also, in effect, restore a section of the Roman Catholic Missal omitted from the English Prayer Book, which must seriously qualify any attempt to portray English Arminians as merely latter-day Edwardian Protestants.[28]

We have dwelt on Andrewes because Laud and his circle regarded him as an intellectual father figure. Indeed the thinking of Andrewes underlies many of the more salient religious developments of the 1630s. Although he passed through a number of bishoprics and ended up a Privy Councillor, only at the very end of the reign of James I did the views of Andrewes come to pose a major threat to Calvinist hegemony. Probably Andrewes achieved the height of his effective influence under the new King, Charles I, and during the last eighteen months of his life. Hence it is significant that Laud was promised the succession to the archbishopric of Canterbury, by Charles, in October 1626 – the month after the death of Andrewes.[29]

III

According to one tradition Laud was elevated to the episcopate, in 1621, thanks to the royal favourite Buckingham. Alternatively, he may have owed his promotion to the growing influence at court of his backers among the bishops. Either way, Laud's becoming Bishop of St David's needs to be understood against the changing political background of the time. The Thirty Years War had broken out three years earlier, and King James was anxious to avoid direct military involvement. As a consequence he sought to counter-balance the Calvinist war party at home, by promoting clergy such as Laud. It was a case of peace, and possible toleration of Catholic recusants, against war in the name of the true, Calvinist religion. Whatever Buckingham's role in the initial promotion of Laud, the latter rapidly established a key position in the Buckingham household. This seems to have come about due to the religious wavering of Buckingham's mother, who was tempted to turn Catholic. Her conversion would have been politically embarrassing, and Laud's own brand of moderate Protestantism was required to prevent it. In the process, Laud became the chaplain and confidant of Buckingham in 1622. This was also the occasion of Laud's major published work, the conference with Fisher the Jesuit about the claims of the Roman Catholic Church to religious obedience. Laud conceded that Rome was 'a true Church in essence', although 'corrupt and tainted'. But because of the limited terms of reference of this debate, it tells us little about his wider thought. None the less he did include a quotation from St Jerome to the effect that a Church could not exist without bishops.[30]

Despite this court employment, Laud seemingly failed to win the complete trust of King James. Promotion from St David's only came in 1626. Indeed his career in national politics did not fully take off until 1627 when he became a Privy Councillor, King Charles having come to the throne two years earlier. Moreover Laud always remained first and foremost an ecclesiastic, and comparisons with Cardinal Wolsey or the contemporary Richelieu are misplaced. It was the churchmanship of Laud which primarily attracted the new King. Charles I, like Laud, apparently came to regard Calvinism as fundamentally subversive of the institutional structures of state as well as Church. As early as 1625, Laud can be found claiming that the 'fatal' teachings of Calvinism nullified the 'practice of piety and obedience'; the overweening confidence of the self-styled elect was equally destructive of 'external ministry' in the Church and 'civil government in the commonwealth'.[31]

There was no necessary conflict, however, between Calvinism and divine right monarchy, and what probably tipped the balance was the religious aversion of Charles to this type of Christian evangelism. As we have remarked, he promised Laud Canterbury in 1626 – when the Calvinist Abbot still had seven years to live. That June saw the issue of a royal proclamation banning the subject of predestination from press and pulpit, in the name of the 'peace and quiet' of the English Church. This was elaborated during late 1628, in a declaration prefacing a reissue of the Thirty-nine Articles. The impact was felt immediately at Cambridge University, and rather more gradually elsewhere. A precedent, of course, had been established here by the Jacobean directions to preachers in 1622, although these had proved largely inoperative. But a ban on all predestinarian teaching was something which anti-Calvinists like Andrewes had also sought back in the 1590s. Then, as now, Calvinists complained that this penalised orthodoxy. Like them, we should not necessarily take the proclaimed peacemakers at face value. To forbid a body of established teaching, because of some opposition to it, is in fact a classic means of altering the *status quo*. Public opposition to Calvinism at this date was mainly confined to the writings of Richard Montagu, who in his *A New Gagg* of 1624 and *Appello Caesarem* of 1625 had gone much further than the remarks of Laud in 1622. Yet behind Montagu was a powerful body of backers, who included Andrewes as well as Laud, Buckeridge and Neile. They in turn successfully pleaded his cause with Buckingham and Charles.[32]

According to Laud, Calvinist theology made of God 'the most unreasonable tyrant in the world' and was also deeply divisive. As he said in 1626, 'divide the minds of men about their hope of salvation in Christ and tell me what unity there will be'. In July 1628 Laud was promoted to the bishopric of London, which gave him a potentially key position in the operation of press censorship – especially of religious books. Laud also vetted in advance the sermons preached at Paul's Cross, the most public pulpit in the land. Here it can be shown that from mid 1628 Calvinist sermons disappeared, and by the following year were being replaced by Arminian ones. Particularly interesting in this connection is Laud's answer to the resolution of the House of Commons, in January 1629, against Arminianism. The Commons had avowed for truth the 'sense' of the Thirty-nine Articles which 'by the general and current exposition of the writers of our Church hath been delivered unto us'. Laud did not attempt to deny that the tenor of 'current' teaching was opposed to Arminianism. But he noted that this was only a 'probable' argument as regards the true nature of English Church teaching. For 'the current exposition of the fathers themselves hath sometimes missed the sense of the Church'. He added that 'consent of writers . . . may, and perhaps do, go against the literal sense' of the Thirty-nine Articles. Consent to an 'article, or canon, is to itself'.[33]

The same year, 1629, Laud had a hand in regulating religious lecturers, at a national level, and in turning afternoon sermons into catechisings. The purpose of lectureships was to provide sermons, and they were often held by clergy with conscientious scruples about conforming. One object of the new instructions was to remove this puritan loophole, by making lecturers read the Prayer Book service before preaching. This policy, like other aspects of the Caroline religious programme, had been foreshadowed in the last few years of King James. It was now revived and extended, the moving spirit apparently being Archbishop Harsnett of York – the senior surviving Arminian cleric. The fact of Harsnett's involvement underlines the collective responsibility of the anti-Calvinist leadership for religious alterations under Charles I. Discussions also took place between Laud and Charles, in December 1629, about revising the Elizabethan Injunctions of 1559. In this connection a document was drawn up comparing them with the Jacobean canons of 1604. Two particular failings in the canons were highlighted, concerning control of printing and the location of the communion table in churches. On this latter topic, the author concluded 'it were to be wished it would please His Majesty by some declaration to take away the scruple which some nowadays make of the placing of the communion table'. Here indeed we seem to have the genesis of the altar policy of the 1630s.[34]

At this point it is necessary to clarify further the relationship between Calvinism and Puritanism. Puritans were generally Calvinists, but only a minority of Calvinists were Puritans in a nonconformist sense. Thus during the 1620s the Archbishops of Canterbury, York and Armagh were all Calvinists. To call George Abbot, Toby Matthew and James Ussher 'Puritan' archbishops would be inappropriate. They were not saboteurs, working to undermine the English Church. Nevertheless Calvinism had provided a shared frame of reference for conformists and nonconformists alike, which was now being dissolved. This is the context of the winding up in the early 1630s of the Feoffees for Impropriations: a group of Puritan-minded clergy and laity who had begun to buy up impropriated tithes in order to increase the stipends of preachers. Laud was convinced that a Puritan 'plot' was afoot, 'to overthrow the Church government', although in earlier days it would probably not have been so regarded. Rightly or wrongly, Laud felt unable to harness the enthusiasm of the feoffees to his own plans for augmenting clerical incomes. The issue was partly one of control, a major objection being that much of the money was earmarked for unbeneficed lecturers. There is also a theological aspect to this, because of the Calvinist stress on sermons.[35]

The full impact of religious change, however, was only felt after Laud became archbishop in 1633. The first few months of his primacy saw both the start of a campaign against strict Sunday observance and a royal ruling in favour of the altarwise position of communion tables. The former involved a reissue of the Jacobean Book of Sports of 1618, which had never been strictly enforced. Whereas during the Elizabethan and Jacobean periods sabbatarianism had increasingly become part of English religious life, from 1633 there was a sustained attempt to reverse the process. One of the arguments adduced in favour was that on Sunday Christians celebrate the fact that Christ died for all mankind without exception and not just the elect. But there was no simple correlation of attitudes here, some notable Calvinists also being opposed to sabbatarianism. At the same time the Book proved a serious stumbling block to Puritans. On the subject of altars Laud and Neile, the latter recently appointed Archbishop of York, had made their views known as early as 1617. Now, however, began the systematic application of the cathedral model at parish level. The start was signalled by the case of St Gregory's-by-St Paul's, in London, which King Charles himself adjudicated in November 1633. The King found in favour of the St Paul's Cathedral authorities and against the parishioners, ordering that the communion table should remain in its new position at the east end of the chancel. Apropos the question whether the moving spirit here was Laud or Charles, the strict answer is neither since we know that Archbishop Neile had already begun converting parish communion tables in the northern province some months previously.[36]

Yet there can be no serious doubt that Laud wholeheartedly, supported the altar policy. During 1634 he commenced a metropolitical visitation of the province of Canterbury, and [by 1635 had] issued instructions to his vicar-general, Sir Nathaniel Brent, in favour of 'the railing in, the setting up at the east end the communion table and the receiving thereat'. Laud, it is true, favoured persuasion rather than coercion, which served to differentiate his position from that of Arminian zealots like Bishop Matthew Wren.[37] The aim, however, was the same, namely to remodel communion practice throughout

England. Laud assumed that a majority of parish churches at the start of the 1630s did not have their communion tables placed altarwise. The subsequent change was probably for many people the most obvious and symbolic religious act of the Caroline regime. It is also clear from the history of his chancellorship of Oxford University that Laud advocated the custom of bowing towards the altar. Both this and the altarwise position of communion tables were to be embodied in the canons of 1640.[38]

Many altars and chancels were further embellished at this time, with pictures of the crucifixion. Decency, order and ecclesiastical status were all factors. But so too was a greatly enhanced view of the importance of the eucharist itself, as the fount of 'eternal life in Christ'. Such 'immaculate, awful, quickening and saving mysteries' almost demanded setting apart in a holy of holies – railed in at the east end of churches. This profound shift of emphasis also spelt redundancy for Calvinist teaching on predestination. By 1632 Calvinism had been silenced at both Oxford and Cambridge Universities. The following year, 1633, the succession of Laud to Canterbury saw a marked tightening of press censorship. Both his own chaplains and those of his protégé Bishop William Juxon of London can be shown to have taken their function as licensers seriously, and at the expense of Calvinists. Conversely, they permitted the publication of Arminian theological views. Neverthless this was essentially secondary to the sacramental reorientation of English religious life now occurring.[39] Certainly in the longer term the future lay with the party of Laud. What however temporarily halted them in their tracks was the political collapse of the Caroline regime, in 1640, following on the Scottish rebellion.

The ostensible cause of the revolt in Scotland was the new Prayer Book of 1637, although Laud claimed that religion merely served as a subterfuge. He also denied direct responsibility for the Scottish Prayer Book, while admitting to approving strongly of its content. Laud said he would have preferred the Scots to have adopted the existing English Prayer Book, as more conducive to uniformity between the three kingdoms. While we may accept this, the sacramental thrust of the new liturgy is none the less extremely revealing. One of the most important departures from that of England concerned the communion service, where the words of administration simply follow those of the first Edwardian Prayer Book: 'the body of our Lord Jesus Christ, which was given for thee', and 'the blood of our Lord Jesus Christ, which was shed for thee, preserve thy body and soul unto everlasting life'. This altered the Elizabethan formula which had subjoined the significantly different wording of the second Edwardian Prayer Book. The initiative here was apparently that of Bishop James Wedderburn of Dunblane, who argued that 'the words which are added since, "take, eat, in remembrance etc.", may seem to relish somewhat of the Zwinglian tenet that the sacrament is a bare sign taken in remembrance of Christ's passion'. Nothing must be allowed to detract from the saving reality of the 'body' and 'blood' of Christ in the eucharist.⁴⁰

'All reformation that is good and orderly takes away nothing from the old but that which is faulty and erroneous'.⁴¹ So Laud generalised from the making of the Scottish Prayer Book. Others, of course, saw such alterations as 'innovation'. Not only the chief executive, Laud was also a leading architect of religious change during the 1630s – working in close alliance with both King Charles and in some cases over-enthusiastic subordinates. From 1633 onwards Laud at Canterbury, Neile at York and Juxon at London oversaw a coherent reform programme centring on doctrine and worship. The intellectual roots ran back to the Elizabethan period, but only came to fruition under Charles I. Eclipsed in the mid-seventeenth century, the movement was to re-emerge at the Restoration as a major directing force.

NOTES

1 A. Grey, *Debates in the House of Commons from the year 1667 to the year 1694* (London, 1769), i, pp. 112–13. For the post-Restoration position of the communion table, see N. Yates, *Buildings, Faith and Worship: the Liturgical Arrangement of Anglican Churches, 1600–1900* (Oxford, 1991), p. 32.

2 H. R. Trevor-Roper. *Archbishop Laud, 1573–1645* (London, 1940), pp. 2–3, 7, 12–22; C. Carlton, *Archbishop William Laud* (London, 1989), pp. 1, 152–3, 228; E. C. E. Bourne, *The Anglicanism of William Laud* (London, 1947).

3 P. Heylyn, *Cyprianus Anglicus* (London, 1668), pp. 50–3, and *Historia Quinqu-Articularis* (London, 1660), pt iii, 74. There appears no evidence, contrary to what is often said, that Heylyn was ever chaplain to Laud.

4 K. Sharpe, 'Archbishop Laud', *History Today* 33 (August, 1983), pp. 26–30, and 'The Personal Rule of Charles I', in H. Tomlinson ed., *Before the English Civil War* (London, 1983), pp. 62–3; J. Davies, *The Caroline Captivity of the Church. Charles I and the Remoulding of Anglicanism* (Oxford, 1992), ch. 6.

5 K. Sharpe, 'Archbishop Laud and the University of Oxford', in H. Lloyd-Jones, V. Pearl and B. Worden eds, *History and Imagination* (London, 1981), p. 161; P. A. Welsby, *George Abbot: the Unwanted Archbishop* (London, 1962), pp. 3, 37–8; K. Fincham, 'Prelacy and Politics: Archbishop Abbot's Defence of Protestant Orthodoxy', *HJ* 61 (1988), 36–64; *CSPD, 1611–18*, p. 533.

6 See pp. 161–2, 164, 174–5 above; Tyacke, *Anti-Calvinists*, chs 2–3 and Appendix i. Whether Heylyn was correct in his assessment of the Elizabethan settlement is a question which I plan to pursue elsewhere. Suffice it to say for the moment that English protestantism had received a major injection of Reformed theology even before the Marian exile. [See also pp. 177–8 above]

7 Laud, *Works*, iii, p. 131; D. Lloyd, *Memoires of the Lives . . . of Excellent Persons that suffered for Allegiance to their Sovereign* (London, 1668), pp. 225–6.

8 J. Young, *A Sermon* (London, 1576), sigs C4v–C5v; S. Clarke, *The Lives of Thirty-Two English Divines* (London, 1677), 38–42. These are my identifications and there is some dispute over the evidence concerning Buckeridge being a prebendary of Rochester: J. Le Neve ed., *Fasti Ecclesiae Anglicanae, 1541–1857*, iii, Canterbury, Rochester and Winchester Dioceses, comp. J. M. Horn (1974), p. 67, n. 1.

9 W. Bradshaw, *A Myld and Just Defense of Certeyne Arguments* (London, 1606), pp. 44–5; G. Powell, *A Rejoynder unto the Mild Defense* (London, 1607), pp. 118–19; H. C. Porter, *Reformation and Reaction in Tudor Cambridge* (Cambridge, 1958), chs 15–17.

10 Laud, *Works*, iv, p. 309; Heylyn, *Cyprianus Anglicus*, 54; Tyacke, *Anti-Calvinists*, 70–1, 266–70.

11 W. H. Stevenson and H. E. Salter, *The Early History of St. John's College Oxford* (OHS, 1939), pp. 197, 353, 356–7.

12 J. Buckeridge, *A Sermon Preached at Hampton Court* (London, 1606), pp. 41–2; J. Strype, *Annals of the Reformation* (Oxford, 1824), i, pt i, pp. 540–1; Tyacke, *Anti-Calvinists*, p. 250.

13 C. Coates, *The History and Antiquities of Reading* (London, 1802), p. 411; PRO, PROB 11/9, fo 117v; R. O'Day, *The English Clergy: the Emergence and Consolidation of a Profession, 1558–1642* (Leicester, 1979), ch. 13.

14 G. Abbot, *The Reasons which Doctour Hill hath brought for the Upholding of Papistry* (Oxford, 1604), pp. 26–71; Heylyn, *Cyprianus Anglicus*, p. 53; A. Clarke ed., *The Register of the University of Oxford* (OHS, 1887), ii, pt i, p. 206. I am grateful to Anthony Milton for discussions on this subject.

15 Laud, *Works*, v, p. 117, vi, p. 704; Tyacke, *Anti-Calvinists*, pp. 11–12, 14.

16 Laud, *Works*, i, p. 26, vi, pp. 689–91; Tyacke, *Anti-Calvinists*, pp. 70–1, 110–13.

17 Laud, *Works*, i, pp. 5–6, 63–4, vi, pp. 57, 119–20.

18 Laud, *Works*, i, pp. 55–7. See also Tyacke, *Anti-Calvinists*, Appendix ii.

19 Laud, *Works*, i, p. 56; O. Chadwick, *John Cassian* (2nd edn Cambridge, 1968), ch. 4. Writers on Laud have strangely neglected this sermon and in particular the vital Cassian reference.

20 The St John's copy of the *Collationes* is a 1606 Lyons edition. I am grateful to Miss A. Williams, the assistant librarian of St John's College, Oxford, for supplying this information.

21 J. P. Kenyon, *The Stuart Constitution* (2nd edn Cambridge, 1986), 128–30; K. Fincham and P. Lake, 'The Ecclesiastical Policy of King James I', *JBS* 24 (1985), 202–6.

22 Laud, *Works*, iv, pp. 233–4, vi, pp. 57, 239–41; Tyacke, *Anti-Calvinists*, pp. xviii, 71, 116–17; C. Oman, *English Church Plate, 597–1830* (Oxford, 1957), pp. 71, 205, 226 and plate 80.

23 PRO, PROB 11/160, fos 16v–17; J. Buckeridge, *A Sermon . . . to which is added a Discourse concerning Kneeling at the Communion* (London, 1618), pp. 68, 96; Laud, *Works*, iv, pp. 441–2.

24 Laud, *Works*, iii, pp. 74–5.

25 Laud, *Works*, iii, p. 196; L. Andrewes, *XCVI Sermons* (London, 1635), sig. Rrrrr5 and 'A Table of the Principal Contents'.

26 L. Andrewes, *XCVI Sermons* (London, 1629), pt i, pp. 299–308. Historians using the nineteenth-century edition of Andrewes's collected works have assumed wrongly that this sermon dates from 1593/4 as opposed to 1594/5, the Old Style year beginning on 25 March. Compare, for example, Porter, *Reformation and Reaction*, 352. My redating allows this sermon by Andrewes to be fitted into the sequence of events unfolding at Cambridge, between February and April 1595. P. Lake, *Moderate Puritans and the Elizabethan Church* (Cambridge, 1982), pp. 201–4. [My 'redating' of this sermon is, alas, incorrect; it was indeed preached in 1594: N. Tyacke, 'Lancelot Andrewes and the Myth of Anglicanism', in P. Lake and M. Questier eds, *Conformity and Orthodoxy in the English Church*, c. 1560–1660 (Woodbridge, 2000), p. 13, n. 26.]

27 Tyacke, *Anti-Calvinists*, 45; J. P. Wilson and J. Bliss eds, *The Works of Lancelot Andrewes* (Oxford, 1841–54), vi, p. 296, xi, pp. xcvii, c, and L. Andrewes, *The Preces Privatae*, ed. F. E. Brightman (London, 1903), p. 121. [Andrewes did in fact preach about predestination in 1599: Tyacke, 'Lancelot Andrewes', p. 13.]

28 F. E. Warner ed., *The Sarum Missal in English* (London, 1911), pt i, pp. 17–19. Compare *The Orthodox Liturgy* (Oxford, 1982), pp. 5–14. The language of these prayers is much more extreme than anything to be found in the English Prayer Book.

29 Laud, *Works*, iii, pp. 160, 196. This revises my earlier argument that up to then Richard Neile was the 'Arminian candidate for Canterbury': Tyacke, *Anti-Calvinists*, p. 123.

30 J. Hacket, *Scrinia Reserata* (London, 1693), pt i, 63–4; Heylyn, *Cyprianus Anglicus*, 85–6, 100–1; Laud *Works*, ii, pp. 144, 147, 194–5, iii, pp. 138–9. I owe the St Jerome reference to Peter Lake.

31 Laud, *Works*, vi, pp. 245–6.

32 Tyacke, *Anti-Calvinists*, 48–51, 76–81, 149; J. Strype, *The Life and Acts of . . . John Whitgift* (Oxford, 1822), ii, pp. 260–1.

33 Laud, *Works*, i, p. 71, vi, pp. 11–12, 133; Tyacke, *Anti-Calvinists*, pp. 182, 249, 263–5.

34 Laud, *Works*, iv, p. 274, v, pp. 307–9, vi, pp. 23–34; Bodl., Rawlinson MS A.127, fo 73r–v. I owe this last reference to the work of Julian Davies.

35 Tyacke, *Anti-Calvinists*, pp. 18–19, 21, 49; Laud, *Works*, iv, p. 303; I. M. Calder ed., *Activities of the Puritan Faction of the Church of England* (London, 1957); see pp. 121–3 above and pp. 278–9 below.

36 Tyacke, *Anti-Calvinists*, pp. 199–209, 222–3; K. L. Parker, *The English Sabbath: a Study of Doctrine and Discipline from the Reformation to the Civil War* (Cambridge, 1988), ch. 7.

37 PRO, SP 16/485, fo 252. The attitude of Laud on this issue has been much debated, but the passage quoted is his own retrospective account of what he recommended. Compare, however, Davies, *Caroline Captivity*, ch. 6.

38 Laud, *Works*, v, pp. 204–7, 624–6, vi, p. 59.

39 Tyacke, *Anti-Calvinists*, pp. xiii, 184–5, 198, 216–18.

40 Laud, *Works*, iii, pp. 335–7, 356–7; G. Donaldson, *The Making of the Scottish Prayer Book of 1637* (Edinburgh, 1954), pp. 200–1.

41 Laud, *Works*, iii, p. 341.

Chapter 9

$\blacklozenge$

Arminianism
and English culture

I

THE notion dies hard that Arminianism in early seventeenth century England was 'a catch-all term of abuse' expressing 'rather vague fears of a group of theologians who, by their emphasis upon the sacraments, ceremonial, and the *iure divino* status of bishops, seemed to be taking the Church back towards Rome'.[1] For such is the combined voice of John Kenyon, in his new Pelican history of Stuart England, and of Andrew Foster the modern biographer of Richard Neile, ultimately Archbishop of York and reputedly a great patron of English Arminian clergy. Yet there exists abundant evidence to show that it was precisely the anti-determinist views of the Dutch Arminius which Englishmen had in mind when they complained, with increasing vehemence, about the emergence of home-grown Arminianism. A good example of this usage is William Prynne's book *The Church of England's Old Antithesis to New Arminianisme*, first published in 1629, which seeks to vindicate the orthodoxy of the English Church from those who intrude 'the Arminian doctrines of free will, the resistability of grace, conditionall, yea mutable election, with total and final apostacie from the state of grace'. According to Prynne, a common lawyer, the very title deeds of 'our salvation' were at stake.[2] Moreover, as we shall see, those Englishmen labelled Arminian by their compatriots did usually espouse the cause of man's free will.

The religious questions raised by Arminius, divinity professor at Leiden, and by his Dutch followers were not of course new to Christianity in the early seventeenth century, but their teaching and even more their published writings launched a debate which threatened to tear Calvinist Europe apart. In England, where a previous challenge to Calvinist determinism had failed,[3] Dutch Arminian developments were followed with close attention. An important early link was Richard or 'Dutch' Thomson, as he is sometimes called, fellow of Clare College, Cambridge, who had known Arminius personally in Holland during the 1590s, a decade when Thomson and those like-minded had tried unsuccessfully to break the virtual monopoly of Calvinism within the English Church. In 1605 Thomson can be found writing of students newly arrived in Cambridge, from Leiden, being cross-questioned about the latest utterances of Arminius.[4] It was Thomson also who in 1611 lent Isaac Casaubon, now settled in England, a copy of the notorious Arminian book by Petrus Bertius – *De Sanctorum Perseverantia et Apostasia*, of which King James wrote that 'the title . . . were enough to make it worthy the fire'.[5] Bertius was among the closest to Arminius of his Leiden disciples and with the posthumous printing, in 1612, of Arminius' own *Examen* of a book on predestination by William Perkins, late fellow of Christ's College, Cambridge, it became public knowledge that Arminius had done literary battle with one of the most popular theologians in Jacobean England.[6] The following year, 1613, saw Hugo Grotius, the newly appointed Pensionary of Rotterdam, at the English Court propagandising in person on behalf of the Dutch Arminian or Remonstrant party.

Ostensibly on a trade mission to England, Grotius had been instructed by Oldenbarnevelt, Advocate of Holland, to canvass support for his policy of tolerating the Dutch Remonstrants. 'Dutch' Thomson had recently died but Grotius was introduced by Casaubon to the two senior English clerics potentially most sympathetic to Arminianism – John Overall, Dean of St Paul's, and Lancelot Andrewes, Bishop of Ely. They in turn helped to procure a private audience with the King. Grotius apparently found James in an eirenic frame of mind, very different from that in which two years earlier he had denounced Arminius as an 'enemie of God'. While the mood of the King was not to last, in Overall Grotius acquired henceforward a particularly warm supporter and collaborator. Overall, for instance, supplied Grotius with a copy of Thomson's tract *De Amissione et Intercisione Gratiae* that had languished in manuscript since the late 1590s. This work by Thomson, which like the *De Sanctorum* of Bertius argued that even the elect could fall from grace, was printed at Leiden in 1616.[7] Thomson was to be answered two years later by Robert Abbot, Regius professor of divinity at Oxford and brother of Archbishop George Abbot of Canterbury, 'burning', as his official biographer put it, 'with zeale both to defend the doctrine of truth and unity in the Reformed Churches'.[8]

Other potential English supporters of the Dutch Remonstrants at the time of Grotius' mission in 1613 were John Richardson, Regius professor of divinity at Cambridge, and Samuel Brooke, Divinity professor at Gresham College in London. Both men were to make plain their Arminian views on free will during the years 1616–17, and Richardson was as a consequence to lose his professorial chair.[9] At Oxford William Laud, the future archbishop, is the first person known to have maintained recognisably Arminian doctrines in the presence of a university auditory. Laud, in the words of his chaplain and biographer, Peter Heylyn, preaching on Shrove Sunday 1615 'insisted on some points which might indifferently be imputed either to Popery or Arminianism, as about that time they began to call it.' It emerges from Heylyn's account that these Arminian 'points' concerned 'free will, justification, concupiscence being a sin after baptism, inherent righteousness and certainty of salvation', and that Laud was indeed contending against 'the Calvinian rigours in the matter of predestination'. This is a very important testimony by a near Oxford contemporary, who was in addition to become an expert on the Arminian controversy, because it has been claimed that the views of Laud apropos free will are 'remarkably obscure'.[10] Laud in fact belonged to an Oxford group which had access to some of Arminius' own writings by 1613 and probably earlier, at a time when, as Heylyn says, the Calvinist predestinarians 'carried all before them'. In so far as Laud had reservations about the teachings of the Dutch Arminians he thought that they were too dogmatic. 'Something about these controversies is unmasterable in this life' was to be his private comment fifteen years later.[11] Another member with Laud of this same Oxford group was Thomas Jackson, fellow of Corpus Christi College. We possess the text of a college sermon preached by Jackson in about 1611, where he attacks 'the fierce current of modern opinions, which deny all possibility of running (in any sort) to God's mercy before grace infused do draw us. The unseasonable overflow of which newly outburst doctrine throughout our land doth more mischief to men's souls than the summer floods do to their fields'. Significantly he also says that his teaching runs the risk of being branded as 'Pelagianism . . . should I utter this doctrine in some public audience'.[12]

Just as the Dutch Remonstrants sought English support so did the Counter-Remonstrants. This involved, among other things, a foray into recent history and saw the publication in 1613 of a two volume collection of documents deriving from the Cambridge predestinarian disputes of the 1590s. The volumes were edited by Anthony Thysius, divinity professor at Harderwijk, who also provided prefatory histories written from a Calvinist point of view. Many of these documents had never been printed before, although Thysius' source remains mysterious.[13] The first volume begins with the *Summa Trium de Praedestinatione* of Peter Baro, Lady Margaret professor of divinity at Cambridge until driven out by the Calvinists in 1596. According to Thysius the growing unorthodoxy of Baro had finally provoked his professorial colleague, William Whitaker, into taking a stand against him. Thus in February 1595 Whitaker delivered his lecture 'adversus universalis gratiae assertores', in the presence of a Cambridge audience which included three earls, five barons and many gentry. This lecture was published by Thysius

with the *Summa Trium*, in which Baro like Arminius rejects absolute predestination, both the supralapsarian and sublapsarian varieties, arguing instead
that election and reprobation are conditional on the behaviour of the individual. There follow refutations of Baro by the continental theologians John
Piscator and Francis Junius the elder. Also included in this volume are the
Lambeth Articles of 1595, so named because they had received their final
form from Archbishop Whitgift at Lambeth Palace in his adjudication of the
Cambridge disputes. Whitgift had sided with the Calvinists as had his fellow
archbishop – Hutton of York, and Thysius' second volume contains a piece
by Hutton defending the Calvinist case. These two books were clearly intended
as ammunition for the Counter-Remonstrant party, but Thysius also expressed
the hope in an unpublished letter of August 1613 that 'si placet quod ago
etiam Ecclesiam Anglicanam ad initia Reformationis revocabo'.[14] He would
seem to imply that anti-Calvinists were again making progress within the
English Church.

Apart from Thomson's tract *De Amissione* no English propaganda comparable to the Thysius volumes was produced by the Dutch Remonstrants.
With the prospect, however, of a national synod to decide the fate of Dutch
Arminianism efforts were made by the Remonstrants, and their supporters,
to influence the choice of the proposed foreign delegations. Oldenbarnevelt
wrote in June 1618 to Noel de Caron, Dutch Ambassador in London, suggesting three English bishops as delegates. The name of John Overall, now
Bishop of Coventry and Lichfield, causes no surprise but that the other two
members of this episcopal trio, suggested by Oldenbarnevelt, should be
Richard Neile of Durham and John Buckeridge of Rochester is a remarkable
tribute to their early Arminian reputations. As it happened none of them
attended the national synod at Dort, King James sending instead a group of
English Calvinists who participated there in the condemnation of Arminianism. Nevertheless the confidence of Oldenbarnevelt and his advisers in the
Arminian sympathies of Neile and Buckeridge is borne out by their later
defence, with their protégé Laud, of the English Arminian Richard Montagu,
whose writings were to be described by Grotius in 1626 as demonstrating
that the doctrines of the English Church and the Synod of Dort differed
radically.[15]

The fortunes of the Dutch Remonstrants were inextricably bound up
with those of Oldenbarnevelt, and his own fall gave rise in England to a considerable popular literature, mostly translations from the Dutch. In one such
work of 1618, entitled *Barnevel's Apology*, the term Arminian or Arminians
occurs over thirty times; 'Arminianisme' is also used. *Barnevel's Apology*
singles out predestination as a key issue and Oldenbarnevelt's view of this
doctrine is labelled Arminian, the author concluding with a predestinarian
prayer directed against the 'Arminian wicked sect'. A further manifestation

of newly aroused lay interest is the London performance, in August 1619, of a play by Fletcher and Massinger called *The Tragedy of Sir John van Olden Barnavelt*. The play draws on the earlier pamphlet literature, and the term Arminian or Arminians is frequently used in the text. The year 1619 also saw the English publication of *The Judgement of the Synode holden at Dort, concerning the Five Articles* of 'predestination and the points thereto annexed.' A preface explains the background to the synod, the Dutch Church having been 'assaulted by one James Harmans, alias Arminius, and his followers, assuming the title of Remonstrants'. This edition of the canons of Dort was produced by the royal printer John Bill. The Oxford press in 1623 and 1624 produced further English language editions of the Dort canons, as confirmed by 'the nationall synode of the Reformed Churches of France' and in the format of a thirty-four page pamphlet. Meanwhile for the *cognoscenti* there were the Latin anti-Arminian lectures of Robert Abbot, published in 1618, and the similar effusions of his successor as Regius professor at Oxford, John Prideaux. At the Oxford Acts between 1616 and 1622 Prideaux lectured against the Arminians concerning reprobation, universal grace, conversion, justification, perseverance and the certainty of salvation. At Cambridge the equivalent anti-Arminian role was played by Samuel Ward, who had been an English delegate at Dort and was now Lady Margaret professor.[16] Arminianism therefore was to some extent a familiar topic when first raised in the House of Commons during May 1624.

The Commons became involved because of a complaint against Richard Montagu's book *A New Gagg*. This complaint took the form of a petition which runs in part as follows.

> It is apparent unto the world how the erroneous and dangerous opinions of Arminius and his sectaries have infested and had brought into great perill the states of the United Provinces, if the King's Majesty by his gracious care, power, piety and providence, had not helped to quench that fire. Notwith-standing, this dangerous doctrine, and other erroneous opinions, hath of late been hatched, and now begins to be more boldly maintained by some divines of this our kingdom, especially by one Mr. Richard Montagu . . .

Reporting the petition from committee, John Pym described Montagu's book as 'full fraught with dangerous opinions of Arminius quite contrary to the articles established [i.e. the Thirty-nine Articles] *in five several points.*' This is almost certainly an allusion to the 'five articles' condemned at Dort, and the parliamentary definition of Arminianism remained equally precise through-out the 1620s. Thus in February 1629 the Commons illustrated 'the doctrine of the Church of England in those points wherein the Arminians differ from us' by 'the resolution of the Archbishop of Canterbury, and other reverend bishops and divines assembled at Lambeth for this very purpose, to declare their opinions concerning these points, *anno* 1595, unto which the Archbishop of York did likewise agree', and 'the suffrage of the British divines sent by our late sovereign King James to the Synod of Dort'.[17] To the extent that Popery was seen as synonymous with Arminianism this was because the teachings on predestination by the Council of Trent were so similar.[18]

At the time of writing *A New Gagg* in 1623 Montagu had not read Arminius as such. Nevertheless he soon repaired this omission, commenting of Arminius in May 1625 that 'the man had more in him than all the Netherlands'. Montagu arrived at his views partly as a result of studying the Greek Fathers of the early Christian Church, but he had also moved in anti-Calvinist circles at Cambridge. For example in the preface to his first book, published in 1610, he thanks 'Dutch' Thomson for providing scholarly assistance. His other most notable link with Dutch Arminianism was John Cosin, former secretary and librarian to Bishop Overall. It was Cosin to whom Montagu sent the manuscript of *A New Gagg* and who in turn supplied him with the works of Arminius. Cosin was now chaplain to Bishop Neile, Overall having died in 1619. Neile emerged as one of the staunchest defenders of Montagu, becoming in effect his patron as he was already of the Oxford Arminian Thomas Jackson. The relations however of Neile with Dutch Arminianism seem to have been less direct than were those of Andrewes and Laud. Grotius, who had kept in touch with Andrewes since his own mission to England in 1613, apparently first made contact with Laud via the Dutch Remonstrant exile Francis Junius the younger. Laud had recommended Junius for the post of librarian to the Earl of Arundel and Junius reciprocated in 1622 with a copy of Grotius' *Disquisitio* on the difference between an ancient Pelagian and a modern Arminian. Junius similarly supplied a copy of the *Disquisitio* to Samuel Harsnett, Bishop of Norwich, who like Andrewes was an anti-Calvinist survivor from Elizabethan days. Grotius also corresponded with Christopher Wren, chaplain to Andrewes, and with Cosin, who as we have noted furnished Montagu with Arminius.[19]

The death of King James in March 1625 found Montagu about to publish a further book in his own defence – *Apello Caesarem*. Within a fortnight after the start of the new reign Laud was sent by the Duke of Buckingham, his patron and the royal favourite, to inquire of Andrewes 'what he would have done in the cause of the Church . . . *especially in the matter of the Five Articles*', that is to say Arminianism. That July, again in the words of Laud, 'it pleased His Majesty King Charles to intimate to the House of Commons that what had been there said and resolved, without consulting him, in Montague's cause, was not pleasing to him'. The following month, at the start of the second session of the 1625 parliament, Laud, Buckeridge and John Howson, Bishop of Oxford, addressed a long letter to Buckingham on behalf of Montagu. In the course of this letter they disassociate the English Church from the 'fatal opinions' enshrined in the Lambeth Articles and more recently promulgated by the Synod of Dort. Interestingly they also stress 'how little' such doctrines agree 'with the practice and obedience to all government'.[20]

These preliminary moves culminated in January 1626 with a royal instruction to Andrewes that he consult with Bishops Montaigne, Neile, Buckeridge, Howson and Laud, 'or some of them', concerning 'Mr. Montague's late book, and deliver their opinions touching the same for the preservation of the truth and the peace of the Church of England'. Predictably, since all these bishops were Arminian sympathisers, they reported that Montagu 'hath not affirmed anything to be the doctrine of the Church of England but that which in our opinion is the doctrine of the Church of England or agreeable thereunto'. They went on to recommend a prohibition of 'any further controverting of these questions'. News of their meeting soon leaked out, the Earl of Clare writing in February that this 'commission by the episcopall decemvirs, regulating doctrine and faith, will reinforce the storm, for this creates the King not only (as heertofore) supreme head of the forme, that is of ecclesiastical discipline, but of the matter, even in all tenets of faith.' Clare went on to say that 'had reformation of error been the object' Arminianism ought to have been referred to 'a generall free councell of all the bishops and other divynes'. The upshot was that King Charles embodied the recommendations of this 'committee of a few selected bishops', as Clare called them, in his proclamation of June 1626 for 'the establishing of the peace and quiet of the Church of England'.[21]

English royal policy, with regard to Arminianism, was much closer than is usually recognised to that which Oldenbarnevelt had earlier sought to implement in the United Provinces. Charles was concerned to protect Montagu and other Arminians, like Jackson, both from the wrath of the laity in Parliament *and* from their fellow clergy in Convocation. It is important to recall here that the Archbishops of Canterbury and York at this time, George Abbot and Toby Matthew, were Calvinists. In 1629 the Calvinist Bishop Davenant, who had been an English delegate at Dort, was still convinced that a free vote in Convocation would result in the condemnation of Arminianism. Although Charles refused to allow any such vote, a member of the lower house of Convocation in 1625 recalled later that 'five and forty of us', led by Daniel Featley, chaplain to Archbishop Abbot, there 'made a solemn covenant among our selves to oppose every thing that did but savour or scent never so little of Pelagianisme or Semi-Pelagianisme'. This is an excellent illustration of the inappropriateness of the term 'High Church' as used by modern historians to describe the English Arminian movement. For in so far as the heresy hunting lower house of Convocation under William and Mary, and Anne, had an early seventeenth-century equivalent it was Featley and his Calvinist band of covenanters rather than bishops like Laud and Neile. Indeed Charles' proclamation of June 1626 is comparable to the resolution of the States of Holland in January 1614 which, as Jan den Tex has written, was feared as a device for tolerating Arminianism while banning orthodox predestinarian teaching.[22] Unlike the Dutch resolution, the English proclamation did not list specific forbidden doctrines but simply prohibited 'any new inventions or opinions' which differed 'from the sound and orthodoxal grounds of the true religion sincerely professed and happily established in the Church of England.'

If we would understand the Calvinist mentality, lay as well as clerical, which Arminianism so much offended, then William Prynne's first book, *The Perpetuitie of a Regenerate Man's Estate*, offers us a guide. It was published in 1626 as one of the many replies to Montagu, all in English and all defining Arminianism in terms of the teachings condemned by the Synod of Dort.[23] After arguing at length 'that such as are once truly regenerated and ingrafted into Christ by a lively faith can neither finally nor totally fall from grace', Prynne turns to the 'use' or application of this doctrine. The 'estate of grace', he points out, is the one true and permanent 'treasure', whereas 'friends, goods, riches, honours ... have their periods and their ends'. When troubles and ultimately death come grace still abides, and 'all the waters of adversitie' cannot extinguish it. Opponents of this doctrine are 'a company of carnall, gracelesse, prophane and dissolute persons'. As for Thomson's book on the subject, the author was 'a Dutchman and a drunken one too', who in his life was 'loose, licentious and voluptuous'. Arminians, Prynne says, are libertines morally as well as intellectually, for 'their very lives and actions do prove their doctrine'. From 1626 to 1629 Prynne wrote three books against Arminianism. He also attacked drink and fashion in *Healthes: Sicknesse* and *The Unlovelinesse of Lovelockes*, both published in 1628. His other target at this time was a devotional work compiled by the Arminian John Cosin, a book imbued with the sacramentalism that was to emerge as an adjunct of English Arminianism in the 1630s.[24]

During June 1628 Laud and Neile were named by the Commons as suspected 'Arminians', and at the end of the year Charles issued his declaration against 'unnecessary disputations, altercations or questions', which to this day still prefaces the Thirty-nine Articles. As supreme governor of the English Church, Charles laid down that

> in these both curious and unhappy differences, which have for so many hundred years, in different times and places, exercised the Church of Christ, we will, that all further curious search be laid aside, and these disputes shut up in God's promises, as they be generally set forth to us in the holy scriptures ...

What this meant can be seen from some of the writings of the Arminian Thomas Jackson, published in the ensuing decade. Christ, says Jackson, died not only for the elect but for 'all mankind', both 'efficiently' and 'sufficiently' without limitation. Similarly, in a sermon preached before King Charles, he castigates the view that God has 'destinated' anyone to 'inevitable destruction before he gave them life or preservation'. On the other, Calvinist side, as the 'root and branch' petitioners complained in 1640, clergy were inhibited from teaching the 'truth of God' concerning 'the doctrine of predestination, of free grace, of perseverance [and] of original sin remaining after baptism', or 'against universal grace, election for faith forseen [and] free will'. They contrasted this with the 'swarming of lascivious, idle and unprofitable books and pamphlets, playbooks and ballads'.[25]

Although many of the other religious changes of the 1630s were related to the temporary triumph of Arminianism critics still tended to distinguish. Thus the new ceremonial emphasis on the sacraments of baptism and the eucharist, as sources of divine grace in lieu of absolute predestination, was usually dubbed 'superstitious' or 'Popish' rather than Arminian.[26] Even the description of the religious community established at Little Gidding, in Huntingdonshire, as an 'Arminian Nunnery' turns out to be accurate with regard to its Arminianism. Nicholas Ferrar, leader of the community, had been exposed to Arminian influences at Clare College, Cambridge. He in turn recommended the works of the Arminian Jackson to a pupil, Barnabas Oley, who later edited them.[27] The *iure divino* theory of episcopacy had little to do with the matter, save only that the bench of bishops came increasingly to be composed of Arminians and was therefore discredited by association. Few eyebrows had been raised earlier when Bishop Carleton, at the Synod of Dort, defended the divine institution of bishops as retained in the English Church.[28] The most impressive witness, however, to the religious centrality of Arminianism in early seventeenth-century England is the Westminster Confession of Faith itself. This summation of English Calvinism produced by the religious arm of the Long Parliament, harks back via the Synod of Dort to the Lambeth Articles and beyond. It was also to prove one of the most enduring monuments of the Puritan Revolution.[29]

II

Something of the wider philosophical implications of the Arminian controversy is evident from the strong denial by Gerhard Vossius in 1614 that the Remonstrants were sowing the seeds of religious uncertainty. The allegation arose in the context of a book by Matthew Slade, attacking the religious policies of the States of Holland and their apologist Grotius. At this time Vossius and Slade, an Englishman, were rectors respectively of the Dordrecht and Amsterdam Gymnasiums. Vossius, discussing Slade's book, distinguishes between permanent suspension of judgement – 'scepticam ac Pyrrhoniam', and doubt as a means of arriving at truth. The Remonstrants, however, remained vulnerable to the charge of scepticism on account of their declared wish to exclude predestination from the category of a fundamental of faith.[30] This was to reopen the debate of Erasmus with Luther and of Castellio with Calvin. It also supports the contention that Arminianism was part of the seventeenth-century Pyrrhonian crisis, as to whether truth can be known and, if so, in what measure. Indeed the Calvinist doctrine of assurance poses the problem of certainty in a particularly acute form, because the true Christian is not only predestinated but must try to convince himself of that fact.[31] The principal source of philosophical scepticism was the Hellenistic writer Sextus Empiricus. Casaubon had made use of his works, in Greek manuscript, when providing notes to the 1593 edition of the *Lives and Opinions of Eminent Philosophers* by Diogenes Laertius. The following year, 1594, 'Dutch' Thomson had written to Casaubon asking to borrow the Greek text of Sextus.[32] To what extent Casaubon and Thomson married up their philosophical interests with their theology remains, however, unclear.

The sceptical attack had soon extended from religious dogmatism to include the whole realm of natural knowledge as well. In England the famous phrase of John Donne about the new philosophy calling 'all in doubt' exemplifies the sceptical response to the astronomical discoveries of Galileo, especially as announced in his *Siderius Nuncius* of 1610.[33] Despite the English interest generated by Galileo greater local excitement was aroused by the comet of 1618. This too inspired a poet, Richard Corbett, who that December addressed a verse letter from Oxford to Thomas Aylesbury at Sion House in London. At this date Corbett, later Bishop of Oxford, was a Student of Christ Church and Aylesbury was secretary to Buckingham, as Lord Admiral. What, asks Corbett, is the astronomical significance of this new star in the sky, and is it compatible with Aristotelian cosmology:

Say, shall the old philosophy be true?

Everyone is discussing the comet, and he appeals to the Sion House experts to resolve the controversy:

By thy rich studyes, and deep Harriot's minde.

Thomas Harriot was the nearest equivalent in England to Galileo, and this response by Corbett to the challenge of new celestial phenomena is markedly different from the stance of Donne earlier. Corbett was certainly an Arminian sympathiser as can be seen from his poem *The Distracted Puritane*, in the course of which he mocks the predestinarian schema of William Perkins.[34] While the religion or irreligion of Harriot and his circle remains a controversial subject Harriot's own interest in Arminianism appears to have gone unremarked. We can document this interest from an extant list of book purchases made by him in 1618. Out of a total of forty-four items, five relate to Arminianism, either for or against, and they include the *De Sanctorum* of Bertius.[35] Among the Harriot papers there also survives part of John Overall's analysis of the differences between Remonstrants and Counter-Remonstrants, as well as some notes by Harriot on Pyrrho and 'his followers called Scepticks which will not affirme or deny any knowledge to be true or false but do still doubt; yet they make there knowledge certayne to doubt assuredly'. There-fore, Harriot argues, 'somethinge' at least is certain even on Pyrrhonian grounds. His own theory of nature was atomistic and it is tempting to see Harriot as having anticipated Pierre Gassendi, the French *libertin érudit*, who combined atomism and free will within a framework of constructive or mittigated scepticism.[36]

Harriot's benefactor was the atomist Henry Percy, ninth Earl of Northum-berland, who emerged in the 1620s as a friend and supporter of the Arminian Montagu. Among the later generation of English atomists, at least as regards the propagandists, Arminianism seems to have been the prevalent mode of religious thought. Their chief patron the Earl of Newcastle was the only peer, apart from the infant Buckingham, to be remembered in Archbishop Laud's will, and the atomists Walter Charleton and John Evelyn were each enthusiastic free willers. Charleton, a medical doctor, defended atomism in 1652 while refuting 'the doctrine of Calvin concerning absolute predestina-tion', which he brackets with the 'fate of the Stoicks'.[37] Similarly Evelyn, a member of the growing class of virtuosi, popularised atomism in his 1656 *Essay* on Lucretius, the follower of Epicurus, having already endorsed the extreme Arminianism of Jeremy Taylor – theologian and later bishop.[38] Evelyn also translated works by the *libertins érudits* François de la Mothe le Vayer and Gabriel Naudé.[39]

The link between atomism and anti-determinism is provided by Epicurus, as can be seen most clearly from the writings of Charleton during the 1650s.[40] Knowledge of Epicurean teaching derived from Lucretius' *De Rerum Natura* and the life of Epicurus, by Diogenes Laertius, which incorporates three of his letters and his maxims. Casaubon, as we have seen, contributed to the 1593 edition of Diogenes. According to Epicurus, 'the whole of being consists of bodies and space'. The smallest constituent parts of bodies are atoms, which are indestructible and 'in continual motion through all eternity'. Man's 'own actions are free, and it is to them that praise and blame naturally attach'.[41] Lucretius explains the compatibility of physical causation with free will by the concept of atomic swerve, which introduces an element of indeterminacy.[42] While in England the new mechanical philosophy of atomism was popularised by Arminians, it has also been argued that there exists an affinity between the mitigated scepticism of theologians like William Chillingworth, Laud's godson, and the scientific attitude of the Royal Society. Chillingworth's book *The Religion of Protestants*, published in 1638, explicitly draws on the idea of Grotius that there are different levels of human certainty, in natural science as well as religion, and all less than absolute. Chillingworth himself rejected Calvinist determinism and was suspected of Socinianism.[43]

Atomism and Arminianism also seem to have coalesced in the case of William Boswell, successively secretary to Lord Herbert of Cherbury and Bishop Williams and then a clerk of the Privy Council. While in the employ of Lord Herbert, Boswell appears to have had a hand in the production of Herbert's book *De Veritate*. Certainly the form in which the manuscript is dedicated to Boswell and George Herbert, the poet, implies a fairly intimate relationship. Friend Boswell and brother George are asked to read the work and expunge anything contrary to good morals or the true Catholic faith.[44] In his autobiography Lord Herbert recalls that he was particularly urged to publish *De Veritate* by Grotius and Daniel Tilenus, the leading French defender of Arminius' teachings. The book is conceived as an answer to the challenge of scepticism generally, and seeks to establish a method for arriving at truth. In the course of it Lord Herbert says that 'free will has been given us for our benefit that we may devote ourselves by our free choice to the means which lead to happiness'. He also warns against 'doctrines of predestination' which issue in 'a kind of Stoic fate'.[45] Boswell, Herbert's secretary, was among the most enthusiastic of English followers of Galileo. He both purchased the works of Galileo and wrote to him, his intermediaries including John Spelman, son of the antiquary Sir Henry. A virtuoso, Boswell was appointed in 1631 to catalogue the royal collection of coins and medals.[46] One of his favourite similes was to compare a situation with the *intermundia* of Epicurus – the spaces between worlds in an infinite universe.[47]

We do not know how far Boswell agreed with the views of Herbert as expressed in *De Veritate*. Furthermore it would be a mistake to underestimate the capacity of early seventeenth-century writers to compartmentalise their thought. In this connexion there exists an instructive letter from Boswell, written in October 1625 to Samuel Collins, provost of King's College, Cambridge, where Boswell refers to 'the old and trewe Pythagorean or Samian philosophie', now revived by Galileo, and goes on to distinguish between the 'metaphysician' and the 'natural philosopher', the latter being simply 'narrator naturae creatae'.[48] Nevertheless it is significant that in 1632 Boswell was sent as English ambassador to The Hague. On religious grounds this was a sensitive diplomatic post. For since the high Calvinist times of the Synod of Dort Arminians had come to dominate the English Church, whereas in the United Provinces only a limited toleration had been extended to the Remonstrants. During the late 1620s two Arminian sympathisers were nominated to succeed the retiring English ambassador Sir Dudley Carleton. The first in point of time was Sir Robert Killigrew, the one-time patron of 'Dutch' Thomson and friend of Casaubon. The other nominee was Richard Spencer, younger son of Baron

Spencer and the Oxford pupil of the Arminian Thomas Jackson. Spencer, to whom Jackson had dedicated a tract on free will, defended Arminianism in the House of Commons in 1629. Although Killigrew and Spencer each received royal warrants for payment as 'ambassador resident' at The Hague neither took up the appointment.[49] Boswell's instructions as ambassador make ritual obeisance to the dominant Counter-Remonstrant party but he was soon collaborating with Vossius, now professor of history at the new Remonstrant Academy in Amsterdam.[50] After the outbreak of the English Civil War, Boswell remained as royalist representative at The Hague. Before his death in 1650 he entrusted certain manuscripts to his friend Isaac Gruter, a schoolmaster and lawyer. These comprised the atomistic writings of William Gilbert and Francis Bacon, which Gruter arranged to have published in the early 1650s. Gruter also edited at this time some of the writings of Grotius, including a discussion with John Overall on the subject of predestination.[51]

The varied interests of virtuosi like Boswell, which so obviously transcend the modern boundary between the 'two cultures' of natural science and the humanities, were characteristic of the Court of Charles I. Lucy Hutchinson, a hostile commentator, acknowledges in the biography of her husband that at the Caroline Court 'men of learning and ingenuity in all arts were in esteeme, and receiv'd encouragement from the King'. Charles was preeminently interested in painting, but 'all' of the arts included the mathematical sciences. Such inclusive royal patronage is symbolised for example in the painting by Gerrit van Honthorst of Buckingham presenting to Charles and Henrietta Maria the seven liberal arts, with Astronomy prominently featured. Charles was later to commission the mathematical practitioner Richard Delamain to construct a giant brass octant and various other scientific instruments.[52] Nor was this an exclusive court culture in the sense of being cut off from the rest of the country. During much of the year courtiers resided on their country estates and the circle around Viscount Falkland at Great Tew in Oxfordshire was only the most famous of similar groups throughout most of England. The households of Cavendish in Nottinghamshire, Hatton in Northamptonshire, Paston in Norfolk, Sandys in Kent, and many more, all played comparable roles.[53] The Court itself operated in part as a cultural entrepôt and even a critic like Mrs Hutchinson found much there to approve, such as music. Moreover she had tried her hand at translating the *De Rerum Natura* of Lucretius, driven by 'youthfull curiositie to understand things I heard so much discourse of'. Later, as Puritanism bit deeper, she came to believe her action sinful in making more available, albeit only in manuscript, 'this dog' Lucretius with his 'foppish casuall dance of attoms'. One major factor however in alienating her from the Court was its evident Arminianism, the 'greate doctrine' of predestination having grown out of fashion with the prelates.[54]

The sacramental aspect of English Arminianism was closely connected with the recrudescence of religious art at this time. New painted glass windows in churches, especially crucifixion scenes, are a marked feature of the 1630s and the best known artist in this medium is Abraham van Linge, originally from Emden.[55] But the Caroline Court is most famous, or infamous, for its patronage of the stage. Although Prynne's monumental attack on the theatre, delivered in his *Histrio-Mastix*, did not appear until 1633 he was gathering material for it, so he says, from the later 1620s – at the same time, that is, as he was writing hundreds of pages against Arminianism. *Histrio-Mastix*, like *The Perpetuitie of a Regenerate Man's Estate*, was licensed for the press by one of Archbishop Abbot's chaplains, the Archbishop sharing with Prynne the same basic hostility to the theatre and Arminianism. In the dedicatory epistle to *Histrio-Mastix* Prynne complains that more and more people are attending plays and that new theatres are being built to meet the demand. Playbooks, says Prynne, are 'now more vendible than the choycest sermons' and they are being printed at the rate of twenty thousand a year. Playhouses are the 'divel's chappels', teaching 'atheisme, heathenisme, pro-phanesse' and that 'Epicurisme' of which he also complains in *Healthes: Sicknesse*. Indeed Prynne suggests that playwrights are preaching an alternative 'libertine' religion which goes hand in hand with the 'Pelagian errors of the times', their plays being the 'grand empoysoners of all grace'. The fallen sons of Adam are merely confirmed in their state of carnal gracelessness by attending the theatre.[56]

An example of the kind of interrelationship envisaged by Prynne is the playwright and clergyman William Cartwright, whose plays slightly post-date *Histrio-Mastix*. The Arminianism of Cartwright is manifest in his writings. Thus in some verses of 1634 to Brian Duppa, Dean of Christ Church and soon to be a bishop, he speaks of:

> Men that do itch (when they have eate) to note
> The chief distinction 'twixt the sheep and goat;
> That do no questions relish but what be
> Bord'ring upon the absolute decree,
> And then haste home, lest they should miss the lot
> Of venting reprobation, whiles 'tis hot.

Cartwright also translated into English the superb elegy of Grotius on Arminius 'searcher of truth's deepest part'. His play *The Ordinary*, which as the title indicates is set in a tavern, contains scoffing references to the 'elect' and includes among the cast some of those 'good-fellow pastors' who were such anathema to Prynne. A comedy, *The Ordinary* is generally ribald and irreverent. Another play by Cartwright, *The Royal Slave*, incorporates a drinking song with the chorus:

> Then laugh we, and quaffe we, untill our rich noses
> Grow red, and contest with our chaplets of roses.[57]

This echoes lines from the Greek collection of poetry known as the *Anacreontea*, particularly two pieces entitled by their later seventeenth-century translators 'Roses' and 'The Epicure'.[58] To put Cartwright's song in perspective, however, we would note that it purports to have been written by a prisoner seeking to keep up his morale.

The Cambridge counterpart of Cartwright, who had been a Student of Christ Church, Oxford, was the layman Thomas Randolph, fellow of Trinity College. The manuscript of *The Drinking Academy*, a play ascribed to Randolph, is prefaced with an unflattering epigram about the Synod of Dort which describes the participants as a 'knot of knaves' and their deliberations as so much 'wind'. Randolph's comedy *Aristippus or the Joviall Philosopher* was published in 1630, and early on in the play one of the characters says that at Cambridge University 'they are all so infected with Aristippus his Arminianism, they can preach no doctrine but sack and red noses'.[59] Although Randolph evidently intends this as a caricature, he none the less implies that a link was thought to exist between the Arminian theology of free will and ancient Epicureanism. Aristippus was the founder of the Cyrenaic school of hedonism, which to some extent anticipated Epicurus. Yet there are marked differences in their moral teaching. Both philosophers hold that pleasure is the aim of life but Epicurus defines this as 'absence of pain in the body and of trouble in the soul', whereas Aristippus means a more positive physical indulgence. Epicurus is particularly concerned to free men from anxiety, by means of 'sobre reasoning, searching out the ground of every choice and avoidance, and banishing those beliefs through which the greatest tumults take possession of the soul'. As an example of the latter he instances the 'yoke of destiny'. Pleasure for Epicurus is 'not an unbroken succession of drinking bouts and of revelry', and he thinks it 'impossible to live a pleasant life without living wisely and well and justly'.[60]

In practice however the two hedonisms of Aristippus and Epicurus are not always easy to distinguish. This can be seen from some of the ballads recorded in the Stationers' Register during the 1630s and intended to reach a much wider audience than the plays. For instance *A Mess of Good Fellowes*, by Martin Parker, extols the virtues of social drinking as conducive to 'heart's ease' and 'a contented mind'. The nineteenth-century editor of this ballad was adamant that it 'is one of that numerous class of productions in which, under the plea of being "jovial blades", "good fellows", and other such rubbish, men sought to excuse themselves for spending all that they had earned towards their own support and that of their families, upon the selfish gratification of drinking to excess'. William Prynne would have agreed with him. But Parker's drinker is concerned to 'recreate his sense' after working hard all day, and furthermore to philosophize:

> He that doth injoy his health,
> and a competent means withall,
> What need he to pine for wealth
> but take what to him doth befall?[61]

With Richard Climsall's *Roaring Dick of Dover* the balance swings more clearly in the direction of Aristippus:

> He that hath aboundant treasure,
>   hence shall nothing beare away:
> Then let's take some part of pleasure,
>   drinke and sing and freely pay.

Nevertheless Dick counsels sensibly that a wife should join her husband in tavern or alehouse rather than become a scold.[62] Given the present state of research into the history of ballads it does not seem possible to say whether Parker and Climsall were being in the least original here, although their hedonistic themes certainly overlapped with those of the Caroline stage. Parker was soon to be dubbed 'the prelat's poet' because of his ballads against the Scots.[63]

The Arminian dramatist Cartwright was a great admirer of Ben Jonson, 'father of poets', as was his patron Duppa who in 1638 edited a volume of poems in honour of Jonson.[64] Their admiration was shared by Sir William Davenant, successor to Jonson in the office of Poet Laureate. Davenant, thanking Duppa in verse for his homage to Jonson, discusses the role of faith and reason and urges him:

> Teach faith to rule, but with such temp'rate law,
> As reason not destroys, yet keeps't in awe.

Later, as part of the long poem *Gondibert*, Davenant expresses views about predestination which are probably his own:

> Doth not belief of being destin'd draw
>   Our reason to presumption or dispaire?
> If destiny be not, like human law,
>   To be repeal'd, what is the use of prayer?

This same poem reveals Davenant to be a supporter of the new natural philosophy, particularly the Baconian variety.[65] Another 'son' of Ben Jonson, if a rather rebellious one, was the court poet Sir John Suckling.[66] In his *Account of Religion by Reason*, dated 1637, Suckling comments on the resurrection of the body: 'it were hard, when we see every petty chymick in his little shop bring into one body things of the same kind, though scatter'd and disorder'd, that we should not allow the great maker of all things to do the same in his own universe'. He contrasts this with the view that 'man corrupted into dust is scattered almost into infinite', apparently opposing Epicurus to Aristotle – atoms versus infinitely divisible matter. Writing in verse to John Hales of Eton, at about the same period, Suckling imagines him debating about 'predestination' or 'reconciling three in one'.[67] This refers to Hales' interest in both the Arminian and Socinian controversies, and it has been well said that 'the morality implicit in court poetry was . . . profoundly related to the religious disputes dividing Caroline England', with Jonson and his comrades of the Devil Tavern, in Fleet Street, ranged firmly against the Calvinists. Jonsonian advocacy of reason, the controller of the passions, complemented the Arminian defence of man as a creature not wholly corrupt. Suckling, however, was also conversant with French *libertin* poetry.[68]

One of the protégés of Suckling was the dramatist Shackerley Marmion, whose plays include *The Antiquary*. Veterano, the character of the title, serves to satirize, albeit in friendly fashion, an aspect of the contemporary virtuoso movement – the passion for collecting antiquities. He is described as gazing all day long at a statue without a nose and an allusion may be intended to the Earl of Arundel, the foremost English collector of antique sculpture. Arundel is often assumed to have been a crypto Roman Catholic, yet he patronised the anti-Calvinist Harsnett, employed the Dutch Remonstrant Junius and supported the Arminian Montagu against his critics.[69] Sculpture was indeed a consuming interest for Arundel. Nevertheless he was on good terms with the mathematician William Oughtred and towards the end of his life planned to colonise Madagascar, 'resolved to goe my selfe in person'. An English settlement on Madagascar was briefly established in 1645, but of Arundel's involvement little more now seems to survive than a fine portrait by Van Dyck. The picture shows the Earl seated beside a large globe and pointing to the island of Madagascar, while the Countess holds a universal ring dial for finding both latitude and time; the librarian Junius stands behind them. Madagascar became a potent myth during the late 1630s, desire for wealth mingling with the idea of a Garden of Eden inhabited by noble savages and contributing thereby to a sense of moral relativism.[70]

Come 1641 the authors of the Grand Remonstrance described their opponents as an unholy alliance of 'Arminians and Libertines', which was being manipulated by 'Papists', and in so doing they intimated the existence of two competing world views. The French term *libertin*, however, describes more accurately than does libertine the nature of the forces arrayed against English Calvinism. For *libertin* thought involves speculative attitudes to religion and science as well as morality. The ideas of Epicurus tend to provide the positive content.[71] Arminianism became the religious ally of English *libertinage* because its exponents sought to rehabilitate natural man by denying predestinarian dogma.[72] Cradled in scepticism, Arminians and *libertins* alike embraced free will.

NOTES

I am grateful to the following for their kind help: Gordon Batho, Stephen Bondos-Greene, Peter Burke, Peter Clark, Patricia Crawford, Basil Greenslade, Shirley Jones, David McKitterick, Victor Morgan, John North, Geoffrey Nuttall, Piyo Rattansi, Ian Roy, Kevin Sharpe, Koenraad Swart and Sarah Tyacke. More generally I am conscious of an intellectual debt to the pioneer in this field – Hugh Trevor-Roper, Lord Dacre of Glanton. To him my essay is dedicated.

1 J. P. Kenyon, *Stuart England* (London, 1978), p. 100; A. Foster, 'The Function of a Bishop: the Career of Richard Neile, 1562–1640', in R. O'Day and F. Heal eds., *Continuity and Change* (Leicester, 1976), p. 54. Cf. pp. 132–55 above.

2 W. Prynne, *The Church of England's Old Antithesis to New Arminianisme* (London, 1629), sigs A4v, C3v. It is perverse of John New to claim that the 'true' concern of this book is with ceremonies and not Arminian teachings about predestination, given that Prynne spends less than a page on the former compared with well over a hundred pages on the latter. J. F. H. New, *Anglican and Puritan* (London, 1964), p. 117.

3 H. C. Porter, *Reformation and Reaction in Tudor Cambridge* (Cambridge, 1958), pp. 344–90. It is also the case that there were Dutch forerunners of Arminius, such as Gellius Snecanus. Anti-Calvinism in both countries was partly a response to growing Calvinist extremism.

4 D. Baudius, *Epistolarum Centuriae Tres* (Leiden, 1620), p. 731.

5 *Isaaci Casauboni Epistolae* (Rotterdam, 1709), pp. 432–3; *His Majestie's Declaration . . . in the Cause of D. Conradus Vorstius* (London, 1612), p. 15. [Tyacke, *Anti-Calvinists*, p. 38.]

6 The index of popularity is provided by the number of editions of Perkins' various works compared with other English theological writers.

7 P. C. Molhuysen and B. L. Meulenbroek eds, *Briefwisseling van Hugo Grotius* (The Hague, 1928–76), i, pp. 230–6, 244; *His Majestie's Declaration*, p. 18; *R. Thomsonis Angli Diatriba de Amissione et Intercisione Gratiae et Justificationis* (Leiden, 1616).

8 R. Abbot, *De Gratia et Perseverantia Sanctorum . . . quibus accesit Eiusdem in Richardi Thomsoni Anglo-Belgici Diatribam . . . Animadversio Brevis* (London, 1618), pp. 83–221. The preface (sig. C4v) provides the evidence for dating Thomson's manuscript to the late 1590s; T. Fuller, *Abel Redevivus* (London, 1651), p. 557.

9 C. R. Elrington ed., *Works of . . . James Ussher* (Dublin, 1847–64), xv, p. 130; CUL, MS Ff/5/25, fos 94–112.

10 P. Heylyn, *Cyprianus Anglicus* (London, 1668), pp. 66–8 and *Historia Quinqu-Articularis: or a Declaration of the Judgement of the Western Churches, and more particularly of the Church of England, in the Five Controverted Points, reproched in these Last Times by the Name of Arminianism* (London, 1660); Kenyon, *Stuart England*, p. 99.

11 OUA, Hyp. B. 20, fos 18r–v; *Laud Works*, iv, p. 319; vi, p. 292.

12 Bodl., Rawlinson MS D. 47, fos 55r–v; T. Jackson, *Works* (Oxford, 1844), viii, p. 256; ix, pp. 441, 444.

13 Thysius' source may have been Laurence Chaderton, master of Emmanuel College, Cambridge: P. Lake, 'Matthew Hutton – a Puritan Bishop?', *History* 64 (1979), 202.

14 *Petri Baronis Summa Trium de Praedestinatione Sententiarum* . . . (Harderwijk, 1613) and *Brevis et Dilucida Explicatio* . . . *de Electione, Praedestinatione ac Reprobatione, Authore Mathaeo, Eboracensis Archiepiscopo* . . . (Harderwijk, 1613), sig. A4, pp. 1–44; BL, Add. MS 22, 961, fo 185.

15 S. P. Haak and A. J. Veenendaal eds, *Johan van Oldenbarnevelt bescheiden betreffende zijn staatkundig beleid en zijn Familie* (The Hague, 1934–67), iii, p. 440. My reading of this document differs from the editor; *Laud Works*, vi, p. 249; Molhuysen and Meulenbroek eds., *Briefwisseling van Hugo Grotius*, iii, pp. 8–9.

16 *Barnevel's Apology: or Holland Mysterie* (London, 1618); W. P. Frijlinck ed., *The Tragedy of Sir John van Olden Barnavelt* (Amsterdam, 1922); *The Judgement of the Synode holden at Dort* . . . (London, 1619), sig. B3; *Articles Agreed on in the National Synode of the Reformed Churches of France* (Oxford, 1623); Abbot, *De Gratia*, pp. 1–82; J. Prideaux, *Lectiones Novem* (Oxford, 1625), pp. 1–22, 49–170; S. Ward, *Opera Nonnulla* (London, 1658), pp. 127–30.

17 J. Yates, *Ibis ad Caesarem* (London, 1626), pt. iii, p. 46. *Commons Journal*, i, p. 788. [My italics]. W. Notestein and F. H. Relf eds, *Commons Debates for 1629* (Minneapolis, Minn., 1921), p. 99.

18 T. A. Buckley ed., *The Canons and Decrees of the Council of Trent* (London, 1851), pp. 30–46.

19 G. Ornsby ed., *The Correspondence of John Cosin* (Surtees Soc. lii, lv, 1868–72), i, pp. 33, 68, 77–9, 90; R. Montagu ed., *Sancti Gregorii Nazianzeni in Iulianum Invectivae Duae* (Eton, 1610), 'Ad Lectorem'; *Jackson, Works*, iv, pp. 303–4; F. Junius, *De Pictura Veterum* (Amsterdam, 1637), sig. *2v; *Nieuw Nederlandsch Biografisch Woordenboek* (Leiden, 1911–37), ix, p. 483; Molhuysen and Meulenbroek eds, *Briefwisseling van Hugo Grotius*, ii, pp. 24–6, 99–101, 241, 246–7.

20 *Laud Works*, iii, pp. 160, 167; vi, pp. 244–6. [My italics].

21 *Ibid.*, iii, pp. 178–9; vi, p. 249; NUL, MS Ne. C. 15, 405, p. 180. The proclamation is printed in J. P. Kenyon, *The Stuart Constitution* (Cambridge, 1966), pp. 154–5.

22 Bodl., Tanner MS 72, fo. 310; W. Loe, *A Sermon Preached at* . . . *the Funerall of* . . . *Daniel Featley* (London, 1645), p. 25; G. Every, *The High Church Party, 1688–1714* (London, 1956); H. Grotius, *Operum Theologicorum* (London, 1679), iii, p. 141; J. den Tex, *Oldenbarnevelt* (Cambridge, 1973), ii, p. 552.

23 H. Burton, *A Plea to an Appeale* (London, 1626); G. Carleton, *An Examination of those things wherein the Author of the Late Appeale holdeth the Doctrines of the Pelagians and the Arminians to be the Doctrines of the Church of England* (London, 1626); D. Featley, *A Second Parallel* . . . *against the Appealer* (London, 1626); A. Wotton, *A Dangerous Plot Discovered* . . . *wherein is proved that Mr. Richard Montague* . . . *laboureth to bring in the Faith of Rome and Arminius* (London, 1626); J. Yates, *Ibis ad Ceasarem* (London, 1626).

24 W. Prynne, *The Perpetuitie of a Regenerate Man's Estate* (London, 1626), pp. 222–5, 405–8, *God no Imposter nor Deluder* (London, 1629), *The Church of England's Old Antithesis to New Arminianisme* (London, 1629), and *A Briefe Survay and Censure of Mr. Cozens his Couzening Devotions* (London, 1628).

25 J. Rushworth, *Historical Collections* (London, 1659–1710), i, p. 621; S. R. Gardiner ed., *The Constitutional Documents of the Puritan Revolution* (Oxford, 1906), pp. 76, 138–9; Jackson, *Works*, vi, p. 109; viii, pp. 217–19.

26 Gardiner ed., *Constitutional Documents of the Puritan Revolution*, pp. 139, 229–30.

27 *The Arminian Nunnery: or a Description of the Late Erected Monasticall Place, called the Arminian Nunnery, at Little Gidding in Huntingtonshire* (London, 1641). Ferrar's tutor was the Arminian Augustine Lindsell, colleague of 'Dutch' Thomson; Jackson, *Works*, i, pp. xxviii–xxix.

28 W. Balcanqual, *A Joynt Attestation, avowing that the Discipline of the Church of England was not impeached by the Synode of Dort* (London, 1626).

29 G. S. Hendry, *The Westminster Confession for Today* (London, 1960).

30 Molhuysen and Meulenbroek eds, *Briefwisseling van Hugo Grotius*, i, p. 353; M. Slade, *Disceptationis cum Conrado Vorstio . . . Pars Altera* (Amsterdam, 1614); Grotius, *Operum Theologicorum*, iii, pp. 111–12.

31 H. R. Trevor-Roper, *Religion, the Reformation and Social Change* (London, 1967), pp. 193–236 and *Edward Hyde, Earl of Clarendon* (Oxford, 1975), pp. 5–8; R. H. Popkin, *The History of Scepticism from Erasmus to Descartes* (New York, 1968), pp. 1–16.

32 Popkin, *History of Scepticism*, pp. 17–43; M. Pattison, *Isaac Casaubon, 1559–1614* (London, 1875), pp. 33–4.

33 J. Donne, *The Epithalamions, Anniversaries and Epicedes*, ed. W. Milgate (Oxford, 1978), pp. 27–8, 140–5. Donne's scepticism is even more pronounced in his 'Second Anniversarie', *ibid.*, pp. 48–9, 165–6.

34 J. A. W. Bennett and H. R. Trevor-Roper eds, *The Poems of Richard Corbett* (Oxford, 1955), pp. 58, 63–5.

35 The list is reproduced in J. W. Shirley ed., *Thomas Harriot: Renaissance Scientist* (Oxford, 1974), pp. 102–3. For a discussion of Harriot's religion see J. Jacquot, 'Thomas Harriot's Reputation for Impiety', *Notes and Records of the Royal Society* 9 (1952), 164–87.

36 BL, Add MS 6789, fos 460, 464; R. H. Kargon, *Atomism in England from Hariot to Newton* (Oxford, 1966), pp. 24–7; J. S. Spink, *French Free-Thought from Gassendi to Voltaire* (London, 1960), pp. 14–17, 85–102.

37 Kargon, *Atomism in England*, pp. 13–14, 63–92; Ornsby ed., *Correspondence of John Cosin*, i, pp. 68, 73; *Laud Works*, iv, p. 443; W. Charleton, *The Darknes of Atheism* (London, 1652), pp. 43–7, 215. Throughout this book Charleton is concerned to purge the atheistic element from Epicurus' teaching.

38 J. Evelyn, *An Essay on the First Book of T. Lucretius Carus . . . interpreted and made English Verse* (London, 1656); C. P. Eden ed., *The Whole Works of . . . Jeremy Taylor* (London, 1850–56), i, pp. xli–ii.

39 F. de la Mothe le Vayer, *Of Liberty and Servitude* (London, 1649) and G. Naudé, *Instructions Concerning the Erecting of a Library* (London, 1661); Popkin, *History of Scepticism*, p. 91.

40 As well as *The Darknes of Atheism* Charleton wrote *Physiologia Epicuro-Gassendo-Charltoniana* (London, 1654) and *Epicurus' Morals* (London, 1656). Together these works purvey a form of Christian Epicureanism. Here it is perhaps suggestive that in 1598 Thomas James, when dedicating his translation of du Vair's *La Philosophie Morale des Stoiques* to Lord Mountjoy, replied to those who denigrated Stoics as 'stockes' by calling them 'wisards'. Much depends, however, on the date when the term 'wizard' was first used to describe members of the Northumberland group. Guillaume du Vair, *The Moral Phylosophy of the Stoicks*, ed. R. Kirk, New Brunswick, NJ, 1951, p. 45.

41 Diogenes Laertius, *Lives of Eminent Philosophers*, ed. R. D. Hicks (London, 1950), ii, 569, 573, 659.

42 Lucretius, *De Rerum Natura*, ed. W. H. D. Rouse (London, 1924), pp. 101–5. I have found particularly helpful here A. A. Long, *Hellenistic Philosophy: Stoics, Epicureans, Sceptics* (London, 1974), pp. 56–61. On the other hand atomism as formulated by Democritus, a precursor of Epicurus, abolishes free will.

43 H. G. van Leeuwen, *The Problem of Certainty in English Thought, 1630–90* (The Hague, 1970), pp. 21–2 and *passim*; R. R. Orr, *Reason and Authority: The Thought of William Chillingworth* (Oxford, 1967), pp. 79–80, 97–9.

44 BL, Sloane MS 3957, fo. 1. The dedication is dated 15 December 1622. For details of Boswell's career I have relied mainly on the revised biographical article by E. S. de Beer in *Corrections and Additions to the Dictionary of National Biography* (Boston, Mass., 1966), pp. 29–30.

45 J. M. Shuttleworth ed., *The Life of Edward, First Lord Herbert of Cherbury* (London, 1976), p. 120; Popkin, *History of Scepticism*, pp. 155–65; E. Herbert *De Veritate*, ed. M. H. Carré (Bristol, 1937), pp. 137, 164.

46 PRO, SP 16/141, fos 139r–v, 143 and SP 16/183, fo 1r–v.

47 PRO, SP 84/146, fo 128; King's College, Cambridge, Provosts' Letter Books, IV, no. 63. Boswell quotes Epicurus in the orginal Greek, from memory.

48 *Ibid.*

49 PRO SP 38/13, fo 132 and SP 38/14, fo 167v; T. Farnaby ed., *M. Val. Martialis Epigrammaton Libri* (London, 1615), sig. A2; J. Russell ed., *Ephemerides Isaaci Casauboni* (Oxford, 1850), ii, pp. 811–12; Jackson, *Works*, ix, pp. 504–8; Notestein and Relf eds, *Commons Debates for 1629*, p. 117.

50 PRO SP 84/144 fos 164v, 167v; R. P. Stearns, *Congregationalism in the Netherlands* (Chicago, IL, 1940), pp. 64–5.

51 Kargon, *Atomism in England*, pp. 52–3; *Hugonis Grotii Quaedam Hactenus Inedita . . .* (Amsterdam, 1652), pp. 236–81.

52 L. Hutchinson, *Memoirs of the life of Colonel Hutchinson*, ed. J. Sutherland (London, 1973), p. 46; O. Millar, 'Charles I, Honthorst and van Dyck', *Burlington Magazine* 96 (1954), p. 37; PRO SP 16/383, fo 66.

53 K. Weber, *Lucius Cary, Second Viscount Falkland* (New York, 1940); J. Jacquot, 'Sir Charles Cavendish and his Learned Friends', *Annals of Science*, 8 (1952), 13–27; *Sir Christopher Hatton's Book of Seals*, ed. L. C. Loyd and D. M. Stenton (Northamptonshire Record Soc., XV, 1950), pp. xxi–xxx; R. W. Ketton-Cremer, *Norfolk Assembly* (London, 1957), pp. 17–40; R. B. Davis, *George Sandys, Poet Adventurer* (London, 1955), pp. 227–54, 265–6. This book has an important appendix entitled 'Sandys and the King's Privy Chamber', pp. 283–5.

54 Hutchinson, *Memoirs*, pp. 28–9, 34; BL, Additional MS. 19, 333, fos 2v, 4r–v.

55 M. Archer, 'English Painted Glass in the Seventeenth Century: The Early Work of Abraham van Linge', *Apollo* (January 1975), p. 30.

56 E. Arber ed., *Transcript*, iv, pp. 188, 207. For Archbishop Abbot's attitude towards plays see PRO. SP 14/80, fo 177v [Today I would be more hesitant in assimilating the views of Abbot and Prynne concerning the theatre]; W. Prynne, *Histrio-Mastix* (London,

1633), sigs *3r–v, **2v, pp. 37, 101, 511–12, 826–7, 961–2, 964, 992 and *Healthes: Sicknesse* (London, 1628), sigs. B7, D4. Examination of the Stationers' Register indicates that during the early 1630s some ten plays per year were being licensed and that Prynne envisages editions of about two thousand copies each.

57 G. B. Evans ed., *The Plays and Poems of William Cartwright* (Madison, Wis., 1951), pp. 223, 283, 299, 455–6, 497–500; W. Prynne, *The Perpetuitie of a Regenerate Man's Estate* (London, 1626), sig. **1.

58 G. M. Crump ed., *The Poems and Translations of Thomas Stanley* (Oxford, 1962), p. 77; R. Hurd ed., *The Works of Mr. A. Cowley* (London, 1809), i, p. 79.

59 H. E. Rollins and S. A. Tannenbaum eds, *The Drinking Academy. A Play by Thomas Randolph* (Cambridge, Mass., 1930), p. 1; W. C. Hazlitt ed., *Poetical and Dramatic Works by Thomas Randolph* (London, 1875), p. 10.

60 W. K. C. Guthrie, *A History of Greek Philosophy* (Cambridge, 1962–78), iii, pp. 490–99; Diogenes Laertius, *Lives of Eminent Philosophers*, ii, pp. 657, 659, 665.

61 H. E. Rollins, *An Analytical Index to the Ballad-Entries (1557–1709) in the Registers of the Company of Stationers of London* (Chapel Hill, Conn., 1924), pp. 152, 199; W. Chappell and J. W. Ebsworth eds, *The Roxburghe Ballads* (Hertford, 1869–99), ii, pp. 142–8.

62 H. E. Rollins ed., *The Pepys Ballads* (Cambridge, Mass., 1929–32), ii, pp. 234–8.

63 H. E. Rollins, 'Martin Parker, Ballad Monger', *Modern Philology*, 16 (1918–19), 125.

64 B. Duppa ed., *Jonsonus Virbius: or the Memorie of Ben Johnson Revived* (London, 1638), p. 34.

65 W. Davenant, *The Shorter Poems, and Songs from the Plays and Masques*, ed. A. M. Gibbs (Oxford, 1972), pp. lii–iii, 79, 196; D. F. Gladish ed., *Sir William Davenant's Gondibert* (Oxford, 1971), pp. 151–69.

66 K. A. McEuen, *Classical Influence upon the Tribe of Ben* (Iowa, 1939), p. 12. Another member of the Jonson circle was Richard Corbett. *Ibid.*, pp. 5–6.

67 L. A. Beaurline and T. Clayton eds, *The Works of Sir John Suckling* (Oxford, 1971), i, pp. 70, 178–9, 265.

68 R. M. Smuts, *The Culture of Absolutism at the Court of Charles I* (Ph.D. thesis, Princeton University, 1976), pp. 231–5; F. O. Henderson, 'Traditions of *Précieux* and *Libertin* in Suckling's Poetry', *Journal of English Literary History*, 4 (1937), 281–8.

69 W. H. Logan and J. Maidment eds, *The Dramatic Works of Shackerley Marmion* (Edinburgh and London, 1875), p. 210; K. Sharpe, 'The Earl of Arundel, his Circle and the Opposition to the Duke of Buckingham, 1618–28', in K. Sharpe ed., *Faction and Parliament* (Oxford, 1978), p. 238; M. A. Tierney, *The History and Antiquities of . . . Arundel* (London, 1834), pp. 431–4; Ornsby ed., *Correspondence of John Cosin*, i, pp. 85, 91.

70 M. F. S. Hervey, *The Life, Correspondence and Collections of Thomas Howard, Earl of Arundel* (Cambridge, 1921), pp. 346, 416–20, 506–8; Davenant, *The Shorter Poems . . .*, pp. 10–21; L. B. Wright, 'The Noble Savage of Madagascar in 1640', *Journal of the History of Ideas*, 4 (1943), 112–18.

71 Gardiner ed., *Constitutional Documents of the Puritan Revolution*, p. 207; Spink, *French Free-Thought*, pp. 75–168.

72 R. Pintard, *Le libertinage érudit dans la première moitié du XVIIe siècle* (Paris, 1943), pp. 49–41, 339–41.

Chapter 10

———◆———

Science and religion at Oxford
before the Civil War

I

WHY did the 'new philosophy', as contemporaries called it, make such
rapid strides in seventeenth-century England? Or, rephrasing the question, what underlying explanation can be offered for such phenomena of the
period as William Harvey, Robert Boyle, and the Royal Society? Historians
of science, in addressing themselves to this problem, have canvassed various
aspects of the environment, religious, institutional, and economic. Puritanism
especially has been seen as integral to the triumph of the new scientific values.
At the same time the importance of institutionalization is widely recognised;
Gresham College in London, with its chairs of astronomy and geometry, and
the similar Savilian professorships at Oxford came into existence respectively
in 1597 and 1619. The mercantile setting of Gresham College has also been
stressed, as well as the college's involvement with navigational instruction
and its different clientele compared to the universities. Christopher Hill has
been an outstanding contributor to the recent debate.[1]

Difficulties of definition, however, have arisen, because Puritanism is
an elastic term. Science too as a concept presents problems, but from 1600
onwards, with the publication of *De Magnete*, we can talk of a 'Gilbert tradition' in England, its hallmarks 'a weakening of confidence in the ancients, a
growing appreciation of the importance of experiment and direct observation, and the spirit of independent thought'. This was accompanied by an
increasingly sophisticated mathematics and an improved instrumentation.[2]
Disagreement about religious identity can moreover be sidestepped by examining the fate of science in a context generally agreed to have been hostile
towards Puritanism. Here a crucial case study is Oxford University, which from
1630 came under the direct Arminian control of William Laud as chancellor.[3]
For if a positive correlation exists between Puritanism and science we would

expect the eclipse of one adversely to affect the other, and the rise to power of Arminianism in the late 1620s to be accompanied by scientific decline or at least stagnation. Therefore this essay concentrates on the Oxford quarter-century which runs from the endowment of new teaching posts in astronomy, geometry, and anatomy, as well as a botanical garden, during the years 1619–24, to the period of the Civil War.

Philosophic reform had its Oxford advocates even before the 1620s, as can be illustrated by two plays performed at Christ Church in February 1618. Both plays are comedies but they also carry reformist messages. *Technogamia*, written by Barten Holyday, concerns the fate of Astronomia and Geometres at the hands of the villains Magus and his wife Astrologia, ending with Magus and Astrologia being exiled from 'the commonwealth of the sciences'. Such treatment is a far cry from the Elizabethan John Dee, who happily mixed magic with science, and it anticipates the debarring by Sir Henry Savile of his astronomy professor from 'professing the doctrine of nativities and all judicial astrology without exception'.[4] The second play, Robert Burton's *Philosophaster*, is an attack on 'pseudo' philosophy. The heroes are Polumathes and Philobiblos, two wandering scholars, while the false philosophers include an Aristotelian logician and are generally identified as those able 'to explain a syllogism'. The only explicit Oxford reference is to the Bodleian Library 'wherein many dead are found, unhappily held by chains'.[5] Burton like Holyday was a Student of Christ Church. Also in 1618 Michael Barkley, on graduation, presented the Christ Church Library with a set of globes, celestial and terrestrial, 'in gratiam studiosorum mathematicae'.[6] That some Christ Church tutors were teaching mathematics at this date is less surprising when we recall that Edmund Gunter, a future Gresham professor of astronomy, had only recently left the college after a residence of fifteen years. Gunter's *Description and Use of the Sector* had circulated in Latin manuscript since 1607, and when an English version was finally published in 1623 one of those who received a presentation copy was Robert Burton.[7]

As regards astronomical theory, Holyday was a conservative who denied both the diurnal rotation of the earth on its axis and its annual rotation about the sun. Burton was more adventurous; in the 1628 edition of his *Anatomy of Melancholy* he says that diurnal rotation is 'most probable' and remarks on his use of an eight-foot telescope to observe the satellites of Jupiter.[8] He was outshone, however, by Brian Twyne, a fellow of Corpus Christi College, who as early as 1613 drew attention to the telescopic discoveries of Galileo, in a volume of verses published by the University. Twyne's copy of the 1610 Venice edition of Galileo's *Siderius Nuncius* is still extant, as are some of his astronomical notebooks.[9] He owed his scientific interests to Thomas Allen of Gloucester Hall, who was to be described at his death in 1632 as 'omnium sui aevi mathematicorum . . . ipsam animam atque solem'.[10] In religion Holyday and Burton were orthodox Calvinists, like most Church of England clergy at this time. Twyne by contrast was a member of the earliest Oxford group conversant with Dutch Arminianism, and probably belonged to that theological school.[11] His scientific mentor Allen inclined to Catholicism.[12]

By 1620 individual scientific enthusiasm of the kind fostered by Allen was gaining a more permanent Oxford base, thanks to the book-acquisition policy of the Bodleian Library. The printed catalogue of that year reveals a considerable holding of recent scientific works, some of them in English. For example, eight separate items by Kepler are listed, while English books include Aaron Rathborne's *Surveyor* and the translation by Edward Wright of Napier's *Logarithmes*, both of 1616, as well as Mark Ridley's *Treatise of Magneticall Bodies and Motions* of 1613. But books on the shelves are one thing, readers are another. Here the new Savilian professorships were of prime importance in providing a regular scientific focus. Attendance at lectures in geometry became compulsory from 1620 for all students in their third to fifth years at university, and astronomy lectures were similarly obligatory on all sixth- and seventh-year students. Both professors were expected to lecture twice weekly in term time.[13]

Explaining the reasons for his munificence to the University, Savile wrote of his desire 'to redeem so far as in me lies, almost from destruction, sciences of the noblest kind'. His subsequent references to surveying, mechanics, and navigation suggest a more practical concern. Indeed as early as 1592, in an Oxford oration delivered before Queen Elizabeth, Savile had argued for the compatibility of philosophy with a life of active soldiering and quoted Plato on the use of mathematics in warfare.[14] Savile in his own life had successfully combined action with scholarship, service to the state with the editing of classical and patristic texts, and his educational ideal would appear to have approximated to that of the virtuoso. Yet England's need for military preparedness was probably also in his mind, a matter made all the more urgent by the outbreak of the Thirty Years War in 1618.[15]

The first Savilian professors were handpicked by the founder. Henry Briggs, appointed from Gresham College to the geometry chair, is mainly remembered for his work on logarithms. His religious position at this date is best described as Puritan; in 1589, as a young fellow of St John's College, Cambridge, he had supported the cause of Puritan nonconformity and his surviving letters from the second decade of the seventeenth century seem to place him firmly in the Puritan camp. Thus he wrote in 1610 of difficulties experienced in getting a religious book printed in England without the 'index expurgatorius, if anything in it do sound suspiciously'. But as the modern historian of Gresham College, Ian Adamson, has written of Briggs, 'it is perhaps more accurate to describe him as a Puritan and scientist than a Puritan scientist'.[16] Savile's other appointment, to his chair of astronomy, was John Bainbridge. In 1619 Bainbridge had published his account of the comet of the previous year, opening with the remark that 'I hope there bee none so farre more precize than wise, as to thinke it unlawfull to looke on this celestiall signe with other then vulgar and pore-blinde eyes: (which were still to maintaine ignorance mother of devotion)'. Later in the same work, discussing the origins of comets, he refers to those 'who have beene scrupulous to conceit any creation since that first saboth'. Such references to preciseness and scrupulosity seem to have Puritans in mind. At the same time Bainbridge's epistolary style is much more secular than that of Briggs.[17]

According to the Savilian statutes the professor of geometry was to expound three set books: Euclid's *Elements*, the *Conics* of Apollonius, and all of Archimedes. In addition he was required to provide classes in surveying and arithmetic, and given the interests of Briggs it is likely that the latter included instruction in the use of logarithms. Certainly Bainbridge assumed knowledge of logarithms when lecturing.[18] The prescribed text in astronomy was Ptolemy's *Almagest*. But there was no archaism involved here for, as F. R. Johnson has pointed out, 'a mastery of the mathematics of the *Almagest* was, until the time of Newton, the necessary foundation of mathematical astronomy for Copernicans as well as for the adherents of the old cosmology'. Furthermore it is clear from his surviving lecture notes that Bainbridge took seriously the Savilian injunction to include in his exposition 'the discoveries . . . of modern writers'. Thus in his inaugural lecture of 9 January 1621 Bainbridge referred to recent telescopic findings concerning the three-bodied appearance of Saturn, the satellites of Jupiter, sun-spots, the phases of Venus, and the mountainous surface of the moon. Similarly in January 1625 he discussed the work of Galileo, Kepler, and Scheiner. Bainbridge also, on 11 May 1621, commenced a series of solar and lunar eclipse observations at Oxford, part of which was communicated to Pierre Gassendi in the 1630s.[19]

Two distinguished products of this new scientific teaching were Henry Gellibrand of Trinity College, who in 1627 succeeded Gunter as Gresham professor of astronomy, and John Greaves of Merton College, who in 1630 became Gresham professor of geometry. The academic references supplied for them by Bainbridge make instructive reading. Gellibrand, he writes, 'was for some yeares a frequent and attentive auditor at my lectures, and hath had many private conferences with me in astronomicall matters, whereby he hath shewed his singular affection to those studies, and his good proficiency in the same'. That Bainbridge did not exaggerate the abilities of Gellibrand is borne out by his later career; as Gresham professor he was, for example, to complete the *Trigonometria Britannica*, which Briggs had left unfinished at the time of his death. Concerning Greaves, Bainbridge wrote that, in addition to attending astronomy lectures he 'hath by many private conferences given me occasion to take notice of his singular skill in the mathematicks, especially in the geometry of Euclide'. During the 1630s Greaves was to make an astronomical expedition to Alexandria, 'a thing that hath beene much desired by the astronomers of this age, but never undertaken by any'. Gellibrand was clearly one of the 'hotter sort' of Protestants, sponsoring in 1630 an almanack with a calendar of saints based on Foxe's *Book of Martyrs*.[20] Greaves, by contrast, became a protégé of Laud and fled to Oxford at the outbreak of the Civil War.

In addition to the specialist labours of Briggs and Bainbridge, a more general Oxford current of philosophic reform continued to flow. Evidence for this comes from a series of books published at Oxford, and therefore licensed by the vice-chancellor. Thus in 1621 there appeared the first edition of Burton's *Anatomy of Melancholy*, a book with important implications for the cult of virtuosity. 'What more pleasing studies can there be', Burton asked, 'then the mathematickes, theorick or practick part?' Or, as he elaborated in a later edition, 'what [is] so intricate or pleasing withall as to peruse Napier's *Logarithmes*, or those tables of artificiall sines and tangents not long since set out by mine old collegiat, good friend and late fellow Student of Christ Church in Oxford, Mr. Edmund Gunter . . . or those elaborate conclusions of his *Sector, Quadrant and Crosse-Staffe*?' Burton was here prescribing mathematics as a cure for 'melancholy', and it is interesting that Robert Boyle later recommended their study in similar terms.[21] But Burton also advocated scientific 'experiments'. Like Boyle too he believed in the practical application of knowledge, his special concerns being inland navigation, fen drainage, and 'industry [which] is a lodestone to drawe all good things'.[22]

The year following the first appearance of Burton's *Anatomy* saw the Oxford publication of *Philosophia Libera* by Nathanael Carpenter. Highly critical of Aristotelian philosophy, the book invites comparison with a similar manifesto published in 1624 by the Catholic Gassendi.[23] Carpenter, a follow of Exeter College, begins by enunciating the principle 'in nullius iuratus verba', and then proceeds to a series of anti-Aristotelian propositions. Like Burton he accepted the daily rotation of the earth, but rejected the idea of a sun-centred universe. In 1625 Carpenter incorporated the astronomical ideas of *Philosophia Libera* in his *Geography Delineated*, which was also produced by the Oxford press.[24] More important, however, than either Burton or Carpenter, as regards breadth of appeal, was George Hakewill, whose *Apologie of the Power and Providence of God in the Government of the World* was published at Oxford in 1627. Dedicated to the university, the book attacked the then widely held belief in the historical decay of intellectual and all other natural powers. On the contrary, says Hakewill, 'not any one man, or nation, or age, but rather mankinde is it which in latitude of capacity answeres to the universality of things to be knowne'. As part of his argument Hakewill instances recent scientific achievements, such as the invention of logarithms, although his book was chiefly significant as a solvent of traditional attitudes. Some idea of its effect is conveyed by the testimonials of various Oxford contemporaries, which preface the 1635 edition; while scientists like Allen and Briggs claim always to have believed the truth of Hakewill's argument that nature remains unimpaired over the centuries, others such as Degory Wheare, Camden professor of history, and Samuel Fell, Lady Margaret professor of divinity, admit to having been converted by him.[25] For the non-specialist the book opened up the prospect of new mental worlds to conquer.

II

Carpenter and Hakewill, like Burton, were Calvinists in their theology.[26] As such they were in accord with the Church of England norm under James I, yet during the 1620s dramatic changes were overtaking official English religious teaching. The crisis centred on the writings of Richard Montagu, who in 1624 publicly denied the credal Calvinism of the English Church. Montagu turned out to have powerful episcopal backers, and within little more than a year of the accession of Charles I Calvinist doctrine was outlawed by royal proclamation.[27] The resulting sense of shock is well illustrated by an entry for 1626 in the diary of Thomas Crosfield, a fellow of Queen's College, Oxford. 'Nota', he wrote, 'quod statim post inaugurationem Regis Caroli, non sine periculo inter orthodoxos, serpebat Pelagianismi cancer a Montagu pestis doctrinae corporis.'[28] A less derogatory and more accurate term than Pelagian to describe the religious views favoured by Charles I is Arminian. The full impact of the Arminian revolution on Oxford was nevertheless delayed some two years thanks to the influence of the university chancellor, the third Earl of Pembroke, who favoured the Calvinist party. But in 1628 Charles I reiterated his earlier ruling against Calvinism, and explicitly included the doctrinal teaching of the universities within his prohibition. Henceforth predestinarian teaching was effectively banned in Oxford as elsewhere,[29] and the term Puritan was now redefined by Arminians to include Calvinism. One of the leading architects of the new Arminian policy was, of course, Laud, who in 1630 succeeded Pembroke as chancellor of Oxford. What, however, is most striking in the scientific context is the *irrelevance* of these religious changes. Far from withering on the bough the scientific movement at Oxford continued to flourish.

Thus in October 1626 Bainbridge can be found writing to Archbishop Ussher, who was interested in astronomy from the point of view of chronology. His letter shows no interest in recent religious changes, despite Ussher being a declared opponent of Arminianism. Instead Bainbridge reports that he has begun a study of Arabic, in order to read mathematical works in that language, and says he is also 'very busy in the fabric of a large instrument for observations, that I may, *mea fide*, both teach and write; and here again I humbly entreat you to take in your consideration my petition at Oxford, that you would, as occasion shall be offered, commend to the munificence of some noble benefactors this excellent and rare part of astronomy, (ὕλη ἀστρονομική), which would certainly commend them to posterity; in the mean time I would not fail to publish their fame unto the learned world.' As well as continuing his series of eclipse observations, it is probable that Bainbridge hoped to witness the predicted transit of Venus across the face of the sun in December 1631. Certainly he discussed the subject in 1630, describing the technique of projecting the solar disc through a telescope and on to a white screen in a darkened room. Unfortunately and, owing to an error in Kepler's tables, unexpectedly, the transit occurred during the European night and was consequently invisible.[30]

But by 1631 Bainbridge was embarked on a far more ambitious project, namely the organization of an astronomical expedition to South America. As before he was on the look-out for a patron, and he found him in Sir Thomas Roe, the distinguished explorer and diplomat. Again the appeal for financial support is couched in terms of the enduring fame that will accrue to the benefactor, whose name, says Bainbridge, 'shall bee resplendent . . . when all other the most precious jewels that ever were brought from either India shall bee consumed and forgotten'.[31] The proposal was to employ the services of a sea captain, Roger Fry, who was already bound on a colonising venture to Guiana. We can show from his own notebook that Fry was at Merton College in December 1626 and December 1627, measuring star altitudes, although there appears to be no trace of him in either the university or college records. Fry also notes a number of sun-spot observations which he made in June and July 1630, using the same method as recommended by Bainbridge in order to observe the transit of Venus.[32] For the Guiana expedition of the following year Bainbridge furnished Fry with a set of detailed astronomical instructions, and clearly one of the objectives was to obtain simultaneous eclipse observations with a view to an improved cartography. More generally Bainbridge hoped that accurate recordings from 'under the aequator or neer thereabouts' would 'clear many doubts in the moste principall poynts of astronomy and bee of singular use in geographye and navigation'.[33] In the event the expedition was attacked by the Portuguese, and Fry was taken as a prisoner to Brazil. But undeterred he proceeded to make a series of astronomical observations at São Luis do Maranhão on the Brazilian coast, and sent the first results back to Oxford in May 1633.[34] Bainbridge, with understandable excitement, announced the news in his lectures, speaking of 'Marenhamiae urbis Brasiliae . . . in quo loco multas observationes caelestes nuper fecit Anglus quidam astronomiae scientissimus'. In particular he cited his and Fry's observations of a solar eclipse which had occurred on 29 March

1633; this indicated that the longitudinal position of São Luis do Maranhão was just under 45° west of Oxford.[35]

At the same time as the Guiana expedition Bainbridge also planned to send a qualified astronomer to Alexandria, in order to check the results of the ancient Greeks.[36] The choice ultimately fell on his former pupil John Greaves, although the latter did not set out until 1637. Finance as ever was a problem, but one of those soliciting funds on behalf of Greaves was Lord Treasurer Juxon, who had succeeded Laud as president of St John's College, Oxford, and then as Arminian Bishop of London. 'This worke', wrote Juxon of the proposed Alexandria expedition, 'I find by the best astronomers, especially by Ticho Brache [sic] and Kepler, hath bynn much desired as tending to the advancement of that science, and I hope it wil be an honour to that nation and prove ours if we first observe it.' He went on to suggest that Greaves's employers should assist 'the advancement of learning' by subsidising his purchase of astronomical instruments.[37] Like Fry, Greaves also hoped to contribute towards solving the problem of longitude on land, by the method of simultaneous eclipse observations. Writing from Constantinople in August 1638, Greaves outlined his preparations: 'the eclipse of the moon in December next will be observed (if it please God) at Bagdad, Constantinople, Smyrna and Alexandria, all which places I have furnished with convenient instruments, and given them instructions according to Tycho Brahe's how they should observe.' From Constantinople Greaves sailed to Alexandria, which was his main astronomical goal, and spent six months there making observations chiefly of the fixed stars.[38]

Medical studies at Oxford were undeniably slower to take off than the mathematical sciences. This was partly due to the fact that the new Tomlins lectureship in Anatomy was held in plurality by the Regius professor of medicine, Thomas Clayton, much of whose time was taken up with transforming Broadgates Hall into Pembroke College. Nevertheless statutory provision was made in 1624 for regular dissections to be performed by a surgeon under the direction of the Regius professor,[39] and one of Clayton's pupils was Edward Dawson who in 1633 publicly maintained the probability of the circulation of the blood, at the annual Oxford Act. Dawson's thesis, which I discovered in 1963, has been described as 'an exceptional concession to contemporary issues, in a period of Galenic supremacy'.[40] Yet it can also be seen as exemplifying the best of Oxford medical science at that time. Dawson was clearly considered an outstanding student, being chosen for instance in July 1621, while a member of Broadgates Hall, to make a speech at the foundation of the Oxford botanical garden.[41] Another Oxford exemplar is George Joyliffe of Pembroke College, who in the 1640s 'exercising himself much in anatomy with the help of Dr. Clayton, master of his college and the King's professor of physic, ... made some discovery of that fourth sort of vessels plainly differing from veins, arteries, and nerves, now called the lympheducts'.[42] Moreover close links existed between medical and mathematical practitioners. Thus Bainbridge in addition to being Savilian professor of astronomy was a licentiate of the College of Physicians and practised medicine, while Clayton in 1622 addressed some verses jointly to Bainbridge and Briggs, 'doctissimos professores mathematicos'. In 1640 both Bainbridge and Clayton contributed letters of recommendation to *Theatrum Botanicum* by John Parkinson, at the same time taking the opportunity to advertise the Oxford botanical garden which was now at long last nearing completion.[43] The following year John Greaves, who was to succeed Bainbridge as Savilian professor in 1643, supplied a prefatory poem for George Ent's *Apologia pro Circulatione Sanguinis*.[44] It is further worth remembering that there existed an experimental tradition among members of the College of Physicians well before Harvey's discovery of circulation, but a tradition of experiment in magnetism not anatomy, outstanding names being Gilbert and Ridley. We would therefore expect medicine to lag somewhat behind other sciences at Oxford, as elsewhere in England. Later, during the Civil War, Harvey was to come in person to Oxford and head a group working on embryology.[45]

Meanwhile in the mid 1630s Archbishop Laud had begun to take a direct interest in the advancement of Oxford science. As part of his building programme at St John's College, he projected a mathematical library which was designed to reinforce the Savilian lectures at collegiate level. He envisaged a special collection of 'mathematical books and instruments', and expressed the wish in October 1635 that 'the younger fellows and students' of St. John's would 'give themselves more to those [mathematical] studies'. Some two and a half years later, in May 1638, he wrote to the president and fellows of the College 'I am glad to hear from you that my mathematical library is in such forwardness.'[46] By now donations were beginning to arrive; for example William Oughtred's *Circles of Proportion and the Horizontall Instrument*, both the book and the brass instrument, were presented this year by George Barkham, son of a member of Laud's household.[47] At about the same time the library acquired a pair of globes and a quadrant, and John Speed, son of the map-maker, gave a pair of human skeletons.[48] In 1634 Laud had also purchased a number of books probably with the intention of giving them to the St John's mathematical library. These books included Napier's *Logarithmes*, in the English translation by Edward Wright, Harriot's *Ars Analytica Praxis*, and atlases by Bertius, Mercator and Ortelius.

The foundation by Laud of an Arabic lectureship in 1636 also had a related scientific purpose. For it was hoped that the Muslim world would yield a rich harvest of mathematical manuscripts. The first holder of the post, Edward Pococke, accompanied John Greaves to the Middle East in 1637, and his Oxford duties were undertaken temporarily by Greaves's brother Thomas, who began his course, on 19 July 1637, with an oration entitled *De Linguae Arabicae Utilitate et Praestantia*. 'Utilitas' for Thomas Greaves comprehended algebra, arithmetic, and astronomy. Such subjects, together with the growing importance of the Arabic language for trade, had been stressed by Pococke's teacher William Bedwell as early as 1612, when dedicating his edition of the Arabic version of St. John's Epistles to the Arminian Lancelot Andrewes. Pococke too, as former chaplain to the Turkey merchants at Aleppo, would be aware of the significance of the Levant in these years for English commerce.[49] The idea of utility also occurs in such a seemingly unlikely place as the imprimatur affixed in 1634 to Captain Luke Foxe's account of his search for a North-West Passage. The licence by Samuel Baker, chaplain to Bishop Juxon, runs 'resensui librum hunc . . . in quo nihil reperio quo minus cum utilitate publica imprimatur'.[50]

The book-acquisition policy of the Bodleian Library continued to favour the growth of science at Oxford, as can be seen from the supplementary catalogue published in 1635. New arrivals included Harvey's *De Motu Cordis et Sanguinis* of 1628 and Gassendi's *Mercurius in Sole Visus et Venus Invisa* of 1632, as well as ten further works by Kepler. Examples of recent English scientific works listed are Richard Norwood's *Trigonometrie* of 1631 and Oughtred's *Circles of Proportion and the Horizontall Instrument* of 1632.[51] Similarly colleges like Merton and Christ Church maintained their scientific interests. In 1632 at Merton, the college to which the Savilian professorships were attached, John Greaves and Hugh Cressy respectively answered in the affirmative the thesis questions 'An mathesis sit scientiarum praestantissima?' and 'An scepticorum dubitantia praeferenda sit peripateticorum thesibus?' Greaves was already Gresham professor of geometry and kept in touch with his 'friends at Merton College' even when in the Middle East during the late 1630s. Cressy had delivered an oration at the funeral of Henry Briggs in 1630 and subsequently became chaplain to the Earl of Strafford, ending his days as a Benedictine monk.[52] At Christ Church Burton was now librarian and remained abreast of astronomical developments, possessing not only Gassendi's account of the transit of Mercury across the face of the sun in November 1631 but also the related commentaries by Hortensius and Schickard. He also owned a set of 'surveighing books and instruments', 'two crosse staves', and a collection of 'Englishe bookes of husbandry', whose authors included Gabriel Plattes the agricultural improver.[53]

Whether Burton gave formal instruction in scientific subjects is unclear,[54] although John Gregory, chaplain of Christ Church at this time, apparently did, to judge from his posthumously published 'Description and Use of the Terrestrial Globe . . . [and] of Maps and Charts Universal and Particular'. This certainly reads as if originally delivered in lecture form. It also draws on recently published scientific material. Thus Gregory cites Gellibrand's work on magnetic variation, published in 1635, and illustrates a discussion of longitude with the simultaneous observation of a lunar eclipse on 29 October 1631, by Gellibrand at London and Captain Thomas James at Charlton south of Hudson Bay. He refers as well to the 'use of the celestial and terrestrial spheres by the supposition of Copernicus per terram mobilem'. Gregory subsequently became domestic chaplain to Bishop Duppa, dying near Oxford in 1646 his circumstances financially reduced.[55] His departure from Christ Church in about 1639 was marked by the return of Robert Payne, who had migrated in 1624 to Pembroke College as one of the original fellows. Payne had then left Oxford for service with the Earl of Newcastle, assisting him in his laboratory experiments and in 1636 translating into English Galileo's *Della Scienza Mecanica*.[56] As canon of Christ Church he presented the college in 1642 with Galileo's *Systema Cosmicum* and a brass instrument by Gunter. In 1648 Payne was purged by the Parliamentary Visitors, along with the Savilian professors John Greaves and Peter Turner.[57]

At a more popular philosophic level during the 1630s new editions of Burton, Carpenter, and Hakewill were all produced by the Oxford press. Over the same period Copernican theory was becoming more widely accepted. We can tell from Bainbridge's lecture notes that he positively recommended the heliocentric hypothesis to his audience,[58] but in 1635 a particularly bold step was taken. Codification of the university statutes had recently been completed, and it was now further decided to print the university syllabus in diagrammatic form. The resulting sheet, dedicated to Laud, shows the day and hour of each lecture, by means of a series of concentric circles with a sun in the middle; the moon, representing Monday, and a clock are so placed in relation to the sun as to indicate that the motif is Copernican.

The most likely author was Turner, who had succeeded Briggs as Savilian professor of geometry in 1630 and was a protégé of Laud. Turner had earlier devised a proctorial cycle which was similarly illustrated by a circular diagram, and he was instructed by Laud in 1634 to 'review' the draft of the new statutes. The vice-chancellor's accounts of 1635–36 record a payment to Turner of £40 for three journeys to London 'about the university statutes'.[59] One result seems to have been the *Encyclopaedia seu Orbis Literarum*, as it was called, and in 1638 this Copernican diagram was bound up with an abridged version of the university statutes intended for student use.[60] Therefore we can say, with pardonable exaggeration, that from the late 1630s every Oxford undergraduate carried a Copernican system in his pocket.

The sun at the centre of the 1635 *Encyclopaedia* may in addition be intended to represent King Charles I, since Copernican sun-king imagery can be found two years earlier in a collection of verses published by the university. Entitled *Solis Britannici Perigaeum*, the volume marked the occasion of Charles's journey to Scotland in 1633. Thomas Lockey, one of the contributors

FIGURE 2   Centre detail from *Encyclopaedia seu Orbis Literarum*
(Oxford, 1635)

and a Student of Christ Church, had written that with the King 'ticed from
his sphere . . . our shine with him' England 'wandered in shadow darke' and
'walk't in night'. Use of the terms wander and walk, together with a reference to Queen Henrietta Maria as the moon, indicate that Lockey was here
extending the analogy of the king as sun to that of the state as planet earth
in orbit around the sun. Silenced in 1651, Lockey returned to Oxford at
the Restoration as librarian of the Bodleian; the inventory taken at his death
in 1679 notes, among items 'in the summer house', a 'telescope with some
other mathermaticall instruments'.[61] Of a piece with the increasing vogue
for Copernicanism at Oxford during the chancellorship of Laud is the fact
that in February 1640 John Wilkins's *Discourse Concerning a New Planet* was
licensed by a chaplain of Juxon *and* by Accepted Frewen, vice-chancellor of

Oxford University and as such deputy to Laud.[62] This book was the first full-scale English defence of Copernicanism and the author, who had recently left Magdalen Hall, both sought and got the official approval of his alma mater.

In some ways, however, the philosophic climax of this Laudian decade was the Oxford publication in 1640 of Francis Bacon's *Advancement and Proficience of Learning*. This was a translation by Gilbert Watts, fellow of Lincoln College, from the 1623 Latin edition. Dedicating his efforts to King Charles and the Prince of Wales, Watts claimed that 'it is only the benigne aspect and irradiation of princes that inspires the globe of learning, and makes arts and sciences grow up and florish', and he described Bacon as 'the first that ever joynd rationall and experimentall philosophy in a regular correspondence'. The title-page is an adaptation of the one found in Bacon's *Novum Organum* of 1620 which shows the ship of human intellect sailing through the Pillars of Hercules. In the 1640 version the pillars are transformed into spires, the one labelled Oxonium and the other Cantabrigia, each resting on volumes by Bacon. Above float two spheres, the 'mundus visibilis' and the 'mundus intellectualis', joined by two hands: 'ratione et experientia foederantur'. The legend from Daniel 12. 4, 'multi pertransibunt et augebitur scientia', occurs in both versions.[63] Such a prophecy had already begun to be realised literally in the astronomical expeditions organised from Oxford by Bainbridge during the 1630s and the phrase 'advancement of learning' was now part of the vocabulary of educated Englishmen. Bishop Juxon, as we have remarked, used the phrase in 1637 and so did Bainbridge in 1629.[64] But the novelty of Bacon lay primarily in his call for the systematic construction of a 'natural history' of observations and experiments, as the basis of a 'new philosophy'. This looks forward to the work of the Oxford philosophical 'clubb' in the early 1650s and ultimately to that of the Royal Society.[65]

Watts, the translator of Bacon, was presented by the King to an Essex living in 1642, which was subsequently sequestered by Parliament. Before his death in 1657 he had begun work on an elaborate edition of the works of Charles I.[66] Enthusiasm for the philosophy of Bacon was shared by many of the royalist gentry gathered in Oxford during the Civil War, men like Justinian Isham and Sir Christopher Hatton. By 1639 Isham had made an 'abridgement' of Bacon's ideas concerning scientific advance, and earned the compliment from William Rawley, former secretary to Bacon, that 'of our nation your self is the second, or third man, that I know of who hath addicted himself [to] or profitted by those studies'. At about the same time Hatton provided Samuel Hartlib, the pansophical reformer, with an unpublished Bacon manuscript.[67] Isham was a committed defender of the English Prayer Book, while Hatton was a patron of the Arminian Jeremy Taylor.[68] They were to become fellows of the Royal Society in 1663. Thus it would seem that no particular religious or political group had a majority interest in Bacon.

Close scrutiny then of scientific developments at Oxford, in the decades before the Civil War, indicates a negative correlation between religion and science. Despite Arminianism, the upward movement of science continued unabated. At the same time we can detect the growth of new values. Concepts like advancement and utility emerged during these years, as did the ideal of the virtuoso. Clearly the institutional endowment of science played a central role. But in a wider context the fortunes of Oxford science reflected changes in the English economy. Oxford efforts to grapple with the problem of longitude, 'the major practical problem of the science of the day', paralleled the work in France of Nicolas Peiresc and in the United Provinces of Willem Blaeu.[69] For it was no accident that the countries moving into the commercial leadership of Europe were also those in the scientific vanguard. In England we must take account too of changes in land management and the accompanying rise of the estate surveyor. The religious background, however, remained pluralistic, embracing all manner of Protestants *and* Catholics. To this evolving pattern of seventeenth-century science, European as well as English, Laudian Oxford made a significant contribution.

NOTES

An earlier version of this essay was read to a Monday seminar at the Institute of Historical Research, and I am especially grateful to Piyo Rattansi and Basil Greenslade for their comments. Inspiration to break what is for me new historical ground has come mainly from my wife, Sarah Tyacke. John Cooper, Roger Highfield, Theo Moody, John North, and Keith Thomas have also kindly helped in various ways, and I am particularly indebted to the following librarians and archivists: at Dublin William O'Sullivan of Trinity College, at Oxford David Cooper of Corpus Christi College, Charles Morgenstern of St John's College, Helen Powell of The Queen's College, David Vaisey of the Bodleian Library, and John Wing of Christ Church, and at Mercers' Hall, London, Jean Imray.

1 C. Hill, *Intellectual Origins of the English Revolution* (Oxford, 1965), esp. pp. 14–84, 301–14, and in C. Webster ed., *The Intellectual Revolution of the Seventeenth Century* (London, 1974), pp. 243–53, 280–3.

2 R. F. Jones, *Ancients and Moderns* (Berkeley, Cal., 1965), p. 84; E. G. R. Taylor, *The Mathematical Practitioners of Tudor and Stuart England* (Cambridge, 1970), pp. 49–83 and *passim*; D. W. Waters, *The Art of Navigation in England in Elizabethan and Early Stuart Times* (London, 1958), pt ii.

3 The disastrous consequences for Puritanism stemming from the Arminianisation of the Church of England are discussed above, pp. 132–55.

4 B. Holyday, *Technogamia*, ed. M. J. C. Cavanaugh (Washington, D.G., 1942), pp. 104–5; P. J. French, *John Dee: The World of an Elizabethan Magus* (London, 1972), esp. pp. 89–125; G. R. M. Ward ed., *Oxford University Statutes* (London, 1845–51), i, p. 274.

5 R. Burton, *Philosophaster*, ed. P. Jordan-Smith (Stanford, Cal., 1931), pp. 53, 211.

6 CL, Donors' Book, fo 55. A pair of globes was also donated to Trinity College, in the mid 1620s, by Devorox Frogg: Trinity College, Oxford, Benefactors' Book, no. 28. For earlier globes see E. Craster, 'Elizabethan Globes at Oxford', *Geographical Journal* 117 (1951), 24–6.

7 E. Gunter, *The Description and Use of the Sector* (London, 1623), p. 143. The copy of Gunter's *Description* owned by Burton, and now in Christ Church Library, is inscribed 'ex dono authoris'.

8 B. Holyday, *A Survey of the World* (Oxford, 1661), pp. 1–2, 8; R. Burton, *The Anatomy of Melancholy* (Oxford, 1628), pp. 239–40.

9 *Justa Funebria Ptolemaei Oxoniensis* (Oxford, 1613), p. 115; R. F. Ovenell, 'The Library of Brian Twyne', *Oxford Bibliog. Soc.*, new ser., 4 (1952), 24; M. H. Curtis, *Oxford and Cambridge in Transition, 1558–1642* (Oxford, 1959), pp. 120–1.

10 A. Wood, *Athenae Oxonienses*, ed. P. Bliss (London, 1813–20), ii, p. 543; [W. Burton and G. Bathurst], *In Thomae Alleni . . . exequiarum . . . Orationes Binae* (London, 1632), p. 6.

11 B. Holyday, *Of the Nature of Faith* (London, 1654), pp. 16–17; R. Burton, *Anatomy* (Oxford, 1628), p. 641. [As late as 1610, Twyne was an orthodox Calvinist: Tyacke, *Anti-Calvinists*, p. 67.]

12 A. Wood, *History and Antiquities of the University of Oxford*, ed. J. Gutch (Oxford, 1792–6), ii, p. 232. I am grateful to Alan Davidson for this reference.

13 T. James, *Catalogus Universalis Librorum in Bibliotheca Bodleiana* (Oxford, 1620), pp. 278–9, 414, 424, 533; Ward ed., *Statutes*, pp. 275–6.

14 Ward ed., *Statutes*, pp. 272–4; H. Savile, *Oratio Coram Regina Elizabetha Oxoniae Habita* (Oxford, 1658), p. 6. On this same occasion Savile argued for the abolition of astrology, *ibid.*, pp. 8–9.

15 W. E. Houghton, 'The English Virtuoso in the Seventeenth Century', *Journ. Hist. Ideas*, 3 (1942), 51–73, 190–219; Curtis, *Oxford and Cambridge*, pp. 126–9, 258–60, 263–5. Discussing Roman warfare, Savile wrote that 'no state may looke to stand without notable molestation and danger of ruine, much lesse to enlarge, which in any kind of service, on foote, or on horsebacke, or by sea is quite defective and utterly disfurnished': *Annotations upon . . . Tacitus* (Oxford, 1591), p. 71.

16 H. C. Porter, *Reformation and Reaction in Tudor Cambridge* (Cambridge, 1958), p. 188; J. Ussher, *Works*, ed. C. R. Elrington (Dublin, 1847–64), xv, p. 62; I. Adamson, 'The Foundation and Early History of Gresham College London, 1596–1704' (Ph.D. thesis, Cambridge Univ., 1976), p. 133.

17 J. Bainbridge, *An Astronomicall Description of the Late Comet* (London, 1619), pp. 1, 24; Ussher, *Works*, xv, pp. 62–4, 89–90, 213, 351–3, 394, 447–8.

18 Ward ed., *Statutes*, pp. 272–4; TCD, MS. 386(5), fo 67. I was alerted to the existence of the Bainbridge papers at Dublin by R. G. Frank, 'Science, Medicine and the Universities of Early Modern England: Background and Sources', *History of Science*, 11 (1973), 203 and n. 25.

19 Ward ed., *Statutes*, p. 273; F. R. Johnson, *Astronomical Thought in Renaissance England* (Baltimore, 1937), p. 270; TCD, MS. 382, fos 27r–v, 122–4; *ibid.*, MS. 386(4), 13–14; P. Gassendi, *Opera Omnia* (Lyons, 1658), vi, pp. 424–5.

20 Mercers' Hall, London, Gresham Repertory, ii, pp. 3, 23; PRO, S.P. 16/381/75: John Greaves to Peter Turner, 10 Feb. 1637. This letter has previously been dated incorrectly to 1638; W. Prynne, *Canterburies Doome* (1648), p. 182.

21 R. Burton, *Anatomy* (Oxford, 1621), p. 352 and (Oxford, 1628), p. 264; R. E. W. Maddison, *The Life of the Honourable Robert Boyle* (London, 1969), pp. 17–18.

22 Burton, *Anatomy* (1621), pp. 51–8, and (Oxford, 1632), pp. 280–1; Jones, *Ancients and Moderns*, pp. 202–4.

23 P. Gassendi, *Exercitationum Paradoxicarum Adversus Aristoteleos* (Grenoble, 1624).

24 N. Carpenter, *Philosophia Libera* (Oxford, 1622), 'Ad Florentissimam Oxoniensis Academiae Iuventutem Praefatio' and *passim*; id., *Geography Delineated* (Oxford, 1625), bk. i, pp. 75–97.

25 G. Hakewill, *An Apologie* (Oxford, 1627), sigs. b3, Ooo 2v, and (Oxford, 1635), sigs. cr–v, c2.

26 N. Carpenter, *Achitophel, or the Picture of a Wicked Politician* (London, 1629), pp. 13–14, 30–4; G. Hakewill, *An Answere to . . . Dr. Carier* (London, 1616), pp. 284–92.

27 This proclamation 'for the establishing of the peace and quiet of the Church of England' was issued on 14 June 1626 and is reprinted in J. P. Kenyon, *The Stuart Constitution* (Cambridge, 1966), pp. 154–5. For the official and anti-Calvinist interpretation put upon it, see Bishop Neile's letter to the vice-chancellor of Cambridge University, dated 16 June 1626: CUA, Royal Letters of Charles I, no. 6.

28 QCL, Oxford, MS. 390, fo 19.

29 [In fact the last Calvinist thesis to be maintained at the Oxford Act, before the Civil War, was in 1631: Tyacke, *Anti-Calvinists*, p. 81.]

30 Ussher, *Works*, xiii, p. 351; xv, p. 352; Bodl., Smith MS. 92, p. 23; B. H. Woolf, *The Transits of Venus* (Princeton, NJ, 1959), pp. 10–12.

31 TCD, MS. 386(1). fos 43r–v. [What appears to be the figure of Fame, with a trumpet, surmounts the monument of Sir Henry Savile in Merton College chapel: N. Tyacke ed., *The History of the University of Oxford, IV: Seventeenth-Century Oxford* (Oxford, 1997), pp. 458–9, plate 9.]

32 *Ibid.*, MS. 443, fos 23v, 25v, 28v, 40.

33 *Ibid.*, MS. 386(1), fos 43–44v.

34 Roger Fry to Bainbridge, 10 May 1633: *ibid.*, MS. 382, fos 105r–v. The subsequent fate of Fry is at present unknown, but J. A. Williamson is clearly mistaken when he writes that Fry was killed by the Portuguese in 1631: *English Colonies in Guiana and on the Amazon, 1604–1688* (Oxford, 1923), p. 139.

35 TCD, MS. 386(5), fos 48, 101v.

36 William Hakewill to Bainbridge, 5 April 1631: *ibid.*, MS. 382, fo 98.

37 Bishop Juxon to the Gresham Committee, 30 April 1637: PRO, T. 56/13, fo 2v. I owe this reference to the kindness of Tom Mason.

38 J. Greaves, *Miscellaneous Works* (London, 1737), ii, pp. 437–8, 443–4. According to David Gregory, writing in 1697, Greaves's observations were not superseded until those made by Halley and Hevelius: Bodl., Smith MS. 93, pp. 165–7.

39 Ward ed., *Statues*, pp. 289–90.

40 C. Webster, *The Great Instauration: Science, Medicine and Reform, 1626–60* (London, 1975), pp. 125, 139. [C. Hill, 'William Harvey and the Idea of Monarchy', *P and P* 27 (1964), 59, n. 30]

41 R. W. T. Günther, *Oxford Gardens* (Oxford, 1912), p. 2.

42 Wood, *Athenae*, iii, p. 351.

43 W. Munk, *Roll of the Royal College of Physicians* (London, 1878), i, pp. 175–6; Bodl., Rawlinson MS. letters 41, fos 3–36; *Ultima Linea Savilii* (Oxford, 1622), sig. F2r–v; J. Parkinson, *Theatrum Botanicum* (London, 1640), sig. a.

44 G. Ent, *Apologia pro Circulatione Sanguinis* (London, 1641), sig. A4v.

45 R. G. Frank, 'John Aubrey, F.R.S., John Lydall, and Science at Commonwealth Oxford', *Notes and Records of the Royal Society*, 27 (1972–73), 195.

46 Laud, *Works*, vii, pp. 192, 434. Unless otherwise stated, information concerning items in the St. John's College Library is derived from inscriptions in the extant books.

47 SJL, MS. 37, fos 163–4. The book and instrument are at present divided between the St. John's College Library and the Oxford Museum of the History of Science; it is to be hoped that they will one day be reunited.

48 W. C. Costin, *The History of St. John's College Oxford, 1598–1860* (OHS, 1958), p. 76; St. John's College Archives, Oxford, Computus Annuus, 1640–41, fo 38; Wood, *Athenae*, ii, p. 660 (I owe this reference to John Fuggles).

49 T. Greaves, *De Linguae Arabicae* (Oxford, 1639), pp. 9, 12; W. Bedwell, *D. Johannis Apostoli et Evangelistae Epistolae Catholicae Omnes Arabicae* (Leiden, 1612), sig. A2; *DNB s.n.* Pococke, Edward; R. Davis, 'England and the Mediterranean, 1570–1670' in F. J. Fisher ed., *Essays in the Economic and Social History of Tudor and Stuart England* (Cambridge, 1961).

50 M. Christy ed., *The Voyages of Captain Luke Foxe of Hull, and Captain Thomas James of Bristol* (Hakluyt Soc., 1894), ii, p. 445. [There is a danger here of glossing the term 'utilitas' in anachronistically modern terms.]

51 J. Rous, *Appendix ad Catalogum Librorum in Bibliotheca Bodleiana* (Oxford, 1635), pp. 78, 89, 105–6, 135.

52 Merton College, Oxford, Register, ii, p. 310; Bodl., Smith MS. 93, pp. 137–8; Wood, *Athenae*, ii, p. 492; *DNB s.n.* Cressy, Hugh.

53 W. Osler *et al.*, 'Robert Burton and the *Anatomy of Melancholy*', *Oxford Bibliog. Soc.* 1 (1927), 219–20, 230, 233–4, 240.

54 Among those to whom Burton bequeathed mathematical instruments in August 1639 was the Earl of Downe, who had matriculated two months previously: *ibid.*, p. 220.

55 J. Gregory, *Gregorii Posthuma* (London, 1649), pp. 272, 281, 289. My attention was drawn to John Gregory by Anthony Turner; *DNB s.n.* Gregory, John (1607–46).

56 J. Jacquot, 'Sir Charles Cavendish and his Learned Friends', *Annals of Science*, 8 (1952), 21; B. D. Greenslade, 'The Falkland Circle: a Study in Tradition from Jonson to Halifax' (M.A. thesis, University of London, 1955), pp. 153–9. Basil Greenslade has most generously made available to me his information concerning Payne.

57 CL, Donors' Book, fo 94; M. Burrows ed., *The Register of the Visitors of the University of Oxford, 1647–58* (Camden Soc., N.S. xxix, 1881), p. lxxxii.

58 TCD, MS. 386(3), fo 22v.

59 F. Madan, *The Early Oxford Press, 1468–1640* (OHS, 1895), pp. 145, 186–7; Wood, *Athenae*, iii, p. 307; Laud, *Works*, v, p. 99; OUA, W.P.B. 21(4), 233.

60 Madan, *Oxford Press*, pp. 208–9. Samuel Boyes of Magdalen Hall, who had matriculated in 1637, paid 1s. 4d. for his copy of the *Statuta Selecta* in 1638: SJL.

61 *Solis Britannici Perigaeum* (Oxford, 1633), sig. Liv; *DNB s.n.* Lockey, Thomas; OUA, Hyp. B. 15.

62 Arber ed., *Transcript*, iv, p. 472.

63 F. Bacon, *Of the Advancement and Proficience of Learning* (Oxford, 1640), sigs ¶2v, ¶3v. [The printer presented a copy to the St John's College Library.]

64 See p. 251 above; Ussher, *Works*, xv, p. 447.

65 H. W. Robinson, 'An Unpublished Letter of Dr. Seth Ward Relating to the Early Meetings of the Oxford Philosophical Society', *Notes and Records of the Royal Society*, 7 (1950), 69.

66 R. Newcourt, *Repertorium* (London, 1708–10), ii, p. 668; *DNB s.n.* Watts, Gilbert; Corpus Christi College, Oxford, MS. 326.

67 Northants RO, MS. I.C. 228; Sheffield Univ. Lib., Hartlib MSS. 44/2/1, 44/29.

68 G. Isham ed., *The Correspondence of Bishop Brian Duppa and Sir Justinian Isham, 1650–60* (Northants Rec. Soc., xvii 1955), p. xxxix; F. Madan, *Oxford Books* (Oxford, 1912–31), ii, pp. 165, 342–3.

69 S. L. Chapin, 'The Astronomical Activities of Nicolas Claude Fabri de Peiresc', *Isis*, 48 (1957), 13–29; P. H. J. Baudet, *Notice sur la part prise par W. J. Blaeu . . . dans la determination des longitudes terrestres* (Utrecht, 1875).

Chapter 11

—◆—

Religious controversy during the
seventeenth century: the case of Oxford

I

Two spectres, often indistinguishable, haunted many English theologians during the seventeenth century. They called one Popery and the other by the names of Arminianism and Socinianism, seeing their embodiment in particular individuals or groups. Those so accused sometimes replied in kind, but more usually they resorted to a counter-charge of Puritanism. Truth, half-truth and falsehood were all involved in this labelling. Although the focus of concern altered with circumstances, most of the ingredients can be found present in Oxford from the late Elizabethan period onwards; broadly speaking, an obsession with Roman Catholicism was increasingly paralleled by alarm about a novel rationalising tendency in religion. An important milestone in this development was the Oxford publication, in 1638, of *The Religion of Protestants*, by William Chillingworth. An ex-Catholic, Chillingworth was widely suspected of both Arminianism and Socinianism.[1] Although they were, strictly speaking, anti-Trinitarians, Socinians were also deemed guilty, even more than Arminians, of subverting Christian orthodoxy through an exaggerated emphasis on the powers of both human reason and spiritual free will.

By contrast the character of Oxford divinity, until the reign of Charles I, was militantly Protestant, generally Calvinist, in the sense of adhering to the Reformed theology of grace,[2] and strongly evangelical. This tradition had been established in the later sixteenth century, thanks especially to the shared outlook of successive deans of Christ Church and Regius professors of divinity, whose names provide an impressive roll-call of Calvinists, continuing in unbroken succession from the 1570s to the 1620s. Deans Toby Matthew, William James, Thomas Ravis, John King and William Godwin soldiered side by side with Laurence Humfrey, Thomas Holland, Robert Abbot and John Prideaux as Regius professors of divinity. Prideaux, Regius professor from 1615, was also a canon of Christ Church and the son-in-law of Dean Godwin. Other leading Calvinist evangelicals were George Abbot, Henry Airay, Sebastian Benefield, and John Rainolds.[3]

Some of these men were undoubtedly Puritans. Thus Rainolds emerged as the champion of nonconformity at the Hampton Court Conference in 1604, while earlier, during the 1580s, he had advocated the institution of lay elders. Puritan sympathies also got Henry Airay into trouble in 1602.[4] But they also included in their ranks two future archbishops, George Abbot and Toby Matthew, and five future bishops, Robert Abbot, William James, John King, John Prideaux and Thomas Ravis. We need in fact to distinguish here between episcopalians, who were basically satisfied with the polity and forms of worship of the English Church, and Puritan critics of the establishment. The similarities, as well as the differences, can be illustrated by a comparison of the writings of George Abbot and Henry Airay, dating from the turn of the century. (Abbot and Airay were chosen master of University College and provost of Queen's College in 1597 and 1598 respectively.)

Both Abbot and Airay assumed that salvation came via preaching. Abbot defined this as a 'commission to be executed in God's name' for 'saving the soules of men', and Airay similarly spoke of it as the 'ordinarie meanes whereby the Lord worketh faith in the hearts of his children'. In addition they exhibit a shared belief in what has been called experimental predestinarianism, teaching that the elect should strive for personal certainty of their salvation. According to Abbot, 'either youth or age, life or death, in him that is elected, shall apprehend the promises. Be it the ninth houre, or the eleventh houre, yet there shal be a time.' This 'it is which bringeth comfort unto the wounded soule and afflicted conscience – not that Christ is a saviour, for what am I the better for that, but a saviour unto me' and 'mine inheritance [is] with the saints'. Similarly Airay maintained 'our labour and endevour must be that we may know ourselves to be the sonnes of God . . . elect and chosen in Christ Jesus before the foundation of the world'. For 'howsoever wee can helpe nothing unto our election . . . yet may wee know whether we be elected . . . by the fruits of the spirit'. Opponents of such doctrine were branded by them as 'Papists'. Furthermore each took it as axiomatic that the Pope was Antichrist.[5]

But Airay combined these views with a much harsher judgement than Abbot of the religious *status quo*. Referring to disputes between 'Puritans' and 'Protestants', about 'ceremonies' and 'discipline', Airay concluded 'let us no longer halt betweene God and Baal, Christ and Antichrist, religion and superstition'. Meanwhile Abbot professed 'I do not yet find anything, either expressly or by consequent, directly to be drawne throughout the whole booke of God for the leaving or refusing of this or that garment, and so of other circumstances'. Again, when attacking separatists, Airay did not seek to extenuate the faults of the English Church. Abbot, however, countered separatism by arguing that 'the spouse is blacke while she remaineth on earth'. Accordingly a degree of ecclesiastical imperfection was inevitable, and a few years later he expressed his own ceremonial ideal in terms of 'seemely conformity'. Furthermore the two disagreed on the subject of bishops, Abbot holding the office to be apostolic whereas Airay could discern no trace of it in the New Testament. Any temptation therefore on our part simply to conflate Puritanism and Calvinism must be resisted, because conformity especially remained a divisive issue.[6]

Yet conformity itself came in different guises. A much more abrasive variety than that of Abbot was purveyed by John Howson, a Student and latterly canon of Christ Church, for whom three sermons survive preached between 1597 and 1602. In these sermons Howson attacked what he saw as an undue stress on preaching among fellow English protestants. 'The end and use of churches is the publike service and worship of God', being 'comprehended under the name of prayer' which 'excels all other religious actions'. But nowadays *oratoria* are turned into *auditoria*, oratories into auditories' and 'the chief place' is 'given to preaching'. Howson associated himself with those slandered under the name of 'formalists', for 'diligently' observing 'the rites and ceremonies commanded by the Church and received from all antiquity', and complained bitterly of the state of parish churches. The latter, in country districts, were 'little better than hog-styes', and in towns merely 'white-limed' or 'at the best wainscotted'. His indictment of the current religious scene also included instances of judaisers, 'which wil see their neighbour perish before they wil relieve him on the sabboth day'. Nevertheless even Howson was still a doctrinal Calvinist at this time, as emerges from his remarks, in 1602, limiting the extent of Christ's atonement. The 'general and admirable benefite of our redemption . . . was sufficient for the whole world, but efficient to al the elect of God'.[7]

Between them, Abbot, Airay, and Howson exemplify the three main schools of religious thought present in Oxford, at the beginning of the seventeenth century. Moreover, as holders of the vice-chancellorship between 1600 and 1607, all three were involved in university politics at the highest level. In terms of age a mere five years separated the eldest, Howson, from the youngest, Abbot. Howson was only a canon of Christ Church when he was appointed vice-chancellor in 1602, although good precedent existed for this.[8] The choice of Howson was officially that of the chancellor, Lord Buckhurst, but it may well be that it was on the recommendation of Archbishop Whitgift. For since the death of Chancellor Leicester in 1588 there had been a series of attempts at enforcing a more rigorous conformity in the university; the firm views of Howson on such matters would have been widely known because of his published sermons. Announcing his appointment as vice-chancellor, in July 1602, Buckhurst wrote

I hartely pray and requier you all in generall, but especially you the proctors and heades of houses, unfeinedly to be assistinge and obedient unto him therein, whose good example whilst the inferiour sort and such as under your severall governments shall behold they doubtless will the more easely subscribe, and be conformed unto all good orders.

The terms subscribe and conform, as used by Buckhurst, seemingly have a religious connotation. Certainly by November Howson was involved in conflict with Oxford Puritans, and early the following year he persuaded congregation to adopt a stiffer form of clerical subscription.[9]

Tension is also likely to have been heightened at this time by the fact that George Abbot was under a temporary cloud, and therefore not in the best position to mediate between the Oxford parties. Although chaplain to Chancellor Buckhurst, he had fallen out with Bishop Bancroft of London over the proposed renovation of Cheapside Cross. Wittingly or not, Abbot was sucked into a quarrel between leading London Puritans and their diocesan – itself part of a long-running saga going back at least twenty years. Periodic instructions concerning Cheapside Cross had been issued to the London corporation, in the name of Queen Elizabeth, to make good the ravages of time and vandalism, the latter perhaps ideologically motivated. Resistance came to a head in 1601, with the Puritans wanting to replace the now ruinous cross with some secular emblem. As in the past, they sought to exploit differences within the highest ranks of the Established Church over what constituted idolatry. Asked for his opinion Abbot, in his capacity as Oxford vice-chancellor, condemned Cheapside Cross because it incorporated representations of the Holy Spirit and of God the Father, as well as being a 'crucifix'. He was supported in his judgement of January 1601 by the Oxford Puritans Henry Airay and John Rainolds – a further instance of intellectual affinity.[10]

II

The death of Queen Elizabeth in March 1603 was the signal for a renewed national campaign by the Puritans on behalf of a further reformation of the English Church. It was crucial to their strategy to win the sympathy of King James, first with a fairly detailed statement of grievances and then by more general lobbying. What is known to history as the Millenary Petition, presented to the King that April, appeared to achieve the first of these aims. Pressure was thereafter kept up by soliciting support on a countrywide basis. The Puritan leader Henry Jacob wrote to Oxford on 30 June, seeking signatures to a petition in the name of members of the university, a development which seems finally to have provoked a response from the university authorities. They were probably already aware of a grace passed by Cambridge University, on 9 June, threatening with suspension anyone who publicly opposed the 'doctrine or discipline' of the English Church. But the Oxford *Answere*, a point-by-point reply to the Millenary Petition, was not published in print until October, after George Abbot had succeeded Howson as vice-chancellor.[11] Thus Abbot was closely associated with this public rebuff to the Puritans, which no doubt also helped in restoring him to the favour of Bishop Bancroft. Nevertheless there are grounds for thinking that the alliance between Abbot and Howson was at best an uneasy one, although they had not yet openly quarrelled. In addition one of the proctors involved, his 'zeal against the Millenary Petition' still remembered twenty years later, was William Laud, then a fellow of St John's College, and the first known religious disagreement between Abbot and Laud occurred in about 1603 – concerning the visibility of the true Church.[12]

The Oxford *Answere* assumes that the authors of the Millenary Petition have presbyterian ambitions. Attention is first drawn to the form of local petition proposed by Henry Jacob, 'that the present state of our Church may bee farther reformed in all things needefull' and 'agreeable to the example of other reformed Churches, which have restored both the doctrine and discipline as it was delivered by our saviour Christ and his holy apostles'. The deduction made from this is that 'they wil never have an end, till they have set up the presbitery'. Again, commenting on the Millenry Petition itself, the *Answere* describes the real aim as 'the utter overthrow of the present church government and in steed thereof the setting up of a presbitery in every parish'. The case for reform, however, is dismissed as groundless in terms reminiscent of Howson rather than Abbot. For example Bible-reading, set forms of prayer, and printed homilies are recommended in lieu of sermons, as 'ordinarie effectual meanes to continue and increase . . . true faith'. A concluding reference to sacrilege also has the mark of Howson about it. It would appear, therefore, that the hard-line conformists were in the ascendant within the university at this point.[13]

A veil of secrecy, however, shrouded the making of the Oxford *Answere*, through which two members of Corpus Christi College, Ralph Barlow and Henry Mason, attempted to pierce in advance of publication. According to their subsequent depositions, they had heard rumours that some such work was in the press and went to see for themselves at the printing house. Barlow admitted that he succeeded in reading the title and 'heare and there in the treatise itselfe'. Related discussions also took place at Corpus, as to how far the university seniors had been unanimous in condemning the Millenary Petition. Some said 'all saving twoe' approved the *Answere*, probably referring to Airay and Rainolds. Others named 'a third' – Thomas Singleton, the principal of Brasenose College, who had allegedly refused his consent because the *Answere* defended clerical non-residency. More generally the Barlow group impugned the *Answere* as unrepresentative, disliking 'that anie such thinge shold be sett forth by a few men in the name of the whole universitie'. One of the sources of their information was Laud's fellow proctor, Christopher Dale, of Merton College, who had reportedly seen and read the *Answere* but 'did not think it shold come publicklie in printe'. Dale had in fact been the recipient of Henry Jacob's letter of 30 June, canvassing Puritan support in Oxford. Jacob assumed that Dale was 'well affected' to the cause of further reformation, and added as a postscript 'I could wishe you to conferre with Dr. Airay about this matter'. Either Jacob was misinformed or Dale lost his nerve. At any rate no Oxford Puritan campaign developed.[14]

Our knowledge of the activities of Barlow and Mason, and the conversations at Corpus Christi College, derives from an investigation launched this same October 1603 by the pro-vice-chancellor and Dean of Christ Church, Thomas Ravis. It is unlikely to have been mere coincidence that the president of Corpus was also the Puritan leader John Rainolds. His name does not occur in the depositions, although the latter indicate the existence of two factions within the college. John Boate and Henry Hindley are to be found siding with Barlow and Mason, against Walter Browne, Gilbert Hawthorn, and George Seller. The subsequent careers of the first group, however, do not suggest that any of them were strong Puritans: Ralph Barlow, for instance, became Archdeacon of Winchester in 1609. On the other hand Browne was probably already a member of the Howson–Laud circle, and soon to be defamed as a 'Papist'.[15] Despite the evident worries of the university authorities, Oxford Puritans kept a low profile at this time. Indeed of the three probable Puritan heads in 1603 Airay was a conformist by 1606, when he was appointed vice-chancellor, Buckhurst writing privately to him the previous year that he understood him now to be 'conformable to the ecclesiastical discipline established in this land . . . whatsoever heretofore hath been surmised or suggested to the contrarye'. Singleton had already served as vice-chancellor in 1598–99, and did so again in the years 1611 to 1614. Only Rainolds may have remained obdurate, still refusing full subscription in 1605. George Abbot's successor as vice-chancellor, in 1604, was John Williams, principal of Jesus College and someone in the same religious mould as John Howson.[16] But it was churchmen of the type of Abbot who occupied the Oxford middle ground in these years, Abbot himself serving as vice-chancellor three times between 1600 and 1606, by the end of which period the Calvinist evangelicals had regained the initiative in the university and Howson's reputation was in eclipse.

Moreover anti-Catholic polemic continued to be *de rigueur* and it remained a Jacobean commonplace that the Pope was Antichrist. The latter thesis was from time to time maintained by doctors of divinity at the annual Oxford Act, and conformists such as Gabriel Powell published whole treatises to the same effect. Nevertheless the point has been well made that Puritans tended to dwell with special intensity on the subject. The same preoccupation with Popery which led Puritans to criticise the English Church as insufficiently reformed impelled them to attack with greater force the Roman seat of Antichristian error. Paradoxically this also had the effect of narrowing the gap between Puritans and many of their Protestant opponents.[17] Here a good illustration is provided by John Terry's book *The Trial of Truth*, the first part of which was published at Oxford in 1600. It is subtitled *A Plaine and Short Discovery of the Chiefest Pointes of the Doctrine of the Great Antichrist*. Terry, a graduate of New College, had left Oxford in the 1580s. Dedicating the work to his diocesan, Bishop Henry Cotton of Salisbury, he refers to Antichrist as the 'capitall enemy' and urges his fellow ministers to sink any disagreements with the bishops, about 'government and ceremonies', in their fight against the common foe. At the same time he asks those in 'higher place' not to 'hastely adjudge' as 'factious and mutinous' all who 'differ a little' from them.[18]

The heads of Antichristian doctrine, as listed by Terry, included the denial of assurance on the part of the faithful that they are justified, prayer to saints as mediators between God and man, the teachings that God 'in no respect willeth sinne' and that free will concurs 'with God's grace in our conversion', transubstantiation, justification by works, the lawfulness of images, the continuing occurrence of miracles, works of supererogation, the perpetual visibility of 'the church of Christ' and the inclusion within it of the reprobate as well as the elect, the possibility of fulfilling God's law, and belief in purgatory and the papal supremacy. Terry has a final section identifying biblical allusions to Antichrist with the 'Bishop of Rome'. His account is informed throughout by generally Calvinist assumptions. This becomes even clearer in *The Second Part of The Trial of Truth*, published at Oxford in 1602 and dedicated to the warden of New College, George Ryves. Here Terry writes that 'the certainty of our election to eternall life, and the assurance that we are the children of God and have our names written in Heaven', is traduced, by 'the servants of Antichrist', as 'the mother of pride and presumption and of carnal security'.[19]

Not everyone, however, endorsed such an anti-Catholic stance. Many years later William Laud recalled his distaste on reading the claim by Gabriel Powell, published in 1605, that he was 'as certain that the Pope is Antichrist as that Jesus Christ is the son of God and redeemer of the world'. Powell was a member of St Mary Hall in Oxford and his book *De Antichristo*, which described the various notes of Antichrist and his Church, apparently had the approval of the Regius professor of divinity, Thomas Holland. There is, however, evidence that John Williams, Lady Margaret professor of divinity as well as principal of Jesus College, dissented. During an acrimonious exchange with John Howson in 1615, George Abbot said that the late Williams 'was

Popishly affected . . . and defended that the pope was not Antichrist'. Such chance remarks enable a picture to be built up of those in Jacobean Oxford who now came increasingly to question the dominant religious views of the day.[20]

Anti-Calvinists at Cambridge had, in the mid-1590s, challenged current teaching on predestination. But they had elicited no support from the sister university. Rather, Oxford theologians had rallied to the Calvinist cause – asserting the unconditional nature of election and reprobation, the limited extent of Christ's atonement, and the inevitable perseverance of the saints. The first datable case of unequivocally anti-Calvinist views being entertained at Oxford is that of Thomas Jackson, then a fellow of Corpus Christi College. Even in this instance, however, we are dependent on later personal testimony. Writing more than twenty years afterwards, Jackson stated that it was about 1605 when he decided, still as a young man, against the doctrine of 'absolute' predestination. Yet, because he did not air his opinion in print until 1628, historians have assumed that he was a Calvinist throughout the Jacobean period. Humfrey Leech, a chaplain of Christ Church, was probably an earlier anti-Calvinist. His suggestion that true believers could finally fall from grace emerged only incidentally during 1607, when he was in trouble for advocating works of supererogation. The next year he became a Roman Catholic, which is likely to have had an inhibiting effect on any sympathisers. Nevertheless the latter, by Leech's own account, included John Buckeridge, president of St John's College, John Howson and John Williams.[21]

Serious opposition to Calvinism in fact developed relatively late at Oxford, and the first decade of the seventeenth century was mainly taken up with other disputes which did not follow clear party lines. Two such questions concerned Christ's descent into hell and the right to remarry after divorce. The first revolved around the meaning of this article of the creed. In what sense had Christ 'descended into hell'? During the later sixteenth century, particularly under the influence of Calvin, a metaphorical interpretation had gained wide acceptance. Archbishop Whitgift, for example, sanctioned the view that the 'worde Hel . . . signifieth not the place of everlasting torments' but 'the terrors and torments of the bodie and soule which Christ suffered'.[22] On the other hand a literalist interpretation also had its advocates. This was the position defended by Richard Parkes, in a pamphlet published at Oxford in 1604. Parkes, a graduate of Brasenose College, had left Oxford in the 1580s. In an expanded version of his argument, published at London in 1607, he identifies his opponents as 'puritans'. The lines of division, how-ever, remained blurred because of a third and linguistic interpretation, which rendered the Greek *hades* and the Hebrew *sheol* as the place of the dead, not the damned. This last won continuing support across a wide religious spectrum, including the Puritan Henry Jacob in the 1590s and the Arminian

Henry Hammond in the 1650s.[23] Likewise the question of remarriage after divorce was not a straight party issue, despite John Rainolds arguing in favour and John Howson against. Howson's views were propounded as a doctoral thesis at the Oxford Act in 1602 and published the same year. But a reply to Howson was licensed for the London press in June 1603 by John Buckeridge, who later emerged as a leading anti-Calvinist and is generally regarded as having had a formative influence on William Laud. The latter in 1605 conducted a marriage service between the Earl of Devon and the *divorcée* Lady Penelope Rich, while her former husband was still living.[24] Rumblings of a further controversy more directly involving Laud are detectable in 1608, when for one of his Act theses he argued that only bishops could ordain ministers and by implication unchurched most continental protestants. Two years later Ralph Barlow, who had been under suspicion of Puritanism in 1603, can be found at the Act defending the legitimacy of the 'Reformed' ministry as well as that of the English Church. Laud's views on this issue, however, would appear to have been thoroughly untypical at the time.[25]

As regards the development of anti-Calvinism, the writings of the Dutch theologian Jacobus Arminius were more important as a defining label than as a direct source. In his *Declaratio* or *Verclaringhe*, published posthumously in 1610, Arminius provided a classic anti-Calvinist statement. Rejecting unconditional election and reprobation, whether before or after the fall of Adam, he affirmed that God 'decreed to receive into favour those who repent and believe . . . but to leave in sin, and under wrath, all impenitent persons and unbelievers'. Grace, both 'sufficient and efficacious', can be resisted, and perseverance is not guaranteed. Clearly it was unnecessary to have read Arminius in order to hold such views – witness the Cambridge anti-Calvinists of the 1590s. Similarly Thomas Jackson almost certainly came to reject Calvinist predestinarianism quite independently of any Dutch religious influence. Nevertheless Walter Browne, Jackson's mentor, owned four books by Arminius at the time of his own death in 1613. Indeed by 1611 the university authorities were taking note of Arminianism as such. Two years later Robert Abbot, the recently appointed Regius professor of divinity, denounced the new phenomenon at the Act – the most public academic event of the Oxford calendar. His target on this occasion was the teaching of the Dutch Arminian Petrus Bertius, apropos falling from grace. Abbot spoke too of the corrupting influence in England of Arminian doctrine. He countered with an orthodox Calvinist exposition, maintaining that 'God's election cannot be frustrated'. Apart from the Bible, the main source cited is St Augustine. In 1614 and 1615 Abbot broadened his attack to encompass Arminian teachings on grace more generally. True grace, he maintained, is neither universal nor resistible, being the gratuitous gift of God to the elect and the cause of belief. At least one fellow Calvinist, Richard Field, was 'much offended' by Abbot making 'matters of opinion into matters of faith', adding that 'Oxford hath hethertoo bin free from these disputes, though Cambridge hath bin much disquieted with them'.[26]

By early 1615 Robert Abbot had identified Laud as in effect an Arminian. This particular accusation, however, was incorporated within a more all-embracing charge of Popery, a charge which Abbot also levelled against Howson. Laud and Howson responded by suggesting that both Abbot and his brother George, now Archbishop of Canterbury, were Puritan fellow-travellers. According to Howson Oxford could only boast three or four 'suspected' Roman Catholics, whereas Puritanism had 300 'supporters'. Ten years later Laud and Howson were indeed to join in condemning the teaching of the Synod of Dort, having by then clearly broken with the Calvinist beliefs which they had both once held. But no evidence is known to exist that either of the Abbots ever inclined towards nonconformity although Robert, like George, was a Calvinist evangelical, who characterised preaching as 'the very aire whereby we take the breath of spirituall and heavenly life'.[27] Nevertheless, such name-calling is indicative of a growing polarisation of views. Moreover Puritanism in Jacobean Oxford had been at best contained and certainly not eliminated. The strategy adopted by John Ley of Christ Church, appointed to a college living in 1616, was probably not untypical. He was willing to conform to 'the ceremonies' of the English Church 'if I may not enjoy my ministry without them', while respecting the conscientious scruples of others. Apparently more radical was William Crompton, who left Brasenose College for a Buckinghamshire lectureship in 1623. Two years later he was in trouble for maintaining the 'parity' of ministers and casting aspersions on the sign of the cross.[28]

Another Brasenose Puritan, more similar to Ley than Crompton, was Robert Bolton, who was presented to a Northamptonshire benefice in about 1609. His biographer, writing in the early 1630s, remarked that he tempered 'zeale' with 'discretion', but it is to Bolton that we owe a remarkable account of an Oxford Puritan deathbed. Thomas Peacock, a fellow of Brasenose, had been instrumental in Bolton's own religious conversion, although when he was dying in 1611 came to believe himself a reprobate. Those who wrestled for the soul of Peacock included John Dod, the deprived rector of Hanwell in Oxfordshire, and Henry Airay, telling him that 'whom God loveth once he loveth to the end'. Peacock's 'patron', Sir Robert Harley, also sent messages of encouragement and their combined spiritual ministrations were finally successful. This account, preserved by Bolton, is a practical essay in experimental predestinarianism, yet the prominent part played by Dod, who paid the dying man at least four visits, as well as the role of Harley, entitles us to label the episode Puritan rather than simply Calvinist. On the other hand Bolton's supporters included John King, who became Bishop of London in

1611.'[29] Similarly the following year John Ley found a theological ally in James Ussher, the future Archbishop of Armagh. Even Crompton, after being admonished in person by King James, was dismissed with a bag of gold.[30]

A Puritan of an earlier generation who maintained close links with Oxford, after his departure for a Cheshire lectureship in 1603, was William Hinde. The protégé of John Rainolds at Queen's College, he arranged for the Oxford publication in 1613 and 1614 of two works by his former teacher, dedicating them to Airay whom he described as the 'nearest and dearest friend' of Rainolds. Hinde was also the leading Puritan in the diocese of Chester by the time of Bishop Morton's appointment in 1616. His nonconformity emerges from a published refutation by Morton, Hinde objecting to wearing the surplice, to using the sign of the cross in baptism, and to kneeling at communion.[31] The spirit of Rainolds lived on in Hinde, yet the patronage of the now conformist Airay lent a measure of respectability to his radicalism. Airay in turn was intimately associated with his predecessor as provost of Queen's College, Bishop Henry Robinson of Carlisle. On his memorial brass Airay is likened to Elisha hastening after Elijah (Bishop Robinson), the two both dying in 1616.[32]

An Oxford Puritan tradition also survived at Corpus Christi College, where Rainolds had been president between 1598 and 1607. The ringleader within the college by the early 1620s was Robert Barcroft, who had graduated BA from Corpus in 1605. About the year 1616 he got into serious trouble for teaching that it was 'lawfull to excommunicate the King and to deprive him of his royall authority'. Barcroft was forced to recant and was suspended from his fellowship for a year. That he also failed to conform to the 'rites and religious ceremonies' of the established church emerges from a presentment made in 1621, by some of the parishioners of Warborough, near Dorchester in Oxfordshire. Barcroft had allegedly refused to wear a surplice when administering communion and had allowed some of those receiving to remain in their pews. More remarkably he had altered the words of the communion service, holding up the communion cup to the 'publique view of the congregation' and saying 'this is a token and signe of the blood of our Saviour Jesus Christ'. He similarly described the communion bread. His 'disciples' at Corpus included Thomas Norwood, Richard Thompson, and Benedict Webb – all much younger men. In addition the group was apparently in touch with John Sprint, an Oxford Puritan from late Elizabethan days, who had finally announced his decision to conform in a published work of 1618. Sprint argued that it was better to conform than to be deprived, while confessing 'my unwillingness thereto if by any means I might avoide it'. The preaching ministry had, in the last resort, to take precedence over such scruples of conscience. 'For as it pleaseth God to save them that beleeve by preaching, so where no vision is the people perish.' Barcroft, who proceeded to the degree of DD at Oxford in 1623, may well have employed a comparable casuistry; for one of his doctoral theses he also maintained that the Pope was Antichrist. As for Sprint, he dedicated his book to Dean Godwin and the canons of Christ Church – an act in part of filial piety towards the college where he had originally studied.[33]

The continuance of this broad alliance of Calvinist evangelicals was, however, threatened by the growing influence of anti-Calvinists at the royal court, dating from the later years of King James. The brothers Abbot in fact failed to curb the Oxford activities of Laud and Howson, or to hinder their ecclesiastical promotion. Laud, who was already president of St John's College, became Dean of Gloucester in 1616 and Bishop of St David's in 1621. The fortunes of Howson underwent a more dramatic improvement. After many years in the wilderness, he was consecrated Bishop of Oxford in 1619. His predecessor was the staunchly Calvinist John Bridges. The deanery of Christ Church also fell to an Arminian, Richard Corbett, in 1620. The changing climate manifested itself most obviously in the royal directions sent to Oxford in January 1617. These involved a tightening up of subscription and conformity, but they also attempted to alter the basis of university religious teaching. 'Young students in divinity' were 'directed to study such books as be most agreeable in doctrine and discipline to the Church of England, and excited to bestow their time in the Fathers and Counsels, schoolmen, histories and controversies, and not to insist too long upon compendiums and abbreviators'. The compilers of this clause seemingly had in mind Calvinist commentaries, including Calvin's own *Institutes*. It is probable that one consequence was the effective abandonment from this date of the Oxford catechetical statute, of 1579, which had specified the Heidelberg Catechism and the *Institutes*, among other works, as yardsticks of orthodoxy.[34]

The ethos of the anti-Calvinist movement now gaining ground in Oxford can be inferred from the poems of Richard Corbett, which circulated in manuscript during the second decade of the seventeenth century. Much of this verse evinces a nostalgia for the pre-Reformation past combined with hostility to modern 'Puritans', and by extension Calvinists, who are convicted of irrationality. Corbett's poem 'The Distracted Puritane' has a stanza attacking Calvinist teaching on reprobation. Laud was later to write of this same doctrine that it made God into 'the most fierce and unreasonable tyrant in the world'. An associated anti-Calvinist hermeneutic can also be deduced from a sermon preached before the university, by John Hales, at Easter 1617. Hales, who at the time was Regius professor of Greek, alluded to the recent royal directions, advising 'young students' not 'to think themselves sufficiently provided upon their acquaintance with some *notitia* or systeme of some technicall divine'. His general theme concerned 'the abuses of obscure and difficult places of holy scripture', particularly the epistles of St Paul,

Hales laying down the rule that the meaning of a biblical passage should be self-evident if it was to bind dogmatically. Silence constituted his remedy for the proliferation of controversy on such subjects as 'predestination', disputants often raising questions which were both unnecessary and incapable of human resolution.[35]

Yet Calvinism at Oxford was not in fact dethroned until the end of the 1620s. Partly this was because of the Dutch Arminian dispute and the decision of King James to intervene on the Calvinist side, culminating with the sending of a British delegation to the Synod of Dort in 1618. This gave fresh momentum to the English Calvinist cause. At the Oxford Act between 1612 and 1617 eleven doctors of divinity handled the predestinarian question, all from a Calvinist viewpoint. Thereafter there was some lessening of interest, although no fundamental alteration occurred until the chancellorship of Laud. Moreover in January 1623 Gabriel Bridges of Corpus Christi College was forced to make a public recantation of Arminian positions which he had taught in a university sermon concerning predestination, grace and free will. Calvinism indeed would appear still to have been strongly represented in the university.[36] Meanwhile, however, religious change was beginning on other fronts. In the wake of the royal Book of Sports in 1618, strict sabbatarian views were subjected to increasing criticism. At the theoretical level the debate centred on the extent to which the fourth commandment – to keep holy the sabbath day – was still morally binding. The practical issue concerned Sunday recreation. Hostility towards sabbatarianism was to be a marked feature of the Arminian ascendancy during the 1630s, but leading Calvinists were themselves not agreed on this issue. Thus for his Act oration of 1622 John Prideaux claimed that the fourth commandment was now in large measure abrogated. As a consequence, 'wee are permitted recreations of what sort soever, which serve lawfully to refresh our spirits and nourish mutuall neighbourhood amongst us'. On the other hand Prideaux did not cite the Book of Sports or specify what he meant by lawful recreations. This Latin oration was to be republished in English translation, by the Arminian Peter Heylyn, in 1634.[37]

The early 1620s also saw a striking new departure in church décor, with the glazing of the east window of Wadham College chapel. Completed in 1623, this depicted the crucifixion and other scenes from the life of Christ. Indeed a series of side windows, portraying the apostles and prophets, had been begun in 1613. By contrast, during the Elizabethan period such glass was the target of officially sponsored iconoclasm and the genre had effectively died out. For example Archbishop Abbot recalled the taking down of a picture of Christ from a window in Balliol College chapel during the 1580s, and at the Act as late as 1614 his chaplain William Westerman maintained that 'Images should not be set up in churches'. The Wadham east window was the work of Bernard van Linge and paid for by Sir John Strangeways, a co-heir of the founder. Clearly a section of Oxford opinion was becoming less concerned about the perils of idolatry, although this revived fashion for religious painted glass would contribute to an iconoclastic reaction in the 1640s.[38]

Much more explosive at the time, however, was an Oxford sermon preached in April 1622 by John Knight, formerly of Broadgates Hall, who argued that inferior magistrates might take up arms against their ruler in the cause of 'true religion'. His remarks need to be understood in the context of the Thirty Years War which had broken out in 1618, and the attempt to involve England on religious grounds. When subsequently interrogated, he cited as his authority the exposition of Romans 13 by the Heidelberg divine David Pareus and also instanced the support of King James for the French Huguenot rebels. Knight was imprisoned and his propositions condemned by the university authorities, while the works of Pareus were publicly burnt. The topic of Knight's sermon was a highly sensitive one given the current negotiations for an Anglo-Spanish marriage treaty and the likelihood that toleration of Catholicism would be a condition. Moreover the resulting furore was especially embarrassing for Calvinists, since Pareus was an editor of the Heidelberg Catechism. Significantly King James took the opportunity to reiterate his directions concerning the course of divinity studies, and Pareus was branded a 'Puritan'.[39]

Protestant anxieties intensified during 1623, with the journey to Spain of Prince Charles in pursuit of a Spanish bride. A volume of Oxford verse published that April, in celebration of the prince's safe arrival in Spain, illustrates the delicacy of the situation; all the contributions were anonymous and the place of publication was London. When Charles came home empty-handed in October there was a return to normalcy, *Carolus Redux* being published at Oxford with every contributor of verse identified by name or initials. Moreover there were at least three times as many authors involved in the latter volume. Nevertheless the continuing potential for disagreement is indicated by a university sermon preached the following April 1624. Parliament was now sitting and members of the House of Commons were pressing King James to intervene militarily against Spain. The preacher Thomas Lushington was, like Knight, a graduate of Broadgates Hall but his stance was very different. He referred to 'the peasant' who 'under pretence of his priviledge in parliament . . . would dispose of kings and commonwealths', and went on to say that 'nothing now contents the commonalty but war and contention'. In the event Lushington was censured for these words and made to preach a recantation sermon. That August John Randol of Brasenose College returned to the question of foreign policy. His sermon was largely taken up with the domestic repercussions of diplomatic alliances, especially with regard to religion. Randol warned of 'matrimonially' dividing the nation against itself and stated that there was no 'excuse for tolerating two religions in one kingdome'. The sermon proved sufficiently acceptable to be published at Oxford the same year.[40]

III

James I died in March 1625. Thomas Crosfield, a fellow of Queen's College, noted in his diary that 'immediately' after the accession of King Charles the 'cancer of Pelagianism', that is to say extreme free will doctrine, began to spread. Crosfield particularly had in mind the Arminian views of Richard Montagu, published in the years 1624–25, and the fact that these appeared increasingly to have the support of the supreme governor of the English Church. Allowing for hyperbole and a certain foreshortening of perspective, his assessment was broadly correct: revolutionary religious changes were in the offing. A younger contemporary at Queen's, Thomas Barlow, elaborated in retrospect that 'the Church of England and all her obedient sons till 1626 or 1628' did 'approve' the teachings of the Synod of Dort. Up until then, that is to say, the English Church was doctrinally Calvinist. On the basis of a royal proclamation of June 1626 and a further declaration in late 1628, prefacing the Thirty-nine Articles, Calvinism was curbed nationally.[41] Preaching in February 1629 John Doughty, a fellow of Merton College, said that 'the orthodox religion stands now betwixt Papistry and semi-Pelagianism' – the latter being an ancient equivalent of modern Arminianism. At the same time he spoke of 'schismaticks' who 'whilst they labour a breach in Christianity . . . make shew of a desired unity and peace', an allusion to the declaration of 1628. Thus 'Arminius, even then when hee was forging those opinions upon which such endlesse troubles have ensued, compos'de a treatise touching a generall reconcilement . . . at once hee offers embraces to the Church and stabs it'. Doughty dedicated his remarks to Nathaniel Brent, warden of Merton. Barlow, Crosfield, and Doughty can none of them meaningfully be called Puritan. Indeed Doughty, in this same sermon, attacked those who while orthodox on 'doctrinal grounds' nevertheless dissented from the established Church concerning 'externall rites'. Of course Laud, and those who thought like him, saw matters differently. They distinguished between the 'literal' meaning of the Thirty-nine Articles and their 'exposition'. Calvinism was opposed by them as being both divisive and without legal authority; in less guarded moments, they also categorised Calvinist teaching as positively erroneous.[42]

Doughty's sermon was printed not later than March 1629, and was one of the last such Calvinist statements to pass the Oxford censor until the 1640s. As far as the university was concerned the election of Laud as chancellor, in April 1630, was a very important religious watershed. Calvinism completely disappeared from the Act after 1631, and by 1634 Arminian views were being both preached and printed at Oxford. The reversal was not total, however, the preferred method of Laud being silence rather than counter-assertion. Thus Arminianism was never maintained at the Act itself and Arminian preachers still had to tread carefully, for it was always possible to overstep the permitted bounds. Moreover, the demise of Calvinism was only part of a complex of religious developments occurring at this time; in 1627, for example, Peter Heylyn maintained during a university divinity disputation that the visible succession of the English Church derived from that of Rome, thereby reviving on a more public stage Laud's teaching of twenty-four years earlier.[43] It was probably in 1628 that Gilbert Sheldon, the future Archbishop, created something of a sensation at Oxford by denying that the Pope was Antichrist.[44]

In 1630, William Prynne, a graduate of Oriel College and already on a collision course with the Caroline regime, published under the tide *Anti-Arminianisme* a second edition of his book claiming that historically the English Church under Elizabeth and James I had been Calvinist in doctrine. He now included 'an appendix concerning bowing at the name of Jesus', which elaborated on his interpretation of Philippians 2. 10 – 'at the name of Jesus every knee shall bow'. According to Prynne this was 'onely meant of a universall subjection and obedience of all creatures' to 'the irresistable all-subduing scepter of Jesus Christ', and 'not of any corporall genuflexion'. From this point of view, it was to be understood as a Calvinist proof text for the 'irresistibility of God's grace in the hearts of the elect'. But Prynne went on to reject the practice of genuflexion as such, and in so doing revealed his Puritan sympathies. For the 1604 canons had laid it down that when the name of Jesus was mentioned during church services 'due and lowly reverence shall be done by all persons present'. What seems to have made the subject particularly topical by 1630 was the growing fashion for converting communion tables into altars and doing reverence towards them. Indeed Prynne explicitly recognised the connection when he wrote that 'bowing to idolized altars' is 'a practize much in use of late among some Romanizing Protestants'. He also witnessed to the emergence of a specifically English Arminian synthesis whereby the grace of the sacraments, especially as conveyed via the eucharist, effectively replaced that of predestination. Moreover this changing scenic apparatus of worship and its attendant ceremonial marked the culmination of criticisms voiced from the 1590s onwards, by John Howson and others, concerning English church practice. One of the earliest such altars to be set up in Oxford was at Magdalen College, in 1631 – an event which helped spark a series of university sermons against Arminianism that summer. The preachers were all disciplined as a result, and John Prideaux was threatened with the loss of his Regius chair for encouraging them. That an establishment figure like Prideaux should be associated with such a challenge to higher authority is indicative of the profound religious alteration now under way; two years earlier, at the Oxford Act, he had been provoked into exclaiming that 'wee are concluded under an anathema to stand to the Synod of Dort against the Arminians.'[45]

As well as the new altar at Magdalen the chapel itself was elaborately refurbished at this time, with Christ's 'birth, passion, resurrection and ascension . . . very largely and exquisitely set forth in colours' at 'the upper end of the choir'. The relationship, however, between aesthetics and theology remained a complex one. That there was no necessary connection is clear from the chapel-building activities of Bishop John Williams at Lincoln College, which included the installation of an east window depicting the crucifixion. Certainly Williams was no Arminian. On the other hand Richard Corbett, now Bishop of Oxford, turned the Lincoln consecration ceremony of September 1631 into an Arminian occasion, speaking out against Oxford preachers who condemned 'reverence' to the altar as 'apish cringing'.[46] The early 1630s also saw a revival of the sabbatarian question, with the publication at Oxford of two treatises by Edward Brerewood. The author was long dead and his writings had remained in manuscript for almost twenty years. Brerewood sought to exonerate servants who worked on Sunday from any personal blame, and this was evidently now deemed grist to the anti-sabbatarian mill. In 1633 the Jacobean Book of Sports was reissued and moreover generally enforced, which had not been the case earlier.[47]

Among the arguments deployed against sabbatarianism was that the Sunday round of sermons, Bible study and discussion represented a covert form of Puritan organization at the parish level. The allegation was an old one but acquired new force with the demotion of preaching and its replacement with a more sacrament-centred form of piety. This same alteration in perspective helps to explain the attack launched by Peter Heylyn against the 'Feoffees for buying in Impropriations', during an Oxford sermon, on Act Sunday 1630. Rightly grasping that a prime objective of this London-based group of clergy, lawyers and merchants was the funding of stipendiary lectureships, the purpose of which was the provision of sermons, Heylyn claimed that a Puritan plot was involved to 'undermine' the English Church. His diagnosis was accepted by Laud, now Bishop of London, and the Caroline government proceeded to suppress the feoffees in the years 1632–33. Heylyn also said that part of the money collected by the feoffees had been used 'for the support of silenced ministers during their lives' and 'of their wives and children also after their decease'. Other evidence exists which tends to bear him out on this point, and thus confirms the genuinely Puritan nature of the enterprise. Calvinist episcopalians, however, had they still been in a position to influence events, might well have been prepared to give the feoffees the benefit of the doubt. As it was, such clerical leaders were obliged to adapt themselves to the new situation.[48]

Between 1616 and 1622 Prideaux, as Regius professor, had lectured regularly at the Act against Arminianism and these lectures were published at Oxford in 1625, during his second period as vice-chancellor. (He had been rector of Exeter College since 1612.) For the remainder of the 1620s, however, his main preoccupation was with Roman Catholicism. A further shift occurred in 1632 and from then to 1637 Prideaux, in his Act lectures, was chiefly concerned with Socinianism. 'What will it profit us', he asked, 'to have relinquished Popery only to fall into Socinianism?' Faustus Socinus himself had died in 1604 and the views of his co-religionists can be most readily gathered from the Racovian Catechism, which was published the following year. Socinianism, narrowly defined, was a form of anti-Trinitarianism: God is 'but one person'. At the same time Socinian teaching on predestination overlapped with that of the Arminians, while elevating spiritual free will to new heights. 'The predestination of God in the scriptures signifieth no other thing than such a decree of his concerning men, before the foundation of the world, that to those who would believe in him and be obedient to him he would give eternall life; and punish them with eternal death and damnation, who would refuse to believe him and be obedient to him.' Therefore the decision of Prideaux to lecture against Socinianism at this time was partly tactical, since refuting Arminianism as such had become taboo. However, his lecture of 1636, concerning original sin, made clear the link – implicating as it did Dutch Arminian authors. Yet there are grounds too for thinking that Socinianism was now beginning to make some genuine inroads. For example John Webberley, a fellow of Lincoln College, seems by 1642 to have become a Socinian.[49]

People had been burnt in England for denying the Trinity as recently as 1612. All the more startling then to find William Page, in 1639, urging a common Christian accord between Protestant, Papist, Grecian, Lutheran, Calvinist, Arminian *and* Socinian. Such 'differences of opinion', he said, should be contained within the bounds of 'charity'. Page was now chaplain to Bishop Walter Curle of Winchester, and these remarks come from the preface to his Oxford edition of *The Imitation of Christ* by Thomas à Kempis. But it does not follow that Page was a Socinian; rather, he belonged to what has been called an 'Oxford school of rational theologians', whose other members included William Chillingworth, John Hales, and Christopher Potter. Like Page, they all made the point that anti-Trinitarians were fellow Christians. Their recipe for religious harmony, and one which they shared with Socinians, involved a minimal Christian creed and the rational discussion of doctrinal differences in the light of scripture. The latter trait is particularly evident in Chillingworth's book, *The Religion of Protestants*, published at Oxford in 1638.

'Naturall reason', Chillingworth wrote, 'is the last resolution, unto which the Churches authority is but the first inducement.' This sounds very similar to Prideaux's description, in 1637, of Socinians who 'make reason their tribunal' for deciding controversies of faith. Moreover in the closing pages of *The Religion of Protestants* Chillingworth indicated his Arminian sympathies, as regards the doctrine of predestination. An imprimatur by Prideaux is nevertheless to be found at the front of the book.[50]

This seal of approval by Prideaux puzzled many contemporaries and requires an explanation. Thomas Sixsmith, a fellow of Brasenose College, read *The Religion of Protestants* soon after publication. He described it, in a private letter, as 'an od booke, some things very well done but at others I cannot but boggle'. Chillingworth 'overthrowes the Popish cause but [on] grounds which indanger the shakinge of our owne . . . I conceive him to smell too much of the Socinian, to talke of natural reason for grace, [and] never to mention originall sinne, nor grace neither (havinge so often occasion) in the true notion of it'. Sixsmith also 'had much parlee' with Prideaux, as to why he licensed the book. He reported that Prideaux 'now much dislikes it' and 'his best excuse is that they have dealt fouly with him in printinge passages which he expunged'. Under pressure from Laud to license Chillingworth's book, Prideaux seems to have agreed on condition that certain changes were made in the manuscript. His stipulation, however, would appear not to have been observed. Furthermore there are signs that Prideaux may even have been blackmailed into acquiescence. A document survives among the English state papers, endorsed as 'Exceptions to Dr. Prideaux his sermons', which comprises passages extracted from Prideaux's collected sermons, published at Oxford in 1636. Most of the extracts consist of generalized remarks about the failings of clerics and courtiers, but in one of these passages Prideaux had linked the growth of Puritanism to 'the statelinesse of some, so different from apostolicall humility'. Such talk was decidedly dangerous in the wake of William Prynne's attacks on bishops as 'lordly prelates', published the same year. No formal proceedings were instituted against Prideaux, although their possibility is likely to have influenced his conduct.[51]

By the late 1630s Prideaux was a rather isolated figure in Oxford. On probation ever since the sermon campaign of 1631 against Arminianism, he had been reported to Laud in 1633 for allegedly making derogatory remarks about the nature of the Church. Prideaux had indeed described the definition of the Church propounded by Heylyn, for one of his DD theses, as a 'mere chimera'. Three years later, in 1636, Prideaux can be found attempting to tone down some of the more fulsome praises in an official letter from the university to Laud, about the new statutes. Among much verbal sparring in convocation, Prideaux said 'we do not recognise any legate *a latere*' – an allusion to Cardinal Wolsey which was probably not lost on his audience. In addition a satire circulating at this time, which likened the individual Oxford colleges to ships, labelled Exeter College the 'Repulse' because Rector Prideaux 'shall suffer the repulse if hee sue for bishoprickes'. Prideaux's position was made even more difficult by the appointment as Lady Margaret professor of divinity, in 1638, of the Arminian Thomas Lawrence.[52]

Thanks to surviving letters from Francis Cheynell, fellow of Merton College, we are thus able to penetrate behind the outwardly civil relations obtaining between Laud and Prideaux during the 1630s. Cheynell also reveals the *avant-garde* nature of Oxford theology in these years. In October 1636 he preached a fast sermon before the university which 'displeased' many of his hearers,

> because I touched upon a doctrine which hath beene often preached at Saint Maryes with equall confidence and blasphemy, that the heathens might bee saved by conforminge their lives to the light of nature, without the knowledge of Jesus Christ our only Lord and Saviour. I told them that it was a doctrine condemned by Fathers, censured by Councells, cursed by our Church [and] confuted by Scripture.

Elsewhere it emerges from his correspondence that Cheynell probably had especially in mind Christopher Potter, the provost of Queen's College, who was now regarded by Calvinists as a turncoat for embracing Arminianism. Potter touched briefly on 'charitable' assumptions concerning the salvation of heathens in his book *Want of Charitie*, published at Oxford in 1633 as a reply to the Jesuit Edward Knott.[53] *The Religion of Protestants* was a continuation of this Protestant–Catholic exchange, Knott having replied to Potter. Chillingworth's book was, of course, first and foremost directed against Roman Catholicism – especially the doctrine of papal infallibility. As such it was greatly admired by Edward Hyde, the future Earl of Clarendon, who graduated from Magdalen Hall in 1626. The book promoted the Bible, interpreted by reason, as an alternative authority to the Pope. This new-style Protestant propaganda, however, was equally subversive of Calvinist orthodoxy, for Chillingworth argued, like Hales earlier, that Christians are only bound to believe things 'evidently contained' in scripture. The reaction of Thomas Sixsmith, discussed above, was mild compared to that of Cheynell; indeed Sixsmith would remain in Oxford until ejected in 1648, by Cheynell and his fellow Parliamentary Visitors. Looking back on the 1630s, Cheynell described the religion patronised by Laud as 'a hotchpotch of Arminianisme, Socinianisme and Popery' – yet one in which the appeal to 'reason' was a significant ingredient. At the time Cheynell had been prominent among those opposed to the new practice of bowing towards the altar, while moving in definitely Puritan circles.[54]

But without events in Scotland the likes of Cheynell or Prynne, the latter locked up in the Channel Islands from 1637, might well have remained impotent. In June 1638 the Oxford vice-chancellor Richard Baylie, an Arminian protégé of Laud, allowed as an Act thesis the question 'Do the additions and alterations in the Scottish liturgy give just matter for scandal?'. Naturally the official answer was in the negative. Any public discussion of this matter, however, struck Laud as unwise and the thesis was subsequently withdrawn on his order. None the less the escalation of the Scottish Prayer Book Rebellion into open war almost certainly lies behind two theses maintained at the Act in 1639. Thomas Weekes, a chaplain of Bishop William Juxon, there denied that 'temporal dominion is founded in grace', while Bruno Ryves, formerly of Magdalen College, rejected the view that 'an impious person forfeits dominion'. Both theses, which are without known precedent at the Act, allude to possible Calvinist justifications for rebellion. That such fears had some substance is illustrated by Prynne's interpretation, in 1642, of Psalm 105. 15 – 'Touch not mine anointed' – as a resistance text. The 'anointed' are, Prynne argued, the 'elect' and have the right to defend themselves by force of arms. By this latter date the Calvinist alliance, which had been so characteristic of the English Church under both Elizabeth and James I, was manifestly in ruins; cracks in the edifice already detectable during the 1590s had so widened as to bring bishops themselves tumbling down, amidst rival and mutually reinforcing accusations of Popery and Puritanism.[55]

IV

For Oxford University the meeting of the Long Parliament, in November 1640, involved a realignment of religious groupings. More specifically John Prideaux was able to come in from the cold, as King Charles sought to woo the moderates among his critics. The following October 1641 Prideaux again became vice-chancellor, the fourth Earl of Pembroke having replaced Laud as chancellor, and in November he was elected Bishop of Worcester. This latter promotion gratified an episcopal ambition on his part dating back to the 1620s. At the same time Prideaux and his former ally the Puritan John Wilkinson, principal of Magdalen Hall, now drew apart. During the anti-Arminian disturbances of 1631 Prideaux and Wilkinson had been the two seniors chiefly involved. Wilkinson, however, was to abandon Oxford in the early 1640s, only returning after the Civil War in 1646.[56] But this should not blind us to certain underlying continuities. Thus the collected Act lectures of Prideaux, in which he berated Arminians, Papists and Socinians, were published at Oxford in a handsome folio edition of 1648 – under parliamentary rule. Moreover, as we shall see, the old doctrinal divisions were to surface again after the Restoration and theological battle was to be resumed, albeit over the relationship of faith and works rather than grace and free will, with Thomas Barlow as the standard-bearer of Oxford Calvinism and George Bull cast in the role of a latter-day Richard Montagu.

In the short term, however, episcopalians of every hue banded together in defence of the institutional being of their Church. They did so the more easily because Prideaux was succeeded as Regius professor by Robert Sanderson, a man of moderate Calvinist credentials. Yet the most extreme defence of episcopacy published at Oxford was that by the Arminian Jeremy Taylor, in 1642. According to Taylor, late fellow of All Souls, the apostleship instituted by Christ is 'all one' with episcopacy, and thus the power of bishops over presbyters has 'divine' origins. He also argued in the strongest terms against the validity of non-episcopal ordinations, dismissing the traditional argument advanced in their defence: 'Necessity may excuse a personall delinquency, but I never heard that necessity did build a church.' Other apologists tended to omit the argument for the 'immediate divine institution' of episcopacy, treating the apostles as effective originators. That various shades of Oxford opinion in fact existed on this issue emerges most clearly from the *Reasons* adduced by the university in 1647 for refusing to subscribe to the Solemn League and Covenant. These *Reasons*, which were approved by Oxford convocation, comment rather tortuously on episcopacy that

> it is if not *iure divino* in the strictest sense, that is to say expressly commanded by God in his word, yet of apostolical institution, that is to say was established in the Churches by the apostles according to the mind and after the example of their master Jesus Christ, and that by vertue of their ordinary power and authority derived from him as deputed by him governors of his Church. Or at least that episcopal aristocracy hath a fairer pretention, and may lay a juster title and claime to a divine institution, then any of the other forms of church-government can doe; all which yet do pretend thereunto, viz. that of the papal monarchy, that of the presbyterian democracy and that of the independents by particular congregations or gathered churches.

Such apologists assumed that the fortunes of episcopacy and monarchy were linked, along the lines of 'no bishop, no king'.[57] Nevertheless a similar diversity of not always strictly compatible claims on behalf of kingship can be found in Oxford publications of the early 1640s. Thus Griffith Williams, the exiled Bishop of Ossory, argued, in a treatise of 1644, that 'the institution of kings is immediately from God' and 'Adam the first king of all men'. On the other hand Henry Ferne, another refugee, had written in 1643 that monarchy is '*ductu naturae*, by nature leading men from paternall to regall government, and *exemplo divino* . . . by divine example, but not *iure divino*, by divine precept commanding all nations to be so governed'. Patriarchy and monarchy therefore are not the same. But Ferne was also concerned to deny the existence of any 'agreement or contrivement of the people'. Here a different case was advanced by Dudley Digges the younger, a former fellow of All Souls and apparently a layman. Digges accepted a contractualist origin of government, while arguing that no residual right of resistance remained. This was the price which subjects paid to escape from a state, 'wherein each single person look't upon the world as his enemy'. The same view can also be found in the writings of Henry Hammond, appointed a canon of Christ Church in 1645.[58]

This plurality of voices, raised in defence of Church and King, did not, however, extend to the doctrinal sphere. Nor did power swing back to the Oxford Calvinists. The true nature of the situation is revealed by Hammond's *Practicall Catechisme*, which was published at Oxford in 1645 and, significantly, found favour with Charles. For this catechism is demonstrably based on Arminian premises. Under the second covenant, grace is granted 'sufficient to perform what is necessary'. Providing 'we make use' of these 'talents', God promises 'more grace' and a final 'crowning'. Hammond goes on to argue that 'faithfull actions' are 'the condition of justification'. But 'if I doe repent no power of heaven or earth, or hell, no malice of Satan, *no secret unrevealed decree* shall ever be able to deprive me of my part in the promise'. In late 1646, after the surrender of the Oxford garrison, Francis Cheynell took up with Hammond, among other points, his teaching on justification. He alleged that Hammond was guilty of 'confounding faith and works', and saw correctly that a prior assumption was involved here about how grace operates in 'the elect'. According to Cheynell, 'God doth by his free and effectuall grace worke the hearts of his elect to receive Christ that they may be justified; not by their own obedience, or vow of obedience, but by the obedience of Christ alone, freely imputed by God and rested on by faith only'. Hammond replied that God requires of 'the unregenerate man . . . a readinesse to obey his call, not to resist but receive his grace when hee bestows it on him, and having received it, what degree soever it be, to cherish and make use of it'. Cheynell was now a Presbyterian, but the Calvinist episcopalian Thomas Barlow later claimed that Hammond's was the first English work to corrupt the doctrine of justification by faith alone, through introducing the condition of 'obedience'.[59]

Arguably, however, a book such as the *Practicall Catechisme* conceals as much as it reveals about the nature and range of the author's views. Any attempt, indeed, to reconstruct a body of thought simply from what was published is subject to a number of disadvantages, hence the importance of private papers, where they survive. Such material, it transpires, exists in abundance for one forgotten member of the group of royalist and Arminian divines driven out of Oxford by the Parliamentary Visitors in the late 1640s. Tristram Sugge was expelled from his Wadham College fellowship in 1648, at the age of about thirty-seven. He returned at the Restoration, only to die in 1661. Nothing from his pen apparently got into print, save some verses celebrating the birth of a daughter to Charles I. Nevertheless a number of his manuscript notebooks are to be found in the Allestree Library at Christ

Church. Their authorship was long lost to view and has had to be recovered from the volumes themselves. Some of these can be dated internally to the 1650s, after Sugge's expulsion, and all were probably bequeathed by the author to Richard Allestree, who became Oxford Regius professor of divinity in 1663.[60]

Sugge covers a wide range of questions, exhibiting throughout an unusual frankness. Moreover his alienation from the official religion of the Interregnum was profound. Thus he writes that 'the Church of England may recover again; it may be all this while that the carpenter's son is making a coffin for Julian [the Apostate]'. Yet this alienation sprang from deeper sources than simply the defeat of the episcopalian cause. For Sugge had serious reservations about the English Reformation itself, commenting that 'as the Church of England hath been disobedient to her parent [Rome] so hath shee met with disobedient children'. In England, 'our first reformers' were 'lustfull, ambitious and sacrilegious persons'. Therefore, 'if the lust of Henry 8 or the impotencie of Edward 6, or the interest of Queen Elizabeth did transport us too far, it is fit that we recede to a mediocritie'. This 'mediocritie', or *via media*, involved recognition of the Pope as 'lieutenant-general of the churches in the west'. Sugge wanted the Pope restored to his original primatial 'right' of calling general councils, receiving appeals from bishops, and determining controversies. Historically the Roman Church has 'usurped' beyond its rights, but 'our reformers' are open to the charge of 'schisme' by their 'utter refusall' of papal authority. One might well jump to the conclusion from these passages that Sugge was a crypto-Papist. That, however, would be mistaken as his own use of party labels makes clear:

> The name of Protestant was rashly imposed and unadvisedly received by us, we being none of those Lutherans who protested against the edict of Charles the emperor and the Diet at Spires *anno* 1529. A Reformed Catholike, or a Catholike of the English Reformation had been a name more agreeable and more honourable.

Sugge in fact rejected Roman Catholic teaching on both the eucharist and purgatory. Nevertheless he defended prayer for the dead, on the grounds that there are 'sins remissible' at the day of judgement, and went on by extension to criticise the dissolution of the monasteries.

> Whereas religious houses were built and endowed with this proviso that the inhabitants should pray for the soules of their founders and benefactors, the demolishers of those houses, and the impropriators of those revenues, did first perswade the people that prayer for the dead was superstitious and vain.

There are some similarities here with the thought of Herbert Thorndike, although this does not seem to have been a major influence.[61]

Sugge also emerges from his notebooks as a thorough-paced Arminian, with no time at all for 'absolute' predestination: 'St Paul saith of his fellow labourers that their names were written in the booke of life: Philippians 4. 3. Of these fellow labourers Demas was one: Colossians 4. 14, Philemon 24. Yet Demas proved an apostate: 2 Timothy 4. 10.' God makes 'them that beleeve vessels of honour and mercie', whereas 'them that beleeve not' are made vessels of wrath as a consequence of their 'demerit'. Grace is 'universall' and 'all men have grace . . . not to offend, otherwise their offences were no sins'. His treatment of the seemingly opposite teaching of Romans 9 recalls that of John Hales: 'it is altogether unequall that this obscure passage should be alleaged against so many clear texts that evince the contrarie'. In addition Sugge identifies with Jeremy Taylor on the subject of original sin. 'The name of originall sin was never heard of till St. Austin's tyme.' Moreover, like Henry Hammond, he argues for the role of works in justification. 'Justification by faith is but conditional, and the condition is this that in due season wee also bring forth the fruit of good life.' Sugge goes on to make quite explicit the relationship between justification and predestination:

> Faith and the purpose of good life doe precede our justification, and so long as we beleeve and live accordingly wee are in a justified condition. But if then wee put away a good conscience, or make shipwrack of this faith, wee are no longer justified but . . . wee are made reprobates untill wee do repent.

Given too the tendency to link accusations of Arminianism with ones of Socinianism, it is intriguing that Sugge admits to doubts about the Trinity. The 'doctrine of a personall trinitie in a numericall unitie doth imply a contradiction: for it implyeth that there are but three persons and yet a fourth person, as also that there are three persons and yet but one person'. Again, Sugge points out that God the father is said to be 'unbegotten', whereas God the son is 'begotten'.[62]

In his political thought Sugge was influenced by the views of Sir Robert Filmer. Thus he can be found making excerpts from 'a manuscript intitled *Patriarcha*, borrowed of Mr. Ashwell'. What appears to be the same copy of *Patriarcha* still survives in the Allestree Library. The 'Mr. Ashwell' concerned was almost certainly George Ashwell, who like Sugge was a former fellow of Wadham College. Sugge, however, combined patriarchalism with a defence both of remarriage after divorce, for adultery, and the practice of usury. On these issues he was in agreement with Hammond. Moreover as regards charitable giving, Sugge reveals an even more unexpected radicalism. 'There is a kind of justice that we should be liberall to the poore [person], because our riches are an occasion of his povertie; for were the blessings of God but proportionably divided there would be enough for all. But one ingrosseth so much that another is in want.' The conventional view, by contrast, was that poverty is God-given rather than man-made. None the less it is as a Christian eirenicist that Sugge deserves especially to be remembered, and there survives what looks to be a draft title-page of his projected Latin treatise on this subject. As translated, it reads 'the kiss of peace and truth, by the mediation of Tristram Sugge of Wadham [College], Oxford: renovation not innovation, unity in fundamentals, liberty in matters doubtful, and charity in everything'. Yet we should also note that this was an eirenic which seemed to leave no room for Calvinists.[63]

After his expulsion from Wadham College, Sugge may well have continued to reside in the Oxford area. As we have seen, he probably borrowed a copy of Filmer's *Patriarcha* from his fellow collegian George Ashwell. In the 1650s Ashwell came to live at Hanwell in Oxfordshire. So too did Richard Allestree, who subsequently acquired Sugge's notebooks. This would appear to link Sugge with the famous trio of Allestree, John Dolben and John Fell, three expelled members of Christ Church who continued to hold clandestine Prayer Book services in Interregnum Oxford – their act of defiance later immortalized in a painting by Peter Lely.[64] Expulsion, however, was by no means the general fate of erstwhile Oxford royalists. During the war all had advocated non-resistance to the monarch, but with the surrender of the King issues of conscience became less clear. What measure of obedience was owed to usurpers now emerged as a leading question, and in the event many college fellows managed to survive.[65] It is difficult to generalise about those who remained; nevertheless, Oxford University during the 1650s was to prove a relatively congenial place for Calvinist episcopalians like Thomas Barlow.

The position of such episcopalians was also made easier by the effective stalemate between Presbyterians and Independents. Plans to Presbyterianise the Oxford colleges, in 1648, were overtaken by the increasing role of the military in politics and the consequent need to accommodate Independency. As early as March 1650 the Presbyterian Francis Cheynell can be found urging a 'union' between 'godly Presbyterians and Independents'. Any remaining hopes of imposing Presbyterianism on Oxford were further dashed by the election of Oliver Cromwell as university chancellor in 1651. Cromwell appointed as his vice-chancellor the Independent John Owen, who held office continually from 1652 to 1657. In addition there was the challenge of the sects. Cheynell himself had clashed at Oxford in late 1646 with the Seeker William Erbery, who denied the need for an ordained ministry. A more formidable threat, however, was posed by the Baptists. In 1652 John Tombes learnt that Henry Savage, the master of Balliol College, was due to defend infant baptism at the forthcoming Act. Tombes, a Baptist and former member of Magdalen Hall, managed to wangle his way into the position of opponent and thereby injected an element of unwelcome realism into the disputation.[66] Two years later Quaker missionaries began to arrive in Oxford. One of them, Elizabeth Fletcher, 'went naked through the streets . . . as a sign against that hypocritical profession they then made there, being then Presbyterians and Independents, which profession she told them the Lord would strip them of'. Fletcher and her companion also interrupted church services, for which they were arrested and taken before the vice-chancellor and city magistrates. The two Quakers were sentenced to be whipped out of town, although the mayor of Oxford, who was himself a Baptist, opposed their punishment.[67]

In these circumstances, respectable Puritans and Calvinist episcopalians tended to rediscover important things in common. Here one of the most striking Oxford features of the 1650s, is the re-establishment of Calvinist orthodoxy. The same thing happened at Cambridge, both universities reverting to a situation which had obtained prior to the accession of Charles I. This can be seen particularly clearly from the divinity theses maintained at the Oxford Act and the Cambridge Commencement. Conscious continuity was also provided by the life and writings of the Oxonian John Prideaux. Thus in 1648 the newly appointed Oxford Regius professor of divinity, Joshua Hoyle, spoke in glowing terms of him during his inaugural address. The following year saw the Oxford publication of the *Fasciculus Controversiarum Theologicarum* by Prideaux. We have already remarked on the publication at Oxford in 1648 of his collected Act lectures, including those against Arminianism. Similarly in the *Fasciculus* Prideaux maintains that election and reprobation are both 'absolute', and denies that 'grace sufficient to salvation' is granted to everyone. But the latter book also comments, at considerable length, on the questions of church government and liturgy. Furthermore the episcopal status of Prideaux is made quite explicit, the *Fasciculus* being prefaced with a dedication by him to his Worcester diocesan clergy in which he exonerates bishops from the charge of being Antichristian and invokes the memory of Cranmer, Latimer, Ridley, Jewel, and Whitgift. In the body of the book Prideaux argues that episcopacy is 'a distinct and superior order to presbytery', deriving from 'the institution of Christ or of the apostles'. He also defends the English Prayer Book as being in conformity with the Bible, albeit going on to gloss its doctrinal teaching in Calvinist terms. Thus the reference to baptised infants as being 'regenerate' is a 'charitable' assumption, not a statement of fact, for neither is grace granted universally nor can it be lost. In addition Prideaux denies that 'subjects' have any right to resist their 'king'. A second edition of the work was published at Oxford in 1652.[68]

But given some of the views contained in the *Fasciculus*, how are we to explain its original publication at Oxford? Had the work been published at London there would be no real problem, because censorship in the capital was in a state of almost total collapse. Yet this was not the case at Oxford. In

1649 the vice-chancellor – the official licensing authority – was Edward Reynolds. Reynolds was a moderate, who resigned from Oxford in 1650 and shortly after the Restoration accepted a bishopric. The *Fasciculus* seemingly reflects the enduring significance of Calvinist episcopalianism, despite the rise of Arminianism having in the eyes of many served to discredit bishops by the eve of the Civil War. For those unhappy with the subsequent experiments of the 1640s, Prideaux stood for an alternative tradition of church government which was nevertheless impeccably orthodox in doctrine. The relevance of this latter consideration is clear from the general tenor of Oxford divinity during the Interregnum. At Oxford the Act had been in abeyance throughout the 1640s but was revived in 1651. That year John Conant, the rector of Exeter College, maintained three related Act theses. First, 'Grace sufficient to salvation' is not granted to 'everyone'. Secondly, God's grace in the conversion of a sinner is 'irresistible' and, thirdly, it cannot thereafter be 'utterly forfeited'. Next year Obadiah Grew, formerly of Balliol College, denied that Christ had died 'equally' for all. In 1654 Conant, this time as an incepting doctor of divinity, argued that 'the decree of election and reprobation' was 'absolute', while John Wallis, Savilian professor of geometry, opposed the view that election depended on 'foresight'. The same year George Kendall, late fellow of Exeter College, maintained that 'neo-Pelagian doctrine' was inimical to Christian faith, piety and consolation. The views of Conant are particularly to the point, because he became Regius professor of divinity in 1654.[69]

A similar Calvinist picture emerges from the theological works printed at Oxford in this decade. Indeed some of the Act material itself ended up in print – for example John Wallis's thesis of 1654. The previous year had seen the publication of *The Riches of God's Love*, by William Twisse. This was a posthumous work from an Oxford-educated Calvinist and constitutes a reply to an English Arminian treatise of 1633. Twisse's book, which defends Calvinist teaching on reprobation, is prefaced with a testimony by John Owen, the vice-chancellor. In 1654 Owen produced an anti-Arminian treatise of his own – *The Doctrine of the Saints Perseverance*. A response to the Independent John Goodwin's *Redemption Redeemed* of 1651, it witnesses to the development of a small Arminian minority within Puritanism.[70] George Kendall also wrote two books against Goodwin, which appeared in 1653 and 1654, concerning the doctrines of election and perseverance. Although printed in London, both these books by Kendall are dedicated to his alma mater Oxford University and contain references to the 'learned' and 'illustrious' John Prideaux. In addition they each have an imprimatur by Owen, as Oxford vice-chancellor, and by the two Oxford professors of divinity: Joshua Hoyle and Henry Wilkinson. (Wilkinson succeeded Cheynell as Lady Margaret professor in 1652.) Not content with this endorsement the publisher of the second volume included an 'attestation' from Bishop Joseph Hall, lest Kendall's views be dismissed as 'puritanicall'. Hall was the last surviving English delegate to the Synod of Dort, and provided an important plank in the Calvinist case for historical legitimacy.[71]

The full text of the Act theses maintained by Kendall in 1654 is extant in print. He there brackets John Goodwin and the episcopalian Henry Hammond as the two leading English neo-Pelagians or Arminians. Kendall singles out Hammond's treatise *Of Fundamentals,* published that same year. This work does indeed contain a most forthright condemnation, by Hammond, of 'the irrespective decrees of election and reprobation', as hindrances to the 'superstructing of Christian life'. Kendall published his Act theses, as part of a larger work, at Oxford in 1657. Two years later Edward Bagshaw the younger and Henry Hickman broadened the Calvinist counter-attack to include the Arminian episcopalians Thomas Pierce, Jeremy Taylor, and Laurence Womock. Bagshaw was a former member of Christ Church and Hickman a fellow of Magdalen College. Interestingly Hammond, Pierce, Taylor, and Womock were all published at London by the royalist bookseller Richard Royston. Both parties invoked the past, Hickman for instance transcribing the Oxford recantation of Arminianism, in 1623, by Gabriel Bridges.[72]

The 1650s also witnessed an analogous Oxford concern with Socinianism, in its anti-Trinitarian aspect. Francis Cheynell, as Lady Margaret professor of divinity, and John Owen each produced works on this subject in 1650 and 1655 respectively. Cheynell was particularly concerned with the writings of John Fry whereas Owen directed his fire against the more formidable John Bidle. Fry was a Member of Parliament, but had not apparently attended university. Bidle on the other hand was a graduate of Magdalen Hall and an ex-schoolmaster, who both translated Socinian works, including the Racovian Catechism, and wrote a series of anti-Trinitarian tracts. Bidle and Fry belonged to the world of Puritanism, yet a section of episcopalian opinion continued to be suspected of Socinian sympathies in these years. Owen's answer to Bidle included a 'vindication of the testimonies of scripture, concerning the deity and satisfaction of Jesus Christ, from the perverse expositions and interpretations of them by Hugo Grotius', contained in his *Annotations* on the Bible. The previous year, 1654, Henry Hammond had defended Grotius on precisely this issue. Now Owen took up that challenge. At about the same date John Conant, as newly appointed Regius professor of divinity, similarly devoted his lectures to 'critical exercitations' on the *Annotations* of Grotius, 'in which he vindicated the scriptures from such of his expositions as the Socinians had taken any advantage'.[73]

Grotius, and to a lesser extent Hammond, were practitioners of a new style of biblical criticism in the post-Reformation context. They approached their subject-matter philologically and historically rather than regarding it as an arsenal of dogmatic truths, and the results were decidedly alarming to more fundamentalist minds. This, incidentally, helps explain Owen's hostility to the Polyglot Bible, completed in 1657, the final volume of which drew on the work of Grotius. How far the eirenical Grotius finally advanced beyond his earlier Arminianism is unclear. But while pursuing the elusive goal of Christian reunion he can be found corresponding amicably with both Socinians and Roman Catholics, and by the early 1640s had come to pin his hopes on a Gallican oecumenical initiative. Grotius died in 1645, still a Protestant but of doubtful orthodoxy. Inevitably he was a suspect figure to Oxford's theological leaders in the 1650s, not least because of a continuing strain of virulent anti-Catholicism. Thus for example Thomas Tully of Queen's College maintained as an Act thesis in 1655 that the 'pseudo-Catholic Roman Church' is not 'truly Christian'.[74] Unlike Owen and Conant, however, Tully was to survive the upheavals of the Restoration and emerge as an important Calvinist voice within the re-established Church.

V

The political undoing of the Interregnum in 1660 is a familiar story. So too, at one level, is the religious settlement which followed. An uncompromising episcopalianism triumphed over attempts at 'comprehension' and 'indulgence'. These developments are, to some extent, reflected in Oxford publications between 1659 and 1662. Hence in 1659 there appeared *Monarchy Asserted* by Matthew Wren – a layman although the son of his namesake the bishop. The work, which is dedicated to John Wilkins the warden of Wadham College, represents the culmination of a long-running debate between Wren and the republican James Harrington. Like the earlier treatises by Digges and Hammond, Wren's defence of monarchy assumes an original but irrevocable contract. Harrington is criticised for deriving 'empire' from the 'balance of dominion in land', since there are many other sources of wealth. For Wren governmental 'perfection' consists in a 'supream' monarch ruling through an hereditary nobility and backed up by a militia, and he looks forward to such an English outcome. In 1662 John Barbon's defence of the prayer book was also published at Oxford. Among other things it explicitly rejects the type of Calvinist reading earlier provided by Prideaux, on the subject of baptismal regeneration. The regenerate and justified can indeed finally fall from grace.[75] Barbon was a product of Exeter College in the 1640s and his rebellion against Rector Prideaux's teaching is particularly striking. Meanwhile Richard Allestree, recently restored as a canon of Christ Church, delivered a sermon at Westminster Abbey, in January 1661, on the occasion of the episcopal consecrations of Gilbert Ironside, Nicholas Monck, William Nicholson, and Edward Reynolds. All four of these new bishops were Oxonians and, moreover, represented a wide variety of theological opinion. Addressing them as 'holy fathers', Allestree described Christ as the 'founder and God of your order'. He also spoke of the miraculous 'resurrection' of the English Church.

> And truely 'twas almost as easie to imagination how the scattered atomes of men's dust should order themselves and reunite, and close into one flesh, as that the parcels of our discipline and service that were lost in such a wild confusion, and the offices buried in the rubbish of the demolisht churches, should rise again in so much order and beauty.[76]

But how was the ambiguous legacy of the English Church now generally to be interpreted, and after what image was episcopacy to be remade? More specifically in which of the two rival traditions, Arminian or Calvinist, was the restored ecclesiastical regime effectively to follow? With a different king and an almost completely new bench of bishops since the 1630s, the answer was not immediately obvious. At Oxford Thomas Barlow, provost of Queen's College, rapidly emerged as a leading figure among the surviving heads of house. Appointed Lady Margaret professor of divinity in 1660, from then until his departure for the bishopric of Lincoln in 1676 he wielded considerable religious influence. Barlow had lived through all the Oxford changes since the 1620s, but there is no question of his essential loyalty to episcopacy and Prayer Book. He regarded the former as 'iure apostolico' and described the latter as 'the best liturgy in the world', going on to speak of the 'fanatique zeale', of those who rejected it as 'unsound and superstitious'. At the same time, however, Barlow was a committed Calvinist. The fullest statement of his views on the predestinarian question is to be found in a manuscript notebook dating from the 1660s. 'Election and reprobation' are not 'from foresight of faith or infidelity'. Christ did not die 'for each and everyone'. The 'operation of grace' is 'irresistible' and 'the truly faithful' cannot 'fall away finally and totally'. Barlow also notes that 'the Arminians did not, durst not appeare in Kinge James his time'.[77]

In September 1661 Barlow wrote a critique of the Prayer Book, which was probably prepared for the committee of bishops discussing liturgical reform at this date. He argued that no human document is perfect, and one of his main suggestions was to bring the wording of the baptismal services more closely into line with Calvinist teaching. What this implies about the original Edwardian framers of the Prayer Book is not something which Barlow here tackles. Nevertheless he does say that the logical implication that children 'really regenerated' in baptism afterwards 'fall away', and 'eternally perish', is a doctrine which 'in all the time of Queen Elizabeth and King James was believed to be erroneous, and condemned as such by the reverend bishops [and] the publique professors in both the universities'. According to Barlow the Prayer Book ascribes too much to baptism, which is 'not necessary to salvation'. Nor is the Bible correctly cited in its support. Barlow also made a number of other suggestions for change, but all proved stillborn as regards the revised Prayer Book of 1662.[78]

That members of the government were aware of the danger of renewed Arminian–Calvinist conflict is clear from a passage in the royal directions to preachers, issued in October 1662. They were 'admonished not to spend their time and study in the search of abstruse and speculative notions, especially in and about the deep points of election and reprobation, together with the incomprehensible manner of the concurrence of God's free grace and man's free will'. The justifiable complaint in the past had been that such rulings were not applied even-handedly, to the resulting detriment of Calvinists.[79] Yet this earlier pattern was not repeated in Restoration Oxford, both Arminian and Calvinist preachers enjoying there a degree of practical toleration. An illustration of the new situation, drawn from among the Oxford Calvinists, is provided by John Wallis. Puritan seems not too strong a term for Wallis, who had been secretary of the Westminster Assembly before his appointment to the Savilian chair of geometry in 1649. At the Restoration he conformed and retained his various Oxford posts. Among his surviving sermons, two preached before the university in 1676 and 1681 are particularly revealing. They were published together at London in 1682 and entitled *The Necessity of Regeneration*. Wallis dedicated them to the Earl of Radnor, lord president of the council, 'being made acquainted that they would not be unacceptable to your lordship'. (Radnor is better known as Lord Robartes, who fought for the parliamentary cause in the Civil War and had studied at Exeter College during the 1620s.) Wallis went on to claim that 'I have therein purposely waved, as I alwaies do, all nice disputes of speculative subtilties in controversal points . . . as more tending to disturb the peace of the Church than to promote piety'. Nevertheless the sermons themselves indicate the Calvinist bias of their author. 'To become the sons of God by regeneration is the beginning of our sanctification.' Whom God 'designed to be happy he designed to be holy, and whom he did thus predestinate them he called, them he justified and them he glorified'. Wallis also clearly distinguishes between regeneration and baptism. 'Our Church presumes of infants that they be at least some of them regenerate when baptised', but 'nor is the Holy Ghost less able to work effectively afterwards.'[80]

Another and even clearer example of Calvinist preaching in Restoration Oxford is afforded by the sermons of Robert South. Educated at Oxford in the 1650s, South became a Student and then, from 1670, a canon of Christ Church. He was also public orator of the university, between 1660 and 1677. During the Interregnum he is said to have used the Prayer Book, and in 1698 publicly identified himself with those described as 'High-Churchmen'.

None the less he remained a Calvinist. Preaching at Christ Church in March 1668 South spoke of an 'eternal covenant made between the Father and the Son, by which the Father agreed to give both grace and glory to a certain number of sinners'. On this 'alone . . . is built the infallibility of the future believing, repenting and finally persevering of such as Christ from all eternity undertook to make his people'. In the same venue, some ten years later and handling the subject of 'preventing grace', South asked rhetorically: 'doe we not sometimes see in persons of equal guilt and demerit, and of equal progress and advance in the ways of sin, some of them maturely diverted, and took off, and others permitted to go on without check or controll, till they finish a sinful course in final perdition?' Such grace, if vouchsafed, works 'by main force'. Both these sermons were published at London, during the 1690s.[81]

Similar bending of the rules, this time by an Oxford Arminian, is apparent in the preaching of Richard Allestree, who became Regius professor of divinity in 1663. Most of his sermons were posthumously printed at Oxford in a collected edition of 1684, prefaced with a life by John Fell – now Bishop of Oxford. Fell writes of Allestree as 'never intermedling with the unfathomable abyss of God's decrees, the indeterminable five points [of Arminianism], which in all times and in all countries, wherever they have happen'd to be debated, past from the schooles to the state and shock'd the government and public peace'. Allestree, however, made plain his Arminian sympathies when preaching. In a sermon at Whitehall, probably dating from the early 1660s, he described the sinner whose

> will is grown too strong for the Almightie's powerful methods and frustrates the whole counsel of God for his salvation, neglects his calls and importunacies whereby he warns him to consult his safety, to make use of grace in time, not to harden his heart against his own mercies and perish in despight of mercy.

Such 'persevering obstinacy does deserve Hell and make it just'. In December 1665 Allestree returned to the theme of God's 'everlasting council', as regards sinners. This sermon was preached at Christ Church, where the pulpit clearly provided a variety of doctrinal fare. 'O do not thus break decrees, frustrate and overthrow the everlasting counsel of God's will for good to you. He set, ordain'd this child [Christ] for your rising again. Do not throw yourselves down into ruin in despite of his predestinations.' In another, undated, sermon Allestree remarked that 'the inheritance of the kingdom of God' is not 'entail'd'. An heir can be disinherited and 'we read of many that were cast off'. For God's 'promises' are 'conditional', on repentance and belief.[82]

The rules, however, could only be bent so far. Thus at Oxford in April 1679 Thomas Smart of St John's College was censured for preaching 'very unadvisedly . . . concerning God's decrees, contrary to the king's commands in that case, and in irreverent and unseemly language'. According to Anthony Wood, Smart's sermon was a 'bold and desperat' one 'against the Calvinists'.[83] In the case of Oxford religious teaching more generally, after 1660 it seems to have been assumed that Charles I's declaration of 1628, silencing the predestinarian dispute, still applied. Such questions again disappear from the Act; they are also absent from the run-of-the-mill disputes in the divinity school, records of which survive in the congregation registers from the 1660s onwards. Nevertheless two other recurring Act topics appear to reflect divergent emphases in Oxford theology during the later seventeenth century. On the one hand the Roman Catholic Church was branded as simply 'idolatrous', while on the other a distinction was drawn between 'the ancient practice of prayer for the dead' and belief in 'Romish purgatory'. First to maintain these respectively intransigent and meliorist theses, *vis-à-vis* Catholicism, were the Calvinist Thomas Barlow and the Arminian Richard Allestree, both in 1661.[84]

There were comparable limitations on airing the Arminian–Calvinist dispute in print at Oxford, although not apparently as regards previously published works. Thus the *Fasciculus* of John Prideaux was reprinted at Oxford in 1664. (We have already remarked on Prideaux's unremitting Calvinism). Similarly in 1671 *A Correct Copy of Some Notes Concerning God's Decrees, especially of Reprobation* by Thomas Pierce, now president of Magdalen College, was also reprinted at Oxford. Pierce makes his Arminian stance abundantly clear throughout: election and reprobation are both 'conditional' and grace, which is 'universal', can be resisted. By contrast, in terms of new publications, nothing really equivalent to these two works was produced in Restoration Oxford.[85] The religious balance of forces, however, remained a delicate one. For example in January 1673 William Richards, chaplain of All Souls College, preached at the university church and is said, by Wood, to have 'insisted much on the Arminian points'. According to the same source, Richards was questioned for this by Thomas Barlow, as pro-vice-chancellor. Yet no record of any official censure survives.[86]

Oxford did, however, produce a more united front against Cambridge Platonism. This might seem surprising, given the earlier Platonist sympathies of the Arminian Thomas Jackson, but the arguments advanced by Henry More and his circle provoked hostile reactions across a wide theological spectrum – not least because they claimed to cut through the Arminian–Calvinist disputes.[87] Here More's use of the patristic writer Origen, concerning the pre-existence of souls, proved especially controversial, being refuted in a divinity disputation at Oxford as early as 1663. This was followed up with a two-part contribution by Samuel Parker, published at Oxford in 1666 and with the imprimatur of the vice-chancellor, Robert Saye. Parker rejected Platonic 'metaphysical theologie' as a whole and Origenism in particular, with its attempt to explain sin in terms of the fall of free pre-existent souls as opposed to that of Adam. Parker was probably already an Arminian, yet the Calvinist Barlow found the teaching of Origen on this subject equally objectionable.[88]

Barlow himself left a mass of manuscript theological writings which are still extant – mainly at Queen's College, Oxford. The two posthumously published volumes of his occasional pieces barely begin to tap this reservoir of material. He also had a tendency to annotate his printed books, many of which are now in the Bodleian Library.[89] From these sources it is possible to reconstruct his views on a great variety of issues, and thereby also to recover a neglected strand in Restoration religious thinking. For Barlow Socinianism posed a comparable threat to Arminianism. Indeed, at the Act in 1661 he argued that Socinian teachings were 'destructive alike of church and state'. Barlow was in addition a sabbatarian, who deplored the Caroline Book of Sports, and he unhesitatingly identified the Pope as Antichrist. He claimed too that communion tables had anciently stood in the middle of chancels, rather than at the east end, and that the English Church had rightly reverted to this practice after the Reformation; as Bishop of Lincoln Barlow appears to have operated on the same principle, while furthermore revealing his opposition to all images whatsoever in churches. He was widely regarded as an oracle on such questions, and many of his writings originated as letters in reply to correspondents. A notable example of this genre is his 'answere to some queries proposed by Mr. W. A.', in 1671, on the subject of lay baptism. Barlow concluded that such baptism is invalid, and where it was known to have occurred the ceremony should be performed again by an ordained clergyman. Commenting on the fact that until the Jacobean revision of 1604 the Prayer Book had permitted lay baptism, he wrote that Archbishop Cranmer and his assistants had 'lived in the twilight and dawn of learninge and reformation, and 'tis much more to be wondered at that they saw and reformed soe many errors then that they oversaw this one'. Such views earned Barlow the title of 'Puritan' in some quarters.[90] But he remained personally opposed to the schemes for toleration and comprehension which emerged in the late 1660s; moreover when toleration was finally achieved, in 1689, Barlow vented his impotent fury in pen and ink on a printed copy of the act.[91]

Fascinating though the views of Barlow are, we should nevertheless note that some of them were now becoming deeply unfashionable in episcopalian circles. Thus, for example, in 1683 Anthony Wood recorded that Exeter was unique among Oxford college chapels in not having its communion table set altarwise. Furthermore, despite Calvinism remaining influential at Oxford, research has revealed that at Cambridge Arminianism was in process of sweeping the board.[92] As regards Restoration Oxford, however, the rival camp to that of Barlow was probably led by Richard Allestree and John Fell, Regius professor of divinity and Dean of Christ Church respectively. Fell was the biographer of both Allestree and Hammond, which certainly appears to identify him with the Oxford Arminians. At national level the Barlow group looked for support from Bishop George Morley of Winchester, whereas the Allestree–Fell group had a similar patron in Archbishop Gilbert Sheldon, and these alignments provide the background to the great religious *cause célèbre* of the early 1670s, stemming from the published teachings of George Bull on the doctrine of justification. Bull's *Harmonia Apostolica* was licensed in April 1669, from 'Lambeth House', by a chaplain of Sheldon; a subsequent defence by Bull was likewise licensed in October 1675. Conversely two of the replies to Bull, published in 1674 and 1676, were dedicated to Morley. Each of these latter books, by Thomas Tully and John Tombes, the Baptist, was published at Oxford. According to Bull's biographer and younger contemporary, Robert Nelson, Morley also issued a 'pastoral charge' to the clergy of his diocese forbidding them even to read the *Harmonia*.[93]

Bull's book was published at London in 1670. Among the surviving copies is one heavily annotated by Barlow, and judging from his remarks there had been an earlier attempt to publish at Oxford, during the vice-chancellorship of Robert Saye, between 1664 and 1666. Saye, who was provost of Oriel College and another survivor from the 1650s, had apparently refused a licence.[94] Bull himself had very briefly attended Exeter College in 1648, but is likely to have acquired his mature views subsequently. The *Harmonia Apostolica*, as the title implies, is an attempt to reconcile the apparently contradictory teaching of St Paul and St James on faith and works. At the outset Bull made quite clear that his target was 'solifidianism'. He argues that 'faith and works are jointly prescribed as the only condition of justification'. Those who deny this, like 'Luther and most of our own divines after his time', are in error. Moreover their teaching leads to 'libertinism'. The core of Bull's case is that St Paul and St James use the term 'works' in different senses. The works which St Paul 'excludes from justification' are those required under Mosaic and natural law. By contrast, 'moral works arising from the grace of the Gospel' are 'absolutely necessary' to justification. This, claims Bull, is the true meaning of the eleventh of the Thirty-nine Articles, and therefore St James is correct in saying that 'by works a man is justified and not by faith only'. He also indicates that his solution to the problem is incompatible with 'the irresistible operation of grace'. A person once justified can indeed fall from grace and be damned, because there is no 'absolute' decree of predestination.[95]

Bull wrote in Latin, yet it is not difficult to understand the shock waves generated by his book. Among fellow Church of England clergy the task of replying in print was undertaken by Thomas Tully, principal of St Edmund Hall. In his *Justificatio Paulina* of 1674 Tully reasserted the doctrine of justification by faith alone. Among other arguments, he maintained that St Paul spoke of a 'living' faith and St James of a 'dead' one. Tully claimed that Bishop Morley had read and approved *Justificatio Paulina* in manuscript. He also sent a copy of the published version to Sir Joseph Williamson, one of the two secretaries of state and a colleague at Queen's College during the 1650s.[96] Behind Tully, however, loomed the figure of Thomas Barlow, with whom he had almost certainly planned his public response to Bull. Previously the involvement of Barlow has been known mainly from Nelson's biography of Bull, where it is recorded that he lectured at Oxford against the *Harmonia Apostolica*. In fact four stout volumes of related lectures survive in Barlow's holograph. They are collectively entitled by Barlow 'De Conciliatione Pauli et Jacobi', and cover a period of almost five years. The opening shots were fired in the form of an Act lecture, on 8 July 1671. Barlow described his task as both 'arduous' and 'full of danger', in clearing the subject from the misinter-pretations of Socinians and Papists. Bull's book is identified by name as an English Socinian product, because of the role it assigns to works in justifica-tion. (The Socinians did indeed so teach, but there was also an anti-Trinitarian smear involved here.) Barlow argues at length that the works rejected by St Paul are indeed those performed under the Christian gospel. They are the fruits of obedience not the cause of justification, and it is to these necessary fruits that St James refers. This intervention by Barlow came not a moment too soon. Two days previously, on 6 July, William Thornton of Wadham College had, for one of his divinity school theses, denied that 'faith alone justifies'. Given that Thornton's topic would have been approved in advance, the at least tacit support of Richard Allestree, in his capacity as Regius pro-fessor, seems highly probable.[97]

Barlow returned to the subject of justification, in his ordinary lectures, on 19 October 1671. But not until November 1673 was Bull again mentioned directly, being bracketed then with Faustus Socinus. Barlow took his stand on the Thirty-nine Articles, going on to invoke by name John Davenant, Richard Hooker, John Jewel, John Rainolds, and William Whitaker, as well as all other English Protestant writers on the topic – up to the 1640s. He again attacked Bull in the following December, exclaiming 'good God that we should live to see such times'. Further hostile references to Bull occur in February 1674, when the *Harmonia* is described as an act of 'parricide' against the Church of England, and also in the ensuing October, November and December. Apart from a few mentions in January and February, however, Barlow apparently fell silent during 1675 on the subject of the 'Harmonist'. Finally there are some brief references to Bull in January and April 1676.[98] By this last date Barlow had already been Bishop of Lincoln for over nine months, having received consecration at the hands of Bishop Morley the pre-vious June. Among those gracing the associated festivities was the university chancellor, the Duke of Ormonde. Sir Joseph Williamson seems to have played a major part in Barlow becoming a bishop and the original plan was that Thomas Tully should succeed him as Lady Margaret professor of divinity, but in the event this was prevented by Tully's death. The year 1676 also saw the publication at Oxford of a further reply to Bull, by John Tombes. His *Animadversiones*, as we have noted, were dedicated to Morley and they also bear the official imprimatur of Ormonde – a most unusual feature.[99]

The Bull affair sheds a fresh light on the nature of religious faction within the Restoration Church, not least because Morley and Sheldon are normally thought of as being on the same side. In terms of the history of English religious ideas, however, perhaps the most remarkable aspect was the published response by Bull to Tully. This was appended to Bull's *Examen Censurae*, which appeared in 1676. Although printed at London, the work was undertaken on behalf of the Oxford bookseller Richard Davis. Bull describes his opponents as Calvinists, who subscribe to the canons of the Synod of Dort. Against them, he identifies with the most forthright defenders of the Arminian Richard Montagu during the 1620s – the Oxonians Buckeridge, Howson, and Laud. According to Bull, it was all part of the same battle for the mind of the Church of England – conditional justification and conditional predestination going together. 'In truth, for the first four centuries no Catholic ever dreamed about that predestination which many at this day consider the basis and foundation of the whole Christian religion.' We should also recall here Morley's complaint back in the 1630s that all the best bishoprics and deaneries were held by Arminians. Yet unlike Montagu earlier, Bull did not earn preferment by his anti-Calvinist writings. The rewards went instead to his opponents, Tully becoming Dean of Ripon and Barlow a bishop.[100]

This, combined with the fact that most of the controversy about justification was conducted in Latin, helps explain why the orthodoxy of the English Church did not become a major political issue during the increasingly stormy 1670s, despite the hostile comments of Dissenters such as Lewis du Moulin. The latter's pamphlet about the 'several advances the Church of England hath made towards Rome' was published in 1680, at the height of the attempt to exclude James Duke of York from the succession. Du Moulin was an Independent who lost his Oxford post as Camden professor of history at the Restoration, but had clearly kept up with religious developments in the university. Thus he singled out recent events at Oxford, mentioning both Bull and Tully by name, to illustrate the threatened inundation of 'Pelagianism, Socinianism and Popery'.[101] Accusations of Popery, however, were uncomfortably close to the mark in this context, given the publication at Oxford in 1675 of an anonymous volume of annotations on St Paul's epistles. As Barlow pointed out in his lectures, they adopt an essentially similar line to Bull –

defending 'justification by works of the law, performed by the assistance of God's grace'. Often ascribed to Obadiah Walker, fellow and subsequently master of University College, these annotations were in significant part the work of Abraham Woodhead who was a Roman Catholic by the mid-1660s. Walker, the long-standing collaborator and close personal friend of Woodhead, was probably mainly responsible for the second half of the volume. Richard Allestree and John Fell also played a role, perhaps largely editorial.[102] Both Walker and Woodhead had come to entertain grave doubts about Protestantism, in any form, during the 1650s at latest. Although restored to his University College fellowship in 1660, Woodhead was thereafter granted regularly renewed leaves of absence. His college emoluments were forwarded to him in London, apparently by Walker, where he spent much of his time in composing Roman Catholic apologetic until his death in 1678.[103] Walker meanwhile remained at University College, and only declared himself a Roman Catholic after James II came to the throne.

The religious evolution of Obadiah Walker is indeed difficult to fathom, but some clues lie embedded in his edition of John Spelman's life of King Alfred. Published at Oxford in 1678, this was ostensibly part of a fundraising exercise for rebuilding University College – Alfred being claimed as founder both of the college and of the university. Nevertheless in the context of the time, with the Roman Catholic James as heir to the English throne, the story of Alfred's relations with the Papacy also had considerable relevance. Most importantly, at least in this account, Alfred was 'anointed' by the Pope and yet remained 'supreme' over the English Church. Walker subsequently erected statues at University College of Alfred and James II.[104] His religious position may originally have approximated to that of Tristram Sugge, although the association with Woodhead suggests the early adoption of a more extreme stance. Walker arranged for the Oxford publication of another work by Woodhead in 1680, but the more avowedly Romanist writings had to await the changed circumstances of James II's reign. Even then, however, it proved necessary to set up a special printing press in University College. During 1678 Walker had been named in the House of Commons as a suspected Papist, and in July 1680 Francis Nicholson, a former member of University College, was ordered to recant an Oxford sermon 'tending to establish the Popish doctrines of purgatory and penance'. Nicholson at the time was preaching in Walker's stead.[105]

However, the failure of the parliamentary attempts to exclude the duke of York from the succession between 1679 and 1681 was followed by a rallying of royalist ranks. At Oxford this first manifested itself in reaction to an exclusionist tract by Samuel Johnson, entitled *Julian the Apostate* and published in London in 1682. The author was a beneficed Church of England clergyman and chaplain to the Whig Lord William Russell. Not content with advocating exclusion, Johnson had gone on to defend active resistance and even tyrannicide: quoting a comment on the supposedly Christian assassin of Julian that 'you can hardly blame him who shews himself so couragious for God and for that religion he approves'. The reader was clearly meant to draw an analogy here between the cases of pagan Julian and Catholic James. During 1682 *Julian the Apostate* was rebutted in a series of Oxford sermons. Henry Aldrich, canon of Christ Church, John Mill, principal of St Edmund Hall, George Royse, fellow of Oriel College, and William Wyatt, the university orator, were among those who preached against it. At the Act Mill also maintained the thesis that 'confederacies entered into under the pretext of religion, and without the consent of the supreme magistrate, are clearly repugnant both to the practice of the primitive church and the principles of the reformed faith'.[106]

Yet this response was as nothing compared to that elicited by the revelation of the Rye House Plot the following June 1683. An apparent attempt to assassinate both Charles II and the Duke of York, the plot was seemingly predicated on the kind of teaching to be found in *Julian the Apostate*. That July twenty-seven propositions were formally condemned by Oxford University as 'destructive of the kingly government, the safety of his majestie's person, the public peace, the laws of nature and bonds of humane society'. Instead there was inculcated a 'submitting to every ordinance of man for the Lord's sake', and this to be 'absolute and without exception'. The mixed collection of propositions rejected include: the popular origin of 'civil authority', the idea of a 'mutual compact', that 'the soveraignty of England is in the three estates', the right of resistance to 'tyrants' and religious persecutors, the denial of hereditary right of succession to the crown, the lawfulness of making religious 'covenants', 'self-preservation' as the 'fundamental law of nature', no obligation passively to obey commands 'against the laws', 'possession and strength give a right to govern', 'the state of nature is a state of war', the right of self-defence 'against force', the unlawfulness of oaths, 'dominion is founded in grace', 'the powers of this world are usurpations upon the prerogative of Jesus Christ', 'presbyterian government is the scepter of Christ's kingdom', and that 'wicked kings and tyrants ought to be put to death'. This list was mainly the work of William Jane, the Regius professor of divinity. Various books were also ordered to be burnt, among them the *Leviathan* of Thomas Hobbes and Johnson's *Julian*. At the Act in 1684 Arthur Charlett, fellow of Trinity College, identified patriarchalism with monarchy, while denying any contractual basis for sovereignty.[107]

Nevertheless there were those even in Oxford who dared to take a contrary view. In June 1682 Strange Southby, now of Magdalen Hall, was denied his master's degree for arguing *inter alia* that 'it is lawfull to take arms against the king'. A better-known case is that of James Parkinson, fellow of Lincoln

College, who was expelled for his 'Whiggisme' in September 1683. Parkinson was accused of defending the teachings of *Julian the Apostate*, as well as many of the other propositions condemned by the university. Interestingly he was initially protected by the rector of Lincoln College, Thomas Marshall. But Parkinson and Southby were small fry compared with John Locke, who was expelled from his Christ Church Studentship in November 1684. A draft of his *Two Treatises of Government* was almost certainly now in existence. Although nothing was directly proved against Locke, he had in fact already left England for Dutch exile.[108] At the same time royalism itself came in a variety of strengths. Timothy Halton, provost of Queen's College and pro-vice-chancellor, having in October 1683 licensed an English translation of *The Lives of Illustrious Men* by Cornelius Nepos, forbade its sale in January because of additional matter 'against the late parliaments'. Leopold Finch, in a dedication to the Earl of Abingdon, had denied the 'power of parliament' to alter 'the lineal succession' and described the exclusionists as republican 'fanaticks'. In 1687 Finch, a younger son of the Earl of Winchilsea, was to be appointed warden of All Souls, on the basis of a royal mandamus from James II.[109]

VI

By the early 1680s a widespread assumption seems to have been that the accession of James would make little religious difference, and in particular that he would not seek markedly to improve the position of his fellow Catholics. Charles II died on 6 February 1685, and the first months of the new reign reinforced the impression of business as usual. Indeed as late as March 1686 James II reissued his brother's directions to preachers, with the clause about avoiding the 'deep points of election and reprobation'. For Oxford University at least the predestinarian question was still a live issue, because the Regius and Lady Margaret chairs of divinity were both now occupied by Calvinists – albeit of very different kinds. William Jane had succeeded Richard Allestree as Regius professor in 1680. According to Edmund Calamy, 'though fond of the rites and ceremonies of the Church', Jane was 'a Calvinist with respect to doctrine' and 'plainly showed this in his public lectures'. Like the Calvinist Robert South, however, he was also a High-Churchman in his ecclesiastical politics and played a leading part in the rejection of comprehension by convocation in 1689.[110] John Hall, master of Pembroke College, had followed Thomas Barlow as Lady Margaret professor in 1676. Calamy, who attended his lectures, recalls that 'he could bring all the catechism of the Westminster Assembly out of the catechism of the Church of England'. In 1689 Hall actively co-operated with the Williamite regime as a member of the commission on Prayer Book and related reforms, aimed at winning back Dissenters. He became Bishop of Bristol in 1691 and his position appears similar to that of John Wallis, who also is said to have harboured episcopal ambitions.[111]

This Calvinist monopoly of the divinity chairs at Oxford had its dangers, not least because of the rapidly growing strength of Arminianism in the English Church at large. Yet, in the short term, the challenge posed by Roman Catholicism came to overshadow all else. On 26 July 1685 Nathaniel Boyse, fellow of University College, preached a thanksgiving sermon for the defeat of Monmouth's Rebellion. According to his subsequent recantation of 1 August, his sermon had included certain remarks 'tending to popery'. The following autumn Obadiah Walker himself attracted attention by the publication of a further work by Abraham Woodhead, concerning the life of Christ. William Jane had censored some passages in the manuscript, 'savouring of popery', but Walker went ahead and published the original version. On 13 October Anthony Wood records an interview at Whitehall between Boyse and James II, in which the King commended both his sermon and the recent Woodhead publication – wondering 'how anyone shall find fault'.[112]

In May 1686 Walker, Boyse and Thomas Deane, another fellow of University College, received royal permission to withdraw from Church of England worship and set up a Roman Catholic chapel instead. They were joined by John Barnard, fellow of Brasenose College. This was a propaganda *coup* out of all proportion to the small numbers actually involved. At the same time Walker also obtained a royal licence to print Woodhead's remaining unpublished manuscripts.[113] Moreover, restraints were now imposed on anti-Catholic preaching, a special example being made of George Tullie whose Oxford sermon of 24 May, against the 'idolatrous practices of the Romish communion', led to his suspension after Walker complained. Tullie, a former fellow of Queen's College and currently sub-dean of York, had sought to refute the 'modern palliators and expositors' of 'image worship' such as Bishop Bossuet. His reference to the 'worship of babies', by which he presumably meant representations of the infant Jesus, may particularly have angered Walker because this was the subject of the recently commissioned east window of University College chapel. Although Walker had ceased to attend the Protestant services of the college chapel, he wrote to the benefactor in 1687 that 'we there salute the morning light . . . meditating on the shepherds and the angells adoring the true son, and that holy service and prostration, by your singular favour, is continually proposed as to our sight and consideration'.[114]

Successive editions of *An Exposition of the Doctrine of the Catholic Church* by Bossuet were printed at London in 1685 and 1686. His moderate explanation of Tridentine teaching was calculated at least to mollify Protestant critics. Whether it achieved any success in this respect is difficult to know. Most of the Protestant fellows of University College apparently disassociated themselves from Walker's letter about the new chapel window. On the other hand, the alacrity with which the Dean and Chapter of York agreed to suspend George Tullie may in part reflect a distaste for his aggressive brand of Protestantism. Again, as we have seen, there looks to have been a strand of Protestant religious thought at Oxford loath to label the Roman Catholic Church 'idolatrous'.[115] But whereas during the reign of Charles II a mere trickle of anti-Catholic works was published at Oxford, in the years 1687 and 1688 this turned into a small flood. The renewed polemic was almost entirely directed against the writings of Abraham Woodhead, as published by Obadiah Walker at his University College press and many of them with the distinctive King Alfred's head imprint.

Henry Aldrich, Francis Atterbury, and George Smalridge produced replies to Woodhead in 1687. They were reinforced in 1688 by James Harrington, who is not to be confused with the republican of the same name, and George Tullie. Aldrich, Atterbury, Harrington and Smalridge were all members of Christ Church, and were no doubt outraged by the installation of the Roman Catholic John Massey as Dean in 1686. (Massey was Walker's former pupil.) Short of a similar appointment to the Regius chair of divinity, it is difficult to conceive of a greater affront to the Oxford religious establishment. Matters were subsequently compounded by the transformation of Magdalen College into a Roman Catholic seminary under Bonaventure Gifford. Such actions rendered ineffective the plea of James II, at Oxford in September 1687, for 'love and charitie' among Christians.[116] The fact that both Atterbury and Smalridge were later to become Jacobites further underlines the inept tactics of the King. An attack on vested interests was guaranteed to unite the Church of England against him.

One of the polemical techniques employed by Woodhead was, in Walker's words, 'to shew the incertitude and inconstancy of the Church of England in her doctrine and practices'. This is particularly evident in his *Two Discourses concerning the Adoration of our Blessed Saviour in the Holy Eucharist*, which sought to demonstrate the existence of alternative schools of eucharistic thought in the various English Prayer Books. At the same time Woodhead very much played down the Roman Catholic doctrine of transubstantiation. Part of the object of the exercise was to indicate a common middle ground shared by moderate Protestants and Catholics. Henry Aldrich, however, would have none of this. There was, he said, no English 'Zwinglian' tradition; the essential distinction remained between the Protestant 'real' as opposed to the Roman Catholic 'corporal' presence of Christ in the eucharist.[117] In his discourse *Concerning the Spirit of Martin Luther*, Woodhead similarly suggested that English Protestants disagreed over the doctrine of justification. To which Francis Atterbury countered that the teaching of Luther on justification by 'faith alone' is 'now the Church of England's doctrine'. 'Good works are inseparable attendants upon this justifying faith, but they contribute nothing to the act of justification: they make not just, but are allwaies with them that are made so.' Even more striking is the claim by Atterbury that Luther's view of what Woodhead calls the 'servitude of man's will and inability to do good even in the regenerate' is 'when fairly expounded, the same' as that of the English Church.[118] The expression of such views confirms the powerful position of Oxford Calvinism at this juncture. Meanwhile it fell to George Smalridge to rebut *A Relation of the English Reformation* by Woodhead, which characterised the Henrician supremacy as a usurpation of state over church and had remarkably little to say about the Pope. As with the issue of transubstantiation, Woodhead's keynote here was moderation.[119]

The following year, 1688, James Harrington and George Tullie replied to Woodhead on the subjects of charity and clerical celibacy. Roman 'sodalities', or confraternities, were weighed in the balance with the English poor law, and the pros and cons of a married clergy debated.[120] Although the Protestant pamphleteers generally derided the arguments advanced by Woodhead, he was far from being the puny opponent that they liked to claim. Furthermore the Protestant Samuel Parker, who in 1686 succeeded John Fell as Bishop of Oxford, took much the same line as Woodhead in his *Reasons for Abrogating the Test*, published in 1688. Transubstantiation was an 'Aristotelian' formulation, about which laymen especially should not bother their heads. By contrast, both the patristic writers and 'the true old protestants . . . unanimously asserted the corporeal and substantial presence' of Christ in the eucharist. Again, argues Parker, it is the Zwinglians who are the exception. But by the time his tract appeared in print Parker was dead and the regime visibly crumbling.[121] Clearly the issue of religion was one of the reasons for the unopposed invasion of William of Orange in November 1688. That same month John Massey and Obadiah Walker both decamped from Oxford. Yet the flesh-and-blood realities of Roman Catholicism in the mid-1680s had served to mask the beginning of a new upsurge in Protestant heterodoxy, especially as regards the doctrine of the Trinity.[122] This latter question now rapidly took the religious centre stage, as can be seen from William's directions of 1696 for 'preserving of unity in the Church, and the purity of the Christian faith, concerning the Trinity'. By then Oxford University itself had been racked by controversy on this issue, following in the wake of Arthur Bury's notorious book *The Naked Gospel*, first published in 1690. The title echoes that of an earlier work by Bishop Herbert Croft of Hereford, *The Naked Truth*, which appeared in 1675 and was also designed to advance the cause of reconciliation with Dissenters. But whereas Croft had been mainly concerned with the question of conformity the goal of Bury, rector of Exeter College, was doctrinal comprehension. On the face of it, the sexagenarian Bury, who had fallen victim to the Parliamentary Visitors back in 1648, came from an impeccable episcopalian and royalist background. Moreover, in a sermon of 1662 he had accused English Presbyterians of being at least indirectly responsible for the death of Charles I. Among the very few recent authorities cited in *The Naked Gospel* is *The Religion of Protestants* by William Chillingworth, which helps locate its intellectual pedigree; nevertheless, both the appeal to 'reason' and the sheer theological daring on the part of Bury are far greater. Bury argued that much of what passed for orthodoxy was in fact the imposition of clerics living in the centuries after Christ. Therefore the completion of the sixteenth-century Reformation required that these theological accretions be stripped away, so that the 'primitive gospel' could shine forth. 'Simplicity of mind is its beauty, as was Eve's nakedness in her innocency, and simplicity of doctrine is the glory of the Gospel, as is the nakedness of the sun in its brightness.'[123]

For Bury the doctrine of the Trinity was a prime example of later obfuscations of religious truth, although he also claimed to resolve the perennial dispute about the relationship of faith and works: 'they are both the same under different aspects, and in their comprehensive latitude either containeth the other'. Faith in Christ as a saviour, however, did not require belief in the 'eternity of his Godhead'. Thus the dispute between Arius and Athanasius on this issue was 'fruitless', and so too were the subsequent ramifications. The man who believes in Christ

> as the traveller doth in the light shall in the end as certainly attain eternal life, as the traveller doth his journey's end; though concerning our Lord's person he may be as much mistaken as the ignorant but industrious traveller, who knoweth nothing of the greatness of the sun's body or the nature of its light.

It was necessary, Bury claimed, to break through the tangled web spun by theologians, to the simple gospel message which had originally swept the world. This reborn Christianity would serve both to heal internal divisions among believers and win new converts.[124]

Bury was inspired to his ultimately Icarian attempt by the prospect of Prayer Book reform in 1689, because the most potentially offensive statements concerning the Trinity were to be found embedded in the English liturgy – notably the Athanasian creed. The reform commission set up by King William did indeed discuss the matter and recommended a new rubric. In the event, however, any hope of change was blocked in the Canterbury Convocation, and *The Naked Gospel* became the victim of a conservative backlash. The book was burnt by the Oxford authorities in August 1690, and various statements extracted from it were formally condemned. As for the author, his alleged heterodoxy featured among charges contemporaneously levelled against him by the visitor of Exeter College, Bishop Jonathan Trelawney. Bury was deprived of his rectorship but won a reprieve by going to common law. Hence he can be found preaching before the university on

New Year's Day 1692, about the 'danger of delaying repentance'. As well as rebutting the charge of Socinianism, Bury maintained, apparently against Calvinists, that 'the question is not concerning God's secret but his declared will', and 'that ordinary rule whereby he professeth to judge the world'. The 'day of grace is shorter than the day of life' and 'there is a measure of iniquity beyond which God's spirit will not strive with man, but leave the reprobate to his own ways wherein he must certainly perish'. God woos, threatens and 'at last' deserts 'the obstinate and therefore perishing fool' (Henry Hammond had argued similarly in a tract published over forty years earlier). Not until 1695 did Bury finally leave Exeter College, the House of Lords having upheld his original deprivation by Bishop Trelawney.[125]

Meanwhile the reverberations from *The Naked Gospel* continued to be felt, producing a series of related Trinitarian defences including one by William Nicholls of Merton College. Conversely Bury's book was enthusiastically received in the radical intellectual circles frequented by John Locke. On the continent the Arminian Jean Le Clerc reviewed Bury sympathetically in his *Bibliotheque Universelle* and the Calvinist Pierre Jurieu wrote against him, the latter provoking a Latin reply from Bury entitled *Latitudinarius Orthodoxus* and published in 1697.[126] Amidst all the clamour of controversy, however, a remarkable sea change had by now occurred – silent and largely unremarked. Calvinism might still survive in Oxford, but elsewhere Arminianism had emerged supreme. During the 1660s an aggressive brand of anti-Calvinism had rapidly become established at Cambridge University, and Archbishop Sheldon increasingly lent his authority to such views in the English Church more generally. Meanwhile the public affirmation of the English Calvinist heritage was left almost exclusively to Dissenters, such as the Oxonian Henry Hickman. The apotheosis of this long-term development was achieved in the 1690s with the triumph of a religious 'Latitudinarianism' which was clearly Arminian in its theological emphases. In this context Bishop Gilbert Burnet's *Exposition* of the Thirty-nine Articles, published in 1699, both outlined the rise and fall of English Calvinism and set a seal on the new Arminian dispensation.[127]

Yet Oxford too contributed to this transformation in a very important and practical manner, by means of a body of popular Arminian devotional literature. This emanated from the Allestree–Fell group and its best-known product is *The Whole Duty of Man*. First published in 1658, with a prefatory letter from Henry Hammond, by 1700 the book had run through twenty-five recorded editions. Still bearing the scars of the Interregnum, *The Whole Duty of Man* calls for religious renewal in terms of an Arminian reading of the Prayer Book. The sacrament of communion and works of charity are held forth as the twin poles of the Christian life, which is to be led along lines later made famous under the label of the 'Protestant ethic'.

For there is a husbandry of the soul as well as of the estate, and the end of the one as of the other is the increasing and improving of its riches; [and] when it is remembered how great a work we have here to do, the making our calling and election sure ... it will appear our time is that which of all other things we ought most industriously to improve.

But this 'husbandry' was premissed on the free co-operation of the will of man with the grace of God; the basic requirement was 'an honest and hearty endeavour to do what we are able'. Thus, having flown the academic nest, Arminianism was already well on the way to establishing a significant following among the English laity.[128]

Much of the earlier anxiety was also now ebbing out of the religious situation. Despite the *frisson* engendered by the policies of James II his reign had exposed as myth the idea of a mass of secret Papists, merely waiting for an opportune moment at which to emerge. Similarly the growing institutionalisation of Dissent served gradually to exorcize the threat of Puritanism, a process advanced by the Toleration Act of 1689 which ushered in a new age of denominational pluralism.[129] For over a century Oxford and Cambridge had found themselves in the front line, as successive English regimes struggled to contain the rivalries unleashed by the Reformation, but the Civil War and its aftermath had marked the beginning of the end of that role. Paradoxically, however, the tolerance which was thenceforward increasingly forced upon the nation turned the English universities into more rather than less exclusive institutions – many of the potential misfits simply going elsewhere. Greater peace of mind had been bought at the price of a certain disengagement from the intellectual challenges of the coming era.[130]

NOTES

I am most grateful to my former colleague Peter Lake, now of Princeton University, for commenting extensively on a draft of this chapter. Fred Trott has similarly given me the benefit of his advice on the Interregnum section, as has James Burns on political thought.

1 W. Chillingworth, *The Religion of Protestants: A Safe Way to Salvation* (Oxford, 1638); F. Cheynell, *The Rise, Growth and Danger of Socinianisme. Together with a Plaine Discovery of a Desperate Designe of corrupting the Protestant Religion, whereby it appeares that the Religion which hath been so violently contended for (by the Archbishop of Canterbury and his Adherents) is not the True Pure Protestant Religion, but a Hotchpotch of Arminianisme, Socinianisme and Popery* (London, 1643), pp. 28–31, 34–5, 72–3; see pp. 279–80 above.

2 Seventeenth-century contemporaries called this body of predestinarian doctrine 'Calvinist', yet the sources were multifarious – including the writings of the early Luther. In a specifically English context, the teachings of Martin Bucer and Peter Martyr were especially important.

3 Tyacke, *Anti-Calvinists* pp. ix, 18–19, 21–3, 59, 61–2, 72–4, 115. For the views of William Goodwin, see a Paul's Cross sermon preached by him on 5 November 1614: London, Dr Williams's Library, MS 12.10, fos 7v–8.

4 P. Collinson, 'The Jacobean Religious Settlement: the Hampton Court Conference', in H. Tomlinson ed., *Before the Civil War* (London, 1983), pp. 38–44; J. Rainolds, *The Prophecie of Haggai interpreted and applied in Sundry Sermons* (London, 1649), pp. 4–5, 16–18; C. M. Dent, *Protestant Reformers in Elizabethan Oxford* (Oxford, 1983), pp. 213–17.

5 G. Abbot, *An Exposition upon the Prophet Jonah* (London, 1600), pp. 231, 267, 632, 635; H. Airay, *Lectures upon the Whole Epistle of Saint Paul to the Philippians* (London, 1618), 265, 294–5, 431–2; G. Abbot, *The Reasons which Doctour Hill hath brought for the Upholding of Papistry* (Oxford, 1604), 9 and *passim*.

6 Airay, *Lectures*, pp. 4, 17, 292–5; Abbot, *An Exposition*, pp. 36, 240; Abbot, *The Reasons*, p. 102; G. Abbot, *Quaestiones Sex* (Oxford, 1598), pp. 187–8. The editor of Airay's lectures, Christopher Potter, dedicated them to Abbot, by then Archbishop, in 1618.

7 J. Howson, *A Sermon preached at St Maries in Oxford, the 17 Day of November, 1602* (Oxford, 1602), pp. 5–6, 17, 25; J. Howson, *A Second Sermon preached at Paules Crosse, the 21 of May, 1598* (London, 1598), pp. 23, 39–40; J. Howson, *A Sermon preached at Paules Crosse, the 4 of December, 1597* (London, 1597), p. 7.

8 Apart from Howson, six Elizabethan canons of Christ Church became vice-chancellors: J. Le Neve, *Fasti Ecclesiae Anglicanae*, ed. T. D. Hardy (Oxford, 1854), iii, p. 476.

9 A. Wood, *The History and Antiquities of the University of Oxford*, ed. J. Gutch (Oxford, 1792–6), ii, pp. 237–8, 242, 258–9, 261; OUA, NEP/supra/II, register M, fo 70; Dent, *Protestant Reformers*, pp. 209–12, 217–18.

10 Corporation of London Record Office, Repertories 20, fos 216r–v, Repertories 25, fos 2v, 24, 262v; *APC 1599–1600*, p. 27, *ibid. 1600–1601*, p. 44; G. Abbot, *Cheapside Crosse Censured and Condemned* (London, 1641), pp. 2–3, 12; M. Aston, *England's Iconoclasts* (Oxford, 1988), i, pp. 294–342.

11 J. P. Kenyon ed., *The Stuart Constitution, 1603–1688* (2nd edn, Cambridge, 1968), pp. 117–19; P. Collinson, *The Elizabethan Puritan Movement* (London, 1967), pp. 452–9; C. Burrage, *The Early English Dissenters in the Light of Recent Research (1550–1641)* (Cambridge, 1912), ii, pp. 146–7; C. H. Cooper, *Annals of Cambridge* (Cambridge 1842–1908), iii, p. 2; *The Answere of the Vicechancelour, the Doctors, both the Proctors, and other the Heads of Houses in the Universitie of Oxford . . . to the Humble Petition of the Ministers of the Church of England* (Oxford, 1603). Subsequent editions of *The Answere* incorporate a letter from Cambridge University, dated 7 October and said to have been received 'immediately after' the first printing.

12 N. Cranfield and K. Fincham eds, 'John Howson's Answers to Archbishop Abbot's Accusations at his "Trial" before James I at Greenwich, 10 June 1615', *Camden Miscellany* xxix (Camden Soc. 4th ser. xxxiv, 1987), 335. J. Hacket, *Scrinia Reserata: a Memorial offer'd to the Great Deservings of J. Williams . . . Archbishop of York* (London, 1693), pt 1, p. 64; P. Heylyn, *Cyprianus Anglicus: or the History of the Life and Death of . . . William [Laud] . . . Archbishop of Canterbury* (London, 1668), pp. 53–4.

13 *The Answere*, sigs ¶¶–¶¶2, pp. 15–16, 23, 31.

14 BL, Add. MS 28, 571, fos 181–6; Burrage, *The Early English Dissenters*, ii, pp. 146–7.

15 BL, Add. MS 28, 571, fos 181–6; Tyacke *Anti-Calvinists*, 65–6.

16 Bodl., Rawlinson MS a. 289, fo 6; HMC *Salisbury MSS*, xvii, pp. 422–3, 431; Tyacke, *Anti-Calvinists*, p. 64. I am grateful to Kenneth Fincham here for advice on dating.

17 Clark ed., *Register*, pt i, pp. 195, 199–200, 204, 213; Bodl. Wood MS 276 A, fo 414; OUA, NEP/supral/14, register o, fo 240v, G. Powell, *Disputationum Theologicarum et Scholasticarum de Antichristo et eius Ecclesia* (London, 1605); C. Hill, *Antichrist in Seventeenth-century England* (London, 1971), pp. 3–33; P. Lake, 'The Significance of the Elizabethan Identification of the Pope as Antichrist', *JEH*, 31, (1980).

18 J. Terry, *The Trial of Truth* (Oxford, 1600), sigs a2–a3.

19 *Ibid.*, sigs a2–a3, pp. 8–31, 35–40, 42, 49–59, 66–8, 76–8, 88–108, 114, 127–8, 150–9; J. Terry, *The Second Part of the Trial of Truth* (Oxford, 1602), sig. C. The third part of Terry's *Tryall of Truth* was published at Oxford in 1625.

20 Laud, *Works*, iv, p. 309; Powell, *De Antichristo*, p. 341; Cranfield and Fincham eds, 'John Howson's Answers', p. 336.

21 Tyacke, *Anti-Calvinists*, pp. 60–4, 66–7; Dent, *Protestant Reformers*, pp. 234–7; A. Kenny ed., *The Responsa Scholarum of the English College of Rome*, pt 1, *1598–1621* (Catholic Record Soc. liv, 1962), p. 212. Examination of a xerox of the original manuscript confirms that 'Hensonum' should read 'Housonum'. I am grateful to Anthony Kenny for his help on this subject.

22 T. Rogers, *The English Creede Consenting with the True, Auncient, Catholique and Apostolique Church* (London, 1585), pt 1, p. 10. This work was licensed by Archbishop Whitgift: 43. Arber ed., *Transcript*, ii, p. 436.

23 R. Parkes, *A Brief Answere unto Certaine Objections and Reasons against the Descension of Christ into Hell* (Oxford, 1604); Richard Parkes, *An Apologie of Three Testimonies of Holy Scripture, concerning the Article of our Creed, 'He descended into Hell'* (London, 1607), pt 2, sig. Aa3; D. D. Wallace, 'Puritan and Anglican: The Interpretation of Christ's Descent into Hell in Elizabethan Theology', *Archiv für Reformationsgeschichte*, 69 (1978), 274–5, 282.

24 A. R. Winnett, *Divorce and Remarriage in Anglicanism* (London, 1958), ch. 6; J. Howson, *Uxore Dimissa propter Fornicationem aliam non licet superinducere* (Oxford, 1602); J. Rainolds, *A Defence of the Judgement of the Reformed Churches. That a Man may law-fullie not onlie put awaie his Wife for her Adulterie, but also marrie Another* (n.p., 1609); T. Pie, *Epistola ad Ornatissimum Virum D. Johannem Housonum* (London, 1603): Arber ed., *Transcript*, iii, p. 238; Tyacke, *Anti-Calvinists*, pp. 67–8, 70, 174, 266–7.

25 Clark ed., *Register*, pt i, pp. 206–7; N. Sykes, *Old Priest and New Presbyter* (Cambridge, 1950), p. 101.

26 J. and W. Nichols eds, *The Works of James Arminius* (London, 1825–75), i, p. 589; Tyacke, *Anti-Calvinists*, pp. 65–7, 72; R. Abbot, *De Gratia et Perseverantia Sanctorum* (London, 1618), pp. 1, 4, 18–20, 25; N. Field, *Some Short Memorials concerning the Life of . . . R. Field*, ed. J. Le Neve (London, 1717), p. 22.

27 Tyacke, *Anti-Calvinists*, pp. xi, 70, 266–71; Cranfield and Fincham eds, 'John Howson's Answers', pp. 322–7, 330; R. Abbot, *The Exaltation of the Kingdom and Priesthood of Christ* (London, 1601), p. 26. In 1612 Howson had also preached a notorious Oxford sermon, accusing the annotators of the Genevan Bible of inculcating anti-Trinitarianism: Bodl., Rawlinson MS d. 320, fos 46v–7.

28 J. Ley, *Sunday a Sabbath* (London, 1641), sigs b2r–v, D. Featley, *Cygnea Cantio or Learned Decisions and . . . Pious Directions for Students in Divinitie, delivered by . . . King James, at White Hall a Few Weekes before his Death* (London, 1629), pp. 12–14, 16–21.

29 E. Bagshaw, *The Life and Death of Mr Bolton* (London, 1639), pp. 17, 27; R. Bolton, *The Last Conflicts and Death of Mr Thomas Peacock* (London, 1646), sig. A2v, pp. 4–6, 21, 30–1, 36, 44, 54. A postscript notes that this tract was refused a licence for printing during the 1630s, as being 'too precise for those times': ibid., sig. D4v; J. Eales, *Puritans and Roundheads: the Harleys of Brampton Bryan and the Outbreak of the Civil War* (Cambridge, 1990), p. 50.

30 Ley, *Sunday a Sabbath*, sig. b; Wood, *Athenae Oxoniensis*, ed. P. Bliss (London, 1813–20), iii, p. 570; Tyacke, *Anti-Calvinists*, pp. 69–70; Featley, *Cygnea Cantio*, p. 9.

31 J. Rainolds, *The Prophecie of Obadiah opened* (Oxford, 1613), sig. A4; J. Rainolds, *The Discovery of the Man of Sinne* (Oxford, 1614); T. Morton, *A Defence of the Innocencie of the Three Ceremonies of the Church of England* (London, 1618); R. C. Richardson, *Puritanism in North-West England: a Regional Study of the Diocese of Chester to 1642* (Manchester, 1972), pp. 23–4, 30–1.

32 Collinson, *The Elizabethan Puritan Movement*, p. 459; K. J. Höltgen, 'Richard Haydocke: Translator, Engraver, Physician', *The Library*, 5th ser., 33 (1978), 26–7; K. C. Fincham, *Prelate as Pastor: The Episcopate of James I* (Oxford, 1990), p. 195.

33 Lincolnshire Archives Office MS Ciii/13/2/24, pp. 1–4, 9, 11–13: I owe my knowledge of this Barcroft material to Kenneth Fincham, who kindly provided me with a microfilm of the original manuscript; OUA, register o, fo 240v; J. Sprint, *Cassander Anglicanus* (London, 1618), sigs ¶3, *3.

34 Tyacke, *Anti-Calvinists*, pp. 108–9, 113–14; P. Lake, *Anglicans and Puritans? Presbyterianism and English Conformist Thought from Whitgift to Hooker* (London, 1988), pp. 103, 121; Wood, *History of the University*, ii, pp. 323–4; S. Gibson ed., *Statuta Antiqua Universitatis Oxoniensis* (Oxford, 1931), pp. 412–13.

35 J. A. W. Bennett and H. R. Trevor-Roper eds, *The Poems of Richard Corbett* (Oxford, 1955), pp. 13, 24–5, 33, 36, 46–7, 52–9; Laud, *Works*, vi, p. 133; J. Hales, *A Sermon preached at St Maries in Oxford upon Tuesday in Easter Weeke, 1617* (Oxford, 1617), pp. 3, 6, 9, 19, 24–5, 32–3, 39–40. On the evidence of this sermon, Hales was already in process of bidding Calvin 'good night' even before the Synod of Dort: *Golden Remains of the Ever Memorable Mr John Hales, of Eton College* (London, 1673), sig. A4v.

36 Tyacke, *Anti-Calvinists*, pp. 72–5, 87–105.

37 J. R. Tanner ed., *Constitutional Documents of the Reign of James I* (Cambridge, 1930), pp. 54–6; T. Broad, *Three Questions Answered* (Oxford, 1621); J. Prideaux, *Orationes Novem Inaugurales* (Oxford, 1626), pp. 135, 147; J. Prideaux, *The Doctrine of the Sabbath* (London, 1634), pp. 13, 39; cf K. L. Parker, *The English Sabbath* (Cambridge, 1988), pp. 164–7.

38 T. G. Jackson, *Wadham College, Oxford* (London, 1893), pp. 163–70; M. Archer, 'English Painted Glass in the Seventeenth Century: The Early Work of Abraham van Linge', *Apollo*, 101 (1975); Abbot, *Cheapside Crosse*, pp. 6–7; Clark ed., *Register*, pt i, p. 210; Wood, *Athenae*, ii, p. 142; Aston, *England's Iconoclasts*, pp. 74–95.

39 Wood, *History of the University*, ii, pp. 341–7. Wood gives Knight's Christian name as William, but cf. *CSPD 1619–23*, p. 400.

40 *Votiva, sive ad Serenissimum, Potentissimumque Jacobum, Magnae Britanniae, Franciae et Hiberniae Regem etc. De Auspicato Illustrissimi Caroli, Walliae Principis etc. in Regiam Hispanicam Adventu, Pia et Humilis Oxoniensum Gratulatio* (London, 1623); *Carolus Redux* (Oxford, 1623); T. Lushington, *The Resurrection of our Saviour Vindicated* (London, 1741), pp. viii, 19; J. Randol, *A Sermon Preach't at St Marie's Oxford, the 5 of August 1624, Concerning the Kingdome's Peace* (Oxford, 1624), pp. 7–11; T. Cogswell, *The Blessed Revolution: English Politics and the Coming of War, 1621–1624* (Cambridge, 1989), pp. 273–6.

41 QCL, MS 390, fo 19; Tyacke, *Anti-Calvinists*, pp. 48–50, 147–63; J. Goodman, *A Serious and Compassionate Enquiry* (London, 1674), p. 7: Bodl. press mark 8°. A. 43. Linc., annotated by Thomas Barlow. I owe this last reference to John Spurr.

42 J. Doughty, *A Discourse Concerning the Abstruseness of Divine Mysteries* (Oxford, 1628/9), pt 2, pp. 8, 15–16, 22 [By 1640 Doughty was in conflict with a group of Puritan parishioners: D. Oldridge, *Religion and Society in Early Stuart England* (Aldershot, 1998), p. 27]; Tyacke, *Anti-Calvinists*, pp. x–xi, 266–70.

43 Tyacke, *Anti-Calvinists*, pp. 78–83, 248–9, 263–5; P. Heylyn, *Examen Historicum* (London, 1659), pt 2, appx, sigs P3v–P4. The relative novelty of the position adopted by Heylyn in 1627, concerning ecclesiastical visibility, can be gauged by comparing it with his own published views of the same year, where he locates 'our church before the time of Luther' among the Albigensians: P. Heylyn, *Microcosmos* (Oxford, 1627), p. 113. I owe this last reference to Anthony Milton.

44 Heylyn, *Cyprianus Anglicus*, p. 126: Bodl. press mark NN. 118. Th., annotated by Thomas Barlow; T. Barlow, *The Genuine Remains* (London, 1693), p. 192. I owe these references to Robert Beddard.

45 W. Prynne, *Anti-Arminianisme or the Church of England's Old Antithesis to New Arminianisme* (London, 1630), pp. 183, 192, sig. qq*3; E. Cardwell ed., *Synodalia* (Oxford, 1842), i, p. 255; Tyacke, *Anti-Calvinists*, pp. 78, 82, 84; Wood, *History of the University*, ii, pp. 372–80; E. Calamy, *The Nonconformists Memorial* (London, 1802–3), ii, p. 27.

46 J. R. Bloxam ed., *A Register of . . . Magdalen College* (Oxford, 1853–81), ii, p. xcvi; Archer, 'English Painted Glass', p. 31; Tyacke, *Anti-Calvinists*, pp. 209–10; *Collectanea* (OHS, 1905), iv, pp. 147–8.

47 E. Brerewood, *A Learned Treatise of the Sabaoth* (Oxford, 1630); E. Brerewood, *A Second Treatise of the Sabbath* (Oxford, 1632); Parker, *The English Sabbath*, pp. 154–60, 191–214.

48 P. Heylyn, *The History of the Sabbath* (London, 1634), pt 2, pp. 250–9; G. E. Gorman, 'A Laudian Attempt to "Tune the Pulpit": Peter Heylyn and his Sermon against the Feoffees for the Purchase of Impropriations', *Journal of Religious History*, 8 (1975), 342–3; Heylyn, *Cyprianus Anglicus*, pp. 198–200; see pp. 113–14, 121–3 above.

49 J. Prideaux, *Lectiones Novem de Totidem Religionis Capitibus* (Oxford, 1625); J. Prideaux, *Viginti-Duae Lectiones* (Oxford, 1648), pp. 299, 330; *The Racovian Catechisme* (London, 1652), pp. 18, 146–7; H. J. McLachlan, *Socinianism in Seventeenth-Century England* (Oxford, 1951), pp. 103–7.

50 McLachlan, *Socinianism*, pp. 31–2, 72, 85–7; Thomas à Kempis, *The Imitation of Christ*, ed. W. Page (Oxford, 1639), sigs *11, ***2; Chillingworth, *The Religion of Protestants*, pp. 65, 406–7; C. Potter, *Want of Charitie* (Oxford, 1633), pp. 113–16; Prideaux, *Vigintiduae lectiones*, p. 347.

51 Brasensse College Library, Oxford, MS B2. a. 38, p. 35; PRO SP 16/406, fos 167–8; W. Prynne, *A Looking-Glasse for All Lordly Prelates* (n.p., 1636) and *The Unbishoping of Timothy and Titus* (Amsterdam, 1636).

52 Laud, *Works*, v, 87–8; NUL, MS Cl. *c.* 73, MS Cl. *c.* 84b; Tyacke, *Anti-Calvinists*, p. 83.

53 NUL, MS Cl. *c.* 75, MS Cl. *c.* 84b; Tyacke, *Anti-Calvinists*, pp. 79–81; Potter, *Want of Charitie*, pp. 44–5. John Prideaux had argued the same case as Cheynell in his Act lecture of 1624: Prideaux, *Lectiones Novem*, p. 192.

54 *The Life of Edward Earl of Clarendon* (Oxford, 1827), i, p. 48; McLachlan, *Socinianism*, p. 83; Cheynell, *The Rise, Growth and Danger of Socinianisme*, pp. 28–9, 40–1; Laud, *Works*, v, pp. 205–6; NUL, MS Cl. *c.* 78, MS Cl. *c.* 84b. [Richard Cust kindly supplied the foregoing material from the Clifton papers at Nottingham University Library.]

55 Laud, *Works*, v, pp. 198–9; Tyacke, *Anti-Calvinists*, p. 183; OUA, register of congregation 1634–47, NEP/*supra*/16, register Q, fo 180; W. Prynne, *A Vindication of Psalm 105. 15* (London, 1642).

56 Le Neve, *Fasti*, iii, pp. 66, 469, 587; A. Wood, *Fasti Oxonienses*, ed. P. Bliss (London, 1815–20) pt 2, p. 2; G. Ornsby ed., *The Correspondence of John Cosin* (Surtees Soc. lii, lv, 1868–72), i, pp. 96, 98, 100; Laud, *Works*, v, p. 56.

57 Apparently Sanderson did not take up his Oxford post until 1646: P. Lake, 'Serving God and the Times: The Calvinist Conformity of Robert Sanderson', *JBS*, 27 (1988), 108–9 and *passim*; J. Taylor, *Of the Sacred Order and Offices of Episcopacy, by Divine Institution, Apostolicall Tradition, and Catholike Practice* (Oxford, 1642), pp. 12–15, 38, 193; *Reasons of the Present Judgement of the University of Oxford, Concerning the Solemne League and Covenant* (Oxford, 1647), pp. 8, 13–14.

58 G. Williams, *Jura Majestatis, the Rights of Kings both in Church and State* (Oxford, 1644), p. 14; H. Ferne, *Conscience satisfied that there is no Warrant for the Armes now taken up by Subjects* (Oxford 1643), pp. 7–8; D. Digges, *The Unlawfulnesse of Subjects taking up Armes against their Soveraigne, in what Case soever* (Oxford, 1643), pp. 2–4; R. Tuck, *Natural Rights Theories: their Origin and Development* (Cambridge, 1979), pp. 103, 108.

59 T. Herbert, *Memoris of the Two Last Years of the Reign of that Unparallell'd Prince of Ever Blessed Memory, King Charles I* (London, 1702), pp. 43, 131; H. Hammond, *A Practicall Catechisme* (Oxford, 1645), pp. 8, 12, 47, 56. My italics; H. Hammond, *A Copy of Some Papers past at Oxford, betwixt the Author of the Practicall Catechisme and Mr. Ch.* (London, 1647), pp. 20, 68–9, 118; QCL, MS 266, fo 27; the Arminianism of Hammond is further confirmed by his *Severall Tracts* (London, 1646), pp. 37–70, and p. 290 above.

60 F. Madan, *Oxford Books* (Oxford, 1895–1931), ii, p. 136; CL, MS M.3.13 [fo 2], MS M.3.15 [fo 167]: I identified Sugge's notebooks during the summer of 1986, and must thank John Wing and Jane Wells for all their help in this connection.

61 CL, MS M.3.6, fos 10, 19–22v, 90, 97v, 137–40, 144–5; *The Theological Works of Herbert Thorndike* (Oxford, 1844–56), iv, pp. 440–2, 722–3, 815; v, p. 380.

62 CL, MS M.3.8 ('Analecta ad Loca Scripturae Difficiliae': Acts 13. 48, Romans 9. 11, 22), MS M.3.15, fos 21, 88–9, MS M.3.6, fos 77–8, 116, 131–2v, 149r–v. For the views of Jeremy Taylor concerning original sin, see especially his *Deus Justificatus* (London, 1656).

63 CL, MS M.3.6, fos 62, 183v, MS M.3.20 ('Patriarcha'), MS M.3.15, fos 126v–8, [167]; Hammond, *A Practicall Catechisme*, pp. 192–5; H. Hammond, *Large Additions to the Practicall Catechisme* (London, 1646), pp. 9–10; R. B. Schlatter, *The Social Ideas of Religious Leaders, 1600–1688* (Oxford, 1940), pp. 146–7.

64 Wood, *Athenae*, iii, p. 1270; iv, p. 396; R. L. Poole, *Catalogue of Portraits in the Possession of the University, Colleges, City, and County of Oxford* (Oxford, 1912–25), iii, pp. 30–1.

65 R. Sanderson, *De Juramenti Promissorii Obligatione Praelectiones Septem* (London, 1647); I. Roy and D. Reinhart, 'Oxford and the Civil Wars', in N. Tyacke ed., *The History of the University of Oxford, IV: Seventeenth-century Oxford* (Oxford, 1997). pp. 728–31.

66 F. Cheynell, *The Divine Triunity of the Father, Son, and Holy Spirit* (London, 1650), sigs B4–B5v; *Truth triumphing over Error. Or a Relation of a Publike Disputation at Oxford . . . between Master Cheynell a Member of the Assembly and Master Erbury the Seeker and Socinian* (London, 1646); H. Savage, *Quaestiones Tres, in Novissimorum Comitiorum Vesperiis Oxon discussae* (Oxford, 1653), sig. A2v, p. 24; J. Tombes, *Refutatio positionis . . . ab Henrici Savage . . . propositae* (London, 1653), sig. A2v.

67 W. C. Braithwaite, *The Beginnings of Quakerism* (London, 1912, 2nd edn, 1955), p. 158; R. Hubberthorne, *A True Testimony of the Zeal of Oxford Professors and University Men, who for Zeal Persecute the Servants of the Living God* (London, 1654), pp. 1–4; *VCH Oxon.*, iv, p. 417.

68 Tyacke, *Anti-Calvinists*, pp. 37–49, 62–81; OUA, NEP/*supra*/17, register Qa, fos 150–4; BL, Harleian MS 7038, pp. 108–9; Wood, *History of the University*, ii, p. 607; J. Prideaux, *Fasciculus Controversiarum Theologicarum* (Oxford, 1649), sigs ¶2–¶4, pp. 136–9, 204–17, 221–30, 235–44, 273–6.

69 OUA, register Qa, fos 150–2v.

70 J. Wallis, *Mens Sobria Serio Commendata: Concio . . . accederunt eiusdem Exercitationes* (Oxford, 1657), 110–35; W. Twisse, *The Riches of Gods Love . . . consistent with his Absolute Hatred . . . of the Vessels of Wrath* (Oxford, 1653); S. Hoard and H. Mason, *God's Love to Mankind, manifested by disprooving his Absolute Decree for their Damnation* (n.p., 1633); J. Owen, *The Doctrine of the Saints Perserverance, explained and confirmed* (Oxford, 1654); D. D. Wallace, *Puritans and Predestination: Grace in English Protestant Theology, 1525–1695* (Chapel Hill, Conn., 1982), pp. 144–57.

71 G. Kendall, *A Vindication of the Doctrine commonly received in the Reformed Churches concerning God's Intentions of Special Grace and Favour to his Elect in the Death of Christ* (London, 1653), sigs aa, *****3, G. Kendall, *Sancti Sanciti: or the Common Doctrine of the Perseverance of the Saints* (London, 1654), sigs A2, *4v; Tyacke, *Anti-Calvinists*, pp. 212–13.

72 G. Kendall, *Fur pro Tribunali . . . accesserunt Oratio de Doctrina Neo-Pelagiana* (Oxford, 1657), pt 2, pp. 1–60; H. Hammond, *Of Fundamentals in a Notion referring to Practise* (London, 1654), pp. 108, 126–8; E. Bagshaw, *A Practicall Discourse concerning Gods Decrees* (Oxford, 1659); H. Hickman, *A Justification of the Fathers and Schoolmen: shewing that They are not Selfe-Condemned for denying the Positivity of Sin* (2nd edn, Oxford, 1659), sigs b4–b5v, Wallace, *Puritans and Predestination*, pp. 120–30, 140–2.

73 Cheynell, *The Divine Triunity*; J. Owen, *Vindiciae Evangelicae, or the Mystery of the Gospel vindicated and Socinianisme examined* (Oxford, 1655), sigs A–A3, pp. 152–347, 521–56; McLachlan, *Socinianism*, pp. 163–217, 239–49; H. Hammond, *An Answer to*

the *Animadversions on the Dissertations touching Ignatius's Epistles* (London, 1654), pp. 125–37; J. Conant, *The Life of the Reverend and Venerable John Conant, D.D.* (London, 1823), p. 20.

74 H. J. de Jonge, 'Hugo Grotius: exégète du Nouveau Testament', in *The World of Hugo Grotius (1583–1645)*, Royal Netherlands Academy of Arts and Sciences (Amsterdam and Maarssen, 1984), pp. 97–155; J. Owen, *Of the Divine Originall, Authority, Self-Evidencing Light and Power of the Scriptures . . . Also a Vindication of the Purity and Integrity of the Hebrew and Greek Texts of the Old and New Testament, in Some Considerations on the Prolegomena and Appendix to the late Biblia Polyglotta* (Oxford, 1659); H. R. Trevor-Roper, *From Counter-Reformation to Glorious Revolution* (London, 1992), pp. 48, 73–8; OUA, register Qa, fo 153.

75 M. Wren, *Monarchy Asserted, or the State of Monarchicall and Popular Government in Vindication of the Considerations upon Mr. Harrington's Oceana* (Oxford, 1659), pp. 19–20, 77, 91, 107; J. Barbon, *Liturgie a Most Divine Service* (Oxford, 1662), pp. 125–8.

76 R. Allestree, *A Sermon preached in St. Peter's Westminster on Sunday Jan. 6, 1660* (London, 1660/1), pp. 35–7. [Cf. pp. 232–4 above.]

77 QCL, MS 340, p. 1, MS 279 ('Considerations concerninge the Common Prayer Booke'), p. 1, MS 260 ('Controversiae Arminianae, Pelagianae [et] Socinianae'), pp. 2, 90, 158, 324, 411.

78 *The Life of Edward Earl of Clarendon*, ii, p. 118; QCL, MS 279 ('Considerations concerninge the Common Prayer Booke'), pp. 1–18: this manuscript is dated 23 September 1661.

79 D. Wilkins ed., *Concilia Magnae Britanniae et Hiberniae* (London, 1737), iv, p. 577; Tyacke, *Anti-Calvinists*, pp. 50–2, 81–3, 181–5, 263–5.

80 J. Wallis, *The Necessity of Regeneration* (London, 1682), sig. A, pp. 18–19, 35.

81 G. Reedy, *Robert South (1634–1716): An Introduction to his Life and Sermons* (Cambridge, 1992), pp. 11–13; R. South, *Sermons* (London, 1692–1717), i, pp. 498, 501, 508–10, iii. sig. A3, p. 450. See also pp. 302 above and pp. 333–4 below.

82 R. Allestree, *Forty Sermons* (Oxford, 1684), sig. ev, pt 1, pp. 61–2, 161–4, pt 2, pp. 93–4.

83 OUA, NEP/*supra*/28, register Tb, fo 3v, A. Wood, *Life and Times*, ed. A. Clark (OHS, xix, xxi, xxvi, xxx, 1891–95) ii, p. 448.

84 OUA, NEP/*supra*/18, register Qb, fo 173.

85 T. Pierce, *A Correct Copy of Some Notes concerning God's Decrees, especially of Reprobation* (Oxford, 1671), pp. 32, 75, 78, 82. London publishing in these same years, however, was much more of a doctrinal free-for-all.

86 Wood, *Life and Times*, ii, p. 258.

87 S. Hutton, 'Thomas Jackson, Oxford Platonist, and William Twisse, Aristotelian', *Journal of the History of Ideas*, 39 (1978); S. Hutton ed., *Henry More (1614–1687): Tercentenary Studies* (Dordrecht, 1990), pp. 7–9, 62–5.

88 OUA, register Qb, fo 39; S. Parker, *A Free and Impartial Censure of the Platonick Philosophie* (Oxford, 1666), pp. 52–115; S. Parker, *An Account of the Nature and Extent of the Divine Dominion and Goodnesse, especially as they refer to the Origenian Hypothesis concerning the Pre-Existence of Souls* (Oxford, 1666), pp. 18–22, 44–112; Wallace, *Puritans*

    and Predestination, p. 167; G. Rust, *A Letter of Resolution concerning Origen and the Chief of his Opinions* (London, 1661), pp. 21, 58, 60: Bodl., press mark A. 4. 9. Linc., annotated by Thomas Barlow.

89 T. Barlow, *Several Miscellaneous and Weighty Cases of Conscience* (London, 1692); T. Barlow, *The Genuine Remains* (London, 1693). I am most grateful to Helen Powell for all her help concerning the very important Barlow papers at Queen's College, Oxford. Paul Morgan has similarly assisted me with Barlow's printed books in the Bodleian Library.

90 OUA, register Qb, fo 173; Heylyn, *Cyprianus Anglicus*, title-page, pp. 77, 126: Bodl., press mark NN. 118. Th., annotated by Thomas Barlow; Barlow, *The Genuine Remains*, pp. 191–3; QCL, MS 278 ('De Templis, eorum Antiquitate et Fabrica etc.') [fos 19–21], MS 278 ('An Answere to some Queries proposed by Mr W. A. 1671'), p. 6 and *passim*; Barlow, *Cases of Conscience*, pt 6; J. H. Pruett, *The Parish Clergy under the Later Stuarts; The Leicestershire Experience* (Urbana, Ill., 1978), p. 26.

91 '[Tracts] for and against Toleration anno 1667, 1668', pp. 71, 84, 86: Bodl. press mark B. 14. 15. Linc., annotated by Thomas Barlow; Bodl. MS Eng. lett. *c.* 328, fo 509; QCL, MS 280, fo 251v. The *DNB* claim that Barlow 'endorsed' plans for comprehension in 1667–68 confuses a narrative account of these events written by Barlow with his own personal views: '[Tracts] for and agains Toleration anno 1667, 1668', pp. 4–14. Previously, however, in the peculiar circumstances of 1660, Barlow *had* adopted a more tolerant stance: Barlow, *Cases of Conscience*, pt 1.

92 Wood, *Life and Times*, iii, p. 53; see pp. 320–39 below.

93 G. Bull, *Harmonia Apostolica, seu Binae Dissertationes* (London, 1670), sig. Av; G. Bull, *Examen Censurae: sive Responsio ad Quasdam Animadversiones* (London, 1676), sig. Av; T. Tully, *Justificatio Paulina sine Operibus ex Mente Ecclesiae Anglicanae* (Oxford, 1674), dedication; J. Tombes, *Animadversiones in Librum Georgii Bull, cui Titulum fecit Harmonia Apostolica* (Oxford, 1676), dedication; R. Nelson, *The Life of Dr George Bull, Lord Bishop of St David's* (London, 1713), p. 102.

94 Bull, *Harmonia Apostolica*, sig. a: Bodl. press mark B. 7. 11. Linc., annotated by Thomas Barlow.

95 G. Bull, *Harmonia Apostolica: or Two Dissertations*, trans. (Oxford, 1842), pp. ix–x, 20–1, 34, 71–6, 178, 194, 196–7, 213, 218–19; A. E. McGrath, *Iustitia Dei: a History of the Christian Doctrine of Justification* (Cambridge, 1986), ii, pp. 107–11.

96 Tully, *Justificatio Paulina*, sig. a3v, p. 138; *CSPD 1673–5*, p. 400.

97 Nelson, *Life of Dr George Bull*, pp. 102–3; QCL, MS 239, fo 140, 148–9; OUA, NEP/ supra/19, register Bd, fo 15v.

98 QCL, MS 240, MS 233, pp. 6–7, 116, 119, 229–33, 437, 489, MS 234, fos 2, 14, 26, 38. Barlow's surviving lectures may well be incomplete.

99 W. Stubbs, *Registrum Sacrum Anglicanum* (Oxford, 1897), p. 127; E. S. De Beer ed., *The Diary of John Evelyn* (Oxford, 1955), iv, pp. 66–7; *CSPD 1675–6*, pp. 78–9, 138; Tombes, *Animadversiones*, title-page verso.

100 I. M. Green, *The Re-establishment of the Church of England 1660–1663* (Oxford, 1978), pp. 23, 93, 97, 213; G. Bull, *Examen Censurae: or an Answer to Certain Strictures*, trans. (Oxford, 1843), pp. 230–3, 342–3; *The Life of Edward Earl of Clarendon*, i, p. 56; Tyacke, *Anti-Calvinists*, pp. 161–2, 266–8; *CSPD 1673–5*, pp. 527, 532.

101 L. du Moulin, *A Short and True Account of the Several Advances the Church of England hath made towards Rome* (London, 1680), p. 31; see also W. Jenkyn, *Celeusma seu Clamor ad Theologos Hierarchiae Anglicanae* (London, 1679), pp. 66–7, 83, 97.

102 W. Jacobson ed., *A Paraphrase and Annotations upon all the Epistles of St Paul* (Oxford, 1852), pp. iii–iv, 3–6; QCL, MS 234, fos 72v–73; Leeds, Yorkshire Archaeological Society, Woodhead papers, MS 51, fos 100r–v; M. Slusser, 'Abraham Woodhead (1608–78): Some Research Notes, Chiefly about his Writings', *Recusant History*, 15 (1981), 409, 412. I am grateful to Alan Davidson for bibliographical advice concerning Woodhead.

103 Woodhead papers, MS 45, pp. 54, 60, MS 51, fo 47v; UCA, registrum i (1509–1722), fos 40–51v, UCA, general account B (1668–1706). I am indebted to David Sturdy for help concerning the relations of Walker and Woodhead with University College.

104 J. Spelman, *Aelfredi Magni Anglorum Regis Invictissimi Vita Tribus Libris Comprehensa* (Oxford, 1678), sig. av pp. 4–6, 70–1; *VCH Oxon.*, iii, p. 177.

105 A. Woodhead, *Of the Benefits of our Saviour Jesus Christ to Mankind* (Oxford, 1680); Slusser, 'Abraham Woodhead', pp. 413–14; Wood, *Life and Times*, ii, pp. 421, 488; HMC, *Twelfth Report*, appx vii, p. 150; OUA, register Tb, fos 191r–v.

106 S. Johnson, *Julian the Apostate: being a Short Account of his Life, the Sense of Primitive Christians about his Succession, and their Behaviour towards Him* (London, 1682), pp. 59–61; Wood, *Life and Times*, iii, pp. 18–19; OUA, NEP/supra/20, register Be, fo 202v.

107 D. J. Milne, 'The Results of the Rye House Plot and their Influence upon the Revolution of 1688', *TRHS*, 5th ser., 1 (1951); *The Judgement and Decree of the University of Oxford . . . July 21 1683* (Oxford, 1683); OUA, register Be, fo 205v.

108 Wood, *Life and Times*, iii, pp. 19–20, 68–72, 117; P. Laslett, 'The English Revolution and Locke's *Two Treatises of Government*', *Cambridge Historical Journal*, 12 (1956); R. Ashcraft, *Revolutionary Politics and Locke's* Two Treatises of Government (Princeton, NJ, 1986), pp. 430–5.

109 Wood, *Life and Times*, iii, pp. 86, 208 (Halton had conducted the proceedings against James Parkinson); *The Lives of Illustrious Men. Written in Latin by C. Nepos and done into English by Several Hands* (Oxford, 1684), dedication; *CSPD 1686–7*, no. 1358.

110 *CSPD 1686–7*, no. 227; *Directions concerning Preachers* (London, 1685/6); E. Calamy, *An Historical Account of my own Life*, ed. J. T. Rutt (London, 1830), i, p. 272; G. V. Bennett, 'Loyalist Oxford and the Revolution' in L. S. Sutherland and L. G. Mitchell eds, *The History of the University of Oxford, V: the Eighteenth-Century* (Oxford, 1986), pp. 27–9.

111 Calamy, *An Historical Account of my own Life*, i, 275; T. J. Fawcett, *The Liturgy of Comprehension 1689* (Alcuin Club liv, 1973), pp. 29, 160–76; Wood, *Life and Times*, ii, p. 489.

112 OUA, NEP/subtus/29, register Bb, fo 3; A. Woodhead, *An Historical Narration of the Life and Death of our Lord Jesus Christ* (Oxford, 1685); Wood, *Life and Times*, iii, pp. 164–6.

113 Wood, *Life and Times*, iii, pp, 182–3, 198; *CSPD 1686–7*, nos 342, 492–3, 899; *Collectanea Curiosa*, ed., John Gutch (Oxford, 1781), i, pp. 288–9.

114 Wood, *Life and Times*, iii, p. 186; *CSPD 1686–7*, no. 679; G. Tullie, *A Discourse concerning the Worship of Images* (London, 1689), sig. A2r–v, pp. 13–14, 35; UCA,

copy of letter from Obadiah Walker to Dr John Radcliffe [1687]; *VCH Oxon.*, iii, pp. 68, 79.

115 J. B. Bossuet, *An Exposition of the Doctrine of the Catholic Church in Matters of Controversie . . . Done into English from the Fifth Edition in French* (London, 1685, 2nd edn, London, 1686); UCA, copy of letter from Obadiah Walker to Dr John Radcliffe [1687], endorsed: 'this letter not being much approved of had another from the fellows that privately accompanied it'; Wood, *Life and Times*, iii, p. 186; see p. 295 above.

116 Wood, *Life and Times*, iii, pp. 197–8, 201, 239; *CSPD 1686–7*, nos 1203, 1427; J. R. Bloxam ed., *Magdalen College and King James II 1686–1688* (OHS, vi, 1886) L. Brockliss, G. Harris, and A. Macintyre eds, *Magdalen College and the Crown: Essays for the Tercentenary of the Restoration of the College 1688* (Oxford, 1988).

117 A. Woodhead, *A Compendious Discourse on the Eucharist, with Two Appendixes* (Oxford, 1688), p. 191; A. Woodhead, *Two Discourses concerning the Adoration of our Blessed Saviour in the Holy Eucharist* (Oxford, 1687), pt 1, pp. 1–4, 16–20, 32; H. Aldrich, *A Reply to Two Discourses. Lately printed at Oxford concerning the Adoration of our Blesssssed Saviour in the Holy Eucharist* (Oxford, 1687), pp. 26, 37.

118 A. Woodhead, *Two Discourses. The First, concerning the Spirit of Martin Luther, and the Original of the Reformation. The Second, concerning the Celibacy of the Clergy* (Oxford, 1687), pt 1, pp. 13, 100; F. Atterbury, *An Answer to Some Considerations on the Spirit of Martin Luther and the Original of the Reformation* (Oxford, 1687), pp. 10–11, 60.

119 A. Woodhead, *Church-Government Part V. A Relation of the English Reformation and the Lawfulness thereof examined by the Theses delivered in the Four Former Parts* (Oxford, 1687); G. Smalridge, *Animadversions on the Eight Theses laid down and the Inferences deduced from them, in a Discourse entitled* Chuch-Government Part V (Oxford, 1687).

120 A. Woodhead ed., *Pietas Romana et Parisiensis, or a Faithful Relation of the Several Sorts of Charitable and Pious Works eminent in the Cities of Rome and Paris* (Oxford, 1687); A. Woodhead, *Two Discourses . . . The Second concerning the Celibacy of the Clergy* (Oxford, 1687); J. Harrington, *Some Reflexions upon a Treatise called* Pietas Romana et Parisiensis (Oxford, 1688); G. Tullie, *An Answer to a Discourse concerning the Celibacy of the Clergy* (Oxford, 1688).

121 S. Parker, *Reasons for Abrogating the Test, imposed upon all Members of Parliament anno 1678* (London, 1688), pp. 10–23, 36–7, 51–2.

122 Wood, *Life and Times*, iii, pp. 282, 285; G. Ashwell *De Socino et Socinianismo Dissertatio* (Oxford, 1680), dedication to Bishop Barlow.

123 Wilkins, *Concilia*, iv, pp. 625–6; H. Croft, *The Naked Truth. Or the True State of the Primitive Church* (London, 1675); A. Bury, *The Bow: or the Lamentation of David over Saul and Jonathan, applyed to the Royal and Blessed Martyr King Charles the I* (London, 1662), p. 44; A. Bury, *The Naked Gospel. Discovering i. what was the Gospel which our Lord and his Apostles preached, ii. what Additions and Alterations Latter Ages have made in it, iii. what Advantages and Damages have thereupon ensued* (London, 1690), preface and p. 17.

124 Bury, *The Naked Gospel*, pp. 9, 20, 40.

125 Fawcett, *The Liturgy of Comprehension*, pp. 66, 200–1; *Judicium et Decretum Universitatis Oxoniensis . . . contra Propositiones quasdam Impias et Hereticas, exscriptas et citatas ex Libello quodam . . . cui Titulus est* The Naked Gospel (Oxford, 1690); J. Harrington, *An Account of the Proceedings of . . . Jonathan Lord Bishop of Exeter in his late Visitation of*

Exeter College in Oxford (Oxford, 1690), pp. 22–3, 32, 55; A. Bury, *The Danger of Delaying Repentance* (London, 1692), pp. 7, 13, 16; H. Hammond, *Several Tracts* (London, 1646), pp. 37–70; C. W. Boase ed., *Registrum Collegii Exoniensis* (OHS, 1894), pp. cxxix–cxxx.

126 W. Nicholls, *An Answer to a Heretical Book called* The Naked Gospel (London, 1691); E. S. De Beer ed., *The Correspondence of John Locke* (Oxford, 1976–89), iv, pp. 12, 22, 150–1; A. Bury, *Latitudinarius Orthodoxus . . . contra Ineptias et Calumnias P. Jurieu* (London, 1697).

127 See pp. 324–5 below H. Hallywell, *Deus Justificatus: or the Divine Goodness vindicated and cleared, against the Assertors of Absolute and Inconditionate Reprobation* (London, 1668): this anti-Calvinist work was licensed by a chaplian of Archbishop Sheldon; H. Hickman, *Historia Quinq-Articularis Exarticulata, or Animadversions on Dr Heylyn's Quinquarticular History* (London, 1673); G. Burnet, *An Exposition of the Thirty-nine Articles* (London, 1699), pp. 148–52.

128 *The Works of the Learned and Pious Author of the Whole Duty of Man* (Oxford, 1684), sig. A3, pp. 63, 77; P. Elmen, 'Richard Allestree and the *Whole Duty of Man*', *Library*, 5th ser., 6 (1951); C. J. Sommerville, 'The Anti-Puritan Work Ethic', *JBS* 20:2 (1981).

129 See pp. 71–83 above.

130 The growing threat of anti-Trinitarianism, however, generated a series of Oxford responses from the 1690s onwords.

Chapter 12

Arminianism and the theology
of the Restoration Church

I

CURRENT understanding of Restoration religious thought remains, it has to be said, at a fairly primitive stage. Partly this reflects a failure to penetrate behind the printed sources, but a more fundamental problem is the conventional terminology of 'Latitudinarian' and 'High-Church' – which obscures rather than clarifies the questions at issue. Difficulties are further compounded by a comparative indifference to and even positive hostility towards theology. Thus it has been said that

> the sixteenth-century Anglican reformers, in contrast to their opposite numbers on the continent, were mercifully deficient in ideas and had little taste for speculative theology. Their methods were opportunist and hand to mouth, and they had no logical theory for what they were trying to do. The English Church consequently escaped the fate that befell so many Protestant bodies on the continent, of being saddled with some dominant theological idea which was to prove a mental and spiritual incubus to future generations.[1]

Although dating from the early 1940s, these words of Dean Addleshaw epitomise a still influential historiographical tradition. Yet just as such assumptions have now been challenged for the earlier seventeenth century,[2] so a similar case can be made for revising traditional views about the later Stuart period, and replacing an essentially Anglo-centric framework with a more international one which gives due weight to ideas.

Despite claims to the contrary, the English Reformation was from the outset indebted to the continent. At first the debt was largely informal, as for example with the famous Tyndale New Testament which drew heavily on the teachings of Luther.[3] During the reign of Edward VI, however, Archbishop Cranmer issued invitations to leading European theologians to come and help forward the English reformation process. Among those who accepted were

Martin Bucer and Peter Martyr, between them contributing significantly to the Reformed bias which came to characterise the Church of England.[4] The Marian exile and subsequent restoration of Protestantism reinforced this Reformed or 'Calvinist' orientation of English theology. Furthermore those who stood out against the trend also drew sustenance from continental sources.[5] At the same time this internationalism was rooted in the early Christian past, involving not just new critical editions of the Bible but of the patristic writers as well. Yet the native English contribution was distinctly limited and the rather unflattering picture which suggests itself, of England as an intellectual off-shore island, contains considerable truth. Of course the ideas flowing in from abroad were refracted by local circumstances, but the agenda was to a considerable extent determined elsewhere.

The nature of the English anti-Calvinist reaction which set in during the last decade of Elizabeth's reign has been much disputed, although all parties to the modern controversy would probably acknowledge an international component. One of the key questions, however, concerns the inspiration for those who increasingly distanced themselves from Calvinism. Did they do so on the basis of a better appreciation of the English Reformation, as informed by extensive borrowings from Catholic sources, or were they rather sucked into a contemporary European debate? As is well known, that debate centred on the theology of grace and none of the major Christian denominations of the time remained immune.[6] At its heart lay contested interpretations of St Augustine's writings against the Pelagians, and even more of St Paul's epistles. It was difficult, if not impossible, to remain disengaged since Paul and Augustine between them constituted so much of the Reformation bedrock.[7] Nevertheless, various and by no means mutually exclusive routes could lead one to adopt an anti-Calvinist stance. Reading of the New Testament as a unity might encourage a relatively optimistic view of humanity's role in the salvific process, as did many patristic authors other than Augustine.[8] Medieval and (to an even greater extent) post-Reformation Catholicism was also potentially subversive. Then there were the second-generation Lutherans or Melanchthonians, and from the 1590s onwards the Dutch Arminians or Remonstrants. They were soon joined by the more radical Socinians, with their base of operations in Poland.[9] All these Protestant groups proved hostile to doctrinal assertions about the unconditional nature of divine predestination. Thus Calvinists had an almost embarrassingly wide range of terms available with which to label their opponents, and as a consequence strict accuracy was often sacrificed in the interests of polemical impact. Yet it does not follow that the Calvinists can therefore be convicted of creating a world of illusions which had no basis in reality.

Irenicists, then and later, deplored all the name-calling and internecine strife.[10] Those in authority also sought to muzzle the warring factions at home, although contamination from outside was difficult to prevent even in a country as centralised as England. None the less English Calvinists were curbed under Charles I and discussion of the theology of grace was generally discouraged. Indeed it remains a question how far a coherent anti-Calvinist or Arminian body of thought existed in England at this juncture. Certainly up until the late 1620s Calvinist doctrine continued to ring out loud and clear. But in so far as its purveyors assumed a domestic foe were they merely mistaken? On the contrary, the suspicion must be that their refutations were increasingly hitting home. Moreover there are definite signs of a growing Arminian faction at both English universities during the 1630s. This decade also saw some of the first allegations of Socinianism, both in the strict anti-Trinitarian meaning and in the more general rationalizing sense which also served as an encoded synonym for Arminianism.[11] These developments, however, were cut short by the onset of the Civil War and the defeat of the royalists. Calvinism swept back in the wake of the parliamentarian victories, and Arminianism was banished from the high ground which it had begun to assume under Archbishop Laud. On the other hand a new sectarian Arminianism sprang up, while episcopalians found a fresh weapon with which to counter Calvinism in the form of Antinomianism – an extreme rendition of the consequences of absolute election. The Cambridge Platonists also began to sap Calvinist orthodoxy from within, during the 1650s.[12]

Much of the foregoing is fairly familiar terrain. From the Restoration period onwards, however, guides become fewer and less certain – based almost exclusively as they are on a sampling of the contemporary printed literature. Modern accounts tend to give the lion's share of attention to so-called 'Latitudinarianism', defined as a religious stance 'which sought to minimize doctrinal discord by emphasizing the role of natural rather than revealed theology'. Breadth of doctrine is supposed to have gone hand in hand with toleration of Dissent, as well as providing a mindset sympathetic to the new science – the 'religion of reason' over that of 'grace'. Those dubbed 'High-Church', by contrast, are conceived of as being on the other side of this religious divide, although the positive doctrinal content of their views remains imprecise.[13] But here we should heed the recent suggestion that the 'Latitudinarian' theology in question was 'commonplace' rather than exceptional, involving a widespread rejection of Calvinist soteriology by members of the Restoration Church, at the same time noting how few initially were the advocates of toleration. Nevertheless the extent to which these Restoration 'Arminians', as Dissenters were quick to call them, came to represent a 'new theological consensus' within the late seventeenth-century Church remains unclear, as does their relationship to the at least superficially similar pre-Civil War developments. Again, how far can this new 'consensus' be assimilated to Arminianism as such? Alternatively should we think, as has been suggested, of a distinctively English 'middle way' ?[14] More problematic still is the connection with Socinianism. Is there any truth in the frequent allegations?[15]

Answers to these and related questions are unlikely to be found simply by further trawling through the printed literature, even with a more finely meshed net. Although historians, particularly those who neglect the archives, sometimes complain of an almost fetishistic approach to manuscripts by certain of their colleagues, a counter-case exists, from the early-modern period onwards, concerning the tyranny of print. For it is widely assumed that every-thing of importance to contemporaries, at least in the realm of thought, will have survived in either book or pamphlet form. This, however, betrays a very naive trust in market forces, which can inhibit as well as liberate potential authors. In addition, during the seventeenth century, there would appear to be a growing disjunction between Latin manuscript and vernacular print. Other constraints also, such as censorship, are known to have operated. Therefore, wherever possible, we must cross-check and supplement print with manuscript.

As regards the Restoration Church, two major surviving manuscript archives comprise the papers of Thomas Barlow, Lady Margaret professor of divinity at Oxford University from 1660 to 1676, and those of Joseph Beaumont, Regius professor of divinity at Cambridge University from 1674 to 1699.[16] These collections have the added attraction that their original owners belonged to the two rival theological wings of the Established Church of the day: Barlow was demonstrably a Calvinist, while Beaumont by his own admission was a 'Remonstrant' or Arminian. Partly on the basis of these papers, Barlow and Beaumont can also be located more widely in their uni-versity contexts. By this period the English clergy were an almost entirely graduate profession, which meant that the vast majority had at least a first degree from either Oxford or Cambridge. Those with a more serious interest in theology went on, via the MA, to the degree of BD and perhaps ultimately a DD as well. For them the outlook of the professoriate was of potentially great importance, helping to shape and direct their own courses of study. Manuscript texts of many of the lectures given by both Barlow and Beaumont survive, and in the case of the latter a very full list exists as well of divinity theses determined by him at Cambridge during the twenty-five year period of his tenure. It is possible to supplement these divinity theses from the papers of Beaumont's predecessor as Cambridge Regius professor from 1661 to 1674, Peter Gunning.[17] An equivalent list for Oxford University, covering the last four decades of the seventeenth century, can in addition be reconstructed from entries in the university registers[18] – a source not available for Cam-bridge. All this material consists of Latin manuscript.

One of the most startling conclusions to emerge from a comparison of the Barlow and Beaumont papers, as well as other related documents, is the marked difference between Oxford and Cambridge theology in the years after 1660. While traces of such a divergence are present before the Civil War,[19] they subsequently become much more obvious. Broadly speaking, Oxford continued the cautious approach pioneered by Archbishop Laud; controversial topics, especially in relation to Arminianism, were on the whole avoided and a rather bland diet of divinity disputations was provided. At Cambridge, by contrast, any such inhibitions were rapidly shed and by the mid 1670s at the latest a full-blooded Arminianism emerged as the order of the day; indeed what had passed for orthodoxy under King James I was now stood on its head. No attempt was made at balancing rival points of view, and disagreement, where it existed, had to be shrouded in silence. These differences are all the more striking in that at both universities during the 1650s Calvinism had been the official orthodoxy, as can be seen from the divinity theses maintained respectively at the Oxford Act and Cambridge Commencement.[20] Nor did either university experience a major change of personnel as a consequence of the Restoration.

Clearly there was a contingent element in the theological divergence of the two universities after 1660, not least the death in 1661 of the Cambridge Lady Margaret professor of divinity – Richard Love. The latter was a Calvinist episcopalian survivor from the pre-Civil War period, who had remained in Cambridge during all the changes of regime.[21] Moreover he was probably behind the publication at Cambridge in 1660 of Samuel Gardiner's Latin treatise *De Efficacia Gratiae Christi Convertentis*. Based on a Cambridge DD thesis of 1658, it argued at length against the Remonstrants and in favour of the irresistibility of grace. Gardiner jointly dedicated his efforts to Love, the master of his former college, and to Anthony Tuckney, the Regius professor of divinity.[22] Tuckney was deprived in June 1661, for nonconformity, but Love was in high favour at the time of his death that February. Their professorial replacements were Peter Gunning and John Pearson. Gunning's views have to be recovered from a series of surviving volumes of chaotic scribblings – commonplaces, sermon notes and disputations now bound together roughly by topic. They include what appear to be divinity theses determined by Gunning as Cambridge Regius professor, and as such indicate that the Cambridge Arminian pattern was already established during the 1660s. Although dates and names of disputants are generally lacking, the frequent numbering '1' and '2' implies that these were originally pairs of divinity theses now broken up by subject matter. (At Cambridge, theology candidates invariably maintained two theses consecutively when they came to dispute formally.)

Many of these theses among Gunning's papers concern the key doctrine of perseverance and all are phrased in an anti-Calvinist sense, as for example, 'The truly regenerate and justified can fall totally and finally'. There are also some related sermon notes, in which Gunning refutes the notion of

'Calvinisticall indefectibility'.[23] Other theses link faith and works in the process of justification: 'Good works are a necessary condition of our justification in the eyes of God'.[24] From further notes of his, Gunning can be shown to hold that divine election is conditional on faith and works as well as grace. His position appears identical to that maintained by John Pearson in his surviving 'Lectiones de Deo et Attributis', delivered in the early 1660s.[25] There is in fact no trace here, nor later in the voluminous writings of Beaumont, of the 'middle way', which combined belief in the absolute election of a minority with the conditional fate of a majority who might or might not choose to co-operate with God's grace.[26] As we shall see, such was more often the doctrinal position of ex-Calvinists unable to emancipate themselves entirely from their previous assumptions.

At Oxford the Calvinist equivalent of Richard Love was Thomas Barlow, with the important difference that Barlow survived. But grounds also exist for thinking that more than accident was at work here. For there are signs of a Calvinist presence among the highest Oxford echelons until at least the end of the century; indeed between 1680 and 1691 both the Regius professor, William Jane, and the Lady Margaret professor, John Hall, were reputedly Calvinists.[27] In this light, Barlow's appointment as Lady Margaret professor at Oxford in 1660 was less eccentric than it otherwise appears. Yet Oxford too had a strong Arminian lobby, which included the Regius professor of divinity from 1663 to 1680, Richard Allestree, as well as Thomas Pierce, president of Magdalen College. (Pierce had published prolifically in defence of Arminianism during the 1650s.)[28] The net effect at Oxford was something approaching stalemate. Not only was the Arminian controversy avoided in disputations, but Barlow also eschewed it in his lectures. Whether Allestree did so too is not known, although his Arminian views can be deduced from his published sermons.[29] Nevertheless it was during the 1660s that Barlow compiled a manuscript volume entitled 'Controversiae Arminianae, Pelagianae [et] Socinianae', which makes abundantly plain the depth of his commitment to Calvinism. In an historical preface, Barlow describes the 1620s as a crucial turning point when the English Arminians first dared to show their heads.[30] Barlow's bracketing of Arminianism and Socinianism is also suggestive. The two bodies of teaching overlapped considerably, yet it was possible to attack Arminianism under the guise of Socinianism. Barlow indeed did just this in the course of his lectures during the early 1670s, pillorying the English theological writer George Bull as a Socinian. In his book *Harmonia Apostolica* (1670) Bull had linked works together with faith as part of justification, while providing broad hints of a more generally anti-Calvinist stance as regards predestination.[31]

At Cambridge, on the other hand, Bull's views probably now counted as orthodox. There the Calvinist flame appears to have been kept alive largely by

John Edwards, who had resigned his St John's College fellowship in the 1660s and by the late 1690s was a private Cambridge resident. Most of Edwards's published Calvinist writing dates from after the turn of the century, although it was clearly in gestation during the previous decades. Judging by his various autobiographical remarks, Edwards found very few like-minded spirits among leading Cambridge academics.[32] Ironically, however, greater tensions seem to have existed between Arminians, like Gunning and Beaumont, on the one hand, and Cambridge Platonists like Henry More on the other, and this despite the fact that the Dutch Remonstrants were from the early 1660s in contact with both groups. Thus a letter from the Remonstrant Arnold Poelenburg to Isaac Vossius in 1664 sent greetings to Gunning and More at Cambridge and Pierce at Oxford, in the context of a scheme whereby it was hoped the English Church would extend fraternal recognition to the Dutch Remonstrants.[33] The situation is further complicated by the fact that in strict theological terms More was less close to the Dutch Remonstrants than were those of the school of Gunning and Beaumont. Thus More was an exponent of the 'middle way' concerning predestination and considered the Remonstrants to be generally over-optimistic in their view of human nature. At the same time More largely shared Remonstrant views on toleration, which were anathema to churchmen such as Gunning and Beaumont. More was already identified as a man of 'latitude', on the strength especially of his book *An Explanation of the Grand Mystery of Godliness*, which had been published at the Restoration. *An Explanation* argues in passing for an extremely comprehensive religious settlement, that would allow most Dissenters to join the new establishment, as well as advocating 'liberty of conscience'. More was somewhat vague over legal details, although he clearly envisaged modifications both of episcopal government and ceremonial requirements.[34]

Latitudinarianism in the context of More's circle, however, had additional connotations to those of comprehension and toleration. For as well as wishing to restrict further the fundamentals of faith, More held a number of other positive and highly idiosyncratic doctrines concerning the soul. Here it is noteworthy that Beaumont in his published objections to More of 1665 asks, apropos the reuniting of body and soul at the resurrection, 'are the words in the Creed to be understood figuratively or properly? I hope not figuratively: this would let the *latitudinarians* loose to make rare sport with all the articles of our faith'.[35] The speculations of More about the soul struck many of his readers as heterodox, although this was a grey area doctrinally in terms of most official formularies. Particularly controversial was More's teaching on the pre-existence of the soul. Deriving their views from the patristic writer Origen, the mid-seventeenth-century advocates of pre-existence explicitly linked it to the Arminian–Calvinist controversy. As early as 1659, in his

The Immortality of the Soul, More wrote of pre-existence as being a 'key' to unlock the mystery of God's providence.[36] Instead of explaining sin as a consequence of the fall of a single individual, namely Adam, holders of the Origenist 'hypothesis' postulated the lapse of myriads of free pre-existent souls. This was their explanation of the manifold presence of evil in the world, and one which claimed both to resolve the apparent contradiction of immaculate souls in sinful bodies and to vindicate God's essential goodness.

At least two works by other writers elaborated More's teaching on pre-existence in the years 1661–62. *A Letter of Resolution* (1661), attributed to George Rust, while rejecting the Calvinist doctrine of absolute reprobation argued that the Arminians had not entirely vindicated God from the charge of being the author of sin. The point was reiterated by Joseph Glanvill, in his *Lux Orientalis* (1662). Pre-existence 'supposeth us to have sinned and deserved all the misery we suffer . . . before we came hither'. Significantly, the opening sentence of Glanvill's preface to *Lux Orientalis* reads: 'It is none of the least commendable indulgences of our Church that she allows us a *latitude* of judging in points of speculation'.[37] Despite the general tendency of Oxford University to fight shy of controversy, in May 1663 Nicholas Meese of Trinity College, for one of his divinity theses, denied that the 'pre-existence of souls, which the Origenists assert, is consonant with Holy Scripture'.[38] Three years later, in 1666, Samuel Parker, also of Trinity College, published at Oxford to the same effect, his views licensed by the vice-chancellor, Robert Saye. As part of his opening section on 'God's dominion', Parker endorsed the Dutch Remonstrant Simon Episcopius's interpretation of Romans 9 – the crucial biblical text for Calvinist teaching on absolute election and reprobation.

Parker, following Episcopius, contended that Romans 9 does not relate to 'God's eternal decrees' but instead refers to 'the rejecting of the Jews, because of their obstinate adherence to the Mosaick Law', and the 'calling of the Gentiles, because of their faith and closing with the gospel'. Not content with refuting pre-existence, Parker rejected Platonic metaphysics as a whole. An enthusiast for the new science, he was also implacably opposed to Dissenter requests for toleration. Traditionally Parker has been categorised as 'High-Church', but his case provides an object lesson in the difficulties of the rival term 'Latitudinarian' as it has come to be used by modern historians. For if the 'religion of reason' means anything then surely Parker was an exponent of it. 'Those men that have laid aside the free and impartial use of their reasons are just as fit for religion as sheep and oxen', is how he put it in 1666, and this refrain runs through his subsequent writings against the Dissenter 'herd', who in their turn objected that Parker had collapsed 'evangelical grace' into 'moral virtue'. To which he replied that the 'Christian institution is not for the substance of it any new religion, but only a more perfect digest of the eternal rules of nature and right reason'. Parker was to use some of the same arguments later, when refuting 'atheism'.[39]

II

Both Arminians and Socinians were accused of placing excessive reliance on reason. The Calvinist John Edwards, for example, in a published work of 1711 wrote of Arminians 'giving way to the suggestions of mere human reason, and preferring these to the infallible oracles of the scriptures'. Conversely the Arminian Beaumont, in an undated manuscript sermon, commented that "tis most unreasonable for reasonable men to expect that God should preserve them whether they will or no, or force them to injoy the benefits of that grace which they willfully neglect'. But reason misapplied could lead to heresy. Thus, in another unpublished sermon, Beaumont invited his auditory:

> View but an old Arian, or a young Socinian, birds of a fether – onely the later is the blacker and nearer the infernal colour. View him well and tell me yf his proud and therfore mistaken reason yoaks him not to all the strange fancies that sceptical imaginacion can produce, yf his floating principles lead him not by vicissitude to beleve contraries, and be of as many religions as he is of apprehensions. Of all madness the most unhappy and incurable is that *quando cum ratione insanis*, and to this disease is the wretched heretik yoked. For reason itself, if fairly deduced and built up from its own bottom, opens a direct way to the Catholik faith and to none but that.

In this same sermon, Beaumont went on to refer to the Fifth Monarchists, who had recently rebelled in the name of King Jesus, as suffering from 'a madness so exorbitant that the professors of it can pretend no argument in its defence but wilde enthusiasmes, more irrational than the logik of Bedlam'.[40]

As has been pointed out, the apostles of rational religion in these years were generally concerned to counter the twin threats of Puritan 'enthusiasm' and secular freethinking. Meanwhile the theme of reason was also handled in divinity disputations at both Oxford and Cambridge. Certainly by the 1690s it was being maintained at Oxford that God is 'knowable by the light of reason'. At the same time Christian dogma itself was held to be a matter of revelation. Similar arguments are to be found considerably earlier at Cambridge, where in December 1675 James Leigh of Christ's College maintained that 'We derive our first notions of God's existence from the created order'. As at Oxford, however, it was denied that human reason could be the rule of faith. Determining a thesis to this effect, in November 1690, Beaumont argued that Christian mysteries were beyond the sphere of 'right reason'. The latter he elsewhere defined as the 'law of the mind', as opposed to that of 'the members'.[41] It would be wrong, however, to assume that Calvinists, unlike Arminians, were precluded from using such arguments, since both parties shared a belief in the existence of innate ideas on which depended the notion of right reason. Preaching at the Cambridge Commencement in July 1699, the Calvinist Edwards took as his subject 'the eternal and intrinsick reasons of good and evil'. His sermon, as published, carried a joint *imprimatur*, including Beaumont as Regius professor. Among other propositions, Edwards taught that 'religion and virtue are ingrafted in our very nature, and are every waies suited to the frame of rational creatures'. Edwards also quoted Plato on the 'idea and pattern of all goodness'. The 'innate principles of good and evil thus implanted in us are a certain and unquestionable eviction of the intrinsick excellency of the moral religion'. A prime target of these remarks turns out to be John Locke, who in his *Essay Concerning Human Understanding* (1690) had delivered a body blow to the concept of innate ideas.[42]

Interestingly the *Essay* found some of its warmest supporters among the Dutch Remonstrants, into whose company Locke had gravitated during his exile of the 1680s. The initial attraction was partly a mutual belief in toleration, but also a common theology. The latter emerges particularly clearly from the paraphrase and notes of Locke on St Paul's epistles, which he wrote at the end of his life. He remarks, for instance, of Romans 9 that

> what is said of God's exerciseing of an absolute power, according to the good pleasure of his will, relates onely to nations or bodys politique of men incorporated in civil societies . . . but extends not to their eternal state in an other world considered as particular persons, wherein they stand each man by himself upon his own bottom and shall so answer separately at the day of judgement.

His brand of Arminianism, however, was a radical one which served further to distance him from pillars of the establishment such as Beaumont. Indeed Locke was, in this respect, much closer to the sectarian Arminianism of the Interregnum.[43] Some of these differences are highlighted by the first set of lectures which Beaumont gave as Regius professor in 1674, under the title 'De Libertate Christiana'. In the course of these lectures, Beaumont attacked Simon Episcopius for extending such liberty beyond the proper bounds. Beaumont singled out two of Episcopius's arguments. The first concerned the laity, both men and women, being allowed to administer the eucharist in case of necessity. From Beaumont's point of view this undermined the ordained ministry. Secondly Episcopius had argued for the toleration of religious meetings by groups outside the Established Church, which for Beaumont amounted *ipso facto* to schism. Despite recognising the doctrinal disagreement between Remonstrants and Counter-Remonstrants, Beaumont could not endorse the effective separatism of the former. Moreover he made no comment here on the merits of their respective views concerning predestination.[44]

In these lectures on Christian liberty, Beaumont defined his own position *vis-à-vis* the English Dissenters. Six months later, however, he turned to the more weighty business of St Paul's Epistle to the Romans. This series of lectures was to last from October 1674 to October 1693, and comprises Beaumont's *magnum opus* in a very real sense. The model adopted is analogous to that of the sermon-lecture, Beaumont doggedly proceeding verse by verse from the beginning to the end during this nineteen-year period. His method involved drawing on a group of ancient and modern guides, between them providing something of a cross-section of opinion. Perhaps not surprisingly, of the many patristic writers quoted it is Chrysostom who features most prominently. The schoolmen, by comparison, are largely absent. Among post-Reformation commentators Gulielmus Estius represents the Roman Catholics, while Beza's New Testament version balances that of Erasmus. The pronounced Augustinianism of Estius, a Jesuit from the Spanish Netherlands, might also be thought to provide a counter-weight to Chrysostom. On the other hand, the citation of Grotius's *Annotations* on the Bible was almost *de rigeur* for a serious scholar. Nevertheless, it still comes as a shock to find that the other principal commentary used by Beaumont was that of the Socinian Johann Crell or Crellius.[45]

To some extent Crell and Estius were employed as foils by Beaumont, in countering Socinian denials of the Trinity and certain Roman Catholic doctrines. Yet he clearly also regarded them as learned authors in their own right, whose explanations of the text were worthy of serious consideration. Thus Beaumont referred to the 'happy and excellent acumen' of Crell, his Socinian 'dogmata' excluded. Apart from refuting their anti-Trinitarianism, Beaumont only took serious issue with the Socinians over the claim that God was ignorant of future contingents; heaping them with ironic praise, he accused the Socinians of being too clever by half in this attempt to vindicate human free will.[46] Therefore it seems legitimate to infer that in the absence of an available Remonstrant commentary on Romans at this date, Crell's work served Beaumont, at least in part, as a substitute. Clearly Beaumont was not a Socinian in the strict sense. Nonetheless his open resort to such a commentary was an act of considerable boldness, rendering him liable to charges both of heresy and of corrupting his auditory. Whether he was in any sense 'guilty' is an interesting question. At the same time the thrust of these lectures by Beaumont is Arminian or Remonstrant, although he avoids using either term. Thus Romans 9 is interpreted in a sense favourable to the Arminians, and the concomitants of conditional election and falling from grace are affirmed.[47] But it is the divinity theses determined by Beaumont as Regius professor which throw his Arminianism into starkest relief; even as bare assertions they are dramatic enough, although in most cases we possess his actual arguments as well.

The tone was set as early as June 1674, when Benjamin Johnson of Sidney Sussex College maintained that 'God under the Gospel does not deal with men like an absolute lord, but by means of a covenant and contract'. In his own determination, Beaumont took the opportunity to interpret Romans 9 in an anti-Calvinist sense – arguing that Esau and Jacob stood respectively for the Jews and the Gentiles. The following February 1675 Robert Peachey of Pembroke Hall chose the thesis 'The justified persevere by means of grace freely accepted'. That June Joseph Johnson of St John's College argued that 'St Paul in Romans 7 does not describe the state of a regenerate person'. Precisely this Arminian interpretation had proved a major *cause célèbre* at Cambridge during the reign of James I, when in 1617 the Regius professor at the time, John Richardson, had been forced to resign as a consequence.[48] Now apparently the same teaching was considered orthodox. In January 1676 Peachey's thesis on perseverance was endorsed by Thomas Lovett of Christ's College, who maintained that 'The faithful and regenerate can fall from grace'. Beaumont in his comments claimed that this was in line with the sixteenth of the Thirty-nine Articles, adding that not simply falling but 'final' falling from grace was involved. Moreover he went even further – citing the cases of David in the Old Testament and Peter in the New Testament, whom he described as being of the 'elect' when they fell.[49]

In May 1676 Edward Duncon of Pembroke Hall can be found arguing for the 'necessary efficacy' of works in justification. Equally daring, that June Richard Salter of Jesus College asserted that 'Faith is rightly resolved into the moral motives of believers'. In his determination Beaumont distinguished between internal and external motives, the former consisting of the 'energy' of God's grace and the latter of morals alone. It was Benjamin Calamy of St Catherine's Hall, however, who really took the Calvinist bull by the horns in November 1676, with the thesis that 'The ninth chapter of Romans does not deal with the absolute election of individual persons to salvation or the rejection of the same'. Although describing it as the 'most vexed question of questions', Beaumont agreed with him. As for predestination, he said it depended on belief or its lack and was therefore conditional not absolute. Many of these topics were to recur. Thus falling from grace was maintained in March 1677 by John Allen of Trinity College, while in January 1680 James Crompton of Jesus College carried the attack on absolute predestination to new heights: 'The decrees of God concerning the eternal state of individuals are conditional'. Beaumont made it clear that both election and reprobation were meant, and neither here nor elsewhere is there any mention of a predestinarian 'middle way'. The 'irresistible' operation of 'efficacious' grace was also denied by James Clark of King's College in November 1681, and

Calvinist teaching on perseverance came under further pressure in May 1683 when John Sturges of Christ's College maintained that 'True believers can fall from faith both totally and finally'. Similarly the role of works in justification was stated increasingly baldly, as by Henry Firebrace of Trinity College in May 1684: 'Good works are necessary conditions to justification'. Nevertheless there were limits to this assault; the doctrine of original sin, for instance, was reaffirmed in these years. Furthermore anti-Calvinism was not apparently voiced at the Commencement itself until July 1697, when George Stanhope, a future Dean of Canterbury, offered an Arminian interpretation of Romans 8, 9 and 11. Nor was it the practice of Beaumont to name Calvinists and Arminians as such: he simply spoke of the 'adversarii'. Only during the last year of his life, in February 1699, did he break this rule – coming, as it were, out of the closet and stating that, in his opinion, 'God is a Remonstrant' in matters of grace. This was how he concluded his determination of a thesis by Daniel Duckfield of Christ's College, who had denied the irresistibility of God's grace in 'conversion'.[50]

Yet, countervailing factors existed even at Cambridge. We have already remarked on the presence of John Edwards and his somewhat ambiguous relations with the university. In addition, as late as 1691 a Calvinist commentary on the Thirty-nine Articles, by Thomas Rogers, was printed at Cambridge by John Hayes – printer to the University. This work, in its revised form, dated back to 1608 and represented a Jacobean response to emergent anti-Calvinism.[51] Originally published at Cambridge and running through numerous early editions, after the Restoration it was first reprinted there in 1675, and again in 1681 and 1691. For whatever reasons, not apparently until the early 1690s did the Cambridge Arminians seek to cut off this rival Calvinist source in their midst. By 1694, however, they had seemingly persuaded Hayes to reprint a commentary on the Thirty-nine Articles more favourable to Arminianism. This was John Ellis's *Defensio*, first published at London in 1660. Reprinted with it, as an appendix, was another and earlier tract of 1651. The latter contained a very critical history of the notorious Lambeth Articles of 1595, by means of which Cambridge Calvinists of an earlier day had sought to fasten their teachings more firmly on the English Church. Archbishop Whitgift is described by the author as only agreeing to the Lambeth Articles 'thro' easiness and a fear of disagreement, since he could not make good his own opinion'. Here we do indeed encounter the 'middle way' doctrine of predestination, in the views of John Overall which are also included, as well as the full Arminian *avant la lettre* teaching of Peter Baro.[52] The combined work would therefore seem calculated to appeal to a broad range of anti-Calvinist opinion. As printed at Cambridge in 1694, it carried a joint *imprimatur* which featured Joseph Beaumont as Regius professor, and a new preface stated that the book was especially intended for use by ordination candidates. Two years later, in 1696, this edition was reprinted at Amsterdam.

The situation at Oxford is more difficult to plumb, but as already indicated a powerful Calvinist presence probably persisted there into the 1690s and beyond. The evidence at present is hearsay concerning the Calvinism of William Jane, Regius professor of divinity at Oxford from 1680 to 1707. We can, however, approach nearer to the true state of affairs through the pages of a remarkable book published at Oxford in four parts between 1693 and 1698. Entitled *A Preservative against Socinianism*, the author was Jonathan Edwards, principal of Jesus College, Oxford, and not to be confused with John Edwards of Cambridge. The book carries the *imprimatur* of Henry Aldrich, Dean of Christ Church, in his capacity as vice-chancellor of Oxford. Ostensibly directed against Socinianism, as the title implies, the approach of the book is reminiscent of that adopted earlier by the Calvinist Thomas Barlow. According to Edwards, Socinianism represents a melding together of the old Arian and Pelagian heresies, concerning the Trinity and free will respectively, and he goes on quite explicitly to include the Dutch Remonstrants Simon Episcopius and Philippus van Limborch in his general indictment. Episcopius and Limborch are described as 'friends to the Socinians' and 'in some notions' agreeing with them. They are also said to 'follow' both Pelagius and 'reason rather than revelation'. Limborch's *Theologia Christiana* (1686) is characterised as 'one of the corruptest' systems of divinity that 'has been published of late years'. Edwards avoids plainly declaring his own doctrinal position, although he appears to identify with the views of the British delegation to the Synod of Dort in 1618–19. (The latter were unquestionably Calvinist, albeit moderate.) Moreover the Socinians and Remonstrants are together ridiculed by Edwards for over-reacting against the doctrine of God's eternal decrees, and as a consequence involving themselves in endless contradictions.[53] He does also refute the anti-Trinitarian teaching of the Socinians, but his target is clearly much broader.

Oxford and Cambridge, however, differed in other ways as well as over their treatment of the Arminian question. While disputants at both universities, from time to time, maintained that episcopacy was *iure divino*, Cambridge men went further and argued that the sacraments were only normally valid when administered by episcopally ordained clergy. This, for example, was one of the theses chosen by John Millington of Magdalen College in June 1685. Along with this exalted view of the priesthood, went an emphasis on ceremonies at Cambridge where, unlike Oxford, 'adoration towards the altar' was intermittently defended as a thesis, in April 1676 by Andrew Baron of Peterhouse, in March 1677 by John Allen of Trinity College and in June 1687 by Alexander Bickerton – again of Peterhouse. Here we should note in passing that Beaumont was master of Peterhouse as well as Regius professor, and had begun his career there before the Civil War under Matthew Wren and John Cosin when the new Peterhouse chapel was variously regarded as the ceremonial glory or scandal of the university.[54] On the other hand both Oxford and Cambridge disputants continued to describe Dissenters as 'schismatics', even after the passing of the Toleration Act in 1689. Furthermore the Calvinist Thomas Barlow, now Bishop of Lincoln, covered his own printed copy of the Toleration Act with splenetic graffiti to the same effect. He added that Parliament had no right to legislate on such matters, which were the province of the clergy in Convocation.[55]

III

But can one deduce from any of this the existence of a distinctive 'High-Church' position? If historians are to continue using the category, then at the very least it will be essential to distinguish sharply between theology and ecclesiology. For the Oxford evidence, in particular, suggests that it was possible to combine doctrinal Calvinism with a highly exclusive view of the Church. Barlow apart, it was William Jane, as prolocutor of the lower house of Convocation in November 1689, who pronounced the deathly words 'nolumus leges Angliae mutare', which spelt an effective end of the comprehension proposals to reconcile at least some Dissenters to the English Church. Jane was supported in his obstructionist attitude by Dean Aldrich of Christ Church and Principal Edwards of Jesus.[56] Yet the terminological difficulty goes much deeper because of the realignments brought about by the political *fait accompli* of the Toleration Act. Overt supporters of toleration among the established clergy were very thin on the ground before the momentous events of 1688–9. Even someone like Gilbert Burnet appears to have embraced toleration rather late in the day, and probably not before the 1680s. Many other future supporters of toleration dragged their feet considerably longer. Thus the fall-out from the Catholicising policies of James II benefited Dissenters much more than any clerical lobby.[57]

This issue is important because, as we have noted, attitudes to toleration are deemed to be a major distinguishing mark between 'High-Church' and 'Latitudinarian' positions. At the same time Latitudinarians of a post-1689 vintage appear to have been almost universally Arminian in their theology. Hence it was no accident that the Dutch Remonstrants identified so strongly with the leadership of the English Church as it emerged under William III.[58] For many years indeed they had tended to make approving remarks about bishops, especially in an English context, and Limborch had gone so far as to dedicate the second volume of Episcopius's *Opera* (1665) collectively to the English clerical establishment. Yet the connecting thread between Henry More's circle and the Latitudinarian leadership after the Williamite revolution appears rather tenuous, and the religious terms which were in fashion from the 1690s onwards are of dubious use in helping to interpret the history of the previous decades. Surviving traces of an earlier usage must not be allowed to obscure the very real novelty of the post-revolutionary situation.

It was particularly in the pamphlet wars sparked by ecclesiastical party politics during the 1690s that the terms 'Latitude' and 'High-Church' began their modern careers. Complicated jurisdictional questions jostled with the issues of toleration and comprehension, as well as increasingly frequent aspersions of heresy. The exchanges between Richard West and Henry Sacheverell at the end of William III's reign are fairly symptomatic. Despite Sacheverell entitling his pamphlet of 1702 *The Character of a Low-Churchman*, this description never really displaced the term Latitudinarian – which he also hurled at his opponents. The same year, 1702, William Jones dedicated to Archbishop Thomas Tenison his translation of Limborch's *Theologia Christiana*. Claiming to be a follower of Bishop Burnet, Jones singled out 'toleration' as a key issue distinguishing 'High-Churchmen' from 'Latitudinarians'. Of his own efforts he wrote, 'To the best of my judgement, I have in copying Limborch followed the dictates of right reason and the clear light of sacred writ'. Already, in 1699, Burnet had published his own *Exposition* of the Thirty-nine Articles, in which he sought to demonstrate their various possible meanings while admitting to being an Arminian himself. His book was dedicated to King William and claimed to have the blessing of both Archbishop Tenison and his predecessor John Tillotson; not surprisingly it featured prominently in the subsequent exchanges between West, who was Burnet's chaplain, and Sacheverell. Replying to Sacheverell's accusation that Latitudinarians or Low-Churchmen interpreted each one of the Thirty-nine Articles in thirty-nine different ways, West wrote that 'if I think the scriptures most favour the Arminian tenets, as they are called, I am sure I can't honestly assent to them [the Articles] in a Calvinistical sense'.[59]

Just as Burnet had been accused of Socinianism or worse, so West here implied that the Oxonian Sacheverell and his backers were Calvinists. But the issue of toleration had already transformed the debate.[60] On the other hand there are also underlying continuities across the 1690s. Cambridge Arminianism, especially in the venerable person of Joseph Beaumont who died aged eighty-four in 1699, dated back at least to the 1630s. Oxford Calvinism as represented by Thomas Barlow was of course part of a much hoarier tradition, although Barlow's ecclesiological and ceremonial stance almost certainly needs to be distinguished from the school of William Jane and Jonathan Edwards.[61] As for the future, eighteenth-century Cambridge came increasingly to be identified with Latitudinarianism and Oxford with High-Church reaction.[62] Although it is likely that the pervasive Arminianism of Cambridge made the transition into the coming age significantly easier, the 'Latitudinarian' heroes of the traditional story appear to have played a subordinate role. Isolated advocates of toleration in their day, Henry More and the Cambridge Platonists had been reluctant to embrace Arminianism and opted instead for the effective blind alley of the soul's pre-existence. By contrast the far more numerous supporters of toleration thirty years later followed the Arminian trail already blazed by Beaumont and his reputedly 'High-Church' colleagues. It was this latter and unsung Cambridge group who had borne the theological heat and burden over the previous decades.

Essentially derived from a later and different period, the terms 'Latitudinarian' and 'High-Church' are unhelpful in analysing the religious history of the English Church during the reigns of Charles II and James II. The solution, however, is not to take refuge in an undifferentiated notion of 'Anglicanism'. On the contrary, more apposite terms are required of which Arminianism and Calvinism are only two. Yet this was no mere replay of earlier doctrinal disputes, for the world had moved on and the theologians with it. The new Arminianism was a much sturdier and more intellectually developed growth, which proved capable of combinations scarcely dreamt of earlier. Or, putting the matter differently, the previously separate English and Dutch Arminian movements now increasingly converged.

NOTES

I am indebted to Peter Lake and John Spurr for their comments on draft versions of this essay. My thanks also are owed to Pam Cremona, Edward Kenney and Roger Lovatt, concerning the Beaumont papers at Peterhouse, Cambridge, and to Helen Powell for her help over the years that I have been working on the Barlow papers at Queen's College, Oxford.

1 G. W. O. Addleshaw, *The High Church Tradition: A Study in the Liturgical Thought of the Seventeenth Century* (London, 1941), pp. 22–3.

2 Tyacke, *Anti-Calvinists*.

3 E. G. Rupp, *Studies in the Making of the English Protestant Tradition* (Cambridge, 1947), pp. 49–50.

4 W. P. Stephens, *The Holy Spirit in the Theology of Martin Bucer* (Cambridge, 1970), pp. 23–41; J. P. Donnelly, *Calvinism and Scholasticism in Vermigli's Doctrine of Man and Grace* (Leiden, 1970), pp. 124–69.

5 I. Breward ed., *The Work of Willam Perkins* (Abingdon, 1970), p. 84.

6 H. C. Porter, *Reformation and Reaction in Tudor Cambridge* (Cambridge, 1958), pp. 282–4.

7 A. E. McGrath, *The Intellectual Origins of the European Reformation* (Oxford, 1987), pp. 178–88; H. Bluhm, 'Luther's *German Bible*', in P. N. Brooks ed., *Seven-Headed Luther* (Oxford, 1983), pp. 184–7; E. G. Rupp, *The Righteousness of God: Luther Studies* (London, 1953), chs 6, 8.

8   A. Kenny, *Reason and Religion: Essays in Philosophical Theology* (Oxford, 1987), pp. 103–20.

9   H. Jedin, *A History of the Council of Trent*, trans. E. Graf (London, 1957–61), ii, pp. 239–316; C. L. Manschrek ed., *Melanchthon on Christian Doctrine: Loci Communes, 1555* (New York, 1965), pp. 187–91; C. Bangs, *Arminius: A Study in the Dutch Reformation* (Nashville, Tenn., 1971), pp. 138–49, 186–205; E. M. Wilbur, *A History of Unitarianism* (Cambridge, Mass., 1945–52), i, pp. 408–19.

10   J. Platt, 'Eirenical Anglicans at the Synod of Dort', in D. Baker ed., *Reform and Reformation: England and the Continent, c. 1500–1750* (Oxford, 1979), pp. 221–43.

11   Tyacke, *Anti-Calvinists*, pp. 50–3, 79–84, 249; H. J. McLachlan, *Socinianism in Seventeenth-Century England* (Oxford, 1951), pp. 41–3, 80–1, 104–7.

12   D. D. Wallace, *Puritans and Predestination: Grace in English Protestant Theology, 1525–1695* (Chapel Hill, Conn., 1982), pp. 104–57.

13   J. Gascoigne, *Cambridge in the Age of the Enlightenment: Science, Religion and Politics from the Restoration to the French Revolution* (Cambridge, 1989), pp. 4–5, 27–33, 40–4, 52–3, 63–5; I. Rivers, *Reason, Grace and Sentiment: A Study of the Language of Religion and Ethics in England, 1660–1780* (Cambridge, 1991), chs 2–3; see also R. L. Colie, *Light and Englightenment: A Study of the Cambridge Platonists and the Dutch Arminians* (Cambridge, 1957).

14   J. Spurr, '"Latitudinarianism" and the Restoration Church', *HJ* 31 (1988), 61–2, 66–7, 77–8, 80–2.

15   Wallace, *Puritans and Predestination*, pp. 163–7.

16   The papers of Thomas Barlow and Joseph Beaumont are to be found respectively at Queen's College, Oxford, and Peterhouse, Cambridge. Transcripts of Beaumont's lectures and determinations also exist at the Cambridge University Library.

17   The papers of Peter Gunning are located among the Rawlinson manuscripts in the Bodleian Library, Oxford. I owe my knowledge of them to the kindness of Anthony Milton.

18   From the Restoration period onwards, the Oxford congregation registers include theses disputed 'pro termino' as well as at the annual Act. The result is a very considerable increase of data.

19   Tyacke, *Anti-Calvinists*, pp. 50–2, 81–2. 85–6.

20   OUA, NEP/*supra*/17, register Qa, fos 150–4; BL, Harleian MS 7038, pp. 108–9.

21   *DNB*, s.n. Love, Richard; D. Hoyle, 'A Commons Investigation of Arminianism and Popery in Cambridge on the Eve of the Civil War', *HJ* 29 (1986), 419–25.

22   S. Gardiner, *De Efficacia Gratiae Christi Convertentis . . .* (Cambridge, 1660).

23   Bodl., Rawlinson MS C.622, fos 128, 142, 176.

24   *Ibid.*, Rawlinson MS C.614, fo 55.

25   *Ibid.*, Rawlinson MS C.615, fos 40–41v; E. Churton ed., *The Minor Theological Works of John Pearson, DD* (Oxford, 1844), i, pp. 255–67.

26   Rivers, *Reason, Grace and Sentiment*, p. 74.

27   E. Calamy, *An Historical Account of My Own Life*, ed. J. T. Rutt (London, 1830), i, pp. 272, 275.

28 Wallace, *Puritans and Predestination*, pp. 123–6.

29 R. Allestree, *Forty Sermons* (Oxford, 1684), pt. i, pp. 61–2, 97, 163–4.

30 QCL, MS 260, pp. 2, 90, 158, 324, 411.

31 *Ibid.*, MS 233, pp. 2–6; G. Bull, *Harmonia Apostolica*, trans. (Oxford, 1842), pp. 11, 20–1, 34, 178, 215–19.

32 J. Edwards, *Veritas Redux* (London, 1707), p. 555; J. Edwards, *The Arminian Doctrines Condemn'd by the Holy Scriptures* (London, 1711), pp. 114–15.

33 Bodl., D'Orville MS 470, pp. 50–1; L. Simonutti, 'Reason and Toleration: Henry More and Philip van Limborch', in S. Hutton ed., *Henry More (1614–1687) Tercentenary Studies* (Dordrecht, 1990), pp. 201–5.

34 H. More, *An Explanation of the Grand Mystery of Godliness* (London, 1660), pp. 502–3, 515–21, 1535–46; M. Nicolson ed., *Conway Letters* (London, 1930, revised edition by S. Hutton, Oxford, 1992), p. 220.

35 J. Beaumont, *Some Observations upon the Apologie of Dr Henry More for his Mystery of Godliness* (Cambridge, 1665), p. 31. My italics.

36 H. More, *The Immortality of the Soul* (London, 1659), pp. 240–5; J. Henry, 'Henry More versus Robert Boyle: the Spirit of Nature and the Spirit of Providence', in Hutton ed., *Henry More*, pp. 62–5, 73–4.

37 G. Rust, *A Letter of Resolution* (London, 1661), pp. 26–35; J. Glanvill, *Lux Orientalis* (London, 1662), sigs A6, Cr–v. My italics. *Conway Letters*, p. 194.

38 OUA, NEP/*supra*/18, register Qb, fo 39.

39 S. Parker, *An Account of the Nature and Extent of the Divine Dominion and Goodnesse, especially as they refer to the Origenian Hypothesis concerning the Preexistence of Souls* (Oxford, 1666), pp. 18–20; S. Parker, *A Free and Impartial Censure of the Platonick Philosophie* (Oxford, 1666), sigs A3v–A4, pp. 45, 47, 52; Rivers, *Reason, Grace and Sentiment*, p. 123; S. Parker, *A Discourse of Ecclesiastical Politie* (London, 1670), sig. A2v, S. Parker, *A Defence and Continuation of the Ecclesiastical Politie* (London, 1671), pp. 301, 315; S. Parker, *Disputationes de Deo . . .* (London, 1678).

40 Edwards, *Arminian Doctrines Condemn'd*, p. 113; Peterhouse, MS. 448, Sermon II, pp. 21–2, Sermon VII, pp. 4, 7.

41 J. Spurr, '"Rational Religion" in Restoration England', *Journal of the History of Ideas* 49 (1988), 564–9; OUA, NEP/*supra*/21, register Bf, fos 12v, 23, 40; Peterhouse, MS 439, [fo 14v], MS 429.4, fo 193, MS 429.5, fo 23.

42 J. Edwards, *The Eternal and Intrinsick Reasons of Good and Evil* (Cambridge, 1699), pp. 2–3, 7, 26–8; Spurr, '"Rational Religion" in Restoration England', 570–3.

43 J. W. Yolton, *John Locke and the Way of Ideas* (Oxford, 1956), pp. 1–5; E. S. de Beer ed., *Correspondence of John Locke* (Oxford, 1976–89), iv, pp. 133, 295; A. W. Wainwright ed., *A Paraphrase and Notes on the Epistles of St. Paul . . . by John Locke* (Oxford, 1987), ii, pp. 560–1; Wallace, *Puritans and Predestination*, pp. 130–2.

44 Peterhouse, MS 429.1, fos 83–106.

45 I have worked mainly from the transcript of these lectures in the Cambridge University Library: MSS Kk.iii. 1–16. For their date of delivery, see Peterhouse, MS 429.16, fo 1, and MS 438, [fo iv].

46 CUL, MSS Kk.iii.6, fo 242, Kk.iii.8, fos 189–92, Kk.iii.9, fos 52–5. For a refutation of Estius, see CUL, Add. MS 8689, fo 91.

47 Gascoigne, *Cambridge in the Age of the Enlightenment*, p. 43; CUL, MSS Kk.iii.9, fos 61–8, Kk.iii.10, fos 78–80, Kk.iii.11, fos 40–1.

48 Peterhouse, MS 429.2, fos 15–19, MS 439, [fo 13v]; Tyacke, *Anti-Calvinists*, pp. 41–4.

49 Peterhouse, MS 429.2, fos 99–102.

50 Peterhouse, MS 429.2, fos 141–5, 154–8, MS 429.3, fos 131–6, MS 429.5, fos. 150–3, MS 439, [fos 14v, 15v, 17r–v, 18, 19v, 21v].

51 T. Rogers, *The Faith, Doctrine and Religion, Professed and Protected in the Realm of England* (Cambridge, 1691), pp. 73–86; Tyacke, *Anti-Calvinists*, pp. 25–7.

52 J. Ellis, *Articulorum XXXIX* (Cambridge, 1694), pt i, pp. 60–4, pt ii, pp. 3–5, 55–75. I have followed the 1700 English translation.

53 J. Edwards, *A Preservative against Socinianism* (Oxford, 1694–1703), pt i, pp. 3–4, 18–28, pt iv, pp. 89–91 and index. I have used a copy in the Dr Williams's Library, London: shelf mark 1011. M. 10(1).

54 Peterhouse, MS 439, [fos 14v, 15v, 17v–18]; OUA, NEP/*supra*/19, register Bd, fo 59v, NEP/*supra*/20, register Be, fo 204; T. A. Walker, *Peterhouse* (Cambridge, 1935), pp. 11–12, 55–9, 127–9.

55 OUA, NEP/*supra*/21, register Bf, fo 183; Peterhouse, MS 439, [fos. 19–20]; QCL, MS 280, fo 251v.

56 G. V. Bennett, 'Loyalist Oxford and the Revolution', in L. S. Sutherland and L. G. Mitchell eds, *The History of the University of Oxford. V: the Eighteenth-Century.* (Oxford, 1986), pp. 27–9.

57 See pp. 76–7 above; Spurr, '"Latitudinarianism" and the Restoration Church', 77–8; T. E. S. Clarke and H. C. Foxcroft, *A Life of Gilbert Burnet, Bishop of Salisbury* (Cambridge, 1907), pp. 145–79. For advice concerning Burnet's views, I am indebted to Tony Claydon.

58 H. Grotius, *De Veritate Religionis Christianae* (Amsterdam, 1709), sigs *2–*4, pp. 305–52. The Dutch Arminian Jean Le Clerc dedicated this edition to Archbishop Tenison, while also adding a new section of his own and various testimonies concerning Grotius. Le Clerc implies that the purest form of Christianity is now to be found in the English Church. [Note, however, the 'middle way' position of Archbishop Tillotson: pp. 3–4 above.]

59 G. V. Bennett, 'The Era of Party Zeal, 1702–1714', in Sutherland and Mitchell eds, *The Eighteenth Century*, pp. 63–4; P. van Limborch, *A Compleat System or Body of Divinity*, trans. W. Jones (London, 1713), i, pp. xxiv–xxvi (I have not traced a first edition of this book); G. Burnet, *An Exposition of the Thirty-nine Articles* (London, 1699), pp. i–ii, vi and *passim*; R. West, *The True Character of a Churchman . . . Together with the Character of a Low-Churchman . . . with Remarks* (London, 1702), pp. 17–21.

60 West, *The True Character of a Churchman*, pp. 26–7, 34–5, 51–4.

61 Barlow maintained that bishops were 'iure apostolico', rather than 'iure divino', and argued against the altarwise position of communion tables. QCL, MS 340, p. 1, MS 278, 'De templis' [fos 19–21].

62 Gascoigne, *Cambridge in the Age of the Enlightenment*, chs 4–5; Sutherland and Mitchell eds, *The Eighteenth Century*, chs 3–4.

Index

Note: 'n' after a page reference indicates a note number on that page.

Gardiner, Samuel, chaplain to Archbishop
Abbot 135
Gardiner, Samuel (*d.* 1686) *De Efficacia
Gratiae Christi Convertentis* 324
Gardiner, Stephen 43
Gaskarth, John 22
Gasquet, Aidan, *The Eve of the Reformation*
38
Gassendi, Pierre 232, 247, 248; *Mercurius in
Sole Visus et Venus Invisa* 253
Gee, H. 56 n7
Gellibrand, Henry 15, 247, 248, 253, 254
Gifford, Bonaventure 304
Gilbert, William 234, 252
Glanvill, Joseph, *Lux Orientalis* 327
Glasgow Assembly (1638) 152
Gloucester Cathedral 142, 211
Godwin, William 262, 273
Goodman, Christopher 151
Goodman, Edward 104; children (named) of
105
Goodwin, John 69, 70, 127, 290; *Redemption
Redeemed* 289
Goodwin, Thomas 123
Gore, John 169
Gouge, William 116, 122
Gower, Be-thankful 100
Gower, Edmund 100, 101
Gower, Stanley 19
Grafton, Richard 42, 47
Gramelin, Matthieu 42
Greaves, John 15, 247, 248, 251–4
Greaves, Thomas 252–3
Gregory 208
Gregory, John 253, 254
Grew, Obadiah 289
Grindal, Edmund, archbishop of Canterbury
138, 178, 205
Grotius, Hugo 163, 223, 225, 227, 230, 233,
290, 291; *Annotations* 290, 330; *Disquisitio*
227
Gruter, Isaac 234
Gualter, Rodolph 26
Gunning, Peter 158, 324, 326
Gunter, Edmund 245, 248, 254; *Desription
and Use of the Sector* 245, 248
Guy, John 181

Haddon, Walter 178, 183
Hadleigh, Suff. 41
Haigh, Christopher 38, 39, 51
Hakewill, George 248, 249, 254; *Apologie of
the Power and Providence of God in the
Government of the World* 248
Hales, John (*d.* 1572) 49–51

Hales, John (*d.* 1656) of Eton 238, 273, 274,
279, 281, 286, 311 n35
Hall, John, bishop of Bristol 25, 302, 325
Hall, Joseph, bishop of Norwich 187, 290
Haller, William 9, 132; *Leveller Tracts* 61;
*Liberty and Reformation in the Puritan
Revolution* 61; *The Rise of Puritanism* 9, 61,
66; *Tracts on Liberty in the Puritan
Revolution* 61
Halliday, William 117
Halton, Timothy 302
Hammond, Henry 22, 270, 284, 286, 290,
291, 297, 307; *Of Fundamentals* 290;
Practicall Catechisme 284
Hampton Court, Middx. 213
Hampton Court Conference (1604) 11, 111,
166, 185
Harbord, Sir Charles 73
Harley, Lady Brilliana 18
Harley, Sir Robert (*d.* 1656) 18, 68, 271
Harley, Sir Robert (*d.* 1724) 82
Harman, Richard 45
Harrington, James 304, 305
Harrington, James, republican 27 n2, 291,
304
Harriot, Thomas 231–2; *Ars Analytica Praxis*
252
Harsnett, Samuel, archbishop of York,
previously bishop of Norwich 150, 165,
184, 216, 227, 238
Harte, Negley 8
Hartlib, Samuel 256
Harvey, William 244, 252; *De Motu Cordis et
Sanguinis* 253
Harwood, Sir Edward 120
Harwood, George 121
Hastings, Sir Francis 65
Hatton, Sir Christopher 256
Hawkins, William 23
Hawthorn, Gilbert 267
Hayes, Middx. 149
Hayes, John 332
Heads of Proposals (1647) 69
Hearne, Thomas 81
Heathfield, Sussex 91, 92, 96–7
Hell, Christ's descent into 269–70
Helwys, Thomas 65, 68
Hely, Thomas 33 n67, 92, 93, 96, 105;
children (named) of 96
Hemmingsen, Niels 156, 157, 163, 178, 181, 184,
189, 190; *Tractatus de Gratia Universali* 163
Hendley, From-above 93
Hendley, Thomas 93
Henrietta Maria, queen consort of Charles I
255

Pym, John 11, 66, 67, 134, 136, 141, 143, 145–7, 168, 196, 226
Pyrrho 232

Quakers 288

Rabson, Richard 127
Radnor, John Robartes, 1st earl of 293
Rainolds, John 116, 263, 265, 267, 270, 272, 298
Randol, John 275
Randolph, Thomas (d. 1635) 236; *Aristippus or the Joviall Philosopher* 236; *The Drinking Academy* 236
Randolph, Thomas (d. 1783) 24
Ranke, Leopold von 6
Rathbone, Aaron, *Surveyor* 246
Ravis, Thomas 164, 262, 263, 267
Rawley, William 256
Rayment, Thomas 193
Reeve, Edmund 169, 191; *The Communion Booke Catechisme* 149, 189
Reformatio Legum Ecclesiasticarum 182
Remonstrance (Dutch Arminian) 156–7, 180, 181, 188
resistance theory 301–2
Reve, Richard 98
revisionism: and English Civil War 7–8, 18, 29 n26, 61; and English Reformation 25, 36 n111, 37–9
Reynolds, Edward, bishop of Norwich 289, 291
Rich, Lady Penelope 209, 270
Richards, William 295
Richardson, Charles, *The Repentance of Peter and Judas* 164
Richardson, John 223, 331
Richelieu, cardinal 215
Ridley, Mark 252; *Treatise of Magneticall Bodies and Motions* 246
Ridley, Nicholas 40, 288
Roberts, Sir Thomas 118
Robinson, Henry, bishop of Carlisle 272
Robinson, William 208
Roe, Sir Thomas 250
Rogers, John 42
Rogers, Thomas 185, 332
Rolvenden, Kent 93
Roman Catholicism: 25, 27, 53–4; at Oxford 299–300, 303–5; and science 32 n62
Romney, Lady Rebecca 117
Romney, Sir William 114, 115
Romsey, Hants. 103
Roots, Richard, *St Paul's Epistle to the Romans . . .* 23

Roper, Mary 95
Rose, Thomas 41, 44
Rotterdam, English church at 123
Rous, Francis 11, 136, 146, 165, 168; *Testis Veritatis* 166
Rowley, Repent 105
Royal Society 256
Royse, George 301
Royston, Richard 290
Rugge, William, bishop of Norwich 45
Rupp, Gordon 25; *The Righteousness of God* 17
Russell, Conrad 5, 6; *The Crisis of Parliaments* 6; *The Origins of the English Civil War* 6–8
Rust, George 327; *A Letter of Resolution* 327
Ryves, Bruno 282
Ryves, George 268

sabbatarianism 217, 274, 278, 296
sacramentalism 13–14, 21, 23, 141–2, 144, 191, 211–14, 218–19
Sacheverell, Henry 79–81, 335; *The Character of a Low-Churchman* 335
St Albans, archdeaconry of 192
St Antholin's lectures 19, 20
St John, Charles Powlett, styled lord 74
St John, Oliver 146, 147
Salehurst, Kent 92–3
Salisbury, Wilts. 195
Salisbury, Robert Cecil, 1st earl of 137
Salter, Richard 331
Sanderson, Robert 283
Sandys, Edwin, archbishop of York 53, 134, 135
Savage, Henry 287
Savile, Sir Henry 14, 15, 245, 246
Savile, Sir John 114
Savilian professors 14–15, 246–51
Saye, William Fiennnes, 1st viscount 144, 147
Saye, Robert 295, 297, 327
Scarisbrick, J. J. 38; *The Reformation and the English People* 38
scepticism 230–3
scientific expeditions 250
Scheiner, Christoph 247
Schickard, Wilhelm 253
Seaver, Paul 139
Sedgwick, Richard 115
Seller, George 267
separatism 65, 68–9
Sevenoaks, Kent 16
Sextus Empiricus 231
Shaftesbury, Anthony Ashley Cooper, 1st earl of 74
Sharpe, Kevin 193–6; *The Personal Rule of Charles I* 193